S0-BHR-833

Perspectives on Marriage
—— A Reader ——

THIRD EDITION

REGIS COLLEGE LIBRARY
100 Wellesley Street West
Toronto, Ontario
Canada M5S 2Z5

BX
2250
P474
2007

Edited by

Kieran Scott
Fordham University

Michael Warren
St. John's University

New York   Oxford
OXFORD UNIVERSITY PRESS
2007

Oxford University Press, Inc., publishes works that further Oxford University's
objective of excellence in research, scholarship, and education.

Oxford   New York
Auckland   Cape Town   Dar es Salaam   Hong Kong   Karachi
Kuala Lumpur   Madrid   Melbourne   Mexico City   Nairobi
New Delhi   Shanghai   Taipei   Toronto

With offices in
Argentina   Austria   Brazil   Chile   Czech Republic   France   Greece
Guatamala   Hungary   Italy   Japan   Poland   Portugal   Singapore
South Korea   Switzerland   Thailand   Turkey   Ukraine   Vietnam

Copyright © 2007 by Oxford University Press, Inc.

Published by Oxford University Press, Inc.
198 Madison Avenue, New York, New York, 10016
http://www.oup.com

Oxford is a registered trademark of Oxford University Press

REGIS COLLEGE LIBRARY

All rights reserved. No part of this publication may be reproduced,
stored in a retrieval system, or transmitted, in any form or by any means,
electronic, mechanical, photocopying, recording, or otherwise,
without the prior permission of Oxford University Press.

Library of Congress Cataloging-in-Publication Data

Perspectives on marriage : a reader / edited by Kieran Scott, Michael Warren.—3rd ed.
     p. cm.
  Includes bibliographical references.
  ISBN-13: 978-0-19-531346-8
  ISBN-10: 0-19-531346-1
    1. Marriage—Religious aspects—Catholic Church. 2. Catholic Church—Doctrines.
I. Scott, Kieran. II. Warren, Michael, 1935–

BX2250.P415 2007
248.4—dc22   2006048800

9 8 7 6 5 4 3

Printed in the United States of America
on acid-free paper

To Ellen

CONTENTS

PART FOUR

Attitudes toward Sexuality

PART FIVE

Communication, Conflict, and Change

PART SIX

Issues Impacting Marriage

PART SEVEN

Commitment, Divorce, and Annulment

PART EIGHT

Spirituality of Marriage

PART NINE

Religious Traditions: Perspectives on Marriage

REGIS COLLEGE LIBRARY
100 Wellesley Street West
Toronto, Ontario
Canada M5S 2Z5

Acknowledgments

Robert Miller, executive editor at Oxford University Press, encouraged us to embark on this third edition and patiently navigated us through it. Emily Voigt, Aleksandra Florek, and Sarah Calabi, editorial assistants, were dedicated professionals in assisting us in the project. Celeste Alexander, project editor for this edition, skillfully and gracefully nurtured the book to completion. Drs. Rosemary Bertocci, Brian Doyle, Peter Feldmeier, Patricia Beatty Jung, and Arvin Vos offered invaluable suggestions for deletions and additions. Ellen O'Rourke worked tirelessly in assembling the final manuscript. Without their generous help, this revised third edition would never have come to fruition.

REGIS COLLEGE LIBRARY
100 Wellesley Street West
Toronto, Ontario
Canada M5S 2Z5

Introduction

Kieran Scott
Michael Warren

With the wide use of *Perspectives on Marriage*, especially in college- and university-level courses on marriage, we have been asked for a third edition, updated with important new material in the four years the 2001 edition had been in print. It now appears the reader itself has sparked renewed academic interest in the question of marriage and in the endless search for wisdom on marriage issues.

Readers familiar with the first and second editions will find we have maintained much material from the second edition and reinstated some important essays from the first edition. In doing so, we have been directed by the many teachers who have given us critical feedback on the previous two editions. Research by Oxford University Press into this book's actual use was invaluable to us in constructing this new third edition.

Perspectives on Marriage remains a "reader" that would be of interest to anyone concerned with marriage at the start of a new millennium. Teachers know this as they read and reread chapters they have already assigned to previous classes and are now assigning them once more. In our view this book has particular energy for those teaching "the course on marriage." Students seem to flock to such a course, spurred on by their own relationship difficulties and their desire to understand better the ecstatic yet difficult "love relationship." There is so much distortion about erotic relationships today that some who come to our classes come as "relationally wounded," searching for solace and wisdom.

Some teachers find the marriage course unfolds easily and often leads into intense discussions about the nuances of relationship. The readings here offer grounding in research and careful reflection for those discussions. Our hope is that the material we have provided will be, in reality, an intellectual gift from the writers whose ideas and opinions are found here. The readings provide a solid platform for informed talk about relationships, and even about their being a marvelous gift from a loving God.

Most teachers of the university-level course in the theology of marriage see their efforts as an academic enterprise, not a ministerial or church one. They seek to disclose historical traditions, including religious ones, affecting marriage, while attending to recent social and cultural shifts in attitudes toward the practice of marriage. Still, an academic course dealing with the religious dimensions of marriage will have some things in common with church efforts in ministry to marriage. One of these is concern for marriage preparation.

Despite the fact that more and more young people have come to question whether a "legal" or formal marriage is necessary or even advisable, students continue to crowd into the theology of marriage courses looking for insight and wisdom about a troubled institution. They know the stakes for them in this enterprise—however they may choose to approach it—are quite high. Bristling in the midst of our students are all the important dilemmas about what it means to be alive at this moment in history. Our goal in this reader is to press them with radical questions and humanizing perspectives that have important consequences for their futures. If they become more thoughtful about the issues and more constructive about their decisions, our efforts will be well rewarded.

Any course that puts marriage in a religious perspective has the possibility of contesting some currents in contemporary culture that are hostile to enduring commitments—hostile to the kind of love ethic needed for successful parenting over the long haul and hostile to the wider networks of support needed for families in the future. While some religious assumptions about marriage need critique, many religious convictions offer a radically humanizing view of the marital relationship, quite different from some of the depictions of marriage found in current film and television fare.

The readings in this collection contest various assumptions about marriage, including many recently created by a consumerist culture and some being challenged from within religious traditions themselves. Careful reading will spark earnest, if not heated, discussion and some conflicts over basic points of view. Many of the underlying, larger issues cannot be settled in a semester.[1] We expect many students will leave their courses with lingering questions needing continuing reflection: the seeds of emancipatory practice.

We recognize the variety of academic levels in what we have gathered here. Some readings are historically "dense" and will need careful preteaching before being read. Others make use of theologically sophisticated concepts that will also need explanation before becoming accessible to many students. Other fare is less weighty but not less important. We have included several popularizations of first-rate social science scholarship. The ideas and issues in such essays should not be dismissed as "magazine pop psychology" since they make accessible for serious and informed discussion sophisticated research conducted, in some cases, over several years.

Our hope is that the resources and ideas found here provide some part of a foundation for joyous, and struggling, life commitments.

Those familiar with the first two editions of *Perspectives on Marriage* will immediately note both what has been carried over from these editions and the deletions and additions that make up this new edition. In some cases readings have been restored to full length, simplified, or even moved to a different section. Each reading continues to be followed by questions for discussion and, in some cases, titles for further study.

Part 1, "Marriage in Historical Perspective," brings together a rich set of materials on marriage in the Jewish and Christian traditions. This material is indispensable for acquiring a developmental sense of religious teaching on marriage.

Part 2, "Contemporary Perspectives on the Theology of Marriage," presents marriage as a basic Christian sacrament, a sign of God's presence.

Part 3, "Marriage: Meanings and Transitions," raises some questions young people have about marriage and offers an approach to marriage as a process of growing together.

Part 4, "Attitudes toward Sexuality," is the longest section, with several provocative readings on the basic assumptions we bring to our relationships.

Part 5, "Communication, Conflict, and Change," is presented as a key section on the issue of conflict and conflict resolution in marriage. All students are familiar with the problems it sets out, but not so many will have considered the kinds of changes in attitudes and behavior it calls for. The difference between conflict and violence is a key matter in these readings.

Part 6, "Issues Impacting Marriage," looks at some recent scientific research on romantic love and the role of money in the wedding industry.

Part 7, "Commitment, Divorce, and Annulment," acknowledges the failure, at times, of the marital ideal and its effects on people's lives. Canonical and theological perspectives on divorce and remarriage are offered, and the dilemma remarriage poses for Catholics seeking ecclesial belonging is probed.

Part 8, "Spirituality of Marriage," explores what it might mean to actually live out a deeply religious marriage in a time of consumerism.

Part 9, "Religious Traditions: Perspectives on Marriage," is offered for the many students living in an increasingly multicultural and multireligious nation who bring to the marriage course questions about interreligious marriage.

Our metaphor for this third volume is also the wedding feast, a moment of hope and joy that unity is possible, that the spirit of God can reveal itself through human self-gifting. These readings themselves represent for us a kind of intellectual feast on the question of marriage, a question at the heart of what it means to be human.

NOTE

1. See the wise overview of marriage preparation from a religious perspective found in: Pontifical Council for the Family, "Preparation for the Sacrament of Marriage," *Origins* 26:7 (4 July 1996): 97/99–109. A key point in this document is its recognition that marriage preparation starts in infancy and continues right up to marriage.

PART ONE

Marriage in Historical Perspective

CHAPTER 1

Marriage in the Bible

Michael G. Lawler

We all have attitudes toward marriage that have been socially shaped for us within our own lifetime. We can easily tend to think of marriage as it is today— or even as it is depicted for us today in movies and television. Marriage has been imagined for us by our own parents, by the behavior of other married people we know, and by the many literary, TV, and film depictions of it.

The following essay is an account of the religious imagination of marriage, particularly the Jewish and the Christian imagination of what it could and should be. Some will find the account unbelievable, perhaps almost shocking. Not all those who call themselves Jews or Christians are aware of the quite radical approach to the marriage relationship their faith calls for.

This essay calls for careful reading. The best way to read it is to have read immediately beforehand the passages from the Old and New Testaments the author refers to and then to have them open before you while reading this important account of the profound Jewish and Christian understanding of marriage.

Questions for Discussion

1. The author stresses the differences between Israel and its neighbors in their understanding of sexuality and marriage. What differences are highlighted here, and exactly why are they so different?

2. Of the Israelite understanding of marriage, do you find any features that are still not widely accepted today—say, in the way marriage is presented in movies and on television?

3. Is the author claiming that marriage is the analogy for understanding our relation to God or that our relation to God is the analogy for understanding marriage?

4. Were Hosea living today, some would say he was "hung up" on Gomer or, in more psychological terms, "obsessed" by her. Obsession is not a beautiful thing. How would you explain the beauty of Hosea's commitment to Gomer, and what is its religious significance?

5. In more than one place, the author stresses that covenant love in the Bible is "not the same as a passionate affection for a person of the opposite sex." Does the author's approach make covenant love seem dull or unexciting? What is his point in this emphasis?

6. In dealing with New Testament passages about marriage, the author spends the most time dealing with several verses in Ephesians. Why does he see these verses as so significant? If the ideas of these verses were actually lived out, what difference would they make in the way people "love" one another?

7. Mutual giving way is an important concept here. What might be some examples of this mutual giving way in an actual marriage? Could you describe five situations in which it might take place?

8. What did you make of the author's claim "If marital love exists only inchoately on a wedding day, as it surely does, indissolubility also exists only inchoately. Marital love is . . . a task to be undertaken"?

A s in all other matters, the biblical teaching on marriage should be seen in the context of the Near Eastern cultures with which the people of the Bible had intimate links, specifically the Mesopotamian, Syrian, and Canaanite. It is not my intention here to dwell on these cultures and their teachings on marriage and sexuality. They were all quite syncretistic, and a general overview sufficiently gives both a sense of the context and their specific distinctions from the Jewish Bible.

Underlying the themes of sexuality, fertility, and marriage in these cultures are the archetypal figures of the god-father and the goddess-mother, the sources of universal life in the divine, the natural, and the human spheres. Myths celebrated the marriage, the sexual intercourse, and the fertility of this divine pair, legitimating the marriage, the intercourse, and the fertility of every earthly pair. Rituals acted out the myths, establishing a concrete link between the divine and the earthly worlds and enabling men and women to share not only in the divine action but also in the efficacy of that action. This is especially true of sexual rituals, which bless sexual intercourse and ensure that the unfailing divine fertility is shared by man's plants and animals and wives, all important elements of his struggle for survival in those cultures.[1] In Mesopotamia, the divine couple is Ishtar and Tammuz; in Egypt, Isis and Osiris; in Canaan, Ashtarte (or Asherah) and, sometimes, Eshmun. After the Hellenization of Canaan, Eshmun is given the title of Adonis.

MARRIAGE IN THE OLD TESTAMENT

The biblical view of sexuality, marriage, and fertility makes a radical break with this polytheistic perspective. The Old Testament, whose view of marriage I do not intend to treat fully here but only as it provides the basis for the New Testament view of Christian marriage, does not portray a god–goddess couple, but only Yahweh who led Israel out of Egypt and is unique (Deuteronomy 6:4). There is no goddess associated with him. He needs no

Reprinted with permission from *Secular Marriage: Christian Sacrament*, pp. 5–22, copyright © 1985 by Michael G. Lawler, published by Twenty-Third Publications, P.O. Box 180, Mystic, CT 06355.

goddess, for he creates by his word alone. This God created man and woman, "male and female he created them and he named *them 'adam*" (Genesis 5:2). This fact alone, that God names male and female together *'adam* (that is, earthling or humankind), founds the equality of man and woman as human beings, whatever be their distinction in functions. It establishes them as "bone of bone and flesh of flesh" (Genesis 2:23), and enables them "therefore" to marry and to become "one body" (Genesis 2:24). These details are taken from the early Yahwist creation account. But the much later priestly account which we find in Genesis I also records the creation of male and female as *'adam* and the injunction given them to "be fruitful and multiply and fill the earth" (Genesis 1:28).

Equal man and woman, with their separate sexualities and fertilities, do not derive from a divine pair whom they are to imitate. They are called into being by the creative action of the sovereign God. Man and woman *'adam,* their sexuality, their marriage, their fertility are all good, because they are the good gifts of the Creator. Later Christian history, as we shall see, will have recurring doubts about the goodness of sexuality and its use in marriage, but the Jewish biblical tradition had none. As gifts of the Creator God, who "saw everything that he had made and behold it was very good" (Genesis 1:31), sexuality, marriage, and fertility were all good, and belonged to man and woman as their own, not as something derived from some divine pair. When looked at within this context of creation-gift, all acquired a deeply religious significance in Israel. That is not to say that they were sacred in the sense in which the fertility cults interpreted them as sacred, namely, as participation in the sexuality and sexual activity of the divine pair. In that sense they were not sacred, but quite secular. But in another sense, the sense that they were from God and linked man and woman to God, they were both sacred and religious. "It was not the sacred rites that surrounded marriage that made it a holy thing. The great rite which sanctified marriage was God's act of creation itself."[7] It was God alone, unaided by any partner, who not only created *'adam* with sexuality and for marriage but also blessed him and them, thus making them inevitably good.

Man and woman together are named *'adam.* They are equal in human dignity and complementary to one another; there is no full humanity without both together. Human creation, indeed, is not complete until they stand together. It is precisely because man and woman are equal, because they are *'adam,* because they are "bone of bone and flesh of flesh," that is, because they share human strengths and weaknesses, that they may marry and become "one body" (Genesis 2:24). Among the birds of the air and the animals of the field there "was not found a helper fit" for the man (Genesis 2:20), and it is not difficult to imagine man's cry of delight when confronted by woman. Here, finally, was one who was his equal, one whom he could marry and with whom he could become one body.

That man and woman become one body in marriage has been much too exclusively linked in the Western tradition to one facet of marriage, namely, the genital. That facet is included in becoming one body, but it is not all there is. For *body* here implies the entire person. "One personality would translate it better, for 'flesh' in the Jewish idiom means 'real human life.'"[3] In marriage a man and a woman enter into a fully personal union, not just a sexual or genital one. In such a union they become one person, one life, and so complement one another that they become *'adam*. They enter into a union which establishes not just a legal relationship, but a blood relationship which makes them one person. Rabbis go so far as to teach that it is only after marriage and the union of man and woman into one person that the image of God may be discerned in them. An unmarried man, in their eyes, is not a whole man.[4] And the mythic stories,[5] interested as always in aetiology, the origin of things, proclaim that it was so "in the beginning," and that it was so by the express design of God. There could be for a Jew, and for a Christian, no greater foundation for the human and religious goodness of sexuality, marriage, and fertility. Nor could there be a secular reality better than marriage for pointing to God and his steadfastly loving relationship with Israel. That was the next step in the development of the religious character of marriage.

MARRIAGE AS COVENANT SYMBOL

Central to the Israelite notion of their special relationship with God was the idea of the covenant. The Deuteronomist reminded the assembled people: "You have declared this day concerning Yahweh that he is your God and Yahweh has declared this day concerning you that you are a people for his own possession" (Deuteronomy 26:17–19). Yahweh is the God of Israel; Israel is the people of Yahweh. Together Yahweh and Israel form a community of grace, a community of salvation, a community, one could say, of one body. It was probably only a matter of time until the people began to imagine this covenant relationship in terms drawn from marriage, and it was the prophet Hosea who first did so. He preached about the covenant relationship of Yahweh and Israel within the biographical context of his own marriage to a harlot wife, Gomer. To understand his preaching, about marriage and about the covenant, we must first understand the times in which Hosea lived.

Hosea preached around the middle of the eighth century B.C. at a time when Israel was well established in Canaan. Many Israelites thought that the former nomads had become too well established in their promised land, for as they learned their new art of agriculture they learned also the cult of the Canaanite fertility god, Baal. This cult, which seriously challenged their worship of Yahweh, was situated in the classic mold presented earlier, that of the god–goddess pair, with Baal as the Lord of the earth, and Anat as his wife (and sister). The sexual intercourse and fertility of these two were looked upon as establishing the pattern both of creation and of the fertile intercourse of every human pair. The relationship of human intercourse and its fertility to that of the divine couple was acted out in temple prostitution, which required both *kedushim* and *kedushoth*, that is, male and female prostitutes. These were prohibited in the cult of Yahweh (Deuteronomy 23:18), and any

Jewish maiden participating in temple prostitution was regarded as a harlot. It was such a harlot, Gomer, that Hosea says Yahweh instructed him to take for his wife (1:2–3).

It is quite irrelevant to the present discussion whether the book of Hosea tells us what Hosea did in historical reality, namely, took a harlot-wife and remained faithful to her despite her infidelity to him, or whether it offers a parable about marriage as steadfast covenant. What is relevant is that Hosea found in marriage, either in his own marriage or in marriage in general, an image in which to show his people the steadfastness of Yahweh's convenantal love for them. On a superficial level, the marriage of Hosea and Gomer is just like any other marriage. But on a more profound level, it serves as prophetic symbol, proclaiming and realizing and celebrating in representation the covenant relationship between Yahweh and Israel.

The names of Hosea's two younger children reflect the sad state of that relationship: a daughter is Not Pitified (1:6), and a son is Not My People (1:9). As Gomer left Hosea for another, so too did Israel abandon Yahweh in favor of Baal and become Not Pitied and Not My People. But Hosea's remarkable reaction proclaims and makes real in representation the remarkable reaction of Yahweh. He buys Gomer back (3:2); that is, he redeems her. He loves her "even as Yahweh loves the people of Israel, though they turn to other gods" (3:1). Hosea's action towards Gomer reveals and makes real in representation the action of Yahweh's unfailing love for Israel. In both cases, that of the human marriage symbol and of the divine covenant symbolized, the one body relationship had been placed in jeopardy. But Hosea's posture both is modeled upon and models that of Yahweh. As Hosea has pity on Gomer, so Yahweh "will have pity on Not Pitied," and will "say to Not My People 'you are my people,'" and they will say to him, "Thou art my God" (2:23). The covenant union, that between Hosea and Gomer as well as that between Yahweh and Israel, is restored. A sundering of the marital covenant relationship is not possible for Hosea because he recognized that his God is not a God who can abide the dissolution of covenant, no matter what the provocation. He believed what the prophet Malachi would later proclaim: "I hate divorce, says Yahweh, the God of Israel . . . so take heed to yourselves and do not be faithless" (2:16).

There are two possibilities of anachronism to be avoided here. The first is that overworked word *love*. In its contemporary usage, it always means a strong affection for another person, frequently a passionate affection for another person of the opposite sex. When we find the word in our Bible it is easy to assume that it means the same thing. But it does not. Covenant Love, of which Hosea speaks and which we read of first in Deuteronomy 6:5, is not a love of interpersonal affection but a love that is "defined in terms of loyalty, service and obedience."[6] When we read, therefore, of Hosea's steadfast love for Gomer and of Yahweh's faithful love for Israel, we ought to understand loyalty, service and obedience, and not interpersonal affection. The second possibility of anachronism rests in the hatred of divorce proclaimed by Malachi. "In the circumstances addressed by Malachi, what God hates is the divorce of Jew and Jew; there is silence about the divorce of Jew and non-Jew."[7] The post-exilic reforms of Ezra and Nehemiah require the divorce of all non-Jewish wives and marriage to Jewish ones. Malachi speaks for this period. The divorce of Jewish wives is hated, but the divorce of all non-Jewish ones is obligatory. As we shall see, Paul will adapt this strategy to the needs of his Corinthian church, and it continues to be a crucial factor in the Catholic strategy toward divorce in our day.

What ought we to make of the story of his marriage that Hosea leaves to us? There is a first, and very clear, meaning about Yahweh: he is faithful. But there is also a second, and somewhat more mysterious, meaning about human marriage: not only is it the loving union of a man and a woman, but it is also a prophetic symbol, proclaiming and making real in representative image the steadfast love of Yahweh for Israel. First articulated by the prophet Hosea, such a view of marriage recurs again in the prophets Jeremiah and Ezekiel. Ultimately, it yields the view of Christian marriage that we find in the New Testament.

Both Jeremiah and Ezekiel present Yahweh as having two wives. Israel and Judah (Jeremiah 3:6–14). Oholah-Samaria and Oholibah-Jerusalem (Ezekiel 23:4). Faithless Israel is first "sent away with a decree of divorce" (Jeremiah 3:8), but that does not deter an even more faithless Judah from "committing adultery with stone and tree" (Jeremiah 3:9). Israel and Judah are as much the harlots as Gomer but Yahweh's faithfulness is as unending as Hosea's. He offers a declaration of undying love: "I have loved you with an everlasting love; therefore, I have continued my faithfulness to you" (Jeremiah 31:3; cf. Ezekiel 16:63; Isaiah 54:7–8). The flow of meaning, as in Hosea, is not from human marriage to divine covenant, but from divine covenant to human marriage. The belief in and experience of covenant fidelity creates the belief in and the possibility of fidelity in marriage, which then and only then becomes a prophetic symbol of the covenant. Yahweh's covenant fidelity becomes a characteristic to be imitated, a challenge to be accepted, in every Jewish marriage. Malachi, as we saw already, puts it in a nutshell: "I hate divorce, says Yahweh . . . so do not be faithless" (2:16).

MARRIAGE IN THE NEW TESTAMENT

The conception of marriage as a prophetic symbol, a representative image of a mutually faithful covenant relationship is continued in the New Testament. But there is a change of dramatis personae, from Yahweh–Israel to Christ–Church. Rather than presenting marriage in the then-classical Jewish way as an image of the covenant union between Yahweh and Israel, the writer of the letter to the Ephesians[8] presents it as an image of the relationship between the Christ and the new Israel, his church. This presentation is of such central importance to the development of a Christian view of marriage and unfortunately has been used to sustain such a diminished Christian view that we shall have to consider it here in some detail.

The passage in which the writer offers his view of marriage (EPH.5:21–33) is situated within a larger context (EPH.5:21–6:9) which sets forth a list of house-hold duties that exist within a family at that time. This list is addressed to wives (EPH.5:22), husbands (EPH.5:25), children (EPH.6:1), fathers (EPH.6:4), slaves (EPH.6:5), and masters (EPH.6:9). All that concerns us here is, of course, what is said of the pair, wife/husband. There are two similar lists in the New Testament, one in the letter to the Colossians (3:18–4:1), the other in the first letter of Peter (2:13–3:7). But the Ephesians' list is the only one to open with a strange injunction. "Because you fear Christ subordinate yourselves to one another"[9]; or "give way to one another in obedience to Christ"[10]; or, in the weaker translation of the Revised Standard Version, "be subject to one another out of reverence for Christ."[11] This junction, most commentators agree, is an essential element of what follows.

The writer takes over the household list from traditional material, but critiques it in 5:21. His critique challenges the absolute authority of any one Christian group over any other, of husbands, for instance, over wives, of fathers over children, of masters over slaves. It establishes a basic attitude required of all Christians, an attitude of giving way or of mutual obedience, an attitude which covers all he has to say not only to wives, children, and slaves, but also to husbands, fathers, and masters.[12] Mutual submission is an attitude of all Christians, because their basic attitude is that they "fear Christ." That phrase probably will ring strangely in many ears, clashing with the deeply rooted Augustinian-Lutheran claim that the basic attitude toward the Lord is not one of fear, but of love. It is probably for this reason that the Revised Standard Version rounds off the rough edge of the Greek *phobos* and renders it as *reverence*. But *phobos* does not mean reverence. It means fear, as in the Old Testament aphorism: the fear of the Lord is the beginning of wisdom (Proverbs 1:5; 9:10; 15:33; Psalms 111:10).

The apostle Paul is quite comfortable with this Old Testament perspective. Twice in his second letter to the Corinthians (2 Cor. 5:11 and 7:1) he uses the phrase *fear of God*. In his commentary on Ephesians, Schlier finds the former text more illuminating of Ephesians 5:21.[13] But I am persuaded, with Sampley, that the latter is a better parallel.[14] Second Corinthians 6:14–18 recalls the initiatives of God in the covenant with Israel and applies these initiatives to Christians, who are invited to respond with holiness "in the fear of God" (2 Cor. 7:1). The fear of God that is the beginning of wisdom is a radical awe and reverence that grasps the mighty acts of God and responds to them with holiness. In 2 Corinthians 6:14–17 that holiness is specified as avoiding marriage with unbelievers; in Ephesians 5:21 it is specified as giving way to one another. That mutual giving way is required of all Christians, even of husbands and wives as they seek holiness together in marriage, and even in spite of traditional family relationships which permitted husbands to lord it over their wives.

As Christians have all been admonished to give way to one another, it comes as no surprise that a Christian wife is to give way to her husband, "as to the Lord" (EPH.5:22). What does come as a surprise, at least to the ingrained male attitude that sees the husband as supreme lord and master of his wife and appeals to Ephesians 5:22–23 to ground and sustain that un-Christian (superior) attitude, is that a husband is to give way to his wife. That follows from the general instruction that Christians are to give way to one another. It follows also from the specific instruction about husbands. That instruction is not that "the husband is the head of the wife" (which is the way in which males prefer to read and cite it), but rather that "in the same way that the Messiah is the head of the church is the husband the head of the wife."[15] A Christian husband's headship over his wife is in image of, and totally exemplified by, Christ's leadership over the Church. When a Christian husband understands this, he will understand the Christian responsibility he assumes toward the woman-gift he receives in marriage as his wife. In a Christian marriage, spouses are required to give way mutually, not because of any inequality between them, not because of any subordination of one to the other, not because of fear, but only because they have such a personal unity that they live only for the good of that one person. Mutual giving way, mutual subordination, and mutual obedience are nothing other than total availability and responsiveness to one another so that both spouses can become one body.

The way Christ exercises headship over the church is set forth unequivocally in Mark 10:45: "The Son of Man came not to be served but to serve, and to give his life as a ransom (redemption) for many." *Diakonia*, service, is the Christ way of exercising authority, and our author testifies that it was thus that "Christ loved the church and gave himself up for her" (Ephesians 5:25). A Christian husband, therefore, is instructed to be head over his wife by serving, giving way to, and giving himself up for her. Headship and authority modeled on those of Christ does not mean control, giving orders, making unreasonable demands, reducing another human person to the status of servant or, worse, slave to one's every whim. It means service. The Christian husband-head, as Markus Barth puts it so beautifully, becomes "the first servant of his wife."[16] It is such a husband-head, and only such a one, that a wife is to fear (v. 33b) as all Christians fear Christ (v. 21b).

(In this section of Ephesians) the reversal of verses 22 and 25 in verse 33 is interesting and significant. Verse 22 enjoined wives to be subject to their husbands and verse 25 enjoined husbands to love their wives. Verse 33 reverses that order, first commanding that husbands love their wives and then warmly wishing that wives fear their husbands. This fear is not fear of a master. Rather it is awe and reverence for loving service, and response to it in a love-as-giving way. Such love cannot be commanded by a tyrant. It is won only by a lover, as the church's love and giving way to Christ is won by a lover who gave, and continues to give, himself for her. This is the author's recipe for becoming one body, joyous giving way in response to, and for the sake of, love. It is a recipe echoed unwittingly by many a modern marriage counselor, though we need to keep in mind that the love the Bible urges upon spouses is not interpersonal affection but loyalty, service, and obedience. That such love is to be mutual is clear from v. 21, "Be subject to one another," though it is not stated that a wife is to love her husband. The reasons that the writer adduces for husbands to love their wives apply to all Christians, even those called wives!

Three reasons are offered to husbands for loving their wives, all of them basically the same. First of all, "husbands should love their wives as [for they are] their own bodies" (v. 28a); secondly, the husband "who loves his wife loves himself" (v. 28b); thirdly, "the two shall become one body" (v. 31b), a reading which is obscured by the Revised Standard Version's "the two shall become one." There is abundant evidence in the Jewish tradition for equating a man's wife to his body.[17] But even if there was no such evidence, the sustained comparison throughout Ephesians 5:21–33 between Christ–Church and husband–wife, coupled with the frequent equation in Ephesians of church and body of Christ (EPH.1:22–23; 2:14–16; 3:6; 4:4–16; 5:22–30), clarifies both the meaning of the term *body* and the fact that it is a title of honor rather than of debasement.

Love is always essentially creative. The love of Christ brought into existence the Church and made its believers "members of his body" (v. 30). In the same way, the mutual love of a husband and a wife brings such a unity between them that, in image of Christ and Church, she may be called his body and his love for her, therefore, may be called love for his body or for himself. But it is only within the creative love of marriage that, in the Genesis phrase, "the two shall become one body" (Gen. 2:24). Prior to marriage, a man did not have this body, nor did a woman have this head. Each receives a gift in marriage, a complement neither had before, which so fulfills each of them that they are no longer two separate persons but one blood person. For each to love the other, therefore, is for each to love herself or himself.

The second reason offered to a husband for loving his wife is that "he who loves his wife loves himself" (EPH. 5:28B, V. 33A). Viewed within the perspective I have just elaborated, such reasoning makes sense. It makes even more Christian sense when one realizes that it is a paraphrase of the great commandment of Leviticus 19:18, cited by Jesus in Mark 12:31: "You shall love your neighbor as yourself." Ephesians, of course, does not say that a husband should love his neighbor as himself, but that he should so love his wife. Where, then, is the link to the great commandment? It is provided through that most beautiful and most sexual of Jewish love songs, the Song of Songs, where in the Septuagint version the lover addresses his bride nine separate times as *plesion*, neighbor (1:9, 15; 2:2, 10, 13; 4:1, 7; 5:2; 6:4). "The context of the occurrence of *plesion* in the Song of Songs confirms that *plesion* is used as a term of endearment for the bride."[18] Other Jewish usage further confirms that conclusion, leaving little doubt that the author of Ephesians had Leviticus 19:18 in mind when instructing a husband to love his wife as himself.

The great Torah and Gospel injunction applies also in marriage: "you shall love your neighbor as yourself." As all Christians are to give way to one another, so also each is to love the other as himself or herself, including husband and wife in marriage. The paraphrase of Leviticus 19:18 repeats in another form what had already been said before in the own-body and the one-body images [of Ephesians]. What the writer [of Ephesians] concludes about the Genesis one-body image, namely "This is a great mystery, and I mean in reference to Christ and the church" (v. 32), will conclude our analysis of this central teaching of the New Testament on marriage.

"*This* is a great mystery," namely, as most scholars agree, the Genesis 2:24 text just cited, "the two shall become one body." The mystery, as the Anchor Bible translation seeks to show, is that "this (passage) has an eminent secret meaning," which is that it refers to Christ and the Church. All that has gone before about Christ and the Church comes to the forefront here: that Christ chose the Church to be united to him, as body to head; that he loved the Church and gave himself up for her; that the Church responds to this love of Christ in fear and giving way. Christ who loves the Church, and the Church who responds in love, thus constitute one body, the Body of Christ (Ephesians 1:22–23; 2:14–16; 3:6; 4:4–16; 5:22–30), just as Genesis 2:24 said they would. The writer is well aware that this meaning is not the meaning traditionally given to the text in Judaism, and he states this forthrightly. Just as in the great antithesis of the Sermon on the Mount, Jesus puts forward his interpretations of biblical texts in opposition to traditional interpretations ("You have heard that it was said to the men of old . . . but I say to you"), so also here the writer asserts clearly that it is his own reading of the text ("*I* mean in reference to Christ and the church," v. 32b).

Genesis 2:24, "That is why a man leaves his father and mother and clings to his wife, and the two of them become one body," was an excellent text for the purpose the writer had in mind, for it was a central Old Testament text traditionally employed to ordain and legitimate marriage. He acknowledges the meaning that husband and wife become one body in marriage; indeed, in v. 33, he returns to and demands that husband and wife live up to this very meaning. But he chooses to go beyond this meaning and insinuate another. Not only does the text refer to the union of husband and wife in marriage, but it refers also to that union of Christ and his church which he has underscored throughout Ephesians 5:1–33. On one level, Genesis 2:24 refers to human marriage; on another level, it refers to the covenant union between Christ and his Church. It is a small step to see human marriage as prophetically representing the covenant between Christ and his Church. In its turn, the union between Christ and Church provides an ideal model for human marriage and for the mutual conduct of the spouses within it.

Ephesians is not, of course, the only New Testament passage to speak of marriage and of the relationship between husband and wife. Paul does so in 1 Corinthians 7, apparently in response to a question which the Corinthians had submitted to him. The question was: "Is it better for a man to have no relations with a woman?" (7:1). The answer is an implied yes, but not an absolute yes. "Because of the temptation to sexual immorality, each man should have his own wife and each woman her own husband" (7:2). Marriage is good, even for Christians, he seems to say, as a safeguard against sexual sins, a point he underscores again in vv. 5–9. I do not wish to dwell, however, on this unenthusiastic affirmation of marriage. I wish only to highlight the equal relationship Paul assumes in marriage between a husband and a wife, a relationship he makes explicit in vv. 3–4. "The husband should give to the wife her conjugal rights, and likewise the wife to her husband. For the wife does not rule over her own body, but the husband does; likewise the husband does not rule over his own body, but the wife does."

A modern Christian might seize (as did medieval canonists seeking a precise legal definition of marriage) on Paul's dealing with marital sexual intercourse as an obligation owed mutually by the spouses to one another. But his contemporaries would have seized on something else, something much more surprising to them, namely, his assertion of strict equality between husband and wife in this matter. As Mackin puts it, correctly: "A modern Christian may wince at finding the apostle writing of sexual intercourse as an obligation, or even a debt, owed by spouses to one another, and writing of husbands' and wives' marital relationship as containing authority over one another's bodies. But Paul's contemporaries—at least those bred in the tradition of Torah and of its rabbinic interpreters—would have winced for another reason. This was Paul's assertion of equality between husbands and wives, and equality exactly on the juridical ground of authority and obligations owed."[19]

The author of 1 Timothy 2:8–15 also has something to say about the attitudes of men and women, laying down somewhat disproportionately what is expected of men (v. 8) and women (vv. 9–15). Of great interest in this text are the two traditional reasons he advances for the authority of men over women and the submission of women to men. The first is that Adam was created before Eve, and the other that it was Eve, not Adam, who was deceived by the serpent. Here the submission of women to men, and therefore of wives to husbands, is legitimated by collected stories of the mythical first human pair. For his part, the author of 1 Peter 3:1–6 requires that wives be submissive to their husbands "as Sarah obeyed Abraham" (v. 6). Such widespread views on such Old Testament bases were common in the Jewish world in which the Christian church originated, which makes the attitude of the writer to the Ephesians all the more surprising.

The Old Testament passage that the writer chooses to comment on is one which emphasizes the unity in marriage of the first pair, and therefore of all subsequent pairs, rather than their distinction. He embellishes it not with Old Testament references to creation and to fall, but with New Testament references to the Messiah and to his love. This leads him to a positive appraisal of marriage in the Lord that was not at all customary in the Jewish and Christian milieu of his time. While he echoes the customary *no* to any form of sexual immorality (5:3–5), he offers a more–than–customary *yes* to marriage and sexual intercourse. For him marriage means the union of two people in one body, the formation of a new covenant pair, which is the gift of both God who created it and his Christ who established it in the love he has for the church. So much so that the Christian marriage between a man and a woman becomes the prophetic symbol of the union that exists between Christ and the Church.

This doctrine does not mythicize marriage as an imitation of the marriage of some divine pair, nor does it idealize it so that men and women will not recognize it. Rather it leaves marriage what it is, a secular reality in which a man and a woman seek to become one person in love. What is added is only this, simple and yet mysteriously complex. As they become one body-person in love, they provide through their marriage a prophetic symbol of a similar oneness that exists between their Christ and their Church.

QUALITIES OF CHRISTIAN MARRIAGE

The qualities of Christian marriage already appear from our biblical analysis. The root quality, the one that irradiates all the others, is the fulfillment of the great Torah and Gospel injunction: "You shall love your neighbor as yourself" (Leviticus 19:18; Mark 12:31; Matthew 19:19). The Apostle Paul instructed the Romans that every other commandment was "summed up in this sentence, 'You shall love your neighbor as yourself'" (13:9). It is an instruction that holds true even, perhaps especially, in marriage. *Love,* of course, is a reality that is not easy to specify in words. It has a variety of different meanings. In Christian marriage love between the spouses, in fulfillment of the great commandment, is so radically necessary that in our time the Roman Rota, the Supreme Marriage Tribunal of the Roman Catholic Church, has ruled that where it is lacking from the beginning a Christian marriage is invalid.[20] That is how important Christian love is between Christian spouses.

We recall here that covenant love in the Bible is a love that is defined in terms of loyalty, service, and obedience, not in terms of interpersonal affection. The Letter to the Ephesians specifies that the love that is demanded in a Christian marriage is that kind of love. It is, first, love as mutual giving way, love as mutual obedience. The love of the spouses in a Christian marriage is a love that "does not insist on its own way" (1 Corinthians 13:4), a love that does not seek to dominate and control the other spouse. Rather it is a love that seeks to give way to the other whenever possible, so that two persons might become one body. There are individuals whose goal in life appears to be to get their own way always. The New Testament message proclaims that there is no place for such individuals in a marriage, least of all in a Christian marriage. That is not to say that there is no place in a marriage for individual differences. It is to say only that spouses who value getting their own way always, who value the domination of their spouses, who never dream of giving way, will never become one person with anyone, perhaps not even with themselves. In a Christian marriage, love requires not insisting on one's own way, but a mutual empathy with and compassion for the needs, feelings, and desires of one's spouse, and a mutual giving way to those needs, feelings, and desires when the occasion demands for the sake of, and in response to, love. Love that is exclusively *eros* is not the kind of love that is apt to ensure that two persons should become one body.

Love in a Christian marriage is, secondly, love as mutual service. All Christians are called to, and are sealed in baptism for, the imitation of Christ, who came "not to be served but to serve" (Mark 10:45). It cannot be otherwise in Christian marriage. In such a marriage there is no master, no mistress, no lady, no lord, but only mutual servants, seeking to be of service to the other, so that each may become one in herself/himself and one also with the other. This is required not just because it is good general counsel for marriage, but specifically because these Christian spouses are called in their marriage both to be imitators of Christ their Lord and to provide a prophetic symbol of his mutual servant-covenant with his church. For Christian spouses their married life is where they are to encounter Christ daily, and thereby come to holiness.

The love that constitutes Christian marriage is, finally, steadfast and faithful. The writer to the Ephesians instructs a husband to love his wife "as Christ loved the church." We can be sure that he intends the same instruction also for a wife. Now Christ loves the Church as Hosea loves Gomer, steadfastly and faithfully. A Christian husband and wife, therefore, are to love each other faithfully. This mutually faithful love, traditionally called fidelity, makes Christian marriage exclusive and permanent, and therefore an indissoluble community of love. On the question of indissolubility I want my position to be clear. Christian marriage is indissoluble because Christian love is steadfast and faithful. Indissolubility is a quality of Christian marriage because it is, first, a quality of Christian love. If marital love exists only inchoately on a wedding day, as it surely does, indissolubility also exists only inchoately. Marital love, as mutual giving way, as mutual service, as mutual fidelity, as mainspring of indissoluble community, is not a given in a Christian marriage but a task to be undertaken. It has an essentially eschatological dimension. *Eschatological* is a grand theological word for simple and constant human reality, namely the experience of having to admit "already, but not yet." Already mutual love, but not yet steadfast; already mutual service, but not yet without the desire to control; already one body, but not yet one person; already indissoluble in hope and expectation, but not yet in full human reality; already prophetic representation of the covenant union between Christ and his church, but not yet totally adequate representation. For authentic Christian spouses, Christian marriage is always a challenge to which they are called to respond as followers of the Christ who is for them the prophetic symbol of God.

SUMMARY

Four things we have seen in this chapter need to be underscored. First, human marriage is not an imitation of the eternal marriage of some divine couple, but a truly human, and therefore truly secular, reality which man and woman, *'adam*, hold as their own as gift from their Creator-God. In the giving and receiving of this gift, the Giver, the gift and the recipient are essentially and forever bound together. Secondly, this bond is explicated by the prophet Hosea, who brings into conscious focus the fact that marriage between a man and a woman is also the prophetic symbol of the covenant union between Yahweh and his people. Thirdly, the author of the letter to the Ephesians further clarifies the symbolic nature of marriage by proclaiming "a great mystery."

The great mystery is that as a man and a woman become one body-person in marriage, so also are Christ and his Church one body-person, and that the one reflects the other. From such thinking Roman Catholic theologians will be led slowly to declare that *human* marriage, on occasion, may be also *Christian* sacrament. Fourthly, Christian marriage is both a covenant and a community of love between a man and a woman, love that does not seek its own, love that gives way, love that serves, love that is steadfastly faithful. Because it is a covenant and a community of steadfast love, it is a permanent and exclusive state and a prophetic symbol of the steadfast covenant and community of love between Christ and his Church. That Christian marriage is such a reality, though, is not something that is to be taken blindly as being so. Rather it is something that in steadfast continuity is to be made so. Permanence is not a static, ontological quality of a marriage, but a dynamic, living quality of human love on which marriage, both human and Christian, thrives.

QUESTIONS FOR REFLECTION AND DISCUSSION

1. In your judgment, what is the radical distinction between the ancient Jewish mythology about sexuality, marriage, and fertility and that of the peoples surrounding them in the ancient Near East? Does that distinction make any contribution to the mythology you hold about those same realities?

2. If you believed that sexuality and marriage were gifts of God, would that be enough for you to say that they related you to God? If you believed they were gifts of God, would that be enough for you to say that they were sacramental? If yes, in what sense?

3. Do you look upon marriage as sacramental? What does *sacramental* mean to you?

4. The two great commandments in Judaism and Christianity prescribe the love of God and the love of neighbor. According to the letter to the Ephesians, how are these commandments to be lived in a Christian marriage?

5. What does it mean to you to say that a man and a woman become one body in marriage? Do you understand their one-body relationship to be a legal or a kind of blood relationship? If it were a kind of blood relationship, how would you go about getting a divorce?

NOTES

1. For more detailed information see M. Eliade, *Patterns in Comparative Religion* (London: Sheed and Ward, 1979); E. O. James, *The Cult of the Mother-Goddess* (London: Thames and Hudson, 1959).

2. E. Schillebeeckx, *Marriage: Secular Reality and Saving Mystery*, Vol. 1 (London: Sheed and Ward, 1965), 39.

3. F. R. Barry, *A Philosophy from Prison* (London: SCM, 1926), 151. Cp. Schillebeeckx, *Marriage*, 43; Markus Barth, *Ephesians: Translation and Commentary on Chapters Four to Six. The Anchor Bible* (New York: Doubleday, 1974), 734–738; X. Leon—Dufour (ed.), *Vocabulaire de Theologie Biblique*, 2nd ed. rev. (Paris: Cerf, 1970), 146–152.

4. See Richard Batey, "The *mid sarx* Union of Christ and the Church," *New Testament Studies* 13 (1966–67), 272.

5. For a discussion of whether the term *myth* should be applied to any biblical passage, and for a suggestion of alternative language, see John McKenzie, "Myth and the Old Testament," CBQ 21 (1959), 265–282.

6. William L. Moran, "The Ancient Near Eastern Background of the Love of God in Deuteronomy," CBQ 25 (1963), 82.

7. Bruce J. Malina, *The Testament World: Insights from Cultural Anthropology* (Atlanta: John Konox, 1981), 110.

8. It is of no interest to any thesis in this book whether the Apostle Paul was or was not the author of Ephesians, and so I do not deal with that disputed question, referring only to *the writer*. Those who require information on the question may consult any of the modern commentaries.

9. Markus Barth, *Ephesians*, 607.

10. *The Jerusalem Bible* (London: Darton, Longman and Todd, 1966).

11. *The Holy Bible: Revised Standard Version* (London: Nelson, 1959).

12. Barth, *Ephesians*, 609.

13. Heinrich Schlier, *Der Brief an die Epheser* (Düsseldorf: Patmos, 1962), 252.

14. J. Paul Sampley, *And the Two Shall Become One Flesh: A Study of Traditions in Ephesians* 5:21–33 (Cambridge: Cambridge University Press, 1971), 119–121.

15. Barth, *Ephesians*, 607.

16. Ibid., 618.

17. Cf. Sampley, *Two Shall Become One Flesh*, 33.

18. Cf. Ibid., 30. See 30–34; cp. Barth, *Ephesians*, 704–708.

19. Theodore Mackin, *What Is Marriage?* (New York: Paulist, 1982), 56.

20. Cited in Paul F. Palmer, "Christian Marriage: Contract or Covenant?" TS 33 (1972): 647–648.

CHAPTER 2

The Primitive Christian Understanding of Marriage

Theodore Mackin, S.J.

Most people understand marriage only within the customs of their own day and are thus unable to consider the arbitrariness of many marriage customs. Thus, our own socially determined customs take on a kind of sacredness unable to be questioned. Theodore Mackin's description of the Jewish marriage customs of Jesus' day helps us see how differently various societies can go about the tasks and duties of marriage. Even more important, this account helps us understand the way Jesus himself would have thought of marriage and then suggests how unusual his contemporaries would have found the fact that he himself did not marry.

The specific roles of women and men in marriage, the role of families in determining whom one would marry, and the centrality of having children are all matters that make the following essay fascinating. This essay could open up discussion of the subtle ways some of these ideas, attitudes, and customs are still with us in a time when they seem so foreign.

Further Reading

In Mackin's book, *What Is Marriage?*, readers will find an equally fascinating description of a later period: "Christian Marriage in the Roman Empire," pp. 67–79.

S ince it is accurate enough to date the establishing of the community of Jesus' followers as a church within the decade 27–37 A.D., we may put the end of the second Christian generation at the turn of the first century. By that time two major traditions, the Jewish and the Hellenistic-Roman, had formed the character of early Christian life in community. By the end of these sixty years the confluence of these two traditions in Christianity was complete. Each had had time to make its contribution to Christian life in full strength. Each had conditioned the other. And even though the first communities of Jesus' followers in Palestine had been destroyed, or at least dispersed, during

Reprinted from *What Is Marriage?* by Theodore Mackin, S.J. Copyright © 1982 by Theodore Mackin, S.J. (New York: Paulist Press). Used by permission of Paulist Press.

the devastation of Judea and the siege of Jerusalem by the Roman army under Vespasian and then Titus in 68–70, the Jewish influence continued past that date because the first Christian communities outside Palestine had been formed mainly from the synagogue communities scattered around the eastern half of the empire. Consequently, though the Hellenistic-Roman character eventually overwhelmed at least Jewish custom as the Jewish portion of the Christian population dwindled, the Jewish vision of marriage left its effect in the early Christian consciousness. It is this vision that we must seek to understand first.

PALESTINIAN JEWISH MARRIAGE CUSTOM

Among Jesus' people marriage was regarded as obligatory. The male who had reached eighteen years but had not yet married could be compelled by a court to do so. While girls, as also boys, could not be married before puberty, the former were ordinarily married as soon as they reached it, which was set at twelve years and six months. Thirteen was the earliest age at which a boy might marry. These early ages for marrying hint clearly at the meaning of Jewish marriage in Palestine at that time. It was for family decisively and in multiple ways. The principal motive for marrying was to provide children so as to preserve the husband's family, to keep his and his father's name from dying out, to keep the tribe, the nation itself as the people of God in existence— withal to honor the ancient covenant commitment with Yahweh to be a light to the nations. Since infant mortality was high and life expectancy low even for those who survived until adulthood, it was important that the childbearer marry at the onset of puberty so as to bear as many children as possible.

Hesitant belief in personal survival beyond death reinforced this tradition. If a man had no heirs, even if he had daughters but no sons, he risked having his name die out; the memory of him might vanish and be lost to his people forever and in every way. Hence marriage was before all else what Christian tradition would later call an *officium*, a dutiful vocation, a vocation motivated by *pietas*, loyal loving concern for one's parents and one's people. The Jewish people itself had already been given and had accepted the *officium* mentioned earlier, to be a light to the nations. Obviously it could be faithful to this vocation only if its sons and daughters bore and nurtured children.

The Jewish people of Jesus' time were not a defining people in the Western sense of assigning an entity to generic and specific categories of existence. But if one were to ask in terms of these categories about the essence of marriage among this people, no more exact answer could be given than that it was an abiding relationship between a man and a woman intended mainly although not exclusively for children.

Although the negotiations between the two families to settle the dowry and the *mohar* (the bride-price given by the husband-to-be to the girl's father) were contractual in form, the marriage itself was not thought of as a contract. For one thing an element essential to a contract was missing. The mutual consent by the contracting parties themselves to the exchange of a contractual good was deemed functionally necessary. Jewish fathers in consultation with their wives negotiated their children's marriages; the wills of the fathers held good for those of their children. The latters' marital consent was more an obedient acceptance of the partners chosen for them, although loving parents took their children's desires into consideration, especially if the desire were against the tentatively chosen partner. Thus the marriage was a covenant between two families. It was made orally by the parents, but by Jesus' time the covenant was confirmed legally in writing.

The preferred source wherein to search for spouses for one's children was one's own relatives, within those forms and degrees of kindred permitted marriage by Torah and the traditions of the fathers. Marriage between uncle and niece was not uncommon; the girl's father found a husband for her among his own brothers. Marriage of cousins was common. This marrying within the family gained two understandable advantages. One could be less uncertain about the quality of a spouse in the uncertain human enterprise of marrying. And there was less likelihood of divorce if a dissatisfied husband had to answer to his brother for dismissing the latter's daughter from his house. And if she did fall victim to divorce, there was considerable comfort for her in having to fall back only to a family she had never really left.

When the girl married she became a member of her husband's family. Since he owed obedience to his father as long as the latter lived, so too did his wife. She became in effect her father-in-law's newest daughter. Often enough the newly married pair, especially if they were quite young, lived in the paternal household. When they did, the young wife took her place as an added daughter in the household managed by her mother-in-law under her father-in-law's authority.

THE RELIGIOUS REALITY OF JEWISH MARRIAGE

Was this marriage a religious reality or was it secular? The question would have been meaningless for a Jew of Jesus' time, for he simply recognized no division in life between these two realms. All of life for him was religious because all the world came from the hand of God. Getting married was one form of faithful response to God's covenant invitation to his people Israel. Marriage in turn was God's gift to men and women as part of his creation. According to the creation poem of Genesis his work of creating came to its climax in the sexually differentiated pair who were given the *officium* of using their sexuality in order to populate the earth and rule it. According to the Genesis parable of the garden the sexually different and therefore desirable creature, the woman, was given to the man as God's gift to him to relieve his loneliness. He made them two and sexually different expressly so that they could become one—even "one flesh," one person before God and the people. The sexual uniting was holy because it was God's creation and given as his gift. Yet it was of this world and worldly, not sacred in the sense of the ancient fertility cults' sexuality interpreted as participation in genital activity of the gods. It was not sacred precisely because it was created and therefore creaturely in substance. It was created by a supra-sexual deity, therefore by one who could not be imitated sexually and in this way bribed by sexually magic ritual.

Because in the parable of the garden God "brought the woman to him" (the man) as a gift to relieve his loneliness, marriage at least in this ancient tradition could only with difficulty be constructed as a contract. An added difficulty against this was the fact that the most excellent religious model for the husband-wife relationship proposed by the prophetic tradition could hardly be contractual. This was the husband-bride relationship of God to Israel pictured by the prophets Hosea (1:1–3:35), Jeremiah (2:1–2), and Ezekiel (16). Common acceptance of this religious metaphor as a normative model, where it was done, overweighed the husband's authority in the marriage severely. The model presumed the wife's infidelity and need to be disciplined; it gave the husband a divine warrant to discipline her. But for this reason alone the model blocked the possibility of seeing Jewish marriages as contracts. As the bride Israel could not negotiate with God, could not in justice hold him to contractual conditions, neither could the Jewish wife with her husband. She could expect and demand that he care for her, protect her, forgive her, but none of these as obligations in justice. As God had promised these to Israel only out of love and in sovereign freedom, so, according to this model, the wife could expect these from her husband only as a gift of his love freely given.

I have said that the marriage itself was not understood as a contract, and that where this prophetic model was in the forefront of awareness, any temptation to understand a marriage contractually was suppressed. But given the contractual nature of the marriage arrangements, especially as these were detailed in the *ketuba*, the inclination to think of the relationship as contractual must have been strong. But since the pre-marital agreement had been struck not between the spouses but between the families, the inclination was to think of these as the contractors.

The solemnization of the Jewish marriage was, in the senses I have explained above, both religious and nonsacral. The *kiddushin*, the year-long trial period (literally "the sanctification"), was sealed and begun with the handing over of the *mohar* to the bride's father. The boy and girl were dedicated to one another and held to sexual fidelity. The bride's intercourse with a third person during that year, but only hers, was considered adultery. In the northern Israel the two were forbidden intercourse with one another until after the wedding feast. In the south, in Judea, betrothal and marriage were in effect the same in permitting intercourse.

The wedding feast lasted a week. All of it was deemed religious, as I have said, but the core of the "liturgical" part of the celebration was a series of seven benedictions read by the father of the groom. No part of the feast took place in either temple or synagogue. No priest, levite, or rabbi had a part in it as an exercise of his office. It was a family affair, supervised and conducted by parents. It was private in that sense but thoroughly public in the sense that the entire village might join in the celebration. Since the groom's father presided over the celebration, it ordinarily took place in his home. The bride's father gave her away, and the groom's father took her for his son. The ceremony ended and climaxed with the groom's leading his bride in procession to his home. If he was quite young, this would be his parents' home.

Joachim Jeremias supplies more detail when describing the condition of women and wives in Jesus' time:

> The wife's first *duties* were household duties. She had to grind meal, bake, wash, cook, suckle the children, prepare her husband's bed and, as repayment for her keep . . . to work the wool by spinning and weaving. . . . Other duties were that of preparing her husband's cup, and of washing his face, hands and feet. . . . These duties express her servile relationship with her husband; but his rights over her went even further. He laid claim to anything his wife found . . . as well as any earnings from her manual work, and he had the right . . . to annul her vows. . . . The wife was obliged to obey her husband as she would a master—the husband was called *rab*—indeed this obedience was a religious duty. . . . This duty of obedience went so far that the husband could force a vow upon his wife, but any vows which put the wife in a discreditable position gave her the right to demand divorce before the court. . . . Relationships between children and parents were also determined by the woman's duty of obedience to her husband; the children had to put respect for their father before respect for their mother, for she was obliged to give a similar respect to the father of her children. . . .
>
> Two facts are particularly significant of the degree of the wife's dependence on her husband:
>
> (a) Polygamy was permissible; the wife had therefore to tolerate concubines living with her. Of course, we must add that for economic reasons the possession of several wives was not very frequent. Mostly we hear of a husband taking a second wife if there was dissension with the first, but because of the high price fixed in the marriage contract, he could not afford to divorce her. . . .
>
> (b) The right to divorce was exclusively the husband's. . . . In Jesus' time (Matt. 19:3) the Shammaites and Hillelites were in dispute over the exegesis of Deut. 24:1, which gives, as a reason for a man divorcing his wife, a case where he finds in her "some unseemly thing," *'erwat dabar.* The Shammaites' exegesis was in accord with the meaning of the phrase, but the Hillelites explained it as, first, the wife's unchastity' (*'erwat*) and, secondly, something (*dabar*) displeasing to the husband; either gave him the right to put away his wife. . . . In this way the Hillelite view made the unilateral right of divorce entirely dependent on the husband's caprice. From Philo (*De spec. leg.* III, 30) and from Josephus (*Ant.* 4.253), both of whom knew only the Hillelite point of view and championed it, it appears that this must already have been the prevailing view in the first half of the first century A.D. However, reunion of the separated parties could take place; also by reason of divorce there was a public stigma on the husband as well as on the wife and daughters . . . ; then, too, when he divorced his wife, the husband had to give her the sum of money prescribed in the marriage contract; so in practice these last two facts must often have been obstacles to any hasty divorce of his wife. As for his

wife, she could occasionally take things into her own hands and go back to her father's house, e.g., in the case of injury received. . . . But in spite of all this, the Hillelite view represented a considerable degradation of women.

. . . to have children, particularly sons, was extremely important for a woman. The absence of children was considered a great misfortune, even a divine punishment. . . . As the mother of a son the wife was respected; she had given her husband the most precious gift of all.

As a widow too a woman was still bound to her husband, that is, if he died without leaving a son. . . . In this case she had to wait, unable to make any move on her side, until the brother or brothers of her dead husband should contract a levirate marriage with her or publish a refusal to do so; without this refusal she could not remarry.

The conditions we have just described were also reflected in the prescriptions of religious legislation of the period. So from a *religious* point of view too, especially with regard to the Torah, a woman was inferior to a man. She was subject to all the *prohibitions* of the Torah (except for the three concerning only men . . .), and to the whole force of civil and penal legislation, including the penalty of death. . . . However as to the *commandments* of the Torah, here is what was said: "The observance of all the positive ordinances that depend on the time of the year is incumbent on men but not on women."

As a woman's religious *duties* were limited, so were her religious *rights*. According to Josephus, women could go no further in the Temple than into the Courts of the Gentiles and of the Women. . . . During the time of their monthly purification, and also for forty days after the birth of a son . . . and eighty days after the birth of a daughter . . . they were not allowed even into the Court of Gentiles. . . . By virtue of Deut. 31:12 women, like men and children, could participate in the synagogue service . . . but barriers of lattice separated the women's section. . . . In the liturgical service, women were there simply to listen . . . Women were forbidden to teach. . . . In the house, the wife was not reckoned among the number of persons summoned to pronounce a benediction after a meal. . . . Finally we must record that a woman had no right to bear witness, because it was concluded from Gen. 18:15 that she was a liar. Her witness was acceptable only in a few very exceptional cases, and that of a Gentile slave was also acceptable in the same cases . . . e.g., on the remarriage of a widow, the witness of a woman as to the death of the husband was accepted.

On the whole, the position of women in religious legislation is best expressed in the constantly repeated formula: "Women, (Gentile) slaves and children (minors)." . . . like a non-Jewish slave and a child under age, a woman has over her a man who is her master . . . and this likewise limits her participation in divine service, which is why from a religious point of view she is inferior to a man.

From a distance of nineteen and a half centuries it is impossible to know with certainty how much this subservant condition of wives in Jesus' time among his people was due simply to the customs of a patriarchal culture, and how much was the consequence of husbands' asserting the lordship they had found granted them in Genesis 3:16b. No doubt the two causes converged and reinforced one another; custom and inclination were justified by what was taken to be a divine decree. And insofar as the decree was understood to be a warrant to punish, the punishment was thought in turn to be for the violation of a covenant. That the violation was also thought to have the first husband's manipulable need as one of its contributing causes could not have diminished the inclination to punish.

CHAPTER 3

Marriage: A Historical Survey

Joseph Martos

The history of marriage in the Christian church is as complicated as it is important. Marriage was influenced by shifts in society, in philosophy, in theology,
and in church organization. Joseph Martos's detailed examination of this history is worth careful study for the light it sheds on the questions religious people still ask about marriage today. Martos shows us where certain ways of
thinking about marriage came from, helping us reflect on them in the light of
these origins.

Here, this historical survey has been broken into three sections: I: Early
Roman, Jewish, and Christian Understandings of Marriage; II: Marriage in the
Western Churches; III: Marriage from the Reformation to the Present. Headings
have been added to make the sections easier to follow. In some ways, each of
these sections would be best explained in detail before being read and further
reflected upon.

Section I, "Early Roman, Jewish, and Christian Understandings of Marriage," shows how marriage could be at the same time religious but not under
ecclesiastical control. This section highlights shifts in marriage celebrations. It
also shows Jesus' teaching on marriage as in opposition to the major religious
teachers of his day. Finally, it surveys marriage in the first eight centuries of the
church.

Section II, "Marriage in the Western Churches," explains the gradual shift
from secular to ecclesiastically governed marriages. In part, the conflict between Roman and Germanic marriage traditions led to more church control. As
differing understandings of what constituted a marriage had to be resolved, so
did various understandings of what the sacrament of marriage meant. These
matters were settled only to an extent, since we find these controversies still
with us today. Understanding these origins helps us reexamine marriage today.

Section III, "Marriage from the Reformation to the Present," explains how
the Reformation's attack on abuses of authority in the Church, including arbitrary annulments for the wealthy, led to a questioning of marriage as a sacrament under clerical control. Luther, Calvin, and other reformers saw marriage
as a civil, not a church, matter, with divorce permissible under certain conditions. In response, the Roman Catholic Church reaffirmed its power over marriage as a sacrament and took special action against secret marriages. Marriage
was a public act, able to be affirmed by witnesses. Forthcoming marriages were
to be publicly announced and then officially entered into church records.

However, questions persisted about exactly what made up the sacrament. These differing Protestant and Catholic positions on marriage were later complicated by civil laws requiring all persons to go through nonchurch weddings and by the question of marriages between Catholics and non-Catholics.

Closer to our own day, changes in social attitudes toward marriage have continued both to challenge the church and to call for reexamining the older understandings of marriage. These challenges and resulting reexaminations have led to new insights into the reality of marriage but also to new questions posed by the complexity of human personality and behavior.

I: EARLY ROMAN, JEWISH, AND CHRISTIAN UNDERSTANDINGS OF MARRIAGE

Relatively early in the history of Christianity, marriage was regarded as a sacrament in the broad sense, but it was only in the twelfth century that it came to be regarded as a sacrament in the same sense as baptism and the other official sacraments. In fact, before the eleventh century there was no such thing as a Christian wedding ceremony, and throughout the Middle Ages there was no single church ritual for solemnizing marriages between Christians. It was only after the Council of Trent, because of the need to eliminate abuses in the practice of private marriages, that a standard Catholic wedding rite came into existence.

Parallel to the absence of any church ceremony for uniting Christians in marriage was the absence of any uniform ecclesiastical regulations regarding marriage during the early centuries of Christianity. As long as the Roman empire lasted—and it lasted longer in the east than in the west—church leaders relied primarily on the civil government to regulate marriage and divorce between Christians and non-Christians alike. It was only when the imperial government was no longer able to enforce its own statutes that Christian bishops began to take legal control over marriage and make it an official church function. In the west, church leaders eventually adopted the position that marriages between Christians could not be dissolved by anything but death; in the east they followed the civil practice of allowing the dissolution of marriages in certain cases. To safeguard the permanence of marriage, Roman Catholicism gradually developed an elaborate system of church laws and ecclesiastical courts, which was challenged by the Protestant reformers as being unscriptural and unnecessary. Today some Catholic theologians and canon lawyers are themselves asking whether it might be better to let the legal regulation of marriage revert back to civil control, without denying that church weddings are important communal celebrations or that Christian marriages are sacramental.

Excerpted from *Doors to the Sacred* by Joseph Martos, expanded edition published by Triumph Books. Copyright © 1981, 1982, 1991 by Joseph Martos. Reprinted with permission.

PARALLELS AND PRECEDENTS

The origins of marriage are as obscure as the origins of the human race itself. Certainly they both started sometime and somewhere since they are both here today. But whether humankind began with an original pair or with a widely scattered population is not known and perhaps never will be known with certainty. And whether marriage began with promiscuity or fidelity, monogamy or polygamy, matriarchy or patriarchy is a historical question that likewise may never be answered.

In prehistoric and ancient cultures, however, marriage in some form or other was already well established as part of the network of relationships that bound people together in kinship and friendship, by occupation and social position. As an accepted custom it had a variety of forms in different parts of the world at different times, and marriage practices through the ages seem to have been just as diverse as the cultures in which they were found. But whether marriages were permanent or temporary, headed by men or women, joining clans or individuals, marriage was always a socially institutionalized way of defining relationships between the sexes, of establishing rights and responsibilities for parents and offspring, of providing for cohesiveness and continuity in society. Such things were important in every culture whether it was nomadic or sedentary in its lifestyle, hunting or farming for its existence, tribal or urbanized in its organization. And since social relationships were so important, the marriage customs that surrounded and supported them were usually revered and sacred, and in that broad sense, religious.

In early Rome, for example, marriage was a religious affair, but the religion was that of the family; there was as yet no official state religion uniting the various clans that lived in central Italy. The father of each family acted as priest and preserver of his household religion, which included reverence for the gods of the home and respect for the spirits of departed ancestors. Besides leading his family in worship, one of the Roman father's chief duties was to provide children (primarily sons) to continue the family religion. In primitive times girls had been captured from neighboring clans to continue the family line, but eventually this practice gave way to a less violent one of arranged marriages: fathers obtained wives for their sons in exchange for a "bride-price" which compensated the girl's family for the loss of a skilled and fertile member. After she was escorted by her father to her new home, the bride was now only ritually abducted by the husband, who carried her over the threshold of his home and fed her a piece of sacred cake, which inducted her into her new religion and established her communion with her husband's family gods.

At the beginning the Roman family was absolutely patriarchal: the father was not only the head of the household but he also possessed all of his family's legal rights; his wife and children had none. He could beat and punish them as he saw fit; he could sell his children into slavery and even put them to death; his wife's personal property became his, and he could divorce her if she did not live up to his expectations, especially if she failed to provide him with male heirs. And although such extreme exercises of paternal power may have been rare because of social pressure, they were legally permissible and they were in fact practiced.

What changed the social status of women and children as well as the institution of marriage was war. When the Romans began to extend their republic throughout Italy and build their empire in the Mediterranean, men were often away for long periods of time, and sometimes they did not return home. Women learned to manage their family's affairs and children began to make decisions that used to be made for them. The older family values were replaced by more nationalistic ones, and the individual religion of hearth and home gave way to a state religion of glory and gods. Many of the traditional wedding customs were kept, like handing over the bride and eating the cake, but they no longer had the religious meaning that they had in the past. The wedding was still primarily a family affair, but now a betrothal ring rook the place of the bride-price, and the marriage was based on the mutual consent of the partners themselves and not on the consent of their parents. At the wedding ceremony the bride was usually dressed in white with a red veil and perhaps a garland of flowers in the fashion of the Greeks, and when she and her husband gave their consent to each other it was customary for them to join their right hands, but there was no legal formula they had to use and there was no special religious significance attached to this action. If they invited a Roman priest to their wedding it was only to offer a sacrifice to the gods or to divine their prospects for a happy future, and if they got married without a family celebration Roman law presumed they were husband and wife if they lived together for a year. But marriage by consent also implied divorce by consent, and by the second century B.C. divorces were not uncommon at least among the upper classes. And like marriage, divorce was a private affair which could be initiated and carried out by either partner; it did not require the approval of any civil authority or the judgment of any court.

But women in the Roman world were never entirely equal to men before the law, nor were they socially equal to men in the Middle East, which was also largely patriarchal. In ancient Israel marriage was a family matter that was arranged by fathers for their children usually when they were adolescents. The Jewish scriptures say little about marriage customs and nothing at all about wedding ceremonies, since marriages were private agreements and weddings were not public religious functions. Most Israelite men had only one wife, but those who could afford the bride-price and maintenance of more than one sometimes had more. Women had few legal rights, and when they were married off they in effect were transferred from the property of their father to that of their husband. Adultery was forbidden by the Torah, for example, not because it was sexually immoral but because it violated the property rights of the woman's father or husband, and even the "ten commandments" placed coveting a neighbor's wife on the same footing as coveting his goods (Exodus 20:17).

At the height of the Israelite kingdom in the tenth century B.C., much of the early Hebrew folklore was collected into books, including the Genesis story of the first man and woman. At the time, however, this story was not taken as a divine endorsement of monogamy since Solomon and other kings had many wives and concubines. But after the conquest of the kingdom by Assyria and Babylonia, the later Israelite prophets pondered the lesson to be learned from that tragedy, and they began to propose that Yahweh had punished his people for not living up to their calling as a chosen people. They were supposed to be a holy people with high moral standards, being just and merciful to all, and not chasing after the false gods of wealth and power. And as part of the new morality that they preached, some of the prophets began to propose that the moral ideal in marriage was faithful love between a husband and one wife. Ezekiel 16 described the relationship between Yahweh and Israel as the marriage of a man who had given his wife everything, only to be deserted by her, and Hosea 1–3 portrayed Israel as a faithless prostitute married to Yahweh, who was still faithful to her and longed to take her back. The Song of Songs extolled the ecstasy of love between a bride and her beloved, and Tobit 6–8 presented the perfect marriage as one bound by the love of one man for one woman. The wisdom literature of Sirach 25–26 described the dangers and rewards of domestic life, and the book of Proverbs 5–7, 31 praised the virtues of the perfect wife and advised husbands against adultery.

The prophet Malachi (2:16) denounced the men who divorced their Jewish wives to marry daughters of the conquerors, but apart from this divorce was an accepted even if regretted way to end an unhappy marriage. If a wife had sexual relations with another man her husband could divorce her, and if he caught her in the act he could have her stoned to death (Deuteronomy 20:22–24). Jewish law was fair-minded inasmuch as it also called for the death of the male accomplice in adultery, but in the case of divorce only the husband had a legal right to demand it. A woman who wanted to be freed from her husband had to ask him to grant her a divorce, and if he refused she was obliged to stay with him. Divorce in the ancient world always included the possibility of remarriage, but in Jewish law there was an exception to this: a woman who was divorced a second time could not remarry her first husband (Deuteronomy 24:1–4).

The Torah allowed a man to give his wife a writ of dismissal if she was guilty of "impropriety," and at the beginning of the Christian era there were two schools of thought about how serious the misconduct had to be for her husband to justifiably divorce her. The followers of Rabbi Shammai authorized divorce only for blatantly shameful behavior, such as adultery; the followers of Rabbi Hillel permitted divorce for almost anything she did that displeased her husband.

EARLY CHRISTIAN MARRIAGE

Jesus said very little about marriage and divorce, but what he did say put him squarely in opposition to both rabbinical schools. In Luke's gospel Jesus' denunciation of divorce and remarriage is apodictic: "Everyone who divorces his wife and marries another is guilty of adultery, and the man who marries a woman divorced by her husband commits adultery" (16:18). Mark's gospel contains the same short statement by Jesus, but attaches it to an argument between Jesus and Jewish religious leaders on the question of divorce (10:1–12). Against their insistence that the Torah permitted divorce, Jesus replied that Moses had allowed it only because the Israelites in his day were so hardhearted. Using the book of Genesis as the basis of his own teaching, Jesus went on: "But from the beginning of creation God made them male and female. This is why a man must leave his father and mother, and the two become one body. They are no longer two, therefore, but one body. So what God has united, man must not divide." In the opinion of most scripture scholars today, what Jesus taught about the permanence of marriage was a radical departure from the traditional Jewish acceptance of divorce.

But then how do the scholars explain the fact that Matthew's gospel contains both the short statement by Jesus (5:31–32) and his argument with the Jewish leaders (19:3–9), but that in both of these places Jesus seems to allow divorce and remarriage (at least for the husband) in certain cases? In Matthew's version of the argument the religious leaders question Jesus about the possible grounds for divorce, apparently trying to get him to side with either Shammai or Hillel. Jesus' first answer is that God never intended the separation of men and women, but then he goes on to say that remarriage after divorce is tantamount to adultery except in the case of immorality.

The texts in Matthew raise a number of questions. Are the passages written by Luke and Mark closer to the words of Jesus, or the passages written by Matthew? What is the reason for the difference between the texts? And what is the immorality referred to?

Many if not all scholars, both Catholic and Protestant, agree that the original teaching of Jesus is found in Luke and Mark. That is to say, Jesus taught that divorce was wrong, that God did not intend it to happen, and that he himself saw it as falling far short of moral perfection. Jesus' standards of morality were high, his call to perfection was revolutionary, and he often presented his teachings in radical, absolute statements. In his "sermon on the mount," for example, Jesus proclaimed that anger is a capital offense, that lust is equivalent to adultery, that swearing oaths is wrong, and that loving one's enemies is right. No less forthrightly he commanded his followers to do good only in secret, to renounce wealth, to avoid judging prople, and to cut off any part of their body that sins (Matthew 5–7). In this manner, then, Jesus also preached an ideal of lasting fidelity in marriage, and he proposed it as a norm for all those who heeded his call to moral perfection.

The book of Matthew was written in its present form around the year 80, and when it was composed its final author (who was not the apostle Matthew) modified the earlier, stark saying of Jesus by adding the words, "except for immorality," to Christ's apodictic condemnation of divorce. Many scholars theorize that the author was a Jewish Christian writing for other Jewish converts, and that he simply wrote down the teaching of Jesus as it was understood at that time in his Jewish Christian community, which allowed divorce in certain cases and believed that it was in conformity with Christ's teaching.

But what were those cases? The Greek word *porneia* can be translated as "immorality" or "indecency," but it can also be translated as "adultery" or "fornication." and some scholars believe that the Jewish Christians continued in the tradition of Rabbi Shammai and allowed husbands to divorce their wives for serious sexual misconduct. Other scholars suggest that the early community continued the Jewish practice of not allowing a pagan convert to Judaism to keep his wife if she had been related to him before they were married. The Torah regarded marriages between certain close relatives as indecent (Leviticus 18:6–18), and according to this interpretation the author of Matthew is indicating that he did not believe that Jesus prohibited divorce in this situation, which might arise if a pagan wished to join a community of Christians who still followed the Law of Moses. No matter which interpretation is accepted, however, it seems that at least some Christians allowed divorce for certain reasons at the time that the gospels were written.

Paul, too, stressed the ideal of marital fidelity, but he also allowed divorce in certain situations. On the one hand he acknowledged that according to Christ, "a wife must not leave her husband—or if she does leave him she must remain unmarried or else make it up with her husband—nor must a husband send his wife away" (I Corinthians 7:10–11; Romans 7:2–3). On the other hand, he viewed marriages to non-Christians as fraught with spiritual dangers, and he ventured the opinion that if a Christian brother or sister was married to an unbeliever who wanted a divorce, he or she might grant it and be free to marry again (I Corinthians 7:12–16; II Corinthians 6:14–18). Ideally the Christian spouses should be a source of salvation for their marriage partners; but Paul reluctantly admitted that this might not always be possible.

Much of what Paul had to say about marriage is found in I Corinthians 7, but it has to be read in the light of his belief that "the world as we know it is passing away" (7:31) and that the second coming of Christ would happen soon. Thus Paul advised the Christians in Corinth not to make any great changes in their lives and to devote their full attention to the things of the Lord. Those who were married should stay married; and if they abstained from intercourse it should be only for a time, to devote themselves to prayer, and only by mutual consent. Those who were single should stay single; it was no sin to get married, but it was better to remain celibate. The same advice applied to widows: it was better for them to remain free, but if they could not get along without a man they should marry again.

About five years later Paul wrote to the community at Ephesus, and this time he devoted a section of his letter to the way husbands and wives should behave toward one another (Ephesians 5:21–33). He accepted the patriarchal marriage system of his own day, including the notion that the relationship of wife to husband was not the same as the relationship of husband to wife. But he saw no reason why those relationships could not be lived "in the Lord," the way Christ gave himself in love to the church and the way the church submitted in love to Christ. Wives should regard their husbands as their head, and be obedient to them in all things; husbands should regard their wives as their own body, caring for them and looking after them. So in the marriage relationship between husband and wife Paul saw an image of the spiritual relationship between Christ and the church. It was, he said, "a great mystery," for it was a reflection of an even greater mystery.

Paul's standard of Christian marriage was echoed in I Peter 3:1–7, and apart from this there is not much more in the New Testament explicitly about marriage. In one of his later letters Paul spoke again about widows, but this time he advised that the younger ones should remarry (I Timothy 5:14). He no longer urged celibacy for those who were engaged in the Lord's work; instead he insisted that the leaders in the church should be men of character, who were faithful to their wives and able to manage their households (I Timothy 3:1–13).

Little is known about Christian wedding and marriage customs in the decades that immediately followed the writing of the New Testament. Most Christians were adult converts from Judaism and other religions, and presumably many of them were married according to their own customs before they were baptized. Some of them were not, however, and around the year 110 Ignatius of Antioch wrote in a letter that "those who are married should be united with the consent of their bishop, to be sure that they are marrying according to the Lord and not to satisfy their lust" (*To Polycarp* 5). But there is no indication that this was a widespread practice; probably most young people needed only the consent of their parents, and Roman law allowed those who were old enough to give their own consent. Still, the idealism of the first generations of Christians was high, and evidently Jesus' statement against divorce continued to be taken as a moral norm.

THE FIRST EIGHT CENTURIES

During the first three centuries of Christianity, then, the fathers of the church did not say much about marriage, but when they did they talked about it as an important aspect of Christian life, not as an ecclesiastical institution. When Christians married they did so according to the civil laws of the time, in a traditional family ceremony, and often without any special church blessing on their union. The early Christian writers implicitly accepted the government's right to regulate marriage and divorce, and when they spoke about marriage they usually limited themselves to pastoral matters, affirming the goodness of marriage, urging Christians to marry within their own community, and warning them not to get drunk and unruly at wedding feasts. The bishops did not approve of divorce but they did not absolutely prohibit it, and they even allowed remarriage in some places that we know of and perhaps others.

Even after the edict of toleration by the emperor Constantine in 313, the great patristic writers said little about marriage compared to the amounts they wrote about other liturgical and doctrinal matters. For one thing, there was no liturgical ceremony for marriage as there was for baptism and the eucharist, and so nothing had to be said to explain or defend it. For another, the Christian teaching on marriage was not complicated, and apart from the periodic bouts with gnostic sects, there were no great doctrinal controversies over marriage to call forth a flood of literature on the subject. All of the bishops agreed that sexual licentiousness and easy divorce were wrong, and they sometimes spoke out against what they perceived as the pagan immorality of the Roman world. They all agreed that marriage was a divine institution sanctioned by Christ, and they sometimes cited the biblical account of creation and Jesus' miracle at the wedding at Cana to prove their point. But by and large they continued to regard marriage as a mundane matter in which Christians were expected to follow the norms of the gospels and epistles no less than in their other daily affairs.

This meant that the legal regulation of marriage and divorce was left to the government, and even though Constantine gave bishops the authority to act as civil magistrates, there is little indication that they were given any marriage cases to decide. Marriage under Roman law was still by the mutual consent of the parties involved (which in rural areas often meant the consent of the parents), and divorces came into court only when they were contested or involved property litigation. But the Roman government itself was concerned about marriage for its own reasons, and since the time of the emperor Augustus it had passed laws to discourage the childless marriages which were becoming more frequent among the aristocracy, and to encourage larger families by means of financial and other legal incentives. Now the emperor Constantine tried to eliminate the injustice of many one-sided divorces by making it illegal for men or women to reject their spouses for trivial reasons. In 331 he passed a law that allowed a woman to be left only if she were an adulteress, a procuress, or a dealer in medicines and poisons, and that allowed a man to be left only if he were a murderer, a dealer in medicines and poisons, or a violator of tombs. Those who abandoned their spouses for other reasons could lose their property and their right to remarry, but the law said nothing and imposed no sanctions against the traditional practice of divorce by agreement.

REMARRIAGE AND THE DOUBLE STANDARD

The Christian bishops, on the other hand, recognized only adultery as grounds for divorce. The local council of Elvira in Spain in the early 300s prohibited a woman from remarrying if she left an unfaithful spouse but said nothing prohibiting a man from doing so. A similar council at Arles in France in 314 declared that young men who caught their wives in adultery should be counseled not to remarry, though it was not forbidden. Later in the century an unknown Christian author in Italy wrote that it was clear from the scriptures that a woman who was divorced for adultery could not marry again, but that nothing prevented the husband from doing so. Thus in the west, many churchmen recognized infidelity as grounds for divorce, and some even allowed injured husbands to remarry.

The same situation—and the same double standard—existed for Christians in the eastern part of the Roman empire. Writing around 375, Basil of Caesaria summarized the current church regulations on marriage and divorce that he was aware of, and offered some of his own suggestions to a fellow bishop. According to Basil, "The Lord's statement that married persons may not leave their spouses except on account of immorality should, according to logic, apply equally to both men and women. However, the custom is different, and women are treated with greater severity" (*Letters* 188). For example, the wife of an unfaithful husband was obliged to remain with him, but the husband of an unfaithful wife could leave her. It was true that a man who committed adultery had to enroll in the order of the penitents, but she could not leave him and remarry even if he physically abused her. If she did so she was considered an adulteress and had to do penance for her sin, but the man she left could remarry without any further ecclesiastical penalty. Even a man who abandoned his wife just to marry another woman could be readmitted to the ranks of the faithful after doing penance for seven years. Furthermore, a woman who was unjustly deserted by her husband would be regarded as an adulteress if she remarried, but a man who was unjustly deserted by his wife could be forgiven if he remarried. Noted Basil, "It is not easy to find a reason for this difference in treatment, but such is the prevailing custom" (*Letters* 199).

Even if divorce and remarriage in the case of adultery was not universally taught during the patristic era, many bishops accepted it particularly in the eastern empire, although they sometimes imposed a period of penance on the persons involved. Those who took advantage of their civil right to divorce by consent and then remarry, for example, were often treated as adulterers in the penitential system, but their second marriage was generally recognized as legal and binding. This is not to say that divorces were frequent among Christians, but it does show that they were possible and that there was no universally recognized prohibition against divorce at this time. In any case, churchmen during this period had no legal say in the matter of marriages, divorces, and remarriages, and so they had to deal with these happenings as pastoral rather than legal matters.

Many of the church fathers were against second marriages of any sort even by widows and widowers, not only because of Paul's advice against it but also because the gnostic movements sometimes tried to prove their moral superiority by rigorously forbidding them. Promiscuity, prostitution, and lewd public entertainments in the cities even led Roman philosophers of the period to insist that the only legitimate purpose of sex was to found a family, and so Christian writers were sometimes hard put to defend why people should remarry if they already had children. Gradually, sexual abstinence became increasingly associated with moral perfection, but most bishops tended to follow Paul's lead by only discouraging and not denouncing second marriages. The sole exception to this trend was divorce and remarriage by converts to Christianity. Paul had sanctioned separation by mutual consent if pagan husbands or wives strongly opposed their spouse's new religion, and bishops still allowed Christians who were divorced under these circumstances to marry again.

Even after Christianity was made the official religion of the Roman empire in 380, there was no great change in the civil marriage laws, though some

Christian writers continued to denounce the ease with which people could obtain divorces even under a Christian emperor. It was not until 449 that Theodosius II passed a law prohibiting consensual divorce, but at the same time he expanded the list of legitimate grounds for leaving one's spouse to include robbery, kidnapping, treason, and other serious crimes, and for the first time it became legal for a woman to divorce her husband for adultery. This change in the law reflected a growing tendency among bishops in the east to interpret the *porneia* of Matthew 19:9 as any kind of gross immorality, as well as their concern that innocent wives should not suffer because of the sins of their husbands.

The outlawing of divorce by mutual consent did not last, however, and later Christian emperors made it possible again. Then, in the sixth century, Justinian brought about a sweeping reform in the laws of the eastern empire, including the laws on marriage and divorce. According to the Code of Justinian the basis of marriage was mutual affection between the sexes, but like any other human contracts marriages should be able to be made and unmade according to law. The code provided for nearly equal grounds for divorce by either husbands or wives, and for the first time in Roman law the children of dissolved marriages were specifically provided for. The traditional grounds for one-sided divorce were reaffirmed, and to them was added impotence, absence due to slavery, and "the renunciation of marriage" by entering a monastery. Couples could also divorce by mutual consent if one of them wanted to pursue the spiritual perfection of the monastic life. In short, permanent marriage was still regarded as the ideal, but the law provided practical norms for those who could not or would not live up to it.

This late Roman attitude was generally accepted by the churches of Greece, Asia Minor, Syria, Palestine, and Egypt, which had already become more involved in the marriage practices of those regions. On the whole marriage was still primarily a family and secular affair with the bride's father playing the chief role in the wedding ceremony. Though there were local variations, the usual custom was that on the wedding day the father handed over his daughter to the groom in her own family's house, after which the bridal party walked in procession to her new husband's house for concluding ceremonies and a wedding feast. The principal part of the ceremony was the handing over of the bride, during which her right hand was placed in the groom's, and the draping of a garland of flowers over the couple to symbolize their happy union. There were no official words that had to be spoken, and there was no ecclesiastical blessing that had to be given to make the marriage legal and binding.

Late in the fourth century, however, it became customary in some places in the east for a priest or bishop to give his blessing to the newly wedded couple either during the wedding feast or even on the day beforehand. This blessing was usually considered something of an honor, showing the clergy's approval of the marriage, and it was not given if the bride or groom had been married before. Then, in the fifth century, especially in Greece and Asia Minor, the clergy began to take a more active role in the main ceremony itself, in some places joining the couple's hands together, in other places putting the

garland over them, and in others doing both. Gradually the wedding ceremony developed into a liturgical action in which the priest joined the couple
in marriage and blessed their union, but still this ceremony was not mandatory and through the seventh century Christians could still get married in a
purely secular ceremony.

By the eighth century, liturgical weddings had become quite common,
and they were usually performed in a church rather than in a home as before.
New civil legislation was passed recognizing this new form of wedding ceremony as legally valid, and in later centuries other laws required that a priest
officiate at all weddings. Marriage in the Greek church (for by this time the
rest of the eastern empire had been conquered by the Moslems) thus became
an ecclesiastical ceremony, and in the view of eastern theologians the priest's
blessing was essential for the joining of two people in a Christian, sacramental marriage.

This same view persists in the Orthodox churches today, for which marriage is a sacrament of Christian transformation, a transition ritual from one
state in life to another which both effects that transition and symbolizes its
spiritual goal. Just as baptism both initiates a person into the kingdom of God
and symbolizes the sinless way that life in the kingdom should be lived, so
marriage unites and consecrates two persons in fidelity to each other and
symbolizes the love and respect that married people should always have for
each other. That relationship, as Paul said, is like the relationship between
Christ and his church, and so just as by baptism Christians enter into and participate in the mystery of the redemption, so also by marriage Christians
enter into and participate in the mystery of union with Christ. It is a true
earthly union of one man with one woman, which both symbolizes and takes
place within the spiritual union of the one Lord with the one church.

It sometimes happens, however, that Christians do not live up to their
spiritual calling, that they do not live up to what was symbolized and initiated in their baptism and marriage, and it sometimes happens drastically and
publicly as in the case of apostasy or divorce. When it does happen the
church does not approve of it but it does recognize it as a fact. Christians
should not renounce their faith, and they should not be divorced, but when
these things happen they must be recognized as realities, and ways must be
found to deal with the persons involved justly and mercifully. In the case of
lapsed Christians, the way is always left open to reconciliation with the
church, and in the case of divorced Christians the way is left open to reconciliation with each other or, if that is not possible, to remarriage.

Orthodox churches, therefore, do not grant divorces but they do allow for
the possibility that Christians might receive a civil divorce and later want to
remarry. Rather than exclude the innocent and repentant from communion in
the church, then, they allow divorced Christians to remarry in the church as
a concession to human needs and imperfections even though this second
marriage cannot symbolize, as the first one did, the union between the one
head and the one body of the church. Thus this second marriage is recognized as a real marriage but it is not regarded as a sacramental marriage, for

it is not a full sign of the unique and eternal commitment that the first one promised to be. It is an approach to marriage which focuses on the liturgical aspects of the sacrament rather than on its juridical aspects, for that is the early church tradition out of which it grew.

II: MARRIAGE IN THE WESTERN CHURCHES

There was, however, another church tradition regarding marriage. It developed not in the east but in the western half of the Roman empire, and it developed along quite different lines.

Initially in the west, as in the east, marriage between Christians involved no distinct wedding ceremony. A Christian marriage was simply one that was contracted between two Christians by their mutual consent and lived "in the Lord." In the fourth century, however, once Christians could practice their religion openly, bishops and priests were sometimes invited to wedding feasts and to bestow their blessing on the newly wedded couple after the family marriage ceremonies were concluded. Sometimes this blessing was given instead during a eucharistic liturgy a day or more after the wedding itself. As in the east, the priest's blessing was usually given as a favor to the family or as a sign of his approval on the marriage; it was not a standard or universal practice. In some places the bishop or priest occasionally participated in the wedding ceremony itself by draping a veil over the newly united couple, a custom that was parallel to the practice of garlanding in the east. Bishop Ambrose of Milan even insisted that "marriage should be sanctified by the priestly veil and blessing" (*Letters* 19), but there is no other evidence that the veiling was ordinarily done by a cleric during this period.

Shortly before the end of the fourth century, however, Pope Siricius ordered that all clerics under his jurisdiction must henceforth have their marriages solemnized by a priest, and Innocent I at the beginning of the next century issued another decree to the same effect. Around the year 400, then, the only Christians who had to receive an ecclesiastical blessing on their marriage were priests and deacons.

AMBROSE AND AUGUSTINE

Ambrose was also the first Christian churchman to write that no marriage should be dissolved for any reason, and to insist that not even men had the right to remarry as long as their wives were alive. "You dismiss your wife as though you had a right to do this because the human law does not forbid it. But the law of God does forbid it. You should be standing in fear of God, but instead you obey human rulers. Listen to the word of God, whom those who make the laws are supposed to obey: 'What God has joined together, let no man put asunder'" (*Commentary on Luke* VIII, 5). Ambrose would not even allow divorce and remarriage in the case of adultery. And his firm stand on the permanence of marriage was taken up by one of his converts to Christianity, Augustine, later the bishop of Hippo in North Africa and one of the greatest influences on the early schoolmen in the Middle Ages.

Augustine's attitude toward marriage was an ambivalent one. On the one hand he viewed it as a beneficial social institution, necessary for the preservation of society and the continuation of the human race, and sanctioned by God since the creation of the first man and woman. On the other hand he saw sexual desire as a dangerous and destructive human energy which could tear society apart if it were not kept within bounds. As a young man he had had two mistresses and a child by one of them, but he had also been attracted by the moral asceticism of the Manichean religion, to which he had belonged for a time. He was the first and only patristic author to write extensively about sex and marriage, and in the end he affirmed that marriage was good even though sex was not.

It was an attitude that was common among the intellectuals of his day. The stoic philosophers taught that strong impulses should be controlled in order to have peace of soul and harmony in society, and that the only justification for intercourse was to produce offspring. The Manicheans and other gnostics were often sexual puritans, condemning sensuality as evil and even forbidding marriage among the devout members of their sects. Christian ascetics like the hermits and monks of the desert sought to quench the desires of the flesh in order to free their minds for prayer and meditation. A number of the fathers of the church, including Gregory of Nyssa and John Chrysostom, taught that intercourse and childbearing were the result of Adam and Eve's fall from grace, and that if they had not sinned God would have populated the earth in some other way. Virginity for both men and women was extolled as the way of perfection for those who sought first the kingdom of God and wished to devote themselves to the things of the Lord. In Augustine's mind sexual desire was evil, a result of original sin, so those who gave in to it cooperated with evil and committed a further sin, even in marriage: "A man who is too ardent a lover of his wife is an adulterer, if the pleasure he finds in her is sought for its own sake" (*Against Julian* II, 7).

According to Augustine, therefore, only those who remained unmarried could successfully avoid the sin that almost always accompanied the use of sex. Those who were married usually committed at least a slight sin when they engaged in sexual intercourse, but they could be excused if they did it for the right reason. "Those who use the shameful sex appetite in a legitimate way make good use of evil, but those who use it in other ways make evil use of evil" (*On Marriage and Concupiscence* II, 21). And for Augustine, as for the stoics, the only fully legitimate reason for having sexual relations was to produce children.

Children were thus the first of the good things in marriage which counterbalanced the necessary use of sex. Another was the faithfulness that it fostered between a man and a woman, so that they did not seek sex for pleasure with other partners. These two benefits could even be found in pagan marriages, said Augustine, but Christians also received a third benefit, which was mentioned by Paul in one of his epistles: it was a sacred sign, a *sacramentum*, of the union between Christ and the church. Augustine read the New Testament in Latin, not Greek, and in Ephesians 5:32 Paul's word *mysterion* had been translated into Latin as *sacramentum*. Augustine took it to mean that marriage was a visible sign of the invisible union between Christ and his spouse, the church. But he also saw a deeper meaning in the word by understanding it in the sense that a soldier's pledge of loyalty was called a *sacramentum*: it was a sacred pledge of fidelity. In this sense it was something similar to the sacramental character that Christians received in baptism. Just as baptism formed the soul in the image of Christ's death and resurrection, so marriage formed the soul in the image of Christ's fidelity to the church; and just as Christians could not be rebaptized and receive another image of Christ, so spouses could not remarry and receive another image of his fidelity. The *sacramentum* of marriage was therefore not only a sacred sign of a divine reality but it was also a sacred bond between the husband and wife. And like the *sacramentum* of baptism, it was something permanent, or nearly so: "The marriage bond is dissolved only by the death of one of the partners" (*On the Good of Marriage* 24).

It was this invisible *sacramentum*, argued Augustine, that reminded Christians that they should be faithful even to a partner who was not. Marriage between Christians therefore should not be disrupted even in the case of adultery; instead, like the prophet Hosea in the Old Testament, Christians should try to win back their erring spouses. If it happened that the visible sign of this union was broken by their being separated, they still had no right to remarry, for the invisible sign of their union, the bond that was formed in the image of Christ's union with the church, remained. And if they did take another partner while their first spouse was still living, the *sacramentum* of their first marriage marked them as adulterers.

Augustine presented a strong theological case for the prohibition of divorce and remarriage, and the council of Carthage which he attended in 407 reflected his position by forbidding divorced men as well as divorced women to remarry. It would be some centuries, however, before the Latin church would turn to Augustine's writings to justify an absolute prohibition against remarriage by either spouse while the other remained alive.

Jerome, a scripture scholar and contemporary of Augustine, spoke out strongly against remarriage after divorce, but he spoke out much more strongly in the case of women than men. He took Christ's words in the Bible as an absolute prohibition for women: "A husband may commit adultery and sodomy, he may be stained with every conceivable crime, and his wife may even have left him because of his vices. Yet he is still her husband, and she may not remarry anyone else as long as he lives" (*Letters* 55). But for men who had divorced unfaithful wives he had a different warning: "If you have been made miserable by your first marriage, why do you expose yourself to the peril of a new one?" (*Commentary on Matthew* 19). He even insisted on scriptural grounds that a man should not continue to live with an adulterous woman, although he was equally insistent that nothing but adultery was a valid reason for separation.

In the opinion of Innocent I, those who divorced by mutual consent as the civil law allowed were both adulterers if they remarried, regardless if they were men or women. He was equally clear in affirming that a woman who had been legally dismissed for adultery could not remarry as long as her husband was alive, but he apparently held that a husband in that case could remarry. Around the year 415 he wrote to a Roman magistrate about a woman who had been carried off by barbarian invaders sometime before and had returned later, only to find her husband remarried. Claiming to be his rightful wife, she appealed to her bishop and Innocent agreed with her: "The arrangement with the second woman cannot be legitimate since the first wife is still alive and she was never dismissed by means of a divorce" (*Letters* 36). Presumably if her husband had divorced her (since women in captivity were usually violated) Innocent would have considered the second marriage legitimate.

Later in the century bishops began to get even more involved in marriage cases as the Germanic invasions led to a breakdown of Roman civil authority. The council of Vannes in France decided that husbands who left their wives and remarried without providing proof of adultery should be barred from communion. And a similar council at Adge in 506 imposed the same penalty on men who failed to justify their divorce before an ecclesiastical court before they remarried. At the close of the patristic period in the west, then, Christian bishops were becoming legally involved with marriage, and there was still no universally recognized prohibition against divorce and remarriage for both sexes. And apart from Augustine, no one spoke of marriage as a sacrament.

FROM SECULAR TO ECCLESIASTICAL MARRIAGE

With the coming of the dark ages in Europe after the fall of the Roman empire, churchmen were called upon more and more to decide marriage cases. Centuries before, Constantine had given them authority to act as judges in certain civil matters, and now that authority grew as the regular judicial system collapsed. Bishops also began to issue canonical regulations about persons who should not marry because they were too closely related. Initially the churchmen simply adopted the prevailing Roman customs, although they sometimes added prohibitions that were found in the Old Testament. Later they incorporated the customs of the invading Germanic peoples into the church's laws. These customs varied somewhat from tribe to tribe, but generally speaking persons who were more closely related than the seventh degree of kinship (for example, second cousins) were not allowed to marry legally.

Moreover, just as the bishops had earlier accepted Roman wedding customs, so they now also accepted the marriage practices of the Germanic peoples who settled within the old Roman provinces. Again these varied from tribe to tribe, although they, too, followed a general cultural pattern. Marriages were basically property arrangements by which a man purchased a wife from her father or some other family guardian to be his wife. The arrangement involved a mutual exchange of gifts, spoken and sometimes written agreements between the groom and the bride's guardian. In many places brides were betrothed ahead of time in return for a token of earnestness such as a small sum of money or a ring from the prospective husband, which would be forfeited if the marriage did not take place as agreed. On the wedding day the guardian handed over the woman and her dowry of personal possessions to her new husband, and received the bride-price as compensation for the loss her family incurred by allowing her to leave it. After the wedding feast that was celebrated by the relatives and other witnesses to the marriage, the bride and groom entered a specially prepared wedding chamber for their first act of intercourse, which formally sealed the arrangement.

Throughout this early period, then, marriage was still a family matter similar to what it had been in the Roman empire, and the clergy were not involved in wedding ceremonies except as guests. Bishops in their sermons and letters tried to impress their people with the Christian ideal of marriage found in the New Testament, and they sometimes urged them to have their marriages blessed by the clergy, but again this blessing was not essential to the marriage itself. In some places it was given during the wedding feast, in others it was a blessing of the wedding chamber, and in others it was a blessing during a mass after the wedding. Some bishops in southern Europe also suggested that the Roman custom of veiling the bridal couple should be done by a priest, but it was not a very common practice.

Just as churchmen were not officially involved in weddings, so also they were not officially involved in divorces when they occurred. However, some divorces ran counter to accepted Christian practices, and when they occurred those who were responsible for them had to confess their sin and do penance for it. The penitential books from the early Middle Ages show that divorce was more accepted in some places than others, but almost all allowed husbands to dismiss unfaithful wives and marry again. An Irish penitential book written in the seventh century instructed that if one spouse allowed the other to enter the service of God in a monastery or convent, he or she was free to remarry. The penitential of Theodore, archbishop of Canterbury in the same century, gave the following prescriptions: a husband could divorce an adulterous wife and marry again; the wife in that case could remarry after doing penance for five years; a man who was deserted by his wife could remarry after two years, provided he had his bishop's consent; a woman whose husband was imprisoned for a serious crime could remarry, but again only with the bishop's consent; a man whose wife was abducted by an enemy could remarry, and if she later returned she could also remarry; freed slaves who could not purchase either spouse's freedom were allowed to marry free persons. Other penitential books on the continent contained similar provisions.

The penitential books contained only unofficial guidelines to be followed in the administration of private penance, but conciliar and other church documents contained more official regulations. Again here these were not uniform, and ecclesiastical practices during this period ranged from extreme strictness to extreme laxness, but at least they show that there was no universal prohibition against divorce. In Spain the third and fourth councils of Toledo in 589 and 633 invoked the "Pauline privilege" in allowing Christian converts from Judaism to remarry. Irish councils in the seventh century allowed husbands of unfaithful wives to remarry, and although the council of Hereford in England advised against remarriage it did not forbid it. In eighth-century France the council of Compiègne allowed men whose wives committed adultery to remarry, and it allowed women whose husbands contracted leprosy to remarry with their husband's consent. In 752 the council of Verberie enacted legislation which allowed both men and women to remarry if their spouses committed adultery with a relative, and it prohibited those who committed the sin from marrying each other or anyone else. It also permitted a man to divorce and remarry if his wife plotted to kill him, or if he had to leave his homeland permanently and his wife refused to go with him. Pope Gregory II in 726 advised Boniface, the missionary bishop to Germany, that if a wife were too sick to perform her wifely duty it was best that her husband practice continence, but if this was impossible he might have another wife provided that he took care of the first one. Boniface himself recognized desertion as grounds for divorce, as well as adultery and entrance into a convent or monastery. Other popes of the period, however, protested against what they considered to be unlawful divorces, and the Italian council of Friuli in 791 strictly forbade divorced men to remarry even if their wives had been unfaithful.

One reason why churchmen became involved in marriage and divorce cases, especially after the popes started sending missionaries into northern Europe, was the difference between Roman and Germanic marriage customs. According to Roman tradition marriage was by consent, and after the consent was given by either the spouses or their guardians the marriage was considered legal and binding. In the Frankish and Germanic tradition, however, the giving of consent came at the betrothal, and the marriage was not considered to be completed or consummated until the first act of intercourse had taken place. Moreover, it was customary for parents to consent to the marriage of their children months and even years before they would begin to live together as husband and wife. This was particularly prevalent among the nobility, who often arranged such marriages as a means of securing allies or settling territorial disputes between them. But it sometimes happened that one of the betrothed spouses would undermine the parental arrangement by marrying someone else before the arranged marriage could be consummated. Bishops who were asked to settle these and similar cases could follow either the Roman or the Germanic tradition in coming to their decision. Under Roman law the arranged marriage was the binding one and the subsequent marriage was adultery, but according to Germanic custom the arrangement between the parents was only a nonbinding betrothal and the second marriage was the real one. Even before any marriage was arranged young people might consent to marry and then claim that they were not free to marry the partners their parents picked out for them, whereupon the parents might appeal to the episcopal court for a decision. In still other cases people sought to rid themselves of unwanted spouses by claiming that they had secretly contracted a previous marriage, which would make their present marriage unlawful. The legal question that had to be decided in each case was: Which marriage was the real marriage? And underlying the practical matters was the more theoretical question: Are marriages ratified by consent or by intercourse? For a long time there was no uniform answer to that theoretical question, and both episcopal and royal courts decided the practical matters according to which tradition they were accustomed to follow.

As Charlemagne initiated legal reforms in his European empire, both church and civil governments made an effort to impose stricter standards for marriage. Late in the eighth century the regional council of Verneuil decreed that both nobles and commoners should have public weddings, and a similar council in Bavaria instructed priests to make sure that people who wanted to marry were legally free to do so. In 802 Charlemagne himself passed a law requiring all proposed marriages to be examined for legal restrictions (such as previous marriages or close family relationships) before the wedding could take place. When the false decretals of Isidore were "discovered" in the middle of the ninth century, they contained documents purportedly from the patristic period aimed against the practice of secret marriage. A decree attributed to Pope Evaristus in the second century read, "A legitimate marriage cannot take place unless the woman's legal guardians are asked for their consent, . . . and only if the priest gives her the customary blessing in connection with the prayers and offering of the mass." Another decree represented the third-century pope Calixtus as saying that a marriage was legal only if it was blessed by a priest and the bride-price was paid. The proponents of reform in the Frankish empire used these spurious documents to support their efforts to outlaw secret marriages, and they were partially successful. Laws were passed making marriages legal only if guardians gave their consent and were present at the wedding.

In the meanwhile, however, Rome continued to follow its own tradition. In 866 Pope Nicholas I sent a letter to missionaries in the Balkans who had asked about the Greek church's contention that Christian marriages were not valid unless they were performed and blessed by a priest. In his reply Nicholas described the wedding customs that had become prevalent in Rome: the wedding ceremony took place in the absence of any church authorities and consisted primarily in the exchange of consent between the partners; afterward there was a special mass at which the bride and groom were covered with a veil and given a nuptial blessing. In Nicholas' opinion, however, a marriage was legal and binding even without any public or liturgical ceremony: "If anyone's marriage is in question, all that is needed is that they gave their consent, as the law demands. If this consent is lacking in a marriage then all the other celebrations count for nothing, even if intercourse has occurred" (*Letters* 97). According to Rome, then, it was the couple's consent, not their betrothal by their parents or their blessing by a priest, which legally established the marriage.

Charlemagne had wanted Roman practices to become normative in his empire, and in the years that followed, a Roman-style nuptial liturgy sometimes began to be included in the festivities that followed a wedding, though it was never very prevalent. Moreover, the pope's insistence that only consent constituted a marriage was initially ignored or largely unknown in the rest of Europe. Hincmar, the bishop of Rheims during this period, decided a number of marriage and divorce cases among the Frankish nobility, and he generally followed the opinion of the false decretals that legal marriages had to be publicly contracted. He also followed the Germanic tradition in ruling that marriages had to be consummated by sexual intercourse, and he allowed that people who had been given in marriage but who had not yet lived together could be legally divorced.

For a while, divorce regulations in northern Europe became more stringent under the impetus of ecclesiastical reform. As early as 829 a council of bishops at Paris decreed that divorced persons of both sexes could not remarry even if the divorce had been granted for adultery. By the end of the century a number of other councils in France and Germany passed similar prohibitions, and the penitential books were revised accordingly. But at the same time in Italy, popes and local councils continued to allow divorce and remarriage in certain circumstances, especially adultery and entering the religious life. Then in the next two centuries the trend in northern Europe reversed itself, and councils at Bourges, Worms, and Tours again allowed remarriages in cases of adultery and desertion.

During this same period, moreover, ecclesiastical courts were slowly gaining exclusive jurisdiction over marriage and divorce cases. As Charlemagne's short-lived empire dissolved into a disunited array of local principalities, more and more marriage cases were appealed to church tribunals. Eventually the secular courts came to be bypassed altogether, and by the year 1000 all marriages in Europe effectively came under the jurisdictional power of the church.

CHURCH CONTROL OF MARRIAGE CEREMONY

There was as yet no obligatory church ceremony connected with marriage, but in the eleventh century this began to change. In order to insure that marriages took place legally and in front of witnesses, bishops invoked the texts of Popes Evaristus and Calixtus in the false decretals to demand that all weddings be solemnly blessed by a priest. It gradually became customary to hold weddings near a church, so that the newly married couple could go inside immediately afterward to obtain the priest's blessing. Eventually this developed into a wedding ceremony that was performed at the church door and was followed by a nuptial mass inside the church during which the marriage was blessed. At the beginning of this development the clergy were present at the ceremony only as official witnesses and to give the required blessing, but as the years progressed priests began to assume some of the functions once relegated to the guardians and the spouses themselves, and many of the once secular customs in the wedding ceremony became part of an ecclesiastical wedding ritual.

By the twelfth century in various parts of Europe there was an established church wedding ceremony that was conducted entirely by the clergy, and although there were numerous local variations it generally conformed to the following pattern. At the entrance to the church the priest asked the bride and groom if they consented to the marriage. The father of the bride then handed his daughter to the groom and gave him her dowry, although in many places the priest performed this function instead. The priest then blessed the ring, which was given to the bride, after which he gave his blessing to the marriage. During the nuptial mass in the church itself the bride was veiled and blessed, after which the priest gave the husband the ritual kiss of peace, who passed it to his wife. In some places the priest also pronounced an additional blessing over the wedding chamber after the day's festivities had concluded.

Along with the church's liturgical and legal involvement in marriage came a growing body of ecclesiastical laws about premarriage kinship, the wedding ceremony itself, and the social consequences of marriage and divorce. The medieval system of government and inheritance emphasized property rights and blood relationships arising from marriage, making it important for ecclesiastical judges to know who was legally free to marry, who was married to whom, and who could have their marriage legally dissolved. In the eleventh century the discovery and circulation of the Code of Justinian led to increasing acceptance of the idea that marriage came about by the consent of the partners, and this idea was reflected in the new rituals for church wedding in which the priest asked the bride and groom, not their parents, for their consent to the marriage. But the growth of the consent theory also led to an increase in the number of secret marriages, which brought legal difficulties about the legitimacy of children and their right to inherit their father's property, as well as pastoral difficulties when women and children were deserted by men who claimed they had never intended to establish a marriage.

In response to these difficulties some church lawyers defended a different theory about when a marriage legally took place, based on the old Germanic notion that intercourse was needed to ratify a marriage. As it was taken up and developed by the law faculty at the University of Bologna, this theory proposed that a real marriage did not exist unless and until the couple had sexual relations. But the opposing theory, that consent alone made a marriage, also had its staunch defenders, mainly at the University of Paris.

Around 1140 Francis Gratian published his collection of canonical regulations known as the *Decree* in which he tried to bring some order into the sometimes conflicting decrees and decisions of popes and councils dating back to the patristic era. He was aware of the two schools of thought about what constituted a marriage, and he tried to harmonize them by suggesting that the consent of the spouses or their parents (in the case of betrothal) contracted a marriage and that sexual intercourse completed or consummated it. His opinion was that a marriage could be legally dissolved before it was consummated but not afterward, and in this respect he sided with the Bologna school. But he also agreed with the Paris school's contention that a binding marriage could be made in secret, without any public ceremony or priestly blessing. In his opinion such a marriage would be illicit or illegal because it flouted the laws of the church, but it would nonetheless be a real marriage, initiated by consent and consummated by intercourse.

Gratian's work clarified but did not settle the issue. In Italy, for example, church courts continued to dissolve marriages if it could be proven that no sexual relations had taken place, but in France the courts refused to dissolve any marriage once the partners' consent had been given. It was not until later in the twelfth century, when a noted canon lawyer of the period became Pope Alexander III, that a definitive solution was worked out and legislated for the whole Latin church. Because it offered a clearer criterion of an intended marriage between two individuals, Alexander sided with the ancient Roman practice that was defended by the Paris school, and he decreed that the consent given by the two partners themselves was all that was needed for the existence of a real marriage. This consent was viewed as an act of conferring on each other the legal right to marital relations even if they did not occur, and so from the moment of consent there was a true marriage contract between the two partners. In and of itself it was an unbreakable contract, but since the church had jurisdiction over it by the power of the keys, it could also be nullified or annulled by a competent ecclesiastical authority if sexual relations between the spouses had not yet taken place.

The decision of Alexander III became the legal practice of the Catholic church. It was reinforced by further papal decrees in the thirteenth century and has remained in effect in canon law through the twentieth century. With the exception of the "Pauline privilege" by which non-Christian marriages could be dissolved if one of the spouses converted to Catholicism, henceforward the church would grant no divorces whatever. Henceforward the marriage bond would be considered indissoluble not only as a Christian ideal but also as a rule of law. Henceforward if Catholics wanted to be freed from their spouses they would have to prove that their marriage contract could be nullified, declared to be nonexistent, either for lack of intercourse or for some other canonically acceptable reason.

But the pope's decision and the support it received in subsequent centuries did not rest only on the practical needs of ecclesiastical courts. Rather, the indissolubility of Christian marriage in the mind of Alexander and later churchmen rested also on a firm theological ground, the sacramentality of Christian marriage. For it was precisely around this time—the late twelfth century and the early thirteenth century—that marriage came to be viewed as one of the church's seven official sacraments.

MARRIAGE AS A SACRAMENT

What Francis Gratian did for canon law in his *Decree*, Peter Lombard did for theology in his *Sentences*. Lombard's collection of theological texts did not solve many of the theological problems of the Middle Ages but it did go a long way toward defining what they were and how they should be treated. Marriage was treated in the section on the sacraments, for by this time in midtwelfth-century France there was an established Christian ritual for marriage which was not unlike the other rituals that Lombard classified as sacramental.

When the book of *Sentences* was first published, however, many theologians still had difficulty in accepting the idea that marriage was a sacrament in the strict sense which was then being developed, and Lombard himself believed that it was different from the other six sacraments in that it was a sign of something sacred but not a cause of grace. One reason for the difficulty was that marriages involved financial arrangements, and if marriage was counted as a sacrament like the others it looked like grace could be bought and sold. Another reason they hesitated to call marriage a sacrament was that it obviously existed before the coming of Christ, and so it could hardly be said to be a purely Christian institution like the other seven. But the third reason was the most crucial, and it was that marriage involved sexual intercourse.

Throughout the early Middle Ages most churchmen held virginity in higher esteem than marriage. On the one hand Christians could not deny that God had told Adam and Eve to increase and multiply, and so marriage itself had to be good. But on the other hand marriage, as Paul said, distracted one from the things of the Lord, and he seemed to suggest that people should marry only if they could not quench the fire of sexual desire. So marriage in the Middle Ages was often viewed negatively as a remedy against the desires of the flesh rather than positively as a way to become holy, and those desires themselves were viewed as sinful or at best dangerous. Some bishops who blessed newly married couples recommended that they abstain from intercourse for three days out of respect for the blessing; others told them not to come to church for a month after the wedding, or at least not to come to communion with their bodies and souls still unclean from intercourse. Most writers held that sexual activity which was motivated by anything but the desire for children was sinful, but most of them also believed that even here children could not be conceived without the stain of carnal pleasure.

So the western theological tradition through the eleventh century taught that marriage was good even though sexual activity was usually sinful. Three things happened in that century, however, which forced them to reexamine that view. The first was the rise of a religious sect in southern France which, like the Manicheans in the patristic period, taught that matter was evil and so marriage was sinful because it brought new material beings into the world. The Albigensians did not accept the Christian concept of God, they denied the value of church rituals, and their leaders attacked the Catholic clergy as corrupt, so they were first denounced and later burned as heretics. And in combating the Albigensian view of marriage Christian writers began to propose more strongly than before that intercourse for the sake of having children was positively good. The second thing that happened during this century was the development of a Christian wedding ritual which, by the presence of the clergy and the blessing they gave, implied that the church officially sanctioned sexual relations in marriage. And the third thing was the rediscovery of the writings of Augustine on marriage in which he developed the idea that marriage was a *sacramentum*. To the early schoolmen it seemed to suggest that marriage was a sacrament in the same way that baptism and the eucharist were sacraments.

Augustine had taught that marriage was a *sacramentum* in two ways. It was a sign of the union between Christ and his church, and it was also a sacred pledge between husband and wife, a bond of fidelity between them that could not be dissolved except by death. It was something like a character on the souls of the spouses which permanently united them, and it was this permanence of their union which symbolized the eternal union of Christ and the church. It seemed to the schoolmen, therefore, that the Christian marriage ritual should be open to the same kind of analysis that they gave to the other sacraments, namely that in marriage there was a *sacramentum*, a sacred sign, a *sacramentum et res*, a sacramental reality, and a *res*, a real grace that was conferred in the rite. It took most of the twelfth century for the scholastics to satisfactorily fit marriage into this scheme, but by the time they did it the Catholic concept of sacramental marriage had become the theological basis for the canonical prohibition against divorce.

DEFINING THE SACRAMENT

But what was the *sacramentum*, the sacramental sign in marriage? At the beginning it seemed to many of the schoolmen that it should be the priest's blessing since in the wedding ritual it corresponded to the part that was played by the priest in the other sacramental rites. Later, others suggested that it should be the physical act of intercourse between the spouses since this physical union could be taken as a sign of the spiritual union between the incarnate Christ and his spouse, the church. Still others felt it should be the spiritual unity of the married couple since this union of wills was closer to the actual way that Christ and the church were united with each other. However, each of these suggestions met with difficulties and had to be abandoned. It was objected that the priest's blessing could not be the sacramental sign because some people were truly married even though they never received the blessing, for example, people who married in secret. The schoolmen who still believed that sexual relations even in marriage were venially sinful objected to intercourse's being considered the sign because this would paradoxically raise a sinful act to the dignity of a sacrament. And it was objected that the union of wills in the married life could not be the sacramental sign because sometimes this spiritual unity was minimal at the beginning of a marriage and altogether lacking later on.

Eventually, because of the growing acceptance of the consent theory of the canon lawyers, the *sacramentum* in a sacramental marriage came to be viewed as the consent that the spouses gave to each other at the beginning of their married life. This mutual consent was something that had to be present in all canonically valid marriages, even those that were unlawfully contracted in secret. Both the canonists in Paris and Pope Alexander in Rome insisted that a real marriage existed from the moment that the consent was given, and theologians such as Hugh of St. Victor argued that a real marriage would have to be possible even without consummation in intercourse since according to tradition Joseph and the Virgin Mary had been truly married even though they had never had sexual relations. In addition, locating the *sacramentum* in the mutual consent kept it within the wedding ritual for most Christian marriages, and it made it possible to look upon the union of wills in a happy married life as a "fruit" of the sacrament even if it was not the sacrament itself.

But the greatest theological consequence of seeing the act of consent as the *sacramentum* in marriage was that it made it possible to regard the marriage contract or bond as the *sacramentum et res*. According to canon law the bond of marriage was a legal reality which came into existence when the two spouses consented to bind themselves to each other in a marital union. Now, in theology, the bond of marriage could also be understood as a metaphysical reality which existed in the souls of the spouses from the moment that they spoke the words of the sacramental sign. Following the lead of Augustine, the scholastics argued that this metaphysical bond was unbreakable, since it was a sign of the equally unbreakable union between Christ and the church. It was not, as in the early church, that marriage as a sacred reality *should* not be dissolved; now it was argued that the marriage bond as a sacramental reality *could* not bedissolved. According to the church fathers the dissolution of marriage was possible but not permissible; according to the schoolmen it was not permissible because it was not possible. Thus the absolute Catholic prohibition against divorce arose in the twelfth century both as a canonical regulation supported by sacramental theory, and as a theological doctrine buttressed by ecclesiastical law. The two came hand in hand.

Even through the beginning of the thirteenth century, however, many theologians found it hard to admit that marriage as a sacrament conferred grace like the other sacraments. The traditional view of marriage was that it was more of a hindrance than a help toward holiness, a remedy for the sin of fornication rather than a means of receiving grace. Many theologians accepted Augustine's idea that original sin was transmitted from one generation to the next through the act of intercourse, and so even sexual relations for the sake of having children were often seen as a mixed blessing. Alexander of Hales was the first medieval theologian to reason that since marriage was a sacrament and since all the sacraments bestowed grace, then marriage must do so as well. But William of Auxerre believed that if any grace came from marriage it must be only a grace to avoid sin, not a grace to grow in holiness. William of Auvergne and Bonaventure both agreed that the effect of the sacrament must be some sort of grace, but both of them also held that the grace came through the priest's blessing.

Nevertheless, under the influence of reasoning like Alexander's and the desire to fit all the sacraments into a single conceptual scheme, theologians from Thomas Aquinas onward admitted that the sacrament gave a positive assistance toward holiness in the married state of life. That grace was first of all a grace of fidelity, an ability to be faithful to one's marriage vow, to resist temptations to adultery and desertion despite the hardships of married life.

It was also even more positively a grace of spiritual unity between the husband and the wife, enabling him to love and care for her as Christ did the church, and enabling her to honor and obey him as the church did her Lord. It was true, of course, that even non-Christians could be faithful to one another and achieve marital harmony, but for Aquinas Christians were called to an ideal of constant fidelity and perfect love which could not be attained without the supernatural power of God's grace.

Aquinas also realized as did the other scholastics that marriage existed long before the coming of Christ, but for him this was no different from the fact that washing existed before the institution of baptism or that anointing existed before the sacraments that used oil. It was thus, like the other sacraments, something natural that had been raised in the church to the level of a sacramental sign through which grace might be received. But this also meant for Aquinas that the *sacramentum* in marriage was not just the act of mutual consent in the wedding ritual but the marriage itself, which came into existence through the giving of consent, was sealed by the act of intercourse, and continued for the remainder of one's life. As a sacramental sign it was therefore permanent, as was the sacramental reality of the marriage bond which was created by consent and made permanent through consummation. As a natural institution marriage was ordered to the good of nature, the perpetuation of the human race, and was regulated by natural laws which resulted in the birth of children. As a social institution it was ordered to the good of society, the perpetuation of the family and the state, and was regulated by civil laws which governed the political, social, and economic responsibilities of married persons. And as a sacrament it was ordered to the good of the church, the perpetuation of the community of those who loved, worshipped, and obeyed the one true God, and was regulated by the divine laws which governed the reception of grace and growth in spiritual perfection. The "matter" of the sacrament was therefore the human reality of marriage as a natural and social institution since this was the natural element, like water or oil, out of which it was made. And the "form" of the sacrament consisted of the words of mutual consent spoken by the spouses, since these were what signified the enduring fidelity which would exist between them, just as it existed between Christ and the church.

Most of the other things that Aquinas had to say about marriage—and this was true of the other schoolmen as well—had to do with the ecclesiastical regulation of marriage, with the laws governing who may and may not lawfully marry, with regulations regarding betrothal and inheritance, and so on. For marriage in the Middle Ages was viewed not so much as a personal relationship but as a social reality, an agreement between persons with attendant rights and responsibilities. Thus Aquinas and the other thirteenth-century scholastics occasionally spoke of marriage as a contract, and in the centuries that followed the legal terminology of canon law was further incorporated into the sacramental theology of marriage.

John Duns Scotus, for instance, conceived of marriage as a contract which gave people a right to have sexual relations for the purpose of raising a family, and from this he drew the inference that intercourse in marriage was legitimate not only for begetting children but also for protecting the marriage bond. A woman was bound in justice to give her husband what was his by right, he reasoned, and so she had to grant his requests lest he be tempted to bring discord into the marriage by satisfying his desires with someone else. Other theologians in the fourteenth and fifteenth centuries also came to accept this argument, and by the sixteenth century it was commonly taught that not every act of intercourse had to be performed with the intention of having children. Married people could ask for sex without blame, provided they did it not out of lust but only to relieve their natural needs.

Scotus was also the first theologian to teach that the minister of the sacrament was not the priest but the couple that was getting married. According to canon law people who wed without a priest were validly married even though they went about it illegally, and according to theology people who were validly married received the sacrament. It followed, therefore, that the bride and groom had to be the ones who administered the sacrament to each other when they gave their consent to the marriage. In the fourteenth and fifteenth centuries this view became more widely accepted, but even in the sixteenth century some theologians still maintained that the priest was the minister of the sacrament, for in many places the priest not only handed over the bride to the groom during the wedding ceremony but he also said, "I join you in the name of the Father and of the Son and of the Holy Spirit."

One thing that did not change, however, was the official prohibition against divorce. In the decree that was drawn up for the Armenian Christians during the Council of Florence in 1439, marriage was listed among the seven sacraments of the Roman church and explained as a sign of the union between Christ and the church. It adopted Augustine's summary of the goods of marriage as the procreation and education of children, fidelity between the spouses, and the indissolubility of the sacramental bond. It granted that individuals might receive a legal separation if one of them was unfaithful, but denied that either one of them could marry again "since the bond of marriage lawfully contracted is perpetual."

Nonetheless. Christians in certain cases did separate and remarry. The hierarchy no longer allowed divorces but ecclesiastical courts were now empowered to grant annulments to those who could prove that their present marriage was invalid by canonical standards. If a married person could show, for example, that he had previously consented to marry someone else, the court could decide that the first marriage was valid even though unlawful and that the present marriage was therefore null and void. Marriage within certain degrees of kinship was also regarded as grounds for an annulment even after years of marriage. But the closeness of prohibited relationships varied in different parts of Europe, and so a marriage that might be upheld in one country might be annulled in another. And if the blood relationship or secret marriage was difficult to prove, ecclesiastical courts were sometimes open to being persuaded by financial considerations, generously but discreetly offered.

III: MARRIAGE FROM THE REFORMATION
TO THE PRESENT

The granting of annulments in dubious cases, for the wealthy and the nobility in particular, was one of the scandals in the Renaissance that led the early reformers to protest against the hierarchy's regulation of marriage. It was not that they denied the sacredness of marriage or disagreed with the practice of church weddings, but they did revolt against the complex canonical legislation that determined who could and could not marry, and they did doubt the justice of the legal system, that allowed dispensations from the law and annulments of established marriages. They could find no justification in the scriptures for most of the ecclesiastical laws about marriage, and when humanist scholars discovered that the early church did not have civil jurisdiction in marriage cases some of the reformers even charged that Rome had turned it into a sacrament just in order to get legal control over it. Most of them called for a more biblical attitude toward marriage, which usually meant a return to allowing divorce in certain cases.

RE-DEFINING MARRIAGE AS NONSACRAMENT

According to Martin Luther, since marriage existed since the beginning of the world, "there is no reason why it should be called a sacrament of the new law and the sole property of the church" (*Babylonian Captivity of the Church* 5). Marriage existed even among non-Christian peoples, and there was no record of any such sacrament's being instituted in the New Testament. The Latin text of Ephesians 5:32–33 could not be used to prove the existence of the sacrament, he argued, because *sacramentum* in that text was only a translation of the Greek word *mysterion,* and in that passage Paul was speaking metaphorically about the mysterious union of Christ and the church, not literally about the marriage bond between men and women. So there was no reason to believe that people received any special grace from God just because they were married.

Marriage certainly was instituted by God, said Luther, but not as a sacrament in the Roman sense. Rather it was a natural and social institution which accordingly fell under natural and civil law, not church law. "No one can deny that marriage is an external and secular matter, like food and clothing, houses and land, subject to civil supervision" (*On Matrimonial Matters*). Thus the church should "leave each city and state to its own customs and practices in this regard" (*Short Catechism,* Preface). The role of the clergy should be to advise and counsel Christians about marriage, not to pass laws about it and judge marriage cases. Civil governments, on the other hand, had a right to make marriage laws because all authority ultimately came from God, and so in the secular world they acted in his name. They could not be expected to pass laws that were in strict conformity with the ideals of the gospel, but at the same time they were morally obliged to keep within the bounds set by the laws of nature in enacting legislation for the good of society.

Luther said that he personally detested divorce, but that as a Christian he had to admit that Christ allowed divorce in the case of adultery, and that as a pastor he was inclined to permit it in other serious cases that seemed to have a scriptural justification. Paul, for instance, had allowed the Christian spouses of unbelievers to remarry, and Luther believed this principle could also be followed if a person acted like an unbeliever and deserted his family. Why, he argued, should the innocent suffer for their spouse's wickedness? In his own eyes he saw more harm done to innocent individuals by ecclesiastical annulments, and he saw a greater violation of Jesus' injunction not to sever what God had joined together when the church courts nullified marriages not on moral grounds but on legal technicalities.

John Calvin, like Luther, agreed that marriage was not a sacrament. "It is not enough that marriage should be from God for it to be considered a sacrament, but it is required that there should also be an external ceremony appointed by God for the purpose of confirming a promise," such as the promise of salvation that was confirmed by baptism (*Institutes of the Christian Religion* IV, 19, 34). But in the case of marriage there was no such ceremony and no such promise mentioned in the New Testament. Calvin also believed, therefore, that marriage laws fell within the jurisdiction of civil and not ecclesiastical authorities, but unlike Luther he contended that governments were morally obliged to make marriage and divorce laws in strict conformity with Christian principles. As far as he could see, the only two scriptural grounds for divorce were adultery and acting like a pagan by deserting one's family. Moreover, in these cases only the innocent spouse should be allowed to remarry.

Despite the divorces of Henry VIII which were granted after the English church's break from Rome, Anglican canon law prohibited divorce and remarriage until the middle of the nineteenth century. Nonetheless, English theologians generally agreed with the other reformers that divorce was possible in certain cases, and so when civil courts granted them from the seventeenth century those who were divorced were allowed to remarry in the church. Initially only adultery, deliberate desertion, prolonged absence, and cruelty were recognized as legitimate grounds for divorce, but in later centuries these grounds were expanded. Throughout all this time, however, marriage continued to be commonly regarded as a sacrament, though only as a sacrament of the church which was not instituted by Christ. The English church also continued to uphold the validity of secret marriages, as the Roman church had, until the British parliament passed a law in 1754 requiring weddings to be celebrated in a church, with few legal exceptions.

ROMAN CHURCH'S RESPONSE

The response of the Roman church to the views of the reformers was slow but deliberate. The Council of Trent did not take up the question of marriage until its last session in 1563, but when it did it attempted to vindicate both the sacramentality of marriage and the church's right to regulate it. In a brief statement presenting the Catholic doctrine on marriage, the bishops of the council affirmed that God had made the bond of marriage unbreakable when he made the first man and woman, and that Christ had both reaffirmed this and made marriage a sacrament whose grace raised natural love to perfect love. Thus Christian marriage was superior to other marriages, and for this reason "our holy Fathers, the Councils and the tradition of the universal Church have always taught that marriage should be counted among the sacraments of the New Law." To this doctrinal statement the bishops then added a series of canons condemning anyone who taught the following heresies: that marriage was not a sacrament instituted by Christ which gave grace; that the church does not have the power to regulate who can and cannot legally marry, and to grant dispensations from these regulations; that ecclesiastical courts cannot annul unconsummated marriages or render judgments about other marriage cases; that the church was wrong in teaching that the marriage bond cannot be dissolved for any reason including adultery, or in forbidding remarriage, or in permitting spouses to legally separate without remarrying.

But the bishops also saw that the reaffirmation of traditional doctrine was not all that was needed to make sure that the sacrament was respected and properly administered. The greatest threat to the sacredness of marriage was the continuing practice of secret marriages that enabled people to enter unions which they later renounced, and that allowed them to seek annulments of public marriages on sometimes doubtful grounds. And so the bishops at Trent decided to take a drastic step. In a separate decree they recognized the validity of all previous secret marriages but declared that henceforth no Christian marriage would be valid and sacramental unless it was contracted in the presence of a priest and two witnesses. Those who tried to contract a marriage in any other way would be guilty of a grave sin and treated as adulterers. Furthermore, all marriages now had to be publicly announced three weeks in advance and entered into the parish records afterward in order to be considered canonically legal.

The bishops' decree effectively put an end to secret marriages in the Catholic church, but their institution of a legal requirement for valid marriages—the giving of consent before a priest and two witnesses—raised additional questions for theologians and canon lawyers.

The first was the reappearance of an old question, namely, who was the minister of the sacrament of marriage? In the Middle Ages the possibility that marriages could be contracted without a church ceremony and even without any witnesses led most theologians to conclude that the ministers of the sacramental bond were the couple themselves, although some theologians continued to think otherwise. These argued that the priest was the minister of the sacrament, and so secret marriages were real but not sacramental since no priest joined them in marriage or blessed their union. Then, in the sixteenth century, a Spanish theologian named Melchior Cano developed a theory that in marriage the mutual consent of the partners was the "matter" of the sacrament, while the priest's blessing was the "form." This implied that people could validly marry (as in Protestant countries) even though they did not receive a valid sacrament (since the required form was not followed). It also implied that the priest was the minister of the sacrament since without his presence, which the Catholic church now demanded, the marriage was nonsacramental.

According to Cano's theory, then, the marriage contract was something separate and distinct from the sacrament, and it continued to be defended by Catholic theologians in the seventeenth and eighteenth centuries who wanted to agree that civil governments had the right to make laws governing the secular aspects of marriage even though the church's hierarchy had sole jurisdiction over the sacramental aspects of marriage. These theologians were in the minority, however, for the hierarchy had had complete control over all aspects of marriage for so long that most theologians and canonists continued to assert that only the church had the right to make marriage laws for Christians. Even though Protestant heretics disobeyed those laws they were not really freed from them, the majority argued, for by their baptism they belonged to the church, and the one true church was the Roman Catholic church. This church's laws, therefore, applied to all baptized persons whether or not they acknowledged and followed them.

CIVIL MARRIAGES

Those who were not under the control of the Catholic hierarchy, however, thought and acted differently. At the beginning of the Protestant era other Christian churches developed their own wedding ceremonies and considered them valid, and as a matter of fact for over two centuries afterward almost all marriages in Europe were church marriages. But late in the eighteenth century this picture began to change. In France the revolution of 1789 brought an end to the ecclesiastical control of marriage, and the Napoleonic Code of 1792 made civil weddings mandatory for all French citizens. During the next century almost all other countries in Europe began to allow people to marry before a civil magistrate rather than a priest or minister, even though most of them did not require it as the French did. And of course governments also continued to regulate the other secular aspects of marriage and divorce (legal registration, inheritance rights, and so forth), as they had done even before the French revolution.

These developments forced the Catholic hierarchy to reexamine the official teaching on marriage and determine more precisely when and how the sacrament was conferred. Technically, according to canon law, all baptized persons who were not married in accordance with Trent's decree were living in sin because their marriages were not canonically valid. But Catholic bishops in Protestant countries began complaining to Rome that this put them in the awkward position of having to regard all Christians who were not married in the Catholic church as adulterers and their children as illegitimate. The popes by this time realized that the Protestant reformation and the civil regulation of marriage were not going to be reversed, and they allowed that the Tridentine decree should be taken as applying only to those who were baptized Catholics and thus still under the legal jurisdiction of the hierarchy.

But what of non-Catholic marriages? Were they, too, sacramental? Even though Rome had reluctantly relinquished control over many of the secular aspects of marriage to other authorities, it did not see how it could surrender its position on the sacramentality of Christian marriage. The church had long recognized that baptisms even by heretics and schismatics were sacramentally valid, and now Rome followed a similar course with regard to non-Catholic marriages. In 1852 Pope Pius IX reacted to the claim of civil governments that all marriages between their citizens were legally dissolvable by declaring that since sacramental marriage was instituted by Christ, "There can be no marriage between Catholics which is not at the same time a sacrament; and consequently any other union between Christian men and women, even a civil marriage, is nothing but shameful and mortally sinful concubinage if it is not a sacrament" (Address, *Acerbissimum vobiscum*). In other words, marriages between Christians were either both valid and sacramental or else they were not marriages at all. The same position was reaffirmed by Leo XIII in 1880: "In Christian marriage the contract cannot be separated from the sacrament, and for this reason the contract cannot be a true and lawful one without being a sacrament as well" (Encyclical, *Arcanum divinae sapientiae*).

One of the reasons why the popes could be confident that the sacrament was identical with the marriage contract was that by this time historical research had shown that through the early Middle Ages the priest's blessing did not have to be given for a marriage to be valid; all that was needed was the mutual consent of the couple. This consent, then, established the contract or bond between the two parties, and so at the same time it had to be the act which established the marriage as sacramental. The theory that the sacrament was conferred by the priest was therefore no longer tenable. Since the contract was established through the giving of consent, the sacrament had to be administered by the bride and groom to each other. And since the sacrament was administered by the bride and groom, even non-Catholic Christians would confer the sacrament on each other whenever they contracted a valid marriage.

But this conclusion raised even further questions for canon lawyers. Were marriages between Christians and non-Christians sacramental as well? If non-Christians became Catholics did they have to be married again, or did their prior marriage automatically become a sacramental one in virtue of their baptism? If non-Catholic Christians divorced and remarried, was their second marriage valid, sacramental, both, or neither? Could a legally divorced non-Catholic validly marry a single Catholic? Could a divorced non-Christian do this? Suppose a Christian of another denomination became a Catholic and was divorced because of this by the non-Catholic spouse. Could the "Pauline privilege" be applied to this case so the Catholic could remarry? Or suppose that two non-Christians were married and divorced, and later became Catholics. Were they free to remarry or was their previous non-

Christian union now sacramental and indissoluble in virtue of their baptism? Questions such as these were actually raised before Catholic marriage courts. They were sent to Rome from countries wherever Catholicism was established, but especially from bishops in Protestant and mission countries. They were cases that had to be decided, and the decisions set precedents for future cases. The ecclesiastical regulation of marriage was becoming more complex than it had ever been.

At the same time, however, the Catholic theology of marriage remained relatively simple. Marriage was a sacrament instituted by Christ in which two legally competent persons became permanently united as husband and wife. The *sacramentum* was the giving of consent, the external rite in which they agreed to the marriage and took each other as their spouse. The *sacramentum et res* was the marriage contract, the sacramental reality which both symbolized the permanent union between Christ and the church and permanently united the couple in the bond of marriage. The *res* was the grace that the couple received to be faithful to each other as Christian spouses, and to fulfill their duties as parents. The primary purpose of marriage was the procreation and education of children; its secondary purpose was the spiritual perfection of the spouses by means of the grace of the sacrament, the mutual support they gave to each other, and the morally permissible satisfaction of their sexual needs.

MARRIAGE IN CONTEMPORARY CATHOLICISM

Through the beginning of the twentieth century the medieval concept of marriage remained relatively unchallenged in the Catholic church. Whatever challenges there were came from without, and for the most part church leaders reacted by regarding them as dangers to the sacredness of Christian marriage. The Protestant rejection of the sacramentality of marriage was one such challenge; civil governments' regulation of marriage and acceptance of divorce was another. The romantic movement in the eighteenth century exalted erotic love over marital fidelity, and popular writers in the nineteenth century applauded the idea of marrying for no other reason but love. To some extent the church adapted, admitting the rights of governments when it could no longer deny them, and allowing that sexual relations in marriage had some secondary purpose besides conceiving children. But for the most part the official Catholic attitude toward marriage continued to emphasize legal rights and social responsibilities, for that had been the European attitude toward marriage during the centuries when the official doctrines were formed.

During the twentieth century, however, western society began to undergo a change the likes of which it had not seen since the fall of the Roman empire and the rise of medieval society. Its roots were found in the Renaissance humanism of the sixteenth century, the rise of secular nations in the seventeenth century, the industrial revolution in the eighteenth century, and the expansion of the natural and social sciences in the nineteenth century, but it was not until the present century that these developments and the changes they caused began to noticeably alter the basic values and norms of western civilization.

Until the twentieth century Catholics could officially ignore the social transformation that was going on around them. The majority lived mainly in the nonindustrialized countries of Europe and in religious isolation elsewhere. Their intellectuals studied and taught the philosophy and theology of the Middle Ages, and critiqued modern ideas from that perspective. Their church leaders concerned themselves with ecclesiastical affairs and remained aloof from the things of this world. But in the present century this social transformation reached into the everyday lives of Catholics, and it affected the ideas and attitudes of Catholic intellectuals and church leaders alike. Now the challenge to the medieval concept of marriage came from within the church itself, and it could not be ignored.

But during the twentieth century the nature and function of marriage in the west began to change. Before, it was a social duty; now, it was an individual right. Before, it was done in compliance with parents' wishes; now, it was done for personal love. Before, love was expected to begin after the wedding; now, it was expected to precede it. There were parallel changes in the nature and function of the family. Before, it was an extended family with three generations of relatives living in the same house, or at least close to one another; now, it was a nuclear family with parents and children having less and less contact with uncles and aunts, grandparents and cousins. Before, the family was the basic unit of society: families lived and worked together; children were educated, trades were learned, recreation was provided, and most human needs were met, all within and by the family. Now, the family was becoming but one social unit among many: people had jobs that took them away from the people they lived with, children went to schools, most occupations could no longer be learned from one's parents, recreation was brought in by printed or electronic media or sought outside the home, and most human needs except the most basic ones of nurturing and affection were met by people outside the family. In short, marriage was coming to be seen mainly as an expression of love between a man and a woman, and the family was no longer needed to educate children the way it used to be.

After the Second World War Catholic thinkers who were influenced by existentialist and personalist philosophy began to reappraise the traditional teaching that marriage was primarily for the procreation and education of children. Contemporary experience suggested that this was no longer so, and social sciences like psychology and sociology suggested that sex had a much deeper significance in human life than biological reproduction. Catholic personalists primarily in Germany proposed that Christian marriage should therefore be redefined to better fit the contemporary experience and understanding of marriage. As Herbert Doms and others saw it, marriage and sex had meaning in themselves, and so they did not have to get their meaning or justification from the children that resulted from intercourse. The meaning of marriage was the unity of two persons in a common life of sharing and commitment, and the meaning of intercourse was the physical and spiritual self-giving that occurred in the intimate union of two persons in love. Thus the primary purpose of marriage was the personal fulfillment and mutual growth of the spouses, which occurred not only through their sexual relations but through all the interpersonal relations of their married life. Children were thus secondary to the meaning and purpose of marriage, and even though they were to be loved and nurtured for their own sake, neither children nor the absence of children affected the primary meaning of marital and sexual union.

Rome's overall response to this inversion of the traditional Catholic teaching was negative, and various Vatican offices reaffirmed the doctrine that the primary purpose of marriage was the begetting and raising of children. But Pope Pius XII saw some merit in the personalist approach to marriage, and in some of his speeches he granted that interpersonal values like commitment and fulfillment were essential even if they were secondary in Christian marriage. Taking this as an official acceptance of their efforts if not always of their views, other theologians such as Josef Fuchs and Bernard Häring continued to explore the long-neglected personal aspects of marriage in their writings. Some tried to avoid the classic dichotomy between primary and secondary ends in marriage and preferred a more integrated approach. Others tried to translate the traditional scholastic teaching into more contemporary language. All of them tried to move away from a legalistic theology of marriage and sex and toward one that was more scriptural, more personal, and more related to contemporary married life.

MARRIAGE IN VATICAN II

This change in attitude was reflected in the documents of Vatican II. The council devoted an entire chapter of its pastoral statement on *The Church in the Modern World* to problems of marriage and the family, and although it did not reverse the traditional Catholic teaching on marriage, it did adopt a more personalistic perspective toward sex. In particular, the council avoided speaking of marriage as a contract or legal bond and instead referred to it in sociological, personal, and biblical terms. It spoke of marriage as a social and divine institution, an agreement between persons, an intimate partnership, a union in love, a community, and a covenant.

Thus on the one hand the council reasserted that "By their very nature, the institution of matrimony and conjugal love are ordained for the procreation and education of children" (*Church in the Modern World* 48). But on the other hand it affirmed that love between spouses is "eminently human" and "involves the good of the whole person." This total love "is uniquely expressed and perfected through the marital act," for sexual relations "signify and promote that mutual self-giving by which spouses enrich each other with a joyful and thankful will" (49). It was because marriage was such a noble and sacred calling that "Christian spouses have a special sacrament by which they are fortified and receive a kind of consecration in the duties and dignity of their state." Through this sacrament "they are penetrated with the

spirit of Christ" which "suffuses their whole life with faith, hope and charity" (48). The sacramental nature of marriage, the unity of love, and the welfare of children all imply that marriage is indissoluble. "Thus a man and a
woman, who by the marriage covenant of conjugal love 'are no longer two
but one flesh,' render mutual help and service to each other through an intimate union of their persons and actions. Through this union they experience
the meaning of their oneness and attain to it with growing perfection day by
day. As a mutual gift of two persons, this intimate union, as well as the good
of the children, imposes a total fidelity on the spouses and argues for an unbreakable oneness between them" (48).

In other documents the council also referred to the traditional analogy
from Paul's letter to the Ephesians. Thus, "Christian spouses, in virtue of the
sacrament of matrimony, signify and partake of the mystery and fruitful life
which exists between Christ and the Church" (*The Church* 11). And in its decree *The Apostolate of the Laity* the council spoke of the sacramentality of marriage in an even broader sense, saying that Christian couples should be signs
to each other, their children, and the world of the mystery of Christ and the
church by the testimony of their love for each other and their concern for
those in need.

As with the other official sacraments, the Catholic marriage rite was revised to allow greater flexibility in different circumstances and more adapt-
ability to personal preferences. Since 1969 couples may choose from a variety
of scriptural passages to be read if the wedding is celebrated during a nuptial mass, and they may use a number of different formulas to express their
consent to each other in marriage. In some places they are allowed to include
poems and other nonscriptural readings which have a special meaning for
them, and even to compose their own marriage vows as long as they express
the basic Christian understanding of marriage. Bishops in mission countries
are encouraged to incorporate native customs into the wedding ceremony as
far as possible, and even to draw up new rituals which express the meaning
of Christian marriage in the symbols and gestures of their own culture. And
church regulations have been revised so that non-Catholics in interfaith marriages may have their own minister as well as a priest preside at their wedding in the Catholic church, a practice that was prohibited in the past.

Since the time of the council in the mid-1960s the theology and the ecclesiastical regulation of Catholic marriage have both tended to become even
more liberal, moving away from a uniformly legalistic understanding of marriage and toward a more person-centered theory and practice. In theology
there has been a shift away from the nineteenth-century identification of the
sacrament with the marriage bond or contract and toward a more liturgical
and scriptural identification of the sacrament with the marriage itself. According to Edward Schillebeeckx the wedding ritual should be an occasion
for personally encountering the felt reality of divine love in and through the
human love that two people have for each other, and for affirming the meaning of Christian marriage as a union in covenant and cooperation. But beyond that, the marriage itself should continue to be a sacramental sign of

God's redeeming activity in human life and of the fidelity and devotion between Christ and the church. Karl Rahner takes this a step further and sees Christian marriage as a unique sign of the incarnation, of the mystery that the transcendent reality of God became flesh in the person and life of Christ, just as men and women incarnate the transforming reality of divine grace in their total love for one another. Marriage is therefore a way in which the church, as Christ's continued presence on earth, comes into being; it is an actualization of the nature of the church in and through the everyday incarnate love that married persons have for each other. For Bernard Cooke, too, love in the family is a sacrament of divine love in the same way that Jesus was a sacrament of God to those who knew him, and in the same way that the early Christian community was a sacrament of Christ to the ancient world. On the one hand sexual love is a natural symbol of the life-giving power of divine love in that it is full of vitality and leads to the creation of new life. On the other hand the fidelity and care that two persons have for each other symbolizes the transcendent meaning that God's love has for all persons, and in the measure that that meaning shines forth from the shared life of married persons their marriage is a sacrament to others of the transforming power of grace.

Other theologians and even canonists have been asking about the practical implications of this new sacramental view of marriage. Is it still necessary to say, for example, that the sacrament is identical with the marriage contract, as Pius IX claimed, and that all the sacramental effects of marriage come from giving one's consent in the wedding ceremony? And is it necessary to hold that the bond of marriage is a metaphysical entity as Augustine and the medieval theologians believed, which cannot be broken except by the death of one of the spouses? If it is not, is the indissolubility of Christian marriage a moral ideal rather than a divine law, as scholars suggest that it was at the time of Jesus and during the first centuries of Christianity? Some have proposed a return to the tradition of the fathers which has been preserved in the Orthodox churches, which regard the permanence of marriage as a norm that allows exceptions in certain cases. Others have proposed even more radically that a marriage is sacramental when it embodies and expresses the kind of love that exists between Christ and the church, and that such a marriage would necessarily be permanent because the love within it would be faithful, forgiving, and self-sacrificing. But if the marriage no longer embodied and expressed that kind of love, it would in fact be no longer sacramental, and by the same token it would be liable to end in divorce.

DIVORCE AMONG CATHOLICS

Married Catholics, however, have not waited for such theological suggestions to win official church approval, and the divorce rate among American Catholics, for example, is now almost as high as it is for other Americans. Nevertheless, according to present canon law they are not free to remarry and so if they do they are automatically excluded from the sacraments and denied reconciliation until they renounce their adultery. For many of them the matter simply ends there, and they cease being Catholics. But others who have wanted to be reinstated into full membership in the church have tried in increasing numbers to have their first marriage officially annulled.

From the time of the Council of Trent the grounds for annulment were quite well defined and they were interpreted rather strictly. Marriage contracts could be declared null and void only if one of the parties did not fully consent to the marriage (for example, if they were coerced), or if they were not able to fulfill their marital obligations (for example, if they were impotent), or if they had not received a dispensation from one of the canonical impediments to a valid marriage (for example, if they were too closely related). In recent years, however, ecclesiastical courts have been interpreting the grounds for annulment more broadly to mean that if a person was psychologically unable to give a full and mature consent or was emotionally incapable of making a lifetime commitment to another person, then a valid marriage may not have existed from the very beginning. But these broader grounds are quite vague, and they are now in fact sometimes used to nullify marriages which have fallen apart for many of the same reasons that civil courts recognize in granting divorces.

At the present time, then, the only way that Catholics can remarry and remain in the church is to have their first marriage annulled. It is a lengthy and involved process, and despite the willingness of canon lawyers to examine every case for possible grounds, most legally divorced Catholics are either unaware that they might be able to obtain an annulment, or they are unwilling to put themselves through the equivalent of another divorce trial, this time in an ecclesiastical court. Over and above this, canonists themselves have noted that if more Catholics petitioned to have their marriages annulled the courts would simply be unable to handle the case load. Some have questioned the way that marriages are now sometimes annulled through what amounts to legal loopholes in canon law, and have been wondering whether the Catholic hierarchy should recognize that church annulments are often being used to legitimate civil divorces. Still others, a minority, have questioned the value and relevance of the whole ecclesiastical judicial system which researches and tries marriage cases, and have recommended that it be dismantled. They would allow marriage and divorce to revert back to civil control, as in the early church, and have the clergy concern themselves only with the pastoral and religious aspects of Christian marriage.

There does not seem to be an easy way out of the dilemma. For the past eight hundred years or so the Catholic church has vigorously maintained that a validly contracted marriage is indissoluble not only by church law but also by divine law. It has become a part of Catholic doctrine, and to change it would call into question the infallibility of the church. During the same period of time the church's judicial system has grown into an elaborate structure of laws and courts intended to safeguard the integrity of marriage. It has become a part of the institutional church, and so to change it would call for a more radical reappraisal than the one that occurred at Vatican II. On the other hand, the historical justification for the present doctrine and judicial system has been called into question by biblical and patristic research. The theological justification for the metaphysical permanence of the marriage bond has been lost in the shift from scholastic to personalist philosophy, and it has been called into question by the view that the sacrament of marriage is not a legally binding contract but a living relationship between two married people. And the practical justification for the impossibility of divorce has been called into question by the fact that the prohibition no longer deters Catholics from obtaining divorces but rather prevents them from remaining Catholics.

But if the dilemma cannot be resolved, steps can be taken to avoid it. The Catholic church has been doing much more than in the past to prepare its members for marriage. In America, for example, Catholic high schools and colleges teach courses not only on the theology of marriage but also on the practical requirements and consequences of being married. Catholic dioceses offer "Pre-Cana Conferences" for engaged couples, and parish priests counsel them about the duties and responsibilities of marriage as well as help them prepare their wedding liturgy. The Christian Family Movement, Marriage Encounter, and similar organizations offer group support for maintaining married and family life. Yet at the same time, these official and unofficial programs reach only a fraction of the Catholics who are about to be married or who are already married. It would seem that much remains to be done if the dilemma is to be averted.

CONCLUSION

And what of marriage as a "door to the sacred"? Is it that now? Or has it ever been that? It is, and it has been, despite the fact that much of the history of marriage in the Catholic church has been a legal history, and despite the fact that the sacramental theology of marriage was for a long time formulated in juridical terms. Marriage has been a sacrament in the broad sense in two different ways. One of them began in the patristic period, the other in the Middle Ages.

In the very first centuries, Paul's passage on marriage in Ephesians was not used to exemplify the union between Christ and the church, but rather Christ's sacrifice for the church and the church's obedience to Christ were used to exemplify how husbands and wives would behave toward one another. Thus marriage was considered to be sacred but not sacramental since the starting point of the analogy was the divine relationship, which was then used to illustrate the human relationship. Augustine, however, took the analogy both ways: he saw the human relationship as a sign of the divine relationship, and the divine relationship as a sign of the human relationship. Still, his emphasis was on the latter, and so he used the everlasting union between Christ and the church to argue for a permanent union between husband and wife. In the Middle Ages the Pauline analogy continued to be taken mainly in this way, but once marriage was understood to be a sacrament in the strict Catholic sense theologians also began to view it also as a sacrament in the broader sense of being a sign of the incarnate spiritual union of Christ and the church. This way of looking at marriage continued in the modern church, and in recent times it has even been emphasized by Catholic theologians who want to affirm the sacramentality of marriage while avoiding the legalism of earlier sacramental theology. Today the analogy is used in books and sermons to bring Catholics to a deeper awareness of what their relationship to Christ and to each other is and ought to be.

The second way in which marriage has been and remains a sacrament in the broad sense is in the sacramental wedding ceremony. It began in the Middle Ages, evolved through a variety of forms, became stabilized during the Tridentine reforms, and is now evolving again. But wedding ceremonies are always sacramental, at least in the broad sense of being celebrations of the sacred value of marriage, whatever it may be in a given culture, as well as in the sense of being rituals of initiation to a new style of life which is honored and meaningful, supported by social custom and religious tradition. In these same ways Christian wedding ceremonies have always been sacramental, for they have celebrated the sacred value of marriage in a Christian culture, and they have initiated men and women into a style of life that was to be modeled on the relationship between Christ and the church. In medieval and modern times that life-style was often understood to be authoritative and faithful on the part of the husband and submissive and dutiful on the part of the wife, for Christ was seen as Lord and master and the church was seen as servant and mistress. In contemporary times that life-style is more often understood to be one of constant self-giving on the part of both husband and wife, for Christ and the church are both seen as incarnations of transcendent love. But however the value and meaning of Christian marriage are understood, the wedding ceremony is always an important and meaningful occasion. Its words and gestures, even the bearing and expressions of its participants, symbolize to the bride and groom and the others who are present the meaning and importance of what is happening and what is about to happen to this couple. They are being transformed, and they are going to be transformed even further. And the wedding is a door through which they enter into that sacred transformation.

PART TWO

Contemporary Perspectives on the Theology of Marriage

CHAPTER 4

Christian Marriage: Basic Sacrament

Bernard Cooke

It was only in the late twelfth and early thirteenth centuries that marriage came to be officially regarded as a sacrament. The Council of Trent (1563) and Vatican II (1962–65) reaffirmed this official teaching. However, relatively early in the history of Christianity, marriage was regarded as a sacrament in the broader sense. The marriage ceremony was only one important element within a larger sacramental process. Bernard Cooke retrieves this ancient perspective, which receded with the legalism of the Counter-Reformation.

The starting point for sacramental reflection is the human context of love and friendship. In filial and loving relationships, God's presence unfolds. Marriage is a paradigm of human friendship and personal love. It touches the most basic level of life. It is, as the author suggests, the basic sacrament of God's presence to human life. In their relationship to one another, the couple are a sacrament for each other, for their children, and for all who come to know them. They "give grace" to one another.

The reader will find in this essay the best of personalistic philosophy, the sacraments viewed as process, and marriage contextualized in a redemptive setting of love and friendship.

Questions for Discussion

1. What is meant by "uncreated grace"?
2. Why can we say that human love is the most basic sacrament?
3. What is the revelation expressed in Gen 1:10?
4. How do we know that God is personal? What does "personal" mean when applied to God?
5. When and how was the sacrament of Christian marriage instituted?
6. The Christian couple are the sacrament of marriage. Explain.

I n the traditional short definition of Christian sacrament, the third element is a brief statement about the effectiveness of sacraments: "Sacraments are

Reprinted with permission from *Sacraments and Sacramentality*, pp. 79–94, copyright © 1985 by Bernard Cooke, published by Twenty-Third Publications, P.O. Box 180, Mystic, CT 06355.

sacred signs, instituted by Christ, to give grace." Sacraments are meant to do something. What they do is essentially God's doing; in sacraments God gives grace. Before looking at the sacramentality of human friendship and of marriage in particular, it might help to talk briefly about the kind of transformation that should occur through sacraments.

In trying to explain what sacraments do, we have used various expressions: celebrants of sacraments "administer the sacraments" to people; people "receive sacraments" and "receive grace" through sacraments; sacraments are "channels of grace." The official statement of the Council of Trent, which has governed Catholic understandings for the past four centuries, is that "sacraments contain and confer grace."

The traditional understanding of grace and sacraments would include at least the following. The grace given was won for us by the death and resurrection of Jesus. Without depending upon misleading images such as "reservoir" or a "bank account," it seems that there must be some way that the graces flowing from Jesus' saving action are "stored up" so that they can be distributed to people who participate in sacraments. The grace given in sacramental liturgy is, at least for baptized Christians, a needed resource if people are to behave in a way that will lead them to their ultimate destiny in the life to come.

Beneath all such formulations—which we are all familiar with in one form or another—there lurks a basic question: What is this "grace" we are speaking about? It is all well and good to say that we receive the grace we need when we come to sacramental liturgy, and that we receive it in proportion to our good will. But what do we have in mind when we use this word "grace"? We have already begun to see that "sacrament" should be understood in a much broader sense, one that extends far beyond the liturgical ceremony that is the focus of a particular sacramental area. Now, with grace also, a deeper examination leads us to the conclusion that grace touches everything in our lives; it pervades everything we are and do.

In trying to get a more accurate notion of grace, it might help to remember a distinction that was sometimes made in technical theological discussions, a distinction that unfortunately received little attention and so was scarcely ever mentioned in catechetical instructions about grace. This is the distinction between "uncreated grace" and "created grace."

"Uncreated grace" refers to God himself in his graciousness towards human beings; "created grace" refers to that special ("supernatural") assistance God gives to humans to heal and strengthen them and to raise them to a level of being compatible with their eternal destiny. For the most part, our previous theological and catechetical explanations stressed created grace as a special help that enabled persons to live morally good lives, an assistance to guide and support them when they faced temptations. There was also a frequent reference to "the state of grace," the condition of being in good relationship to God and therefore in position to move from this present earthly life to heaven, rather than to hell. But there was practically no mention of uncreated grace.

During the past few decades, there has been a renewed interest in and study of grace. We have learned to pay much more attention to uncreated grace, that is, to the reality of God who in the act of self-giving and precisely by this self-giving transforms and heals and nurtures our human existence. Along with this new emphasis on God's loving self-gift as *the* great grace, there has been more use of the notion of "transformation" to aid our understanding of created grace. Under the impact of God's self-giving, we humans are radically changed; this fundamental and enduring transformation of what we are as persons is created, sanctifying grace.

In various ways, sacraments—in their broader reality as well as in their liturgical elements—are key agencies for achieving this transformation. Though the effectiveness of the different sacraments is quite distinctive, each area of sacramentality touches and changes some of the significances attached to human life. As these significances are transformed, the meaning of what it is to be human is transformed; our human experience is therefore changed, and with it the very reality of our human existing.

This process of transformation is what we now turn our attention to, hoping to discover what sacraments are meant to accomplish in the lives of Christians.

SACRAMENT OF HUMAN FRIENDSHIP

Explanation of the individual sacraments traditionally starts with baptism. Apparently it is the first sacrament Christians are exposed to, and the one all the others rest upon; it is the one that introduces the person to Christianity, etc. However, as we attempt to place the sacraments in a more human context, there is at least the possibility that we should begin with another starting-point. Perhaps the most basic sacrament of God's saving presence to human life is the sacrament of human love and friendship. After all, even the young infant who is baptized after only a few days of life has already been subjected to the influence of parental love (or its lack), which in the case of Christian parents is really the influence of the sacrament of Christian marriage.

Sacraments are meant to be a special avenue of insight into the reality of God; they are meant to be words of revelation. And the sacramentality of human love and friendship touches the most basic level of this revelation. There is a real problem in our effort to know God. Very simply put, it seems all but impossible for humans to have any correct understanding of the divine as it really is. God is everything we are not. We are finite, God infinite; we are in time, God is eternal; we are created, God is creator. True, we apply to God the ideas we have drawn from our human experience; we even think of God as "person." But is this justified? Is this the way God is?

Some fascinating and important discussion of this problem is going on today among Christian philosophers, but let us confine our approach to those insights from the biblical traditions. As early as the writings of the first chapter of Genesis (which is part of the priestly tradition in Israel that found final form around 500 B.C.), we are given a rich lead. Speaking of the creation of humans by God, Genesis 1:19 says that humans were made "in the image and likeness of God." That is to say, somehow the reality of human persons gives us some genuine insight into the way God exists. But the passage continues—and it is an intrinsic part of the remark about "image and likeness"—"male and female God made them." This means that the imaging of God occurs precisely in the relationship between humans, above all in the interaction of men and women. To put it in our modern terms, some knowledge of the divine can be gained in experiencing the personal relationship of men and women (and one can legitimately broaden that to include all human personal relationships).

The text provides still more understanding, for it points out that from this relationship life is to spread over the earth; humans in their relation to one another (primarily in sexual reproduction, but not limited to that) are to nurture life. And humans are to govern the earth for God; they are to image and implement the divine sovereignty by this nurture of life that is rooted in their relationship to one another. As an instrument of divine providence, human history is meant by the creator to be effected through human community, through humans being persons for one another.

Though the first and immediate aspect of the relationship between Adam and Eve as life-giving is their sexual partnership, the text does not confine it to this. Rather, Genesis goes on to describe the way Adam's own human self-identity is linked with Eve's. As Adam is given the chance to view the other beings in God's creation, he is able to name them, but he is unable to name himself until he sees Eve. The very possibility of existing as a self is dependent upon communion with another.

Implicit in this deceptively simple biblical text is a profound statement about the way human life is to be conducted. If life is to extend to further life, either by creating new humans or by creating new levels of personal life in already-existing humans, it will happen on the basis of people's self-giving to one another. And, if women and men are truly to "rule" the world for God, they will do this by their love and friendship, and not by domination. To the extent that this occurs, the relationship of humans to one another will reveal the fact that God's creative activity, by which he gives life and guides its development (in creation and in history), is essentially one of divine self-gift. Humans have been created and are meant to exist as a word, a revelation, of God's self-giving rule; but they will function in this revealing way in proportion to their free living in open and loving communion with one another.

Whatever small hint we have regarding the way God exists, comes from our own experience of being humanly personal. Our tendency, of course, is to think of the divine in human terms, even carrying to God many of the characteristics of our humanity that obviously could not apply directly to God, for example, changing our minds as to what we intend to do. Excessive anthropomorphism has always been a problem in human religious thinking and imagination; we have always been tempted by idolatry. Even today, when our religious thinking has been purified by modern critical and scientific thought, we still fall into the trap of thinking that God exists in the way we think God does. This does not mean, however, that we must despair of ever knowing God. On the basis of biblical insights (like those in Genesis 1:19 and even more in New Testament texts grounded in Jesus' own religious experience) we can come to some true understanding of God by reflecting on our own experience of being personal.

For us to be personal—aware of ourselves and the world around us, aware that we are so aware, relating to one another as communicating subjects, loving one another, and sharing human experience—is always a limited reality. We are personal within definite constraints of time and place and happenings. Even if our experience as persons is a rich one, through friends and education and cultural opportunities, it is always incomplete. For every bit of knowledge there are immense areas of reality I know nothing about; I can go on learning indefinitely. Though I may have a wide circle of friends, there are millions of people I can never know; I can go on indefinitely establishing human relationships. There are unlimited interesting human experiences I will never share. In a sense I am an infinity, but an infinity of possibilities, infinite in my completeness. Yet, this very experience of limitation involves some awareness of the unlimited; our experience of finite personhood points toward infinite personhood and gives us some hint of what that might be.

GOD REVEALS SELF AS PERSONAL

What lets us know the divine is indeed personal in this mysterious unlimited fashion is the fact (which as Christians we believe) that this God has "spoken" to humans; God has revealed, not just some truths about ourselves and our world, but about God's own way of being personal in relation to us. God in the mystery of revelation to humans is revealed as someone. What this means can be grasped by us humans only through our own experience of being human together. In our love and concern for one another, in our friendships and in the human community that results, we can gain some insight into what "God being for us" really means. These human relationships are truly insights into God, but not just in the sense that they are an analogue by which we can gain some metaphorical understanding of the divine. Rather, humans and their relationships to one another are a "word" that is being constantly created by God. In this word God is made present to us, revealing divine selfhood through the sacramentality of our human experience of one another.

One of the most important results of this divine revelation and genuinely open relationships to one another is the ability to trust reality. This might seem a strange thing to say, for reality is a given. Yet, the history of modern times has been one of growing uncertainty and strong distrust of the importance and goodness and even the objective reality of the world that surrounds us, the world of things and especially the world of people. Great world wars, among other things, have made many humans cynical about human existence and have made many others unwilling to admit that things are as they are. There is abundant evidence that our civilization is increasingly fleeing towards fantasy, taking refuge in a world of dreams, so that it does not have to face the real world. It is critically important, perhaps necessary for our sanity, that we find some basis for trusting life and facing reality optimistically and with mature realism.

Most radically, a culture's ability to deal creatively with reality depends on its view of "the ultimate," of God. We must be able to trust this ultimate not only as infinitely powerful but also as infinitely caring, as compassionate and concerned. The only ground, ultimately, for our being able to accept such an incredible thing—and when we stop to reflect, it is incredible—is our experience of loving concern and compassion in our human relationships. If we experience the love and care that others have for us, beginning with an infant's experience of parental love, and experience our own loving concern for others, this can give us some analogue for thinking how the ultimate might personally relate to us. Jesus himself drew from this comparison. "If you who are parents give bread and not a stone to your children when they ask for food, how much more your Father in heaven. . . ."

Experiencing love in our human relationships makes it possible for us to accept the reality of our lives with a positive, even grateful attitude. And this in turn makes it possible for us to see our lives as a gift from a lovingly providential God. If we have friends, life has some basic meaning; we are important to them and they to us. What happens to us and them makes a difference; someone cares. If love exists among people, there is genuine, deep-seated joy, because joy shared by people is the final dimension of love. If this is our experience of being human, then our existence can be seen as a good thing and accepted maturely and responsibly.

All of this means that our experience of being truly personal with and for one another is sacramental; it is a revelation of our humanity at the same time that it is a revelation of God. This experience of human love can make the mystery of divine love for humans credible. On the contrary, if a person does not experience love in his or her life, only with great difficulty can the revelation of divine love be accepted as possible. Learning to trust human love and to trust ourselves to it is the ground for human faith and trust in God.

To say that human love is sacramental, especially if one uses that term strictly (as we are doing), implies that it is a mystery of personal presence. Obviously, in genuine love there is a presence of the beloved in one's consciousness; the deeper and more intimate the love, the more abiding and prominent is the thought of the beloved. To see this as truly sacramental of divine presence means that human love does more than make it possible for us to trust that God loves us. The human friendships we enjoy embody God's love for us; in and through these friendships God is revealing to us the divine self-giving in love. God is working salvifically in all situations of genuine love, for it is our consciousness of being loved both humanly and divinely that most leads us to that full personhood that is our destiny. Such salvation occurs in our lives to the extent that we consciously participate in it, in proportion to our awareness of what is really happening and our free willingness to be part of it.

It is instructive to note that when Jesus, immediately after being baptized by John, was given a special insight into his relationship to God as his Abba, the word used in the gospel to describe his experience of his Father's attitude towards him is the Greek *agapetos*, "my beloved one." This was the awareness of God that Jesus had, an awareness of being unconditionally loved, an awareness that became the key to human salvation. And John's Gospel describes Jesus at the last supper as extending this to his disciples. "I will not now call you servants, but friends."

MARRIAGE, PARADIGM OF FRIENDSHIP

Among the various kinds of human friendship and personal love, the one that has always been recognized as a paradigm of human relationship and love, and at the same time a ground of human community, is the relation between husband and wife. There is considerable evidence that humans have never been able to explain or live this relationship satisfactorily, basic and universal though it is. In our own day, there is constant and agitated discussion of the way men and women are meant to deal with one another, and there is widespread talk of a radical shift taking place in the institution of marriage. As never before, the assumptions about respective roles in marriage are being challenged. Marriage is seen much more as a free community of persons rather than as an institution of human society regulated for the general benefit of society; equality of persons rather than respect for patriarchal authority is being stressed. And with considerable anguish in many instances, people are seeking the genuine meaning of the relation between women and men, and more broadly the relationship of persons to one another in any form of friendship.

Questioning the woman–man, and especially the husband–wife, relationship is not, of course, a new phenomenon. As far back as we can trace, literature witnesses to the attempt to shed light on this question. What complicates the issue is the merging of two human realities, sexuality and personal relatedness, in marriage, a merging so profound that people often are unable to distinguish them. We know, however, that in many ancient cultures there was little of what we today consider love between spouses; marriage was a social arrangement for the purpose of continuing the family through procreation. In not a few instances, there was so pronounced a cleavage between love and sexuality that the wife was considered the property of her husband and she was abandoned if she proved unable to bear him children. If men sought human companionship, they sought it outside the home. Apparently the marriages in which something like a true friendship existed between wife and husband were relatively rare.

SACRAMENTALITY OF MARRIAGE IN ISRAEL

In ancient Israel an interesting development began at least eight centuries before Christianity. Surrounded as they were by cultures and religions that worshipped the power of human sexuality, the Israelites assiduously avoided attributing anything like sexuality to their God, Yahweh. At the same time, these neighboring erotic religions were a constant temptation to the Israelites; the great prophets of Israel lashed out repeatedly against participation by Israel's women and men in the ritual prostitution of the Canaanite shrines. In this context it is startling to find the prophet Hosea using the example of a husband's love for his wife as an image of Yahweh's love for his people Israel.

Apparently, Hosea was one of those sensitive humans for whom marriage was more than a family arrangement; he seems to have had a deep affection for his wife, Gomer. The love was not reciprocated; his wife abandoned him for a life of promiscuity with a number of lovers; perhaps she became actively involved in some situation of shrine prostitution. At this point, Hosea was obliged by law to divorce her, which he seems to have done. But then "the word of the Lord came to Hosea," bidding him to seek out and take back his errant wife. And all this as a prophetic gesture that would reveal Yahweh's forgiveness of an adulterous Israel that had gone lusting after false gods.

Once introduced by Hosea, the imagery of husband–wife becomes the basic way in which the prophets depict the relationship between Yahweh and the people Israel. Tragically, the image often has to be used in a negative way. Israel is the unfaithful spouse who abandons Yahweh to run off with "false lovers," the divinities of the surrounding fertility religions. Yet, despite this infidelity on Israel's part, Yahweh is a merciful God who remains faithful to his chosen partner. "Faithful" becomes a key attribute of this God of Israel. Yahweh is a faithful divinity who keeps his promises to Israel. And the husband–wife relation becomes in the prophetic writings an alternative to the king–subject relation that the rulers of Israel and Judah (for their own purposes) preferred as a way of describing the covenant between Yahweh and Israel.

Our particular interest, however, is not the manner in which the use of the husband–wife imagery altered Israel's understanding of the covenant between people and God. Rather, it is the manner in which, conversely, the use of imagery began to alter the understanding of the relation between a married couple. If the comparison husband–wife/Yahweh–Israel is made, the significance of the first couplet passes into understanding the significance of the second couplet, but the significance of the second passes also into understanding the first.

The understanding the people had of their god, Yahweh, and of his relationship to them, the depth and fidelity of his love, the saving power of this relationship, slowly became part of their understanding of what the marriage relationship should be. Thus, a "Yahweh-significance" became part of the meaning of married relatedness. The sacramentality of the love between husband and wife—and indirectly the sacramentality of all human friendship—was being altered. It was, if we can coin a term, being "yahwehized." The meaning of God in his relationship to humans became part of the meaning of marriage, and marriage became capable of explicitly signifying and revealing this God. This meant that human marriage carried much richer significance than before; it meant that the personal aspect of this relationship was to be regarded as paramount; it meant that the woman was neither to be possessed as property nor treated as a thing; it meant that the marital fidelity was expected of both man and woman. Thus the "institution of the sacrament of marriage" begins already in the Old Testament.

MARRIAGE AS A CHRISTIAN SACRAMENT

With Christianity another dimension of meaning is infused into this relation between wife and husband, the Christ-meaning that comes with Jesus' death and resurrection. Several New Testament passages could be used to indicate this new, deeper meaning, but the key passage probably is the one in Ephesians that traditionally forms part of the marriage liturgy.

> Be subject to one another out of reverence for Christ. Wives, be subject to your husbands as to the Lord; for the man is the head of the woman, just as Christ also is the head of the Church. Christ is indeed the savior of the body; but just as the Church is subject to Christ, so must wives be subject to their husbands. Husbands, love your wives, as Christ also loved the Church and gave himself up for it, to consecrate it . . . In the same way men are bound to love their wives, as they love their own bodies. In loving his wife, a man loves himself. For no one hates his own body: on the contrary, he provides and cares for it; and that is how Christ treats the Church, because it is his body, of which we are living parts. Thus it is that (in the words of scripture) "a man shall leave his father and mother and shall be joined to his wife, and the two shall become one flesh." (5:21–32)

In dealing with this text it is important to bear in mind what the author of the epistle is doing. As so often in the Pauline letters, the purpose is neither to challenge nor to vindicate the prevailing structures of human society as they then existed. Just as in other cases the Pauline letters do not argue for or against an institution like slavery, the passage in Ephesians takes for granted the commonly accepted patriarchal arrangements of family authority without defending or attacking them; in a patriarchal culture all authority is vested in the husband–father. However, Ephesians insists that in a Christian family this authority structure must be understood and lived in an entirely new way. The relation between the risen Christ and the Christian community must be the exemplar for a loving relationship between the Christian couple.

This text contains a rich treasure of sacramental and Christological insight that has scarcely been touched by theological reflection. Mutual giving of self to one another in love, not only in marital intercourse but also in

the many other sharings that make up an enduring and maturing love relationship, is used in this passage as a way of understanding what Jesus has
done in his death and resurrection. He has given himself to those he loves.
His death was accepted in love as the means of passing into a new life that
could be shared with those who accept him in faith. Jesus' death and conse-
quent resurrection was the continuation of what was done at the supper
when Jesus took the bread and said, "This is my body (myself) given for
you." Ephesians 5 tells us that we are to understand this self-giving of Jesus
in terms of the bodily self-giving in love of a husband and wife, and vice
versa, we are to understand what this marital self-gift is meant to be in terms
of Jesus' loving gift of self in death and resurrection.

One of the most important things to bear in mind in studying this text is
that Jesus' self-giving continues into the new life of resurrection. Actually, his
self-giving is intrinsic to this new stage of his human existence. The very purpose and intrinsic finality of his risen life is to share this life with others. The
risen Lord shares this resurrection life by sharing what is the source of this
life, his own life-giving Spirit. For Jesus to exist as risen is to exist with full
openness to and full possession of this Spirit. So, for him to share new life
with his friends means giving them his own Spirit. What emerges from this
Spirit-sharing is a new human life of togetherness, a life of unexpected fulfillment, but a life that could not have been reached except through Jesus
freely accepting his death. So also, a Christian married couple is meant to
move into a new and somewhat unexpected common existing, which cannot
come to be unless each is willing to die to the more individualistic, less
unrelated-to-another, way of life that they had before.

Christ's self-giving to the church is more than the model according to
which a man and woman should understand and live out their love for each
other. The love, concern, and self-giving that each has for the other is a
"word" that expresses Christ's love for each of them. The fidelity of each to
their love is a sign that makes concretely credible their Christian hope in
Christ's fidelity. In loving and being loved, each person learns that honest
self-appreciation which is the psychological grounding for believing the
incredible gospel of God's love for humankind. In their relationship to one
another, and in proportion as that relationship in a given set of circumstances
truly translates Christ's own self-giving, the couple are a sacrament to each
other and a sacrament to those who know them.

In this sacramental relationship, a Christian man and woman are truly
"grace" to one another; they express and make present that uncreated grace
that is God's creative self-giving. Though there certainly is mystery in this loving divine presence, it is revealed in the new meanings discovered in the lived
relationship between Christian wife and husband. The trust required by their
unqualified intimacy with one another and the hope of genuine acceptance by
the other, which accompanies this intimacy, help bring about a new level of
personal maturity. But this trust and hope are grounded in the Christian faith
insight that open-ended love can lead to new and richer life. Perhaps even
more basically, a Christian couple can commit themselves to this relationship,

believing that it will not ultimately be negated by death. Instead, Christian hope in risen life supports the almost instinctive feeling of lovers that "love is stronger than death."

Psychological studies have detailed the ways a truly mature married relationship, one that integrates personal and sexual love, fosters the human growth of the two people, and it is not our intent to repeat such reflections here. But these same studies point also to the indispensable role that continuing and deepening communication with each other plays in the evolution of such a relationship. In a Christian marriage the communication is meant to embrace the sharing of faith and hope in that salvation that comes through Jesus. The Christian family is meant to be the most basic instance of Christian community, people bonded together by their shared relationship to the risen Jesus.

All of us can think of marriages where this ideal has been to quite an extent realized, where husband and wife have over the years supported and enriched one another's belief and trust in the reality and importance of Christianity. Various challenges can come to Christian faith, if it is real faith and not just a superficial acceptance of a religious pattern. These challenges can change shape over the years, they can come with suffering or disappointments or disillusionment or boredom, they can come to focus with the need to face the inevitability of death. At such times of crisis, when faith can either deepen or weaken, the witness of a loved one's faith and hope is a powerful and sometimes indispensable preaching of the gospel.

Perhaps the most difficult thing to believe over the course of a lifetime is that one is important enough to be loved by God. Nothing makes this more credible than the discovery of being important to and loved by another human. The fidelity of one's lover, not just in the critically important area of sexual fidelity but also in the broader context of not betraying love by selfishness or exploitation or pettiness or dishonesty or disinterestedness or insensitivity, makes more credible the Christian trust in God's unfailing concern.

One could go on indefinitely describing how a Christian couple "give grace" to each other, because the contribution to each other's life of grace (their being human in relation to God) involves the whole of their life together. The sacrament of Christian marriage is much more than the marriage ceremony in the church; that ceremony is only one important element in the sacrament. Christian marriage is the woman and the man in their unfolding relationship to each other as Christians; they are sacrament for each other, sacrament to their children, and sacrament to all those who come to know them. The meaning of what they are for each other should become for them and others a key part of what it means to be a human being.

SUMMARY

If we restrict "sacrament" to certain liturgical rituals, it is logical to think of baptism as the initial sacrament. If, however, we realize the fundamental sacramentality of all human experience and the way Jesus transformed this sacramentality, there is good reason for seeing human friendship as the most basic sacrament of God's saving presence to human life. Human friendship reflects and makes credible the reality of God's love for humans; human friendship gives us some insight into the Christian revelation that God is a "self."

Within human friendship there is a paradigm role played by the love between a Christian wife and husband. Building on the transformation of a marriage's meaning that began with the Israelitic prophets, Christianity sees the love relationship of a Christian couple as sacramentalizing the relationship between Christ and the church, between God and humankind. God's saving action consists essentially in the divine self-giving. This is expressed by and present in the couple's self-gift to each other; they are sacrament to each other, to their children, and to their fellow Christians. This sacramentality, though specially instanced in Christian marriage, extends to all genuine human friendship.

CHAPTER 5

"Nuptial Pentecost":
Theological Reflections on the
Presence and Action of the Holy Spirit in
Christian Marriage

Julie McCarty

In this prize-winning essay, Julie McCarty retrieves and re-presents marriage as a way of the Spirit. The daily interaction of spouse and children can encourage ongoing metanoia. It can be a means for inner transformation of oneself and outer transformation of the world.

McCarty presents a theology of marriage rooted in the love of God. She calls for a renewed awareness of the role of the Spirit in sacramental marriage. Initially, she theologically grounds her perspective in wedding liturgies, modern church documents, and the sacred quotidian of married life. The article proceeds to explore three images of the Spirit. These images give rise to new insights and contribute to a renewed theology of marriage.

McCarty's wonderfully suggestive images are (1) the Spirit as "bonding agent" of Christian marriage, the principle of communion, making us one without destroying our unique personhood; (2) the Spirit as "breath," the life-giver in marriage, breathing life in marital relations, giving life to children, and pouring life out toward others in community; (3) the Spirit as "fire," when open to the workings of the Spirit, marriage can be holy ground. It can be a purifying and sanctifying agent, like gold that is "tested by fire" (1 Pet. 1:7). It is the place to practice Christian virtues and to live the evangelical counsels. We can speak, then, of the "gift of marriage." In light of this renewed awareness of the presence of the Spirit in Christian marriage, McCarty concludes her essay with some creative pastoral suggestions for liturgists, homilists, theologians, and pastoral ministers.

Questions for Discussion

1. How can we, with the assistance of the Spirit, negotiate a communion of persons that protects and fosters a healthy diversity in marriage?
2. From a spiritual point of view, what do we mean when we claim that marriage is an ascetical feat?

3. Can we say of marriages that end in divorce that the relationship "died"? The breath of the Spirit no longer animates them?

4. What are some examples of ongoing metanoia in marriage? Ongoing sanctification?

Try this experiment sometime: Ask a Catholic couple with a good, stable relationship how the Holy Spirit helps them with their marriage. Ask several couples. Next, ask a priest, pastoral minister, or even a theology professor how the Spirit is present in the sacrament of marriage. If your results resemble mine, chances are the reactions to these questions will range from puzzlement to a thoughtful, silent stare. After a time, you may receive a vague reply about God being the "third partner" of the marriage.

Whether working with engaged couples in a parish marriage preparation program or talking with seasoned married couples in my parish, I am often struck by how little awareness there is that marriage is a *spiritual* way of life, a means both for inner transformation of oneself and for outer transformation of the world. When a parish committee working on long-range goals for "family ministry" suddenly awoke to the idea that *ministry* is, for them, something to be done inside their own homes and not just on church property, bells and whistles went off. They expressed surprise in the realization that listening lovingly to their spouses or reading stories to their children were forms of *ministry*. They began to connect the sacraments of the home, such as forgiving one another, breaking bread together, and caring for each other in sickness, with the Church's seven sacraments.

The excitement that this group felt came from seeing that *spiritual* or holy things were happening in their lives at home and not just at church. The realization that they were loving God through loving their families made them understand that they were not second-class citizens in the kingdom of God.

Marriage is called "sacrament," a word grounded in the word "sacred," or "holy." Yet, it is my belief that we have yet to uncover the theological riches embedded in marriages that are permeated with the living love of Christ. We Catholics still subconsciously think of celibacy as the way to holiness, and marriage as a concession to human weakness, a fleshly, worldly affair. Yet, I believe that the path of religious celibacy is only as holy as a given person makes it. The same can be said of marriage. There are those who marry and live destructive lives, and there are those with marriages steeped and overflowing with sanctity.

Marriages that are truly *sacramental* contain a good deal of theological meaning that has yet to be fully explored. Far from being a "lesser state," marriage has its origins in God's own creativity when the Creator designed man and woman to be harmonious partners. The disharmony between the sexes

---

Julie McCarty is a freelance writer and the author of *The Pearl of Great Price: Gospel Wisdom for Christian Marriage* (Liturgical Press, July 2007). "Nuptial Pentecost" originally appeared in *New Theology Review*, 16, 1 (February 2003) 57–67. Reprinted with permission of the author.

erupted after sin entered the scene and the blaming game began. The redemptive work of Christ that restores us to grace also works to heal the brokenness between the sexes in the sacrament of marriage (Evdokimov 1995, 32).

Yet, in our theology of marriage, we have virtually overlooked the presence and the action of the Holy Spirit in any genuinely *Christian* marriage. We relate marriage to the Father's creative action or to the sacrificial love Christ has for the Church, but we have yet to ponder the rich meaning of the Spirit dwelling in the hearts of Christian spouses by virtue of their baptism.

Keeping in mind that the persons of the Trinity work together, how does the Spirit help couples to live marriages permeated with the love of God? After a brief theological grounding, this article explores three images of the Spirit: the Spirit as "bonding agent" (principle of *communio* in marriage), the Spirit as "breath" (life-giver in marriage), and the Spirit as "fire" (sanctifying agent in marriage). These images lead to new insights that contribute to our theology of marriage and have practical implications for pastoral ministry.

THE "NUPTIAL PENTECOST" IN THE WEDDING LITURGY

Traditional theology texts on pneumatology or sacramental theology—or even very current ones—generally lack any specific references to the dynamic action of the Spirit in Christian marriage. Nevertheless, a careful examination of Christian marriage rites reveals that this idea was not completely unknown.

In the Eastern Orthodox tradition, the wedding ceremony culminates in the crowning ceremony, during which the priest places garlands or gold crowns upon the heads of both the bride and the groom. Among the many spiritual meanings associated with the crowning, theologians identify this moment as the *epiclesis* (invocation of the Spirit) of the sacrament (Congar 1999, 269; Evdokimov 1995, 153; Petras 1981, 232–34). Orthodox theologian Paul Evdokimov describes the crowning as the "nuptial Pentecost," the outpouring of the Spirit for the good of this particular couple:

> In the Gospel, every work of Christ reaches completion in glory; its Fulfillment is manifested and glorified by the Holy Spirit. Standing in the presence of Christ, the betrothed receive the glory that achieves the establishment of their unique being, and the priest raises them to this glory through the invocation (*epiclesis*) of the sacrament: "O Lord our God, crown them with glory and honor." This is the effective moment of the sacrament, the time of the nuptial Pentecost, the descent of the Holy Spirit making a new creation (1995, 153).

In the Coptic marriage rite, this "nuptial Pentecost" is also evident in the anointing of the bride and groom with oil. Here, the prayers and songs describe the oil as the "oil of sanctification for your servants." Gifts associated with this "oil of holy spirits" are many, among them truth, justice, purity, beauty, happiness, strength, and "renewal and restoration in body, soul and spirit" (Searle and Stevenson 1992, 70, 92–93). This anointing of the couple is "a sign that marriage is a Christian vocation, and therefore an extension of baptism" (Stevenson 1999, 180).

In the Western Church, the need for the assistance of the Holy Spirit in the sacrament of marriage was not completely unknown. Kenneth Stevenson notes that in medieval Europe, some northern rites interspersed prayers from the Votive Mass of the Trinity with prayers of the nuptial Mass. A similar interplay of the Votive Mass of the Holy Spirit and the marriage rite occurred in some French and Spanish dioceses. In fact, the Metz rite of 1543, local to a bilingual area of France, ends with the song *Veni Creator* (1987, 204).

Italian theologian Carlo Rocchetta relates that the "Mass of the Holy Spirit" was allowed in pre- and post-Tridentine times as *preparation* for the sacrament of marriage. Rocchetta also observes that some rituals "referred to a form of *epiclesis* or invocation of the Spirit to be made over the wedding rings, [and] at other times there was reference to a blessing with the laying of hands on the heads of the spouses to evoke the consecrating action of the Spirit" (1998, 175).

THE "NUPTIAL PENTECOST" IN THE MODERN CATHOLIC CHURCH

The Holy Spirit's role in marriage has been quietly seeping into the collective church consciousness in recent years. The Vatican II teachings on marriage include a subtle reference to the Spirit's presence in marriage in *Gaudium et Spes* (The Church in the Modern World), using the phrase "spirit of Christ," a phrase that theologian Yves Congar notes is Vatican II shorthand for the Holy Spirit (1999, 167). In a section dealing with marital love, the spouses are described as consecrated for marriage and "penetrated with the spirit of Christ" (no. 48).

One sometimes finds references to the wedding *epiclesis* in newer church writings. In his 1981 apostolic exhortation *Familiaris Consortio* (The Role of the Christian Family in the Modern World), Pope John Paul II notes that "the Holy Spirit who is poured out in the sacramental celebration offers Christian couples the gift of a new communion of love that is the living and real image of that unique unity which makes of the Church the indivisible Mystical Body of the Lord Jesus" (no. 33). In his 1994 Letter to Families, Pope John Paul II refers at least four times to the *epiclesis* of the wedding ceremony (nos. 4, 7, 11, 20). The *Catechism of the Catholic Church* teaches, "In the epiclesis of this sacrament [marriage] the spouses receive the Holy Spirit as the communion of love of Christ and the Church. The Holy Spirit is the seal of their covenant, the ever-available source of their love and the strength to renew their fidelity" (no. 1623).

The *epiclesis* to which the *Catechism* refers is found in the *Ordo Celebrandi Matrimonium* (Order of Celebrating Marriage), the officially approved, revised marriage rite of 1991. Although not yet available in English, this rite reveals a renewed awareness of the pneumatological dimension of marriage. Jan Michael Joncas gives us these rough translations of the revised nuptial blessings:

> Form A: ". . . send forth upon them the grace of the Holy Spirit, so that, with your love diffused in their hearts, they may remain faithful in the conjugal covenant" (1996, 219).
>
> Form B: "Upon these servants of yours (N. and N.) we pray, extend your [right] hand and pour out the power of the Holy Spirit in their hearts . . ." (1996, 223).
>
> Form C (Version 1, 2): "May your copious blessing come down upon this bride N., Lord, and upon her partner for life, N., and may the power of your Holy Spirit inflame their hearts from above . . ." (1996, 225).
>
> [Form C, Version 3, and Form D involve a lay presider and therefore do not contain an explicit *epiclesis*.]

Theologians Michael Joncas, German Martinez, and Carlo Rocchetta have determined that these nuptial blessings contain "explicit epicleses," that is, we are asking the Holy Spirit to pour out gifts upon this bridal couple for the good of their marriage (Joncas 1996, 220, 223, 226; Martinez 1995, 129; Rocchetta 1998, 176).

The inclusion of explicit *epicleses* in the 1991 rite indicates that we believe that the Holy Spirit acts in sacramental marriage. Keeping in mind that marriage is an ongoing process flowing beyond the wedding day, how is the Spirit a dynamic part of the couple's daily married life?

THE "NUPTIAL PENTECOST" IN THE DAILY LIFE OF MARRIED COUPLES

Theologizing about the role of the Holy Spirit in marriage is a task that has barely begun in the Western Church (Rocchetta 1998, 175). Because of this, I propose that certain parameters be drawn for venturing into this new territory.

First, when I use the term *sacramental marriage* in this article, I am referring to marriages in which both partners are baptized and actively engaged in following Christ. This is not to imply that the Spirit is completely absent from other marriages; rather, it is to provide a starting point for theological reflection.

Second, when I speak of "marriage," I am not talking about the wedding day but rather the couple's relationship, with its own historic unfolding in time, tentatively initialized in courtship, formally entered into on the wedding day, tested and deepened in the years that follow.

Third, nothing written herein is meant to imply that the Spirit works apart from the other two persons of the Trinity. It is only for the sake of theological meditation that we are looking at the Spirit distinctly.

Fourth, it is worth noting that any comparisons between created things (the images of "bonding agent," "breath," and "fire") and the Holy Spirit will not by any means exhaust the richness of the Spirit. The Fourth Lateran Council reminds us that our comparisons between created realities and God will always fall short of the awesome mystery of God.

Finally, as Patricia O'Connell Killen and John de Beer explain in *The Art of Theological Reflection*, images can help us discover new meanings. As they note, when images are considered in the light of Scripture, tradition, and life experience, new discoveries and ideas for active, positive steps emerge.

THE SPIRIT AS THE "BONDING AGENT" OF CHRISTIAN MARRIAGE

A bonding agent is something that gathers two or more objects together, like glue, a cord, or a ligament. The Holy Spirit is the "bonding agent" of the Church, the love that gathers us together into one ecclesial Body of Christ. However, this "bonding" is not a side-by-side type of gathering, but rather an interpenetration of persons that exist in *communio*. This type of bonding agent penetrates and permeates the persons being gathered, like the liquid ingredients in a cake mix penetrate and gather all the dry ingredients into one batter to be baked. As *Lumen Gentium* reminds us, the Holy Spirit is the principle of communion, the person of the Trinity sent forth as the crowning act of Christ's paschal mystery to draw together the followers of Christ into one ecclesial Body of Christ (no. 13). This *communio of persons* is a unity that protects and fosters a healthy diversity of gifts and cultural expressions, maintaining a harmonious balance between the uniqueness of the human individual and a healthy communal whole.

The Christian tradition has often portrayed the Spirit as the bond of love or *nexus* that exists in the pure, mutually giving and mutually loving relationship of the Father and the Son (Congar 1999, 85–90). One example of this is found in Augustine's reflections upon the idea that God *is* love in Scripture (1 John 4:8). He reasons that love between two persons is a kind of "coupling" and that love cannot exist without the *other*. This coupling of two brings about the third reality of "love." Augustine relates his reflections on Lover–Beloved–Love to the trinitarian Father–Son–Spirit, with the Spirit as the one who is the *nexus* or *bond of love* (Augustine 1991, 255).

The Spirit that bonds the ecclesial community together also works to unite husband and wife, the "domestic Church," into a *communion of persons*. Pope John Paul II repeatedly refers to marriage as a *communion of persons*, a phrase that carries with it the theological understanding of *communio* as a unity that is not uniformity and does not destroy the distinctive quality of the human person, and *person* as one who discovers true identity in relationship with others.

Marriage therapists Patrick and Claudette McDonald emphasize three important aspects of marriage: "I" (my distinct self), "You" (my spouse), and "We" (our shared self). In healthy marriages, the "We" that is the unified married couple does not destroy the healthy "I" and "You" of the marriage. Marriage is a constant interplay of these three realities (McDonald and McDonald 1999, 71–76; Law and Law 2002, 97–108).

Heribert Mühlen observes that the Holy Spirit can be associated with the "we" of the "I–Thou" relationship of the Father and the Son, and this Spirit is also associated with the "we" of the Church community, and the "we" of husband and wife in marriage (1975, 27–29). Carlo Rocchetta describes this "communion in difference" as a "synthesis" that the Spirit brings about in marriage:

> The Spirit is poured out on the spouses so that they may be in a position to realize themselves in a communion that avoids two potential but opposite dangers: that of eliminating differences, beginning with the man–woman specificity, or that of sharpening the differences and so shattering the communion. The Spirit wants to mould the marital community as communion in the image of the Trinity (1998, 179).

The Spirit is the "bonding agent," the One bringing about true *communio* over the long haul, as couples negotiate the ever-changing waters of "good times and bad."

THE SPIRIT AS THE "BREATH" OF CHRISTIAN MARRIAGE

Breath is critical for human life. Without air, without breath, we die. In the Gospel of John, when the Risen Christ appeared to the disciples, he "breathed on them and said to them, 'Receive the Holy Spirit'" (20:22). In the Acts of the Apostles, the coming of the Spirit at Pentecost is described as accompanied by "a noise like a strong driving wind" (2:2). This association of the Spirit with breath, blowing, or wind signifies a dynamic energy that is a life-giving force (Theological Committee 1997, 31). Like the breath of God that brought the first earthling to life from the clay, the coming of the Spirit *animates* believers, giving them new life in Christ.

The Holy Spirit, the "Lord and Giver of Life," breathes life into the marital community in at least three ways: the Spirit animates the marital relationship, the Spirit is present in giving life to children, and the Spirit brings life to the larger community through the sacrament.

First, the Spirit breathes life into the relationship of this particular couple. Rocchetta calls the Holy Spirit the "invisible protagonist" of sacramental marriage (1998, 174). This silent Advocate encourages the couple to make good choices about their relationship from the moment of initial meeting.

The Spirit inspires little acts that nurture the life of the conjugal relationship: the tender caress, the squeezed hand that says, "I support you," and the flowers that say, "I'm sorry." We sometimes say of marriages that end in divorce that the relationship "died." Sacramental marriages are animated by the breath of the Spirit.

Healthy marriages are not turned inward in a type of joint self-centeredness. The abundant life of the conjugal relationship normally overflows into the creation of children, when not impeded by biological circumstances. Theologians remind us that this fruitfulness of marriage is much more than mere biological reproduction; it involves not only procreation but also the ongoing, demanding commitment of nurturing this new life with generativity (Gaillardetz 2002, 102–03; Lawler 1993, 103). The Spirit strengthens parents for this ascetical feat of love.

This generativity is not limited to the confines of the home. The superabundance of love found in sacramental marriage pours beyond the family, in generous acts toward others in the community. While infertile couples may perhaps have more time and energy to devote to acts of charity and justice, all married couples are called to community outreach. As Gaillardetz says, "A spirituality of marriage would be horribly defective if it did not recognize the generativity of marriage as a call to mission and service in the church and world" (2002, 103).

THE SPIRIT AS THE "FIRE" OF CHRISTIAN MARRIAGE

The image of "fire" in Scripture often signifies the purifying, transforming, and mysterious presence of God. Moses experiences God's presence in the burning bush. The Lord's "breath sets coals afire; a flame pours from his mouth" (Job 41:13). "For the LORD, your God, is a consuming fire" (Deut 4:24). In Isaiah's vision, the burning coal from the altar of the Lord purifies his lips for the mission of prophesying (Isa 6:7). John the Baptist proclaims that the Messiah will "baptize you with the Holy Spirit and fire" (Matt 3:11; Luke 3:16). The letter to the Hebrews reminds us: "For our God is a consuming fire" (12:29).

The death and resurrection of Jesus Christ brings about the outpouring of the Holy Spirit at Pentecost, in the appearance of "tongues of fire which parted and came to rest on each one of them" (Acts 2:3). The frightened and insecure disciples, hiding behind closed doors, are *transformed* by this spiritual "fire" to go forth, boldly proclaiming the Gospel despite persecution and suffering.

In sacramental marriage, the Spirit transforms the ordinary relationship of a man and woman who "like" and "love" each other into a Christian marriage that is increasingly permeated with God's presence and action. If monks choose monastery living because it helps them draw close to God, Christian *believers* choose marriage because conjugal love is also a path to holiness. All are invited to saturate their lives with the kenotic love of Christ, that is, the love that empties self for the sake of others. The Spirit, called the

"Sanctifier," works to sanctify the spouses. St. John Chrysostom reminds us that Christ addressed his Gospel words to all people, not just monks, and it follows that

> the monk and the layperson must attain the same heights [of holiness], and if they fall they inflict the same wounds upon themselves. . . . You are entirely mistaken if you think that there are certain things required of seculars, and others for monks. . . . They will have the same account to render. . . . And if any have been hindered by the marriage state, let them know that marriage is not a hindrance, but their purpose which made ill use of marriage. Use marriage *chastely*, and you shall be the first in the Kingdom of Heaven (Evdokimov 1995, 67).

When open to the Spirit's work, marriage itself contains the necessary elements for becoming holy. Opportunities to practice Christian virtues abound. Christian marriage allows for the practice of the evangelical counsels of poverty as detachment from material things, chastity as right use of sexual giftedness, and obedience as loving, mutual deference to each other (McCarty 1999, 84–85). Interaction with spouse and children encourages ongoing *metanoia* through the daily deaths-to-self for the sake of another, bringing with that its own asceticism (Gaillardetz 2002, 62–63). Gaillardetz explains: "My relationship with my wife and my children is indeed the spiritual 'place' wherein I will work out my salvation" (2002, 62). He goes on to explain that salvation is, of course, a gift of God; yet, it is up to us to respond to grace, to put forth the necessary human effort. Marriage is "a mystery in which, by the working of the Holy Spirit, one man and one woman sacrifice their own lives to become one flesh and are united and divinized by God's love" (Petras 1981, 231).

One sometimes hears the phrase the "gift of celibacy," but we can also speak of the "gift of marriage" as a gift given by the Spirit for the good of the marital partners and the good of the Church (Rocchetta 1998, 174–75). Pope John Paul II asserts, "It is extremely urgent to *revive awareness of conjugal love as a gift*" ("Revive Awareness," 9). This conjugal love—perhaps begun as mere physical attraction—will mature over the years, deepening and expanding as the Spirit purifies and sanctifies the couple, like gold that is "tested by fire" (1 Pet 1:7). The expression "golden anniversary" is most appropriate: the couple of fifty years has had their love tried, tested, and purified in the crucible of married life by the Spirit, transformed into the deep, ecstatic communion of trinitarian love.

"NUPTIAL PENTECOST": PASTORAL IMPLICATIONS

These reflections invite us to consider practical ways to foster awareness of the presence and action of the Holy Spirit in Christian marriage.

Regarding the wedding liturgy, those given the authority to provide us with the revised rite of marriage in English are encouraged to complete this task so that we may all benefit from the explicit *epiclesis* of the sacrament.

Liturgists might consider the use of appropriate songs, such as Marty Haugen's "Send Down the Fire," Bob Hurd's *"Envia Tu Espíritu,"* Taizé Community's *"Veni Sancte Spiritus,"* or David Haas's "Send Us Your Spirit" during the wedding liturgy. Homilists could include the pneumatological dimension of marriage in their reflections. The Hispanic custom of the *lazo* might be encouraged as a sign of the two-yet-oneness of marriage. Both Joncas and Stevenson suggest that the wedding rite of the future might be enriched with the anointing of the couple with chrism (Joncas 1996, 237; Stevenson 1999, 197).

Marriage preparation and enrichment programs might be redesigned to include discussion of the Spirit's active presence in marriage. Theologians and pastoral ministers need to look for ways to gather the experiences of married couples for the further development of the theology of marriage. Given enough time, perhaps when couples are asked, "How does the Holy Spirit help you build a strong marriage?" they will readily respond, based upon experiential awareness: the Spirit makes us one without destroying our personhood, the Spirit brings life, and the Spirit sanctifies our conjugal love.

REFERENCES

Augustine. *The Trinity.* Ed. John E. Rotelle. Trans. Edmund Hill. Brooklyn, N.Y.: New City Press, 1991.

Congar, Yves. *I Believe in the Holy Spirit.* Trans. David Smith. 3 vols. New York: Crossroad Publishing, 1999.

Evdokimov, Paul. *The Sacrament of Love: The Nuptial Mystery in the Light of the Orthodox Tradition.* Trans. Anthony P. Gythiel and Victoria Steadman. Crestwood, N.Y.: St. Vladimir's Seminary Press, 1995.

Gaillardetz, Richard R. *A Daring Promise: A Spirituality of Christian Marriage.* New York: Crossroad, 2002.

John Paul II. *Familiaris Consortio* (The Role of the Christian Family in the Modern World). Boston: Pauline Books, 1981.

———. *Letter to Families,* Feb. 2, 1994. http://www.vatican.va.

———. "Revive Awareness of Conjugal Love as Gift of the Spirit through the Sacrament of Marriage" (Address given on 7 Nov. 1988). *L'Osservatore Romano* 49 (5 December 1988) 8–9.

Joncas, Jan Michael. "Solemnizing the Mystery of Wedded Love: Nuptial Blessings in the *Ordo Celebrandi Matrimonium* 1991." *Worship* 70 (1996) 210–37.

Killen, Patricia O'Connell, and John de Beer. *The Art of Theological Reflection.* New York: Crossroad, 1994.

Law, Maureen Rogers, and Lanny Law. *God Knows Marriage Isn't Always Easy: 12 Ways to Add Zest.* Notre Dame, Ind.: Sorin, 2002.

Lawler, Michael G. *Marriage and Sacrament: A Theology of Christian Marriage.* Collegeville, Minn.: The Liturgical Press, 1993.

McCarty, Julie. "Marital Spirituality and the Quest for Poverty, Chastity, and Obedience." *Spiritual Life* 45 (1999) 84–94.

McDonald, Patrick J., and Claudette M. McDonald. *Marital Spirituality: The Search for the Hidden Ground of Love.* New York: Paulist Press, 1999.

Martinez, German. "The Newly Revised Roman Rite for Celebrating Marriage." *Worship* 69 (1995) 127–42.

Mühlen, Heribert. "The Person of the Holy Spirit." In *The Holy Spirit and Power: The Catholic Charismatic Renewal.* Ed. Kilian McDonnell. Garden City, N.Y.: Doubleday, 1975.

Ordo celebrandi matrimonium. Editio typica altera. [Order of Celebrating Marriage. Revised ed.] Vatican City: Libreria Editrice Vaticana, 1991.

Petras, David M. "The Liturgical Theology of marriage." *Diakonia* 16 (1981) 225–37.

Rocchetta, Carlo. "The Holy Spirit and Marriage." *INTAMS Review* [International Academy for Marital Spirituality] 4:2 (1998) 174–84.

Searle, Mark, and Kenneth Stevenson. Documents of the Marriage Liturgy. Collegeville, Minn.: The Liturgical Press, 1992.

Stevenson, Kenneth W. To *Join Together: The Rite of Marriage.* New York: Pueblo, 1987.

———. "The New Marriage Rites: Their Place in the Tradition." In *To Glorify God: Essays on Modern Reformed Liturgy.* Ed. Bryan Spinks and Iain Torrance. Edinburgh: T & T Clark, 1999.

Theological Historical Committee for the Great Jubilee of the Year 2000. *The Holy Spirit, Lord and Giver of Life.* Trans. Agostino Bono. New York: Crossroad, 1997.

Vatican Council II: The Conciliar and Post Conciliar Documents. Revised ed. Ed. Austin Flannery. Collegeville, Minn.: The Liturgical Press, 1992.

PART THREE

Marriage: Meanings and Transitions

CHAPTER 6

Marriage versus Living Together

Jo McGowan

Students will find the following essay interesting and controversial. Jo McGowan lays out the two positions—i.e., that marriage is an outdated formality and that it is for several reasons an important step. She makes clear her own position about the importance of marriage as a public and communal act.

Questions for Discussion

1. Why does the author claim that living together is like taking on all that is difficult in marriage without taking the helps that marriage offers?
2. The author says that living together implies that the central relationship of one's life is nobody's business but one's own. Why would you agree or disagree?
3. How accurate are the things the author says about the typical wedding?
4. How common in North America is the author's conviction that marriage (not just the wedding) is a communal matter?
5. What are your reasons for accepting or not accepting the author's conviction "What the community does not bless, it doesn't feel responsible for"?

Some months ago we had a beautiful young woman from India (my husband is also from India) staying with us. At dinner, the conversation turned to the question of marriage versus simply living together. Smita, the Indian woman, maintained that marriage was nothing more than a convenience, a way to avoid the censure of society; that if two people were willing to commit their lives to each other, then marriage was an unnecessary formality, signifying nothing.

To engage in the kind of discussion that followed is to risk sounding foolish. One talks of "marriage" as an institution and yet it is apparent that one is talking out of personal experience that cannot help but be narrow and unimposing compared to the subject itself. Having been married not very long myself, I realized how presumptuous it is to say almost anything (even at the dinner table, let alone in print) about marriage in general. But when

Copyright © 1981, Commonweal Foundation. Reprinted with permission.

will it become *not* presumptuous—after five years, ten, twenty, fifty? The more years pass, I also realize, the more changes in social and cultural conditions will separate me from those entering marriage then, and so perhaps my reflections would take on a presumptuousness of a different sort. In any case, the discussion that evening was so enlightening to me that I decided to risk my dignity and write down some of the thoughts that emerged.

Apart from anything else, marriage is simply a very practical institution. It is an institution which recognizes and makes allowances for human failings. Since constancy is a virtue that very few of us possess at all times, it is important that we see marriage as something beyond ourselves. The very nature of marriage insists that we see it so: when we marry, we create new life; we go beyond ourselves. We create responsibilities, the weight of which our marriages must be strong enough to bear. Marriage is one of those peculiar things (like God!) which make immense demands of us while simultaneously giving us the strength to meet those demands. It is precisely because marriage is so difficult that we must see it as permanent. It is precisely because we are so likely to give it up that we must promise—at the outset, when everything is wonderful—that we are in it for life. (This is one reason, then, why the extreme prevalence of divorce is so troubling. It not only destroys the marriages of those individuals who choose to separate, but it erodes the *concept* of the permanence of marriage. It makes it that much easier for the next couple to give up.)

Simply living together, without "benefit of marriage," does not provide the security of knowing that this is forever. But if you need that security, our friend Smita says, then the relationship can't be that strong to begin with. Smita and I are both in our early twenties, still young enough to believe in the power of love to overcome all odds. And I do believe that. What I don't believe is that a wife and husband always love each other enough to stay married. There are times when love fails, and in those times, many people just take a deep breath and stay married because they *are* married. And when they come through to the other side, their marriages are stronger and more firmly rooted in love.

Smita grew up in India where divorce is practically unheard of—I grew up in an America where *marriage* is practically unheard of. She can perhaps afford to take marriage for granted. I can't. I have seen far too many of my friends—and even my parents' friends—divorce. I have taken care of too many children whose parents are separated. I have seen the scars that divorce inevitably leaves—the pain and near-despair in grownups; the bewilderment and insecurity in the children. I'm not saying that these couples didn't have problems; I'm sure they did. But no human relation is without problems. And if one enters into marriage, one should do it knowing full well that this is the case and that *in spite of it*, the marriage is forever. Living together does not carry with it the weight of a centuries-old tradition. The content of the relationship—a woman and a man living together sexually—contains all the elements that are present in a marriage, but without its form. It is like taking on all that is difficult in a marriage without taking the helps that marriage can offer. Simply knowing that one is married, that one has promised—before God and the human community—that this is forever, puts a different light on the inevitable problems that one faces. One is more likely (given, of course, a belief in the permanence of marriage) to slog through, to get past whatever it is in the way, to stay together.

Constancy, of course, is not limited to those couples who are formally married. Many of my friends are living together. They have made serious commitments to each other, they have children and, for all practical purposes, they might as well be married. Indeed, several of them have relationships that I consider to be closer to the ideal of marriage than that of most of the married couples I know. But that, I think, is more a function of the kind of people they are, and not of the form of their living arrangements. They are extraordinary people who would probably make a success of any relationship.

Even so, there is, it seems to me, something missing. I wouldn't presume to judge what goes on between two people who have committed themselves to each other—in whatever form they have chosen. I can only look at their relationship as it is perceived by the rest of the human community. It is here, I think, that the strongest argument for marriage as opposed to living together can be made.

Let us assume two couples: One married, one living together. Both have promised a lifetime commitment, both have children, both are trying to live with each other as lovingly, gently, and non-violently as they can. What is the difference?

The difference, as Ravi and I pieced it together that night with Smita, is this: one is a community-building act from the very beginning and the other is not.

To marry, to celebrate a love and a commitment publicly, in the presence of family and friends, is to say that the meaning of one's life can only be found in the context of a community. It is to acknowledge one's part in the human family, to recognize that one's life is more than one's own, that one's actions affect more than oneself. It is to proclaim that marriage is more than a private affair between one woman and one man.

To live together seems to me to imply that the central relationship of one's life is nobody's business but one's own. To live together is a decision reached privately and put into motion alone. There is no community blessing or celebration of the decision.

And what the community does not bless, it does not feel responsible for. Couples who are living together often find themselves quite alone when problems arise in their relationships. Their community may quite properly feel that such problems are none of its business. It was not asked for advice, or even congratulations, at the outset; why should it feel any responsibility now that things are going badly? On the other hand, a community which is asked to witness and bless the beginning of a marriage is far more likely to feel a sense of responsibility to the couple as their marriage grows and develops. I grant that most couples who do actually marry do not ask this of their community. Indeed, most couples think of the people at their wedding simply as guests who have to be fed, and not as participants in a community celebration. More on that in a bit.

The need for privacy, for individualism, looms extraordinarily large in American culture. We have been brought up to believe that it is a sign of weakness to admit that we need others. We have made a virtue of going it alone. Our ideal family is composed of a mother, a father, and one or two children. Grandparents, aunts, uncles, and cousins are all kept at a safe distance, and even neighbors are required, by zoning laws, to be at least an acre away. That this should be reflected in young people's choosing to live together, an essentially private choice, is not surprising. What *is* perhaps surprising is the extent to which most *marriages* are also quite private affairs, all the while purporting to be community events.

Most weddings say very little about the two individuals marrying—or about the community witnessing the union. Most weddings say something about the amount of money the participants have to throw about. They say something about fashion. They say something about respect for authority, in the form of the State, which issues the license, for a fee.

Most wedding ceremonies take place on an altar—so far from the guests who, theoretically, are there to witness the union of these two, that no one but the priest can hear the vows they exchange.

Most weddings are the occasion for bitter arguments: over relatives one cannot abide but invite anyway, seating arrangements at the reception, who pays for what, how many guests each family is allowed. . . . It goes on and on until many couples wish they *had* just decided to live together and skip all the hassle.

What is most telling, though, is the fact that so many weddings do not welcome children. Indeed, many outright discourage them. The phrase "No children, please" can be found frequently on wedding invitations and hard are the judgments passed on parents who dare to bring them anyway. Children, the hope and the future of any community, are an interruption, a noisy distraction, an additional and unnecessary expense—they take away from what is really important.

And what is really important, apparently, is that two grownups want to live together, but before they can, they have to get married.

This alienation of the community from the wedding ceremony, this lack of identification with the bride and groom—who seem more like actors playing prearranged roles than two people expressing their love for each other—serves to depersonalize the celebration. There is a boring sameness to weddings—one goes because one has to, because it is expected. The community is not asked to take part, and it does not. And the wedding sets the tone for the community's role in the marriage itself. The message is clear: It should limit its involvement to making appearances at the appropriate times, giving gifts on the appropriate occasions. Nothing more.

When Ravi and I married, we wanted a community celebration, one involving as many of our friends and families as possible. We wanted our wedding to reflect our religious (Catholic/Hindu) and cultural backgrounds, as well as our social and political concerns; we wanted our wedding to be a celebration of our love, naturally, but also for the community who had come to share our joy.

And it was. What a diversity of talents went into that day—from the wedding invitations and programs we designed, Ravi's side in Hindi and mine in English, to the wedding clothes made by Ravi's cousin and the wedding cake made by my father and a close friend. Ravi's mother performed the Hindu wedding ceremony; two priest friends witnessed the Catholic ceremony. Ravi and I wrote our own vows and selected the readings (from the Hindu and Christian scriptures) that friends and relatives read at the ceremony. Two nuns who had taught me in high school provided their oceanside convent for the day. The vegetarian banquet (both Indian and American foods) was entirely prepared by friends who arrived a few days early to cook . . . and best of all were the children everywhere, behaving exactly as children should behave, especially at a wedding.

It seemed to us then, and it seems even more so now, that our wedding was a symbol of the way we want to live our lives: surrounded by family and friends; giving, and receiving the gifts of time, laughter, advice, and help; sharing food, work, prayer, and celebration; creating a world where children are free and full of joy.

But marriage is a community event. It expresses, in its ideal form, a belief in the goodness of community, a belief in the beauty of two people who love each other coming together to live in communion, a belief in the wonder of human life, a belief so strong that it expressed itself in the creation of new human life.

If two people who say they want to marry do not believe this, then perhaps they should not marry. If they want to "join America"—to live in the suburbs with themselves and their 1.7 genetically screened children, exactly one acre from the nearest neighbor—then perhaps what they want is not marriage but just to live with each other.

If they want to be part of the human community, to start building the kingdom of God here on earth, then marriage is probably what they are seeking. And if it is, then the wedding itself, which is the beginning of marriage, should be an expression of their belief in community.

CHAPTER 7

Marriage Preparation and Cohabiting Couples: Information Report

NCCB Marriage and Family Committee

The report that follows may be the most succinct and comprehensive treatment of what today is a trend among young people: living together (cohabiting), either as a step toward marriage or as a way of saying that a public legal marriage is no longer necessary. This report explores the growing prevalence of living together in North America.

On first reading this report, those students—convinced that marriage as an institution in the twenty-first century is as outmoded as the tooth fairy—may initially rejoice. The report does offer data about a growing trend toward living together outside of marriage, but such data are not the sum total of the report's disclosures.

The report offers facts that should give those involved in or contemplating a cohabiting relationship cause for serious concern, especially those seeking a lifelong relationship. Statistically, there is a greater rate of divorce for those who live together before marriage than for those who do not. Whether they live together as a step toward marriage or not, such persons divorce at a higher rate than those who get to know one another, go through an engagement, marry, and *then* live together.

Unwillingness to take one's time can spell disaster in a committed relationship. Actually, many students are quite aware of the perils of impetuousness, and class discussion often uncovers much wisdom about the issues raised in this report.

Only the report's first part containing social science research is presented here. The second part, which deals with pastoral issues and questions raised by cohabitation, has been omitted.

Questions for Discussion

1. How important is security as a base for growth in an intimate relationship?
2. If there are risks in a cohabiting arrangement, whose risk is greater, the man's or the woman's? If the relationship goes bad, who has the most to lose?
3. If lovers cohabit, who owns the lease? Who owns the furniture? If the relationship falters, who moves out?

4. Consider the following statement: People should do what suits them; they are old enough to make up their own minds and even make their own mistakes.

INTRODUCTION

Today almost half the couples who come for marriage preparation in the Catholic Church are in a cohabiting relationship.[1] Cohabitation, in a commonly understood sense, means living together in a sexual relationship without marriage. Living together in this way involves varying degrees of physical and emotional interaction. Such a relationship is a false sign. It contradicts the meaning of a sexual relationship in marriage as the total gift of one-self in fidelity, exclusivity and permanency.

[Over the past 25 years cohabitation has become a major social phenomenon affecting the institution of marriage and family life.[2] It is also an extremely perplexing issue for priests, deacons and lay pastoral ministers who help couples prepare for marriage in the church.]

In 1988 the National Conference of Catholic Bishops' Committee on Pastoral Practices published *Faithful to Each Other Forever: A Catholic Handbook of Pastoral Help for Marriage Preparation.* The intent of this volume was to be a resource for those involved in marriage-preparation work. It remains a very useful and comprehensive pastoral tool.

Faithful to Each Other Forever discussed (pp. 71–77) the question of cohabitation under two headings: (a) input on cohabitation from personal experiences and the behavioral sciences, and (b) pastoral approaches to cohabiting couples. In this latter section the handbook drew upon the written policies of a few dioceses to present a range of possible options for working with cohabiting couples who come seeking marriage in the church.

Now, nearly 12 years after the original work of *Faithful to Each Other Forever,* the cumulative pastoral experience of ministering to cohabiting couples has broadened and deepened. This is reflected, at least partially, in the increased number of dioceses that now include a treatment of the issue within their marriage-preparation policies.

In this present resource paper the NCCB Committee on Marriage and Family builds upon the foundation provided by *Faithful to Each Other Forever* when it first treated the question of cohabitation. . . .

This paper is neither an official statement of the Committee on Marriage and Family nor of the National Conference of Catholic Bishops. It does not offer formal recommendations for action. It is intended as a resource paper, offering a compilation of resources and a reflection of the present "state of the question" regarding certain issues of cohabitation.

In this way, it wishes to help:

Reprinted by permission of the United States Conference of Catholic Bishops.

1. Bishops and diocesan staff who are reviewing and possibly revising their marriage-preparation policies.

2. Priests, deacons, pastoral ministers and lay volunteers who want to become more informed and effective in working with cohabiting couples who come to marriage-preparation programs.

3. Those who are responsible for in-service and continuing education of clergy and laity who carry out the church's ministry of marriage preparation.

As pointed out in *Faithful to Each Other Forever* (p. 71), the committee acknowledges a distinction between sexual activity outside of marriage and cohabitation. They are not identical matters. One can exist without the other. Couples may engage in sexual intercourse without living together; other couples may share the same residence but not live in a sexual relationship. The focus of this paper, however, is on cohabitation understood as both having a sexual relationship and living together in the same residence.

EMPIRICAL INFORMATION ABOUT COHABITATION AND MARRIAGE

Those couples who are in a cohabiting relationship and who come to the church for marriage preparation represent only a percentage of the total cohabiting population. Nonetheless, to understand and respond to them one must appreciate some aspects of the broader phenomenon of cohabitation. This, in turn, is set within a context of widespread sexual activity outside of marriage. In this section we provide highlights of what social science has discovered about cohabitation in general and with specific reference to cohabiting couples who eventually marry.

1. HOW WIDESPREAD IS COHABITATION?

Cohabitation is a pervasive and growing phenomenon with a negative impact on the role of marriage as the foundation of family. The incidence of cohabitation is much greater than is indicated by the number of cohabiting couples presenting themselves for marriage. Slightly more than half of couples in first-time cohabitations ever marry; the overall percentage of those who marry is much lower when it includes those who cohabit more than once. Cohabitation as a permanent or temporary alternative to marriage is a major factor in the declining centrality of marriage in family structure. It is a phenomenon altering the face of family life in first-world countries.

• Eleven percent of couples in the United States cohabited in 1965–74; today, a little over half of all first marriages are preceded by cohabitation (Bumpass and Lu, 1998; Popenoe and Whitehead, 1999).

• Across all age groups there has been a 45 percent increase in cohabitation from 1970 to 1990. It is estimated that 60 percent to 80 percent of the couples coming to be married are cohabiting (Bumpass, Sweet, and Cherlin, 1991).

• Overall, fewer persons are choosing to be married today; the decision to cohabit as a permanent or temporary alternative to marriage is a primary reason (Bumpass, 1995). The percent of couples being married in the United States declined 25 percent from 1975 to 1995. The Official Catholic Directory reported 406,908 couples married in the Catholic Church in 1974; in 1995, it reported a 25 percent decline to 305,385 couples.

• Only 53 percent of first cohabiting unions result in marriage. The percentage of couples marrying from second and third cohabitations is even lower (Bumpass and Lu, 1998; Bumpass, 1990; Wu, 1995; Wineberg and McCarthy, 1998). Ten percent to 30 percent of cohabitors intend never to marry (Bumpass and Sweet, 1995).

• All first-world countries are experiencing the phenomenon of cohabitation and the corrosive impact it has on marriage as the center of family (Bumpass, 1995; Hall and Zhao, 1995; Thomasson, 1998; Haskey and Kiernan, 1989).

2. WHAT IS THE PROFILE OF THE COHABITING HOUSEHOLD?

The profile of the average cohabiting household is both expected and somewhat surprising. Persons with low levels of religious participation and those who have experienced disruption in their parents' marriages or a previous marriage or their own are likely candidates for cohabitation. Persons with lower levels of education and earning power cohabit more often and marry less often than those with higher education. The average cohabiting household stays together just over one year, and children are part of two-fifths of these households. Men are more often serial or repeat cohabitors, moving from woman to woman, while women tend to cohabit only one time.

• Forty percent of cohabiting households include children, either the children of the relationship or the children that one or both partners bring to the relationship (U.S. Bureau of Census, 1998; Wu, 1995; Schoen, 1992).

• Median duration of cohabitation is 1.3 years (Bumpass and Lu, 1998; Wu, 1995). Previously married persons cohabit more often than never-married [persons]; two-thirds of those separated or divorced and under age 35 cohabit. They are more likely than never-married cohabiting couples to have children in the household, and they are much less likely than never-married [persons] to marry their current partner or someone else (Wineberg and McCarthy, 1998; Wu, 1995; Bumpass and Sweet, 1989).

• Those not completing high school are almost twice as likely to cohabit as those who complete college. Forty percent of college graduates, however, do cohabit at some time. Only 26 percent of women with college degrees cohabit, compared to 41 percent of women without a high school diploma. The higher the level of education, the more likely the cohabitor is to marry the partner (Qian, 1998; Bumpass and Lu, 1998; Thornton, Axinn, and Teachman, 1995; Willis and Michael, 1994).

• Women are likely to cohabit only once, and that with the person they subsequently marry; men are more likely to cohabit with a series of partners (Bumpass and Sweet, 1989; Teachman and Polanko, 1990).

• Individuals, especially women, who experienced disruption in their parents' marriages are more likely to cohabit than those who had parents with stable marriages (Axinn and Thornton, 1992; Kiernan, 1992; Black and Sprenkle, 1991; Bumpass and Sweet, 1989).

• Persons with low levels of religious participation and who rate religion of low importance are more likely to cohabit and less likely to marry their partner than those who consider religion important and practice it. There is no difference in frequency of cohabitation by religious denomination; there is a significant difference in cohabitation frequency by level of religious participation (Krishnan, 1998; Lye and Waldron, 1997; Thornton, Axinn, and Hill, 1992; Liefbroer, 1991; Sweet, 1989).

• In general, those in cohabiting households are more independent, more liberal in attitude and more risk oriented than noncohabitors (Clarkberg, Stolzenberg, and Waite, 1995; Cunningham and Antill, 1994; Huffman, Chang, and Schaffer, 1994; DeMaris and MacDonald, 1993).

3. WHAT ARE THE REASONS FOR COHABITATION?

The declining significance of marriage as the center of family is in large part a result of growing secularization and individualization in first-world cultures. Aversion to long-term commitments is one of the identifying characteristics of these trends and a major reason for cohabitation. Key milestones previously associated with marriage, such as sexual relationships, childbearing, and establishing couple households, now occur without marriage. Individuals choose to cohabit under the influence of these cultural values but also for very individual reasons. Some are seeking to ensure a good future marriage and believe that a "trial marriage" will accomplish this; many are simply living together because it seems more economically feasible or because it has become the social norm. In general, cohabitors are not a homogenous or monolithic group, however fully their general characteristics can be described. The reasons for choosing cohabitation are usually mixed: Cohabitation may be in equal parts an alternative to marriage and an attempt to prepare for marriage.

There are both broad cultural reasons and a range of individual reasons for cohabitation.

• The cultural reasons are descriptive of most first-world countries: changing values on family and decline in the importance of marriage (Bumpass, 1995; Clarkberg, Stolzenberg, and Waite, 1995; Parker, 1990).

• Declining confidence in religious and social institutions to provide guidance (Nicole and Baldwin, 1995; Thornton, Axinn, and Hill, 1992).

• Delaying of marriage for economic or social reasons while sexual relationships begin earlier. Eighty-five percent of unmarried youth are sexually active by age 20. "Marriage no longer signifies the beginning of sexual relationship, the beginning of childbearing or the point at which couples establish joint households" (Bumpass, 1995; Popenoe and Whitehead, 1999; Peplau, Hill, and Rubin, 1993; Rindfuss and Van den Heuvel, 1990).

The individual reasons for cohabitation are varied:

• Fear of or disbelief in long-term commitment (Nicole and Baldwin, 1995).

• Desire to avoid divorce (Nicole and Baldwin, 1995; Thornton, 1991; Bumpass, 1990).

• Desire for economic security (Rindfuss and Van den Heuvel, 1990; Schoen and Owens, 1992).

• Stage of personal development, escape from home, "rite of passage" (Nicole and Baldwin, 1995).

• Desire for stability for raising of children (Wu, 1995; Bumpass, Sweet, and Cherlin, 1991; Manning and Lichter, 1996).

• Pressure to conform to current mores that having cohabiting partner is measure of social success, personal desirability, adult transition (Rindfuss, and Van den Heuvel, 1990; Schoen and Owens, 1992).

• Desire to test the relationship (Nicole and Baldwin, 1995; Bumpass, Sweet, and Cherlin, 1991; Bumpass, 1990).

• Rejection of the institution of marriage and desire for an alternative to marriage (Sweet and Bumpass, 1992; Rindfuss and Van den Heuvel, 1990).

4. WHAT ABOUT COHABITORS AND MARRIAGE?

Overall, less than half of cohabiting couples ever marry. Those who do choose to marry are in some part counterculture to the growing view that it is certainly not necessary and perhaps not good to marry. Those who choose to marry instead of continuing to cohabit are the "good news" in a culture that is increasingly anti-marriage. Those cohabiting couples who move to marriage seem to be the "best risk" of a high-risk group: They have fewer risk factors than those cohabitors who choose not to marry. Even so, they still divorce at a rate 50 percent higher than couples who have never cohabited. They are a high-risk group for divorce, and their special risk factors need to be identified and addressed, especially at the time of marriage preparation, if the couples are to build solid marriages.

Only 50 percent to 60 percent of cohabitors marry the persons with whom they cohabit at a given time. Seventy-six percent report plans to marry their partner, but only about half do. The percentage of couples marrying after second and third cohabitation is even lower (Brown and Booth, 1996; Bumpass and Sweet, 1989).

• Up to 30 percent of cohabitors intend never to marry (Bumpass and Sweet, 1995).

• Twenty percent of cohabiting partners disagree about whether or not they intend to marry (Bumpass, Sweet, and Cherlin, 1991).

• When cohabitors do marry, they are more at risk for subsequent divorce than those who did not cohabit before marriage. In the United States the risk of divorce is 50 percent higher for cohabitors than noncohabitors. In some Western European countries, it is estimated to be 80 percent higher (Bumpass and Sweet, 1995; Hall and Zhao, 1995; Bracher, Santow, Morgan, and Trussell, 1993; DeMaris and Rao, 1992; Glenn, 1990).

• When previously married cohabitors marry, their subsequent divorce rate is higher than that of cohabiting couples who have not been previously married (Wineberg and McCarthy, 1998; Wu, 1995; Bumpass and Sweet, 1989).

• Those who cohabit more than once prior to marriage, serial or repeat cohabitors, have higher divorce rates when they do marry than those who cohabit only once (Brown and Booth, 1996; Stets, 1993; Thomson and Colella, 1991).

• There is some indication that the divorce rate is higher for people who cohabit for a longer period of time, especially over three years. The data on this are mixed (Lillard, Brien, and Waite, 1995; Thomson and Colella, 1991; Bennett, Blanc, and Bloom, 1988).

• Cohabitors who marry break up in the earlier years of marriage. Cohabitors and noncohabitors have the same rate of marriage stability if the marriage remains intact over seven years (Bumpass, Sweet, and Cherlin, 1991; Bennett, Blanc, and Bloom, 1988).

• Cohabitors who do choose to marry appear to be of lesser risk for later divorce than those cohabitors who choose not to marry would be. They appear to be the best risk of a high-risk group (Thomson and Colella, 1991).

5. WHAT ARE THE FACTORS THAT PUT COHABITORS WHO MARRY AT RISK?

Individuals who choose to cohabit have certain attitudes, issues and patterns that lead them to make the decision to cohabit. These same attitudes, issues, and patterns often become the predisposing factors to put them at high risk for divorce when they do choose to move from cohabitation to marriage. The cohabitation experience itself creates risk factors, bad habits, that can sabotage the subsequent marriage. These attitudes and patterns can be identified and brought to the couple preparing for marriage for examination, decision making, skill building, [and] change. Without creating "self-fulfilling prophecies," those preparing cohabiting couples for marriage can help them identify and work with issues around commitment, fidelity, individualism, pressure, [and] appropriate expectations.

Many studies explore why cohabitors are more at risk when they marry. The research suggests that there are two overlapping and reinforcing sources for risk:

- Predisposing attitudes and characteristics they take into the marriage.

- Experiences from the cohabitation itself that create problem patterns and behaviors.

PREDISPOSING ATTITUDES AND CHARACTERISTICS

- Cohabitors as a group are less committed to the institution of marriage and more accepting of divorce. As problems and issues arise to challenge the marriage, they are more likely to seek divorce as the solution (Lillard, Brien, and Waite, 1995; Bracher, Santow, Morgan, and Trussell, 1993; Thomson and Colella, 1991; Bennett, Blanc, and Bloom, 1988).

- "Sexual exclusivity" is less an indicator of commitment for cohabitors than for noncohabitors. In this regard, cohabitation is more like dating than marriage. After marriage, a woman who cohabited before marriage is 3.3 times more likely to be sexually unfaithful than a woman who had not cohabited before marriage (Forste and Tanfer, 1996).

- Cohabitors identify themselves or the relationship as poor risk for long-term happiness more often than do noncohabitors. There is evidence that some cohabitors do have more problematic, lower-quality relationships with more individual and couple problems than noncohabitors. Often this is why they feel the need to test the relationship through cohabitation. There is the probability that some of these significant problems will carry over into the marriage relationship (Lillard, Brien, and Waite, 1995; Thomson and Colella, 1991; Booth and Johnson, 1988).

- Cohabitors tend to hold individualism as a more important value than noncohabitors do. While married persons generally value interdependence and the exchange of resources, cohabitors tend to value independence and economic equality. These values do not necessarily change just because a cohabiting couple decides to move into marriage (Clarkberg, Stolzenberg, and Waite, 1995; Waite and Joyner, 1996; Bumpass, Sweet, and Cherlin, 1991).

- Cohabitors can allow themselves to marry because of pressure from family and others, and because of pressure to provide a stable home for children. While it is generally better for the children in a cohabiting household or a child born to a cohabiting couple to be raised in a stable marriage, this is not by itself sufficient reason for the marriage. While family and friends are often right to encourage marriage for a cohabiting couple, a marriage made under such pressure is problematic unless the couple chooses it for more substantial reasons (Barber and Axinn, 1998; Wu, 1995; Mahler, 1996; Manning and Smock 1995; Teachman and Polanko, 1990).

• Cohabitors are demonstrated to have inappropriately high expectations of marriage that can lead them to be disillusioned with the ordinary problems or challenges of marriage. Cohabitors generally report lower satisfaction with marriage after they marry than do noncohabitors. There is danger that they think they have "worked out everything" and that any further challenges are the fault of the institution of marriage (Brown, 1998; Nock, 1995; Booth and Johnson, 1988).

EXPERIENCES FROM THE COHABITATION ITSELF

• The experience of cohabitation changes the attitudes about commitment and permanence, and makes couples more open to divorce (Axinn and Barber, 1997; Nock 1995; Schoen and Weinick, 1993; Axinn and Thornton, 1992).

• Cohabitors have more conflict over money after they marry than non-cohabitors do. Often they have set patterns of autonomy or competition about making and handling money during the time of cohabitation, and this carries over to the marriage. Many couples have one pattern of money handling in the cohabitation household and have not discussed clearly how one or the other individual expects this pattern to change after marriage (Singh and Lindsay, 1996; Ressler and Walters, 1995; Waite, 1995).

• Domestic violence is a more common problem with cohabitors than with married persons, and this pattern will carry over to a subsequent marriage relationship. Cohabiting partners can have a lesser-felt need to protect the relationship while they are cohabiting because they do not see it as permanent. If this is the case, some will begin dysfunctional patterns of problem-solving. The existence of the partner's children in the relationship [and] stress over the permanency of the relationship are common causes of conflict and sometimes violence (Jackson, 1996; McLaughlin, Leonard, and Senchak 1992; Stets and Straus, 1989).

• Cohabitors who marry are less effective at conflict resolution than those who did not cohabit. Either a fear of upsetting an uncommitted relationship or the lack of need to protect a temporary relationship can be factors that lead cohabiting couples into poor patterns of conflict resolution which they then carry into marriage (Booth and Johnson, 1988).

• Using sex as a controlling factor can be a negative pattern, which cohabiting couples can bring to their subsequent marriage. Reinforcement of negative family of origin patterns can also have occurred in the cohabiting relationship and be carried over to marriage. Both of these patterns are common issues that dating couples carry into marriage, but they can be exaggerated by the cohabitation experience (Waite and Joyner, 1996; Waite, 1995; Thornton and Axinn, 1993).

NOTES

1. In 1995 a national study of Catholic-sponsored marriage preparation found that 43.6 percent of couples were living together at the time of their marriage preparation. The average length of cohabitation had been 15.6 months. See "Marriage Preparation in the Catholic Church: Getting It Right," Creighton University Center for Marriage and Family, 1995, p. 43.

2. In a report titled "The State of Our Unions: The Social Health of Marriage in America" (The National Marriage Project, Rutgers University, 1999), authors David Popenoe, Ph.D., and Barbara Dafoe Whitehead, Ph.D., identify the rise in unmarried cohabitation as partly responsible for the 43 percent decline, from 1960 to 1996, in the annual number of marriages per thousand unmarried women.

REFERENCES

Axinn, William G. and Barber, Jennifer S. "Living Arrangements and Family Formation Attitudes in Early Adulthood." *Journal of Marriage and the Family* 59 (1997) 595–611.

Axinn, William G. and Thorton, Arland. "The Relationship between Cohabitation and Divorce: Selectivity or Causal Influence?" *Demography* 29 (1992) 357–374.

Barber, Jennifer S. and Axinn, William G. "Gender Role Attitudes and Marriage among Young Women." *The Sociological Quarterly* 39 (1998) 11–31.

Bennett, Neil G., Blanc, Ann Klimas, and Bloom, David E. "Commitment and the Modern Union: Assessing the Link between Premarital Cohabitation and Subsequent Marital Stability." *American Sociological Review* 53 (1988) 127–138.

Black, Lenora E. and Sprenkle, Douglas H. "Gender Differences in College Students' Attitudes toward Divorce and Their Willingness to Marry." *Journal of Divorce and Remarriage* 14 (1991) 47–60.

Booth, Alan and Johnson, David. "Premarital Cohabitation and Marital Success." *Journal of Family Issues* 9 (1988) 255–272.

Bracher, Michael, Santow, Gigi, Morgan, S. Philip, and Trussell, James R. "Marriage Dissolution in Australia: Models and Explanations." *Population Studies* 47 (1993) 403–425.

Brown, Susan L. "Cohabitation as Marriage Prelude vs. Marriage Alternative: The Significance for Psychological Well-Being." Unpublished Paper, Bowling Green University, Ohio (1998).

Bumpass, Larry L., Sweet, James A., and Cherlin, Andrew. "The Role of Cohabitation in Declining Rates of Marriage." *Journal of Marriage and the Family* 53 (1991) 913–927.

Clarkberg, Marin, Stolzenberg, Ross M., and Waite, Linda J. "Attitudes, Values and Entrance into Cohabitational vs. Marital Unions." *Social Forces* 74 (1995) 609–634.

Committee on Pastoral Practices, National Conference of Catholic Bishops. *Faithful to Each Other Forever: A Catholic Handbook for Marriage Preparation.* Washington, D.C.: NCCB, 1988.

Creighton University Center for Marriage and Family. "Marriage Preparation in the Catholic Church: Getting It Right." Omaha, Neb.: Creighton University, 1995.

Cunningham, John D. and Antill, John K. "Cohabitation and Marriage: Retrospective and Predictive Comparisons." *Journal of Social and Personal Relationships* 11 (1994) 77–93.

DeMaris, Alfred and MacDonald, William. "Premarital Cohabitation and Marital Instability: A Test of the Unconventionality Hypothesis." *Journal of Marriage and the Family* 55 (1993) 399–407.

DeMaris, Alfred and Rao, K. Vaninadha. "Premarital Cohabitation and Subsequent Marital Stability in the United States: A Reassessment." *Journal of Marriage and the Family* 54 (1992) 179–190.

Forste, Renata and Tanfer, Koray. "Sexual Exclusivity among Dating, Cohabiting and Married Women." *Journal of Marriage and the Family* 58 (1996) 33–47.

Glenn, Norval D. "Quantitative Research on Marital Quality in the 1980s: A Critical Review." *Journal of Marriage and the Family* 52 (1990) 818–831.

Hall, David R. and Zhao, John Z. "Cohabitation and Divorce in Canada: Testing the Selectivity Hypotheses." *Journal of Marriage and the Family* 57 (1995) 421–427.

Haskey, John and Kiernan, Kathleen. "Cohabitation in Great Britain—Characteristics and Estimated Numbers of Cohabiting Partners." *Population Trends* 58 (1989).

Huffman, Terry, Chang, Karen Rausch, and Schaffer, Nora. "Gender Differences and Factors Related to the Disposition toward Cohabitation." *Family Therapy* 21 (1994) 171–184.

Jackson, Nicky Ali. "Observational Experiences of Interpersonal Conflict and Teenage Victimization: A Comprehensive Study among Spouses and Cohabitors." *Journal of Family Violence* 11 (1996) 191–203.

Kiernan, Kathleen. "The Impact of Family Disruption in Childhood and Transitions Made in Young Adult Life." *Population Studies* (1992) 46.

Krishnan, Bijaya. "Premarital Cohabitation and Marital Disruption." *Journal of Divorce and Remarriage* 28 (1998) 157–170.

Liefbroer, Aat C. "The Choice between a Married or Unmarried First Union by Young Adults." *European Journal of Population* 1 (1991) 273–298.

Lillard, Lee A., Brien, Michael J., and Waite, Linda. "Premarital Cohabitation and Subsequent Marital Dissolution: A Matter of Self-Selection?" *Demography* 32 (1995) 437–457.

Lye, Diane N. and Waldron, Ingrid. "Attitudes toward Cohabitation, Family, and Gender Roles: Relationships to Values and Political Ideology." *Sociological Perspectives* 40 (1997) 199–225.

Mahler, K. "Completed Premarital Pregnancies More Likely among Cohabiting Women Than among Singles." *Family Planning Perspectives* 28 (1996) 179–180.

Manning, Wendy and Smock, Pamela. "Why Marry?: Race and the Transition to Marriage among Cohabitors." *Demography* 32 (1995) 509–520.

McLaughlin, Iris G., Leonard, Kenneth E., and Senchak, Marilyn. "Prevalence and Distribution of Premarital Aggression among Couples Applying for a Marriage License." *Journal of Family Violence* 7 (1992) 309–319.

Nicole, Faith Monique and Baldwin, Cynthia. "Cohabitation as a Developmental Stage: Implications for Mental Health Counseling." *Journal of Mental Health Counseling* 17 (1995) 386–397.

Nock, Steven L. "A Comparison of Marriages and Cohabiting Relationships." *Journal of Family Issues* 16 (1995) 53–76.

Parker, Stephen. *Informal Marriage, Cohabitation and the Law, 1750–1989.* New York: St. Martin's Press, 1990.

Peplau, Letitia A., Hill, Charles T., and Rubin, Zick. "Sex Role Attitudes in Dating and Marriage: A 15-Year Follow-Up of the Boston Study." *Journal of Social Issues* 49 (1993) 31–52.

Popenoe, David and Whitehead, Barbara Dafoe. *Should We Live Together?: What Young Adults Need to Know about Cohabitation before Marriage.* New Brunswick, N.J.: The National Marriage Project (Rutgers University), 1999.

Qian, Zhenchao. "Changes in Assortative Mating: The Impact of Age and Education, 1970–1990." *Demography* 35 (1998) 279–292.

Ressler, Rand W. and Walters, Melissa S. "The Economics of Cohabitation." *Ayklos* 48 (1995) 577–592.

Rinfuss, Ronald R. and Van den Heuvel, Audrey. "Cohabitation: A Precursor to Marriage or an Alternative to Being Single?" *Population and Development Review* 16 (1990) 703–726.

Schoen, Robert. "First Unions and the Stability of First Marriages." *Journal of Marriage and the Family* 54 (1992) 281–284.

Schoen, Robert and Owens, Dawn. "A Further Look at First Unions and First Marriages." *The Changing American Family,* ed. Scott J. South and Stewart E. Tolany. Boulder, Colo.: Westview Press, 1992.

Schoen, Robert and Weinick, Robin. "Partner Choice in Marriages and Cohabitation." *Journal of Marriage and the Family* 55 (1993) 408–414.

Singh, Supriya and Lindsay, Jo. "Money in Heterosexual Relationship." *Australian and New Zealand Journal of Sociology* 32 (1996) 57–69.

Stets, Jan E. "The Link between Present and Past Intimate Relationship." *Journal of Family Issues* 14 (1993).

Stets, Jan E. and Straus, Murray A. "The Marriage License as a Hitting License: A Comparison of Assaults in Dating, Cohabiting and Married Couples." *Journal of Family Violence* 4 (1989) 161–180.

Sweet, James A. "Differentials in the Approval of Cohabitation." National Survey of Families and Households, Working Paper No. 8. Center for Demography and Ecology: University of Wisconsin-Madison, 1989.

Sweet, James A. and Bumpass, Larry L. "Young Adults' Views of Marriage, Cohabitation and Family." *The Changing American Family,* ed. Scott J. South and Stewart E. Tolany. Boulder, Colo.: Westview Press, 1992.

Teachman, Jay D. and Polanko, Karen A. "Cohabitation and Marital Stability in the United States." *Social Forces* 69 (1990) 207–220.

Thomasson, Richard. "Modern Swedes: The Declining Importance of Marriage." *Scandinavian Review,* August 1998.

Thomson, Elizabeth and Colella, Ugo. "Cohabitation and Marital Stability: Quality or Commitment." Center for Demography and Ecology: University of Wisconsin-Madison, 1991.

Thornton, Arland. "Influence of the Marital History of Parents on the Marital and Cohabitational Experience of Children." *American Journal of Sociology* 96 (1991) 868–894.

Thornton, Arland and Axinn, William G. "Mothers, Children and Cohabitation: The Intergenerational Effects of Attitudes and Behavior." *American Sociological Review* 58 (1993) 233–246.

Thornton, Arland, Axinn, William G., and Hill, Daniel H. "Reciprocal Effects of Religiosity, Cohabitation and Marriage." *American Journal of Sociology* 98 (1992) 628–651.

Thornton, Arland, Axinn, William G., and Teachman, Jay D. "The Influence of School Enrollment and Accumulation on Cohabitation and Marriage in Early Adulthood." *American Sociological Review* 60 (1995) 762–774.

U.S. Bureau of the Census. "Marital Status and Hiring Arrangements." March 1997 (1998).

Waite, Linda J. "Does Marriage Matter?" *Demography* 32 (1995) 483–507.

Waite, Linda J. and Joyner, Kara. "Men's and Women's General Happiness and Sexual Satisfaction in Marriage, Cohabitation, and Single Living." Unpublished Paper, Population Research Center: National Opinion Research Center and University of Chicago, 1996.

Willis, Robert J. and Michael, Robert T. "Innovation in Family Formation: Evidence on Cohabitation in the United States." *The Family, the Market, and the State in Aging Societies,* ed. J. Ermisch and N. Ogawa. London: Oxford, 1994. 119–145.

Wineberg, Howard and McCarthy, James. "Living Arrangements after Divorce: Cohabitation vs. Remarriage." *Journal of Divorce and Remarriage* 29 (1998) 131–146.

Wu, Zheng. "Premarital Cohabitation and Postmarital Cohabiting Union Formation." *Journal of Family Issues* 16 (1995) 212–232.

CHAPTER 8

Cohabitation and Marriage as a Life-Process

Kieran Scott

In Chapter 7, the first part of the NCCB Marriage and Family Committee report on cohabitation is presented. It documents empirical information about cohabitation and marriage. This chapter addresses pastoral issues and questions raised by the data. However, the framework, analysis, and proposed solution enter a different paradigm from the NCCB report.

This essay steps back from the immediate issue of cohabitation. First, it reframes the issue by setting it in a larger context of a stage theory of marriage. It proceeds to highlight some pertinent social science research. Conventional pastoral responses of the Christian churches to the topic are described. The essay concludes with distinguishing different forms of cohabitation and reevaluating the practice in light of the distinction.

In this previously unpublished essay, Kieran Scott highlights the emergence of a developmental meaning of marriage that has come to the fore in the latter half of the twentieth century. Marriage is interpreted as a process, a series of steps or stages. Enriched by the creative work of Adrian Thatcher, Scott advocates that marriage is sufficiently encompassing to cover premarital cohabitation. By their intention to marry, the couple has already embarked on the process. This step, in turn, can lead to sacramentalizing the marriage. But during this in-between time, their sexual activity can be loving, faithful, and morally responsible.

Questions for Discussion

1. The NCCB report defines cohabitation as "both having a sexual relationship and living together in the same residence." Is this definition adequate? What might be missing in it?

2. Christian marriage in the modern period has accommodated enormous changes. Indicate examples of remarkable flexibility in the areas of ceremony, sacramentality, spheres of love, divorce, equality of partners.

3. Do you find the current response of your church adequate to the widespread practice of cohabitation? Why? Does it distinguish between types of cohabitation? Should it, in its moral evaluation?

4. Should Scott and Thatcher's moral evaluation and pledging ritual be extended to gay and lesbian partners? To postmarried people?

Widespread cohabitation is a fairly recent phenomenon. It has become a major social phenomenon in the past 25 years. Its upsurge spans both sides of the Atlantic Ocean, and even most parts of the Western industrialized world. Churches seem perplexed, if not paralyzed in their response to the phenomenon. Pastoral ministers are still learning how to address the issue in marriage preparation. Many of them identify cohabitation as the most difficult issue they deal with in marriage preparation programs and pre-marriage counseling (NCCB, 2000).

This chapter takes a fresh look at cohabitation. It makes some critical distinctions as a way of seeking a moral re-consideration of the issue. First, a framework is set for our proposal by offering a stage theory of marriage. Second, current social science research is presented on the topic. Third, some traditional pastoral solutions by the churches are described. Finally, a moral reassessment of the issue is proposed in light of historical precedent and contemporary personal and pastoral needs.

A STAGE THEORY OF MARRIAGE

The celebration of a couple's marriage in church is generally the high point of their growing union. It is the point of no return. It solemnizes this union as the couples mutually administer the sacrament. The assumption, however, that marriage *begins* at this point is false. This assumption has gravely weakened our theology of marriage, and the efforts of the churches in commending marriage and ministering to couples in postmodern times. A wide and deep sense of our own Christian history tells us: the marriage nuptial in church is not the beginning of marriage. Contemporary psychological theory, legal proposals and faith development perspectives support this historical perspective.

Evelyn and James Whitehead, in *Marrying Well* (1981), write about the demise of marriage as a state and its survival as a journey. Marriage as a stable state is gone. Divorce functions in our consciousness as one of the outcomes of marriage. Married couples find fidelity a new and unexpected challenge. New resources are needed to navigate the unexpected turns, detours, and passages. These continuing shifts and challenges give marriage the appearance of journeying. It is not a location in life, a place where we live, but rather a relational pattern of movement, a way we travel through life. The Whiteheads capture well this rich developmental psychological perspective. They write: "Understood as an institution, marriage has been a state that one either did or did not inhabit. Legally, a person is either married or not married; there is no in-between. The Christian Church, influenced by this legal orientation toward marriage, came to view marriage as an either/or situation." They proceed to note: "Outside this well defined state no sexual sharing was permitted; once inside this institution, one could even demand one's sexual rights. There seemed no gradualness or development in this commitment; one was either in or out. The period of engagement and of marriage preparation were anomalies; little effective attention and ministry could be given to these 'borderline' events" (1981, 98). The fundamental thesis of the Whiteheads is to oppose this legal framework and to propose marriage as relational process. In theological language, marriage is a personal covenant between individuals.

Some decades earlier Margaret Mead sensed the emergence of some crucial cultural changes that were impacting marriage. In particular, she named shifting attitudes toward sex and commitment. Sex, for most Americans, has become a natural activity, like eating and sleeping. "We have come to believe also," she wrote, "that asking physically mature young people to postpone sex until their middle twenties is neither fair nor feasible. . . . [Also] We believe in commitment, but we do not believe that commitments are irrevocable" (1970, 76–78). The succeeding years would bear out Mead's observations. She discerned an emerging gap between belief and experience, between precept and practice in relation to the style of marriage at the time. She asked: "How can we invest marriage forms with new meaning?" (76). Can we create new patterns that would (1) give young couples a better chance to come to know each other and (2) give children a better chance to grow up in an enduring family? In response to her own questions, Mead proposed marriage in two steps.

We need two forms of marriage, Mead wrote: an *individual marriage* and a *parental marriage*. One can develop into the other, though it need not. Each has its own possibilities and special forms of responsibility.

The first step in marriage would be the *individual marriage*. It might be called a "student marriage" or a "companionate marriage." It would be a licensed union, a serious commitment, entered into in public and validated and protected by law and, for some, by religion. The central obligation of the couple to each other would be an ethical, not an economic, one. Each partner would have a deep and continuing concern for the happiness and well-being of the other as long as they wished to stay together. Children and commitment to future parenting are not part of this marital form. In the individual marriage, the couple has a chance to know each other, grow into each other's life and develop meaningful relationships of choice. It could also open the way to a more complex marital form, namely, a parental marriage, or it may allow the couple to part without guilt or recrimination.

The *parental marriage* is the second step in Mead's analysis of marriage. It is explicitly directed toward the founding of a family. This second type of marriage always follows on an individual marriage—no matter what stage in life. It would have its own license, ceremony and responsibilities. It would be more difficult to contract. The couple needs to demonstrate their economic ability to support a child and marital skills to foster a quality marital relationship. This would be a marriage that looks to a lifetime relationship with links to the wider community.

While I have reservations with some of Mead's proposal, I affirm three aspects of it: (1) her concern that couples have a better chance to come to know each other, (2) her concern that children have a better chance to grow up in an enduring family, and (3) her recognition that marriage is a development journey.

On the canonical and liturgical levels, there has also been a growing awareness of the depth and development of faith in relation to Christian marriage. The issue tends to surface when a baptized Catholic couple requests a nuptial for their church wedding. The couple is ready to enter into the covenant of marriage with each other. However, they may not possess a faith sufficiently alive to affirm that their relationship is a reflection of the love of Christ and the Church. In other words, they are unable to state that their marriage is an explicit participation in that covenant. The only choice facing the couple at this stage is: celebrate a sacrament in which they really do not believe or enter a marriage relationship not recognized by the Christian community.

James Schmeiser (1981) describes a marriage program initiated by the diocese of Autun, France, that permits these baptized Catholic couples a further option in order to respond to this situation. The Autun diocesan pastoral team believes it was important to develop a notion of Church as "catechumenal" or as a "place of welcome and freedom." This would offer each person a way of experiencing himself/herself as he/she is and provide a structure that offers a real choice. The diocese proposed diverse forms of reflection and celebration in accordance with different situations. It would recognize different choices and respond to these choices. No longer would there be only two possibilities: sacramental marriage in the church or civil marriage. The diocese of Autun proposed three forms of marriage.

The first form of marriage is *civil marriage*. The marriage takes place at city hall and is registered with the State. The Church recognizes the value of this commitment and its permanence. The married couples are welcomed publicly in Church. An implicit affirmation or openness to faith is required; in as much as they are one with family and friends, for whom faith is a living reality.

The second form of marriage is *welcomed civil marriage*. This may not be the most appropriate naming, but it follows the civil marriage. In this case, the baptized couple believes in God but is very distant from church practice and is not receptive to celebrating the sacrament of marriage. It has little or no meaning for them. Yet, they desire a religious ethos and a religious manner of expressing their commitment and personal beliefs before family and friends. The Church welcomes and opens itself to the couple, helps them to reflect upon their faith and discover the realities of their love, as it testifies to its own faith. The couple is asked to declare their intentions before the community. The celebration may take place with the full participation of the assembly in the ritual. The ritual has a rich religious dimension to it. But it is not the sacrament of marriage. The marriage, however, is registered in a special church register.

The third form of marriage is *sacramental marriage*. This is celebrated by a couple of deep faith. They wish to symbolize the covenant of Christ and the

Church. The Gospel will guide their married life. It will be a sacrament. The couple celebrates their sacramental love before the community. The community, in turn, commits itself to support them.

In these three forms of marriage, then, a civil marriage is seen as a true and important step; a welcome civil marriage provides a religious ceremony, which is recognized as non-sacramental; and the sacramental marriage is an explicit form of covenantal grace. As Schmeiser notes, "This approach recognizes possible growth within the marital relationship. There is a recognition of various stages of marriage" (33).

SOCIAL SCIENCE RESEARCH AND COHABITATION

As indicated above, the emergence on various levels of a stage theory of marriage sets the framework for an ethical re-assessment of cohabitation. Before we turn to this re-examination, however, we need to get a clear and accurate handle on the scope of cohabitation. The social sciences offer us extensive empirical information on the phenomenon.

Cohabitation is pervasive and growing. In the US, between 1970 and 1980, Census Bureau data recorded a tripling in the number of cohabitating couples to over 1.5 million. Between 1980 and 1990, there was a further increase of 80%, to 2.9 million couples. In 1990, unofficially, there were actually between 3 and 8 million cohabitating couples. Similar figures and trends have been found in the UK (Thatcher, 2002).

Cohabitation is common both before marriage and after it. A little over half of all first marriages are preceded by cohabitation. The trend crosses all age groups and all first world countries. Some additional pertinent data is worth noting:

- Cohabitants are as likely to return to singleness as to enter marriage (Thatcher, 2002, 7).
- Slightly more than half of couples in first time cohabitation ever marry (NCCB, 2000).
- The median duration of cohabitation is 1–3 years. One third of couples cohabit for less than a year. 16% live with their partner for more than 5 years.
- Half of all cohabiting couples are young, unmarried or not yet married, and childless.
- Persons with lower levels of education and earning power cohabit more often and marry less often.
- Some people choose cohabitation as an alternative to marriage, not as a "trial" for it.
- Cohabitation is more likely to occur where religious belief is weak. However, there is no difference in frequency of cohabitation by religious denomination.

- Cohabiters may be more likely to divorce than people who marry directly from the single state. They divorce at a rate of 50% higher.

- Cohabiters with plans to marry report no significant difference in relationship quality to married people.

- The reasons for cohabitation vary: the growing secularization and individualization in first world countries; sexual, social and economic changes; peer pressure; fear of long-term commitment; desire to test the relationship; waiting to conclude higher education.

This cumulative data indicates one striking fact: cohabitation, as a contemporary phenomenon, is having a profound impact on marriage and family in postmodern times. Lost in the data, however, is adequate attention to different forms of cohabitation. Three types can be distinguished. First, there is temporary or casual cohabitation. This is entered with little thought or commitment. The second type is conscious preparation for marriage, a trial run as it were. The third type functions as a substitute for marriage (Thatcher, 1999). These distinctions will be vital in our ethical re-assessment of cohabitation and the needed pastoral responses of the churches. Let us turn first to the traditional responses of religious bodies to cohabiting couples.

TRADITIONAL PASTORAL SOLUTIONS

Cohabitation is disapproved in all the *official* documents of the Christian Churches and by many Christian theologians. The official belief is: people should not have sexual intercourse before they marry. This teaching, however, is widely disregarded by church members (practicing and non-practicing) and, as noted above, almost universally disregarded. In spite of this mismatch between traditional church teaching and the convictions and practices of its members, official church teaching cannot bring itself to sanction cohabitation before marriage. The unanimous teaching of the churches remains: sexual intercourse must be confined to marriage (Thatcher, 2002, 41).

The Roman Catholic Church condemns cohabitation. Such a relationship is seen as a false sign, contradicting the meaning of a sexual relationship. It violates the Church's teaching about sexual love and marriage. It is condemned under the rubric of "free union" and is considered a grave offense against the dignity of marriage. However, there is acknowledgement of the pastoral difficulty in dealing with this issue. Two extremes are to be avoided: (1) immediately confronting the couple and condemning their behavior and (2) ignoring the cohabitation aspect of their relationship. A middle road is suggested as the wisest strategy: integrate general correction with understanding and compassion; use it as a "teachable moment" in such a way as to smooth the path for them to regularize their situation. The assumption is that they are in a disordered state of sexuality, a state of sin (NCCB, 2000).

The Orthodox churches also strongly disapprove of cohabitation. Officially, they are reluctant to raise the question of sexual activity outside of marriage. The response from the evangelical churches is generally the same, and a similar position is taken by the Lutheran, Presbyterian and Episcopalian Churches. They all affirm: sexual intercourse properly belongs exclusively within marriage. Some committee reports, however, from some of these churches seek some pastoral accommodation to living together. However, there is near unanimous consensus in all official teachings: living together before marriage is wrong.

This traditional position is based on a threefold argument:

1. It situates sexual intercourse within the context of the bond of marriage. Any non-marital sexual intercourse then is wrong. Cohabitation, in this situation, is a sign of lack of discipline and giving in to the spirit of the times.

2. Cohabitation is a threat to marriage and family. Marriage, as Christians understand it, is a communal event undertaken with the intention of unlimited commitment. Cohabitation, on the other hand, tends to be private, lacking communal sanction and unlimited commitment.

3. Thirdly, cohabitants tend to create less stable relationships when converted into marriage (Thatcher, 1999, 106).

For a constructive re-assessment of cohabitation, the concerns expressed in this traditional argument need to be heard, given additional consideration, and, at the same time, outweighed by a most persuasive counterargument. This is the task of the rest of this essay.

COHABITATION RECONSIDERED

Contemporary theology (and religious studies) has to perform a double act of listening. It must listen to the voices of its traditions and the voices surrounding those traditions. It must be able to make connections between the Christian tradition and ordinary life—if the gospel is to be capable of touching and transforming people. In light of the topic at hand, a Christian theology of marriage must take seriously both the Christian traditions of marriage and the difficult challenges facing marriage today. High on the list of these challenges is the phenomenon of cohabitation. Adrian Thatcher (1999, 2002) offers a serious, substantive and lucid vision of marriage. What is creative about his proposal is: it incorporates some forms of cohabitation. I am indebted to Thatcher in opening up this new (yet old) perspective in his groundbreaking work.

Key to Thatcher's proposal is his basic distinction between two types of cohabitation. There is a form of cohabitation within which the couple intends to marry. They are engaged and on their way to the altar. This is prenuptial cohabitation. There is also a form of cohabitation where the couple has no plans to marry. Here cohabitation is an alternative to marriage. It is non-nuptial cohabitation. For Thatcher, there is a qualitative difference between the two forms. They are not equal, and there ought to be a corresponding difference in moral judgment about the two types of relationship. It seems unjust to bring those who intend to marry and those who do not under the same rubric, namely, fornication.

However, Thatcher offers a still stronger argument for treating engaged couples in a different category from those who merely live together. His argument is an historical one. We could also call it deeply conservative, i.e., preserving deep strands within the tradition. In Christian history, there are two traditions regarding the beginning of marriage. The traditional or conventional view is that a marriage begins with a wedding. An earlier Christian view, however, is that marriage begins with a pledging and binding of the couple to each other with a promise to marry. (The quaint sounding term betrothal captures the meaning of this view better than our own current term engagement.) This nuptial pledging of the couple was followed later by the marriage ceremony. Sexual experience regularly began after the couple's pledge to marry (i.e. betrothal) and before the wedding ceremony (i.e. the nuptial). This pre-modern distinction between spousal (pledging) and nuptial (wedding) has largely been forgotten today. Yet, it holds the key as to when marriage begins. Does marriage begin with the wedding or is the entry into marriage a staged process, with the wedding marking the "solemnization" of a life commitment . . . already well begun?

Thatcher (1999) offers us a meticulously documented history on the question. The widespread belief that a marriage begins with a wedding, he demonstrates, was not so much a religious or theological issue but a class matter. From the mid-eighteenth century onwards, in England and Wales, the middle and upper classes had the political clout to enforce the new marriage laws requiring the registration and ceremonial ritualization of marriage. Also new courtship procedures in the upper classes required prenuptial virginity of brides—for social rather than moral reasons. However, for most of Christian history marriage did not begin with the wedding. The entry into marriage has been by spousal pledge or/and betrothal ceremony. John Gillis proceeds to note, "Betrothal constituted the recognized rite of transition from friends to lovers, conferring on the couple the right to sexual as well as social intimacy" (1985, 47). Sex began at the moment of engagement. The marriage in church came later, often triggered by the pregnancy. Half of all brides in Britain and North America were pregnant at their weddings in the eighteenth century (Stone, 2001). So pre-marital sex is not simply a modern phenomenon. The only significant difference is: throughout most of Christian history it was mostly and truly pre-marital; i.e., it was part of the process of marrying. But with the current loss of the central importance of the spousal pledge (and betrothal rite), Adrian Thatcher claims, "Gone with it is the sense of entry into marriage as a process, liturgically marked and celebrated and sometimes revocable in cases of serious difficulty or incompatibility. Gone too is much of the social recognition of the in-between status of the couple" (2002, 46).

Thatcher's agenda is to recover this earlier (and biblical) understanding of the entry into marriage. It is essential, he believes, to the future of marriage in the new millennium. It also holds the possibility of transforming the perception of cohabitation with the intention to marry, from the domain of sin and fornication to the domain of marital beginnings of mutual growth and religious development. Crucial, of course, to this transformation is the distinction between forms of cohabitation. It is laissez-faire, promiscuous, non-nuptial cohabitation that is damaging to the couple (and to any children they may have). On the other hand, faithful, committed cohabitants with a clear intention of getting married are qualitatively different. They ought also to be considered, in Christian ethics, morally different.

Finally, Thatcher asks: how can the churches pastorally support this moral reassessment? He proposes the reintroduction of betrothal (the pledging of the couple), as well as the ritual betrothal, and of seeing betrothal as already part of the process of marriage. Thatcher argues: marriage itself is a process and a liturgically celebrated engagement could become a significant symbol of the beginning of that process. This, in many ways, is a pre-modern solution to our post-modern marriage crisis.

The operating assumption in Thatcher's approach, then, is that the meaning of marriage already belongs to premarital cohabiters. By their intention to marry they have already embarked on the process that leads to the solemnization of their marriage. Unlike most cohabitating couples, betrothal was "emphatically premised by the intention to marry." It was never an end in itself. It was open "to the probability of future marriage." It honored the sacredness of marriage.

In pre-modern times, betrothal could last up to two years. It served valuable functions. The couple had the opportunity to grow intimately together. The couple's families and the community came together to support the upcoming marriage. Couples discovered whether their union could produce children. Churches supported these unions. And they also supported breaking them under certain conditions.

Today, however, the formal process around marriage generally only takes one day, the wedding day. The reclaiming of the notion—and the ritual—of betrothal helps us to see marriage again not as a simple event, but as a "process." This, in turn, would enable couples to begin to explore the sacred dimensions of their bond before they solidify their union for life. It would support them in the process of linking the various stages of their relationship. And, of vital importance, it would help couples to weave their relationship into the larger social fabric of family, community and church. In this regard, Adrian Thatcher concludes: "If the entry into marriage were accepted as a process which involved, as steps within it, betrothal and ceremony, the anomalies presented to the church by cohabitees could be more easily handled. Furthermore, the actual availability of a betrothal liturgy or liturgies would help considerably in providing the missing language, which renders cohabitation socially problematic. It would also meet the concern that, while marriages are public, cohabitation is private [McGowan, 2001]. A betrothal ceremony would provide precisely the public language and community dimension which are currently properties of weddings" (Thatcher, 1999, 131). In a word, it would be a public act, with public legitimation.

We can summarize some conclusions from this study:

First Christian morality should not assume that all premarital sex is wrong. It is not. Nor ought we to assume that the nuptial has always been normative. It has not.

Second, to distinguish between pre-nuptial and non-nuptial forms of cohabitation, we must open up the possibility of a moral re-assessment of the issue.

Third, there is no longer any provision for a two-staged entry into marriage, engagement and ritual solemnization. Some current practice of cohabitation could be read as a return to earlier pre-modern sensibilities rather than as a rejection of Christian marriage.

And, finally, reclaiming the notion and the ritual practice of betrothal may be of service to the Christian churches in the construction of a post-modern theology of entry into marriage.

REFERENCES

Gillis, John (1985). *For Better, For Worse: British Marriages, 1600 to the Present*. Oxford: Oxford University Press.

McGowan, Jo (2001). Marriage versus Living Together. In Kieran Scott and Michael Warren (eds), *Perspectives on Marriage*, 2nd Edition. New York: Oxford University Press, 83–87.

Mead, Margaret (1970). Marriage in Two Steps. In Herbert Otto (ed), *The Family in Search of a Future*. New York: Appleton Century Crofts: 75–84.

NCCB Marriage and Family Committee (2000). *Marriage Preparation and Cohabiting Couples: Information Report*. Washington, DC: NCCB.

Schmeiser, James A. (1981). Marriage: New Alternatives. *Worship* 55, 1:23–34.

Stone, Lawrence (2001). Passionate Attachments in the West in Historical Perspective. In Kieran Scott and Michael Warren (eds), *Perspectives on Marriage*, 2nd Edition. New York: Oxford University Press, 129–138.

Thatcher, Adrian (1999). *Marriage After Modernity*. New York: New York University Press.

Thatcher, Adrian (2002). *Living Together and Christian Ethics* Cambridge: Cambridge University Press.

Whitehead, Evelyn and James (1981). *Marrying Well: Possibilities in Christian Marriage Today*. New York: Doubleday.

CHAPTER 9

The Meaning of Marriage

Evelyn Eaton Whitehead
James D. Whitehead

Some unmarried people think of marriage only in terms of a relationship filled with romance, rejecting the social institution of marriage as too rigid, too filled with legal formalities and rigid rituals—basically, too "unromantic." In this essay Evelyn and James Whitehead look at three aspects of marriage: as a relationship, as a commitment, and as a lifestyle.

They see relationship as not one way but mutual. Once they use the term *mutual*, they put the marriage relationship in a line of continuity with all other mutual relationships, like friendship and family. Married love as a relationship of mutuality has these characteristics: romance, sex, friendship, and devotion. None of these characteristics maintains itself automatically. Each must be *intended* and then *attended to*.

It is worth noticing that the model they use for mutual relationships is friendship. They point out how there arise in any friendship tensions and pressures, but especially "the tensions and ambiguities that are inevitable as we attempt to live as complex a relationship as marriage."

This highlighting of "tensions and ambiguities" may be especially encouraging to those with the mistaken notion that "being in love means never having to say you're sorry," but who are going through the inevitable strains of any mutual relationship. These tensions and ambiguities are more a sign of mutuality than a sign of a relationship in danger.

The commitment side of marriage is the one that makes many people most nervous and raises the most questions about whether one is capable of such a commitment. The Whiteheads offer wisdom on two dimensions of commitment: our expectations of exclusivity and our expectations of permanence. This section of the essay might be read in conjunction with Margaret Farley's "The Meaning of Commitment" (chapter 32).

The final section is about the lifestyle of marriage. The authors wisely point out that a lifestyle comes from choices made in a marriage, but also from circumstances. Some choices—like parenthood—are permanent and can't be changed. However, many choices can and must be rethought and remade or unmade and shifted, like our choices about money and time. Readers of this collection may want to give special attention to this last section and the meaning it may have for the choices being made right now.

The word "marriage" refers to many things. We can use the word to mean our own experience of the day-to-day relationship we share. The word can also mean the social institution of matrimony, which has legal definition and rights and duties that are regulated by the state and sanctioned in many religious traditions through special rites and ceremonies. Between these two senses of the word—marriage as my experience and marriage as a social institution—there are other meanings as well. Marriage is a relationship; marriage is a commitment; marriage is a lifestyle.

When we speak of marriage as a *relationship* we focus on the quality of the bond that exists between us, our mutual love. The *commitment* of marriage refers to the promises we make to do "whatever is necessary" to deepen and develop this love and, in this love, to move beyond ourselves in creativity and care. The *lifestyle* of marriage describes the patterns that we develop as we attempt to live out these promises—our choices among values and activities, the organization of our daily life, our patterns in the use of time and money and the other resources we have. These three facets of marriage are overlapping and interrelated. Each contributes richly to the complexity of our life together and to the satisfaction we experience in marriage. And, as we are becoming more aware, none of these aspects of our marriage is ever finished or static. Each is in movement, in an ongoing process of realization and development—or decline.

THE RELATIONSHIP OF MARRIAGE—MUTUAL LOVE

Mutual love is the heart of the process of marriage as we envision it today. This has not always been the case. In patriarchal understandings of marriage the wife is more property than partner. Vestiges of this "wife as possession" are still to be found (often embodied in laws and customs surrounding sexuality in marriage) but the movement toward mutuality continues in the way many married people choose to live and, gradually, in the larger social definitions of marriage as well.

The expectations for love in marriage today are high. The "ideal" of married love for most people includes romance, sex, friendship and devotion. Romance: We want the emotional and physical attraction that we experienced early in our relationship to continue through our married years. Sex: We want our lovemaking to be lively and mutually satisfying, enhanced by a deepening responsiveness to each other's preferences and needs. Friendship: We want to continue to like each other, to enjoy each other's company, to find in each other the sources of comfort and challenge, of solace and stimulation that we need for continuing growth. Devotion: We want to be able to "count on" one another, to give our trust in the deep conviction that it shall not be betrayed, to experience the awesome responsibility and transforming power of holding someone else's well-being as important to us as our own and to know that we, too, are held in such care.

Copyright © 1981 by Evelyn Eaton Whitehead and James D. Whitehead. Reprinted with permission.

These are not easy accomplishments. With these high expectations come equally high demands. In a relationship that is mutual, I must be ready to give these benefits as well as to receive them. And for many of us these emotional benefits are sought and expected only in marriage. We have no other so serious or so sustained an adult relationship.

Marriage did not always carry such high emotional demands. Wives and husbands did not generally expect to be one another's chief companion or best friend. Each could be expected to develop a range of social relationships—in the extended family, in the neighborhood, in the workplace, in clubs and churches and associations—that provided support and a sense of belonging to complement the marriage relationship. Today our involvement in these wider circles seems to have slipped. Economic and geographic mobility can cut into, even cut off, ties with family and neighborhood. The workplace is increasingly competitive; our relationships there seem of necessity to remain superficial. No one wants to take the risk of deeper friendship with a potential rival. And here, too, mobility plays a part in keeping these relationships light. We know it is likely that one or both of us may move to another job. Many associations—political parties, civic groups, churches—seem to have lost the consensus they formerly enjoyed. In these groupings today we are likely to experience polarization rather than a sense of belonging. Now it is often only from my spouse and, perhaps, my children that I expect any deep or continuing emotional response. This expectation has enriched the experience of mutuality in marriage, but it has also added to its strains. There are few of us today who would choose a style of marriage that did not include friendship and mutuality among its chief goals. But we have not given much attention to pressures that are inevitable in the companionate marriage or to the resources that may be required for us to live well this style of mutual love.

Marriage brings us in touch with our incompatible hopes for human life. It is useful to look at some of these incompatibles—the tensions and ambiguities that are inevitable as we attempt to live as complex a relationship as marriage. These tensions exist not simply because I am "selfish" or my spouse is "unreasonable" or "immature." These tensions are built into the experience of relationship—most relationships, but especially relationships as encompassing as marriage.

Security and adventure are both significant goals in adult life. We seek the stability of established patterns, and yet we are attracted by the new and the unknown. Often we sense these goals in opposition; life seems to force our choice of one over the other. To seek adventure means to risk some of the security I have known; to be secure means to turn away from some of life's invitations to novelty and change. Most of us learn to make these choices, but an ambivalence remains. At times, when the pull of security is strong, change may be seen as uninviting or even dangerous. A preference for stability is then easy to sustain. But at other times the appeal of change will be compelling and stability will seem a synonym for boredom and stagnation.

One of the ongoing tensions of marriage concerns this conflict between freedom and security, adventure and stability. I want to deepen the love and life we share, and I want to be able to pursue other possibilities that are open to me, unencumbered by the limits that come with my commitment to you. I need change and novelty and challenge; I need what is predictable and familiar and sure. I want to be close to you in a way that lets me share my weaknesses as well as my strengths, and I want to be strong enough to stand apart from you and from the relationship we share. Again, the presence of these incompatibles is not, of itself, cause for concern. These are normal, expectable, inevitable. But, then, neither is it surprising that the process of mediating among these needs generates considerable stress.

The commitment of marriage takes us to the heart of this ambivalence between stability and change. In marriage we say both "yes" and "no"— "yes" to each other and to the known and unknown possibilities that will be a part of our life together as it unfolds, "no" to the known and unknown possibilities that our life together will exclude. Marriage for a lifetime demands both stability (that we hold ourselves faithful to the promises we have made) and change (that we recognize the changing context in which our promises remain alive). We can anticipate that at different points in our marriage we will experience this ambivalence—sometimes celebrating the new developments in our life together, sometimes resisting these changes; sometimes grateful for the stability of our love, sometimes resenting its "sameness."

Marriage invites me to recognize these ambiguities of my own heart as I attempt to choose a style of life and love in which both to express myself and to hold myself accountable. Without commitment and choices, I know I remain a child, but that realization seldom makes the process of choice any easier.

THE COMMITMENTS OF MARRIAGE—
PRIORITY AND PERMANENCE

The commitments of marriage are the promises we make. In many ways it is these mutual promises that transform our experience of love into marriage— an enduring relationship of mutual care and shared life-giving. Both by our choice and by the momentum of its own dynamics, marriage takes us beyond where we are now. It projects us into the future. Through the hopes we hold for our life together we condition the future—we begin to mold and shape it. We open ourselves to possibilities, we make demands, we place limits, we hold each other in trust.

Our commitments, of course, do not control the future. We learn this mighty lesson as we move through adult life, invited by the events of our days to give up one by one our adolescent images of omnipotence. An illusory sense of the degree to which we can control our own destinies may have once served us well, energizing us to move beyond indecision and enter the complex world of adult responsibility. But maturity modifies both our sense of power and our sense of control. We are both stronger and weaker than we had known. Our promises are fragile, but they still have force. It is on this vulnerable strength of human commitment that we base our hope. And it is through our commitments that we engage the future.

The commitments of marriage are the promises we make—to ourselves, to one another, to the world beyond—to do "whatever is necessary" so that the love that we experience may endure; even more, that it may flourish. Our own relationship of love is, we know, similar to that which other couples share. But it is in many ways special, unique to who we are, peculiar to the strengths and needs and history we have. Our commitments, then, will reflect features in common with most marriages as well as the demands and possibilities that are particularly our own.

Two of the commitments that have been seen to be at the core of marriage are sexual exclusivity and permanence. The social meaning of these commitments has fluctuated across time. Stress on the importance of the woman's virginity at marriage and her sexual availability only to her husband after marriage is particularly strong in cultures where property and social status are transferred according to the male line of descent. It is important here that there be no confusion about paternity. And strict regulation of the woman's sexual experience is one way to keep the facts of paternity clear.

There are other instances where the stress on sexual exclusivity is intended to regulate the wife's behavior but not, or not to the same degree, the husband's. This double standard of sexual morality, which looks with some leniency on a married man's "fooling around" while it castigates a married woman as a wanton or an adulteress, has been tied closely with those understandings of marriage that see the wife as, in some ways, the property or possession of her husband.

In many current marriages the commitment to sexual exclusivity has expanded toward an expectation that neither spouse shall have any emotional involvement outside the marriage itself. By conscious decision or simply by circumstances, the couple or the small family unit depend exclusively upon one another for emotional sustenance. They have become an emotional island, apart. Neither wife nor husband has any other substantive adult friendship; their network of social acquaintances is shifting and somewhat superficial. Each may also feel that to need or seek support from someone other than the spouse is itself a kind of "infidelity." Sometimes this caution in exploring wider friendship is rooted in a fear of the "inevitable" sexual overtones of relationships between women and men. "Better not to start anything than to find this friendship slipping into an affair." Sometimes it responds to real insecurity or jealousy in one or both spouses. Sometimes, however, this insistent emotional exclusivity is more an expression of what couples judge to be "expected" of marriage. Emotions and needs, personal values and concerns—these are of the substance of my "private life." Family is the unit of private life in our society. It is to my family, especially to my spouse, that I retreat from the arbitrary and impersonal "public world." Increasingly, colleagues at work, people in the neighborhood, fellow citizens are all seen as part of the "public world." My relations with them are limited, objective and often hostile. There is little opportunity and less ability to share with them any meaningful part of life. It is in marriage that I expect that my subjectivity will be nourished. Here, and possibly here alone, "who I am" is more important than "what I can do." As the polarization of the subjective and the objective worlds, the realms of the private and the public, increases, so do the pressures for emotional exclusivity in marriage.

Many judge that the pressures of the emotionally exclusive marriage ultimately work against its development and permanence. Permanence is the second of the commitments that have generally described marriage. Here, too, the promise has been experienced differently at different times. Seldom has this expectation been absolute. Cultures and legal systems, while stressing the significance of permanence to the interpersonal experience and the legal contract of marriage, have also stipulated a variety of circumstances under which this commitment can be set aside. Sometimes childlessness was justification, frequently adultery has been sufficient cause. Religious conversion, desertion, physical abuse, psychological immaturity, emotional illness—each has been seen as of sufficient weight to justify the dissolution of marriage, whether through annulment or divorce.

The commitment of permanence has also had different psychological meaning. As recently as a century ago "marriage for a lifetime" often did not last very long. The woman's death in childbirth ended many marriages. An average life expectancy of some fifty years meant that many marriages ended in mid-life. In 1870, for example, a married woman could expect that her husband would die before her youngest child would leave home. Today, increasingly, couples can anticipate some twenty or more years together, alone, after the children have left the family household and are on their own. Movement into this time of "post-parental intimacy" is hard on some marriages. Couples may be surprised to find that, without their shared concern for parenting, they have little left of mutuality. They face the challenge of developing anew a life in common, one that is adequate to the reality of each partner now and to the possibilities that are present in their relationship. Other couples have been aware of a deteriorating relationship and yet have chosen to remain together through the years of their most active family responsibilities. These past, they judge there is no further bond to hold them together.

The strains on permanence can be experienced earlier in marriage as well. The accelerated pace of social change today is reflected in the experience of personal change. As we approach marriage we judge—to some degree correctly, to some degree in error—that we "fit" together, that we shall be able to offer each other the resources of love and support and challenge that will enable us to find and to give life. And then we change, sometimes each of us and in ways that enrich our mutual commitment. Sometimes, though, there is not such synchrony. One of us changes in ways that are threatening or seem unfair to the other. Each of us develops—perhaps gradually, perhaps suddenly—in directions that lead us apart and leave us without a clear sense of how we can be together now. Are there ways we might stay better in touch over the course of change so that we are not so taken by surprise? Or must the loss of our relationship be the price we pay for growth?

There are those who suggest that the prevalence of divorce among us today has dissolved our expectations of permanence in marriage. Young people approaching marriage, it seems, do not expect it to last. And, so the argument goes, married people today consider divorce a ready option, one which they anticipate that they, too, will use. There are, obviously, people of whom this characterization is true. But the effect of the increasing incidence of divorce on the expectations of permanence in marriage is more complex than these attitudes suggest. Permanence is no longer a guarantee of marriage even when it is promised. This awareness permeates our consciousness today. This may lead us to question whether, or under what circumstances, permanence is possible. But it seldom leads us, whether we are beginning a relationship of marriage or ending one, to judge that permanence is not to be preferred. Permanence is not to be preferred to everything, so that under no circumstances will I consider the end of my own marriage. But permanence is to be preferred as the goal and intention of our life together. And it is to be preferred, if it is in any way possible, to the pain of divorce.

Most people want marriage to last. It is in the hope of an enduring relationship that we take the emotional and the practical, legal steps that lead us into marriage. Our standards are high for what constitutes the kind of relationship that we want to endure, and sometimes these criteria are not always clear or compatible. (We may want to be the central figure in each other's life and also want each to be open to continuing growth in new relationships. We may want to start our family now and yet to have each of us pursue the development of our own career without serious interruption.) Each of our goals for marriage, taken alone, may be worthy. But taken together they may place considerable strain on our resourcefulness. While no one of our goals may be incompatible with our marriage flourishing over a lifetime, the combination of goals and priorities that we establish may carry heavy costs. We may find, in living out these patterns that define our marriage, that the strain is taxing. This realization invites us to reconsider—to reexamine what it is we want together, to reassess the strengths and needs we bring to the relationship, to recommit ourselves to its development and continuation.

We may find, especially if it is through a period of pain or deprivation that we come to a sense of the costs of sustaining this relationship, that the price is too high. Our own goals are no longer fulfilled, our resources are spent, our trust is broken. The movement through legal divorce will seem the only reasonable option to terminate a relationship that has already died.

But for many people the prevalence of divorce set against their own hope of an enduring relationship in marriage leads not to taking marriage lightly but to approaching it with greater seriousness, even caution. The expectation of permanence, sometimes experienced as an all too fragile hope, remains. The concern becomes how we shall safeguard and make robust this fragile conviction of our love.

Each marriage today must come to terms with these two dimensions of commitment: our expectations of exclusivity (What is the meaning of the priority in which we hold each other in love? How is this priority expressed?) and our expectations of permanence (What is the significance of our hope that our love shall flourish for our lifetime? How does this hope influence our lives now?).

THE LIFESTYLE OF MARRIAGE

Marriage is love, marriage is commitment, marriage is also a lifestyle—not one lifestyle experienced universally but the many particular lifestyles through which married couples express their love and live out the promises that hold them in mutual care. The lifestyle of marriage is the design or pattern of our life together that emerges in the choices we make. Many people do not experience the patterns of their daily life as open to personal choice. By the time of marriage, and from long before, factors of poverty or class or personality have narrowed the range of those parts of my life over which I have much say. I live out life, but I do not see myself as influencing its design in many important ways. Things happen to me, to my marriage, to my family—and I make the best of them. But I have little conviction that I can initiate changes or take responsibility on my own.

But for most Americans today there is a heightened consciousness of choice. We are aware that there are different ways in which the possibilities of life and of marriage may be lived out. And while our choices are always limited, we are aware that we not only can but must choose among these options for ourselves. The lifestyle of our marriage thus results from both our choices and our circumstances.

The choices that construct the lifestyle of our marriage include the decisions we make about the practical details of living—the routine of our daily activities, how we allocate the recurrent tasks of family and household care. But more basic decisions are involved—the values we hold important, the goals we have for our life together, the ways we choose to invest ourselves in the world.

At the heart of our decision about lifestyle is the question: What is our marriage for? Are we married only for ourselves? Does our life together exist chiefly as a place of personal security and a source of mutual satisfaction? Or is our marriage also about more than just the two of us? Is it a way for us to engage ourselves—together—in a world that is bigger than ourselves?

In previous decades the expectable presence of children in marriage answered this question in part. One of the things our marriage is for is our children. A child is so concrete an expression of the love that exists between us and so insistent an invitation that this love now go beyond itself in care. In parenting we experience the scope of our love widening to include our children. Often this broadening of concern continues, expanding to include more of the world and even the future, in which "our children's children" shall have to find their own way. Married people have always been generously engaged in the world in ways other than as parents, as well. But the central connection between being married and having children has been so clear and so prevalent for centuries that it has been a defining characteristic of the lifestyle of marriage.

Today there is more choice involved in the link between marriage and parenthood. Couples come to the decision to have a child with more consideration given to how many children there shall be in the family, how the births of these children shall be spaced, when in the marriage the commitments of family life shall begin. Some couples who have been unable to have children of their own seek other ways to expand their life together as a family—through adoption or foster care or through the assistance of recent developments in the biological sciences and medical practice. Other couples decide not to have a family and, instead, to express their love beyond themselves in other forms of creativity and care.

A comparable challenge accompanies each of these options—to develop a way of being together in marriage that takes seriously the demands of mutuality in our own relationship as it takes seriously the challenge that we look beyond ourselves in genuine contribution and care. Thus a central choice in marriage concerns our progeny—how shall we give and nurture life beyond ourselves: in our own children? in our friendships and other relationships? in our creative work? in our generous concern for the world? And the decisions that we come to here do much to determine the design of our daily life together.

Beyond this central choice concerning the focus of our creative love, there are other decisions of lifestyle. How shall we use the resources we possess? How, especially, do we allocate our money and our time? Here, again, the questions can be stated simply: What is our money for? What has priority in our time? We can respond to these questions at the practical level, offering the balance sheet of the family budget and our calendar of weekly events. But as an issue in lifestyle the question is more to the core: How are our own deepest values expressed or obscured in how we spend our money and our time?

Most American families today experience both money and time as scarce. There is not enough of either to go around. There seem to be always more possibilities, more demands for each than we feel we can meet. We have little "discretionary" income and even less "free" time. But among the demands that seem both genuine and inevitable there are others that seem to squander us uselessly, leaving us no time to be together or to be at peace and leaving us few resources to use for any purpose beyond ourselves. This sense of overextension characterizes the lifestyle of many marriages. Its prevalence invites us to reflect on our own patterns of money and time, not looking to praise or blame but trying to come to a better sense of the motives and pressures that move us and, in that way, define our lives. How much does our use of money and time revolve around "us," somewhat narrowly conceived—as a couple or a family over against "others"? What are the ways in which our decisions about time and money are more reflective of what our society expects of us than of the values and activities and possessions that make sense to us? Couples and families will differ in their responses to these questions, as they will differ on other issues of value and lifestyle. But the reflective process can lead to a greater congruence between the goals we have for our life together in marriage and the ways that this life is lived on a day-to-day basis.

Establishing our lifestyle in marriage is not done once and for all, but is itself an ongoing process. The lifestyle of our marriage must respond to the movements of development and change in each of us, in our relationship and in our responsibilities.

Marriage for a lifetime, then, is constituted by the interaction of our relationship, our commitments and our lifestyle. Our mutual love is at the core of our marriage. But in marriage we experience our relationship as more than just our love here and now. Marriage is focused by the promises to which we hold ourselves. It is the commitments that we made to one another that ground our love and give it duration. These commitments give us courage to undertake the risks of creative and procreative activity together. It is these commitments that are expressed in the choices and behavior and attitudes that make up the patterns of our lifestyle. And it is, in turn, an important goal of the commitments of our marriage and the lifestyle to which these commitments give shape, to sustain and deepen and mature the relationship of love between us.

It is important to note, as we begin our consideration of marriage for a lifetime, that the relationship and commitment and lifestyle of marriage do not exist in a vacuum. For each of us our experience of marriage is influenced by legal and historical and cultural understandings of what marriage is. In the next chapter we shall examine more closely the ways in which these social understandings of marriage are themselves undergoing change.

REFLECTIVE EXERCISE

These sentence stems may help you to explore your own awareness of the relationship, the commitments and the lifestyle that are marriage today. Complete the sentence begun by each of these phrases. There is no need to force an answer, just respond with what comes to mind at the time. For some phrases you may have several responses; others may call up little for you right now.

The relationship of marriage . . .

For me, mutual love . . .

Romance is a part of marriage . . .

The commitments of married people . . .

Today permanence in marriage . . .

The lifestyle of married people today . . .

Children bring to marriage . . .

Marriage for a lifetime is . . .

After you have completed the sentences, read through your whole list a couple of times to see if there is a dominant theme or tone to your responses.

CHAPTER 10

The Meaning of Marriage: Of Two Minds

Edward C. Vacek

The meaning of marriage today is up for grabs. Until comparatively recently, the meaning of marriage seemed simple. Our taken-for-granted assumption was that the frame of reference was a heterosexual union. This assumption is challenged and the complexity of the question emerges when homosexual unions insist on inclusion in the meaning of the term. What once seemed simple, restrictive, and exclusive in meaning has moved into the realm of the complex, public discourse, and the inclusive.

Edward Vacek's article is valuable to enable us to navigate through this messy thicket and to coolly analyze this hot-button issue. Vacek sets up his analysis in an illuminating manner by contrasting two very different mindsets or positions. These two contrasting worldviews undergird and are central to the current debate. They are the essentialist (premodern) and postmodern worldviews. Each has its own set of assumptions, epistemologies, sensibilities, values, and perspectives on human nature, marriage, and family life. In contemporary lingo, there may not be "a clash of civilizations" here, but there sure is a clash of ways of being in the world.

Vacek brings these contrasting positions to his exploration of the meaning of marriage. In a concise, precise, and brilliant analysis he brings six overlapping criteria into his reflections: (1) male–female difference, (2) reproduction, (3) "unnatural" sex, (4) institutional recognition, (5) purposes of marriage, and (6) parenting. A sincere dialogue about the nature of marriage, Vacek declares, is necessary, within minds and between persons. He tries not to show his cards. But it remains to be seen, he notes, whether homosexual union will deform or develop the meaning of marriage.

Questions for Discussion

1. Which position is most persuasive to you: the mindset of the congregation for the Doctrine of the Faith or the postmodern mindset?
2. Is the legal concept of "domestic partnership" an adequate classification for enduring gay and lesbian relationships?
3. Would (civilly) legalizing and (ecclesially) ritualizing gay marriages weaken or strengthen the family?
4. Could the Christian meaning of marriage (as sacrament) be consonant with life-long lesbian and gay partnerships?

5. Are all sexual forms equal? Or does heterosexual marriage have a special and irreplaceable place at the center of the Christian tradition?

Forty years ago, most Americans considered homosexual activity an abomination and homosexual marriage an impossibility. Now a wide range of U.S. and Canadian citizens are debating whether homosexual marriage may be an idea whose time has come. Appropriately, the Congregation for the Doctrine of the Faith (CDF) has entered the discussion, arguing against recognition of same-sex unions (see "Considerations Regarding Proposals to Give Legal Recognition to Unions between Homosexual Persons," *Origins*, August 14, 2003).

In this essay, I want to explore how something unthinkable only a few decades ago has already been legalized in more than a dozen countries. For the record, I am not arguing for homosexual marriages. Frankly, my early life in the pre-Vatican II church, my Jesuit training, and my study of Thomistic philosophy strongly bias me toward what I will call the essentialist mindset. Thus, I prefer clear and distinct ideas, and I lean toward the view that anything less than the best is not good enough. I usually find the Vatican's moral positions to be intelligently argued. Because of my background, I am predisposed to agree with the church's approach to homosexual unions. Still, as a priest, I have learned that human life is messy and that the best is often the enemy of the good. That is why over the ages priests have supplemented normative ethics with a "pastoral approach." At times, that approach has gradually become the norm.

The essentialist mindset that grounds the CDF position clearly defines the nature of sex; from this, it draws unambiguous conclusions about what marriage is and which sexual acts are morally right or wrong. Contrast that to what I will call the postmodern mindset, which relies on categories with fuzzy boundaries and on fallible human wisdom to deal with the ever-changing mix of reality. The first mindset inhabits the realm of the textbook; the second wanders/wonders in the realm of the morning newspaper. Justice Antonin Scalia, in his dissent against the recent Supreme Court decision invalidating Texas's sodomy laws, noted that, while the law does better with strictly logical thinking, daily life often does better without it.

For the essentialist, the "universe" is well ordered, and there are clear distinctions that must be preserved. In particular, God created the institution of marriage, and so its terms are not open to human modification. Sexual activity is either natural and good, or unnatural and evil. In Scripture, it is abhorrent to God that a woman would wear a man's clothes. Similarly, it is abhorrent for a man to lie with another man as with woman. In the well-ordered cosmos of Thomas Aquinas, offenses against our biological sexuality are direct offenses against God. For the subsequent tradition, all sexual sins, no

© 2003 Commonweal Foundation, reprinted with permission. For subscriptions: www.commonwealmagazine.org.

matter how small, are judged "objective mortal sins" because they attack God's design for the survival of the human race.

To the postmodern mind, our categories are more or less adequate; they are mental groupings of things for pragmatic purposes. Hence the postmodern mind sees similarities between homosexual and heterosexual unions. By contrast, the CDF sees no connection whatsoever: "There are absolutely no grounds for considering homosexual unions to be in any way similar or even remotely analogous to God's plan for marriage and family." To the essentialist, moral evaluations of sexual acts tend to black or white, but to the postmodern mind they are varied in hue and value.

In the fragmented "pluriverse" (to use William James's term) of the postmodern mind, the world is not well ordered, so we (not God or the cosmic order) must decide, always provisionally, which practices and institutions help us live with one another and flourish. At times, we must submit to the limits of our embodied existence and at other times transcend them. For example, we cannot fly, but we can take an airplane. Biological nature is not definitive.

According to the CDF, homosexual unions deserve strong and unequivocal condemnation because they violate human nature and the common good. According to a postmodern mindset, homosexual unions should perhaps be sanctioned so that homosexual persons too can develop their humanity and make a contribution to society. While the essentialist mind of the CDF says that it is wrong to use principles of respect or nondiscrimination to protect what is in fact immoral, the postmodern mind demands respect for the sexual differences in people.

"Marriage" as traditionally defined means that a man and a woman join their lives sexually and bear children. So simple. But history shows that marriage has always been complicated when it comes to real people living in diverse cultures and ages. Such variations incline the postmodern mind to consider expanding the institution of marriage to include one more variation, namely, the union of two persons of the same sex.

I will consider six overlapping criteria commonly used for deciding what is or is not a "marriage": (1) male–female differences; (2) reproduction; (3) "unnatural" sex; (4) institutional recognition; (5) purposes of marriage; and (6) parenting. I hope that these considerations will help overcome the mutual incomprehension that divides the essentialist and the postmodern positions.

DIFFERENCES

According to Cardinal Joseph Ratzinger, prefect of the CDF, the human spirit knows with "certainty that marriage exists solely between a man and a woman." This claim presupposes that men and women are relevantly different. Few things seem more obvious. Yet most people have found it difficult to say what, apart from reproductive capacity, is essentially different in women and men. Some women can do almost anything most men can do, and vice versa. Few men could beat Annika Sorenstam in a round of golf or run Hewlett Packard better than Carly Fiorina. These days, tough-minded wives go to the law office, and gentle husbands stay home to nurture their children. Since we find it so hard to say what the psychological and spiritual differences are between men and women, we also find it hard to say why, on the all-important interpersonal level, the marriage covenant of a man and a woman is significantly different from a covenant between, say, two women.

This lack of decisive difference is significant because most American marriages are primarily whole-life unions of persons and only secondarily genital unions. The poet John Milton, arguing against the idea that adultery is the only grounds for divorce, perceptively wrote that such a restriction perversely implies that sexual intercourse is the core of a marriage. Rather, the complementary way spouses play, argue, and work together is more significant than the way they have sex together. In fact, sexual intercourse ordinarily serves the function of bonding the couple far more than the function of procreation. Since gays can live and sexually bond well with one another, it is hard for postmodern thought to understand why bodily differences legitimate one kind of union but forbid another.

Further, the boundary between males and females has become even more obscure because some people feel they are men trapped in female bodies, and vice versa. I recently listened to a woman complain about a male relative who had become a woman. (She did not complain about the sex change, but rather that this guy, who used to be "ugly as sin," became "drop-dead gorgeous.") I asked myself what moral criteria should be used to decide, first before and then after the surgery, whether he/she should look for a man or a woman to marry.

REPRODUCTION

The standard reason for insisting on one man and one woman in a marriage is, of course, that they fulfill one another reproductively. Based on that difference, the CDF argues that homosexual unions cannot be marriages since they cannot produce children. What could be clearer?

Twenty-five years after the birth of the first test-tube baby, matters are not so clear. Reproductive technology has become so widely accepted that many states require insurance companies to pay for it. Indeed, reproductive medicine has forced us to reevaluate our notion of parenthood. Four different persons may contribute sperm, egg, womb, and gestation in the conception and birth of a child. Embryo splitting and recombination make tracing our origins even more difficult. Adoptive parents quite rightly claim to be real parents. In this context, homosexual parenthood looks less anomalous to the postmodern mind.

The official Catholic position says children should be conceived through sexual intercourse by married couples. The postmodern challenge is not that this position is unreasonable. Rather, the question is why is this the only moral way to have children? My point is not to approve all the variations created by reproductive technology and adoption. Rather, I am trying to explain why the changes of the past twenty years have led the "fuzzy logic" of the postmodern mind to consider sanctioning homosexual families. Whether we as a society should rethink how we have children is a separate question.

NATURE OF SEXUAL ACTS

For the essentialist mind, sex by its very nature requires that the right male organ engage the right female organ in the right manner under the right circumstances and for the right reasons. Anything else is unnatural and therefore immoral.

It is doubtful that most heterosexual married people confine themselves within such limits. Husbands and wives engage in sexual activities such as kissing, fondling, showering together, cunnilingus, fellatio, masturbation, even anal intercourse. Some engage in these acts not just as foreplay, but often as sexual acts chosen for mutual enjoyment. Today, many consider these "unnatural" acts to be within the broad pale of what is acceptable, and so they are hard-pressed to insist that such acts are wrong for homosexual partners.

Actually, the essentialist tradition has long had trouble naming which sexual acts are truly "natural." For Augustine and Aquinas, sexual acts when procreation cannot occur are more sexually "unnatural" than sex with a prostitute when it can. We now know that most sexual acts, including those within marriage, are infertile. By one reading of *Humanae vitae*, "natural" now means something like "not deliberately closed by human intervention to the possibility of procreation." Of course, the same might, tongue-in-cheek, be said of homosexual sex. When, after Vatican II, Catholics began to connect sexual activity more strongly with expressing love than with making babies, it became harder to see how homosexual acts are completely different from heterosexual acts.

LEGAL STATUS

The CDF quite rightly observes that civil law grants institutional recognition to marriage because the succession of generations is a matter of public interest. By this logic, childless heterosexual marriages do not deserve legal recognition. Nevertheless, the church and society have decided that even childless heterosexual marriages are "close enough" to receive important legal benefits and protections. On the other side, some homosexual couples now seek legal recognition precisely to bring legitimacy and stability to their children. Faced with this mix, in 1998 the Vermont Supreme Court decided that gay couples deserve, if not the name "marriage," at least the same privileges.

There are many other functions that current marriages fill: interpersonal commitment, permanence, sexual exclusivity, economic rights. Prima facie, these benefits seem to be as good for homosexual persons as they are for heterosexual persons, and thus they seem to warrant equivalent public recognition.

The CDF quite rightly argues against an understanding of marriage that is too broad. Still, the church itself has always had difficulty naming the necessary features of not only getting married but, more important, of being married. At least some legally married people lack one or more features—they may not live together, not have sexual relations, not have children, not have only one partner, etc. Indeed, the church says that two (civilly divorced) separated persons are still married even though they may have nothing in common except bad memories.

On the other hand, the postmodernist's aversion to exclusive definitions makes it difficult to decide what might count as marriage. If marriage is described, as some do, as an "intimate and lasting human relationship," then a daughter who commits herself to care for her aging mother could marry her. As a consequence, postmodern minds are divided. Some are open to homosexual marriage as just another variation on an evolving institution. Others find a middle ground in "registered partnerships." Still others think that gay unions "cross the line" and at best deserve only tolerance.

PURPOSE

It would be easier to decide whether there is such a thing as "gay marriage" if one could establish the "purposes" of marriage. Unfortunately, over the centuries there has been considerable waffling on this issue. For Augustine and most of the Catholic tradition, the primary purpose of marriage was to have children. John Chrysostom, in his "Homily on Marriage," writes that the primary purpose of marriage was not children but the avoidance of fornication. For many contemporary theologians, the purpose of marriage is to form a covenant of love expressible through sexual intercourse.

Consider the following: Three couples want to get married. The first couple say they don't like one another, but want to bear children. The second say they feel guilty about having sex and want to legitimate it. The third couple love one another and want to share their lives together but, for reasons of their genes, will not bring any children into the world. Although each of these cases isolates one of the standard purposes of marriage, most American Catholics likely would refuse the first couple, strongly discourage the second, and affirm the third. A homosexual union fits the second and third cases.

PARENTING

Finally, who should raise children? The CDF's answer is clear: Children should be raised by their biological parents. Ratzinger writes that it is a gravely immoral act of violence to bring a child into an arrangement where either a father or a mother is missing.

This judgment seems overly restrictive. Historically, wealthy families have "farmed out" their children's care to wet nurses, nannies, other families, or boarding schools. Through divorce, death, or adoption, single parenting is common and viable. The key question is what kinds of parents will negatively affect the child. To Ratzinger, homosexual parenting creates unjustifiable obstacles to a child's development. In the experience of many other people, homosexual parenting gives love and life to those who otherwise would not have these treasures.

Thus, sincere dialogue about the nature of marriage is necessary, within minds and between persons. Otherwise, the clear logic of the CDF will not correspond to the reality experienced by the postmodern mind. And the latter's experience of "reasonableness" will be thought by the CDF to be just sloppy thinking.

Historically, marriage has often been changed by cultural shifts. Some adaptations, such as the requirement that rapists marry their victims, now seem quite inadequate. Others, such as the requirement of a love covenant, now seem quite proper. It remains to be seen whether homosexual unions will deform or develop that most central institution we call marriage.

CHAPTER 11

Same-Sex Marriage: Threat or Aspiration?

Stephen J. Pope

Globalization is no longer restricted to international commerce in goods and services. Ideologies, values, terror, and lifestyles have all become part of our global interchange. Likewise, the question of same-sex marriage has emerged in recent years as a global issue. In the United States and worldwide, the issue has moved into the courts and before state legislatures. Of course, the topic is also a hot-button issue in our political campaigns and church debates. In spite of the heat the topic gives rise to, I find it amazing how far the conversation has developed in the last twenty-five years.

However, what is at stake is the meaning of marriage. Traditionally, our frame of reference for this meaning has been a heterosexual union. On the legal level, the challenge to this restricted meaning continues unabated. Stephen Pope's contribution in this essay is to bring a moral dialogue and ethical analysis to the complexity of the question.

Traditionalists and magisterial teachings see same-sex marriage as a threat to marriage and family. Pope lays out their fourfold objection: (1) marriage would be defined by the "exchange of sex," (2) it would extend marriage to the general category of friendship, (3) it reflects the modern rejection of the inherent ends of marriage and sex, and (4) it denies the primacy of procreation as the first and defining characteristic of marriage. While acknowledging some valid concerns of critics of same-sex marriage, Pope logically, rationally, and skillfully dismantles each of the above objections. He places love and commitment at the center of marriage. Observers with "sympathetic understanding," he proposes, ought to consider the point of view of same-sex couples who aspire to these ideals. These couples, then, could and should be included in the meaning of marriage. They may even improve and enrich its practice.

Discussion Questions

1. Is marriage simply "an exchange of sex" between partners?
2. Is the metaphor of friendship adequate to establish the grounds and boundaries of marriage?
3. What are some of the dangers in looking to technology to provide the best answers to serious moral problems?
4. How could legalizing and canonizing same-sex marriage be viewed as a conservative move?

5. Are the concepts of "domestic partnership" or "civil union" adequate classi-
fications for enduring same-sex relationships? Or are they part of the problem?

The debate over legalizing same-sex marriage has become a worldwide
issue. On Sept. 4 Pope John Paul II denounced the notion to the new Canadian ambassador to the Holy See, Donald Smith. The issue also has been the
subject of court decisions and legislative actions throughout the United States
and was taken up by both presidential candidates in their campaigns. The way
of addressing the issue often seems to be more a matter of political maneu-
vering and power struggles than moral dialogue or ethical analysis, yet occasionally one does find clear arguments advanced by careful thinkers. One
such contribution was offered in the June 7, 2004, issue of *America* in an article
by Msgr. Robert Sokolowski entitled "The Threat of Same-Sex Marriage."

Sokolowski's essay has the virtues of clarity and consistency. Readers
know where he stands, and why, on recent proposals to give legal recognition
to same-sex marriages. His central claims can be summarized as follows:

1. Recognition of same-sex marriages would mean that marriage will be
defined by the "exchange of sex." This is a redefinition of marriage that
breaks with the traditional notion according to which procreation "specifies"
what a marriage is.

2. If marriage is a contract that brings benefits and protections to adults
who are simply friends rather than procreative couples, then it would have
to be extended to all groups of people who wish to be friends. If marriage is
defined more specifically, as a contract that gives legal status to consenting
adults engaged in a specifically sexual relationship, then it would have to include multiple partners rather than just couples. Restricting the contract to
two adults would be arbitrary from the point of view of those who would like
to have legal status granted to polygamous or other multiple-partner sexual
relationships.

3. The desire to detach procreation from marriage reflects the modern rejection of teleology, the ancient principle that the "nature" of things deter-
mines their good and proper functioning. The modern commitment to the
"mastery of nature" by technology explains why many contemporary people
find it possible to believe that marriage and sex do not have inherent purposes rooted in their natures.

4. Sex is "defined as the power to procreate," and the first and defining
characteristic of marriage is the "physical procreation" of children. Mutual
love is not "on a par" with procreation, though the marital relationship ought
to be informed by love or "mutual benevolence." Anyone who separates sexuality from procreation lives an "illusion" and "lies" about the matter, and

Stephen J. Pope "Same-Sex Marriage: Threat or Aspiration" *America*, Dec. 6, 2004. Vol. 191, No.
18, pp. 11–14. Copyright 2005 America Magazine. All rights reserved. Reproduced by permission
of America Press. For subscription information, visit www.americamagazine.org.

these vices lead in turn to a host of other moral problems. "The most obvious truths become obscured."

These four claims capture the essential points, if not all the details, of the ethical argument put forth by Sokolowski against the legal recognition of same-sex marriage. His argument is straightforward, and his moral logic articulates a way of viewing this matter that is expressed by some members of the magisterium and their intellectual collaborators.

The argument contains a number of different kinds of claims. The first is based on a general vision of the place of sex within marriage; the second concerns the extension of marriage to the general category of friendship (i.e., one that is neutral with regard to procreation), joined to a "slippery-slope" argument that begins with an ethic justified by the decisions of consenting adults; the third laments the modern abandonment of final causality as the key point in a cultural context that makes proposals for legal recognition of same-sex marriage plausible to significant proportions of American society; and the fourth claim argues for the return to the traditional belief that marriage is for the sake of procreation.

It is important to note that his argument is based on reason, especially common sense observations of human behavior shaped by a Thomistic view of human nature and its intrinsic "ends." There is little doubt that the modern fascination with the "mastery of nature" has had some destructive effects on society, on the natural world and on social institutions. It connects, in complex ways and in tandem with other cultural and economic factors, to a variety of problems related to sexual ethics: the reduction of sex to a tool for entertainment and recreation and its detachment from love as well as procreation; the legitimation of sexual behavior solely by the choices of consenting adults; and the threat to human dignity, particularly the dignity of unborn life, by the emergence of barely restrained reproductive technology. This having been said, other features of this argument suffer from significant defects.

The first claim, the heart of the argument, maintains that same-sex marriage would "re-define" marriage as the "exchange of sex." Yet those gay people who wish to marry profess to do so because they love each other and want therefore to pledge themselves to each other in a permanent commitment. Many gay people, like many straight people, already "exchange sex" without desiring any such commitment. The argument thus fails to acknowledge the aspirations and ideals that motivate gay people who want to marry. From the point of view of authors like Andrew Sullivan, the civil law ought to extend to gay couples the same legal protection and social support that is already granted to married heterosexual couples. Marriage in this view is not simply about an "exchange of sex"—language that sounds a bit like the old manualist "conjugal debt"—but about intimate, caring, interpersonal love. Sokolowski's emphasis on the primacy of procreation actually represents a reversion to an earlier preconciliar ethic that represents a substantial departure from the more personalist theology of marriage developed by Pope John Paul II.

MORE THAN FRIENDSHIP

It is also important to recognize that marriage is not only about friendship in any very broad sense of the term. It is about a romantic and sexual relationship that joins two people in a lifelong and exclusive bond. The template for this bond is heterosexual—a union of complementary opposites, as John Paul II has described in his many talks. The monogamous and exclusive nature of this love is said to be a reflection of its depth and profundity; it is not the kind of love that a person can share with more than one beloved. Considerations of interpersonal love as well as of justice (and particularly equality) militate against polygamy or other forms of multiple-partner marriage ("polyamory"). Having more than one partner in a marriage necessarily creates an imbalance of power and leaves the relationship structurally open to the destabilizing force of sexual jealousy.

Another plank in the argument holds that the separation of sex and marriage is due to the modern rejection of the inherent ends of marriage and sex. While some readers will doubt that most couples using birth control are avid readers of Bacon and Descartes, Sokolowski is right to point to broad cultural patterns that feed into a pervasive ethos that looks to technology to provide the clearest and best answers to serious moral problems. This desire to dominate nature and humanity is evident not only in the domains of sex and reproduction but also in our military adventures and environmental policies.

Yet it also has to be acknowledged that some advocates of same-sex marriage argue on the basis of natural human ends and not against them. They maintain that the natural ends of sexuality and sexual behavior include love as well as procreation. Primatologists like Francis de Waal of Emory University and Richard Wrangham of Harvard have shown in considerable detail how sexual behavior in our closest primate relatives, the chimpanzees, naturally functions to create social bonds, soothe fractured relationships, provide comfort in times of stress and promote other pro-social goods. Humans are not chimps, obviously, but there are scientific as well as moral reasons for holding that human sexual behavior functions to enhance the emotional and affective bond between lovers. This claim can be read as a claim that endorses rather than repudiates the age-old notion that human nature inclines to certain ends, the achievement of which contributes to human flourishing. Some advocates argue that, though it may not lead to "physical procreation," same-sex marriage provides conditions that satisfy what Pope Paul VI called the "unitive" purpose of sex. Hence arguments against same-sex marriage need to address this "essentialist" rationale—i.e., one based on an account of natural ends—if they are going to be reasonably comprehensive.

NON-PROCREATIVE SEX

Sexual intercourse is the natural way in which humans engage in "physical procreation"; but, as just noted, there are reasons for thinking that procreation is not the primary (let alone exclusive) natural end of sex. Human beings across cultures engage in an enormous amount of nonprocreative sex. Unlike species in which females go into heat and give clear signals to potential mates, the human species is one of the few in which females manifest constant sexual receptivity (when they are already pregnant, for example, or even postmenopausal).

Nor is it obvious that procreation is the dominant end of marriage. Marriage, after all, is a social and cultural institution whose meaning varies in important ways across historical and cultural boundaries. In the past, marriage in most of its forms has been related to child-bearing and child-rearing. Marriage is the context in which procreation has more often than not taken place, and in general it provides a more nurturing, reliable framework for raising children than do the alternatives. Yet this does not mean that the "first and defining character of marriage" is the "physical procreation" of children. The latter phrase sounds as if human beings are like fish, whose main "investment" (as the biologists like to say) is to make sure that the female's eggs are fertilized by the male in the right riverbed before they depart. The vast majority of human procreative energy is expended not in "physical procreation," if by that is meant simple biological reproduction—fertilization, gestation and birth—but in providing children with the proper emotional, moral, social and spiritual upbringing.

This is the broader and more noble sense in which Pope Paul VI spoke about "procreation" in *Humanae Vitae*. The extended period of adult child-rearing, preceded by a profound infantile and childhood dependence, is one of the traits that are uniquely human. Yet this level of child care does not mean that childless married couples are any less married than procreative married couples. Marriage has its own integrity, which does not require validation by procreation. This message is important today, when married couples living into their mid-80's spend the major portion of their life together having nothing to do with procreation.

Furthermore, we are now in a society that gives social recognition to a great variety of relationships outside of marriage. Children are being raised outside of marriage at a higher rate. Middle-class married couples are increasingly delaying childbearing, even into their early 40's.

THE REAL WORLD

Some gay couples are adopting and in this way function as "procreative units," at least in the broad sense of the term that embraces child-rearing and education. This development provides great benefits for children who would otherwise go without loving homes. The desire to return to a "golden age" when marriage "meant" procreation (if it ever really did) is more nostalgic than realistic. Ethical analysis of current proposals to give legal recognition to same-sex marriage thus needs to begin with an acknowledgment of the "real world" status of the social situation in which we find ourselves—and of the real benefits as well as costs that are at stake in it.

Critics of same-sex marriage have a number of valid concerns, of a broad social nature, that need to be subjected to further examination and discussion. But this further discussion needs to be informed by a perspective that acknowledges that love and commitment are at the center of marriage. If observers want to understand the desire to extend marriage to same-sex couples, they ought to consider the point of view of those couples. The absence of this "sympathetic understanding" leads to significant flaws in some ways of viewing same-sex marriage. This is not to say that "sympathetic understanding" provides all the answers, only that it offers a helpful context for conversation. If polemics and political maneuvers have often undermined the possibility of genuine conversation, perhaps Catholics have a duty to examine the issues freshly and without the rancor that so often mars public debate in this country.

CHAPTER 12

Marriage Becomes a Journey

Evelyn Eaton Whitehead
James D. Whitehead

Overlooking the significance of the metaphor the authors use here would be a mistake: marriage as a journey. This metaphor suggests marriage as a much more fluid reality than when it is seen as an institution, an immobile and unmovable edifice, a building fixed in a single place. The new metaphor of journey helps focus on what the Whiteheads call "the necessary instability of marriage." Their explanation of the history of where the institutional image of marriage comes from and what its value has been, is helpful for understanding where the shifts in today's understanding of marriage come from.

Many have found the Whiteheads' explanation of the three psychological transitions in marriage to be a marvel of clarity and insight. When unmarried or newly married persons read it, they do well to ask if they are ready or willing to go through these transitions, which will shift their very sense of self. Looked at from the angle of each person in the marriage, the journey is toward a new way of being a human being, with new commitments and a growing, shifting set of priorities.

Questions for Discussion

1. Of the three psychological transitions in marriage, which one do you think people your own age resist most strongly and why?
2. If the resistance to the transitions is not just in one's head, but especially in one's behavior, what forms does the resistance take? Can you specify any specific resistant behaviors?

FROM INSTITUTION TO JOURNEY

Our view, as we have said, is about the dissolution of marriage as a state in life and its survival as a journey. More precisely it is about the growing awareness of the fluidity and movement that mark marriage today. The

Copyright © 1981 by Evelyn Eaton Whitehead and James D. Whitehead. Reprinted with permission.

changes and transitions which are a necessary part of a maturing marriage give it less the appearance of a stable institution than of a complicated journey. Pope Paul VI turned, in a speech in 1970, to this metaphor of movement:

> The journey of married people, like that of all human lives, has its stages; difficult and sorrowful moments have their place in it, as you know from your experience through the years.

But the Pope then suggested that, though such a journey includes difficulty and sorrow, it ought not to entail anxiety or fear: "But it must be stated clearly that anxiety and fear should never be found in souls of good will." In our discussion of marriage as a journey in the following chapters, we will understand anxiety and fear, not as indicators of a failure of good will, but as expectable perils on the way.

An institution can be imagined as a building that one enters. It is a solid, fixed place. Most everyone is expected to enter this institution and to remain in it. Once inside, a person receives the traditional privileges and obligations that come with residence. The rules that apply here are well known and constant; everyone inside this institution is expected to follow them.

Understood as an institution, marriage has been a state that one either did or did not inhabit. Legally, a person is either married or not married; there is no in-between. The Christian Church, influenced by this legal orientation toward marriage, came to view matrimony as an either/or situation. Christian ambivalence about sexuality found a clear resolution in this institutional view of marriage. Outside this well-defined state no sexual sharing was permitted; once inside this institution, one could even demand one's sexual rights. There seemed no gradualness or development in this commitment; one was either in or out. The periods of engagement and of marriage preparation were anomalies; little effective attention and ministry could be given to these "borderline" events.

The shift in the image of marriage from that of an institution to that of a journey is in line with our experience of marriage today. The commitment of marriage is increasingly seen not as a contract between families but as a personal covenant between individuals. The *necessary instability* of marriage—the changes required as a person approaches it (and when a person must exit from it) and the transitions demanded within such a complex relationship—gives it less and less an institutional appearance.

The continuing shifts and challenges of a maturing marriage give it the appearance of a journey. Marriage as a journey suggests that this relationship is not a location in life but a pattern of movement. Marriage is not a place where we live but a way that we travel through life. The image of journey responds to our sense of the precariousness of marriage. Even after this trek is well begun, we continue to learn new things about ourself and our partner. These are often subtle and confusing things, not covered under the contract or the institutional warranty.

The change in our image of marriage reminds us that new skills and virtues will be needed: different strengths are required to live in an institution and to survive on a journey. More adaptable and even wily skills are called for on a trip that is only partly charted beforehand.

A second concern will be the patterns of movement discernible in this journey of marriage. Are we married people enough alike so that we can expect our marriages to be more than "private trips"? If so, what are the expectable turns, and detours, of this journey? What is the terrain of contemporary marriage? Is it similar enough that we can learn from one another how to become skillful travelers? In this section of the book we will examine the patterns of change in marriage today, especially under the rubric of marriage as a passage. But before turning to the transitions which bring us into marriage and would mature us there, let us recall that the images of institution and journey are both influential in our religious history.

Marriage was seen as an institution during the centuries when the Church itself was becoming a powerful social institution. Especially from the fourth century the Christian Church, originating as scattered groups of believers in Jesus Christ, increasingly pictured itself as an institution. At the beginning of the fifth century St. Augustine captured this self-understanding in the attractive image of the City of God. A city is a sort of institution: a stable, legal entity, it enjoys clear and certain boundaries. The citizens of the City of God were recognizable by their credential of Baptism. These citizens were expected to stay in the institution—to marry other Christians, their own kind. (This would get more complicated after the Reformation when Catholics would banish Protestants from their city, making them religiously "uncivilized" and therefore unmarriable.)

This institutionalizing of religious faith gave great clarity and stability to Christianity. Stability, unfortunately, is sometimes but a few steps from rigidity. The image of the City of God further solidified in the sixteenth-century hymn "A Mighty Fortress Is Our God." This hymn, still popular today, suggests a well-defended, institutional view of God and Christian faith. It also suggests, at least to many Christians today, that we know for certain where God is—with *us*. An institutional view of God tends to locate and even localize God in a definite, defended space. God is enshrined and "tabernacled" as ours. The legalistic management of this institution—be it the Church or marriage—naturally ensues.

Parallel to our recognition of marriage as a journey is our return to this primordial image as a description of our common religious faith. It was in the circuitous trek through the Sinai Desert that our religious ancestors came to their earliest encounters and covenant with God. Journey, then, should be an especially sacred image for us, whether describing our fragile and changing relationship with God or with our marriage partner. The metaphor of journey includes discovery and doubt, detours and new beginnings. It suggests the special set of virtues required for religious faith and for marriage—virtues which help us decide when to settle down and when to keep moving, which way to turn at a fork in the road, how to read the signs that tell us where we are.

The image of faith and of marriage as a journey also suggests a different understanding of our God. Not institutionalized in a shrine or other stable location, God is a presence sensed on the trip. God is a presence that visits our life in strange and unpredictable ways to give it meaning and direction. Religious faith and a Christian marriage require our attentiveness to this subtle and graceful presence.

Attractive as this image of the journey is, marriage today remains an institution as well. Marriage is too important for all of us for it to be reduced to a private affair. Every community has a stake in its marriages and so this commitment must remain public as a legal, social and religious institution. Yet today we are more conscious of marriage as a process, a path pursued, a journey which includes both expected and unexpected events.

THREE PSYCHOLOGICAL TRANSITIONS IN MARRIAGE

Of the many transitions which describe the journey of a growing marriage, three merit special attention here. The first of these is the gradual movement from "I" to "we," the transition into married mutuality.

A couple may bring to marriage very different histories and identities. You are Italian, from a large and demonstrative family; I am English, an only child and unaccustomed to emotional displays. Each of us has lived apart from our families for a few years, establishing our independent ways of work and recreation. Now we would bring together these very separate "I's" into the "we" of marriage. The commonness of this "we" involves more than having the same address and sharing bed and board. It involves the merging of our separate patterns of living into a shared life. The stakes here are high; the risks can be considerable. A life-in-common will involve practical questions of how we use time and money and how we shall establish together the rhythms that make up a lifestyle. And deeper issues are concerned—our priorities and values, our energies and enthusiasms, our patterns of emotional responsiveness and sexual expression. The establishment of such a new life together includes the lengthy process of mutual knowledge and mutual influence. The challenge here is to create a "we" that is an expression of both "I's," where the identity of each is tested and expanded, probably even changed, but not destroyed.

This movement from two separate "I's" toward a shared life as "we" has long been seen as essential to the relationship of marriage. The Bible speaks of this common life in powerful images of union: "bone from my bones and flesh from my flesh" (Genesis 2:23) and "a man leaves his father and mother and joins himself to his wife, and they become one body" (Genesis 2:24). This close union is stressed in English common law statements, an important part of our own legal heritage, that in marriage "the two shall become one."

But what does it mean, that we two shall become one? At one level this image captures a psychological experience that is strong in romantic love—the desire to be together, to share everything, to overcome whatever separates us and to merge ourselves as fully as we can. And this image of union is not limited to early romance. For many who are married, "two becoming one" describes their experience of love growing and tested over time. "And they become one body" may not say all we know about marriage but it expresses both a reality and a hope in which our love is grounded.

Psychologically, then, these images of union ring true, even where they express only part of the larger reality of married love. But marriage is more than a psychological reality; it takes on social forms as well. And these social forms both reflect and influence how we understand the union of woman and man in marriage. In a society in which patriarchy is strong the union of marriage will be understood in terms of the legal preeminence of the husband. Thus an early formulation of English common law states bluntly that "the husband and wife are as one and that one is the husband."

In earlier generations in our own country this union of two-in-one has often been achieved by incorporating the wife—her ambitions, her energies, her values and opinions, often her material resources as well—into the plan and plot of her husband's life. And many women have found personal meaning and genuine fulfillment in this experience of marriage: giving themselves—even somewhat exclusively—to tasks and roles that have served, and often been subservient to, their husbands. But today there are new expectations of mutuality in the "we" of marriage. It is less and less acceptable among women (and, to be sure, among many men) that the "we" of marriage be achieved primarily through the absorption of the wife into her husband's identity and life ambition. So today the process of marriage involves the more difficult—and more rewarding—effort to create a "we" that bears the stamp of both spouses, a "we" that moves beyond each into a larger reality of a common life.

To create a life in common in which both of us survive and continue to grow, together—it is in this hope that couples approach marriage today. To achieve this we must each bring to marriage some beginning sense of confidence and comfort in "who I am." Neither a defended nor an unclear identity can easily move toward mutuality. If I am largely unsure of who I am, I am not able easily to sustain a relationship. If I must defend a fragile sense of self against the demands of change, then flexibility and compromise will be hard. In either case, it will be difficult for me to come close to you without the fear that I will lose myself. And it is this fear, that "we" must mean a loss of "I," that complicates the transition into a common life in marriage.

COMPLEMENTARITY, EQUALITY, MUTUALITY

The mutuality that is a goal in marriage today takes us beyond the understanding of women and men as "complementary." Many couples experience themselves as complementing one another. We "fit" together well. Your dynamism enlivens me; my patience is a useful balance to your enthusiasm. Or, more pragmatically, I like to cook and you like to clean house. But as a cultural image "complementarity" does not celebrate these individual differences. Instead it reinforces the notion of the "innate" differences between all women and all men. In this understanding our complementarity in marriage is not something that we discover between us; it is rather a *given*. "After all, he's a man and she's a woman. It should be clear how their marriage should work." In this view it is not as two particular persons that we complement each other in our marriage; it is rather because each of us falls into one of the two "complementary" categories—male or female. Very often, then, as the image of complementarity actually functions, its appealing nuances of interdependence and exploration are lost. It becomes instead a restatement of a conventional notion of what marriage should be. Many critics judge that the impulse to understand women as "complementary" to men in marriage is similar to that which sees blacks as "separate but equal" in society. Both find their roots in a conviction of "the way things are" that owes more to ideology than to the evidence available.

If mutuality takes us beyond "complementarity" it takes us beyond "equality" as well. "Equality of opportunity" and "equality under the law" are appropriate statements of societal goals. But equality is a tricky objective in close relationships. This is not to say that intimacy always works itself out into some uneven dichotomy—leader–led or dominant–submissive. It suggests rather that quantitative images, such as equality, are not always useful in personal relations. It is difficult to determine "equality" in emotion or concern or generosity. It is hard to measure what is "enough" for each of us to give in order that our love might develop or survive. We must each nurture our own integrity in our marriage, but this will go beyond keeping count of who "gives in" the most. For many of us, these core issues of mutuality—the tension between integrity and interdependence, between autonomy and compromise—are not adequately covered by the term "equality."

Mutuality implies real engagement between people. I am open enough in this engagement to meet *you*, not just my stereotypes of you or my prejudices about *your kind*. In mutuality both of us experience ourselves giving and receiving. We can acknowledge our dependence on one another without guilt or shame; we can celebrate the ways we empower each other, without resentment or control. We each sense that our greatest strength is born of our being together. It is truly my strength, but I owe it to our love. And together *we* are more than either of us is alone.

Establishing this kind of mutuality in our marriage involves the ongoing process of learning more about each other and ourselves and of influencing each other as we develop toward a life together. It is not just a process of the first years of marriage but a continuing dynamic of growth and change over a lifetime. So the "we" of our marriage is to be celebrated now, but we know also that it is still becoming.

FROM ROMANCE TO COMMITTED LOVE

A second transition in marriage today is from romance to committed love. The dominant norm of marriage in America today is self-selection based on the criteria of romantic love. *I* choose whom I shall marry, and I choose to marry someone with whom I have fallen in love. The choice of romantic love is a complicated one, since romance often includes some element of projection. Part of what I see in you is my ideal of "man" or "woman," especially of the woman or man I shall marry. This ideal, itself partly a statement of my values and partly an expression of my needs, may correspond more or less closely to who you really are. So while romance may appear to be a highly personalized love, in many ways it is not. Romance often involves "falling in love with love." In the romantic stimulation of our discovery of love, we are likely to sense that we are perfectly suited to each other: we like the same things, we never argue, we share the same values of marriage and family life. As we live together in our marriage we will each have the chance to examine more closely this ideal. I will learn more about what I really want; I will learn more about who you really are.

The impact of romance in love may be described by the term "enchantment." I am enchanted by the one I love, enthralled by each detail and every mannerism. I am swept off my feet. *This* person, I am convinced, can rescue me at last—from my parents, from my dull job, even from myself. This marvelous power of romance appears in life as a most useful illusion. This larger-than-life, idealized view of the other energizes me to take on the commitments of married life. As an adult career often begins in larger-than-life ambitions of what I will be able to achieve, so romance leads me into marriage with powerful hopes of what our life together will be.

The route from romantic love toward a maturing marriage often goes by way of disenchantment. This is not to suggest that our prince (or princess) must always turn into a frog. It does mean that the enchanted, idealized view of my spouse will likely change as I come to know this person better. Practical decisions we must make about our children, our careers, even our housecleaning, can reveal unknown parts of who we are, to ourselves and to each other. As our life together matures, I am invited to love not just my ideal spouse, but the simultaneously lovely and limited person whom I have married.

"Disenchantment" is an ambiguous term, to be sure. While for many of us it is a necessary stage between romance and a matured love, it is for some an experience simply of falling out of love. Unable to tolerate a non-ideal lover or a growing realization that the person I married is not the person I dated, I may find that for me disenchantment leads to divorce. Or it may lead to my beginning the cycle of romance again, this time in an extramarital affair with a more exciting (because still unknown) partner. Here disenchantment is not part of the maturing of our love into a resilient and personalized commitment but an experience that sets off a cycle of immaturity: needing the enchantment of romance, I seek "someone new," leaving behind the demands and invitations that arise in the familiarity of my experience of my spouse.

The process of maturing in marriage thus requires a movement beyond the exhilarating but largely passive experience of falling in love, to the experience of love as a chosen and cultivated commitment. It is the added element of commitment that transforms romantic love into the love that is able to sustain marriage for a lifetime. Committed love grows as I am able to know and cherish my spouse "as is," beyond the idealized images that may have been a part of our early experience of romance. I come to know you more completely and more clearly, as perhaps more gifted than I had dreamed but also as more flawed than I had hoped. This is a maturing love of choice. In the light of this deepening awareness of who you are and who I really am, I choose anew to love you. I reaffirm the commitment to do "whatever is necessary" so that this relationship in which we hold each other may live and grow.

This is the movement from romantic love to the love of mutual devotion, strong enough to sustain us in the moments of strain and confusion that are inevitably associated with our continuing close contact. Such devotion is possible only if each of us is capable of generous self-disregard.

This dynamic of mutual devotion is one of the most profound movements in marriage. In it the "active" and "passive" sides of love seem to merge in an experience of both caring and being cared for. We are together deeply and we each feel this as a strength. You know me so well . . . and still you love me. You care for me in ways that go beyond what I could ask for. You call me out to what is best in myself. I know you hold my life as important to you as your own. And all these gifts I give to you as well.

Most of us are not capable of this quality of love in adolescence or even in young adulthood. In our twenties few of us have the resources of self-possession and self-transcendence that are needed. Mature inner commitment is the fruit of our married love, not its initial seed. Romance gives us the hope of mutual love, but only the test of time together can bring its realization.

For some this test is too difficult. Romance does not mature into commitment but simply fades, leaving us dissatisfied and disillusioned. The movement beyond romance is expectable—even inevitable—in marriage. But the loss of love is not. The expectation that the quality of our commitment to one another will change does not mean that we must fall out of love. It means rather that we must move into a love that is larger than romance.

THE PROCESS OF SEXUAL MATURING

While the commitment of marriage matures into a love that is larger than romance, it remains a love in which sexuality and affection are central. We approach sexual maturity in our marriage as we develop our capacity for sharing physical affection and genital pleasure. This sexual maturity, too, is more a process than a state. We learn to be good lovers and, for most of us, it takes time.

To give ourselves to this process of sexual maturing we must each be able to move beyond the experience of love play and intercourse as chiefly competitive—an experience of proving myself as a "real" woman or man or "winning out" over my partner. These interpretations of sex keep the focus on "me," making mutuality difficult. And without mutuality, sex is more often a barrier to, than a part of, the larger psychological experience of intimacy.

In contrast with many marriages of a generation ago, couples today generally approach marriage with greater awareness of their own bodies and with more information about genital sex. This intellectual sophistication is a boon to marriage, but it is, again, more a starting point of a satisfying sex life than its guarantee. Married sex is a process through which we both learn to contribute to what is, for us, mutually satisfying shared sexual experience. We learn the physical and emotional nuances that make lovemaking special for us. We develop the patterns of expression that fit us—patterns of frequency, of time and place, of initiation and response. We discover the ways in which passion and affection, humor and intensity, are a part of our own love life.

The exhilaration of sexual discovery is usually strong early in marriage, at least if we are able to move beyond an initial embarrassment. For most of us, it is our spouse who gives us the gift of knowing our sexuality to be beautiful. Loving me in my body, you invite me beyond the shame and guilt I carry still. With you, I am free to explore my passion and to expose my vulnerability and self-doubt. Having risked the self-revelation of sex—and survived—we can approach with greater confidence the other, even more threatening, processes of self-disclosure upon which the quality of our life together will depend.

After this early period of exploration, our sexual life may begin to level off. We have found a pattern that works for us and, especially in the press of the other responsibilities of our lives, this pattern can become routine.

It may be only gradually that we realize in our marriage that, though our love is strong, our lovemaking somehow falls short. Our early sexual sharing was surrounded with an aura of romance. Frequently, this romantic aura made our experiences of sex more satisfying than our lovemaking skills would otherwise justify! Now sex seems to have lost this savor. We know that the substance of our love is more important than our sexual style, but the questions of sexual style and satisfaction may begin to become more important than they were for us earlier in our marriage.

American culture's current interest in sexual techniques reinforces this concern over our own sex life. We are more aware of the richness of human sexuality and of the diversity of sexual expression. This new awareness can work destructively, setting up yet another standard of "success" against which to evaluate our own intimacy. But it need not have this negative effect. Instead it can remind us that the patterns of mutually satisfying sexual experience can be expected to differ from couple to couple. And that it is *we* who can best discover what these patterns are for us. In sex, as in most other aspects of our marriage, to be "mature" does not mean to fit some general criterion of performance but to have a developing (and, perhaps, changing) sense of what is appropriate *for us*, what works *for us*.

Sex research shows the contribution that diversity and surprise make to long-term sexual satisfaction. This realization can be liberating, inviting us to expand the ways in which we celebrate the sexuality of our marriage. This sense of exploration helps us move beyond a point of sexual boredom or routine, stimulating our own creativity in lovemaking. The expanding literature of sexual functioning can assist this process of sexual maturity in marriage, not by giving us a norm of what is "best" but by providing information that can enrich our own experimentation and choice.

THE MOVEMENT FROM "WE ARE" TO "WE CARE"

A third significant transition in the process of marriage is the movement from "we are" to "we care." Here we are involved in balancing the tensions between our own intimacy and the larger responsibilities of our lives. There is the challenge to move beyond our love as a couple in order that we may contribute to, and care for, a larger world. We can experience some strain as we try to learn ways to move beyond ourselves that do not destroy the experience and commitments of mutuality between us. The birth of the first child can be an early experience of this challenge. How shall we be for each other when we now must also be for our child? Job responsibilities and career choices also raise the challenge. Does marriage mean that only one of us may pursue a career? How do I, how do we, manage the multiple demands of being responsible citizen, financial provider, parent and spouse? The question can surface as an issue of social concern. How do we balance our commitments to each other and to our children alongside our responsibility to the needs of the world beyond ourselves?

The dilemma may be posed this way: What is our marriage for? Do we exist as a couple only for ourselves? Or does our being together go beyond ourselves? Are the resources of support and challenge that we generate in our family to be spent solely within our family? Or is there "enough" of us so that we can take the risk of sharing some of our resources (of love or concern or time or goods) with the world beyond? Is the love we share simply "a haven in a hostile world" or is it also a force that frees us to "love our neighbor as ourselves"?

Love is creative beyond itself and it must be so if it is to endure. A love that does not give life beyond itself risks becoming a caricature of intimacy. It is true that there is often a stage of mutual absorption in love, especially in the early experience of romance. The lovers are enthralled with each other. Everything about the other person is engrossing—and there is little beyond this relationship itself that seems worthy of attention. Job responsibilities, school activities, other friends and family—all pale to insignificance. In this timeless present of romance, "you and I" is all there is.

The world tends to be tolerant of this attitude in lovers—at least for a while. Recalling our own experience with romance we overlook much of the bizarre behavior of new love and excuse the rest. We know this shared obsession is but a phase of romance; soon it passes. The romance may mature into a deeper love or it may die from lack of any further substance. But in either case the charmed circle of exclusive fascination will be broken. Soon the lovers shall rejoin us—better, we trust, for the experience.

This early exclusivity in love is normal, an important dynamic of the process of exploration and self-disclosure that contributes to the possibility of commitment. But maturing love moderates this exclusivity. Being *for* one another does not require that each of us must be against everyone else. Indeed, the enrichment we experience in being for one another leads us to be for more than "just us." Our love for one another gives us more of what is best in each of us. We feel the impetus to move beyond ourselves, to share this wealth, to bring others into the power of what our love has given us. This movement of expansion is itself an expectable dynamic of love as it matures. Psychologists are aware of the importance to our love of this impulse beyond ourselves. They warn that the absence of any movement beyond "just us" imperils a love relationship. A "pseudo-intimacy" can result, turning the partners in upon themselves in a way that gradually impoverishes the relationship. What results from this failure to expand our concern is not an intimacy more protected and complete, but stagnation. Having failed to share our love beyond ourselves we soon find that we have little left to give each other.

This truth about love, of concern in current psychology, does not come as news to our religious tradition. Love that does not give life beyond itself will die—Christian wisdom has long proclaimed this sometimes fleeting insight of our own experience. There is an essential connection between loving and giving life. It is, in part, this abiding truth that the Church has tried to share in its celebration of the fruitfulness of marriage.

In our history there has been a tendency to understand this connection in an almost exclusively biological sense—that every act of genital love must be open to the creation of a child, that bearing children is the most important goal of marriage and married love. Many Catholics today, especially married lay persons, find these statements of the connection between marriage and generative love to be at odds with their own experience. But the larger truth, that a maturing love in marriage both wants to and needs to go beyond itself, is reinforced by our experience and our religious heritage.

PART FOUR

Attitudes toward Sexuality

CHAPTER 13

Sex Matters: The Riches of the Catholic Sexual Tradition

Sidney Callahan

Every person who sees the title of this essay will instantly recognize the obvious truth in it. Yes, sex does matter and you don't have to be even twelve to know it in some deep but possibly unarticulated way. Here, Sidney Callahan, for years a leading writer on the most human issues around Christian living, brings to us a heightened sense of the truth that sex does indeed matter.

Not all those quick to talk about sex are willing to look at the conflicts and complications it brings into our lives. Many Christians are likewise unready to embrace the wisdom of the Christian tradition on sexual matters. Before she points out this wisdom, Callahan points to a sex-suspicious, body-denying strain in some Christian teaching. In my classes on marriage, students are ready to admit, some out loud, that the greatest emotion and suffering in their lives so far has come via their sexual encounters. Women seem usually more ready than men to talk about that pain in sexual relationships in the context of a class. Men can be very articulate about their pain but seem to prefer discussing it in a one-on-one situation than in the context of a class.

Here, Callahan celebrates sex, while at the same time naming the many protections needed for sexual happiness. One of these is the ability to keep commitments; another is the capacity to tell the truth to each other. Keeping commitments and telling the truth are not so common as we might like in our society—among people of all ages.

Questions for Discussion

1. If you had to list the three most important sources of emotional pain in sexual relationships, what would they be? Because it may be difficult talking about such pain, writing down in order of painfulness these sources may be a step toward a good class discussion.

2. Do you think women experience more of this pain than men? Or is the pain pretty much the same for both?

3. In your view, which group is better able to name and talk about this pain: men or women?

4. Callahan mentions several points of wisdom in the Christian sexual tradition. Which one seemed most important to you, which least important?

5. Callahan writes:

> Deploring past prejudices of the Church toward sexuality doesn't justify ignoring the present pitfalls in a culture that trivializes, markets, and exploits sexuality. Sexual dangers may have been overemphasized in our past ascetic traditions that disdained sexual embodiment and ecstasy, but then earlier Christians were dealing with Caligula's orgies, slavery, and the horrors of the Roman Empire, which were followed by barbarian invasions. Today, only the naive can deny the harmfulness of sexual abuse, sexually transmitted disease, abortion, prostitution, rape, harassment, and other sexual evils. Yet there is still hope for a better future.

If you agree with her basic point in this statement, how might you apply it to a twelve- to fourteen-year-old young relative or if you became a teacher, how would you raise such issues in a classroom?

What are we going to pass on to future generations when it comes to Christian sexual morality? Many riches exist in our Catholic sexual tradition, but these goods have been obscured by theological infighting.

Conflicts over questions of gender, homosexuality and the morality of reproduction distract us. On the birth of a new millennium, it is vital for the church to clarify issues presented by new medical knowledge and evolutionary biology, but heated arguments aren't edifying. (Full disclosure: I have been a frequent player in these debates.)

Worse still, the horror and shame of the sexual abuse scandal among Catholic clergy can turn Catholics off the whole subject of sexuality. Many Catholics have given up on efforts to reconnect their human sexuality and Christian discipleship. Admittedly the secular culture offers little of substance or spiritual guidance, but (many think) what else is there?

Quite a lot, actually. Our ever-reforming tradition gives us good and heartening news about sexuality, without jettisoning the realistic prudence of the past.

Christians affirm that human sexuality is God's good creation and it matters. We are our bodies. The body–mind unity insisted upon by modern science is no news for Christians. Believers in the resurrection of the body know that human beings are not ethereal souls floating through this life. Human beings are embodied creations that will live forever corporally transformed. No disdain or disregard for the flesh can be accepted by those who believe God becomes fully human in the Incarnation.

Whatever we embodied folk do "in word or work," we do for the glory of God, and sexuality is definitely included. Minute by minute we are cocreating our eternal selves through all of our actions, thoughts and fantasies.

At long last Christians are getting over the old dualistic suspicions of sexuality, emotions and bodily emissions. Jesus spoke against the purity taboos that declared individuals unclean. How could female menstruation and pla-

© 2004 *National Catholic Reporter,* www.NCRonline.org.

centas be considered unclean when Jesus cured the blind and the deaf by prayer and spit?

It was the involuntary nature of embodied sexual responses that most worried St. Augustine and company. Having a new understanding of the way the brain and body work, we see how adaptive much of our involuntary responses can be. Think of the immune system or perceptual processes. Moreover, the best things of life just arrive from God as gifts. Love and pleasure are not achievements of the will.

The involuntary ecstasies of orgasm can now be seen as good; they are not little deaths but signs of the wonder of birth. Once you affirm that God lovingly gives GodSelf to the world in Christ with nothing held back, you validate ecstasy. Total, complete self-giving acts of love imitate God. The high joys and pleasure of loving sexuality can be seen as a preview of the graced communion of heaven. Traditional images of the kingdom as the marriage of the Lamb and a wedding feast affirm this truth.

The marvelous thing about sexual communion is that while it is an on-going conversation, it includes more than words can tell. Love and mutual assent are marked by touch, gesture and shared emotions. Sex can be seen as a form of high play and celebration. Like all communal play, sexuality requires courtesy and tactful care for one another. Before a dive into water, its depth must be assessed. Once in the swim, love can heal the fears of bodily rejection that often wound human lives.

Married people have experienced the truth that unity and love are recreated by sexual intercourse, and now theologians name this process as the recall and celebration of the marital commitment. In an intimate, loving marital friendship, two become one. Just as the celebration of the Eucharist recalls and reinstitutes our essential Christian relationships of communion, so does sexual lovemaking.

The mystery of Christ being one with the whole church and simultaneously living within each individual is also reproduced in marital union. Two individuals give to each other and yet increase and grow as individuals within the common relationship. It is another of God's win–win games. The fidelity and staying power of the marriage commitment give solid ground and enough space and time to get your act together and learn to love.

Naturally one of the greatest gifts of sexuality is children. The wonder of babies begins the world anew. Sex is nature's way to spur evolution onward and to ensure the parental caretaking that higher animals like ourselves require. The sexual pair bonding strengthens mutual parenting and also produces kinship ties. Families formed through mating provide care for the sick and old as well as for survival of the young.

Happily, Christian claims go far beyond a reductive biological focus on (sex as a means of) survival. Humans possess free will and the ability to make promises and stick to them. Only self-conscious selves can practice fidelity, focusing upon the future and the well-being of others. Keeping commitments strengthens the trust of a group. God can be praised for giving married persons the power to be faithful and to keep on loving.

Religiously vowed celibacy for the sake of God's kingdom is also part of the human sexual repertoire. Those who direct all their sexual energies to religious praise and service of God bear fruit in a community's life. Vowed celibacy is a witness to the power of the unseen reality of the Spirit.

In an earlier day dedicated religious celibacy was considered superior to marriage as the best way to holiness. The second-class status of marriage arose partly because of the underlying prejudices against the body and women. This unbalanced view has officially been corrected. But sometimes whiffs of prejudice against marital sexuality waft about in the rhetoric. When theological sources speak of "mere genitality," the phrase resonates with the purity taboos of old. No one who attempts to live a sexual relationship of love and genital generosity is going to use an adjective like "mere." Sometimes celibates seem to deny the specific focused power and programmed development of human sexuality by trying to blur or subsume sex into the larger category of embodiment. Clarity is better served by seeing human bodies as consisting of more than their sexual powers. A mother nursing her child is an act of embodiment but not of sexuality; an aged sick person being fed is partaking in an embodied relationship but not a sexual one.

Another important gift of the Christian sexual tradition, often flouted in practice, has been the assertion of moral equality between men and women in their sexual practices and rights. The body is for God. This demand for equality was a revolutionary move that has taken centuries to become accepted. Christians freed women and men from the bondage of subordinating their sexuality to the family lineage, the state's need for manpower or the market. The vocation of dedicated female virginity was particularly important for giving women's bodies intrinsic dignity. Women flocked to Christianity in response.

The requirement of equal individual assent to marriage also attacked the family and the state's power over sexuality. Of course we are so used to ideals of autonomy, free consent and equality between the sexes that we hardly notice this positive Christian sexual tradition—until we confront cultures where women are controlled and oppressed. And with the concern for women's condition, we are forced to face the dark side of human sexuality.

REALISM AND PRUDENCE

Since sexuality is so good and so central to embodied life, it follows that sexual powers can be distorted and misused. All powers and goods can be abused. Religion, the family, the gift of language can be used for evil ends; and the human condition includes sexual abuse, sexual torture and sexual exploitation of the vulnerable by the dominant. In the same way, selfish aggression, greed, domination, and war have always afflicted humankind. Evils also feed upon each other. AIDS ravages the undeveloped world just as the sexual traffic in women and children exploits a society's sexism and poverty.

The Christian tradition has been realistic about the fact that greed and sexual desire can distort human thought and behavior. The drive for sexual gratification has always produced the self-deception that can affect the will or blind the conscience. It is no accident that ascetics striving for holiness take vows of abstinence as well as poverty and obedience.

Sexually active persons today who seek to reconnect their sexuality with Christian discipleship will have to develop new and appropriate examinations of conscience. To be innocent as a dove, a modern Christian has to be shrewder than a serpent. If sexuality is a fundamental language of the body, can I ask whether I am speaking truth, or even the whole truth? Do I mean what I say and do what I mean? Have I indulged in willful ignorance about the effect of my sexual behavior on myself and others? And so on. As always, the practice of justice, care, courage and responsibility produces sexual virtue.

Deploring past prejudices of the church toward sexuality doesn't justify ignoring the present pitfalls in a culture that trivializes, markets and exploits sexuality. Sexual dangers may have been overemphasized in our past ascetic traditions that disdained sexual embodiment and ecstasy, but then earlier Christians were dealing with Caligula's orgies, slavery and the horrors of the Roman empire, which were followed by barbarian invasions. Today only the naive can deny the harmfulness of sexual abuse, sexually transmitted disease, abortion, prostitution, rape, harassment and other sexual evils. Yet there is still hope for a better future.

MOVING TO A BALANCED FUTURE

A living tradition responds to the Holy Spirit and changes. The authoritative sources for development are scripture, church teachings, reason, liturgical prayer and experience. Certainly, human experiences of the dark side of sexuality have shaped past vigilance and suspicions of sexuality. Christians, especially the parents of adolescents, may have to struggle against their fears in order not to let pessimism rule the day.

Central moral teachings on sexuality reflect the natural consequences inherent in group life. Lies, cheating, adultery and selfish exploitation breed hate, distrust and social chaos. Prostitution soils the spirit; lust degrades; promiscuity debases emotions and breeds disease and motivates abortion.

But the positive experiences of Christian disciples trying to be responsive to the Spirit in active sexual lives have not yet become fully articulated or accessible to the community. Unfortunately, the way the church is currently organized leaves little opportunity for hierarchical celibate leaders to listen to the experience of lay Christians. The sense of the faithful has been more or less silenced.

Another ironic condition that suppresses the good news of Christian experiences of sexuality is tactful courteousness. Mature persons do not wish to publicize their intimate sexual experiences of joyful love. The vulgarity of current tell-all media displays makes this point. Have these poor people no sense of privacy, family loyalty or self-respecting behavior?

Thus, the bad news is publicized and the church hears little of the good news. For example, a point I have never heard mentioned anywhere before is the parental hope that one's adult children have turned out to be good lovers, and tender, playful sexual partners. This particular vindication of one's embodied life and childrearing must remain hidden, since it would violate the privacy appropriate to family life.

But sexual development and marriage preparation will continue in and out of the church and the Spirit blows where it wills. Truth has a way of dispelling falsity while love casts out fear. Perhaps those working out their sexual salvation in new and uncertain sexual situations have the most to give to other seekers. Peers can help peers as various marriage and sexual education programs have found.

After 50 years, I know how to be a faithfully married spouse and I think I understand how one can live a vowed celibate religious life. But what will discipleship mean for the single or young career woman desiring marriage, or a divorced father, or a young gay person? How does one make a transition and search for love while remaining committed to commitment?

Surely the witness and character of those in the Christian community are going to be decisive in the church's achievement of sexual balance. There is also the resource of the creative imagination to be counted on for vicarious experience. Scripture lights up God's core truths, and novels, poetry and movies provide complementary sources of insight, as art always does. The Spirit leads us gradually but surely in every dimension of life. The educated heart learns to laugh, playfully rejoice in sexual gratitude and stay steadfast to the truth of promise keeping.

CHAPTER 14

A Revolution's Broken Promises

Peter Marin

Sex has acquired a prominence in our society unrivaled in past time or in other cultures. Sexual fulfillment, likewise, has been elevated to the highest level in the list of human aspirations. We have witnessed, in the last quarter century, a sea change in sexual attitudes and behaviors. Peter Marin, in this essay, takes a critical look at what came ashore with this sexual revolution in the 1960s.

Marin is one of our favorite writers. He is an insightful and passionate cultural critic. His essay is a severe indictment of what passes for sexual liberation today. With the collapse of most traditional (social and religious) restraints upon sexual freedom, our human lives have become marred by pretense, desperation, and an immense amount of "bad faith." The author chronicles our culture's restless search for the ideal and the demand for instant gratification. The path is inevitably self-defeating and the results ultimately destructive. The essay will spark lively discussion, and its counterculture stance will challenge the student reader.

Questions for Discussion

1. Where do you see people acting out the sexual images and ideas provided for them, projected upon them, by others today?
2. Are these images/ideas liberating toward authentic personhood or a new form of imprisonment to selfishness?
3. Where are the casualties of the sexual revolution displayed today?
4. Are constraints, generosity, and kindness the new taboos in sexual relations?
5. Is sex a private affair, or does it have social and public dimensions?
6. What images/values can our religious traditions offer to the humanizing of sexual activity?

Further Reading

A similar analysis and critique of our sexual lives is made by Rollo May in his classic work *Love and Will* (New York: Norton, 1969), Chapter I.

Mention the sexual revolution to a dozen people, or to 100, and you get a dozen or 100 different analyses, conclusions, and complaints. And mixed in with these responses, there usually is a shrug or a grimace or a bitter smile: "What revolution?" people ask. The response does not mean that changes have not occurred. Obviously, they have. The rueful question means rather that the sexual freedom established during the past couple of decades has not been accompanied by the increase in happiness that many people assumed would follow from a freeing of sexual mores.

There have been obvious and important gains, of course. But there have been losses as well, many of which are suggested by the story of a friend of mine, Colin, who decided in the late '70s to have a sex change. He was then in his middle 30s, recently divorced from his wife, and separated from his son and daughter. One afternoon he showed up at our house and announced that he was going to have a sex change.

Years before, it turned out, he had idly picked up a book about sex and sex changes, and realized that he, too, like the subjects of the book, had felt since childhood as if he were a woman trapped in a man's body. Some time after that, he said, he made an agreement with his wife: When she went out with other men, as she often did, he would dress up in her clothes at home, pretending to be a woman. Then, after he and his wife separated, he met a woman who ran a clothing store for transvestites, and she taught him how to walk and talk and smile like a woman and to relearn, as a woman, all of the things that he did as a man. And now, he explained, he was going to have an operation to change his sex physically: He was going to become a woman.

A year later, one night in a bar in Los Angeles, a tanned, long-haired, muscular young man came up to me and said: "There's someone with me who knows you." At his table I saw a pretty, middle-aged woman, in a cashmere sweater, a string of pearls around her neck. "Hello, Peter," said the woman in a high, rather artificial voice, and I realized that it was my old friend Colin, now become Claire.

I saw him, or her, from time to time after that, and she seemed neither happy nor unhappy, only much the same as before. I remember once being taken aback when, in a discussion of how her sex change affected her children, she said: "Oh, but I just want to be a mother to them."

I did not see her for about a year, when she came again to the house one afternoon with a woman friend who might also once have been—I was not sure—a man. This time Claire was not happy. She was tired, and the feminine surface that she had so carefully cultivated seemed to be slipping. One could almost see through it, as if she was unable to muster the energy required to keep her femininity intact. Her voice kept sliding down into the lower registers; her hair kept coming undone; even her gestures had become again, at least for the moment, a man's. Her operation, it turned out, had not gone well. The doctor had botched it, though I did not get the details; and when I asked her how she was feeling in general, she said: "I had hoped I'd be happier. To tell the truth, I seem to be trapped in any body."

From *Psychology Today* (July 1983): 50–57. Reprinted by permission of the author.

I think of my friend now, and it seems to me that there is a sense in which he or she was trapped in a body—but not one of flesh and bone. It was, instead, an idea of a body that had been sold to him as surely as his car or house had been sold. He was acting out before the operation, and she was acting out afterward, not only a social role defined by others, but also a set of images imposed upon him. The mechanical devices that were now Claire's—the pumped-up silicone breasts, the carved vagina lined with the skin of what had been a penis—were no different, really, from the gadgets hawked in the marketplace: the various objects and accoutrements that we accept without question as a necessary part of our modern lives.

In essence, most of us are no different from Colin-Claire. Everywhere we act out the sexual images and ideas provided for us, projected upon us, by others. Whether it is men with their Marlboro mustaches, lesbians in their bull-dyke janitor's outfits, male homosexuals with their clone look, or adolescent girls in tight jeans, we move somnambulistically through roles and rituals, responding to every whim and wind in the cultural air. We have been liberated from the taboos of the past only to find ourselves imprisoned in a "freedom" that brings us no closer to our real nature or needs.

It is this that explains the grimaces and shrugs when one mentions liberation. For many people, the idea of liberation—whether it is sexual, political, or social—is synonymous with happiness or satisfaction. In the instance of sexual freedom, whether it is the work of Freud or that of myriad insistent sex-rebels exemplified by men and women as varied as Margaret Sanger, Havelock Ellis, John Cowper Powys, and Wilhelm Reich, everything said in support of sexual freedom implied that it would transform and restore all aspects of emotional and relational life. Since the absence of a successful sexual life was taken to be a cause of disease and pain, it followed that its presence would inevitably bring joy in its wake and, ultimately, social happiness.

There is something peculiarly bourgeois and hygienic about this line of thought. Sex, which in the culture's past had been associated with evil, was moved lock, stock, and barrel into the camp of goodness. It became an all-purpose healing instrument, a kind of glorifed patent medicine for everything that might ail us. Eventually, by a continuation of this logic, for Wilhelm Reich and the succeeding generation, the ideal orgasm itself became the wellspring of kindness and human decency.

What most of us currently seem to believe is that once restraints are removed from human behavior, "nature" simply asserts itself, like water filling an empty space. We forget that we bring with us, into any kind of freedom, the baggage of the past, our internalized cultural limits and weaknesses. Thus freedom—in this case sexual freedom—increases choice, but it guarantees nothing, delivers nothing. To the extent that it diversifies and expands experience, it also diversifies and multiplies the pain that accompanies experience, the kinds of errors that we can make, the kinds of harm that we can do to one another.

The simple fact is that many of the obstacles to sexual life are not merely the function of repressive attitudes or mores. They are grounded in the complexities of human nature and in the everyday difficulties of living together.

And all these natural—one is almost inclined to say "eternal"—difficulties are intensified by the disappearance of traditional sexual roles, the proliferation of sexual choices and styles, the permission to introduce, in public life, the full range of sexual fantasies and yearnings to which we are prey and heir.

I cannot here enumerate the various casualties of the sexual revolution, from the young men and women whom I once saw as a therapist and teacher, who, barely out of adolescence, had slept with so many people that they found themselves frigid or unresponsive beside those whom they genuinely loved, to the middle-aged couples who, spurred on by glowing reports of open marriage, pushed one another too far, into the jealousy and fury that they believed they could leave behind. But I think all of us must acknowledge, however reluctantly, that there was something to those "reactionaries"—starting with Freud's colleagues—who argued that deliberate, broad changes in our systems of sexual remissions and taboos would let loose among us as many troubles as they solved.

Sexual life, which ought to begin with, and deepen, a pervasive and genuine sympathy between men and women, seems instead to produce among us a set of altogether different emotions: rage, disappointment, suspicion, antagonism, a sense of betrayal, and sometimes contempt. It is not so much that one cannot find good feelings in many persons or between many lovers; it is, rather, that the sexual realm as a whole seems somehow corrupted. The general feel to it is one of perplexity, even anger; betrayal rather than gratitude pervades it; and though sex no longer seems to us a curse visited upon us by the devil, few of us seem to experience it continuously, or even often, as a gift. It remains for most men and women a world through which they move warily, cautiously, self-protectively—not a home but an alien land.

Ironically, much of this is the result of the shifting of sex from the private to the public world, which is the hallmark of the sexual revolution. Back in the '50s and early '60s, sex could be an alternative to the dominant culture. It constituted a world in which the mores and fashions of the public realm did not hold quite the power that they did elsewhere, and to enter that world on one's own was, in various small rebellious ways, to leave home, to mark out a territory where one could define oneself. Though that had its own costs (making a rebellion out of behavior that should be natural), it also had its advantages, not least of which was that it often made comrades and friends out of lovers; they were, after all, engaged together in creating a private world.

But the popularization of sex has changed much of that. Sex has become almost entirely socialized, invaded by manufactured images and experts; it is no longer a way of retreating from the public world but a way of entering it. The sexual realm has been corrupted by any number of absurd or destructive ideas, almost all of them put forward by people whose main interest is not sex but making money or names for themselves. The nonsense bruited about is unbelievable; the ignorance passing itself off as wisdom is endless; sexual ideas and techniques are hawked incessantly in the marketplace. Creative masturbation, the ideal orgasm, the clitoral orgasm, the G spot, the joys of sex, the virtues of homosexuality, the virtues of bisexuality, the virtues of sex with children, porpoises and disembodied spirits, the good old missionary virtues of heterosexuality—all of these now have their norms, their measures, their proprieties. We do sex filling in the squares laid out for us by others.

Whereas in the more puritanical past, the darkness and mysteries of sex remained outside the order of things, it has now become a sort of vast Club Med, a vacation paradise into which supposedly anyone can venture successfully and without cost. It is crowded with visitors, each of them seeking an identity and an experience that bears no more relation to things as they are than did the old idea of sex as the devil's playground.

Beneath all this there is one crucial point that we often ignore: that many people are far less driven or drawn by sex than we like to think. The cant and fashion of the age imply that sex is fundamentally important to everyone and a powerful, primary source of pleasure for everyone. But if you listen carefully to what moves beneath people's words, it does not really seem so.

The loneliness and dissatisfaction that most people express, the yearnings they articulate, have much less to do with sex than with an unfulfilled desire for good company or good conversation or the intimacy of shared perceptions and interests. I would say that friendship and community seem more important to most people than genuine sexual passion, and what they accept as a decent sexual life has little to do with the turbulence and confusion and adventurous risk required to live out, deeply and fully, the tendings of one's sexual nature. What seems to dominate their concerns about sex when they do surface is a sort of idealized and sugary notion, brought up to date with erotic trimmings—a child's drawing of security extended to include sex: a house with smoke curling from the chimney, a couple hand-in-hand at the door, and behind them, upstairs, the circular mirrored bed into which, after the day's work has been done and the front and back doors locked, they tumble for a riotous good time.

One does not usually find attached to sex these days the curiosity, adventurousness, and the tolerance for disappointment or capacity for camaraderie that once seemed to mark it and that must always accompany any genuine attempt to keep faith with one's nature. Where excitement does exist, it seems as often as not to come not from the pleasures of sex, but from the situation, the cinematic trappings of "affairs." One is tempted to say that we are a nation of romantics, using sex to create idealized scenarios for ourselves, but it is probably more accurate to say that we are sentimentalists, pining—as James Joyce puts it—for emotions for which we are not willing to pay the price of experience.

Do I exaggerate here? Perhaps a bit. There are moments, of course, for most men and women—both those who are genuinely concerned with sex and those who are not—in which the raw truth of some kind of love breaks through the preconceptions that have ringed it round, and desire sweeps all before it, even our notions of romance. Such moments have nothing to do with fantasy or even images. When they occur, they occur, as the wise Greeks understood, in forms and with consequences we have not anticipated or even wanted: A world is revealed—and with it a sweetness and a self we had not imagined.

But how often does it happen? Once, twice, half a dozen times in a lifetime. Sometimes, for some people, it does not happen at all. At my daughter's school, for instance, they teach the children about sex with the help of a child's picture book that describes orgasm as something akin to a sneeze. The book tells its readers that the children can get an idea of sexual pleasure by imagining first a terrible itch and then the relief of scratching it. What kind of adults could have written such a book? Certainly not those for whom sex has *some* importance. Perhaps the authors simply lack a talent for language, but one suspects that there is more to it than that. The sneeze represents the head and the itch stands for surface sensation, and these seem to be the ways in which many men and women experience sex.

We are, after all, a puritanical people still, whose talent or capacity for sexual feeling falls far short of the attention we pay to it. As a result—despite all our rhetoric, all our manuals, all our universal make-believe—the sexual realm is marred by pretense, desperation, and an immense amount of "bad faith," which constitutes a simultaneous betrayal of both the other person and oneself.

It was not always this bad; it was not this bad even recently. I remember coming to California from the East in the very early '60s, a couple of years before the sexual revolution burst into full bloom and "the greening of America" made adolescence into the model for all adult behavior. I was surprised by the quality of sexual life I found there: men and women who seemed to feel at ease with sexuality and with one another. This was true of men and women in their 40s and 50s—something that I had not seen before.

I had grown up in Brooklyn in the '50s, when almost no one had much of a sexual life—not, at least, in terms of real lovemaking. Our adolescence—which was more openly sexual than the life of our elders—was not as terrible as it has since been made out to be. We were romantic, mildly driven, somewhat frustrated, skewed in various trivial sexual ways, but nonetheless we did not have a bad time of it. Sex for us was straightforward; desire was almost always focused on a particular person. There were crushes, attractions, awkwardness, small fiascos, and though we never got to make love (that came later, in college, for us), at least there was a genuine yearning, accumulating and mixing with frustration, forming a preliminary sense of what desire means, of how it might feel.

It was not until I got to California that I came upon large numbers of grown men and women who had about them a casual sexual grace. Remember, these were the early '60s. This was not the California of cranks and encounter groups, idealized sexual abandon, and foolish or apocalyptic zeal. It was an easier and warmer world in which people drank rather than took drugs, and somehow this gave a different tone to things than the one later provided by drugs. There was not the driven sexuality or pornographic desperation back then that would later fill the air.

As a corollary, those who found themselves drawn to sex or one another were more often than not comrades. That seems to me the most significant difference from what now surrounds us. Of course, sex did not often have attached to it, even back then, the deepest intensities, higher kinds of awareness, or the transformative significance that Reich or D. H. Lawrence claimed for it. But it did have kindness and good humor attached, and to meet with someone in the flesh was to enter a shared community of flesh, as if one had met someone far from home with whom one could make at least a temporary home.

That happened to people—by their own accounts—even in casual encounters, not all of the time, but at least part of the time. Men and women seemed capable of tolerating their disappointments and mistakes without holding their failures—as we tend to do now—against those with whom they were involved. If things went wrong in or out of bed, there was little recrimination and much less rage. Expectations were lower, needs not as great; people did not yet think of sex as a panacea, did not expect it to make them whole or pure or healthy in any magical way.

Most important of all was that the only people who bothered with sex were, for the most part, those who liked it. Everyone else left it alone. The mild taboos still intact in those days were not strong enough to discourage those who were genuinely drawn to a sexual life. But they were strong enough to allow those not so drawn to stick to pleasures closer to their own natures. This left the sexual world to those who felt at home in it, whereas today, it is much like the ski slopes on a crowded weekend: mobbed with people who are there for a dozen reasons other than a genuine love of skiing or the slopes.

No doubt it was all too casual, and perhaps it was not all that it seemed. There must have been—there always is—cruelty, exploitation, and pretending, and at the heart of each privacy, the kinds of sorrow, estrangement, and pain familiar to us all. Perhaps women complained less because they did not then have the courage to speak out. But I think there was more to it than that. There was a kind of restraint, as if men and women still understood that what they owed one another, and the way to protect the sexual realm, was not to visit upon one another all of their sorrows and pain.

It is precisely that constraint, a minimal kindness connected to a naturalness of behavior, that is in large part what is missing from the sexual world today. What we have seen on a grand scale during the sexual revolution has been called in another context "the return of the repressed." But what has been repressed for so long is not only animal need. It is also, we have learned as it comes flooding upward to the surface, a raw mix of anger, frustration, bitter disappointment, sullen resentment—the whole underlying plane of feeling that forms itself in those whose world (despite all our talk of liberation) seems to have made no room for their deepest nature. How many, these days, turning to take another person in their arms, have not found themselves confronted by a range of accumulated disappointments, betrayals, and unfulfilled yearning—the living residue left behind not only by mothers, fathers, and lovers, but also the despair engendered by an unlived or falsely lived life?

Caught in the midst of this, people seem to have no one to blame but one another.

What I hear, everywhere around me, are complaints, descriptions of unmet demands, disappointments—that someone has failed them, let them down, is not what they ought to be. This is the strain that runs through much that I have heard as a therapist, teacher, or friend when men and women talk about one another (though men are less articulate, feel less justified than women in their public complaints). Many of these complaints are accurate, of course—we do fail one another. But their accuracy cannot hide the fact that the expectations have less to do with the world as it is or people as they are than with mistaken, preconceived, borrowed or inherited notions about what men and women ought to be or can be. The tone of all this is not merely one of sadness or unanswered yearning; more often than not it is a tone of judgment, impatience, even contempt. It is as if every lover is also an enemy, as if every companion is less an invited guest than an unwanted intruder.

We have come a long way in the sexual revolution. We have left behind us a great many old illusions and delusions; we know more than we did about the kinds of betrayal, guilt, and confusion that we can survive, and the kinds that we cannot. But what we have not learned—and this is the heart of the problem—is how to be kind to one another, how, in the midst of the confusions we ourselves have created, among the congeries of styles and pretenses of sex that surround us—how we can sustain those we find at our sides or in our arms.

The problem is not that sex has been separated from love, as many people have suggested (though there is some truth to this). The more general problem is that sex—along with countless other activities—has been emptied of generosity. There is nothing specifically sexual about such generosity, nor is there anything unique in the place it ought to play in sex. Yet the hardest thing of all in sexual life, more difficult by far than having the world's finest orgasm, is to leave images and dreams behind, and to learn that the person in one's arms is a poor forked creature, subject to the same confusions and alarms as oneself. Beyond all will, beyond all imagining, beyond all sensation—whether a sneeze or an itch—there remains a human reality that yields itself to a kindness of touch but which remains closed to us, despite all our yearnings, until we can somehow learn to bring to sex, through generosity, precisely what it is that we seek there from others, and without which the sexual world remains a kind of limbo.

Unfortunately for all of us, a capacity for generosity may be no more easily learned than a love of sexual life. Here too is an area where manuals or good advice are not likely to save us. It is one thing to be able to explain where the generosity in a particular culture comes from or what tends to destroy it (and I am not sure, really, that we can do even that). But nobody knows how to interject generosity into a culture whose members no longer seem to feel it on their own.

Of course, in spite of all this, the graces of flesh have not vanished completely and will not vanish. Like any other power rooted in nature, they seem capable of reasserting themselves in spite of anything we do or say. There will always be experiences that sweep away our notions derived from therapy or ideology and liberate us even from our notion of liberation.

It is the imperviousness of sex to ultimate understanding, the way it dissolves understanding, that gives rise to both its curses and gifts, its devils and angels. It remains, in the midst of that "revolution" which has provided neither much equality nor liberty nor fraternity, a troublesome but fecund darkness in which, like lost children, we call out to one another in both fear and delight.

CHAPTER 15

Passionate Attachments in the West in Historical Perspective

Lawrence Stone

Lawrence Stone, a historian at Princeton University, uncovers in this essay a rich set of insights with a historical examination of passionate attachments in the West. The two most common passionate attachments explored are: (1) romantic love between two adolescents or adults of different sex, and (2) the caring love-bond between mothers and children. We have undergone a revolution in both sets of attachments in the past century and find ourselves in a unique position today. Stone traces the historical trend in the spread of the cultural concept of romantic love in the West and the evolution in the mother–child relationship. This fascinating material gives us an educational reminder: We cannot assume people in the past thought about romance and parenting the way we do.

Questions for Discussion

1. What is the nature of romantic love?
2. Is it an adequate rationale and basis for marriage?
3. Is there a relationship between romantic love and permanence in marriage?
4. What is the distinction between romance, lust, and committed love?
5. Is there a gender gap in attitudes toward these diverse forms of passionate attachments in our culture?
6. What are some of the possible implications of changing sex roles in marriage on parent–child relationships?

Further Readings

The subject of romantic love is treated with skill and depth analysis by Robert Johnson in his book *We: The Psychology of Romantic Love* (San Francisco: Harper & Row, 1983).

C entral to the argument of this chapter is a proposition put forward by my colleague Robert Darnton:

Reprinted with the permission of The Free Press, a Division of Simon & Schuster, Inc. from *Passionate Attachments: Thinking about Love*, edited by William Gaylin, M.D., and Ethel Person, M.D. Copyright © 1988 by Friends of Columbia Psychoanalytic Center, Inc.

> One thing seems clear to everyone who returns from field work: other people are other. They do not think the way we do. And if we want to understand their way of thinking, we should set out with the idea of capturing otherness.[1]

What this means is that we cannot assume that people in the past—even in our own Western Judeo-Christian world—thought about and felt passionate attachments the way we do.

My remarks will be confined to the two most common of passionate attachments—between two adolescents or adults of different sexes, and between mothers and children. I know there are other attachments—between homosexuals, siblings, fathers and children—but they are not of such central importance as the first two. Before we can begin to examine the very complex issue of passionate attachments in the past, we therefore have to make a fundamental distinction between attachment between two sexually mature persons, usually of the opposite gender, and attachment to the child of one's body.

In the former case, the problem is how to distinguish what is generally known as falling in love from two other human conditions. The first of those conditions is an urgent desire for sexual intercourse with a particular individual, a passion for sexual access to the body of the person desired. In this particular instance the libido is for some reason closely focussed upon a specific body, rather than there being a general state of sexual excitement capable of satisfaction by any promiscuous coupling. The second condition is one of settled and well-tried ties which develop between two people who have known each other for a long time and have come to trust each other's judgment and have confidence in each other's loyalty and affection. This condition of caring may or may not be accompanied by exciting sexual bonding, and may or may not have begun with falling in love, a phase of violent and irrational psychological passion, which does not last very long.

Historians and anthropologists are in general agreement that romantic love—this usually brief but very intensely felt and all-consuming attraction toward another person—is culturally conditioned, and therefore common only in certain societies at certain times, or even in certain social groups within those societies—usually the elite, with the leisure to cultivate such feelings. They are, however, less certain whether or not romantic love is merely a culture-induced sublimated psychological overlay on top of the biological drive for sex, or whether it has biochemical roots which operate quite independently from the libido. Would anyone in fact "fall in love" if they had not read about it or heard it talked about? Did poetry invent love, or love poetry?

Some things can be said with certainty about the history of the phenomenon. The first is that cases of romantic love can be found at all times and places and have often been the subject of powerful poetic expression, from the Song of Solomon to Shakespeare. On the other hand, neither social approbation nor the actual experience of romantic love is at all common to all societies, as anthropologists have discovered. Second, historical evidence for romantic love before the age of printing is largely confined to elite groups, which of course does not mean that it may not have occurred lower down the social scale among illiterates. As a socially approved cultural artifact it began in Europe in the southern French aristocratic courts in the twelfth century, made fashionable by a group of poets, the troubadours. In this case the culture dictated that it should occur between an unmarried male and a married woman, and that it should either go sexually unconsummated or should be adulterous. This cultural ideal certainly spread into wider circles in the middle ages—witness the love story of Aucassin and Nicolette—but it should be noted that none of these models ends happily.

By the sixteenth and seventeenth centuries, our evidence for the first time becomes quite extensive, thanks to the spread of literacy and the printing press. We now have love poems, like Shakespeare's Sonnets, love letters, and autobiographies by women primarily concerned with their love life. All the courts of Europe were evidently hotbeds of passionate intrigues and liaisons, some romantic, some sexual. The printing press began to spread pornography to a wider public, thus stimulating the libido, while the plays of Shakespeare indicate that romantic love was a familiar concept to society at large, who composed his audience.

Whether this romantic love was approved of, however, is another question. We simply do not know how Shakespearean audiences reacted to Romeo and Juliet. Did they, like us, and as Shakespeare clearly intended, fully identify with the young lovers? Or, when they left the theatre, did they continue to act like the Montague and Capulet parents, who were trying to stop these irresponsible adolescents from allowing an ephemeral and irrational passion to interfere with the serious business of politics and patronage? What is certain is that every advice book, every medical treatise, every sermon and religious homily of the sixteenth and seventeenth centuries firmly rejected both romantic passion and lust as suitable bases for marriage.[2] In the sixteenth century marriage was thought to be best arranged by parents, who could be relied upon to choose socially and economically suitable partners who would enhance the prestige and importance of the kin group as a whole. It was believed that the sexual bond would automatically create the necessary harmony between the two strangers in order to maintain the stability of the new family unit. This, it seems, is not an unreasonable assumption, since recent investigations in Japan have shown that there is no difference in the rate of divorce between couples whose marriages were arranged by their parents and couples whose marriages were made by individual choice based on romantic love. The arranged and the romantic marriage each has an equal chance of turning out well, or breaking up.[3]

Public admiration for marriage-for-love is thus a fairly recent occurrence in Western society, arising out of the romantic movement of the late eighteenth century, and only winning general acceptance in the twentieth. In the eighteenth century orthodox opinion about marriage shifted away from subordinating the individual will to the interests of the group and away from economic or political considerations towards those of well-tried personal affection. The ideal marriage of the eighteenth century was one preceded by three to six months of intensive courting, between a couple from families roughly equal in social status and economic wealth, a courtship which only took place with the prior consent of parents on both sides. A sudden falling head over heels in love, although a familiar enough psychological phenomenon, was thought of as a mild form of insanity, in which judgment and prudence are cast aside, all the inevitable imperfections of the loved one become invisible, and wholly unrealistic dreams of everlasting happiness possess the mind of the afflicted victim. Fortunately, in most cases the disease is of short duration, and the patient normally makes a full recovery. To the eighteenth century, the main object of society—church, law, government, and parents— was to prevent the victim from taking some irrevocable step, particularly from getting married. This is why most European countries made marriage under the age of 21 or even later illegal and invalid unless carried out with the consent of parents or guardians. In England this became law in 1753. Runaway marriages based on passionate attachments still took place, but they were made as difficult as possible to carry out, and in most countries were virtually impossible.

It was not, therefore, until the romantic movement and the rise of the novel, especially the pulp novel, in the nineteenth century, that society at large accepted a new idea—that it was normal and indeed praiseworthy for young men and women to fall passionately in love, and that there must be something wrong with those who have failed to have such an overwhelming experience some time in late adolescence or early manhood. Once this new idea was publicly accepted, the dictation of marriage by parents came to be regarded as intolerable and immoral.

Today, the role of passionate attachments between adults in our society is obscured by a new development, the saturation of the whole culture— through every medium of communication—with sexuality as the predominant and overriding human drive, a doctrine whose theoretical foundations were provided by Freud. In no past society known to me has sex been given so prominent a role in the culture at large, nor has sexual fulfillment been elevated to such preeminence in the list of human aspirations—in a vain attempt to relieve civilization of its discontents. If Thomas Jefferson today was asked to rewrite the Declaration of Independence he would certainly have to add total sexual fulfillment to "Life, Liberty and Human Happiness" as one of the basic natural rights of every member of society. The traditional restraints upon sexual freedom—religious and social taboos, and the fear of pregnancy and venereal disease—have now been almost entirely removed. We find it scarcely credible today that in most of Western Europe in the seventeenth century, in a society whose marriage age was postponed into the late twenties, a degree of chastity was practiced that kept the illegitimacy rate—without contraceptives—as low as 2 or 3 percent. Only in Southern Ireland does such a situation still exist—according to one hypothesis, due to a lowering of the libido caused by large-scale consumption of Guinness Stout. Under these conditions, it seems to me almost impossible today to distin-

guish passionate attachment in the psychological sense—meaning love—
from passionate attachment in the physical sense—meaning lust. But the
enormous success today of pulp fiction concerned almost exclusively with
romantic rather than physical love shows that women at least still hanker
after the experience of falling in love. Whether the same applies to men is
more doubtful, so that there may be a real gender gap on this subject today,
which justifies this distinction I am making between love and lust.

To sum up, the historian can see a clear historical trend in the spread of
the cultural concept of romantic love in the West, beginning in court circles in
the twelfth century, and expanding outward from the sixteenth century on. It
received an enormous boost with the rise of the romantic novel, and another
boost with the achievement of near-total literacy by the end of the nineteenth
century. Today, however, it is so intertwined with sexuality, that is is almost
impossible to distinguish between the two. Both, however, remain clearly
distinct from caring, that is, well-tried and settled affection based on long-
term commitment and familiarity.

It is also possible to say something about the changing relationship of
passionate love to marriage. For all classes who possessed property—that is,
the top two-thirds economically—marriage before the seventeenth century
was arranged by the parents, and the motives were the economic and political benefit of the kin group, not the emotional satisfaction of the individuals.
As the concept of individualism grew in the seventeenth and eighteenth centuries, it slowly became accepted that the prime object was "holy matrimony," a sanctified state of monogamous married contentment. This was
best achieved by allowing the couple to make their own choice, provided that
both sets of parents agreed that the social and economic gap was not too
wide, and that marriage was preceded by a long period of courtship. By the
eighteenth and nineteenth centuries, individualism had so far taken precedence over the group interests of the kin that the couple were left more or less
free to make their own decision, except in the highest aristocratic and royal
circles. Today individualism is given such absolute priority in most Western
societies, that the couple are virtually free to act as they please, to sleep with
whom they please, and to marry and divorce when and whom they please to
suit their own pleasure. The psychic cost of such behavior, and its self-
defeating consequences, are becoming clear, however, and how long this situation will last is anybody's guess.

Here I should point out that the present-day family—I exclude the poor
black family in America from this generalization—is not, as is generally supposed, disintegrating because of a very high divorce rate of up to 50 percent.
It has to be remembered that the median duration of marriage today is almost
exactly the same as it was 100 years ago. Divorce, in short, now acts as a functional substitute for death: both are means of terminating marriage at a premature stage. It may well be that the psychological effects on the survivor
may be very different, although in most cases the catastrophic economic consequences for the woman remain the same. But the point to be emphasized is
that broken marriages, stepchildren, and single-parent households were as

common in the past as they are today, the only difference being the mechanism which has brought about this situation.

The most difficult historical problem concerns the role of romantic love among the propertyless poor, who comprised about one-third of the population. Since they were propertyless, their loves and marriages were of little concern to their kin, and they were therefore more or less free to choose their own mates. By the eighteenth century, and probably before, court records make it clear that these groups often married for love, combined with a confused set of motives including lust and the economic necessity to have a strong and healthy assistant to run the farm or the shop. It was generally expected that they would behave "lovingly" towards each other, but this often did not happen. In many a peasant marriage, the husband seems to have valued his cow more than his wife. Passionate attachments among the poor certainly occurred, but how often they took priority over material interests we may never know for certain.[4]

All that we do know is that courting among the poor normally lasted six months or more, and that it often involved all-night sessions alone together in the dark in a room with a bed, usually with the knowledge and consent of the parents or masters. Only relatively rarely, and only at a late stage after engagement, did full sexual intercourse commonly take place during these nights, but it is certain that affectionate conversation, and discussion of the possibilities of marriage, were accompanied by embracing and kissing, and probably also by what today is euphemistically called "heavy petting." This practice of "bundling," as it was called, occurred in what was by our standards an extremely prudish, and indeed sexually innocent, society. When men and women went to bed together they almost invariably kept on a piece of clothing, a smock or a shirt, to conceal their nakedness. Moreover the sexual act itself was almost always carried out in the "missionary" position. The evidence offered in the courts in cases of divorce in the pre-modern period provide little evidence of that polymorphous perversity advocated in the sex manuals available in every bookstore today.

What is certain is that even after this process of intimate physical and verbal courtship had taken place, economic factors still loomed large in the final decision by both parties about whether or not to marry. Thus passion and material interest were in the end inextricably involved, but it is important to stress that, among the poor, material interest only became central at the *end* of the process of courtship instead of at the beginning, as was the case with the rich.

If an early modern peasant said "I love a woman with ten acres of land," just what did he mean? Did he lust after the body of the woman? Did he admire her good health, administrative and intellectual talents and strength of character as a potential housekeeper, income producer, and mother of his children? Was he romantically head over heels in love with her? Or did he above all prize her for her ten acres? Deconstruct the text as we wish, there is no way of getting a clear answer to that question; and in any case, if we could put that peasant on the couch today and interrogate him, it would probably turn out that he merely felt that he liked the woman more because of her ten acres.

Finally, we know that in the eighteenth century at least half of all brides in England and America were pregnant on their wedding day. But this tells us more about sexual customs than about passionate attachments: sex began at the moment of engagement, and marriage in church came later, often triggered by the pregnancy. We also know that if a poor servant girl was impregnated by her master, which often happened, the latter usually had no trouble finding a poor man who would marry her, in return for payment of ten pounds or so. Not much passionate attachment there, among any of the three persons involved.

The second type of passionate attachment is that which develops between the parent, especially the mother, and the child. Here again as historians we are faced with the intractable problem of nature versus nurture, of the respective roles of biology and culture. The survival of the species demands that the female adult should take optimum care of the child over a long period, to ensure its survival. This is particularly necessary among humans since the child is born prematurely compared with all other primates, because of its exaggerated cranial size, and so is peculiarly helpless for an exceptionally long period of time. Moreover, experiments with primates have shown that it is close body contact in the first weeks of life which creates the strong bond between mother and child. A passionate attachment of the mother for its child therefore seems to be both a biological necessity for survival and an emotional reality.

On the other hand recorded human behavior indicates that cultural traditions and economic necessity often override this biological drive. For over 90 percent of human history man has been a hunter-gatherer, and it is impossible for a woman to carry two babies and perform her daily task of gathering. Barring sexual abstention, which seems unlikely, some form of infanticide must therefore have been a necessity, dictated by economic conditions.

Other factors came into play in more recent times. From at least classical antiquity to the eighteenth century it was normal in northwest Europe to swaddle all babies at birth—that is, to tie them up head to foot in bandages, taken off only to remove the urine and feces. This automatically reduced body contact with the mother, and therefore presumably the bonding effect between mother and child. Secondly, all women who could afford to do so put their infants out to wet-nurse from birth to about the age of two. The prime reason for this among the more well-to-do was undoubtedly the accepted belief that sexual excitement spoils the milk. Few husbands were willing to do without the sexual services of their wives for that length of time; hence the reliance on a wet nurse. But this meant that for all except the tiny minority who could afford to take the nurse into the house, the child was removed within a few days of birth and put in the care of a village woman some distance from the home. Under these conditions affection between parents and children could not begin to grow until the child returned to the home at about the age of eighteen months or two years, and the child might well have a more passionate relationship with its nurse than with its mother—as was the case with Shakespeare's Juliet.

In any case, the child's return to its mother would only take place if it did not die while with the wet nurse. There is overwhelming evidence that the mortality rate of children being wet-nursed was very much higher than that of children being breast-fed by their mothers, and contemporaries were well aware of this. It is difficult to avoid the suspicion that one incentive for the practice, particularly for its enormous expansion in France in the nineteenth century, was as an indirect method of infanticide, out of sight and out of mind. This suspicion is reinforced by the huge numbers of children in the eighteenth and nineteenth centuries who were abandoned and deposited in workhouses or foundling hospitals, only a small fraction of whom survived the experience. Whatever the intention, in practice the foundling hospitals of London or Paris acted as a socially acceptable means of family limitation after birth. Few women other than those who gave birth to bastard children practiced infanticide themselves, if only because the risks were too great. But overlaying and stifling by accident while in the same bed during the nights, putting out to wet-nurse, abandoning to public authorities, or depositing in foundling hospitals served the same purpose. Unwanted children of the poor and not so poor were somehow or other got rid of in all these socially acceptable ways.[5]

These common eighteenth and even nineteenth century practices, especially prevalent in France, raise questions about the degree of maternal love in that society. This is not an easy question to answer, and historians are deeply divided on this issue. Some point to evidence of mothers who were devoted to their children and seriously disturbed by their premature deaths. Others point to the bleak statistics of infant mortality: about 25 percent dead before the age of two, a percentage deliberately increased by wet-nursing, abandonment, and infanticide by neglect—practices which have been described as "post-natal family planning." A mid-nineteenth century Bavarian woman summed up the emotional causes and consequences:

> The parents are glad to see the first and second child, especially if there is a boy amongst them. But all that come after aren't so heartily welcome. Anyway not many of these children live. Four out of a dozen at most, I suppose. The others very soon get to heaven. When little children die, it's not often that you have a lot of grief. They're little angels in heaven.[6]

Another question is how kindly children were treated if they did survive. I have suggested that sixteenth and early seventeenth century societies were cold and harsh, relatively indifferent to children, and resorting to frequent and brutal whippings from an early age as the only reliable method of discipline. Calvinism, with its grim insistence on original sin, encouraged parents and schoolmasters to whip children, in order quite literally to beat the Hell out of them. I have argued that only in the eighteenth century did there develop a more optimistic view of the infant as a plain sheet of paper upon which good or evil could be written by the process of cultural socialization. The more extreme view of Rousseau, that the child is born good, in a state of innocence, was widely read, but not very widely accepted, so far as can be seen—for the rather obvious reason that it is contradicted by the direct experience of all observant parents.

To sum up, first there is ample evidence for the widespread practice of infanticide in societies ignorant of contraception, a practice which, disguised in socially acceptable forms, lasted well into the nineteenth century. Second, children, even of the rich, were often treated with calculated brutality in the sixteenth and seventeenth centuries, and again in the nineteenth, in order to eradicate original sin; the eighteenth and twentieth centuries are two rare periods of educational permissiveness. As for the poor, they have always regarded children very largely as potential economic assets and treated them accordingly. Their prime functions have been to help in the house, the workshop, and the field, to add to the family income, and to support their parents in old age. How much room was left over from these economic considerations for passionate attachment, even with the mother, remains an open question.

Passionate attachments between young people can and do happen in any society as a by-product of biological sexual attraction, but the social acceptability of the emotion has varied enormously over time and class and space, determined primarily by cultural norms and property arrangements. Furthermore, though there is a strong biological component in the passionate attachment of mothers to children, it too is often overlaid by economic necessities, by religious views about the nature of the child, and by accepted cultural practices such as wet-nursing. We are in a unique position today in that society, through social security and other devices, has taken over the economic responsibilities of children for their aged parents; contraception is normal and efficient; our culture is dominated by romantic notions of passionate love as the only socially admissible reason for marriage; and sexual fulfillment is accepted as the dominant human drive and a natural right for both sexes. Behind all this there lies a frenetic individualism, a restless search for the sexual and emotional ideal in human relationships, and a demand for instant ego gratification which is inevitably self-defeating and ultimately destructive.

Most of this is new and unique to our culture. It is, therefore, quite impossible to extrapolate from present values and behavior to those in the past. Historical others—even our own forefathers and mothers—were indeed other.

NOTES

1. Darnton, R. *The Great Cat Massacre and Other Episodes in French Cultural History* (New York: Basic Books, 1984), 4.

2. For further discussion of these issues, and references, see my book *The Family, Sex and Marriage in England, 1500–1800* (New York: Harper & Row, 1977).

3. *Journal of Family History,* 8, 1983, p. 100.

4. Flandrin, J. L. *Les Amours Paysannes* (XVI–XIX Siècles) (Paris: Gallimard, 1975).

5. The literature on infanticide (rare), infant abandonment, and early death by deliberate neglect or wet-nursing in Western Europe up to the nineteenth century is now enormous. See, for example:

de Mause, L. *The History of Childhood* (New York: Psychohistory Press, 1974).
Delasselle, C. "Les enfants abandonés à Paris au XVIII siécle," *Annales E.C.S.,* 30, Jan.–Feb. 1975.
Flandrin, J. L. "L'attitude devant le petit enfant . . . dans la Civilisation Occidentale," in *Annales de Demographie Historique,* 1973.
Sussman, G. D. *Selling Mother's Milk: The Wet-nursing Business in France, 1715–1914* (Champaign: University of Illinois Press, 1982).

6. Medick, H. and D. W. Sabean, eds. *Interest and Emotion* (New York: Cambridge University Press, 1984), 91.

CHAPTER 16

Four Mischievous Theories of Sex: Demonic, Divine, Casual, and Nuisance

William F. May

William May's article easily lends itself to constructive classroom discussion and clarification on the topic of sex. The author lays out four conflicting attitudes on sex. While the attitudes are loosely associated with the behavior of different cultural groups, the divergent views can be found in each one of us.

The author's typology is suggestive and stimulating: sex as demonic, divine, casual, and a nuisance. Each category contains an element of truth, but each is also ultimately fallacious. A theological interpretation and analysis is offered of the viewpoints on the basis of the biblical tradition and Christian heritage. The article is a valuable pedagogical tool to facilitate self-examination on this important topic.

Questions for Discussion

1. How do you account for the popularity of the playboy philosophy of sex in the United States? What is the root problem in this attitude? Is there a credible alternative?
2. Is there a place for discipline in sex? How would you justify it? Where does discipline end and repression begin?
3. What is the current dominant attitude toward sex in contemporary music, movies, church?

S everal conflicting attitudes toward sex beset us today. We loosely associate these attitudes with the behavior of different cultural groups. Whether the groups actually behaved in these ways poses a descriptive question that will not preoccupy me for the moment. I am interested more in the attitudes than in the historical accuracy of the symbols. The Victorian prude feared sex as demonic; romantics, such as D. H. Lawrence, elevated sex to the divine; liberals tend to reduce sex to the casual; and the British, as the satirists relent-

Reprinted with the permission of The Free Press, a Division of Simon & Schuster, Inc. from *Passionate Attachments: Thinking about Love*, edited by William Gaylin, M.D., and Ethel Person, M.D. Copyright © 1988 by Friends of Columbia Psychoanalytic Center, Inc.

lessly portray them, pass it off as a nuisance. I will argue that all these views of sex contain an element of truth; all are ultimately mischievous; and most can be found conflicting and concurrent in ourselves.

SEX AS DEMONIC

Those who fear sex as the demon in the groin reckon with sex as a power which, once let loose, tends to grip and destroy its host; it is self-destructive and destructive of others, a loose cannon, as it were, in human affairs. Our movies and drugstore paperbacks relentlessly mock this view, which we tend to assign remotely to our Victorian forebears and proximately to our parents. While parents, in fact, may fear the explosive power of sex in their adolescent children, it is doubtful whether most parents are quite the Victorians their children assume them to be. Children impute this view to their elders because at some level of their being they partly hold to this attitude themselves.

In any event, this pessimism that emphasizes the runaway destructiveness of sex hardly originated with the Victorians. Religiously, it dates back to the Manichaean dualists of the Third Century of the Common Era. Manichaeans divided all reality and power into two rival kingdoms: the Kingdom of God pitted against the Kingdom of Satan, Good versus Evil, Light versus Darkness. They associated the Absolute Good with Spirit and Absolute Evil with Matter. Originally Spirit and Matter existed in an uneasy separation from one another; but through the aggressive strategies of Satan, the present world and humankind came into existence, a sad commingling of them both—Spirit and Flesh. The world is a kind of battleground between these two rival kingdoms. Man's only hope rests in disengaging himself from the pain and confusion and muck of life in the flesh, and allying himself with the Kingdom of Spirit. I say "man" deliberately because the Manichaeans tended to associate women with the intentions of the Devil; that is, with his strategy to perpetuate this present age of confusion and commingling through the device of sex and offspring. Quite literally, marriage in their view is an invention of the Devil, a scheme for perpetuating the human race and the messy world that we know. Man should achieve a final state of metaphysical *Apartheid*, a clean separation from the toils of the flesh, women, and all their issue.

Manichaean sex counselors thus urged on their followers a rigorous ethic of sexual denial—with, however, an antinomian escape clause since not everyone could lead the wholly ascetic life. If one couldn't totally abstain—here is the twist—the Manichaeans believed it was better to engage in "unnatural sex" so as to avoid the risk of progeny. In the Manichaean vision of things, sex is bad, but children are worse. Reproduction should be avoided at all costs, since it only perpetuates the grim, woe-beset world that we know. (The mythology sounds strange to the modern ear, but the Manichaeans have served as a symbol of pessimism in later Western theology, and rightly so. A reluctance to have children usually blurts out the pessimism—whatever its causes—of those who think little of the world's present and future prospects.)

Christianity rejected this Manichaean pessimism, and thereby confirmed the religious vision it derived largely from the Scriptures of Israel and from the New Testament. Its monotheism differs from a dualism that takes evil too seriously and that identifies evil too readily with the flesh. Its scriptures highly esteem sexual love (the erotic Song of Solomon would jar in a Manichaean scripture); it grants a sacramental status to marriage; and it describes the body as the temple of the Lord. The lowly, needy, hungering, flatulent body is nothing less than the real estate where the resurrection will occur.

But dualism kept reappearing in the Western tradition, often nesting in Christianity itself or appearing in an alluring alternative, the cult of romantic love. On the surface, the ideal of romantic love, Denis de Rougemont once shrewdly argued, appears to be sexually vigorous; it celebrates God's good green gift of sex. But, in fact, it secretly despairs of sex; it always directs itself to the faraway princess—not to the partner you've got, but to the dream person, the remote figure not yet yours. Sex slips its focus on actual contacts between people and transposes to the realm of the imagination. To possess her is to lose one's appetite for her. Love, therefore, feeds best on obstacles. "We love each other, but you're a Capulet and I'm a Montague." And so it goes from Romeo and Juliet, backward to the Tristan and Iseult myth, and forward to Noel Coward's "Brief Encounter" and the mawkish *Love Story.* The poignancy of passion depends upon separation, ultimately upon death. The cult of romantic love locates passion in the teased imagination. The flesh kills; the spirit alone endures; thus Manichaean pessimism hides in its alluring garb.

The post-Renaissance world offered a somewhat drabber version of this dualist suspicion of sex. Social diseases assaulted the Western countries and associated sex with forces that abuse the mind and body. Further, a concept of marriage emerged with middle-class careerism that encourages a Manichaean wariness toward sex. The bourgeois family depended for its stability and life on the career and the property of the male provider. Premarital sex, which distracts a man from his career and leads him prematurely into marriage, severely limits his prospects. Extramarital sex spoils the marriage itself and public reputation. And marital sex leads to too many children with a cramping effect on the careers of those already arrived. Thus, all told, sex severely inconveniences a careerist-oriented society that depends throughout on deferred gratification.

But not surprisingly, bourgeois culture produced not only repression, but also a pornographic fascination with sex. Sex became, at one and the same time, unmentionable in polite society but also an unshakable obsession in fantasy. Geoffrey Gorer, the English social anthropologist, in his often plagiarized article, "The Pornography of Death," nicely defined all such pornographic preoccupation with sex as an obsession with the sex act abstracted from its natural human emotion, which is *affection.* This definition helps explain the inevitable structure of pornographic novels and films. Invariably, they must proliferate and escalate the varieties of sexual performance. When the sex act separates from its natural human emotion of affection, it loses its tie with the concrete lives of the two persons performing the act; it becomes *boring*. Inevitably, one must reinvest one's interest in the variety of ways and techniques with which the act is performed—one on one, then two on one, then in all possible permutations and combinations, culminating in the orgy. When affection isn't there, it won't do to have bodies perform the act in the age-old ways. Sad variety alone compensates.

(The oft-cited pornographic preoccupation with death and violence today follows the same pattern of escalation. A pornography of death entails an obsession with death and violence abstracted from its natural human emotion, which is grief. Once again such violence, abstracted from persons, inevitably bores, and therefore one must reinvest interest in the technology with which the act is performed. It won't do for James Bond to drive an ordinary General Motors car (as though it weren't death-dealing an instrument enough); he must have a specially equipped vehicle that jets flames out its exhaust. Spies must be killed in all sorts of combinations and permutations. Violence inevitably escalates.)

This ambivalent attitude toward sex that generates both repression and obsession is basically religious—not Jewish or Christian, to be sure, but religious, specifically Manichaean—in its root. It religiously preoccupies itself with sex as a major evil in human affairs.

SEX AS DIVINE

The second of the four attitudes toward sex also qualifies as religious; in this case, however, one elevates sex from the demonic to the divine. D. H. Lawrence offers the definitive expression of this sex-mysticism; let his views stand for the type. *Lady Chatterley's Lover* is a religious book. That assessment didn't occur to people of my generation who, before laying hands on the book, assumed its title was *Lady Chatterley's Lovers*, and settled down for the inevitable orgy. The book offered, however, religion in a very traditional sense, for religion consists of some sort of experience of sacred power perceived in contest with other powers. The sacred grips the subject as overwhelming, alluring, and mysterious, and eventually orders the rest of life for the person or community so possessed. (Exodus 3, for example, describes the contest between Yahveh, God of the Jews, and the power of the Pharaoh. God liberates his people from Egypt and orders their life at Mt. Sinai; God prevails.)

Just so, the novel focuses on a woman who experiences in her own being a contest of the powers—those opposingly symbolized by Lord Clifford, her husband, and Oliver Mellors, her husband's gamekeeper. Her husband possessed those several powers which the English highly prized—status, money, and talent. He was at once an aristocrat, an industrial captain, and an author—an ironmonger and wordmonger. He wielded economic power and word power. Leaving such a man for his gamekeeper would utterly confound the commitments of Lady Chatterley's class. Lord Clifford's only trouble, his fatal trouble, however, was a war wound that left him dead from the waist down, a state of affairs which was but the natural issue of the kind of destructive power which he wields. Lady Chatterley discovers in the gamekeeper and in the grove where he breeds pheasants, a different kind of power, a growing power in the pheasant and the phallus, and this power prevails.

Lawrence's novel celebrates not random sex but a sex-mysticism. The grove where Lady Chatterley and Oliver meet serves as a sacred precinct removed from the grimy, profane, sooty, industrial midlands of England where men like Lord Clifford ruled. Lawrence explicitly uses the coronation Psalms of Israel to describe the act of sexual intercourse. "Open up, ye everlasting gates, and let the king of glory enter in." In using royal language, Lawrence advocated not sexual promiscuity, as the hungering undergraduates of my generation supposed. Far from it! Lawrence disdained the merely casual affair: he exalted sexual union into a sacred encounter. Tenderhearted sex is the closest we come to salvation in this life. It provides contact with all that nurtures and fulfills. Americans in the 1950s relied on a sentimental marital version of this religious expectation. As the song of the times put it, "love and marriage go together like a horse and carriage." In the oft-called "age of conformity" one tended to look to the sanctuary of marriage to provide respite from the loneliness and pressures of the outer world to which one conformed but which one found unfulfilling.

SEX AS CASUAL

W. H. Auden once observed that the modern liberal offended Lawrence more than the Puritan. The Puritan mistakenly viewed sex as an outsize evil, but the liberal made the even greater mistake of reducing sex to the casual—to one of the many incidental goods that in our liberty we take for granted. Some have called this the drink-of-water theory of sex.

This casual attitude toward sex reflects a liberal industrial culture that prizes autonomy above all else, that reduces nature to raw material to be manipulated and transformed into products of man's own choosing, and that correspondingly reduces the body to the incidental—not to the prison house of the dualists, or to the Lord's temple of the monotheists, or to the sacred grove of the mystics, but to a playground pure and simple.

Some observers argue that this third attitude toward sexual experience dominates our time. Is not D. H. Lawrence, despite his flamboyance, actually somewhat quaint and old-fashioned, the reverse side, if you will, of the Victorian prude? Don't both the prude and the romantic make the mistake of taking sex too seriously? One elevates sex into the satanic, and the other celebrates it as divine. Have we not succeeded in desacralyzing sex and reducing it now to the casual?

This third and apparently prevailing theory of sex today, the so-called new sex ethic, takes two forms. First and most notoriously, its earlier, male chauvinist version converts sex into an instrument of domination. It reduces sex to the casual, by converting women into bunnies and by replacing heterosexuality with a not so latent male orientation. In its magazine formula, it condemns women, flatters the young male, and lavishes on him advice on how to dress, talk, choose his cars, and handle his women—all without involvement. The women's movement has shown proper contempt for this view.

The second version of the new sex ethic avoids the more obvious criticisms of the woman's movement; indeed, it seeks to join it by offering easy access, easy departure, and no long-term ties, but with equal rights for both partners. One of our entertainers best summarized this casual, tentative, experimental attitude toward sex and marriage by referring to his decision to do the "marriage bit"—a phrase from show biz. It suggests that marriage offers a role one chooses to play rather than a relationship by which one is permanently altered—not necessarily a one-night stand, but then not likely, either, to run as long as "Life With Father."

This reading of the social history of our time—from the religious to the secular—only apparently persuades. We are not quite as casual about sex as this analysis would suggest. Our popular magazines—men's and women's—may have evangelized for a cool attitude toward sex; but they would not have sold millions of copies if, underneath it all, in the steamy depths of our desires, we could toy with it that easily.

Denis de Rougemont neatly skewers our irrepressible fascination with sex in *The Devil's Share*, a book that included chapters on such topics as the "Devil and Betrayal," the "Devil and War," and the "Devil and Lying." His first sentence in his essay on the "Devil and Sex" reads, in effect: "To the adolescent amongst my readers who have turned to this chapter first . . ." I read de Rougemont's book when I was 32, but the age makes little difference. There one is—young or old—caught red-handed, eyes riveted, imagination stirred, ready for fresh rivulets of knowledge on that most fascinating of topics. Casual curiosity? Yes. But the lure of mystery as well. Elements of the religious as well as the casual characterize our attitude toward the subject.

SEX AS A NUISANCE

So far, this essay has covered three views of sex; symmetry alone would demand a fourth to complete two sets of paired attitudes. Dualists inflate sex into a transcendent evil; mystics view it as a transcendent good; and casualists reduce it to a trivial good. The demands of symmetry, then, would posit the existence of a fourth group composed of those prosaic folk who dismiss sex as a minor evil, a nuisance. Comic writers have rounded up this particular population and located them in Great Britain under the marquee: "No Sex, Please. We're British." Copulation is, at best, a burdensome ritual to be endured for the sake of a few lackluster goods. One has visions therewith of an underblooded, overarticulate clutch of aristocrats in whom the life force runs thin.

But a report in one of the most popular of American syndicated newspaper columns (in the *Washington Post,* June 14 and 15, 1985) suggests that the number of people occupying the quadrant of petty pessimists may be surprisingly large. Ann Landers asked her reading audience to send a postcard or letter with a reply to the question: "Would you be content to be held close and treated tenderly and forget about 'the act'? Reply YES or NO and please add one line: 'I am over (or under) 40 years of age.' No signature is necessary." Even discounting for the fact that the disgruntled find more time to write than the contented, the percentage of those replying to Landers' inquiry who deemed themselves to be sexually burdened was impressive. More than 70 percent replied YES and 40 percent of those affirmatives were under 40 years of age. Clearly the people who find sex to be a burden transcend the boundaries of the British Isles. Over 90,000 letters poured in from the U.S. and other places where Landers' column appears (in Canada, Europe, Tokyo, Hong Kong, Bangkok, Mexico). This outpouring has exceeded every inquiry that Landers has directed to her readers, except for the pre-fab letter to be sent to President Reagan on the subject of nuclear war. "This sex survey beats . . . the poll asking parents, 'If you had to do it over again, would you have children?'" (Seventy percent said NO.) (Some astute historians of religion have argued that Manichaeaism persists as the ranking heresy in the West.)

Critics of the Landers report have warned that her results are not scientific. Her respondents are self-selective and her question tips the responses negatively. By placing the term for intercourse in quotation marks and calling it "the act," she tends to separate the sex act from tenderness. Still, the grammar of her question does not force an either/or response: tenderness or sex. However parsed, Landers uncovers a great deal of dissatisfaction amongst women . . . "it's a burden, a bore, no satisfaction . . ." Her letter-writers largely blame men for this state of affairs, but her survey and the ensuing discussion leave untouched the question as to whether the male failure to satisfy reflects a deeper masculine version of the experience of sex as a nuisance. One thinks here not of the occasionally impotent male who is agonizingly aware of sex as a nuisance, but, of the robust stallion who prides himself on his efficient performance but who finds foreplay, after-play, tenderness, and gratitude an incomprehensible and burdensome detail.

THEOLOGICAL INTERPRETATION

Since I am a trained Protestant theologian, not a social commentator, I will close with a few comments about each of these four attitudes on the basis of the biblical tradition. In these matters I don't think I stray too far from what my colleagues in the rabbinate and priesthood might say.

1. Whatever criticisms the biblical tradition might deliver against the casualist approach to sex, that approach has an element of truth to it. Not all sexual encounter should carry the weight of an ultimate significance. Sometimes sex is merely recreational, a way to fall asleep, a *jeu d'esprit*, to say nothing of a *jeu de corps*. But at the same time, the interpretation of a particular episode should not exhaust the full meaning of the activity. At first glance, the ideology of the casualist seems virile, optimistic, and pleasure-oriented. But a latent melancholy pervades it. The fantasy of transient pleasure as an interpretation of the full meaning of the act requires a systematic elimination of everything that might shadow the fantasy. The sacred grove trivializes into a playpen. Hugh Hefner's original policy of never accepting a story for his magazine on the subject of death betrays the pathos of the approach. The fact of human frailty and death shatters the illusion upon which Hefner's world depends. By comparison, a sturdy optimism underlies a tradition that invites a couple to exchange vows that can stretch across the stark events of plenty and want, sickness and health, until death parts them. Since life is no playpen, it lets the world as it is flood in upon the lovers in the very content of their pledge.

Further, the casual outlook tends to ignore the inevitable complications of most sexual relationships. It lapses into a kind of emotional prudery. We are inclined to apply the word prudish to those who deny their sexual being. The modern casualist, however, is an emotional prude; that is, he tries to deny those emotions that cluster around his sexual life: affection, but not affection alone, loneliness in absence, jealousy, envy, preoccupation, restlessness, anger, and hopes for the future. The emotional prude dismisses all these or assumes that sincerity and honesty provide a kind of solvent that breaks down chemically any and all inconvenient and messy feelings: You hope for the future? But I never promised you a future. Why complain? I am emotionally clean, drip-dry. Why not you? This antiseptic view overlooks the element of dirt farming in sex and marriage. Caesar ploughed her and she cropped. Put another way, this view overlooks the comic in sex; adopting the pose of the casual it lacks a comic sense. It overlooks the way sex gets out of control. Sex refuses to stay in the playpen. It tends to defy our advance formulae. It mires each side down in complications that need to be respected.

If sex is a great deal more important, complicated, and consequential for the destiny of each partner than the committed casualists are wont to pretend, then it may not be out of place to subject it to a deliberateness, to submit it to a discipline, to let sexual decisions be *decisions* instead of resolving sexual ties by the luck of the draw, opportunity, and drift. The Hebrew tradition emphasized and symbolized the element of deliberateness in sexual life when it imposed the rite of circumcision. The rite does not deny the natural (as castration does with a vengeance) but neither does it accept the natural vitalities without their conforming to purposes that transcend them. Human sexual life is properly itself only when it is drawn into the self's deeper identity. Thus, against those who reduce sex to the casual, the tradition says sex is *important,* and should be subjected to discipline like anything important and consequential in human affairs.

2. The approach of the dualists to sex, either those who elevate it to a transcendental evil or those who reduce it to a doggish burden, hold to an element of truth. Sometimes, sexual activity can be abysmally self-destructive and destructive of others; at other times, it is merely a burdensome obligation. But, from the biblical perspective, both approaches wrongly estimate sexual love: they confuse the abuse of an activity with the activity itself. Sexual love is a good rather than an evil. God created man in his own image, *male and female* created He them. Genesis provides quite an exalted theory of sexual identity. Not divine, but in the image of God.

This differing estimate of sexual love shifts dramatically the meaning and warrants for discipline in one's sexual life. The Manichaeans disciplined sexual activity in the sense that they sought to eradicate it altogether; they justified radical denial on the ground that sex is inherently *evil*. The Jew and Christian, on the other hand, justify discipline on the basis of the goodness of sexual power.

Unfortunately, most popular justifications of discipline, especially in the perspective of the young, rest on the evilness of an activity or a faculty. Discipline the child because he is evil. Renounce your sexuality because it corrupts. This is the Manichaean way.

We may need to recover the vastly more important warrant for discipline that we already recognize in education and that the biblical tradition largely supports. The goodness and promise of the human mind, not its evilness, justifies the lengthy discipline of an education. Because the child has worthwhile potentialities, we consider it worth our while to develop her to the maximum. Because the piano is a marvelously versatile and expressive instrument, we think it worth the labors of the talented person to realize the full potentialities of the instrument rather than trivialize its capabilities with "Chopsticks." Some sexual encounters are not so much wicked as trivial, less than the best.

3. Finally, the sex-mystics also have an element of truth on their side. The event of sexual intercourse does supply us with one of our privileged contacts with ecstasy—the possibility of being beside ourselves, of moving beyond ourselves, experiencing a level of energy and urgency that both suspends and restores the daily round. But when all is said and done, sexuality, though a good, is only a *human* good, not *divine* as such. Despite Lawrence's perorations on the subject of love and the mountains atremble for Robert Jordan and his mate in Hemingway's *For Whom the Bell Tolls,* the act of sexual intercourse falls short of Exodus–Mount Sinai, death-resurrection. Intercourse is not an event of salvation; neither is marriage another name for redemption.

Biblical realism requires us to acknowledge three ways of abusing sex— to malign it with the dualists, to underestimate it with the casualists, but also to overestimate it with the sentimentalists and therefore to get angry, frustrated, and retaliatory when it fails to transcend the merely human. As a sex-ologist, St. Augustine had his faults, but he recognized that people tend to engage in a double torture when they elevate the human into the divine—whether it be sex, marriage, children, or any other creaturely good.

First, they condemn themselves to disappointment; they torture them-selves. If men and women look for the resolution to all their problems in mar-riage, if they look to it for salvation, they are bound to discover that neither sex nor marriage converts an ordinary human being into someone sublime. They let themselves in for a letdown. Second, one not only tortures oneself, one also tortures the partner to whom one has turned. One places on the mate too heavy a burden. Dostoevsky tells of a dream in which a driver flogs a horse, forcing it to drag an overloaded wagon until the horse collapses under too much weight. We similarly overburden another when we look to him for too much. We expect others to function as a surrogate for the divine. Thus parents drive their thwarted ambitions through their children like a stake through the heart. Some marriages break up not because people expected too little from marriage, but because they have expected too much.

This biblical realism need not produce the sort of pessimism that expects little of the world and savors even less. Indeed, it should free us a little for enjoyment. Once we free our relationships to others from the impossible pressure to rescue us or redeem us, perhaps we can be free to enjoy them for what they are. Specifically, we can enjoy without shame and with delight a sexual relationship for the pleasurable, companionable, and fertile human good that it is.

CHAPTER 17

The Neglected Heart: The Emotional Dangers of Premature Sexual Involvement

Thomas Lickona

Most young people I have met are very clear about the following principle: in order to be on a sport's team you have to show some skill at playing the game. You can't just walk onto the field, name yourself as a player, and expect to be handed a uniform. You have to go through tryouts to see if you have developed enough skill to qualify for the team. And then if you do get a spot on the team, you will face endless activities at strengthening your skills, at becoming a team player, and—and this is my main point here—at psychological conditioning for the sport, ensuring that your mind and heart are also ready when you take to the field or the court.

Not all people understand that by its very nature, "sex" is meant to be something more than a physical activity. Understanding this aspect of ourselves seems of great importance. I once heard an astute fifteen-year-old say this about her sex education class: "Today I found out that I was physically fully prepared to be a mother: to conceive a child, to carry that child to term, and to give birth to that child. And today I finally saw that that was the *only* sense in which I was prepared. I am not prepared emotionally, psychologically, educationally, financially, or socially."

The following essay argues that the "skills" of full human sexual functioning are not just the physical "skills" of "doing it." Many twelve-year-olds think that is all there is to it. One can understand that error in one so young. The problem comes when the person over seventeen lives out the same illusion. Thomas Lickona gives us something to think about.

The best way to read this essay may be to ask yourself where the author touches on matters you know to be true.

Questions for Discussion

1. Where does he tell it like it is? After all, some reading this book can tell their own stories about the dangers Lickona touches on.
2. What would I want to say to fourteen-year-olds to help them be aware of the dangers that may lie ahead?

3. Where does the author seem, in your view, to overstate "the dangers of premature sexual involvement."

4. What does that word *premature* mean? Could a particular involvement be premature for a twenty-five-year-old? What would be some examples?

You didn't get pregnant. You didn't get AIDS. So why do you feel so bad?
—*Leslee Unruh, abstinence educator*

There is no condom for the heart.
—*Sign at a sex education conference*

In discussions of teen sex, much is said about the dangers of pregnancy and disease—but far less about the emotional hazards. And that's a problem, because the destructive psychological consequences of temporary sexual relationships are very real. Being aware of them can help a young person make and stick to the decision to avoid premature sexual involvement.

That's not to say we should downplay the physical dangers of uncommitted sex. Pregnancy is a life-changing event. Sexually transmitted disease (STD)—and there are now more than 20 STDs—can rob you of your health and even your life. Condoms don't remove these dangers. Condoms have an annual failure rate of 10 percent to 30 percent in preventing pregnancy because of human error in using them and because they sometimes leak, break, or slip off. Condoms reduce but by no means eliminate the risk of AIDS. In a 1993 analysis of 11 different medical studies, condoms were found to have a 31 percent average failure rate in preventing the sexual transmission of the AIDS virus.[1] Finally, condoms do little or nothing to protect against the two STDs infecting at least one-third of sexually active teenage girls: human papilloma virus (the leading cause of cervical cancer) and chlamydia (the leading cause of infertility), both of which can be transmitted by skin-to-skin contact in the entire genital area, only a small part of which is covered by the condom.[2]

Why is it so much harder to discuss sex and emotional hurt—to name and talk about the damaging psychological effects that can come from premature sexual involvement? For one thing, most of us have never heard this aspect of sex discussed. Our parents didn't talk to us about it. The media don't talk about it. And the heated debate about condoms in schools typically doesn't say much about the fact that condoms do nothing to make sex *emotionally* safe. When it comes to trying to explain to their children or students

Reprinted with permission from the Summer 1994 issue of the *American Educator*, the quarterly journal of the American Federation of Teachers.

how early sexuality can do harm to one's personality and character as well as to one's health, many adults are simply at a loss for words, or reduced to vague generalities such as, "you're too young" or "you're not ready" or "you're not mature enough."

This relative silence about the emotional side of sex is ironic, because the emotional dimension of sex is what makes it distinctively human.

What in fact are the emotional or psychological consequences of premature, uncommitted sex? These consequences vary among individuals. Some emotional consequences are short-term but still serious. Some of them last a long time, sometimes even into marriage and parenting. Many of these psychological consequences are hard to imagine until they've been experienced. In all cases, the emotional consequences of sexual experiences are not to be taken lightly. A moment's reflection reminds us that emotional problems can have damaging, even crippling, effects on a person's ability to lead a happy and productive life.

Let's look at 10 negative psychological consequences of premature sexual involvement.

1. WORRY ABOUT PREGNANCY AND AIDS

For many sexually active young people, the fear of becoming pregnant or getting AIDS is a major emotional stress.

Russell Henke, health education coordinator in the Montgomery County (Maryland) Public Schools, says, "I see kids going to the nurses in schools, crying a day after their first sexual experience, and wanting to be tested for AIDS. They have done it, and now they are terrified. For some of them, that's enough. They say, 'I don't want to have to go through that experience anymore.'"[3]

A high school girl told a nurse: "I see some of my friends buying home pregnancy tests, and they are so worried and so distracted every month, afraid that they might be pregnant. It's a relief to me to be a virgin."

2. REGRET AND SELF-RECRIMINATION

Girls, especially, need to know in advance the sharp regret that so many young women feel after becoming sexually involved.

Says one high school girl: "I get upset when I see my friends losing their virginity to some guy they've just met. Later, after the guy's dumped them, they come to me and say, 'I wish I hadn't done it.'"[4] A ninth-grade girl who slept with eight boys in junior high says, "I'm young, but I feel old."

Girls are more vulnerable than boys because girls are more likely to think of sex as a way to "show you care." They're more likely to see sex as a sign of commitment in the relationship.

If a girl expects a sexual interlude to be loving, she may very well feel cheated and used when the boy doesn't show a greater romantic interest after the event. As one 15-year-old girl describes her experience: "I didn't expect the guy to marry me, but I never expected him to avoid me in school."

Bob Bartlett, who teaches a freshman sexuality class in a Richfield, Minn., high school, shares the following story of regret on the part of one of his students (we'll call her Sandy):

> Sandy, a bright and pretty girl, asked to see Mr. Bartlett during her lunch period. She explained that she had never had a boyfriend, so she was excited when a senior asked her out.
>
> After they dated for several weeks, the boy asked her to have sex with him. She was reluctant; he was persistent. She was afraid of appearing immature and losing him, so she consented.
>
> "Did it work?" Mr. Bartlett asked gently. "Did you keep him?"
>
> Sandy replied: "For another week. We had sex again, and then he dropped me. He said I wasn't good enough. There was no spark.
>
> "I know what you're going to say. I take your class. I know now that he didn't really love me. I feel so stupid, so cheap."[5]

Sandy hoped, naively, that sex would keep the guy. Here is another high school girl, writing to an advice column about a different kind of regret. She wishes she *could* lose the guy she's involved with, but she feels trapped by their sexual relationship.

> I am 16, a junior in high school, and like nearly all the other girls here, I have already lost my virginity. Although most people consider this subject very personal, I feel the need to share this part of my life with girls who are trying to decide whether to have sex for the first time.
>
> Sex does not live up to the glowing reports and hype you see in the movies. It's no big deal. In fact, it's pretty disappointing.
>
> I truly regret that my first time was with a guy that I didn't care that much about. I am still going out with him, which is getting to be a problem. I'd like to end this relationship and date others, but after being so intimate, it's awfully tough.
>
> Since that first night, he expects sex on every date, like we are married or something. When I don't feel like it, we end up in an argument. It's like I owe it to him. I don't think this guy is in love with me, at least he's never said so. I know deep down that I am not in love with him either, and this makes me feel sort of cheap.
>
> I realize now that this is a very big step in a girl's life. After you've done it, things are never the same. It changes everything.
>
> My advice is, don't be in such a rush. It's a headache and a worry. (Could I be pregnant?) Sex is not for entertainment. It should be a commitment. Be smart and save yourself for someone you wouldn't mind spending the rest of your life with.
>
> —Sorry I Didn't And Wish I Could Take It Back[6]

Regret over uncommitted sexual relationships can last for years. I recently received a letter from a 33-year-old woman, now a psychiatrist, who is very much concerned about the sexual pressures and temptations facing young people today. She wanted to share the lessons she had learned about sex the hard way. After high school, she says, she spent a year abroad as an exchange student:

> I was a virgin when I left, but I felt I was protected. I had gotten an IUD so I could make my own decisions if and when I wanted. I had steeled myself against commitment. I was never going to marry or have children; I was going to have a career. During that year abroad, from 17½ to 18½, I was very promiscuous.
>
> But the fact is, it cost me to be separated from myself. The longest-standing and deepest wound I gave myself was heartfelt. That sick, used feeling of having given a precious part of myself—my soul—to so many and for nothing, still aches. I never imagined I'd pay so dearly and for so long.

This woman is happily married now, she says, and has a good sexual relationship with her husband. But she still carries the emotional scar of those early sexual experiences. She wants young people to know that "sex without commitment is very risky for the heart."

3. GUILT

Guilt is a special form of regret—a strong sense of having done something morally wrong. Guilt is a normal and healthy moral response, a sign that one's conscience is working.

In his book for teenagers, *Love, Dating, and Sex,* George Eager tells the story of a well-known speaker who was addressing a high school assembly. The speaker was asked, "What do you most regret about your high school days?"

He answered, "The thing I most regret about high school is the time I singlehandedly destroyed a girl."

Eager offers this advice to young men: "When the breakup comes, it's usually a lot tougher on the girls than it is on the guys. It's not something you want on your conscience—that you caused a girl to have deep emotional problems."[7]

One 16-year-old boy says he stopped having sex with girls when he saw and felt guilty about the pain he was causing: "You see them crying and confused. They say they love you, but you don't love them."

Even in an age of sexual liberation, a lot of people who are having sex nevertheless have a guilty conscience about it. The guilt may come, as in the case of the young man just quoted, from seeing the hurt you've caused other people.

The guilt may come from knowing that your parents would be upset if they knew you were having sex. Or it may stem from your religious convictions. Christianity, Judaism, and Islam, for example, all teach that sex is a gift from God reserved for marriage and that sexual relations outside marriage are morally wrong.

Sometimes guilt about their sexual past ends up crippling people when they become parents by keeping them from advising their own children not to become sexually involved. According to counselor Dr. Carson Daly: "Because these parents can't bear to be considered hypocrites, or to consider themselves hypocrites, they don't give their children the sexual guidance they very much need."[8]

4. LOSS OF SELF-RESPECT AND SELF-ESTEEM

Many people suffer a loss of self-esteem when they find out they have a sexually transmitted disease. For example, according to the Austin, Texas-based Medical Institute for Sexual Health, more than 80 percent of people with herpes say they feel "less confident" and "less desirable sexually."[9]

But even if a person is fortunate enough to escape sexually transmitted disease, temporary sexual relationships can lower the self-respect of both the user and the used.

Sometimes casual sex lowers self-esteem, leading a person into further casual sex, which leads to further loss of self-esteem in an oppressive cycle from which it may be hard to break free. This pattern is described by a college senior, a young woman who works as a residence hall director:

> There are girls in our dorm who have had multiple pregnancies and multiple abortions. They tend to be filled with self-loathing. But because they have so little self-esteem, they will settle for any kind of attention from guys. So they keep going back to the same kind of destructive situations and relationships that got them into trouble in the first place.

On both sides of dehumanized sex, there is a loss of dignity and self-worth. One 20-year-old college male confides: "You feel pretty crummy when you get drunk at a party and have sex with some girl, and then the next morning you can't even remember who she was."

Another college student describes the loss of self-respect that followed his first sexual "conquest":

> I finally got a girl into bed—actually it was in a car—when I was 17. I thought it was the hottest thing there was, but then she started saying she loved me and getting clingy.
>
> I figured out that there had probably been a dozen guys before me who thought they had "conquered" her, but who were really just objects of her need for security. That realization took all the wind out of my sails. I couldn't respect someone who gave in as easily as she did.
>
> I was amazed to find that after four weeks of having sex as often as I wanted, I was tired of her. I didn't see any point in continuing the relation-

ship. I finally dumped her, which made me feel even worse, because I could
see that she was hurting. I felt pretty low.[10]

People aren't things. When we treat them as if they were, we not only
hurt them; we lose respect for ourselves.

5. THE CORRUPTION OF CHARACTER AND THE DEBASEMENT OF SEX

When people treat others as sexual objects and exploit them for their own
pleasure, they not only lose self-respect; they corrupt their characters and
debase their sexuality in the process.

Good character consists of virtues such as respect, responsibility, honesty,
fairness, caring, and self-control. With regard to sex, the character trait of self-
control is particularly crucial. The breakdown of sexual self-control is a big
factor in many of the sex-related problems that plague our society: rape,
promiscuity, pornography, addiction to sex, sexual harassment, the sexual
abuse of children, sexual infidelity in marriage, and the serious damage to
families many of these problems cause. It was Freud who said—and it is now
obvious how right he was—that sexual self-control is essential for civilization.

Sex frequently corrupts character by leading people to tell lies in order to
get sex. The Medical Institute for Sexual Health reports: "Almost all studies
show that many sexually active people will lie if they think it will help them
have sex."[11] Common lies: "I love you" and "I've never had a sexually transmitted disease."

Because sex is powerful, once sexual restraint is set aside, it easily takes
over individuals and relationships. Consider the highly sexualized atmosphere that now characterizes many high schools. A high school teacher in
Indiana says, "The air is thick with sex talk. Kids in the halls will say—boy to
girl, girl to boy—'I want to f—you.'"

In a 1993 study by the American Association of University Women, four
of five high school students—85 percent of girls and 75 percent of boys—said
they have experienced "unwelcome sexual behavior that interferes with my
life" in school.[12] An example: A boy backs a 14-year-old girl up against her
locker, day after day. Says Nan Stein, a Wellesley College researcher: "There's
a Tailhook happening in every school. Egregious behavior is going on."

Another recently reported example of this corruption of character is the
Spur Posse club at Lakewood High School in suburban Los Angeles. Members of this club competed to see how many girls they could sleep with; one
claimed he had slept with 63. Sadly, elementary school-age children are
beginning to mimick such behavior. In a suburb of Pittsburgh, an assistant
superintendent reports that sixth-grade boys were found playing a sexual
contact game; the object of the game was to earn points by touching girls in
private parts, the most points being awarded for "going all the way."

In this sex-out-of-control environment, even rape is judged permissible by many young people. In a 1988 survey of students in grades six through nine, the Rhode Island Rape Crisis Center found that two of three boys and 49 percent of the girls said it was "acceptable for a man to force sex on a woman if they have been dating for six months or more."[13] In view of attitudes like these, it's easy to understand why date rape has become such a widespread problem.

In short, sex that isn't tied to love and commitment undermines character by subverting self-control, respect, and responsibility. Unchecked, sexual desires and impulses easily run amok and lead to habits of hedonism and using others for one's personal pleasure. In the process, sexual intercourse loses its meaning, beauty, and specialness; instead of being a loving, uniquely intimate expression of two people's commitment to each other, sex is trivialized and degraded.

6. SHAKEN TRUST AND FEAR OF COMMITMENT

Young people who feel used or betrayed after the break-up of a sexual relationship may experience difficulty in future relationships.

Some sexually exploited people, as we've seen, develop such low self-esteem that they seek any kind of attention, even if it's another short-lived and demeaning sexual relationship. But other people, once burned, withdraw. They have trouble trusting; they don't want to get burned again.

Usually, this happens to the girl. She begins to see guys as interested in just one thing: Sex. Says one young woman: "Besides feeling cheap [after several sexual relationships], I began to wonder if there would ever be anyone who would love and accept me without demanding that I do something with my body to earn that love."[14]

However, boys can also experience loss of trust and fear of commitment as a result of a broken relationship that involved sex. Brian, a college senior, tells how this happened to him:

> I first had intercourse with my girlfriend when we were 15. I'd been going with her for almost a year, and I loved her very much. She was friendly, outgoing, charismatic. We'd done everything but have intercourse, and then one night she asked if we could go all the way.
>
> A few days later, we broke up. It was the most painful time of my life. I had opened myself up to her more than I had to anybody, even my parents.
>
> I was depressed, moody, nervous. My friends dropped me because I was so bummed out. I felt like a failure. I dropped out of sports. My grades weren't terrific.
>
> I didn't go out again until I got to college. I've had mostly one-night stands in the last couple of years.
>
> I'm afraid of falling in love.[15]

7. RAGE OVER BETRAYAL

Sometimes the emotional reaction to being "dumped" isn't just a lack of trust or fear of commitment. It's rage.

Every so often, the media carry a story about a person who had this rage reaction and then committed an act of violence against the former boyfriend or girlfriend. Read these accounts, and you'll find that sex was almost always a part of the broken relationship.

Of course, people often feel angry when somebody breaks up with them, even if sex has not been involved. But the sense of betrayal is usually much greater if sex has been part of the relationship. Sex can be emotional dynamite. It can lead a person to think that the relationship is really serious, that both people really love each other. It can create a very strong emotional bond that hurts terribly when it's ruptured—especially if it seems that the other person never had the same commitment. And the resulting sense of betrayal can give rise to rage, even violence.

8. DEPRESSION AND SUICIDE

In *Sex and the Teenager*, Kieran Sawyer writes: "The more the relationship seems like real love, the more the young person is likely to invest, and the deeper the pain and hurt if the relationship breaks up."[16] Sometimes the emotional turmoil caused by the rupture of a sexual relationship leads to deep depression. The depression, in turn, may lead some people to take their own lives.

In the past 25 years, teen suicide has tripled. In a 1988 survey by the U.S. Department of Health and Human Services, one in five adolescent girls said they have tried to kill themselves (the figure for boys was one in 10).

This is the same period during which the rate of teenage sexual activity has sharply increased, especially for girls. No doubt, the rise in youth suicide has multiple causes, but given what we know about the emotional aftermath of broken sexual relationships, it is reasonable to suspect that the pain from such break-ups is a factor in the suicide deaths of some young people.

9. RUINED RELATIONSHIPS

Sex can have another kind of emotional consequence: It can turn a good relationship bad. Other dimensions of the relationship stop developing. Pretty soon, negative emotions enter the picture. Eventually, they poison the relationship, and what had been a caring relationship comes to a bitter end.

One young woman shares her story, which illustrates the process:

With each date, my boyfriend's requests for sex became more convincing. After all, we did love each other. Within two months, I gave in, because I had justified the whole thing. Over the next six months, sex became the center of our relationship. . . .

At the same time, some new things entered our relationship—things like anger, impatience, jealousy, and selfishness. We just couldn't talk anymore. We grew very bored with each other. I desperately wanted a change.[17]

A young man who identified himself as a 22-year-old virgin echoes this warning about the damage premature sex can do to a relationship:

I've seen too many of my friends break up after their relationships turned physical. The emotional wreckage is horrendous because they have already shared something so powerful. When you use sex too early, it will block other means of communicating love and can stunt the balanced growth of a relationship.[18]

10. STUNTING PERSONAL DEVELOPMENT

Premature sexual involvement not only can stunt the development of a relationship; it also can stunt one's development as a person.

Just as some young people handle anxieties by turning to drugs and alcohol, others handle them by turning to sex. Sex becomes an escape. They aren't learning how to cope with life's pressures.

Teenagers who are absorbed in an intense sexual relationship are turning inward on one thing at the very time in their lives when they should be reaching out—forming new friendships, joining clubs and teams, developing their interests and skills, taking on bigger social responsibilities.

All of these are important nutrients for a teenager's development as a person. And this period of life is special because young people have both the time and the opportunities to develop their talents and interests. The growing they do during these years will affect them all their lives. If young people don't put these years to good use, they may never develop their full potential.

The risk appears to be greater for girls who get sexually involved and in so doing close the door on other interests and relationships. Says New York psychiatrist Samuel Kaufman:

A girl who enters into a serious relationship with a boy very early in life may find out later that her individuality was thwarted. She became part of him and failed to develop her own interests, her sense of independent identity.[19]

Reflecting on her long experience in counseling college students and others about sexual matters, Dr. Carson Daly comments:

I don't think I ever met a student who was sorry he or she had postponed sexual activity, but I certainly met many who deeply regretted their sexual involvements. Time and time again, I have seen the long-term emotional and spiritual desolation that results from casual sex and promiscuity.

No one tells students that it sometimes takes years to recover from the effects of these sexual involvements—if one ever fully recovers.

Sex certainly can be a source of great pleasure and joy. But as should be amply clear—and youngsters need our help and guidance in understanding this—sex also can be the source of deep wounds and suffering. What makes the difference is the relationship within which it occurs. Sex is most joyful and fulfilling—most emotionally safe as well as physically safe—when it occurs within a loving, total, and binding commitment. Historically, we have called that marriage. Sexual union is then part of something bigger—the union of two persons' lives.

NOTES

1. Susan Weller, "A Meta-Analysis of Condom Effectiveness in Reducing Sexually Transmitted HIV," *Social Science and Medicine,* June 1993, p. 12.

2. See, for example, Kenneth Noller, *OB/GYN Clinical Alert-t,* September 1992; for a thorough discussion of the dangers of human papilloma virus, see "Condoms Ineffective Against Human Papilloma Virus,"*Sexual Health Update* (April 1994), a publication of the Medical Institute for Sexual Health, P.O. Box 4919, Austin, Texas 78765.

3. "Some Teens Taking Vows of Virginity," *Washington Post* (November 21, 1993).

4. William Bennett, "Sex and the Education of Our Children," *America* (February 14, 1987), p. 124.

5. Bob Bartlett, "Going All the Way," *Momentum* (April/May, 1993), p. 36.

6. Abridged from Ann Landers, "A Not-So-Sweet Sexteen Story," *Daily News* (September 23, 1991), p. 20.

7. Eager's book is available from Mailbox Club Books, 404 Eager Rd., Valdosta, Ga. 31602.

8. Carson Daly, personal communication.

9. *Safe Sex: A Slide Program.* Medical Institute for Sexual Health, Austin, Texas: 1992.

10. Josh McDowell and Dick Day, *Why Wait: What You Need to Know About the Teen Sexuality Crisis* (Here's Life Publishers, San Bernardino, Calif.: 1987).

11. Medical Institute for Sexual Health, P.O. Box 4919, Austin Texas 78765.

12. *American Association of University Women Report on Sexual Harassment,* June 1993.

13. J. Kikuchi, "Rhode Island Develops Successful Intervention Program for Adolescents," *National Coalition Against Sexual Assault Newsletter* (Fall 1988).

14. McDowell and Day, op. cit.

15. Abridged from *Choosing the Best: A Values-Based Sex Education Curriculum,* 1993. (5500 Interstate North Parkway, Suite 515, Atlanta, Ga. 30328).

16. Kieran Sawyer, *Sex and the Teenager* (Ave Maria Press, Notre Dame, Ind.: 1990).

17. McDowell and Day, op. cit.

18. Ann Landers, "Despite Urgin', He's a Virgin." *Daily News* (January 15, 1994).

19. Quoted in Howard and Martha Lewis, *The Parent's Guide to Teenage Sex and Pregnancy* (St. Martin's Press, New York: 1980).

CHAPTER 18

Sex, Time, and Meaning:
A Theology of Dating

Jason King
Donna Freitas

Young adults (as well as mid-lifers and the elderly) get little constructive help or guidance in dating in contemporary society. Secular sources (television, movies, books, and the Internet) tend to be mostly useless. They focus on techniques for manipulating relationships to a certain end. Religious sources are just as problematic. They do not provide realistic perspectives on love relationships outside of marriage. Their almost exclusive focus is on the avoidance of premarital sex. This leaves people in dating relationships adrift without wise counsel and forced to reject or, at least, compartmentalize religion as it relates to their loving relationships. This is the premise of Jason King and Donna Freitas's essay. Its purpose, however, is to offer a theology of dating from a Christian perspective. The essay is refreshingly original and imaginative. It should lend itself to rich classroom conversation.

King and Freitas are in search of a framework that can make sense of the variety of dating experiences. We need, they claim, a new understanding, a new story, of dating. Their proposal offers a Christian narrative of dating that takes into account its inherent value, its finitude, sexuality, and meaning. They accomplish this by turning to ancient and contemporary theological and philosophical works on friendship (Aristotle and Wadell), marriage (Cahill and Gaillardetz), and feminist spirituality (Soelle and hooks). They distill from these resources values and visions indispensable for constructing a positive Christian theology of dating. These resources are also important in providing guidelines regarding healthy, Christian relationships.

King and Freitas conclude their essay by offering a two-tiered perspective on dating. The first tier explores the encounter between two people and situates the meaning of dating within a larger life journey. The second tier relates this dating narrative to the Gospel narrative. It makes it intelligible in a Christian perspective. It is seen as part of the larger story of God's redemption and salvation. In a word, dating holds the possibility of being revelatory, of hearing God's call, and of responding to our vocational call.

Questions for Discussion

King and Freitas pose some unanswered questions at the conclusion of their essay:

1. What would a fully developed account of sexuality in dating look like?
2. How do we make sense of the experiences of value and failure in dating?
3. What are the implications of technology, like instant messages, for dating?
4. How does our understanding of dating make sense of the elderly's experience of dating?
5. How do issues of race (e.g., African American, Asian American, Hispanic, white) and sexual orientation (e.g., heterosexual, homosexual, bisexual) bear on this theology of dating?

When we ask people about the meaning of dating, they often respond by asking us first to define dating. Do we mean the three to four year relationships that people have after college, the one night stands or group outings that happen in college, the four to six month relationships of high school, or the single evening chaperoned dates of middle school? These different experiences presumably have different meanings.

If forced to give a definition, we would probably define dating by saying what it is not. Our definition would run something like this: dating is an encounter between two people that is not friendship as it is open to romance and not marriage as it is temporary. If friends are kissing, they are more than friends. If people are saying "I do" to good times and bad, sickness and health, wealth and poverty, then they are more than just dating.

Still the question of definition, while important, is slightly off target. We are not looking to describe what dating is. We are trying to explain what dating can and should mean from a Christian perspective. We want a framework that can makes sense of the variety of dating experiences but also addresses why some of them are particularly problematic. This paper is an attempt to articulate just such a perspective, what we call a theology of dating.

Trying to find Christian resources to do this, however, is not easy. Television, movies, and the internet prove mostly useless. Religious television shows are either Sunday services or prolonged testimonials with heavy make-up and tears. Overtly Christian movies are few, and one of the more recent ones, *Left Behind,* did not address dating and rapidly "left behind" the theatres. Internet sites that address Christian dating focus on providing information on books about dating (courtshipconnection.com), forums where Christians can meet on-line (fusion101.com), or guidelines for Christian dating (christianadvice.com).

If you turn to a Borders or Barnes and Nobles bookstore for a book on Christianity and dating, you will most likely encounter evangelical Protes-

From *Horizons,* 30, 1, Spring 2003: 25–40. Reprinted by permission of *Horizons,* Journal of the College of Theology Society.

tant works such as: *Staying Pure* by Stephanie Perry More, *Wait for Me: The Beauty of Sexual Purity* by Rebecca St. James, and the very popular *I Kissed Dating Goodbye* by Joshua Harris.[1] Harris, for example, argues that the Bible offers young people three options that are only peripherally related to dating: remaining single, "courtship" only when it leads directly to marriage, and, of course, marriage.[2] His view is simple: young people are to save their hearts for "the one" and above all else, God. Each time someone has a relationship that does not lead to marriage, they lose a piece of their heart that they can never get back *and* they turn away from God. If you date a lot, then only a little bit of your heart will be left for your future spouse if any at all.[3] Harris concludes that dating endangers your salvation and can only be acceptable as a prelude to marriage. In other words, the absolute best preparation for marriage is to have no previous relationships whatsoever.

To be fair, Joshua Harris and other evangelical Protestant authors like him take the phenomenon of dating seriously. They know that dating affects us and our relationships with God and others. Yet as a rule, Christian perspectives on dating generally do two things. First, they collapse dating into the issue of premarital sex and appear to ban dating in banning premarital sex.[4] Vincent Genovesi's *In Pursuit of Love* is a good example of this.[5] He has no reference to dating in the book but a whole chapter on pre-marital sex. His topics range from "deep (soul or 'French') kissing" that he finds "unwise," "frustrative," and "dishonest"[6] to premarital sex that he considers "a significant *premoral, ontic, or physical wrong.*"[7] Implicitly, for he never articulates a position, dating is the near occasion for these activities and, consequently, must be carefully circumscribed to avoid such physical episodes.

In addition to equating dating with sex, the Christian perspective on dating tends to promote a view of relationships (both outside of and even within marriage) as characterized by an unhealthy love triangle between us, those whom we date, and God. God, of course, resides at the pinnacle of the triangle, we (the daters) are at one point, and presumably the "other" or person we date (the "datee") is at the third point of the triangle. The primary relationship is always portrayed as between God and ourselves. At least outside of marriage, when an "other" comes into the picture this person is presented as a danger or intrusion in the divine relationship, tearing us away from what God wants and propelling us into the world of sexual temptation. Only when God believes we are ready for marriage can a "third party" be appropriately introduced into the triangle. In marriage the triangle between God, our spouses, and ourselves persists, only this time the relationship is divinely ordained.[8]

The problem we find with religious resources, assuming that those of dating age read them, is three-fold. First, they fail to address the temporary character of dating. Young people are led to believe that the only acceptable outcome of dating is marriage, and if marriage is not the result, dating is at best a failure and at worst a sin. Second, these resources do not have a viable account of sexuality in dating. Almost all physical contact between people is condemned, whether it is kissing or sex. Those who date are left with the

view that all actions—from intercourse to hugging—are equally problematic.
The last and most troubling problem is that religious dating resources offer
no positive meaning to the phenomenon of dating. Many young people stay
single well into their thirties today. By condemning dating and offering
celibacy or married life as the *only* religiously and spiritually sound options
for relationships, a serious and terrible danger is created and perpetuated for
the younger generations: alienation from religion. To offer only the single life,
to present dating as something to fear and protect oneself against is unrealistic in a society where individuals no longer marry at age fifteen. It places
young people in a position to reject religion as a viable narrative altogether
during some of the most difficult and important years of life. Or, at the least,
it encourages people to separate religion and spirituality from their love relationships. They place their "church on Sundays" in one compartment and
their relationships somewhere else, and if somehow they do mix, guilt and
fear result.

We have both watched this happen among our friends and also the college students we interact with through our experiences in Student Affairs.
Christianity does not provide a realistic perspective on love relationships
outside of marriage, so young people who date forget about religion and the
meaning that religion and spirituality can provide in their lives. Instead, they
turn to the secular world and pop culture to find some means of making
sense of dating. Yet, these sources often portray relationships and sex as a
commodity (à la *Cosmo* and *Maxim*), dating as synonymous for sex (*Friends*),
and relationships as simply a frustrating thing that we are inevitably going to
fail at (*Ally McBeal*). If they are ambitious or inquisitive people they may turn
to books to enlighten themselves on dating. A visit to Borders or Barnes and
Noble, though, reveals a strange assortment of texts: *The Rules: Time Tested Secrets for Capturing the Heart of Mr. Right*,[9] *The Complete Idiots' Guide to Dating*,[10]
and, most recently, *The Worst-Case Scenario Survival Handbook: Dating and
Sex*.[11]

Secular sources are just as problematic as the religious ones and, surprisingly, bear a striking resemblance in approach. Neither perspective addresses
the fundamental meaning of dating but rather focuses on techniques for manipulating dating relationships to a certain end. Where meaning is lost, technique triumphs. Thus, Christians might risk hell for dating, but the secular
world risks the much more painful consequence of social awkwardness. Like
the Christian texts, secular works present a fearful disposition toward dating.
The fear stems not from the dangers to one's salvation but from the dangerous mismanagement of one's relationships. In other words, *The Rules*, *The
Idiots' Guide*, and *The Survival Handbook* articulate a method to avoid pain (i.e.,
embarrassment and failure) and instead pursue pleasure (i.e., satisfaction
and sex) in dating. The Christian techniques have similar objectives—avoid
pain (i.e., hell) and pursue pleasure (i.e., Heaven)—and the means are a series of disapprobations against too much intimate contact, physical or interpersonal, with others.[12] Believers are left to view dating not as a manifesta-
tion of love for self, others, or God, but primarily as occasions for sin, mostly

of the sexual variety. The other person is viewed as a danger to one's salvation and to be avoided at all costs unless marriage is imminent. The Christian position on dating is therefore not to date at all.

From a religious perspective, we both worry that if we do not come up with an alternative to the "don't date at all" narrative, one that accounts for the finitude, sexuality, and meaning of dating, we are putting ourselves at risk. Such a negative approach from Christianity forces young people to divorce the potential religious, ethical, and spiritual dimensions from their love relationships and encourages the secular perspective which seeks to manipulate others for one's own benefit to triumph. One thing is clear: young people from teenagers to early thirty-somethings *are* dating and struggling with it. Some are managing well, but many are waking up at twenty-five feeling used and depressed. We need to offer a new understanding, a new story, of dating. Christianity, particularly Catholicism, which has so far said almost nothing about dating, can no longer afford to ignore this need.

With this paper, we hope to provide a new and viable Christian narrative of dating, one that takes into account its tremendous value and addresses its finitude, sexuality, and meaning. Despite the inadequacy of the sources on Christianity and dating, we do not have to start from scratch. There are useful resources from feminist spirituality and theologies of friendship and marriage. These resources at least provide guidelines regarding healthy, Christian relationships and provide a foundation through which we can begin to understand, value, and assess the dating relationship.

One of feminist theology's major contributions is an emphasis on the priority of relationship in human flourishing. This value stands at the foundation of spirituality. Feminist theology, however, does not directly address the meaning and significance of dating. It goes without saying that neither friendship nor marriage relationships are equivalent to dating. The works on friendship, for example, do not address the element of sexuality that is so integral to the modern notion of dating, and those on marriage fail to tackle finitude. Nevertheless, such resources provide important insights for discerning a theology of dating.

WORKS OF FRIENDSHIP

ARISTOTLE'S NICOMACHEAN ETHICS

Chapter eight of the *Nicomachean Ethics* is a foundational text in the study of friendship. In the *Ethics*, Aristotle tells us that friendship is not only good but one of the supreme goods, "for without friends no one would choose to live, though he had all other goods."[13] According to Aristotle, friendship binds people together. It enables people to enjoy the goods they have, help others who do not have the goods, and even acquire goods they may need. These goods are not the capitalist notion of goods —products for consumption—but goods that are important for human existence and flourishing.

Aristotle distinguishes three characteristics that generate friendship, but he maintains that only the third is the perfect type. The first type is utility.[14] People come together and become friends because they are mutually advantageous to one another. The second type is the friendship of pleasure. Like friendships founded on utility, these relationships are often unstable "for it is not as being the man he is that the loved person is loved, but as providing some good or pleasure. Such friendships, then are easily dissolved, if the parties do not remain like themselves; for if the one party is no longer pleasant . . . the other ceases to love him."[15] The perfect kind of friendship according to Aristotle is a friendship founded on virtue.[16] These relationships are stable since they are founded on the person's character and character does not change quickly or often. The friendship based on virtue has many important characteristics. Among the most important are: desiring the good of the other, finding pleasure in the other, and being able to completely trust the other.[17]

This brief presentation of Aristotle on friendship highlights several important issues: what brings friends together and what keeps friends together. People do come together over utility, pleasure, and/or virtue. With respect to dating, probably the most common utilitarian reason is that one is tired of or does not wish to be alone. Dating based on pleasure is perhaps even more prevalent. People date because they make each other laugh, or they share the same interest, or they have a good sex life. Finally, there are people who date because of shared values. Aristotle's categories can assist us in assessing the foundations of dating and, consequently, help to analyze its finite character.

PAUL WADELL'S FRIENDSHIP AND THE MORAL LIFE

Paul Wadell's work on friendship has as its central thesis that the primary relation for understanding the moral life is friendship. This "model" encourages people not only to love themselves and their friends but also the stranger and neighbor.[18] He attempts not only to retain the exclusivity of friendship but also to claim that it is necessary if one is to be able to love others as Christians.

There are three major, relevant themes in Wadell's work on friendship. First, friendships are necessary because without them we have no chance of knowing or becoming good people. Because human existence is relational, we would not be fully human without friendships. Second, friendship is crucial in the formation of the self. Friendships expand our concerns to include others and empower us to overcome our suspicion of others. Friendships move people out of a defensive posture against others to a position where others are viewed as important for one's own existence. Wadell maintains that "selfhood is not gained by overcoming the other, but by being in relationship with them."[19] Hence, friendship is valuable because it enhances our own sense of self-worth.[20] Finally, friendship enables us to view others not as dangerous, but as good. In viewing others as good one understands how another person can enhance a greater understanding of one's own life, the world, and one's place and vocation in community. Friendship enables this new-found orientation toward others because it stands as a witness to what can happen when one views others not as dangerous but as good; for the friend was once a stranger and now is someone who contributes to one's flourishing.

Wadell's notion of friendship raises a challenge to the Christian perspective that dating is dangerous because of sex. If human beings are relational and these relationships shape our existence in the world, then dating, if it is to be considered acceptable to any Christian, must bring about a positive change in the self similar to the way friendship positively affects us. We (Jason and Donna) both have had dating experiences that support this idea and that have led us to a better understanding of ourselves and the world. If Wadell is correct in asserting that relationships are essential for human flourishing, the condemnation of dating and sexuality runs the risk of understanding relationships as extrinsic and not intrinsic to human flourishing. Hence, an adequate Christian understanding has to view dating, and sexuality within dating, as something contributing to the well-being of the people involved.

CONCLUSION: WORKS ON FRIENDSHIP

Both Aristotle's and Waddell's perspectives of friendship raise important issues for any theology of dating. Aristotle pushes the question about what brings people together and keeps them together. This question is extremely relevant for a discussion of dating where people come together for different reasons and often do not stay together for very long. Wadell raises the question about how our relationships impact our reception of others. Dating and sexual activity within dating should not encourage fear, manipulation, and suspicion of another person, but instead, help two people to view one another as good. The above makes sense for a Christian notion of dating, not only because of Wadell's argument, but also because of the Christian call to love others.

WORKS ON MARRIAGE

LISA SOWLE CAHILL'S SEX, GENDER, AND CHRISTIAN ETHICS

Lisa Sowle Cahill begins her approach to marriage by stating that she agrees with much of what the Christian tradition has to say about sex and marriage. She agrees that procreation is an important value in human sexuality and that children should be raised in stable families.[21] She also disagrees with the concept of abortion as a means of birth control.[22] Her problem is not so much with what has been said, but with what has been left out.

Cahill's critique is that Christian churches have focused almost exclusively on procreation and abortion to the neglect of other claims of justice, especially by women, Christians, she claims, focus on procreative issues to the detriment of greater female, and hence human, wholeness. According to Cahill, what the church must do is work to address the greater injustices of women instead of focusing narrowly on sexual issues.[23] Christianity in general and Catholicism in particular need to spend less time condemning sexual sin and more effort and money on rectifying the marginalization and oppression of women. She links this approach to Jesus, who did not condemn the prostitutes and tax collectors, but instead worked to help those on the fringes of society.

Although Cahill directs her attention to women's issues, her critique challenges contemporary conceptions of dating. The focus on sexual sinfulness in dating has led to a virtual condemnation of all dating. As a result, many teenagers and young adults feel marginalized by Christianity. Just as women feel put off by an institution that does not address its deeper claims of justice, so too those who date are alienated since there is little attention paid to the life realities of young people today. Hence, Cahill's perspective challenges us to come up with an understanding of dating that places emphasis on greater human flourishing and justice, instead of primarily on sex.

RICHARD R. GAILLARDETZ' A DARING PROMISE: A SPIRITUALITY OF CHRISTIAN MARRIAGE

What Gaillardetz says about a spirituality of marriage in the context of Christianity is not unusual.[24] He talks of marriage as a call to conversion, as a vocation, as the means through which we work out our salvation, and as an occasion of redemption. Gaillardetz builds on the above perspective by integrating sexual love and redemptive love as an imperative part of the marriage experience. His overall discussion of marriage is accessible and practical for any reader seeking a framework for reflection on the spirituality of marriage.

Gaillardetz' emphasis on marriage as vocational, as a challenge that is the occasion for conversion, and as an institution that can bring us closer to God and redemption is relevant for a theology of dating. These perspectives on marriage assist us in raising questions about the meaning of the dating relationship, about whether dating can be viewed as a vocation, a time of conversion, and an occasion for redemption. By raising these questions regarding the meaning of dating relationships and by exploring the different complexities that are at issue in a dating relationship as opposed to a marital one, we are able to explore the significance of dating as a vocation and as central to the development of our relationship with God.

CONCLUSION: WORKS ON MARRIAGE

Cahill's and Gaillardetz' insights on marriage raise two issues relevant to a theology of dating. Cahill critiques the implications that an overemphasis on sex can have on any theological understanding of relationships. This is especially important for any discussion of dating since theological reflection on dating so often collapses into issues of sexual morality. Gaillardetz points to the need to understand relationships in light of a higher purpose or meaning. He is arguing that marriage should be situated with the broader Christian narrative. By extension, his work implies that any truly Christian conception of dating must also be compatible with the Christian gospel.

RESOURCES FROM FEMINIST SPIRITUALITY

DOROTHEE SOELLE'S TO WORK AND TO LOVE: A THEOLOGY OF CREATION

For Dorothee Soelle, love is foundational to our relationship with God. Our capacity to love is an expression of how we are created in God's image. The experience of love between us humans is essential to our relationship with God because it is through loving others that we also experience God's love and express our love for God. "What happens to us in our work and in our relationships shapes our life with God and is therefore inseparable from our religious life."[25] In other words, God is immanent to our love lives.

Soelle spends a lot of time exploring the sexual dimension in love relationships, including a critique both of how capitalism presents sex as a commodity and how religion is obsessed with the sinful nature of premarital sex. Her interest is to bring us to a more wholistic and healthy perspective on the relation between sexuality, human fulfillment, community, and spirituality. For Soelle, love is by its very nature a political thing. At the foundation of our experience of love in community is the cultivation of loving relationships, particularly relationships that embody both *agape* and *eros*. She believes that Christians have mistakenly separated *eros* from *agape*, thereby devaluing one of the most fundamental ways that humans express and experience love with each other.[26] Soelle's emphasis on the presence of *eros* is not restricted to her discussion of human sexual love within the marital relationship. For Soelle, the physical expression of love between two people is essential to the creation of a loving community.

Soelle's notion of *eros* shifts our understanding of human relation to God from one of transcendence to one of immanence. Thus, the love triangle in which God exists as a third term in tension with a loving human relationship collapses, and, instead, couples cultivate an understanding of human love where divine love is immanent and foundational to the relationship. Hence, Soelle also helps us to provide a view of dating that is compatible—and not competitive—with our relationship to God.

BELL HOOKS' SALVATION: BLACK PEOPLE AND LOVE

Love and justice are inseparable for womanist bell hooks.[27] Only through the *practice* of loving, mutual relationship do we learn redemptive love and lay the foundations for a redemptive community, bell hooks is particularly interested in the topic of love and its relation to race and its centrality to the black community. The practice of respectful, mutual, loving relationship is not the norm among blacks according to hooks. In black communities people denigrate love, there is despair about the possibility of love, and violence and unfaithfulness are the norm.

It is with "lasting love" and sustained commitment that hooks claims that love flourishes. Committed love is the kind that has the potential to transform communities. "We cannot effectively resist domination if our efforts to create meaningful, lasting personal and social change are not grounded in a love ethic."[28] hooks calls us to the "work" that is love.

While she praises marriage as one framework within society that supports a love that fosters justice and communal transformation, she is not convinced that married love is our only means toward achieving redemptive love. Evidence of a lack of committed, healthy, mutual love within marriage abounds, particularly within the black community, a fact that hooks attributes to a general lack of understanding and practical experience of healthy loving relationships, particularly physical ones, among blacks.

hooks' perspective on love is relevant to a theology of dating in several ways. Like Soelle, she affirms that love and redemption are inherently connected to community. Since a loving relation is the hoped for foundation of a dating relationship, this perspective situates dating as a participatory practice in the pursuit of redemptive community. Interestingly, hooks does not view this redemptive, loving relationship that includes the expression of physical love as exclusive to marriage. In fact, according to hooks, it is within marriage that many blacks find the most unhealthy relationships and lack of love. For hooks, marriage is not the signifier of lasting, redemptive love; rather this kind of love is possible in a variety of contexts. Her concern is that we practice love. Thus, dating as a "practice" can be an occasion of love, hooks helps us in understanding how the finite aspect of dating can be participatory in a redemptive community.

CONCLUSION: FEMINIST RESOURCES

The spiritual and relational perspectives raised here are foundationally important for a theology of dating. At the root of feminism is a concern for justice and community, and healthy relationship within community. Resources within feminist spirituality often locate loving, mutual relationship as foundational to community, to healthy human development, and as foundational to our experience of the divine. Loving relationship allows us to experience God not as one who exists apart from the world, but as immanent to human experience of community and others. The practice of loving, mutual relationship teaches us to see God in others, and we believe that the practice of love is possible in dating. Yet if we are not allowed to practice love until marriage, and this includes the practice of physical love, then after twenty years outside of loving relationship, how are we to suddenly know the meaning of loving another, seeing that embodied person as made in God's image?

NARRATIVE SOURCES

The feminist, friendship, and marriage sources we cite provide us with invaluable insights for a theology of dating. These insights, however, are disparate. We need some way of linking them to render dating from a Christian perspective intelligible. We need a narrative of dating that is consonant with the Christian gospel.[29] What follows here is a proposal for a two-tiered narrative of dating: a first tier that makes sense of dating and a second tier that relates this meaning to Christianity.

Many stories can provide a structure for the first-tier of a dating narrative. In Walker Percy's *The Second Coming*,[30] Will Barret is a retired lawyer who has a problem with falling down. He meets Allison, a woman who is good at hoisting things up but has a problem communicating with the outside world. When they come together, Allison is able to keep Will aright and Will is able to bridge the gap between Allison and the rest of society. A similar pattern is discerned in the relationship between Mitsuko and Otsū in Shusaku Endo's *Deep River*.[31] Mitsuko lacks meaning in her life and Otsū is unsure of himself. They meet, date, and then break up, but through their encounter Otsū finds his calling in God and Mitsuko begins a slow discovery of life's meaning. In *Shakespeare in Love*,[32] Shakespeare has writer's block and Viola de Lassep seeks poetry in her life. When they encounter each other, Shakespeare overcomes his difficulties, and Viola experiences poetry. Unfortunately, they must part but are significantly different as a result of their time together. In *Ten Things I Hate About You*,[33] Patrick Verona is viewed as a volatile rebel, and Katerina Stratford is hostile to everyone. Through the various circumstances that bring them together, Kat's view of the world becomes more open and Patrick finds he is capable of tremendous goodness. Finally, the story in *The Long Loneliness*:[34] Dorothy Day learns to love creation and see its beauty through her common-law husband Forster. When she moves from creation to the Creator, Day comes into conflict with Forster. Her encounter with him changed the way she viewed the world, but, in the act of changing, the relationship no longer was viable. Day felt she must leave him in order to be faithful to her self, her vocation, and God.

These stories all share a similar structure and hence provide us with a narrative of dating. The main characters are searching for a solution to their problems, trying to discover meaning in life, or suffering from distortions in their relationships to the world. Whatever the end, the characters are all engaged in what we interchangeably call a quest, a mystery, and a journey. When two people come together, they end up assisting each other in their respective quests. Individuals are opened up to new possibilities through their encounters with another that enable them to progress on their journey. And common to all of these interactions is the question of permanence. Sometimes through the relationship two people not only help each other but also realize that they share a common journey. Hence, Will and Allison get married. Yet, Mitsuko and Otsū turn out to follow different journeys but need each other to unlock them. Without Forster, Dorothy Day had neither child nor love of creation and hence would be hindered on her journey to God.[35] The other person often provides not the end of the journey or the answer to the mystery but acts more as an assistant on the way or as a clue to the answer. Based on this narrative theme, dating is not just a transitional period for marriage but is important for our flourishing.

This first-tier explores the encounter between two people and situates the meaning of dating within a larger life journey or quest. For Christians, this dating narrative needs to be sublated by a second-tier, namely the gospel stories. Hence, the journey or quest can be renamed discipleship. Discipleship involves the ongoing attempt of individuals to love themselves, others, and God in the way that Jesus loved. On the surface, it may seem that discipleship involves a commitment to Jesus that has no parallels with the temporality of dating. However, there are many examples in the gospels where Jesus "encounters" people who come to support him but do not become one of his itinerant followers. In his study of the historical Jesus, John Meier discusses these individuals in a section entitled "The Unclear Boundaries of Discipleship: Supporters of Jesus who did not leave their homes."[36] Meier notes people like Zacchaeus (Lk 19:1–10), Lazarus (Jn 12:1–2), the host of the Last Supper (Mk 14:13–15), Simon the Leper (Mk 14:3), and Martha and Mary (Lk 10:38–42, Jn 11:1–45) who became committed adherers to Jesus' message after their encounter with him but did not leave family, possessions, and livelihood behind. Instead, these figures provided homes, food, and other resources to support Jesus and his fellow travelers. Such "hospitality disciples" were models that the Christian community could imitate. Even though their physical interaction with Jesus was temporary and their encounter with him did not lead to a radical change of life like that of the twelve apostles, their contribution was still valuable and an ideal for the Christian community. By making a comparison between the hospitality disciples and dating, we argue that we can view dating as part of the larger story of God's redemption of humanity, even if dating involves a temporary encounter between two people. Dating is a component of redemption valuable in and of itself regardless of whether it leads to marriage, just as believers who stayed home contributed to the building up of the kingdom even if they did not leave behind their work or family.

CONCLUSION: THE INTEGRATION OF SOURCES

How does the proposed two-tiered narrative utilize the aforementioned resources to address the finitude, sexuality, and meaning of dating? The narrative makes the finite aspect of dating intelligible by situating the insights of hooks and Aristotle within a dating framework. Aristotle argues that individuals must evaluate the foundations and causes of their relationships, hooks advocates that all relationships be viewed as attempts at loving relationships. In applying these insights to dating, we do not lose Aristotle's focus on the role of utility, pleasure, and virtue in shaping relationships nor hooks' emphasis on race and justice. Instead, the dating narrative helps situate these insights in the context of dating. Those who are dating are called to view each other as clues to a mystery, assistance in a journey, or preparation for a quest. The mystery, journey, or quest is a process of discerning each one's response to God's call. Hence, dating must a) be a relationship that is loving since that is the only proper response to mutually exchanged clues, assistance, and preparation, and b) be a relationship that is evaluated in light of God's call.

In the same manner, the dating narrative accounts for sexuality in dating. Wadell's perspective on friendship calls us to view others not as dangerous but as gifts. Cahill insists on the danger of emphasizing sexuality to the detriment of justice. Soelle expresses the role of bodily love in the creation and experience of loving community. All of these perspectives are utilized by the dating narrative's call to view the other as contributing to the flourishing of the self and the redemption of community. Our dating narrative combats the emphasis on sexuality in dating in both the secular and religious perspectives and the negative assessment of sexuality by religion. The proposed narrative focuses on the meaning of dating instead of collapsing the phenomenon into the issue of premarital sexuality, thereby meeting Cahill's demand to focus on the issues of justice and respect. Our narrative also focuses on viewing the other as good—as a clue, assistance, and preparation—and not as the occasion for sexual sin and the endangerment of one's salvation. Hence, we also heed Wadell's call to view others as gifts and Soelle's to view these relationships as essential to loving community.

Finally, and perhaps most significantly, our understanding attempts to make dating intelligible in contemporary and Christian perspectives. We claim that dating is an important, even though temporary, encounter in one's response to God's call. It is meant to illuminate the call of those who date and to strengthen their respective vocations. We are thus making use of Gaillardetz' idea of viewing marriage as a vocation and hence part of the Christian mission by insisting that dating can also be understood as vocational: as part of God's call to conversion and plan for the redemption of the world. We make use of Soelle's emphasis on the immanent God in insisting that God is present and operative—calling us to love self, other, and God—even in our finite, dating relationships. We learn that dating is both vocational and a rich occasion for conversion.

While this narrative accounts for three of the main features of dating, many issues remain to be addressed. What would a fully developed account of sexuality in dating look like? How do we make sense of the experiences of value *and* of failure in dating? What are the implications of technology, like instant messenger, for dating? How does our understanding of dating make sense of the elderly's experience of dating? How do issues of race (e.g., African-American, Asian-American, Hispanic, white), sexual orientation (e.g., heterosexual, homosexual, bisexual), and relationship to Christianity (e.g., Donna as struggling and Jason as accepting) bear on our theology of dating? These issues, some of which we initially knew about and others that were brought to our attention, we hope to address at a later time. We also hope, though, that the many people who are struggling with dating will help us to uncover further and explore the issues necessary for a full and healthy theology of dating.

NOTES

1. Joshua Harris, *I Kissed Dating Goodbye* (Sisters, OR: Multnomah Publishers, 1999).

2. Ibid., chap. 1.

3. Ibid., 17–18.

4. See Ronald Lawler, Joseph Boyle, and William May, *Catholic Sexual Ethics: A Summary, Explanation, and Defense* (Huntington, IN: Our Sunday Visitor, 1998), chap. 6 and 8; Charles E. Curran and Richard McCormick, eds., *Readings in Moral Theology No. 8: Dialogue About Catholic Sexual Teaching* (New York: Paulist, 1993), part 7.

5. Vincent Genovesi, *In Pursuit of Love: Catholic Morality and Human Sexuality* (Collegeville, MN: Liturgical Press, 1996).

6. Ibid., 178.

7. Ibid., 172. He does qualify his position by stating that in certain circumstances (e.g., lack of knowledge, immaturity, slow moral development), people engaging in premarital sex may not be committing subjective sin.

8. Richard Gaillardetz, *A Daring Promise: A Spirituality of Christian Marriage* (New York: Crossroad, 2002), 42–43.

9. Ellen Fein and Sherrie Schneider, *The Rules: Time Tested Secrets for Capturing the Heart of Mr. Right* (New York: Pocket Books, 2002)

10. Judy Kuriansky, *The Complete Idiot's Guide to Dating* (New York: Alpha Books, 1998).

11. Joshua Piven, Jennifer Worick, Brenda Brown, and David Borgenicht, *The Worst-Case Scenario Survival Handbook: Dating and Sex* (San Francisco: Chronicle Books, 2001).

12. Generally, many people brought up in a Christian community leave it during their high school and college years only to return when they are married with children. While we by no means think this is because the Church lacks a theology of dating, we would argue that we facilitate the departure because we offer them no means of making sense of this part of their life other than, "It is dangerous."

13. Aristotle, *Nichomachean Ethics*, 8.1.

14. Ibid., 8.2.

15. Ibid., 8.3.

16. Ibid.

17. Ibid., 8.3–4. See also ibid., 8.13: "for those who are friends on the ground of virtue are anxious to do well by each other . . . each man desires what is good."

18. Paul Wadell, *Friendship and the Moral Life* (Notre Dame, IN: University of Notre Dame Press, 1989), xiii and 152.

19. Ibid., 152.

20. Ibid., 157.

21. Lisa Sowle Cahill, *Sex, Gender, and Christian Ethics* (New York: Cambridge University Press, 1996), 214.

22. Ibid.

23. Ibid.

24. See n. 8.

25. Dorothee Soelle, *To Work and To Love: A Theology of Creation* (Philadelphia: Fortress, 1984), 115.

26. Ibid., 144–45.

27. bell hooks, *Salvation: Black People and Love* (New York: William Morrow, 2001).

28. Ibid., xxiv.

29. On the importance of narrative, see Stanley Hauerwas *A Community of Character* (Notre Dame, IN: University of Notre Dame Press, 1986), 145–51. We believe that narratives can provide paradigmatic examples that assist people in their attempts to understand the meaning, morality, and spiritual dimensions of dating.

30. Walker Percy, *The Second Coming* (New York: Washington Square Press, 1980).

31. Shusako Endo, *Deep River*, trans. Van C. Gessel (New York: New Directions Books, 1994).

32. *Shakespeare in Love*, film directed by John Madden (Miramax Films, 1998).

33. *Ten Things I Hate About You*, film directed by Gil Junger (Touchstone Pictures, 1999).

34. Dorothy Day, *The Long Loneliness* (San Francisco: Harper Collins, 1997).

35. This is not meant to imply that relationships in general are a hindrance to one's relationship with God but only that Day's particular relationship *presented* problems for her *particular* relationship to God.

36. John P. Meier, *A Marginal Jew, vol. 3: Companions and Competitors* (Garden City, NY: Doubleday, 2001), 80–82. We are gratefully to Christopher McMahon, a professor at Mt. Marty College, for providing us with this reference.

CHAPTER 19

Beyond Romance to Human Love

Robert A. Johnson

This chapter complements Lawrence Stone's essay (chapter 15) on the history of romantic love and its emergence as a mass phenomenon in the West. In *We,* Robert Johnson brings a profound Jungian analysis to our understanding of the dynamics of romantic love, the single greatest energy system in the Western psyche. It saturates every facet of popular culture and has become the rationale and basis for marriage. But, if we are honest with ourselves, we have to admit that our approach to romantic love is not working well. We have not yet learned to handle its tremendous power. More often than not, we turn it into tragedy and dead ends rather than enduring human relations.

In this excerpt, Johnson seeks to salvage love from the swamps of romance. The key is to distinguish between human love and romantic love. Romantic love is airy, fantasy, projection, an evanescent high. It is fundamentally egotistical—fixated on its own wants and whims. It can never lay the foundation for personal commitments. Human love, on the other hand, is "stirring-the-oatmeal" love. It is rooted in relatedness, directed toward the good, and attentive to small daily tasks in our lives. Human love affirms the wonderful and flawed person who is actually there. Romance, however, is blind, intoxicating, and illusionary. The question is: will we continue to drink the love potion of romantic love or sober up to establish a new/old substance and basis for enduring human relations?

Questions for Discussion

1. Where in popular culture (movies, music, novels, TV) do you see the ideology of romantic love influence the daily lives of people? Give examples.
2. Comment on the statement: Hindus love the woman they marry, rather than marry the woman they love.
3. Is our culture of divorce connected to the pervasive influence of romance in our society?
4. Compare Johnson's meaning of human love with the Christian meaning of *agape.*
5. What should be the rationale and basis for committed personal relations?
6. What does Johnson mean when he says: "the essence of love is not to use the other to make us happy"?

P eople become so wearied of the cycles and dead ends of romance that
they begin to wonder if there is such a thing as "love." There is. But sometimes we have to make profound changes of attitude before we can see what
love is and make room for love in our lives.

Love between human beings is one of the absolute realities of human
nature. Just as soul—Psyche—was one of the gods of the Greek pantheon, so
was Love: His name was Eros. For the Greeks understood that love, being an
archetype of the collective unconscious, is both eternal and universal in
humankind. And for the Greeks, that qualified Love as a god.

Because love is an archetype, it has its own character, its own traits, its own
"personality." Like a god, love behaves as a "person" in the unconscious, a
separate being in the psyche. Love is distinct from my ego; love was here
before my ego came into the world, and love will be here after my ego departs.
Yet love is something or "someone" who lives within me. Love is a force that
acts from within, that enables my ego to look outside itself, to see my fellow
humans as something to be valued and cherished, rather than used.

Therefore, when I say that "I love," it is not I who love, but, in reality,
Love who acts through me. Love is not so much something I do as something
that I am. Love is not a doing but a state of being—a relatedness, a connect-
edness to another mortal, an identification with her or him that simply flows
within me and through me, independent of my intentions or my efforts.

This state of being may express itself in what I do or in how I treat people, but it can never be reduced to a set of "doings," or acts. It is a feeling
within. More often than we realize, love works its divine alchemy best when
we follow the advice of Shakespeare's Cordelia: "Love, and keep silent."

Love exists, regardless of our opinions about what it ought to be. No matter how many fabrications or how much selfishness we justify in the name of
"love," love still keeps its unchanging character. Its existence and its nature
do not depend on my illusions, my opinions, or my counterfeits. Love is different from what my culture has led me to expect, different from what my ego
wants, different from the sentimental froth and inflated ecstasies I've been
taught to hope for; but love turns out to be real; it turns out to be what I am,
rather than what my ego demands.

We need to know this about love. Otherwise we could never stand to look
honestly at our self-deceptions. At times people say: "Don't make me see my
illusions; if you take away my illusions, there will be nothing left!" We seem
to think of love as "man-made," as though we invented it in our minds. Even
though romantic love has not turned out to be what we thought, there is still
a human love that is inherent in us, and this love will be with us even after
our projections, our illusions, and our artifices have all passed away.

Human love is so obscured by the inflations and commotions of romance
that we almost never look for love in its own right, and we hardly know what

From *We: Understanding the Psychology of Romantic Love* by Robert A. Johnson. Copyright © 1983
by Robert A. Johnson. Reprinted by permission of HarperCollins Publishers, Inc.

to look for when we do search. But as we learn love's characteristics and attitudes, we can begin to see love within us—revealed in our feelings, in the spontaneous flow of warmth that surges toward another person, in the small, unnoticed acts of relatedness that make up the secret fabric of our daily lives.

Love is the power within us that affirms and values another human being as he or she is. Human love affirms that person who is actually there, rather than the ideal we would like him or her to be or the projection that flows from our minds. Love is the inner god who opens our blind eyes to the beauty, value, and quality of the other person. Love causes us to value that person as a total, individual self, and this means that we accept the negative side as well as the positive, the imperfections as well as the admirable qualities. When one truly loves the human being rather than the projection, one loves the shadow just as one loves the rest. One accepts the other person's totality.

Human love causes a man to see the intrinsic value in a woman; therefore love leads him to honor and serve her, rather than to try to use her for his ego's purposes. When love is guiding him, he is concerned with her needs and her well-being, not fixated on his own wants and whims.

Love alters our sense of importance. Through love we see that the other individual has as great a value in the cosmos as our own; it becomes just as important to us that he or she should be whole, should live fully, should find the joy of life, as that our own needs be met.

In the world of the unconscious, love is one of those great psychological forces that have the power to transform the ego. Love is the one power that awakens the ego to the existence of something outside itself, outside its plans, outside its empire, outside its security. Love relates the ego not only to the rest of the human race, but to the soul and to all the gods of the inner world.

Thus love is by its very nature the exact opposite of egocentricity. We use the word *love* loosely. We use it to dignify any number of demands for attention, power, security, or entertainment from other people. But when we are looking out for our own self-styled "needs," our own desires, our own dreams, and our power over people, this is not love. Love is utterly distinct from our ego's desires and power plays. It leads in a different direction: toward the goodness, the value, and the needs of the people around us.

In its very essence, love is an *appreciation*, a recognition of another's value: It moves a man to honor a woman rather than use her, to ask himself how he might serve her. And if this woman is relating to him through love, she will take the same attitude toward him.

The archetypal nature of love is perhaps nowhere better expressed than in the simple language of Saint Paul:

> Love suffers long and is kind; love does not envy; love does not vaunt itself, is not puffed up. . . . Love does not seek her own way, is not easily provoked, is not anxious to suspect evil. . . . bears all things, believes all things, hopes all things, endures all things.
>
> Love never fails: but whether there be prophecies, they shall fail, whether there be tongues, they shall cease, whether there be knowledge, it shall vanish away.

Here is a brief and eloquent statement of the difference between an ego left to its own devices and an ego under the influence of love. My ego is concerned only with itself; but "love suffers long and is kind." My ego is envious, always seeking to inflate itself with illusions of absolute power and control, but "love does not vaunt itself, is not puffed up." My ego, left to its ego-centeredness, will always betray, but "love never fails." My ego only knows how to affirm itself and its desires, but love "seeks not her own way." Love affirms all of life: "bears all things, believes all things, hopes all things."

This is why we have taken exception to romantic love, and this is the main distinction between human love and romantic love: Romance must, by its very nature, deteriorate into egotism. For romance is not a love that is directed at another human being; the passion of romance is always directed at our own projections, our own expectations, our own fantasies. In a very real sense, it is a love not of another person, but of ourselves.

> It should now be clear that to the extent that a relationship is founded on projection the element of human love is lacking. To be in love with someone we do not know as a person, but are attracted to because they reflect back to us the image of the god or goddess in our souls, is, in a sense, to be in love with oneself, not with the other person. In spite of the seeming beauty of the love fantasies we may have in this state of being in love, we can, in fact, be in a thoroughly selfish state of mind.
>
> Real love begins only when one person comes to know another for who he or she really is as a human being, and begins to like and care for that human being.
>
> ... To be capable of real love means becoming mature, with realistic expectations of the other person. It means accepting responsibility for our own happiness or unhappiness, and neither expecting the other person to make us happy nor blaming that person for our bad moods and frustrations. (Sanford, pp. 19–20)

When we are focused on our projections, we are focused on ourselves. And the passion and love we feel for our projections is a reflexive, circular love that is directed inevitably back to ourselves.

But here, again, we run headlong into the paradox of romantic love. The paradox is that we *should* love our projections, and that we should also love ourselves. In romance the love of self becomes distorted; it becomes egocentric and its original nature is lost. But if we learn to seek it on the correct level, the love of self is a true and valid love: It is the second great stream of energy that flows into romantic love, human love's archetypal mate, the other face of Eros.

We need to revere the unconscious parts of ourselves that we project. When we love our projections, when we honor our romantic ideals and fantasies, we affirm infinitely precious dimensions of our total selves. The riddle is how to love one's self without falling into egotism.

As we learn the geography of the human psyche, with its islands of consciousness, its multilayered and multicentered structure, we see that the love of the total self can not be a centering of the universe on our egos. Love of self is the ego's seeking after the other "persons" of the inner world, who hide within us. It is ego's longing for the larger dimensions of the unconscious, its willingness to open itself to the other parts of our total being, and to their points of view, their values, and their needs.

Understood in this way, our love of self is also the "divine" love: our search for the ultimate meaning, for our souls, for the revelation of God. This understanding returns us to the words of Clement of Alexandria:

> Therefore, as it seems, it is the greatest of all disciplines to know oneself; for when a man knows himself, he knows God.

The fault in romantic love is not that we love ourselves, but that we love ourselves wrongly. By trying to revere the unconscious through our romantic projections on other people, we miss the reality hidden in those projections: We don't see that it is our own selves we are searching for.

The task of salvaging love from the swamps of romance begins with a shift of vision toward the inside; we have to wake up to the inner world; we have to learn how to live the "love of self" as an inner experience. But then it is time to redirect our gaze outward again, toward physical people and the relationships we make with them—we must learn the principles of the "human" love.

Many years ago a wise friend gave me a name for human love. She called it "stirring-the-oatmeal" love. She was right: Within this phrase, if we will humble ourselves enough to look, is the very essence of what human love is, and it shows us the principal differences between human love and romance.

Stirring oatmeal is an humble act—not exciting or thrilling. But it symbolizes a relatedness that brings love down to earth. It represents a willingness to share ordinary human life, to find meaning in the simple, unromantic tasks: earning a living, living within a budget, putting out the garbage, feeding the baby in the middle of the night. To "stir the oatmeal" means to find the relatedness, the value, even the beauty, in simple and ordinary things, not to eternally demand a cosmic drama, an entertainment, or an extraordinary intensity in everything. Like the rice hulling of the Zen monks, the spinning wheel of Ghandi, the tent making of Saint Paul, it represents the discovery of the sacred in the midst of the humble and ordinary.

Jung once said that feeling is a matter of the *small*. And in human love, we can see that it is true. The real relatedness between two people is experienced in the small tasks they do together: the quiet conversation when the day's upheavals are at rest, the soft word of understanding, the daily companionship, the encouragement offered in a difficult moment, the small gift when least expected, the spontaneous gesture of love.

When a couple are genuinely related to each other, they are willing to enter into the whole spectrum of human life together. They transform even the unexciting, difficult, and mundane things into a joyful and fulfilling component of life. By contrast, romantic love can only last so long as a couple are "high" on one another, so long as the money lasts and the entertainments are exciting. "Stirring the oatmeal" means that two people take their love off the airy level of exciting fantasy and convert it into earthy, practical immediacy.

Love is content to do many things that ego is bored with. Love is willing to work with the other person's moods and unreasonableness. Love is willing to fix breakfast and balance the checkbook. Love is willing to do these "oatmeal" things of life because it is related to a person, not a projection.

Human love sees another person as an individual and makes an individualized relationship to him or her. Romantic love sees the other person only as a role player in the drama.

A man's human love desires that a woman become a complete and independent person and encourages her to be herself. Romantic love only affirms what he would like her to be, so that she could be identical to anima. So long as romance rules a man, he affirms a woman only insofar as she is willing to change, so that she may reflect his projected ideal. Romance is never happy with the other person just as he or she is.

Human love necessarily includes friendship: friendship within relationship, within marriage, between husband and wife. When a man and a woman are truly friends, they know each other's difficult points and weaknesses, but they are not inclined to stand in judgment on them. They are more concerned with helping each other and enjoying each other than they are with finding fault.

Friends, genuine friends, are like Kaherdin: They want to affirm rather than to judge; they don't coddle, but neither do they dwell on our inadequacies. Friends back each other up in the tough times, help each other with the sordid and ordinary tasks of life. They don't impose impossible standards on each other, they don't ask for perfection, and they help each other rather than grind each other down with demands.

In romantic love there is no friendship. Romance and friendship are utterly opposed energies, natural enemies with completely opposing motives. Sometimes people say: "I don't want to be friends with my husband [or wife]; it would take all the romance out of our marriage." It is true: Friendship does take the artificial drama and intensity out of a relationship, but it also takes away the egocentricity and the impossibility and replaces the drama with something human and real.

If a man and woman are friends to each other, then they are "neighbors" as well as lovers; their relationship is suddenly subject to Christ's dictum: "Love thy neighbor as thyself." One of the glaring contradictions in romantic love is that so many couples treat their friends with so much more kindness, consideration, generosity, and forgiveness than they ever give to one another! When people are with their friends, they are charming, helpful, and courteous. But when they come home, they often vent all their anger, resentments, moods, and frustrations on each other. Strangely, they treat their friends better than they do each other.

When two people are "in love," people commonly say that they are "more than just friends." But in the long run, they seem to treat each other as *less* than friends. Most people think that being "in love" is a much more intimate, much more "meaningful," relationship than "mere" friendship. Why, then, do couples refuse each other the selfless love, the kindness and good will, that they readily give to their friends? People can't ask of their friends that they carry all their projections, be scapegoats for all their moods, keep them feeling happy, and make life complete for them. Why do couples impose these demands on each other? Because the cult of romance teaches us that we have the right to expect that all our projections will be borne—all our desires satisfied, and all our fantasies made to come true—in the person we are "in love" with. In one of the Hindu rites of marriage, the bride and groom make to each other a solemn statement: "You will be my *best friend.*" Western couples need to learn to be friends, to live with each other in a spirit of friendship, to take the quality of friendship as a guide through the tangles we have made of love.

We can learn much of human love by learning to look with an open mind at Oriental cultures and their attitudes.

During the time I spent in India and Japan, I saw marriages and love relationships that are not based at all on romance but on a warm, devoted, and enduring love. Hindus are instinctive masters of the art of human love. I think this is because they have never taken on romantic love as a way of trying to relate to each other. Hindus automatically make the differentiation that we have completely muddled in the West: They know how to worship anima, the archetypes, the gods, as inner realities; they know how to keep their experience of the divine side of life distinct from their personal relationships and marriages.

Hindus take the inner world on a symbolic level; they translate the inner archetypes into images and external symbols through temple art and allegorical ritual. But they don't project the inner gods onto their husbands and wives. They take the personified archetypes as symbols of another world and take each other as human beings; as a result, they don't put impossible demands on each other and they don't disappoint each other.

A Hindu man does not ask of his wife that she be anima or that she take him off to another world or that she embody all the intensity and perfection of his inner life. Since lyrical religious experience is still part of their culture, Hindus do not try to make their marriages and human relationships into a substitute for communion with the soul. They find their gods in the temple, in meditation, or sometimes in the guru; they don't try to make the outer relationship serve the role of the inner one.

At first a Westerner is confused by the Hindu way; their love doesn't seem to be bubbling with enough heat and intensity to suit the Western romantic taste. But if one observes patiently, one is startled out of Western prejudices and begins to question the assumption that romance is the only "true love." There is a quiet but steady lovingness in Hindu marriages, a profound affection. There is stability: They are not caught in the dramatic oscillations between "in love" and "out of love," adoration and disillusionment, that Western couples are.

In the traditional Hindu marriage, a man's commitment to his wife does not depend on his staying "in love" with her. Since he was never "in love" in the first place, there is no way he can fall "out of love." His relationship to his wife is based on loving *her*, not on being "in love" with an ideal that he projects onto her. His relationship is not going to collapse because one day he falls "out of love," or because he meets another woman who catches his projection. He is committed to a woman and a family, not to a projection.

We think of ourselves as more sophisticated than the "simple" Hindus. But, by comparison with a Hindu, the average Western man is like an ox with a ring in his nose, following his projection around from one woman to another, making no true relationship or commitment to any. In the area of human feeling, love, and relationship, Hindus have evolved a highly differentiated, subtle, and refined consciousness. In these matters, they do better than we.

One of the most striking and surprising things I observed among traditional Hindus was how bright, happy, and psychologically healthy their children are. Children in Hindu families are not neurotic; they are not torn within themselves as so many Western children are. They are bathed constantly in human affection, and they sense a peaceful flow of affection between their mother and father. They sense the stability, the enduring quality of their family life. Their parents are committed permanently; they don't hear their parents asking themselves whether their marriage is "going to work out"; separation and divorce do not float as specters in the air.

For us Westerners there is no turning back of the clock. We can't go the way of the Hindus; we can't solve our Western dilemma by doing an imitation of other people's customs or other people's attitudes. We can't pretend that we have an Eastern psyche rather than a Western psyche. We have to deal with our own Western unconscious and our own Western wounds; we have to find the healing balm within our own Western soul. We have drunk the love potion and plunged into the romantic era of our evolution, and the only way out is by the path that leads straight ahead. We can't go back, and we may not linger.

But we can learn from the Eastern cultures to stand outside ourselves, outside our assumptions and our beliefs, just long enough to see ourselves in a new perspective. We can learn what it is to approach love with a different set of attitudes, unburdened by the dogmas of our culture.

We can learn that human relationship is inseparable from friendship and commitment. We can learn that the essence of love is not to use the other to make us happy but to serve and affirm the one we love. And we can discover, to our surprise, that what we have needed more than anything was not so much to be loved, as to love.

REFERENCE

Sanford, John A. *Invisible Partners: How the Male and Female in Each of Us Affects Our Relationships.* New York: Paulist, 1984.

CHAPTER 20

The Transmission of Life

Pope John Paul II

Pope Paul's Encyclical *Humanae Vitae* (1968) caused a firestorm of protest within Roman Catholicism. Its prohibition against artificial means of contraception was a marker point for millions of practicing Roman Catholics. Following one's conscience, continued reception of the sacraments, and informed dissent became the ecclesial way of life for many. And so it is today.

In this excerpt, from his Apostolic Exhortation on "Role of the Christian Family in the Modern World," Pope John Paul II vigorously defends the traditional Roman Catholic teaching. It is truly, he believes, prophetic proclamation. The fundamental task of family life is to serve life by the transmission of new life. The unitive and procreative meanings of the conjugal act can never be *artificially* separated. Natural family planning accepts the natural cycle of the person and expresses the total reciprocal self-giving of the couple. The artificial use of contraceptives, on the other hand, speaks an objectively contradictory language, namely, not giving oneself totally to the other.

In the current social and cultural context, Pope John Paul II acknowledges that this traditional teaching is difficult to understand. An array of forces fosters a contraceptive mentality and antilife dispositions. Some public authorities formulate public policies (contraception, sterilization, abortion) that support this outlook. The church, however, must say "yes" to life in the face of the "no" that assails and afflicts the world. John Paul II's stance is certainly countercultural. Will it win the hearts and minds of the faithful?

Questions for Discussion

1. Is John Paul II's argument against artificial contraception convincing for you? Why?

2. Is there some truth to the claim that a contraceptive mentality holds sway in the lives of some young married couples today?

3. John Paul II's position is: harmonizing conjugal love with the responsible transmission of life must be determined by *objective standards*. Are there objective standards to look to? If so, where?

4. What can you affirm in this papal perspective as a form of prophetic cultural resistance today?

5. Have human beings the right and/or responsibility to shape and reorder expressions of their sexuality? If so, when?

6. Would you agree or disagree with governmental support and financing of contraception, sterilization, and abortion?

COOPERATORS IN THE LOVE OF
GOD THE CREATOR

With the creation of man and woman in His own image and likeness, God crowns and brings to perfection the work of His hands: He calls them to a special sharing in His love and in His power as Creator and Father, through their free and responsible cooperation in transmitting the gift of human life: "God blessed them, and God said to them, 'Be fruitful and multiply, and fill the earth and subdue it.'"[1]

Thus the fundamental task of the family is to serve life, to actualize in history the original blessing of the Creator—that of transmitting by procreation the divine image from person to person.[2]

Fecundity is the fruit and the sign of conjugal love, the living testimony of the full reciprocal self-giving of the spouses: "While not making the other purposes of matrimony of less account, the true practice of conjugal love, and the whole meaning of the family life which results from it, have this aim: that the couple be ready with stout hearts to cooperate with the love of the Creator and the Savior, who through them will enlarge and enrich His own family day by day."[3]

However, the fruitfulness of conjugal love is not restricted solely to the procreation of children, even understood in its specifically human dimension: it is enlarged and enriched by all those fruits of moral, spiritual and supernatural life which the father and mother are called to hand on to their children, and through the children to the Church and to the world.

THE CHURCH'S TEACHING AND NORM,
ALWAYS OLD YET ALWAYS NEW

Precisely because the love of husband and wife is a unique participation in the mystery of life and of the love of God Himself, the Church knows that she has received the special mission of guarding and protecting the lofty dignity of marriage and the most serious responsibility of the transmission of human life.

Thus, in continuity with the living tradition of the ecclesial community throughout history, the recent Second Vatican Council and the magisterium of my predecessor Paul VI, expressed above all in the Encyclical *Humanae vitae*, have handed on to our times a truly prophetic proclamation, which reaffirms and reproposes with clarity the Church's teaching and norm, always old yet always new, regarding marriage and regarding the transmission of human life.

For this reason the Synod Fathers made the following declaration at their last assembly: "This Sacred Synod, gathered together with the Successor of Peter in the unity of faith, firmly holds what has been set forth in the Second Vatican Council (cf. *Gaudium et spes*, 50) and afterwards in the Encyclical *Humanae vitae*, particularly that love between husband and wife must be fully human, exclusive and open to new life (*Humanae vitae*, 11: cf. 9. 12)."[4]

THE CHURCH STANDS FOR LIFE

The teaching of the Church in our day is placed in a social and cultural context which renders it more difficult to understand and yet more urgent and irreplaceable for promoting the true good of men and women.

Scientific and technical progress, which contemporary man is continually expanding in his dominion over nature, not only offers the hope of creating a new and better humanity, but also causes ever greater anxiety regarding the future. Some ask themselves if it is a good thing to be alive or if it would be better never to have been born: they doubt therefore if it is right to bring others into life when perhaps they will curse their existence in a cruel world with unforeseeable terrors. Others consider themselves to be the only ones for whom the advantages of technology are intended and they exclude others by imposing on them contraceptives or even worse means. Still others, imprisoned in a consumer mentality and whose sole concern is to bring about a continual growth of material goods, finish by ceasing to understand, and thus by refusing, the spiritual riches of a new human life. The ultimate reason for these mentalities is the absence in people's hearts of God, whose love alone is stronger than all the world's fears and can conquer them.

Thus an anti-life mentality is born, as can be seen in many current issues: one thinks, for example, of a certain panic deriving from the studies of ecologists and futurologists on population growth, which sometimes exaggerate the danger of demographic increase to the quality of life.

But the Church firmly believes that human life, even if weak and suffering, is always a splendid gift of God's goodness. Against the pessimism and selfishness which cast a shadow over the world, the Church stands for life: in each human life she sees the splendor of that "Yes," that "Amen," who is Christ Himself.[5] To the "No" which assails and afflicts the world, she replies with this living "Yes," thus defending the human person and the world from all who plot against and harm life.

The Church is called upon to manifest anew to everyone, with clear and stronger conviction, her will to promote human life by every means and to defend it against all attacks, in whatever condition or state of development it is found.

Thus the Church condemns as a grave offense against human dignity and justice all those activities of governments or other public authorities which attempt to limit in any way the freedom of couples in deciding about children. Consequently, any violence applied by such authorities in favor of contraception or, still worse, of sterilization and procured abortion, must be altogether condemned and forcefully rejected. Likewise to be denounced as gravely unjust are cases where, in international relations, economic help given for the advancement of peoples is made conditional on programs of contraception, sterilization and procured abortion.[6]

THAT GOD'S DESIGN MAY BE EVER MORE COMPLETELY FULFILLED

The Church is certainly aware of the many complex problems which couples in many countries face today in their task of transmitting life in a responsible way. She also recognizes the serious problem of population growth in the form it has taken in many parts of the world and its moral implications.

However, she holds that consideration in depth of all the aspects of these problems offers a new and stronger confirmation of the importance of the authentic teaching on birth regulation reproposed in the Second Vatican Council and in the Encyclical *Humanae vitae*.

For this reason, together with the Synod Fathers I feel it is my duty to extend a pressing invitation to theologians, asking them to unite their efforts in order to collaborate with the hierarchical Magisterium and to commit themselves to the task of illustrating ever more clearly the biblical foundations, the ethical grounds and the personalistic reasons behind this doctrine. Thus it will be possible, in the context of an organic exposition, to render the teaching of the Church on this fundamental question truly accessible to all people of good will, fostering a daily more enlightened and profound understanding of it: in this way God's plan will be ever more completely fulfilled for the salvation of humanity and for the glory of the Creator.

A united effort by theologians in this regard, inspired by a convinced adherence to the Magisterium, which is the one authentic guide for the People of God, is particularly urgent for reasons that include the close link between Catholic teaching on this matter and the view of the human person that the Church proposes: doubt or error in the field of marriage or the family involves obscuring to a serious extent the integral truth about the human person, in a cultural situation that is already so often confused and contradictory. In fulfillment of their specific role, theologians are called upon to provide enlightenment and a deeper understanding, and their contribution is of incomparable value and represents a unique and highly meritorious service to the family and humanity.

IN AN INTEGRAL VISION OF THE HUMAN PERSON AND OF HIS OR HER VOCATION

In the context of a culture which seriously distorts or entirely misinterprets the true meaning of human sexuality, because it separates it from its essential reference to the person, the Church more urgently feels how irreplaceable is her mission of presenting sexuality as a value and task of the whole person, created male and female in the image of God.

In this perspective the Second Vatican Council clearly affirmed that "when there is a question of harmonizing conjugal love with the responsible transmission of life, the moral aspect of any procedure does not depend solely on sincere intentions or on an evaluation of motives. It must be determined by *objective standards*. These, *based on the nature of the human person and his or her acts*, preserve the full sense of mutual self-giving and human procreation in the context of true love. Such a goal cannot be achieved unless the virtue of conjugal chastity is sincerely practiced."[7]

It is precisely by moving from "an integral vision of man and of his vocation, not only his natural and earthly, but also his supernatural and eternal vocation."[8] that Paul VI affirmed that the teaching of the Church "is founded upon the inseparable connection, willed by God and unable to be broken by man on his own initiative, between the two meanings of the conjugal act: the unitive meaning and the procreative meaning."[9] And he concluded by re-emphasizing that there must be excluded as intrinsically immoral "every action which, either in anticipation of the conjugal act, or in its accomplishment, or in the development of its natural consequences, proposes, whether as an end or as a means, to render procreation impossible."[10]

When couples, by means of recourse to contraception, separate these two meanings that God the Creator has inscribed in the being of man and woman and in the dynamism of their sexual communion, they act as "arbiters" of the divine plan and they "manipulate" and degrade human sexuality—and with it themselves and their married partner—by altering its value of "total" self-giving. Thus the innate language that expresses the total reciprocal self-giving of husband and wife is overlaid, through contraception, by an objectively contradictory language, namely, that of not giving oneself totally to the other. This leads not only to a positive refusal to be open to life but also to a falsification of the inner truth of conjugal love, which is called upon to give itself in personal totality.

When, instead, by means of recourse to periods of infertility, the couple respect the inseparable connection between the unitive and procreative meanings of human sexuality, they are acting as "ministers" of God's plan and they "benefit from" their sexuality according to the original dynamism of "total" self-giving, without manipulation or alteration.[11]

In the light of the experience of many couples and of the data provided by the different human sciences, theological reflection is able to perceive and is called to study further *the difference, both anthropological and moral*, between contraception and recourse to the rhythm of the cycle: it is a difference which is much wider and deeper than is usually thought, one which involves in the final analysis two irreconcilable concepts of the human person and of human sexuality. The choice of the natural rhythms involves accepting the cycle of the person, that is the woman, and thereby accepting dialogue, reciprocal respect, shared responsibility and self-control. To accept the cycle and to enter into dialogue means to recognize both the spiritual and corporal character of conjugal communion, and to live personal love with its requirement of fidelity. In this context the couple comes to experience how conjugal communion is enriched with those values of tenderness and affection which constitute the inner soul of human sexuality, in its physical dimension also. In this way sexuality is respected and promoted in its truly and fully human dimension, and is never "used" as an "object" that, by breaking the personal unity of soul and body, strikes at God's creation itself at the level of the deepest interaction of nature and person.

NOTES

1. Gn 1:28.

2. Cf Gn 5:1–3.

3. Second Vatican Ecumenical Council, Pastoral Constitution on the Church in the Modern World, *Gaudium et Spes*, n. 50.

4. *Propositio* 21. Section 11 of the encyclical *Humanae Vitae* ends with the statement: "The Church, calling people back to the observance of the norms of the natural law, as interpreted by her constant doctrine, teaches that each and every marriage act must remain open to the transmission of life (*ut quilibet matrimonii usus ud vitam humanam procreandam per se destinatus permaneat*)": AAS 60 (1968), 488.

5. Cf 2 Cor 1:19; Rv 3:14.

6. Cf the Sixth Synod of Bishops' Message to Christian Families in the Modern World (Oct. 24, 1980), 5.

7. Pastoral Constitution on the Church in the Modern World, *Gaudium et Spes*, n. 51.

8. Encyclical *Humanae Vitae*, n. 7:AAS 60 (1968), 485.

9. Ibid., 12: loc. cit., 488–489.

10. Ibid., 14: loc. cit., 490.

11. Ibid., 13: loc. cit., 489.

PART FIVE

Communication, Conflict, and Change

CHAPTER 21

How People Change

Allen Wheelis

Allen Wheelis's reflection on how people change has ideas important for those seeking the right marriage partner. It may be the single most important essay in this book. He points out convincingly how our actions eventually make us a particular kind of person, whether we want to admit it or not. Thus, there is a lot more to any person we meet than that person's initial attractiveness. That person's behavior has over time made him or her a particular kind of person. If you want to find out who a person is, look to the person's behavior. Some prefer to look into their own feelings of attraction and to project onto the other person affectionate feelings having nothing necessarily to do with the other person. "Pay attention to the person's behavior rather than to your own feelings only" seems to be Wheelis's insight.

Wheelis's angle is hopeful because he shows convincingly that people can change and they do so by taking in reverse the same steps they took to develop the unhelpful pattern of behavior that plagues them.

Questions for Discussion

1. "We are what we do." In what ways is the author's statement convincing or unconvincing to you?
2. "Freedom as the ability to choose alternatives is contingent on awareness and consciousness." What does this statement mean in dealing with a person whose behavior needs to change?
3. What implications does Wheelis's essay have for people who are dating?
4. At the end, Wheelis explains how we can look at any life in terms of causes and choices. If the life is one's own or that of someone we love, we will emphasize choice. But the deeper question is: Whose choice? What would you say to someone who claims, "If I marry so and so, I will be able to change him or her through my love."

We are what we do . . . Identity is the integration of behavior. If a man claims to be honest we take him at his word. But if it should transpire

From *Commentary*, May 1969, pp. 57–58, 63, 66. Reprinted by permission of *Commentary* magazine.

that over the years he has been embezzling, we unhesitatingly discard the identity he adopts in words and ascribe to him the identity defined by his acts. "He claims to be honest," we say, "but he's really a thief."

One theft, however, does not make a thief. One act of forthrightness does not establish frankness; one tormenting of a cat does not make a sadist, nor one rescue of a fledgling a savior. Action which defines a man, describes his character, is action which has been repeated over and over, and so has come in time to be a coherent and relatively independent mode of behavior. At first it may have been fumbling and uncertain, may have required attention, effort, will—as when one first drives a car, first makes love, first robs a bank, first stands up against injustice. If one perseveres on any such course it comes in time to require less effort, less attention, begins to function smoothly; its small component behaviors become integrated within a larger pattern which has an ongoing dynamism and cohesiveness, carries its own authority. Such a mode then pervades the entire person, permeates other modes, colors other qualities, in some sense is living and operative even when the action is not being performed, or even considered. A young man who learns to drive a car thinks differently thereby, feels differently; when he meets a pretty girl who lives fifty miles away, the encounter carries implications he could not have felt as a bus rider. We may say, then, that he not only drives a car, but has *become* a driver. If the action is shoplifting, we say not only that he steals from stores but that he has *become* a shoplifter.

Such a mode of action tends to maintain itself, to resist change. A thief is one who steals; stealing extends and reinforces the identity of thief, which generates further thefts, which further strengthens and deepens the identity. So long as one lives, change is possible; but the longer such behavior is continued the more force and authority it acquires, the more it permeates other consonant modes, subordinates other conflicting modes; changing back becomes steadily more difficult; settling down to an honest job, living on one's earnings, becomes ever more unlikely. And what is said here of stealing applies equally to courage, cowardice, creativity, gambling, alcoholism, depression, or any other of the myriad ways of behaving, and hence of being. Identity comprises all such modes as may characterize a person, existing in varying degrees of integration and conflict. The greater the conflict the more unstable the identity; the more harmonious the various modes, the more durable the identity.

The identity defined by action is present and past; it may also foretell the future, but not necessarily. Sometimes we act covertly: the eye does not notice the hand under the table, we construe the bribe to have been a gift, the running away to have been prudence, and so conceal from ourselves what we are. Then one day, perhaps, we drop the pretense, the illusion cracks. We have then the sense of an identity that has existed all along—and in some sense we knew it but would not let ourselves know that we knew it—but now we do, and in a blaze of frankness say, "My God! I really am a crook!" or "I really am a coward!" We may then go too far and conclude that this identity is our "nature," that it was writ in the stars or in the double helix, that it transcends experience, that our actual lives have been the fulfilling of a pre-existing pattern.

In fact it was writ only in our past choices. We are wise to believe it difficult to change, to recognize that character has a forward propulsion which tends to carry it unaltered into the future, but we need not believe it impossible to change. Our present and future choices may take us upon different courses which will in time comprise a different identity. It happens, sometimes, that the crook reforms, that the coward stands to fight.

. . . *And may do what we choose.* The identity defined by action is not, therefore, the whole person. Within us lies the potential for change, the freedom to choose other courses. When we admit that those "gifts" were bribes and say, "Well, then, I'm a crook," we have stated a fact, not a destiny; if we then invoke the leopard that can't change his spots, saying, "That's just the way I am, might as well accept it," we abandon the freedom to change, and exploit what we have been in the past to avoid responsibility for what we shall be in the future.

Often we do not choose, but drift into those modes which eventually define us. Circumstances push and we yield. We did not choose to be what we have become, but gradually, imperceptibly became what we are by drifting into the doing of those things we now characteristically do. Freedom is not an objective attribute of life; alternatives without awareness yield no leeway. I open the door of my car, sit behind the wheel, and notice in a corner of vision an ant scurrying about on the smooth barren surface of the concrete parking lot, doomed momentarily to be crushed by one of the thousand passing wheels. There exists, however, a brilliant alternative for this gravely endangered creature: in a few minutes a woman will appear with a picnic basket and we shall drive to a sunny, hilltop meadow. This desperate ant has but to climb the wheel of my car to a safe sheltered ledge, and in a half hour will be in a paradise for ants. But this option, unknown, unknowable, yields no freedom to the ant, who is doomed; and the only irony belongs to me who observes, who reflects that options potentially as meaningful to me as this one to this ant may at this moment be eluding my awareness; so I too may be doomed—this planet looks more like a parking lot every day.

Nothing guarantees freedom. It may never be achieved, or having been achieved may be lost. Alternatives go unnoticed; foreseeable consequences are not foreseen; we may not know what we have been, what we are, or what we are becoming. We who are the bearers of consciousness but of not very much, may proceed through a whole life without awareness of that which would have meant the most, the freedom which has to be noticed to be real. Freedom is the awareness of alternatives and of the ability to choose. It is contingent upon consciousness, and so may be gained or lost, extended or diminished.

Personality is a complex balance of many conflicting claims, forces, tensions, compunctions, distractions, which yet manages somehow to be a functioning entity. However it may have come to be what it is, it resists becoming any-thing else. It tends to maintain itself, to convey itself onward into the future unaltered. It may be changed only with difficulty. It may be changed from within, spontaneously and unthinkingly, by an onslaught of physiological force, as in adolescence. It may be changed from without, again sponta-neously and unthinkingly, by the force of unusual circumstance, as in a Nazi concentration camp. And sometimes it may be changed from within, delib-erately, consciously, and by design. Never easily, never for sure, but slowly, uncertainly, and only with effort, insight, and a kind of tenacious creative cunning.

Personality change follows change in behavior. Since we are what we do, if we want to change what we are we must begin by changing what we do, must undertake a new mode of action. Since the import of such action is change, it will run afoul of existing entrenched forces which will protest and resist. The new mode will be experienced as difficult, unpleasant, forced, un-natural, anxiety-provoking. It may be undertaken lightly but can be sus-tained only by a considerable effort of will. Change will occur only if such ac-tion is maintained over a long period of time.

The place of insight is to illumine: to ascertain where one is, how one got there, how now to proceed, and to what end. It is a blueprint, as in building a house, and may be essential, but no one achieves a house by blueprints alone, no matter how accurate or detailed. A time comes when one must take up hammer and nails. In building a house the making of blueprints may be delegated to an architect, the construction to a carpenter. In building the house of one's life or in its remodeling, one may delegate nothing; for the task can be done, if at all, only in the workshop of one's own mind and heart, in the most intimate rooms of thinking and feeling where none but one's self has freedom of movement or competence or authority. The responsibility lies with him who suffers, originates with him, remains with him to the end. It will be no less his if he enlists the aid of a therapist; we are no more the prod-uct of our therapists than of our genes: we create ourselves. The sequence is suffering, insight, will, action, change. The one who suffers, who wants to change, must bear responsibility all the way. "Must" because as soon as re-sponsibility is ascribed, the forces resisting change occupy the whole of one's being, and the process of change comes to a halt. A psychiatrist may help per-haps crucially, but his best help will be of no avail if he is required to provide a kind or degree of insight which will of itself achieve change.

Should an honest man wish to become a thief the necessary action is ob-vious: he must steal—not just once or occasionally, but frequently, consis-tently, taking pains that the business of planning and executing thefts replace other activities which in implication might oppose the predatory life. If he keeps at it long enough his being will conform to his behavior: he will have become a thief. Conversely, should a thief undertake to become an honest man, he must stop stealing and must undertake actions which replace steal-ing, not only in time and energy, and perhaps also excitement, but which carry implications contrary to the predatory life, that is, productive or con-tributive activities.

Of two equally true accounts of the same life the one we choose will depend upon the consequences we desire, the future we intend to create. If the life is our own or that of someone who has come to us for help, if it involves suffering and there is desire to change, we will elect a history written in terms of choice; for this is the view that insists upon the awareness of alternatives, the freedom to make one's self into something different. If the life in question is one we observe from a distance, without contact or influence, for example a life which has ended, we may elect a history written in terms of cause. In reconstructing a life that ended at Auschwitz we usually ignore options for other courses of individual behavior, locate cause and responsibility with the Nazis; for our intent is not to appraise the extent to which one person realized existing opportunity, but to examine and condemn the social evil which encompassed and doomed him. In considering the first eighteen years in the life of Malcolm X few of us would find much point in formulating his progress from delinquency to rackets to robbery to prison in terms of choice, holding him responsible for not having transcended circumstance; most of us would find the meaning of his story to lie in the manner in which racism may be seen as the cause of his downward course.

Conflict, suffering, psychotherapy—all these lead us to look again at ourselves, to look more carefully, in greater detail, to find what we have missed, to understand a mystery; and all this extends awareness. But whether this greater awareness will increase or diminish freedom will depend upon what it is that we become aware of. If the greater awareness is of the causes, traumas, psychodynamics that "made" us what we are, then we are understanding the past in such a way as to prove that we "had" to become what we are; and, since this view applies equally to the present which is the unbroken extension of that determined past, therapy becomes a way of establishing why we must continue to be what we have been, a way of disavowing choice with the apparent blessing of science, and the net effect will be a decrease in freedom. If, however, the greater awareness is of options unnoticed, of choices denied, of other ways to live, then freedom will be increased, and with it greater responsibility for what we have been, are, and will become.

CHAPTER 22

"Put Down That Paper and Talk to Me!": Rapport-Talk and Report-Talk

Deborah Tannen

In reading the following essay, men may find themselves fidgeting or their attention wandering, while women may read on with attentive fascination. Tannen puts a spotlight on habits men have rarely thought about but that may need changing, while women find Tannen naming things they themselves have noticed but never dared name or bring to attention. It is important to notice she is dealing here with *tendencies*, true enough in general, but not true of all men. However, if she is right about these tendencies, then the essay is especially important for men, because it can help men rethink how ordinary speech helps or hinders intimacy.

Another important point to notice is that Tannen is not blaming either men or women for the communication patterns she outlines. "The real problem is conversational style," she says. Men and women (especially boyfriends and girlfriends) do well to talk over these styles and the entire essay from their own points of view. As Tannen says, these differences in ways of speaking may never be perfectly adjusted for our partner's satisfaction, but *understanding them* takes the edge off complaints.

Some years ago, at the annual meetings of a professional association of professors, feminists began noting how many people of each gender were present at a particular session and how many women spoke and how many men. At the end of a session, they would announce their count. This procedure was transformative for many men in that association, who had never noticed the patterns. It was also transformative for women, who saw their need to speak up more often.

The marriage-course classroom might be an interesting lab for testing Tannen's claims. If someone agreed to do a regular speech analysis, giving at the end of class the ratio of women and men who volunteered observations, personal anecdotes, questions, and so on, all in class would become more conscious of "speaking out" as an important ongoing issue. Such consciousness could provide the spark to ignite very lively discussion of any issue that might arise.

Questions for Discussion

1. From your own point of view as a woman or a man, what single statement of Tannen's do you find most true of your own way of speaking? What statement do you find most true of the opposite sex's way of speaking?

2. What can you point to in her essay as most important for men to understand about their conversational styles? What do you find most important for women?

3. Where in her essay did you find she overstated or exaggerated?

4. If you were pushed to find one point that might change your own behavior, what would it be?

I was sitting in a suburban living room, speaking to a women's group that had invited men to join them for the occasion of my talk about communication between women and men. During the discussion, one man was particularly talkative, full of lengthy comments and explanations. When I made the observation that women often complain that their husbands don't talk to them enough, this man volunteered that he heartily agreed. He gestured toward his wife, who had sat silently beside him on the couch throughout the evening, and said, "She's the talker in our family."

Everyone in the room burst into laughter. The man looked puzzled and hurt. "It's true," he explained. "When I come home from work, I usually have nothing to say, but she never runs out. If it weren't for her, we'd spend the whole evening in silence." Another woman expressed a similar paradox about her husband: "When we go out, he's the life of the party. If I happen to be in another room, I can always hear his voice above the others. But when we're home, he doesn't have that much to say. I do most of the talking."

Who talks more, women or men? According to the stereotype, women talk too much. Linguist Jennifer Coates notes some proverbs:

A woman's tongue wags like a lamb's tail.

Foxes are all tail and women are all tongue.

The North Sea will sooner be found wanting in water than a woman be at a loss for a word.

Throughout history, women have been punished for talking too much or in the wrong way. Linguist Connie Eble lists a variety of physical punishments used in Colonial America: Women were strapped to ducking stools and held underwater until they nearly drowned, put into the stocks with signs pinned to them, gagged, and silenced by a cleft stick applied to their tongues.

Though such institutionalized corporal punishments have given way to informal, often psychological ones, modern stereotypes are not much different from those expressed in the old proverbs. Women are believed to talk too much. Yet study after study finds that it is men who talk more—at meetings, in mixed-group discussions, and in classrooms where girls or young women sit next to boys or young men. For example, communications researchers Barbara and Gene Eakins tape-recorded and studied seven university faculty

Pages 74–99 from *You Just Don't Understand* by Deborah Tannen. Copyright © 1990 by Deborah Tannen. Reprinted by permission of HarperCollins Publishers, Inc.

meetings. They found that, with one exception, men spoke more often and, without exception, spoke for a longer time. The men's turns ranged from 10.66 to 17.07 seconds, while the women's turns ranged from 3 to 10 seconds. In other words, the women's longest turns were still shorter than the men's shortest turns.

When a public lecture is followed by questions from the floor, or a talk show host opens the phones, the first voice to be heard asking a question is almost always a man's. And when they ask questions or offer comments from the audience, men tend to talk longer. Linguist Marjorie Swacker recorded question-and-answer sessions at academic conferences. Women were highly visible as speakers at the conferences studied; they presented 40.7 percent of the papers at the conferences studied and made up 42 percent of the audiences. But when it came to volunteering and being called on to ask questions, women contributed only 27.4 percent. Furthermore, the women's questions, on the average, took less than half as much time as the men's. (The mean was 23.1 seconds for women, 52.7 for men.) This happened, Swacker shows, because men (but not women) tended to preface their questions with statements, ask more than one question, and follow up the speaker's answer with another question or comment.

I have observed this pattern at my own lectures, which concern issues of direct relevance to women. Regardless of the proportion of women and men in the audience, men almost invariably ask the first question, more questions, and longer questions. In these situations, women often feel that men are talking too much. I recall one discussion period following a lecture I gave to a group assembled in a bookstore. The group was composed mostly of women, but most of the discussion was being conducted by men in the audience. At one point, a man sitting in the middle was talking at such great length that several women in the front rows began shifting in their seats and rolling their eyes at me. Ironically, what he was going on about was how frustrated he feels when he has to listen to women going on and on about topics he finds boring and unimportant.

RAPPORT-TALK AND REPORT-TALK

Who talks more, then, women or men? The seemingly contradictory evidence is reconciled by the difference between what I call *public* and *private speaking*. More men feel comfortable doing "public speaking," while more women feel comfortable doing "private" speaking. Another way of capturing these differences is by using the terms *report-talk* and *rapport-talk*.

For most women, the language of conversation is primarily a language of rapport: a way of establishing connections and negotiating relationships. Emphasis is placed on displaying similarities and matching experiences. From childhood, girls criticize peers who try to stand out or appear better than others. People feel their closest connections at home, or in settings where they *feel* at home—with one or a few people they feel close to and comfortable with—in other words, during private speaking. But even the most public situations can be approached like private speaking.

For most men, talk is primarily a means to preserve independence and negotiate and maintain status in a hierarchical social order. This is done by exhibiting knowledge and skill, and by holding center stage through verbal performance such as story-telling, joking, or imparting information. From childhood, men learn to use talking as a way to get and keep attention. So they are more comfortable speaking in larger groups made up of people they know less well—in the broadest sense, "public speaking." But even the most private situations can be approached like public speaking, more like giving a report than establishing rapport.

PRIVATE SPEAKING: THE WORDY WOMAN AND THE MUTE MAN

What is the source of the stereotype that women talk a lot? Dale Spender suggests that most people feel instinctively (if not consciously) that women, like children, should be seen and not heard, so any amount of talk from them seems like too much. Studies have shown that if women and men talk equally in a group, people think the women talked more. So there is truth to Spender's view. But another explanation is that men think women talk a lot because they hear women talking in situations where men would not: on the telephone; or in social situations with friends, when they are not discussing topics that men find inherently interesting; or, like the couple at the women's group, at home alone—in other words, in private speaking.

Home is the setting for an American icon that features the silent man and the talkative woman. And this icon, which grows out of the different goals and habits I have been describing, explains why the complaint most often voiced by women about the men with whom they are intimate is "He doesn't talk to me"—and the second most frequent is "He doesn't listen to me."

A woman who wrote to Ann Landers is typical:

My husband never speaks to me when he comes home from work. When I ask, "How did everything go today?" he says, "Rough . . ." or "It's a jungle out there." (We live in Jersey and he works in New York City.)

It's a different story when we have guests or go visiting. Paul is the gabbiest guy in the crowd—a real spellbinder. He comes up with the most interesting stories. People hang on every word. I think to myself, "Why doesn't he ever tell *me* these things?"

This has been going on for 38 years. Paul started to go quiet on me after 10 years of marriage. I could never figure out why. Can you solve the mystery?
—The Invisible Woman

Ann Landers suggests that the husband may not want to talk because he is tired when he comes home from work. Yet women who work come home tired too, and they are nonetheless eager to tell their partners or friends everything that happened to them during the day and what these fleeting, daily dramas made them think and feel.

Sources as lofty as studies conducted by psychologists, as down to earth as letters written to advice columnists, and as sophisticated as movies and plays come up with the same insight. Men's silence at home is a disappointment to women. Again and again, women complain, "He seems to have everything to say to everyone else, and nothing to say to me."

The film *Divorce American Style* opens with a conversation in which Debbie Reynolds is claiming that she and Dick Van Dyke don't communicate, and he is protesting that he tells her everything that's on his mind. The doorbell interrupts their quarrel, and husband and wife compose themselves before opening the door to greet their guests with cheerful smiles.

Behind closed doors, many couples are having conversations like this. Like the character played by Debbie Reynolds, women feel men don't communicate. Like the husband played by Dick Van Dyke, men feel wrongly accused. How can she be convinced that he doesn't tell her anything, while he is equally convinced he tells her everything that's on his mind? How can women and men have such different ideas about the same conversations?

When something goes wrong, people look around for a source to blame: either the person they are trying to communicate with ("You're demanding, stubborn, self-centered") or the group that the other person belongs to ("All women are demanding"; "All men are self-centered"). Some generous-minded people blame the relationship ("We just can't communicate"). But underneath, or overlaid on these types of blame cast outward, most people believe that something is wrong with them.

If individual people or particular relationships were to blame, there wouldn't be so many different people having the same problems. The real problem is conversational style. Women and men have different ways of talking. Even with the best intentions, trying to settle the problem through talk can only make things worse if it is ways of talking that are causing trouble in the first place.

BEST FRIENDS

Once again, the seeds of women's and men's styles are sown in the ways they learn to use language while growing up. In our culture, most people, but especially women, look to their closest relationships as havens in a hostile world. The center of a little girl's social life is her best friend. Girls' friendships are made and maintained by telling secrets. For grown women too, the essence of friendship is talk, telling each other what they're thinking and feeling, and what happened that day: who was at the bus stop, who called, what they said, how that made them feel. When asked who their best friends are, most women name other women they talk to regularly. When asked the same question, most men will say it's their wives. After that, many men name other men with whom they do things such as play tennis or baseball (but never just sit and talk) or a chum from high school whom they haven't spoken to in a year.

When Debbie Reynolds complained that Dick Van Dyke didn't tell her anything, and he protested that he did, both were right. She felt he didn't tell her anything because he didn't tell her the fleeting thoughts and feelings he experienced throughout the day—the kind of talk she would have with her best friend. He didn't tell her these things because to him they didn't seem like anything to tell. He told her anything that seemed important—anything he would tell his friends.

Men and women often have very different ideas of what's important— and at what point "important" topics should be raised. A woman told me, with lingering incredulity, of a conversation with her boyfriend. Knowing he had seen his friend Oliver, she asked, "What's new with Oliver?" He replied, "Nothing." But later in the conversation it came out that Oliver and his girl-friend had decided to get married. "That's nothing?" the woman gasped in frustration and disbelief.

For men, "Nothing" may be a ritual response at the start of a conversa-tion. A college woman missed her brother but rarely called him because she found it difficult to get talk going. A typical conversation began with her ask-ing, "What's up with you?" and his replying, "Nothing." Hearing his "Noth-ing" as meaning "There is nothing personal I want to talk about," she sup-plied talk by filling him in on her news and eventually hung up in frustration. But when she thought back, she remembered that later in the conversation he had mumbled, "Christie and I got into another fight." This came so late and so low that she didn't pick up on it. And he was probably equally frustrated that she didn't.

Many men honestly do not know what women want, and women hon-estly do not know why men find what they want so hard to comprehend and deliver.

"TALK TO ME!"

Women's dissatisfaction with men's silence at home is captured in the stock cartoon setting of a breakfast table at which a husband and wife are sitting: He's reading a newspaper; she's glaring at the back of the newspaper. In a Dagwood strip, Blondie complains, "Every morning all he sees is the news-paper! I'll bet you don't even know I'm here!" Dagwood reassures her, "Of course I know you're here. You're my wonderful wife and I love you very much." With this, he unseeingly pats the paw of the family dog, which the wife has put in her place before leaving the room. The cartoon strip shows that Blondie is justified in feeling like the woman who wrote to Ann Landers: invisible.

Another cartoon shows a husband opening a newspaper and asking his wife, "Is there anything you would like to say to me before I begin reading the newspaper?" The reader knows that there isn't—but that as soon as he begins reading the paper, she will think of something. The cartoon highlights the difference in what women and men think talk is for: To him, talk is for information. So when his wife interrupts his reading, it must be to inform him of something that he needs to know. This being the case, she might as well tell him what she thinks he needs to know before he starts reading. But to her, talk is for interaction. Telling things is a way to show involvement, and listening is a way to show interest and caring. It is not an odd coincidence that she always thinks of things to tell him when he is reading. She feels the need for verbal interaction most keenly when he is (unaccountably, from her point of view) buried in the newspaper instead of talking to her.

Yet another cartoon shows a wedding cake that has, on top, in place of the plastic statues of bride and groom in tuxedo and gown, a breakfast scene in which an unshaven husband reads a newspaper across the table from his disgruntled wife. The cartoon reflects the enormous gulf between the romantic expectations of marriage represented by the plastic couple in traditional wedding costume, and the often disappointing reality represented by the two sides of the newspaper at the breakfast table—the front, which he is reading, and the back, at which she is glaring.

These cartoons, and many others on the same theme, are funny because people recognize their own experience in them. What's not funny is that many women are deeply hurt when men don't talk to them at home, and many men are deeply frustrated by feeling they have disappointed their partners, without understanding how they failed or how else they could have behaved.

Some men are further frustrated because, as one put it, "When in the world am I supposed to read the morning paper?" If many women are incredulous that many men do not exchange personal information with their friends, this man is incredulous that many women do not bother to read the morning paper. To him, reading the paper is an essential part of his morning ritual, and his whole day is awry if he doesn't get to read it. In his words, reading the newspaper in the morning is as important to him as putting on makeup in the morning is to many women he knows. Yet many women, he observed, either don't subscribe to a paper or don't read it until they get home in the evening. "I find this very puzzling," he said. "I can't tell you how often I have picked up a woman's morning newspaper from her front door in the evening and handed it to her when she opened the door for me."

To this man (and I am sure many others), a woman who objects to his reading the morning paper is trying to keep him from doing something essential and harmless. It's a violation of his independence—his freedom of action. But when a woman who expects her partner to talk to her is disappointed that he doesn't she perceives his behavior as a failure of intimacy: He's keeping things from her; he's lost interest in her; he's pulling away. A woman I will call Rebecca, who is generally quite happily married, told me that this is the one source of serious dissatisfaction with her husband, Stuart. Her term for his taciturnity is *stinginess of spirit*. She tells him what she is thinking, and he listens silently. She asks him what he is thinking, and he takes a long time to answer, "I don't know," In frustration she challenges, "Is there nothing on your mind?"

For Rebecca, who is accustomed to expressing her fleeting thoughts and opinions as they come to her, *saying* nothing means *thinking* nothing. But Stuart does not assume that his passing thoughts are worthy of utterance. He is not in the habit of uttering his fleeting ruminations, so just as Rebecca "naturally" speaks her thoughts, he "naturally" dismisses his as soon as they occur to him. Speaking them would give them more weight and significance than he feels they merit. All her life she has had practice in verbalizing her thoughts and feelings in private conversations with people she is close to; all his life he has had practice in dismissing his and keeping them to himself.

WHAT TO DO WITH DOUBTS

In the above example, Rebecca was not talking about any particular kind of thoughts or feelings, just whatever Stuart might have had in mind. But the matter of giving voice to thoughts and feelings becomes particularly significant in the case of negative feelings or doubts about a relationship. This difference was highlighted for me when a fifty-year-old divorced man told me about his experiences in forming new relationships with women. On this matter, he was clear: "I do not value my fleeting thoughts, and I do not value the fleeting thoughts of others." He felt that the relationship he was currently in had been endangered, even permanently weakened, by the woman's practice of tossing out her passing thoughts, because, early in their courtship, many of her thoughts were fears about their relationship. Not surprisingly, since they did not yet know each other well, she worried about whether she could trust him, whether their relationship would destroy her independence, whether this relationship was really right for her. He felt she should have kept these fears and doubts to herself and waited to see how things turned out.

As it happens, things turned out well. The woman decided that the relationship was right for her, she could trust him, and she did not have to give up her independence. But he felt, at the time that he told me of this, that he had still not recovered from the wear and tear of coping with her earlier doubts. As he put it, he was still dizzy from having been bounced around like a yo-yo tied to the string of her stream of consciousness.

In contrast, this man admitted, he himself goes to the other extreme: He never expresses his fears and misgivings about their relationship at all. If he's unhappy but doesn't say anything about it, his unhappiness expresses itself in a kind of distancing coldness. This response is just what women fear most, and just the reason they prefer to express dissatisfactions and doubts—as an antidote to the isolation and distance that would result from keeping them to themselves.

The different perspectives on expressing or concealing dissatisfactions and doubts may reflect a difference in men's and women's awareness of the power of their words to affect others. In repeatedly telling him what she feared about their relationship, this woman spoke as though she assumed he was invulnerable and could not be hurt by what she said; perhaps she was underestimating the power of her words to affect him. For his part when he refrains from expressing negative thoughts or feelings, he seems to be over-estimating the power of his words to hurt her, when, ironically, she is more likely to be hurt by his silence than his words.

These women and men are talking in ways they learned as children and reinforced as young adults and then adults, in their same-gender friendships. For girls, talk is the glue that holds relationships together. Boys' relationships are held together primarily by activities: doing things together, or talking about activities such as sports or, later, politics. The forums in which men are most inclined to talk are those in which they feel the need to impress, in situations where their status is in question.

MAKING ADJUSTMENTS

Such impasses will perhaps never be settled to the complete satisfaction of both parties, but understanding the differing views can help detoxify the situation, and both can make adjustments. Realizing that men and women have different assumptions about the place of talk in relationships, a woman can observe a man's desire to read the morning paper at the breakfast table without interpreting it as a rejection of her or a failure of their relationship. And a man can understand a woman's desire for talk without interpreting it as an unreasonable demand or a manipulative attempt to prevent him from doing what he wants to do.

A woman who had heard my interpretations of these differences between women and men told me how these insights helped her. Early in a promising relationship, a man spent the night at her apartment. It was a weeknight, and they both had to go to work the next day, so she was delighted when he made the rash and romantic suggestion that they have breakfast together and report late for work. She happily prepared breakfast, looking forward to the scene shaped in her mind: They would sit facing each other across her small table, look into each other's eyes, and say how much they liked each other and how happy they were about their growing friendship. It was against the backdrop of this heady expectation that she confronted an entirely different scene: As she placed on the table an array of lovingly prepared eggs, toast, and coffee, the man sat across her small table— and opened the newspaper in front of his face. If suggesting they have breakfast together had seemed like an invitation to get closer, in her view (or obstructing her view) the newspaper was now erected as a paper-thin but nonetheless impenetrable barrier between them.

Had she known nothing of the gender differences I discuss, she would simply have felt hurt and dismissed this man as yet another clunker. She would have concluded that, having enjoyed the night with her, he was now availing himself of her further services as a short-order cook. Instead, she realized that, unlike her, he did not feel the need for talk to reinforce their intimacy. The companionability of her presence was all he needed, and that did not mean that he didn't cherish her presence. By the same token, had he understood the essential role played by talk in women's definition of intimacy, he could have put off reading the paper—and avoided putting her off.

THE COMFORT OF HOME

For everyone, home is a place to be offstage. But the comfort of home can have opposite and incompatible meanings for women and men. For many men, the comfort of home means freedom from having to prove themselves and impress through verbal display. At last, they are in a situation where talk is not required. They are free to remain silent. But for women, home is a place where they are free to talk, and where they feel the greatest need for talk, with those they are closest to. For them, the comfort of home means the freedom to talk without worrying about how their talk will be judged.

This view emerged in a study by linguist Alice Greenwood of the conversations that took place among her three preadolescent children and their friends. Her daughters and son gave different reasons for their preferences in dinner guests. Her daughter Stacy said she would not want to invite people she didn't know well because then she would have to be "polite and quiet" and put on good manners. Greenwood's other daughter, Denise, said she liked to have her friend Meryl over because she could act crazy with Meryl and didn't have to worry about her manners, as she would with certain other friends who "would go around talking to people probably." But Denise's twin brother, Dennis, said nothing about having to watch his manners or worry about how others would judge his behavior. He simply said that he liked to have over friends with whom he could joke and laugh a lot. The girls' comments show that for them being close means being able to talk freely. And being with relative strangers means having to watch what they say and do. This insight holds a clue to the riddle of who talks more, women or men.

PUBLIC SPEAKING: THE TALKATIVE MAN
AND THE SILENT WOMAN

So far I have been discussing the private scenes in which many men are silent and many women are talkative. But there are other scenes in which the roles are reversed. Returning to Rebecca and Stuart, we saw that when they are home alone, Rebecca's thoughts find their way into words effortlessly, whereas Stuart finds he can't come up with anything to say. The reverse happens when they are in other situations. For example, at a meeting of the neighborhood council or the parents' association at their children's school, it is Stuart who stands up and speaks. In that situation, it is Rebecca who is silent, her tongue tied by an acute awareness of all the negative reactions people could have to what she might say, all the mistakes she might make in trying to express her ideas. If she musters her courage and prepares to say something, she needs time to formulate it and then waits to be recognized by the chair. She cannot just jump up and start talking the way Stuart and some other men can.

Eleanor Smeal, president of the Fund for the Feminist Majority, was a guest on a call-in radio talk show, discussing abortion. No subject could be of more direct concern to women, yet during the hour-long show, all the callers except two were men. Diane Rehm, host of a radio talk show, expresses puzzlement that although the audience for her show is evenly split between women and men, 90 percent of the callers to the show are men. I am convinced that the reason is not that women are uninterested in the subjects discussed on the show. I would wager that women listeners are bringing up the subjects they heard on *The Diane Rehm Show* to their friends and family over lunch, tea, and dinner. But fewer of them call in because to do so would be putting themselves on display, claiming public attention for what they have to say, catapulting themselves onto center stage.

I myself have been the guest on innumerable radio and television talk shows. Perhaps I am unusual in being completely at ease in this mode of display. But perhaps I am not unusual at all, because, although I am comfortable in the role of invited expert, I have never called in to a talk show I was listening to, although I have often had ideas to contribute. When I am the guest, my position of authority is granted before I begin to speak. Were I to call in, I would be claiming that right on my own. I would have to establish my credibility by explaining who I am, which might seem self-aggrandizing, or not explain who I am and risk having my comments ignored or not valued. For similar reasons, though I am comfortable lecturing to groups numbering in the thousands, I rarely ask questions following another lecturer's talk, unless I know both the subject and the group very well.

My own experience and that of talk show hosts seems to hold a clue to the difference in women's and men's attitudes toward talk: Many men are more comfortable than most women in using talk to claim attention. And this difference lies at the heart of the distinction between report-talk and rapport-talk.

REPORT-TALK IN PRIVATE

Report-talk, or what I am calling public speaking, does not arise only in the literally public situation of formal speeches delivered to a listening audience. The more people there are in a conversation, the less well you know them, and the more status differences among them, the more a conversation is *like* public speaking or report-talk. The fewer the people, the more intimately you know them, and the more equal their status, the more it is like private speaking or rapport-talk. Furthermore, women feel a situation is more "public"—in the sense that they have to be on good behavior—if there are men present, except perhaps for family members. Yet even in families, the mother and children may feel their home to be "backstage" when Father is not home, "onstage" when he is: Many children are instructed to be on good behavior when Daddy is home. This may be because he is not home often, or because Mother—or Father—doesn't want the children to disturb him when he is.

The difference between public and private speaking also explains the stereotype that women don't tell jokes. Although some women are great raconteurs who can keep a group spellbound by recounting jokes and funny stories, there are fewer such personalities among women than among men. Many women who do tell jokes to large groups of people come from ethnic backgrounds in which verbal performance is highly valued. For example, many of the great women stand-up comics, such as Fanny Brice and Joan Rivers, came from Jewish backgrounds.

Although it's not true that women don't tell jokes, it is true that many women are less likely than men to tell jokes in large groups, especially groups including men. So it's not surprising that men get the impression that women never tell jokes at all. Folklorist Carol Mitchell studied joke telling on a college campus. She found that men told most of their jokes to other men, but they also told many jokes to mixed groups and to women. Women, however, told most of their jokes to other women, fewer to men, and very few to groups that included men as well as women. Men preferred and were more likely to tell jokes when they had an audience: at least two, often four or more. Women preferred a small audience of one or two, rarely more than three. Unlike men, they were reluctant to tell jokes in front of people they didn't know well. Many women flatly refused to tell jokes they knew if there were four or more in the group, promising to tell them later in private. Men never refused the invitation to tell jokes.

All of Mitchell's results fit in with the picture I have been drawing of public and private speaking. In a situation in which there are more people in the audience, more men, or more strangers, joke telling, like any other form of verbal performance, requires speakers to claim center stage and prove their abilities. These are the situations in which many women are reluctant to talk. In a situation that is more private, because the audience is small, familiar, and perceived to be members of a community (for example, other women), they are more likely to talk.

The idea that telling jokes is a kind of self-display does not imply that it is selfish or self-centered. The situation of joke telling illustrates that status and connection entail each other. Entertaining others is a way of establishing connections with them, and telling jokes can be a kind of gift giving, where the joke is a gift that brings pleasure to receivers. The key issue is asymmetry: One person is the teller and the others are the audience. If these roles are later exchanged—for example, if the joke telling becomes a round in which one person after another takes the role of teller—then there is symmetry on the broad scale, if not in the individual act. However, if women habitually take the role of appreciative audience and never take the role of joke teller, the asymmetry of the individual joke telling is diffused through the larger interaction as well. This is a hazard for women. A hazard for men is that continually telling jokes can be distancing. This is the effect felt by a man who complained that when he talks to his father on the phone, all his father does is tell him jokes. An extreme instance of a similar phenomenon is the class clown, who, according to teachers, is nearly always a boy.

RAPPORT-TALK IN PUBLIC

Just as conversations that take place at home among friends can be like public speaking, even a public address can be like private speaking: for example, by giving a lecture full of personal examples and stories.

At the executive committee of a fledgling professional organization, the outgoing president, Fran, suggested that the organization adopt the policy of having presidents deliver a presidential address. To explain and support her proposal, she told a personal anecdote: Her cousin was the president of a more established professional organization at the time that Fran held the same position in this one. Fran's mother had been talking to her cousin's mother on the telephone. Her cousin's mother told Fran's mother that her daughter was preparing her presidential address, and she asked when Fran's presidential address was scheduled to be. Fran was embarrassed to admit to her mother that she was not giving one. This made her wonder whether the organization's professional identity might not be enhanced if it emulated the more established organizations.

Several men on the committee were embarrassed by Fran's reference to her personal situation and were not convinced by her argument. It seemed to them not only irrelevant but unseemly to talk about her mother's telephone conversations at an executive committee meeting. Fran had approached the meeting—a relatively public context—as an extension of the private kind. Many women's tendency to use personal experience and examples, rather than abstract argumentation, can be understood from the perspective of their orientation to language as it is used in private speaking.

A study by Celia Roberts and Tom Jupp of a faculty meeting at a secondary school in England found that the women's arguments did not carry weight with their male colleagues because they tended to use their own experience as evidence, or argue about the effect of policy on individual students. The men at the meeting argued from a completely different perspective, making categorical statements about right and wrong.

The same distinction is found in discussions at home. A man told me that he felt critical of what he perceived as his wife's lack of logic. For example, he recalled a conversation in which he had mentioned an article he had read in *The New York Times* claiming that today's college students are not as idealistic as students were in the 1960s. He was inclined to accept this claim. His wife questioned it, supporting her argument with the observation that her niece and her niece's friends were very idealistic indeed. He was incredulous and scornful of her faulty reasoning; it was obvious to him that a single personal example is neither evidence nor argumentation—it's just anecdote. It did not occur to him that he was dealing with a different logical system, rather than a lack of logic.

The logic this woman was employing was making sense of the world as a more private endeavor—observing and integrating her personal experience and drawing connections to the experiences of others. The logic the husband took for granted was a more public endeavor—more like gathering information, conducting a survey, or devising arguments by rules of formal logic as one might in doing research.

Another man complained about what he and his friends call women's "shifting sands" approach to discussion. These men feel that whereas they try to pursue an argument logically, step by step, until it is settled, women continually change course in midstream. He pointed to the short excerpt from *Divorce American Style* quoted above as a case in point. It seemed to him that when Debbie Reynolds said, "I can't argue now. I have to take the French bread out of the oven," she was evading the argument because she had made an accusation—"All you do is criticize" that she could not support.

This man also offered an example from his own experience. His girlfriend had told him of a problem she had because her boss wanted her to do one thing and she wanted to do another. Taking the boss's view for the sake of argumentation, he pointed out a negative consequence that would result if she did what she wanted. She countered that the same negative consequence would result if she did what the boss wanted. He complained that she was shifting over to the other field of battle—what would happen if she followed her boss's will—before they had made headway with the first—what would happen if she followed her own.

SPEAKING FOR THE TEAM

A final puzzle on the matter of public and private speaking is suggested by the experience I related at the opening of this chapter, in which a woman's group I addressed had invited men to participate, and a talkative man had referred to his silent wife as "the talker in our family." Following their laughter, other women in the group commented that this woman was not usually silent. When their meetings consisted of women only, she did her share of talking. Why, then, was she silent on this occasion?

One possibility is that my presence transformed the private-speaking group into a public-speaking event. Another transformation was that there were men in the group. In a sense, most women feel they are "backstage" when there are no men around. When men are present women are "onstage," insofar as they feel they must watch their behavior more. Another possibility is that it was not the presence of men in general that affected this woman's behavior, but the presence of *her husband*. One interpretation is that she was somehow cowed, or silenced, by her husband's presence. But another is that she felt they were a team. Since he was talking a lot, the team would be taking up too much time if she spoke too. She also may have felt that because he was representing their team, she didn't have to, much as many women let their husbands drive if they are in the car, but do the driving themselves if their husbands are not there.

Obviously, not every woman becomes silent when her husband joins a group; after all, there were many women in the group who talked a lot, and many had brought spouses. But several other couples told me of similar experiences. For example, when one couple took evening classes together, he was always an active participant in class discussion, while she said very little. But one semester they had decided to take different classes, and then she found that she was a talkative member of the class she attended alone.

Such a development can be viewed in two different ways. If talking in a group is a good thing—a privilege and a pleasure—then the silent woman will be seen as deprived of her right to speak, deprived of her voice. But the pleasures of report-talk are not universally admired. There are many who do not wish to speak in a group. In this view, a woman who feels she has no need to speak because her husband is doing it for her might feel privileged, just as a woman who does not like to drive might feel lucky that she doesn't have to when her husband is there—and a man who does not like to drive might feel unlucky that he has to, like it or not.

AVOIDING MUTUAL BLAME

The difference between public and private speaking, or report-talk and rapport-talk, can be understood in terms of status and connection. It is not surprising that women are most comfortable talking when they feel safe and close, among friends and equals whereas men feel comfortable talking when there is a need to establish and maintain their status in a group. But the situation is complex, because status and connection are bought with the same currency. What seems like a bid for status could be intended as a display of closeness, and what seems like distancing may have been intended to avoid the appearance of pulling rank. Hurtful and unjustified misinterpretations can be avoided by understanding the conversational styles of the other gender.

When men do all the talking at meetings, many women—including researchers—see them as "dominating" the meeting, intentionally preventing women from participating, publicly flexing their higher-status muscles. But the *result* that men do most of the talking does not necessarily mean that men *intend* to prevent women from speaking. Those who readily speak up assume that others are as free as they are to take the floor. In this sense, men's speaking out freely can be seen as evidence that they assume women are at the same level of status: "We are all equals," the metamessage of their behavior could be, "competing for the floor." If this is indeed the intention (and I believe it often, though not always, is), a woman can recognize women's lack of participation at meetings and take measures to redress the imbalance, without blaming men for intentionally locking them out.

The culprit, then, is not an individual man or even men's styles alone, but the difference between women's and men's styles. If that is the case, then both can make adjustments. A woman can push herself to speak up without being invited, or begin to speak without waiting for what seems a polite pause. But the adjustment should not be one-sided. A man can learn that a woman who is not accustomed to speaking up in groups is *not* as free as he is to do so. Someone who is waiting for a nice long pause before asking her question does not find the stage set for her appearance, as do those who are not awaiting a pause, the moment after (or before) another speaker stops talking. Someone who expects to be invited to speak ("You haven't said much, Millie. What do you think?") is not accustomed to leaping in and claiming the floor for herself. As in so many areas, being admitted as an equal is not in itself assurance of equal opportunity, if one is not accustomed to playing the game in the way it is being played. Being admitted to a dance does not ensure the participation of someone who has learned to dance to a different rhythm.

CHAPTER 23

Communication and Conflict

Evelyn Eaton Whitehead
James D. Whitehead

Enriching this section on communication, conflict, and change is the following essay by Evelyn and James Whitehead. Like so many of the other writers in this section, they situate conflict within the context of intimacy. In other words, conflict can be a means for greater intimacy—or, if handled poorly, for greater distance and alienation. The Whiteheads state clearly that any couple "can get better at being married" by getting better at the skills of intimacy. One of these is skill with confrontation and conflict.

This essay may well be a classic for its helpful way of explaining conflict's connection with communication and intimacy. It deserves careful study.

Questions for Discussion

1. What are the skills of intimacy and which of them seems to you most crucial?
2. Why is premature judgment so dangerous in confrontation?
3. How common is it for people to grow up "assuming love does away with conflict, that love and conflict are mutually exclusive"?
4. Do you think most people accept that "conflict is a normal, expectable ingredient in any relationship," including marriage?

In marriage we see intimacy in both its most inviting and its most challenging face. Our daily patterns of life—living together, working together, sleeping together—these are the substance of intimacy. Here we feel ourselves being tested and getting better at being "up close." To live well these "up close" patterns of marriage we need the resources of psychological maturity: a sense of who I am, an openness to others, a capacity for commitment, some tolerance for the ambiguity both in myself and in other people. But these resources may not be enough. Aptitudes for intimacy must be expressed in behavior. We must be able, in the give-and-take of our life together, to develop a lifestyle that is mutually satisfying. Our desire to be close must be expressed

Copyright © 1981 by Evelyn Eaton Whitehead and James D. Whitehead. Reprinted with permission.

in the way we act toward one another. It is encouraging to know that we can get better at being married. We can learn more satisfying ways *for us* to be close; we can learn more effective ways to give and receive the gift of ourselves that is at the core of our married love. And among the most valuable resources for this growth in marriage are the skills of intimate living.

THE SKILLS OF INTIMACY

Over the past two decades there has been much interest in psychology and other disciplines in understanding better what happens in communication between people. As a result we are more clearly aware today of both what helps and what frustrates understanding in close relationships. Values and attitudes are important in our ability to live up close to others, but so, especially, is our behavior. There are skillful—that is, effective—ways to be with and behave toward one another. Interpersonal skills that are especially important to the intimate life of marriage include empathy, self-disclosure and confrontation. Each involves both attitudes and behaviors; each can contribute significantly to marriage for a lifetime.

Empathy enables me to understand another person from within that person's frame of reference. Empathy begins in an attitude of openness which enables me to set aside my own concerns and turn myself toward you. But this basic openness is not always sufficient. My capacity for empathy can be enhanced by my developing a range of behavioral skills. An accepting posture, attentive listening, sensitive paraphrasing—each of these can contribute to my effective presence to you.

My posture can give you important information about who you are to me and how important I judge your communication to be. If I appear distracted or edgy, if I keep glancing at my watch or rush to take an incoming phone call, I am likely to let you feel that you are not very important to me now. In the midst of the hectic schedules of most married couples today, it is often necessary to take steps to ensure the postures of presence: taking the time to sit down together to talk, finding ways to give each other some undivided attention, learning when to hold a personal concern until later and when to "stop everything" in order to deal with an issue now.

Learning to listen well to each other can be the most important skill of our marriage. To listen well is to listen actively, alert to the full context of the message—the words and silences, the emotions and ideas, the context in which our conversation takes place. To listen is to pay attention: paying attention is a receptive, but not a passive, attitude. If I cannot pay attention, it will be difficult for me to hear; if I do not listen, it will be difficult for me to understand and to respond effectively to you. The skills of active listening are those behaviors which enable me to be aware of your full message. This includes my being alert to your words and their nuances. But equally and often even more important are the non-verbal factors involved. Your tone of voice, your gestures, the timing, the emotional content—these may tell me more than the words between us. To listen actively, then, calls for an awareness of the content, the feelings and the context of our communication.

Sensitive paraphrasing is a skill of empathy as well. I show you that I understand you by saying back to you the essence of your message. To paraphrase is not merely to "parrot"—to repeat mechanically what you have just said. Rather I want to show you that I have really heard *you*, that I have been present not just to your words but to their deeper meaning for you. I go beyond the simple assurance that "I understand" by offering you a statement of what I have understood. You can then confirm that, in fact, I have understood you—or clarify your message so that my understanding may be more accurate. In either case, I demonstrate my respect for you and for your message. It is important to me that I understand what you say, and it is to you that I come to check my understanding.

Empathy, then, is my ability to understand your ideas, feelings and values from within your frame of reference. The goal of empathy is to understand; as such, it precedes evaluation. Empathy does not mean that I will always agree with you; it does not require that I accept your point of view as my own or even as "best" for you. I may well have to evaluate your ideas. We may well have to discuss and negotiate as we move toward a decision we can share. But these movements of evaluation and judgment come later in our communication. My first goal is to accurately understand you and what you are trying to say to me. Judgment and decision are not secondary in our communication but they are subsequent to accurate understanding.

Empathy is the practical ability to be present to another person. Its exercise is a discipline: if I am distracted by fatigue or agitated by fear I cannot be present to my spouse. As virtuous behavior, empathy depends on a (relatively) strong sense of my identity and vocation. I do not have to defend myself: being aware of and comfortable with who I am, I can give my full attention to another person. Empathy thus is the stuff of intimacy. Without some skill, some virtue here, it will be difficult for me to express my love for my partner. Finally, to speak of empathy as both a skill and a virtue is to remind us again that we can get better at it. A Christian spirituality or asceticism of marriage will include these efforts to learn to be more effectively present to those we most love.

The open stance of empathy does much to enhance communication in marriage. But communication involves more than receptivity. I must be able to speak as well as to listen; to initiate as well as to understand. Self-disclosure thus becomes an essential skill of intimacy. To share myself with you I must be able to overcome the hesitancy suggested by fear or doubt or shame. But these inhibitions overcome, I must be able to act in a way that gives you access to my mind and heart, in a way that is fitting for me and for our relationship. Appropriate self-disclosure can seem complicated. But I am not limited to my current level of success. I can become more skillful, learning better ways to express my values and needs, my ideas and feelings.

Self-disclosure begins in self-awareness. I must *know* what I have experienced, what I think, how I feel, what I need, what I want to do. This knowledge is not likely to be full and finished; an unwillingness to speak until I am completely sure of myself can be a trap in communication. Self-awareness is rather an ability to know where I am now, to be in touch with the dense and ambiguous information of my own life. Beyond knowing my own insights, needs and purposes, I must value them. This need not mean that I am convinced that they are "the best." It means rather that I take them seriously as deserving of examination and respect, from myself and from others as well. My feelings, my perceptions of myself and of the world—these have worth and weight. By valuing them myself I contribute to the possibility that they can be appreciated by others as well. My needs and purposes exist in a context of those of other people, to be sure. But a conviction that my own ideas and goals are of value is basic to mature self-disclosure.

An important skill of self-disclosure is my ability to speak concretely. I must be able to say "I," to acknowledge my own ideas and feelings. Self-disclosure can be thwarted by a retreat into speaking about "most people"; "everybody knows . . ." instead of "I think that . . ."; "most people want . . ." instead of "I need . . ."; "people have a hard time . . ." instead of "it is difficult for me to . . ." Beyond this willingness to "own" my experience, I can learn to provide more specific details about my actions and emotions. To share myself with you in our marriage I will need, for example, a well-nuanced vocabulary of feelings—one that goes well beyond "I feel good" and "I feel bad." To tell you that "I feel good" is to share some important information about myself but not yet very much. What does this mean for me? Is this good feeling one of confidence? or affection? or physical vigor? Does it result from something I have done or something that has been done for me? Are you an important part of this good feeling for me or are you really incidental to it? My self-disclosure becomes more concrete when I can name my feelings more precisely and when I can describe the events and actions that are part of them for me.

Confrontation, too, makes a critical contribution to intimacy in marriage. For most of us the word "confrontation" implies conflict. And, as we shall see shortly, the ability to deal well with conflict between us is an important skill of marriage. But we use the word "confrontation" here in a meaning that goes beyond its narrow and, most often, negative connotation as interpersonal conflict. The ability to confront involves the psychological strength to give (and to receive) emotionally significant information in ways that lead to further exploration rather than to self-defense. Sometimes the emotionally significant information is more positive than negative. To say "I love you" is to share with you emotionally significant information. And many of us know how confrontive it is to learn of another's love for us. Similarly, to give a compliment is to share emotionally significant information, and there are people who defend themselves against this "good news" as strongly as others of us defend ourselves against an accusation of blame. But most often, to be sure, when confrontation becomes necessary and difficult in our marriage, it is because there is negative information we must share with our spouse. It may be some practical issue of daily life that we must face—the use of the automobile, our bank balance, plans for next summer's vacation. The issues, however, may be more sensitive—the way you discipline the children, my parents' influence in our home, how satisfying is our sex life.

Skills of confrontation are those behaviors that make it more likely that our sharing of significant negative information in these instances will lead us to explore the difficulty between us rather than to defend ourselves against one another. My ability to confront effectively is enhanced when I am able to speak descriptively rather than judgmentally. To tell you that I missed my meeting because you came home late is to *describe*; to call you a selfish and inconsiderate person is to *judge*. While both may be hard for you to hear from me, one is more likely to escalate into a quarrel than is the other. As we have noted before, judgment is not irrelevant in marriage, but premature judgment is likely to short-circuit the process of exploration and mutual understanding. Perhaps there are extenuating circumstances that caused you to be late; perhaps you are genuinely sorry that you inconvenienced me and want to do something to make amends. My attack on your selfishness is not likely to leave room for this kind of response on your side. It is more likely to lead you to defend yourself against my accusation, perhaps by calling up instances of my own selfishness, perhaps by leaving the scene altogether. In neither case has communication between us been furthered.

There are other behaviors that make our confrontation more effective, that is, more likely to further communication between us. These include the ability to accept feelings of anger in myself and in you and the ability to show respect for you even as I must disagree with you or challenge your position. These skills become especially important in dealing with conflict in marriage.

CONFLICT AND LOVE

Conflict is an aspect of Christian marriage about which our rhetoric can be misleading. In ceremonies and sermons about marriage, it is upon images of unity and peace and joy that we dwell. These images of life together in Christian marriage are important and true, but partial. When, as a believing community, we do not speak concretely to the more ambiguous experiences in marriage—experiences of anger, frustration, misunderstanding—we can leave many married people feeling that their marriages are somehow deficient.

Conflict and hostility are not goals of marriage, to be sure. But neither are they an indication that our marriage is "on the rocks." Conflict is a normal, expectable ingredient in any relationship—whether marriage, teamwork or friendship—that brings people "up close" and engages them at the level of their significant values and needs. The challenge in close relationships is not to do away with all signs of conflict or, worse, to refuse to admit that conflicts arise between us. Rather we can learn ways to recognize the potential areas of conflict *for us* and to deal with these issues and feelings in ways that strengthen rather than destroy the bonds between us.

Conflict is normal in interpersonal exchange; it is an expectable event in the intimate lifestyle of marriage. Whenever people come together in an ongoing way, especially if significant issues are involved, we can expect that they will become aware of differences that exist between them. Sometimes these differences will be simply noted as interesting. But often they will involve disagreements, misunderstanding and discord. It is here that the experience of conflict begins.

Marriage engages each of us at a level of our most significant values and needs. My sense of who I am, my convictions, my ideas and ideals, what I hope to make of my life—in our marriage all these are open to confirmation or to challenge and change. In addition, every marriage is a complex pattern of interaction and expectation. We develop our own way of being together and apart; we come to our own understanding of what each of us gives and receives in this relationship. The process through which we develop the patterns of our own marriage is ongoing. We can expect times of relative stability when the rhythms of our life together seem to fit especially well. We can also expect periods marked by significant adjustment and change. The process of marriage includes this continuing exploration, even trial and error, as we attempt to learn more about ourselves and our partner. It is these normal and even inevitable experiences of personal challenge and mutual change in marriage that set the stage for conflict.

Conflict is a response to discrepancy or disparity. "Things are not as I expected or as I want them to be." In interpersonal conflict the other person is seen as somehow involved in, or responsible for, this discrepancy. "You are not as I expected; it is your fault that things are not as I want them to be." Marriage brings us together in so many ways, as friends and lovers as parents and householders, in cooperation and competition, in practical decisions about our money and our time. These overlapping issues give us many opportunities both to meet and to fail each other's expectations. Thus discrepancy and conflict are predictable.

This predictability of conflict in marriage is not simply a cause for concern. Conflict is not "all bad." Its effects in intimacy are not simply or necessarily destructive. As many marriage counselors know, conflict is as often a sign of health in a relationship as it is a symptom of disease. The presence of conflict between us indicates that we are about something that is of value to us both. Conflict thus marks a relationship of some force. This energy can be harnessed; it need not always work against us. A marriage in which there is nothing important enough to fight about is more likely to die than one in which arguments occur. Indifference is a greater enemy of intimacy than is conflict.

Many of us have grown up assuming that love does away with conflict, that love and conflict are mutually exclusive. But this romantic view of love is challenged by our experience of tension in our own marriage. We come to know conflict as a powerful dynamic in our relationship and one with ambiguous effect. For most of us, it is the negative effects of conflict that we know best and fear. Conflict feels bad and seems to have bad results. To be in conflict seems like a move away from intimacy. I am angry or hurt, you feel rejected or resentful. And most often my own past experience reinforces the unpleasant conclusion that conflict leads to the disintegration of relationships. Sometimes the relationship ends immediately; sometimes it continues, but with a burden of bitterness and unhealed grievances that ultimately leads to its death. In the face of this negative sense of the power of conflict, the evidence that it is expectable and even inevitable in our marriage is likely to strike us with alarm.

CONFLICT CAN BE CONSTRUCTIVE

But these negative results of conflict do not give the full picture. Conflict can make a constructive contribution to our marriage. It can bring us to a more nuanced appreciation of who each of us is; it can test and strengthen the bonds that exist between us; it can deepen our capacity for mutual trust.

The experience of conflict points to an area of discrepancy between us. I am uncomfortable with the way you discipline our oldest child; you don't like me to let my new job interfere with our weekends together as a family; I no longer want to be "the perfect housewife and mother," though this is the way you have always seen me; you no longer want to be "the strong and self-sufficient male," though you know it frightens me to see your weakness.

If we are willing to face the conflict, we may be able to learn from the experience of discrepancy that is at its root. Exploring this discrepancy—between what I want from you and what you are able to give, or between who I am and who you need me to be, or between our differing views about money or privacy or sex or success—we can come to know one another more fully. We can grow toward a greater and more respectful mutuality, based on a greater awareness and respect for who each of us really is.

Conflict is not necessarily a part of every development in marriage. Some changes are accompanied more by a sense of fulfillment than frustration. Some couples are open to the processes of mutual exploration in such a way that there is little sense of discrepancy and little experience of conflict between them. But change is frequently a source of confusion and conflict, even if only temporarily. A relationship that cannot face at least the possibility of conflict will soon be in trouble. In order to ensure the conflict will not arise between us, we may decide that our relationship should touch us only minimally, in areas where we are not vitally concerned. Or we may believe that we must be willing to disown our response to the concerns that do matter to us. But to disown conflict does not strengthen a relationship. It tends instead to have us look away from part of the reality that exists between us. But the reality that is there—the troublesome concern that stands beneath the conflict—does not go away. The discrepancy remains, unattended, as a likely source of more serious trouble between us in the future.

We may know from previous experiences that conflict, faced poorly, can lead to resentment and recrimination. But not to face it does not ensure that our marriage will be free of these negative emotions. A more useful stance involves our willingness to face the conflicts that may arise between us, aware of their ambiguous power both to destroy and to deepen the love we share. This willingness to accept conflict as inevitable and even as potentially valuable need not mean that we find it pleasant to be at odds. But it does mean that we are willing to acknowledge and even tolerate this discomfort that conflict brings, in view of the valuable information it provides about our relationship and ourselves.

The experience of facing together the conflicts that arise between us can give greater confidence, an increased security in the strength and flexibility of the commitment between us, since we have seen it tested and found it sufficient to the test. Conflict can have this positive effect in a relationship but it remains a powerful and ambiguous dynamic. Just as the presence of conflict does not necessarily or automatically signal a relationship in trouble, neither does it necessarily or automatically result in new learning or growth. Whether the expectable event of conflict in our marriage will have positive or negative effect is due in large part to how we respond to it. To deal well with the ambiguous power of conflict we must first appreciate that conflict can be more than just negative between us. We must believe that the benefits of working through our conflict are worth the trouble and discomfort that attend. We must both have the resources of personal maturity that enable us to face strong emotion and to look at ourselves anew and possibly change. And we must have the skills that enable us to deal effectively with one another even in the heat of our disagreement.

CHAPTER 24

Communication

Thomas N. Hart
Kathleen Fischer Hart

Thomas and Kathleen Hart begin this essay on communication with a tale of conflict in Tony and Sue's marriage. Their conflicts are similar to those of many couples who are dating or even engaged.

Behind the Harts' eleven hints for communication lies an assumption that we can change our basic patterns of communicating if we are willing to try and if there are others to help us. One of the hardest lessons of life comes in realizing that nobody can force another person to change. You can encourage the person, but change can only come from the person him- or herself. This means that we ourselves have to face our own willingness to change so as to become a more trustworthy and loving gift to others.

The eleven techniques, or "hints," offered here need to be practiced. A person who wants to develop these as skills might ask a close friend to help. They could practice them together. This essay, like so many others in this book, is meant to be shared with those we love and with whom we are trying to improve communication.

Questions for Discussion

1. The authors stress that in marriage two people pledge to each other "the gift of the self," which "always involves the disclosure of feelings," including ones we may find difficult to communicate. This raises the question of whether the disclosure of feelings may be just as difficult before a marriage—say, during dating or engagement—as afterward. Which feelings would you say are most difficult to communicate in dating? Why are these particular feelings so difficult to express?

2. This essay offers eleven hints to help foster the art of communication in intimate relationships. If you were to pick a small number of these—say, five or fewer—that are more important than the others, what would they be and why do you pick them?

3. The Harts seek to make us much more aware of how we actually go about communicating to others. Considering that our patterns of communicating are learned as habits in childhood interaction with parents, what chances do you think we have of changing them? For example, how do you react to the

common defense: "This is how I am; I can't change; you have to accept me as I am"?

W hen Tony and Sue came in for counseling, they had been married five years and had two children. But things were not going at all well. At a recent workshop for couples, the two of them had been asked to recall one or two of the peak experiences of their marriage, and Tony could not think of any. He wondered if he was just so angry that his recall of anything good was blocked. As we talked, the roots of the anger were gradually uncovered. Tony summed up the problem this way: "Sue never understands me, and so she always reacts in the wrong way. But you know, the reason she doesn't understand me is that I have never really let her know me." Sue chimed in and said: "Everything he said is true. What's worse, he doesn't understand me either. And that's my fault, because I've held back too. So you can imagine what our guessing-game interaction is like." They went on to say that it had been like this from the beginning.

This clear analysis of their problem, offered by the couple themselves, set the agenda for counseling. The task was to assist them to begin to talk to one another about what was going on deep inside, to open out their inner worlds to one another. The heart of that was to get them expressing how they felt about themselves, each other, and the myriad situations of their lives. Tony admitted that the reason he held himself in was that he did not like himself very much, and he found it much easier to remain crouched behind his wall sniping at Sue than to come out from behind it and let her see who he was. To do the latter would be to make himself vulnerable, to admit hurt, weakness, inadequacy, and need, and to put the truth in Sue's hands for her to deal with. That required a degree of courage he had long been unable to muster.

We talk in Christian terms of the gift of the self. In marriage, that is what two Christians pledge to one another. It is *the* great gift of love. Many married people stay with one another and serve each other in many ways. But this is not yet the gift of the *self*, which can only be given if one is willing to open one's heart to the other. One can do many external deeds of love and still hold back the really precious gift, the inner self. This gift can be given only through communication. It costs, like all of the better gifts. But union between two persons is hardly possible if they have not let each other into their inner worlds. This always involves the disclosure of feelings.

Some feelings are harder to communicate than others. Some people, for some reason, find it next to impossible to say "I love you." Many people, especially men, find it difficult to admit their fears, their sense of failure, or their sadness. Some find it hard to affirm others, to give positive feedback.

Reprinted from *The First Two Years of Marriage* by Thomas N. Hart and Kathleen Fischer Hart. Copyright © 1983 by Thomas N. Hart and Kathleen Fischer Hart. Used by permission of Paulist Press.

Husbands stop telling their wives that they are beautiful, saying, "She already knows that," or "It would go to her head." We have yet to meet someone who does not need to be told the good things over and over (and even then still doubts it), or whose head is in much danger of an over-swell from too much affirmation. But there is another reason why people hold in their feelings in marriage. They care about their mates and do not want to hurt them. So they do not express dissatisfaction, irritation, or any other uncomfortable feelings.

What happens in an intimate relationship when unconfortable feelings are held in? Terrible outbursts from time to time, when feelings reach the breaking point. A note on the kitchen table announcing the divorce. Or, in milder forms, sarcasm, silence, and various forms of subtle punishment. One thing is certain. If people cannot deal with their anger, they cannot be intimate either. You either have a relationship in which there are angry exchanges at times and warm closeness at others (often shortly after the angry exchange), or you have a relationship in which all is smooth on the surface but the psychological distance is unbridged. In these latter relationships there arc several forbidden subjects and an abundance of silence.

In intimate relationships, communication is the foundational skill. There is none more basic. It is the indispensable condition of union. It is the key to resolving conflict. It is the only way two people can continue growing together, or even living together.

The question is: How do you do it? It is an art, and it takes time to cultivate. The following are eleven hints to point the way.

1. *Use I-statements rather than You-statements.* Talk about yourself rather than your mate. Don't say things like, "*You* never care about anybody but yourself," or "*You* think you know everything all the time," or "*You* never do anything around here." Say instead, "*I* often feel lonely," or "Sometimes *I* feel put down by things you say," or "*I* feel overburdened with household chores and sometimes *I* resent it because it doesn't seem fair to me." Talk about yourself, in other words, and your feelings, in response to concrete behaviors for your mate. Do that instead of making judgments about your mate ("You're always flirting"; "You're so damn sure about everything") or giving commands ("Get out of here"; "Why don't you loosen up once in a while?").

The approach we are suggesting is risky because it exposes you. But it has many distinct advantages. It does not make your mate so defensive, and so it gives you a better chance of getting a hearing and an honest response. It lets your mate in on your inner world, and so reveals important information. It does not pronounce judgment about who is wrong, but leaves the question open. For instance, if I am bothered by the way you socialize at parties, it may indeed be your fault. But it could just as well be mine. Maybe I am very insecure, and cling too much, and am very easily threatened and jealous. Maybe I misinterpret what you are doing. If I find you overly emotional, it may be that you are. But it may also be that I am emotionally repressed and uncomfortable with the expression of feelings, or simply that I feel inadequate to meeting the needs you make known to me. When I stay with my own feelings, owning them and letting you know them, I let you know me and I leave the question open about who should do what. We can work on that together. "I feel uncomfortable around your dad" is not yet a comment about your dad, still less about you. So far, it is just an informative comment about me.

Talking about your mate is legitimate to this extent: As far as possible, tie your feeling statements to your mate's concrete *behaviors*. "When you come in without saying hello, I feel unloved." "I start to feel insecure when I see you having a good time with another man." You are talking here just about concrete *behaviors*, externally observable. You are not guessing at your mate's *feelings* or *intentions*, which are hidden from view.

There are four basic I-statements which carry most of the weight in an intimate relationship. They are: (1) I think, (2) I feel, (3) I want, and (4) I need. All of them are positive steps in self-assertion and indicate an underlying self-respect. All of them make me vulnerable to you. They do not state what is right, nor do they make a demand. They simply tell you who I am and what is going on with me right now. If you are willing to make a similar self-revelation, we have the materials for really learning to care for one another.

2. *Express feelings rather than thoughts.* Not that it is bad to express thoughts. There is plenty of scope for those too. But our feelings reveal more of who we are. One can sit for an entire course before many professors, and know a good deal of their thought and almost nothing of who they are. A wife expressed this eloquently once, saying that everything her husband said to her could be said on television. He was an engineer, and lived much more in the realm of thought than of feeling. He was not untalkative, but she was always left wondering what was going on inside. It is in expressing our feelings that we give the gift of the self. That was the gift she was still waiting for.

People sometimes hide their feelings behind their thoughts. "A woman's place is in the home" is an apparent statement of principle, but it may be a man's way of saying that he feels he has failed as a provider if his wife takes a job outside the home, or that he fears he will lose her if she has much occasion to be with other men. Those are feelings. "Should" statements can also be masks. "You should enjoy sex" is probably best translated "I enjoy sex," or "I feel inadequate as a lover when you don't seem to enjoy sex, or hurt when you turn me down." In more open communication, people just talk about their feelings, not about the eternal order of things (as they see it), or the commonsense truths embraced by all (but you). Most of our feelings, after all, come out of our cultural relativity.

Some people are not very aware of their feelings. You cannot communicate what you do not know. To develop a greater awareness of feelings, it is a helpful exercise to go inside yourself from time to time during the day, inquiring what you are feeling right now. Watch the variations in typical situations: talking with your child, talking with the boss, hearing the phone ring, approaching the front door at home, waking up in the morning, watching TV at night, going about your daily work, getting into bed at night. Move gradually from becoming more aware of feelings to becoming more expressive of them.

3. *Listen attentively without interrupting.* Good communication requires more than good talking. It demands good listening too. Listening is difficult. It requires setting other things aside, even the ruminations of the mind. It is especially hard when we do not like what we are hearing, or when we think we have heard it all before. One of the things a marriage counselor does most frequently is stop married partners from interrupting each other, suggesting instead a three-step process which can revolutionize the way they talk to each other: (a) listen without interrupting; (b) say back what you heard, and check it out; (c) respond to it.

In poor communication, the listeners are working on their responses instead of listening, and cut in to make them as soon as they are ready. In the approach suggested here, you have to listen closely or you will not be able to say back what you heard. This is how you make sure you got the message. There are often surprises here, as the original speaker makes the necessary corrections. Then you can respond. This may seem cumbersome and time-consuming. But if you really get your mate's message, and respond to it rather than to something else, you end up saving time. And your mate has the gratifying feeling of being heard, even if you end up differing. If two people are in the habit of interrupting each other as they argue back and forth, the entire time is probably being wasted. Neither is listening. Neither is open. Nothing is being produced except more bad feeling.

4. *Check out what you see and hear.* Part of this is summarizing what you hear your mate saying and asking if that is the message. It keeps the conversation on track. But there are other parts to this checking out too. Listen for the feelings behind the words, and check those out. Listen for anger and frustration. Listen for loneliness. Listen for fear. And test what you think you hear, saying, for example, "You sound weary," or, "You sound as if this is really hard for you to tell me." This approach is especially useful with people who do not express feelings directly, but prefer to make statements of fact, pronounce judgments of good and bad, and give direct or indirect commands. You cannot get them to play by your rules. If you say, "Don't make judgments; tell me your feelings," you have given them a command instead of expressing your frustration and leaving them free. Even if they persist in their usual ways, you can listen for the feelings behind the words, and check those out.

Checking out can be useful outside of times of conversation. You come home, and seem tired, discouraged, or distant. But I am not sure. Mostly you are silent. If I want to relate to you appropriately—giving you space, encouraging you, or inviting you to unburden yourself—I have to know what you are feeling. I can ask the open question, "How are you doing?" Or I can check out my impressions: "You seem distant." Or, "You look as if you had a hard day."

Such an approach invites mates to express themselves. The ideal situation would be that they would volunteer this information, and ask for what they need. But the situation is not always ideal.

5. *Avoid mind-reading.* Mind-reading is the attempt to reach inside the sanctuary of the other person's psyche and declare what is going on there. You tell others what they are feeling or what their motives are. "You're saying that because you're jealous." "You're just telling me what you think I want to hear." This kind of statement almost always gets an angry reaction. It deserves it. The statement is a violation of the other's privacy, and what is alleged is often inaccurate besides. We have *impressions* of other people's feelings, and *hunches* about their motives. It is legitimate to inquire. It is also all right to voice our impressions, if we do it tentatively, with recognition of our uncertainty. Mind-reading is another matter. It is a violation of the person. It shows disrespect for that person's integrity, destroys trust, and invites retaliation.

6. *Make your needs known.* Sometimes those needs are general: "I need about half an hour's space when I get home from work before I can face any new challenges." "I need relief from child care at least one day a week." Sometimes they are particular: "I need a hug." "I need to get away some weekend soon."

A couple came for counseling. The problem they brought was that the husband was angry much of the time. What came to light was that he expected his wife to anticipate his needs and take care of them, and when she did not, he got angry. He expected her to know when he needed space, and not to talk to him then. He expected her to know when he needed affection, and to be affectionate then. When she guessed wrong and acted unsuitably, he was angry. This is an extreme form of a common fallacy: "If you really loved me, you would know what I am feeling and what I need." Not so. All of us are unfamiliar territory, often even to ourselves, certainly to others. Our only hope of getting our needs met is to be assertive in declaring them. They will not always get met, of course, because others have their needs too and some limitations in their ability to meet ours. But if needs are declared, they can at least be negotiated.

7. *Learn your mate's language of love.* All of us have a language in which we like to be told that we are loved. And one person's language differs from another's. What tells Randy that he is loved is a massage by Betty. But what tells Betty that she is loved is not a return massage by Randy, but just being held by him. What told your mother that your father was sorry was a single red rose, but what tells *your* wife you are sorry is not a rose at all but an apology and an explanation of what was going on inside you at the time of the incident. A woman might express her love by keeping a very clean house, but what would actually speak love to her husband would be her relaxing more with him.

There is usually a lot of love in the first two years of marriage, but sometimes it is spoken in your own language rather than your mate's, and so it does not have much impact. The trick is to learn your mate's language and to speak that. One very ironic situation of our acquaintance was that of a couple who differed in how they wanted to be treated when they were sick. She liked people to come into her room, freshen the air, bring her some orange juice, ask her how she was, and leave some flowers behind. He liked to be left completely alone so he could sleep. So when she was sick, he left her alone. And when he was sick, she visited him often and did all kinds of nice things for him. It took them a while to learn each other's language. It usually does. The Golden Rule here is "Do unto others as they would have you do unto them."

8. *Avoid the words "always" and "never."* This is an easy one to understand, but a hard one to do. "Always" and "never" are very tempting words, especially when you are angry. "You *never* listen." "You're *always* complaining." "You *never* want to do anything but watch TV." Because they are exaggerations, they provoke anger and invite a quick denial. And so the point is missed. Wouldn't "sometimes" be a better word than "always," more accurate and easier for the other person to hear? Then there is "often," and, when you really want to be emphatic, "usually." Never use "never."

9. *Avoid name-calling.* Names usually come into the game in the heat of anger. They hurt (which is why they are used). They stick. That is the problem. The fight ends, you make up, and things are supposed to be all right again. But your mate cannot forget that name you called her. Did you really mean that? If you didn't mean it, why did you say it? You have unwittingly planted a weed, and weeds are very hard to eradicate.

A couple once agreed in marriage counseling to just two contracts with one another. They would not read each other's minds and they would not call each other names. Seventy-five percent of their wrangling dropped away.

10. *Deal with painful situations as they arise.* Have you had the experience of setting off an angry tirade by some simple slip-up, like being five minutes late to pick up your mate? There has probably been some gunnysacking going on, and the sack has just burst. You take it over the head not just for the present offense but for several others stretching back over weeks and months. You didn't know your mate was carrying all this around. You can't even remember the incident they refer to.

If couples would be close, they must learn to deal with anger honestly and constructively. That means handling it by occasions, not allowing it to build. There is no point in trying not to hurt your mate with the bad news that you did not like something. You will harm your mate more in the long run if you hold these things back. You can soften the pain by telling the truth with love each time. That way you avoid the big outburst with white-hot anger, exaggerated statements, name-calling, and sometimes physical violence.

11. *Make time for talk that goes beyond practical problems.* Most couples manage to get the day-to-day problems solved. They communicate enough to get the bills paid, the food bought, the baby taken care of, the guests entertained, the car fixed. But many couples gradually neglect talking about themselves. The very thing that made the courting period such a deeply happy

time, talking about you and about me and about us, gets pushed from the center to the periphery and sometimes dies out altogether. We make love less frequently, and I notice it, but I don't say anything. We do more things separately, and talk about them less. I go to work and muse a lot on the general drift of my life, but I keep these thoughts and feelings to myself. You go off to be with your parents. We keep solving the day-to-day problems, but we do not talk about *ourselves*. And both of us notice in our interaction a growing distance and irritability.

Marriage Encounter has a simple idea to keep marriages going and growing. Each day the couple write each other a short letter, no more than ten minutes' worth, on some subject that draws out feelings. Some couples accomplish the same purpose in other ways. They keep an agreement to do something together one night a week, to be by themselves and talk about things that are important to each of them. It may be a dinner, or it may just be a walk. Other couples commit themselves to a weekend away every few months. These exercises in deliberate cultivation of the relationship are vital. Often all that is needed is to remove the obstacles, the challenges that ordinary living throws in the way of deeper communication. If we can free ourselves from these regularly, the deeper currents can keep flowing and joining. There is an amazing power of resurrection in marital relationships if they are not neglected too long. The coals may seem a little quiet at times, but don't call the fire out. Couples who make a little time and tend the embers see some amazing things happen. The habit of doing this needs to be formed in the first two years.

Communication is the foundational skill, and the key to all the rest of the elements that build a marriage. It is learned over time. Doing some reading about it, and attending marriage enrichment events that foster it, are very helpful in making it grow. It is actually possible for two people to be open and honest with each other, to entrust each other with nothing less than the gift of the whole self, and to become increasingly one instead of increasingly two. It takes courage, but it is one of the most satisfying experiences that life offers.

CHAPTER 25

The Battered Woman: Myths and Reality

Lenore E. Walker

Lenore Walker's report on her research on battered women is, to say the least, alarming. She is quite convincing as she tells of her own interviews with battered women and as she notes what other researchers have written. Her report is written in a very popular style, avoiding theoretical and technical language, in favor of an easy-to-understand style that can speak to those who have not thought much about the problem of physical abuse in intimate relationships. Interested students wishing more detailed statistical information will find ample evidence here to back up her claims.

Consider reading this essay with this hypothesis in mind: physical abuse rarely begins only after the marriage. In most cases, it is present before the wedding in one or other of the abuser's relationships with women. Some researchers have claimed that between 35 and 45 percent of teen women are physically abused by their boyfriends. To make the situation even more frightening, we have the official U.S. crime statistics. Each year the U.S. Department of Justice publishes its *Uniform Crime Statistics Report*, which can be found in most libraries. In the report are the yearly statistics on the number of women murdered that year in the United States, and also the gender of the murderers. In one recent year, 2,751 women were murdered; all but 243 were murdered by men, a total that year of 2,508. That comes out to men being responsible for 91 percent of murders of women that year.

Both women and men do well to consider these facts. And both may want to consider what they, as individuals and by working together, can do to counter the phenomenon of the battered woman.

Questions for Discussion

1. What single point in Walker's essay surprised you the most?
2. What point in her essay were you already convinced of?
3. What information do you, from your own observation and your own listening to what people say, know about this problem?
4. What action can you take about this problem?

T he battering of women, like other crimes of violence against women, has been shrouded in myths. All of the myths have perpetuated the mistaken notion that the victim has precipitated her own assault. Some of them served as a protection against embarrassment. Others were created to protect rescuers from their own discouragement when they were unsuccessful in stopping the brutality. It is important to refute all the myths surrounding battered women in order to understand fully why battering happens, how it affects people, and how it can be stopped.

The battered woman is pictured by most people as a small, fragile, haggard person who might once have been pretty. She has several small children, no job skills, and is economically dependent on her husband. It is frequently assumed she is poor and from a minority group. She is accustomed to living in violence, and her fearfulness and passivity are emphasized above all. Although some battered women do fit this description, research proves it to be a false stereotype.

Most battered women are from middle-class and higher-income homes where the power of their wealth is in the hands of their husbands. Many of them are large women who could attempt to defend themselves physically. Not all of them have children; those who do do not necessarily have them in any particular age group. Although some battered women are jobless, many more are highly competent workers and successful career women. They include doctors, lawyers, corporation executives, nurses, secretaries, full-time homemakers, and others. Battered women are found in all age groups, races, ethnic and religious groups, educational levels, and socioeconomic groups. Who are the battered women? If you are a woman, there is a 50 percent chance it could be you!

MYTH NO. 1: THE BATTERED WOMAN SYNDROME AFFECTS ONLY A SMALL PERCENTAGE OF THE POPULATION

Like rape, the battering of American women is a seriously underreported crime. Data on wife beating are difficult to obtain because battering generally occurs at night, in the home, without witnesses. The statistics on battered women are buried in the records of family domestic disturbance calls to police departments, in emergency room records in hospitals, and in the records of social service agencies, private psychologists, and counselors. The United States Commission on Civil Rights recently completed an investigation which supports the suspicion that police records on battered women are in-

From *The Batterered Woman* by Lenore E. Walker. Copyright © 1979 Lenore E. Walker. Reprinted by permission of HarperCollins Publishers, Inc.

accurately low owing to poor police reporting techniques. My personal estimate is that only one in ten women report battering assaults.

Marjory Fields, a New York City attorney who specializes in battered
women, reports that of 500 women represented in divorce actions in Brooklyn in 1976, 57.4 percent complained of physical assaults by their husbands.
They had suffered these assaults for approximately four years prior to seeking the divorce. Of 600 divorcing wives in Cleveland, according to a study by
Levinger, 36.8 percent reported physical abuse by their husbands. The first
epidemiological study of battered women undertaken in this country, by sociologists Murray Straus, Richard Gelles, and Susan Steinmetz, reported that
a physical assault occurred in 28 percent of all American homes during 1976.
This statistic, nearly one third of all families, is certainly evidence that the battered woman problem is a widespread one.

MYTH NO. 2: BATTERED WOMEN
ARE MASOCHISTIC

The prevailing belief has always been that only women who "liked it and de-
served it" were beaten. In a study of battered wives as recently as twenty
years ago, it was suggested that beatings are solicited by women who suffer
from negative personality characteristics, including masochism. "Good
wives" were taught that the way to stop assaults was to examine their behavior and try to change it to please men: to be less provocative, less aggressive, and less frigid. There was no suggestion that provocation might occur
from other than masochistic reasons, that aggressiveness might be an attempt
to ward off further assault, and that frigidity might be a very natural result of
subjection to severe physical and psychological pain. The burden of guilt for
battering has fallen on the woman, and the violent behavior of the male has
been perpetuated. The myth of the masochistic woman is a favorite of all who
endeavor to understand the battered woman. No matter how sympathetic
people may be, they frequently come to the conclusion that the reason a battered woman remains in such a relationship is that she is masochistic. By
masochism, it is meant that she experiences some pleasure, often akin to sexual pleasure, through being beaten by the man she loves. Because this has
been such a prevailing stereotype, many battered women begin to wonder if
they are indeed masochistic.

MYTH NO. 3: BATTERED WOMEN ARE CRAZY

This myth is related to the masochism myth in that it places the blame for the
battering on the woman's negative personality characteristics. Battered
women's survival behaviors have often earned them the misdiagnosis of
being crazy. Unusual actions which may help them to survive in the battering relationship have been taken out of context by unenlightened medical

and mental health workers. Several of the women in this sample reported being hospitalized for schizophrenia, paranoia, and severe depression. One woman who told of hearing voices which told her to kill her husband had received numerous electroshock therapy treatments. But just listening to her describe her husband's brutal treatment made her hallucination very understandable. Many women reported being given heavy doses of anti-psychotic medications by doctors who were responding to their overt symptoms rather than attempting to understand their family situations. It is not clear whether these women were overtly psychotic at the time of their reported diagnoses. As a clinical psychologist, I can state that at the time I interviewed these women, there was insufficient evidence of such disorders. One woman was interviewed shortly after being released from a state hospital. Arrangements had been made for her to go to a temporary shelter, legal assistance was provided to initiate divorce proceedings, and her batterer was refused knowledge of her whereabouts. Her mental health improved markedly within days. I wonder how many other women who have been mislabeled as mentally ill were really attempting to cope with a batterer. After listening to their stories, I can only applaud their strength in retaining their sanity.

MYTH NO. 4: MIDDLE-CLASS WOMEN DO NOT GET BATTERED AS FREQUENTLY OR AS VIOLENTLY AS DO POORER WOMEN

Most previously recorded statistics of battering have come from lower-class families. However, lower-class women are more likely to come in contact with community agencies and so their problems are more visible. Middle- and upper-class women do not want to make their batterings public. They fear social embarrassment and harming their husbands' careers. Many also believe the respect in which their husbands are held in the community will cast doubt upon the credibility of their battering stories. The recent public focus on battered women has brought many of these middle- and upper-class women out of hiding. The publicity being given the problem is creating a climate in which they think they will finally be believed. They report an overwhelming sense of relief once they have told their stories and find that others will now believe them.

MYTH NO. 5: MINORITY-GROUP WOMEN ARE BATTERED MORE FREQUENTLY THAN ANGLOS

The battered women interviewed in this study were Hispanic, native American, black, Asian, and Pacific American, as well as Anglo. Although each grew up in a culture with different values and different attitudes about male and female roles, none of them was able to make any impact on the kind of

violence she experienced. Anglo and minority women alike told similar battering stories and experienced similar embarrassment, guilt, and the inability to halt their men's assaults. Minority women, however, spoke of having
even fewer resources than Anglos to turn to for assistance.

MYTH NO. 6: RELIGIOUS BELIEFS
WILL PREVENT BATTERING

The Catholic, Protestant, Mormon, Jewish, Eastern, and other religious
women in this study all indicated that their religious beliefs did not protect
them from their assaultive men. Most of the women in my study held religious beliefs. For some, belief in a deity helped them endure their suffering,
offering comfort and solace. Sometimes attending services was the only safe
outside contact they had. However, other women indicated they no longer
practiced their religion, because giving it up eliminated a point of conflict
with their batterer. Still others gave up their religion in disillusionment, feeling that a just and merciful God would not have let them suffer so. Others reported losing faith after having unsuccessfully sought help from a religious
or spiritual leader.

Some women told stories in which their religious adviser suggested they
pray for guidance, become better women, and go home and help their husbands "become more spiritual and find the Lord." Needless to say, these
women did not have time to wait for their husbands to "find the Lord" while
they continued to receive brutal beatings. Other women joyfully told of humane religious advisers who understood their problems and helped them
break out of their disastrous relationships.

MYTH NO. 7: BATTERED WOMEN ARE
UNEDUCATED AND HAVE FEW JOB SKILLS

The education level of the women interviewed ranged from fifth grade
through completion of professional and doctoral degrees. They were homemakers, teachers, real estate agents, lawyers, psychologists, nurses, physicians, businesswomen, politicians, and successful corporation executives.
Some did well at their jobs and some performed poorly. Although many were
successful career women, they stated they would give up their careers if it
would eliminate the battering in their relationships. Most had tried changing
jobs or staying home without any effect on their husbands' behavior. Those
women who chose to be homemakers tried heroically to keep their lives from
falling apart: they struggled to make financial ends meet, kept family chaos
at a minimum, and tried to smooth life for their batterer. Most of them sought
status in their home lives rather than in their careers. Thus, their self-esteem
was dependent on their ability to be good wives and homemakers and was
not well integrated with their successful professional activities.

MYTH NO. 8: BATTERERS ARE VIOLENT
IN ALL THEIR RELATIONSHIPS

Based on the women in my study, I estimate that only about 20 percent of battered women live with men who are violent not only to them but also to anyone else who gets in their way. Unfortunately, this violent group of men has been the most studied. They tend to be poorer and to live outside the mainstream of society's norms. They often have fewer resources or skills with which to cope with the world. Most street crime is committed by such men. They also have the most contact with society's institutions and seem always to be in trouble with the police. They often subsist on welfare payments; their children have behavioral and learning problems in school; they use hospital clinics. Courts send them to treatment facilities in lieu of jail sentences. Because so much of our resources is spent in dealing with these people, it often seems that they are representative of all of the violence in our culture. When it comes to battered women, this is simply not true. Most men who batter their wives are generally not violent in other aspects of their lives.

MYTH NO. 9: BATTERERS ARE UNSUCCESSFUL AND
LACK RESOURCES TO COPE WITH THE WORLD

It has been suggested that men who feel less capable than their women resort to violence. Contrary findings were reported in England, where physicians, service professionals, and police had the highest incidence of wife beating. Most of the professionally successful volunteers in this study have similarly successful husbands. Among the affluent batterers were physicians, attorneys, public officials, corporation executives, scientists, college professors, and salesmen. Many of these men donated a good deal of time and energy to community activities. Often they would be unable to maintain their high productivity level were it not for the support of their wives. In one town, the mayor's wife, whose layers of make-up concealed the serious bruises he had inflicted upon her, regularly assisted him with all his official duties. In some cases, previously successful men lost their effectiveness because of alcohol or emotional problems. Many men were reported as erratic in performance by the women. As a group, however, the batterers in this sample would be indistinguishable from any other group of men in terms of capability.

MYTH NO. 10: DRINKING CAUSES
BATTERING BEHAVIOR

Over half the battered women in this sample indicated a relationship between alcohol use and battering. Many tended to blame the battering incidents on their men's drinking. Upon further questioning, however, it became clear that the men beat them whether or not they had been drinking. But some association between drinking and battering cannot be denied. Exactly what it is is still not known. It does seem reasonable, however, to suggest that in many cases alcohol is blamed as the precipitating factor, whereas it is only a component in the battering relationship. But it is psychologically easier for the battered woman to blame the violence on the batterer's drunkenness. Often the men in this study drank as a way of calming their anxieties. Drinking seemed to give them a sense of power. Many of the women felt that if they could only get their men to stop drinking, the battering would cease. Unfortunately, it just did not happen.

The most violent physical abuse *was* suffered by women whose men were consistent drinkers. Much work still needs to be done on the association between drinking and battering. I strongly suspect that there are specific blood chemistry changes that occur under a generalized stress reaction such as battering. Furthermore, these may be the same chemicals that are found in the blood of alcoholics. It is entirely possible that fundamental changes in brain chemistry cause both cycles. It is hoped that as our scientific technology becomes more precise, we will be able to measure these chemical changes with more accuracy.

MYTH NO. 11: BATTERERS ARE PSYCHOPATHIC PERSONALITIES

If batterers could be considered antisocial and psychopathic personalities, then individual psychopathology could be used to differentiate batterers from normal men. Unfortunately, it is not that simple. The batterers in this sample were reported to have many kinds of personality disturbances other than just being psychopathic. One trait they *do* have in common with diagnosed psychopaths is their extraordinary ability to use charm as a manipulative technique.

The women interviewed all described their batterers as having a dual personality, much like Dr. Jekyll and Mr. Hyde. The batterer can be either very, very good or very, very horrid. Furthermore, he can swing back and forth between the two characters with the smoothness of a con artist. But, unlike the psychopath, the batterer feels a sense of guilt and shame at his uncontrollable actions. If he were able to cease his violence, he would.

MYTH NO. 12: POLICE CAN PROTECT THE BATTERED WOMEN

The women in this study manifestly do not believe this to be true. Only 10 percent ever called the police for help. Of these, most stated that the police were ineffective: when the police left, the assault was renewed with added vigor.

Sociologist Murray Straus, in his studies on violence in the family, labeled such assaults a crime and declared that were the violence to occur in any setting other than the home, it would warrant prosecution. He cites studies indicating that somewhere between 25 and 67 percent of all homicides occur within the family in all societies.

A recently completed study in Kansas City and Detroit indicates that in 80 percent of all homicides in those cities, the police had intervened from one to five times previously. Thus, homicide between man and woman is not a "crime of passion," but rather the end result of unchecked, long-standing violence.

MYTH NO. 13: THE BATTERER IS NOT A LOVING PARTNER

This myth has spawned others, most particularly that of the masochistic wife. Women have been accused of loving the batterers' brutality rather than their kindness because it has been difficult for society to comprehend the loving behavior of batterers. But batterers are often described by their victims as fun-loving little boys when they are not being coercive. They are playful, attentive, sensitive, exciting, and affectionate to their women. The cycle theory of battering described later on explains how the batterers' loving behavior keeps these women in the battering relationship.

MYTH NO. 14: A WIFE BATTERER ALSO BEATS HIS CHILDREN

This myth has some foundation in fact. In my sample, approximately one third of the batterers beat their children. These men were also suspected of seductive sexual behavior toward their daughters. In another third of the cases, battered women beat their children. Although the children of the final third were not physically abused, they suffered a more insidious form of child abuse because of living in a home where the fathers battered the mothers. Those women in my sample who had seen their fathers beat their mothers report psychological scars which never healed. Children whom I encountered while doing this study seemed to be undergoing similar traumas. The National Center for Child Abuse and Neglect has reported a higher percentage of men in battering relationships who also beat their children than those who do not. Their data show that when there is concurrent child abuse in these families, 70 percent is committed by the violent man.

MYTH NO. 15: ONCE A BATTERED WOMAN, ALWAYS A BATTERED WOMAN

This myth is the reason why many people have not encouraged women to leave their battering relationships. They think she will only seek out another violent man. Though several of the women in this sample had a series of violent relationships, this pattern did not hold true for most of those interviewed. While they wanted another intimate relationship with a man, they were extremely careful not to choose another violent one. There was a low rate of remarriage for older women who had left battering relationships. Most of them had left a marriage by going against the advice of their families and friends. They preferred being single rather than trying to make the male–female relationship work again. Women who had received some beneficial intervention rarely remarried another batterer.

MYTH NO. 16: ONCE A BATTERER, ALWAYS A BATTERER

If the psychosocial-learning theory of violent behavior is accurate, then batterers can be taught to relearn their aggressive responses. Assertion rather than aggression, negotiation rather than coercion, is the goal. My theoretical perspective, then, indicates that this myth of once a batterer, always a batterer is just that. The data have not yet been analyzed to prove it false.

MYTH NO. 17: LONG-STANDING BATTERING RELATIONSHIPS CAN CHANGE FOR THE BETTER

Although everyone who believes in the positive nature of behavior change wants to believe this myth, my research has not shown it to be true. Relationships that have been maintained by the man having power over the woman are stubbornly resistant to an equal power-sharing arrangement. Thus, even with the best help available, these relationships do not become battering free. At best, the violent assaults are reduced in frequency and severity. Unassisted, they simply escalate to homicidal and suicidal proportions. The best hope for such couples is to terminate the relationship. There is a better chance that with another partner they can reorder the power structure and as equals can live in a nonviolent relationship.

MYTH NO. 18: BATTERED WOMEN DESERVE TO GET BEATEN

The myth that battered women provoke their beatings by pushing their men beyond the breaking point is a popular one. Everyone can recount a story where the woman seemed to deserve what she got: she was too bossy, too insulting, too sloppy, too uppity, too angry, too obnoxious, too provocative, or too something else. In a culture where everyone takes sides between winners and losers, women who continuously get beaten are thought to deserve it. It is assumed that if only they would change their behavior, the batterer could regain his self-control. The stories of the women in this study indicate that batterers lose self-control because of their own internal reasons, not because of what the women did or did not do. Furthermore, philosophically this myth robs the men of responsibility for their own actions. No one could deserve the kind of brutality reported in these pages.

MYTH NO. 19: BATTERED WOMEN CAN ALWAYS LEAVE HOME

In a society where women are culturally indoctrinated to believe that love and marriage are their true fulfillment, nothing is lost by pretending that they are free to leave home whenever the violence becomes too great. In truth, battered women do not have the freedom to leave after being assaulted. . . . A battered woman is not free to end her victimization without assistance.

MYTH NO. 20: BATTERERS WILL CEASE THEIR VIOLENCE "WHEN WE GET MARRIED"

A small number of women in this sample reported violence in their premarital relationships. They thought that their men would cease their abuse once they were married, because the men would then feel more secure and more confident of the women's exclusive love for them. In every case, the expected marital bliss did not happen. Rather, the batterer's suspiciousness and possessiveness increased along with his escalating rate of violence.

MYTH NO. 21: CHILDREN NEED THEIR FATHER EVEN IF HE IS VIOLENT—OR, "I'M ONLY STAYING FOR THE SAKE OF THE CHILDREN"

This myth shatters faster than some of the others when confronted with the data on the high number of children who are physically and sexually abused in homes where there is such domestic violence. There is no doubt that the ideal family includes both a mother and a father for their children. However, children of abusive parents, compared with children of single parents, all say they would choose to live with just one parent. The enormous relief in living with a single parent expressed by children who formerly lived in violent homes is universal. In this sample, young children from homes where the father beat the mother had severe emotional and educational problems. The women in this sample remained with their batterers long after the children left home, putting to rest the myth that they were staying because it was better for the children. They remained because of the symbiotic bonds of love established over a period of time in such relationships.

Who, then, are the battered women?

COMMON CHARACTERISTICS
OF BATTERED WOMEN

As indicated earlier, the battered women interviewed for this book were a mixed group, representing all ages, races, religions (including no religion), educational levels, cultures, and socioeconomic groups. The youngest was seventeen years old, and the oldest was seventy-six years old. The shortest battering relationship was two months and the longest lasted fifty-three years, when the batterer died from natural causes.

The battered woman in this study commonly:

1. Has low self-esteem.
2. Believes all the myths about battering relationships.
3. Is a traditionalist about the home, strongly believes in family unity and the prescribed feminine sex-role stereotype.
4. Accepts responsibility for the batterer's actions.
5. Suffers from guilt, yet denies the terror and anger she feels.
6. Presents a passive face to the world but has the strength to manipulate her environment enough to prevent further violence and being killed.
7. Has severe stress reactions, with psychophysiological complaints.
8. Uses sex as a way to establish intimacy.
9. Believes that no one will be able to help her resolve her predicament except herself.

Although a few of the women were unmarried and not living with their batterers, most either lived with their batterers or had been legally married to them. Many women reported living with their batterers prior to marriage without experiencing abuse. Abuse usually began in the first six months of marriage. Some women had no children; several had seven or more; a few were interviewed during pregnancy. For many, this was their first marriage; for others, it was their second, third, and, in one case, her fifth. While some of the women were still living with the batterers, others had left the relationship prior to participating in this study. A number of the women began the process of terminating a battering relationship while the interviewers were still in contact with them. Several of the women interviewed were referred while in the hospital recuperating from injuries inflicted by the batterer. To the best of my knowledge, none of the women has died. Four killed their husbands and several others were arrested for assault on their men. The women who talked with us lived in urban environments, in suburbia, and in isolated rural areas. There seemed to be a high concentration of women living in areas which afford anonymity. Many Metropolitan Denver women lived in the foothills of the mountains, where they were isolated, especially in winter.

LOW SELF-ESTEEM

Because of their lowered sense of self-esteem, these women typically under-estimated their abilities to do anything. They doubted their competence and underplayed any successes they had. Those battered women with activities outside the home evaluated their outside performance and skills more real-istically than they could their wifely duties. They were in constant doubt about their abilities as housekeepers, cooks, or lovers. Thus, the man's con-stant criticism of them in these areas adversely affected their judgment. Women in general have not learned how to integrate their home lives and outside lives as men do. They tend to evaluate their performances at home and outside the home according to separate criteria. Battered women tend to be traditionalists about home performance, since that is the basis of their self-esteem. Activities outside the home simply do not figure in their evaluation of how they feel about themselves. Thus, when things are not going well at home, the battered woman considers herself a failure. She has internalized all the cultural myths and stereotypes and assumes the guilt for the batterer's behavior. She agrees with society's belief that the batterer would change his behavior if only she could change her behavior. If she has lived with him for a while, she is aware that although she can often manipulate him to some de-gree, she has, in truth, little control over his behavior. This makes her feel even more of a failure. Most of the women interviewed eventually got around to saying that they were still not completely sure that there was not something they could have done differently that might have made the bat-terer cease his abusive behavior.

TRADITIONALISTS

The traditionalist orientation of the battered woman is evident in her view of the woman's role in marriage. First, she readily accepts the notion that "a woman's proper place is in the home." No matter how important her career might be to her, she is ready to give it up if it will make the batterer happy. Often she does just that, resulting in economic hardship to the family. Even those who believe that women have a right to a career suspect that that very career might be causing the batterer's difficulties. Those women who cannot give up working feel guilty. Although many of the women work because the family needs the money, they also state that the time spent on the job pro-vides a brief respite from the batterer's domination. But the batterer's need to possess his woman totally often causes her to lose or leave her job. The bat-terer batters her with a litany of suspicions about her supposed behavior on the job. Usually, he is jealous of her work relationships, especially those with other men.

Battered women who work often turn their money over to their hus-bands. Even those women who provide the family's financial stability feel their income belongs to their husband. Ultimately, she gives the man the right to make the final decisions as to how the family income is spent. The battered woman views the man as the head of the family, even though often she is the one actually keeping the family together; she makes the decisions concerning financial matters and the children's welfare; and she maintains the house and often a job as well. She goes out of her way to make sure that her man feels he is the head of the home. Some of the women interviewed revealed elaborate deceptions they resorted to to put aside some money—money they saved secretly in order to leave the marriage. Often they did not follow through, but their nest egg helped them cope. Others left the relationship when they had enough money.

KEEPERS OF THE PEACE

Another behavior common among battered women is the attempt to control other people and events in the environment to keep the batterer from losing his temper. The woman believes that if she can control all the factors in his life, she can keep him from becoming angry. She makes herself responsible for creating a safe environment for everyone. One woman interviewed spent an enormous amount of time talking about her efforts to control her mother, his mother, and their children so that none of them would upset her husband. She found that if she kept all these people in check through some interesting manipulations, life was pleasant in their home. The moment someone got out of line, her man began his beatings.

SEVERE STRESS REACTION

The battered women in this sample were hard workers who lived under constant stress and fear. This had physical and psychological effects on them. Although most battered women report being able to withstand enormous amounts of pain during a battering incident, at other times they are often seen by their doctors for a variety of minor physiological ailments. Battered women often complain of fatigue, backaches, headaches, general restlessness, and inability to sleep. Psychological complaints are, frequently, depression, anxiety, and general suspiciousness. Being suspicious and secretive often helps a battered woman to avoid further beatings. Many battered women go to great lengths to find a few moments of privacy from their very intrusive battering husbands. They will often hide things from their men that they fear might precipitate another battering incident.

CHILDHOOD VIOLENCE AND SEX-ROLE STEREOTYPING

I was curious to learn whether or not the women who lived in battering relationships with their husbands had also lived in battering relationships with their parents. Although this was true in a small number of cases, many more women reported that their first exposure to violent men was their husbands. Their fathers were described as traditionalists who treated their daughters like fragile dolls. The daughters were expected to be pretty and ladylike and to grow up to marry nice young men who would care for them as their fathers had. Doted upon as little girls, these women, in their fathers' eyes, could do no wrong. Such pampering and sex-role stereotyping unfortunately taught them that they were incompetent to take care of themselves and had to be dependent on men.

COMMON CHARACTERISTICS OF MEN WHO BATTER

Who are the batterers?

The batterers described were also a mixed group. They represented all ages, races, religions (including no religion), educational levels, cultures, and socioeconomic groups. The youngest was described as sixteen years old and the oldest was seventy-six. They were unrecognizable to the uniformed observer and not distinguished by demographic data.

The batterer, according to the women in this sample, commonly:

1. Has low self-esteem.
2. Believes all the myths about battering relationships.
3. Is a traditionalist believing in male supremacy and the stereotyped masculine sex role in the family.
4. Blames others for his actions.
5. Is pathologically jealous.
6. Presents a dual personality.
7. Has severe stress reactions, during which he uses drinking and wife battering to cope.
8. Frequently uses sex as an act of aggression to enhance self-esteem in view of waning virility. May be bisexual.
9. Does not believe his violent behavior should have negative consequences.

The first three characteristics of the batterers are strikingly similar to those of the battered women. Batterers typically deny that they have a problem, although they are aware of it; and they become enraged if their women should reveal the true situation. These men do not want to discuss the problem, and attempts to learn more about batterers have not been successful. When these men do agree to be interviewed, often as a favor to their women during their contrite and loving phase, they cannot describe the details of an acute battering incident. They evade questions or claim not to remember very much of what did occur. Thus, the knowledge we have of these men comes from the battered women themselves and our few, meager observations.

Researchers Eisenberg and Micklow found 90 percent of the batterers in their study had been in the military. Twenty-five percent received dishonorable discharges. I did not systematically collect such data for this sample, but subjectively it appears that a similarly high percentage were also in the military. Del Martin, feminist author of *Battered Wives*, suggests a correlation between the military as a "school for violence" and subsequent battering behavior in males.

OVERKILL

There is always an element of overkill in the batterer's behavior. For example, he reports he does not set out to hurt his woman; rather, he sets out to "teach her a lesson." He may begin by slapping her once, twice, three times; before he knows it, he has slapped her ten or twelve times, with punches and kicks as well. Even when the woman is badly injured, the batterer often uncontrollably continues his brutal attack. The same is true for his generosity. During his loving periods, he showers the woman with affection, attention, and gifts. Rather than buying his woman a small bottle of perfume, one batterer bought her a three-ounce bottle. In another instance, the woman asked for a pocket calculator to help her to keep their checkbook balanced. The batterer bought her a calculator capable of performing mathematical computations neither of them understood. Several women complained of their husbands' extravagance, stating that they had to work longer and harder to pay off the charge accounts. This quality of overdoing things tends to be a standard characteristic of battering relationships.

EXCESSIVE POSSESSIVENESS AND JEALOUSY

Another staple characteristic is the batterer's possessiveness, jealousy, and intrusiveness. In order for him to feel secure, he must become overinvolved in the woman's life. In some instances, he may take her to work, to lunch, and bring her home at the end of the working day. In others, when he goes to work, he may require her to bring him coffee, lunch, his checkbook, and generally to account for every moment of her time. In one extreme case, the batterer escorted his wife to the door of the ladies' room in any public facility they visited. Despite this constant surveillance of her every activity, the batterer is still suspicious of his woman's possible relationships with other men and women.

A frequent subject for the batterer's verbal abuse is his suspicion that the battered woman is having an affair or affairs. Most of the women interviewed had not had other sexual liaisons. If they did engage in affairs, they were generally of very short duration and represented an attempt to alleviate some of their loneliness and stress. Most battered women do not expect another relationship to be any better than the one they are suffering through. If they had any such hopes, they probably would have left the batterer in search of a new Prince Charming long ago.

CHILDHOOD VIOLENCE AND SEX-ROLE STEREOTYPING

Although battered women typically do not come from violent homes, batterers frequently do. Many of the batterers saw their fathers beat their mothers; others were themselves beaten. In those homes where overt violence was not reported, a general lack of respect for women and children was evident.

These men often experienced emotional deprivation. These reports support the notion of the generational cycle theory that is so popular in our child abuse literature today. Children who were abused or witnessed abuse are more likely to grow up to be tomorrow's abusers.

BATTERERS' RELATIONSHIP WITH THEIR MOTHERS

The women also reported that their batterers have unusual relationships with their mothers. It is often characterized as an ambivalent love–hate relationship. The batterer's mother seems to have a good deal of control over his behavior; yet he will often abuse her, too. In fact, many women report that acute battering incidents are triggered by a visit to the batterer's mother. Often their rages are reminiscent of infantile temper tantrums designed by angry little boys to provoke their mommies. Included in this study are several reports from women being battered by young sons. In one such case, a twenty-one-year-old college honor student beat his sixty-five-year-old mother several times a week. When the mother was ill or simply unavailable to him because of previous batterings, he would beat his twenty-year-old girl friend.

Much more research is needed before we can reach any definite conclusions about the relationship between the batterer and his mother. Psychology has done much damage by casting mothers in a negative light as being responsible for the emotional ills of their children. Still, we must look carefully at the role of the batterer's mother in this problem. Also, we must look at the role of the batterer's father and the father–son relationship. The information that we have collected can serve as a beginning to formulate new questions that need to be answered.

MENTAL STATUS OF BATTERERS

Psychological distress symptoms were often reported in batterers, particularly prior to an acute battering incident. Alcohol and other drugs were often said to calm his nervousness. Although many of the men seemed to have a need for alcohol, few of them were reported addicted to drugs. Those who were had become addicted to hard drugs while in the military, usually in Vietnam.

Personality distortions were frequently mentioned by the women. They said the batterers had a history of being loners and were socially involved with others only on a superficial level. They were constantly accomplishing feats that others might not be able to. They loved to impress their women. For example, one man took his future bride into a furniture store and handed the salesperson two thousand dollars in cash for a bedroom set she admired. This sort of behavior tended to reinforce their women's viewing them as possessing extraordinary abilities.

The men are further described as being extremely sensitive to nuances in other people's behavior. Their attention to minimal cues from others gives them the ability to predict reactions faster than most of us can. Thus, they are helping their women to deal with others in their world when they share their usually accurate predictions of others' behavior. When these men decompensate under stress, their sensitivity becomes paranoid in nature. When they are comfortable, however, the women appreciate and benefit from this protective behavior, since battered women tend to be overly gullible and trusting of others. Much of this seemingly self-protective behavior becomes homicidal and suicidal when the batterer's violence escalates beyond his control.

BRAIN DISEASES

Many of the battered women felt their husbands' violent behavior approximated some kind of brain seizure and that there might be a relationship between neurological disorders and violence. The most common disorder discussed was psychomotor epilepsy. This is a disorder of the brain manifested by sudden, unexplained outbursts of movement. Persons who suffer from such brain disorder often do not remember their episodes, especially if they result in violence. Sometimes an aura or feeling of an impending attack is identifiable but usually precipitation is unknown. Medication is often useful in controlling onset and frequency of attacks, although a cure is most times impossible.

Neurologists are studying the relationship of such brain diseases and violence. It is interesting, though, that seemingly only men, and not women, are so afflicted with such a physical disorder.

Another disease mentioned that may cause violent outbursts was hypoglycemia. This disease is characterized by low blood-sugar levels that cause starvation among body cells. The brain cells become irritable more rapidly than the rest of the body, and such irritability, it is theorized, can trigger violent outbursts. One woman reported that if she sensed a rising tension, she was able to avoid an acute battering incident by feeding her hypoglycemic husband. Although minor battering incidents still occurred, explosions disappeared. This improvement had been stable over the six months prior to her interview and followed a three-year battering history. I wonder how much her nurturing behavior of feeding him also helped to alleviate his explosiveness.

Further support for the theory of neurological or blood chemistry changes in batterers is found in the geriatric population. Some older women report dramatic changes in their husbands' behavior as they age. Senility or hardening of the arteries can cause previously nonviolent men to begin to abuse their wives. One sixty-eight-year-old woman told of her seventy-year-old husband's attacking her with his cane. Other stories indicate the cruel fate that can befall women who have devoted their lives to pleasing their husbands only to find that aging brings on organic brain syndromes that can impel them to violent behavior.

In conclusion, battered women and batterers come from all walks of life. This sample has indicated that they cannot be distinguished by demographic description or stereotypes. They do have some personality characteristics in common, but it is not known how much the victim/offender roles produce such personalities or whether they sought each other out first. Rather than concentrating on the study of individual personality, it appears that the study of the interrelatedness of the sociological and psychological factors may be the way to a solution.

CHAPTER 26

Men Who Make Women Want to Scream

Connell Cowan
Melvyn Kinder

The state of men's lives is troubling and problematic. We seem confused, directionless, and stuck in patriarchal patterns. It has become fashionable in the current situation to engage in male bashing and blame men for all the ills of the world. This is neither therapeutic for men nor helpful to women who may be seeking a suitable life-partner.

The Cowan and Kinder essay offers a suggestive typology that acts as a critical examination of four types of men. Each of the men is initially charming, attractive and intriguing—but all end up infuriating women: The Clam radiates a tough outer mystique; the Pseudo-Liberated male is disarmingly expressive; the Perpetual Adolescent shuns adult responsibilities: and the Walking Wounded wallows in self-pity and vulnerability.

Exploration of the various types should make for interesting, if not provocative, classroom discussion.

Questions for Discussion

1. What is initially attractive about men who display a tough, macho mystique? What is the dark side of this type of masculinity?
2. Emotional expressivity can be a form of narcissism. Why is this so? How can it be a false form of liberation for men?
3. Why do so many men resist adult responsibilities and commitments today?
4. Men carrying a mixture of hurt, bitterness, and rejection can make foolish choices. Why? Is a healing and healthy relationship possible for them?

There are several types of men who very predictably end up infuriating women. Some are charming in the beginning and then change. Others are attractive because of the qualities women hope to find in them. All, sooner or later, make women want to scream in frustration.

From *Smart Women, Foolish Choices* by Dr. Connell Cowan and Dr. Melvyn Kinder. Copyright © 1985 by Connell O'Brien Cowan and Melvyn Kinder. Reprinted by permission of Clarkson N. Potter, Inc., a division of Crown Publishers, Inc.

THE CLAM

Some men radiate a tough mystique that grows out of a basically selfish, withholding, and guarded nature. This kind of man can be as dangerous as he is attractive and intriguing. A woman can be drawn to what she sees as strength in this man's insensitive toughness and may also feel potentially reassured by that "strength." We say "potentially," because she never quite feels part of such a man's strength, since the man doesn't really share or even truly open himself to the woman. He makes the woman do the emotional work for the two of them. He sets the stage and she dances around, attempting to read his mind. She knows she wants the security of feeling close to his strength. But he doesn't ever allow her to get too close. She loves it, she hates it. She knows she is drawn by the very characteristic she is bound and determined to change.

Arlene, 28, is a warm, gregarious bank loan officer. When she met Tom she knew this relationship was "it" for her. She described him as "a bit too emotionally guarded" for her tastes, but she thought all that would change once he realized he could trust her. She thought that she understood Tom's secretive tendencies, which she saw as reflecting his self-control or perhaps shielding an old hurt. He wasn't the least sensitive to her needs, but she talked herself into believing it was only because she hadn't communicated them to him clearly enough, and so it must be her fault.

They married eight months after they met. Arlene felt sure the kind of commitment they were making would open the door to at last feeling loved by Tom. She was absolutely convinced that if she loved him enough, with no holds barred, he would open himself to her. With love as the key, she would open his heart and finally reap the treasure that surely lay within. Tom's tough, controlled outer shell concealed a tough, controlled inner core. Tom claimed he loved Arlene, but she never felt it and he never showed the demonstrative affection she wanted and needed. She divorced him after one painful year.

Arlene made a mistake in the choice of her relationship with Tom. She interpreted his guarded, withholding nature as mystique. What she found was that instead of standing guard over some hidden treasure, he in fact was desperately trying to protect his insecurity from exposure. When Arlene realized this, Tom's strength was transformed in her eyes to brittle crumbling defenses. His wonderful mystique turned to fear.

The Clam either fears his dependency needs or has managed to convince himself that he doesn't have any. He is very attractive to many women, who mistake this trait for strength and self-containment. But problems soon emerge as the woman begins to want more. We all experience love, at least in part, through feeling needed by our partner, "needed" emotionally. The Clam can't allow himself to need anyone enough to form an intimate, satisfying bond. To do so would require confronting his fears of weakness and vulnerability. Ancient, scarred-over hurts may have destroyed his capacity to feel that deeply.

We all need, in a love relationship, to have our partners dependent upon us—not bloodsuckingly so, but needing us emotionally nevertheless. And this man will never allow himself to be dependent enough to be able to form a close, sharing relationship. He functions as a self-contained system. No matter how warm a woman's love, it will never melt his protective shield. It is too tough, too old.

Another necessary bonding agent in the man/woman relationship is trust. Trusting and being trusted. The Clam is recognized by his secretive qualities. The secretive person is protecting something he fears may be lost, betrayed, taken away. Women need to keep in mind when they meet a secretive man that his concealment is a result of his past and has nothing to do with them.

Trust develops through a process of give and take. It involves mutually disclosing deeper and more complex aspects of ourselves. The Clam cannot take a chance on important emotional exposure. He will not risk the danger of looking into old wounds stored away in the locked file of forgotten, painful memories. Most often, he doesn't even know just what it is he is protecting or even that he is, in fact, behaving in a self-protective and distrustful fashion. The Clam cannot trust and he does not open up.

He doesn't know how to love, for the process of giving and loving means exposing his needs and vulnerabilities. If he hasn't learned to love by the time he is an adult, a woman won't be able to teach him—no matter how patient she is. It's foolish to believe otherwise.

What is misguided in the pursuit of this man is the failure to correctly identify his real strengths and weaknesses. If you find yourself with this type, you may believe you possess the magic potion to change him, to release in him what you believe to be a capacity to love, but you don't. In fact, the more a woman loves and cares for this kind of man, the better the chances of driving him away. Intimacy is his enemy—it scares the hell out of him. If he doesn't run away first, you will become so frustrated with having to do all the emotional work, provide all the tenderness, that eventually you will end the relationship—if you're smart.

THE PSEUDO-LIBERATED MALE

At the outset of a relationship, the Pseudo-Liberated Male can be disarmingly attractive to women. He is the living embodiment of the liberated man, the perfect and natural complement to today's woman. He accepts her changes, even encourages them. He seems gentle and sensitive, vulnerable, expressive, revealing—a real dream come true! But it's a dream that frequently turns into a nightmare.

This type of man interpreted the women's movement as an invitation to become more expressive emotionally. He distorts this new "freedom" as a license to whine and a rationalization to express endless fears and personal insecurities, often to the point of utter distraction. The Pseudo-Liberated

Male is certainly quite different from the withholding man described earlier. Many women see him as a welcome change—someone who will share himself, be open with his feelings. That's great, but some of these men go overboard. Even when women begin to get a whiff of his excesses, they frequently don't trust their own instincts—they don't run.

In a way, women have been encouraged and made to feel as if they should like this man. After all, if they expect to be able to explore new and unfamiliar "masculine" parts of themselves, and if they expect men to accept and love them for it, then they, in turn, should be tolerant of men's becoming more expressive and vulnerable.

When Marv and Marlena came in for couples therapy, Marv said they were not having any specific problems living together—they wanted rather to make their relationship as dynamic and positive as possible, and they were both interested in the therapy process as a means of personal growth.

Marv, 32, is a free-lance carpenter and unpublished novelist. Marlena, 34, is an office administrator for an import-export company and the steady wage earner in their household. They're both active in antinuclear and liberal political causes, Marv more so than Marlena because he doesn't work steadily and has more time.

Marv and Marlena are both bright, attractive, and personable. But what became clear in the very first session, as Marv talked on and on, with occasional glances at Marlena for approval, was that Marv is a narcissistic Pseudo-Liberated Male. He wasn't interested in making his relationship with Marlena better. What he wanted was a fresh, larger audience for his seemingly inexhaustible insights about himself.

Marlena revealed that Marv preferred talking about their relationship and himself to just about any other activity. Marlena eventually confessed that she felt exhausted by the constant talk and by his incessant demands for attention and analysis of "where we're at with each other now."

This man hides the fact that he is an emotional drain, that he's a taker. He is so happy and relieved to have a chance to legitimize his insecurity and neediness that he doesn't realize that he is taking without giving. He sincerely believes that his emotional diarrhea is a gift. He hides his fears and passivity beneath a deceptive costume of gentleness and sensitivity—and hopes the woman won't see through his disguises.

During the early stages of the relationship, this man performs dazzlingly. He is a master with words—he may even be poetic. His verbal output is such that a woman thinks she should feel nourished. Instead, she feels drained. He wraps his need for reassurance in a pretty package, one that can make a woman feel privileged, needed. Eventually, she may become aware that all he ever seems interested in talking about is the relationship—or himself! She wants to like him. She thinks she should like him. After all, he is expressive, isn't he? "In touch" with his feelings? Why does he make her want to scream? Perhaps it's because she finally realizes that he would rather talk about a relationship than have one.

These men are sensitive, and that can be a refreshing experience. The problem is that as time goes by, it becomes increasingly apparent that their sensitivity is one-sided, directed consistently toward themselves.

We believe women do want to know how a man feels, but they don't want to hear about it all the time. A relationship with one of these overly emotional types can eventually make them feel crazy. Somewhere along the way, these women may sense they are drawing a curtain of insensitivity about themselves, much as they have accused men of doing in the past. They want to shout, "Will you just shut up and make love to me and stop this endless discussion about us?" "Where we're at" with this man is all too frequently talking about his feelings toward you, toward himself, and toward the relationship—"talking about" rather than letting it just happen.

The Clam is too contained, while the overly sensitive Pseudo-Liberated Male is too uncontained. He wears his insecurities like medals on his chest.

Trying to free this man from his emotional problem can make a woman feel powerful, but it's a trap. They are better left alone. You might even be doing them a favor, for then they would be forced to deal with their insecurities themselves, from the inside out, rather than attempting to foist the responsibility on some woman who will indulge them.

Some men who make women want to scream are fundamentally unredeemable. The smart woman passes on these men, regardless of how interesting or intriguing they may appear on the surface. The Clam and the Pseudo-Liberated Male are such men. Then there are two other types of men who are terribly frustrating to women, but who do have very redeemable features if a woman can tolerate the frustration and make her way through the obstacles they place in her way: the Perpetual Adolescent and the Walking Wounded.

THE PERPETUAL ADOLESCENT

The Perpetual Adolescent stopped developing in what is late adolescence for a man—around the mid-twenties. This man's unspoken and unconscious credo is "I'm going to be 25 forever." This stunted growth is not always easy to detect. It is reflected in his emotional construction and in his diminished capacity to participate fully in relationships rather than in the external surface features of his life.

Outwardly, he has many disarmingly attractive qualities. He may be boyish in a confident, brash way. This man often works with the public and is articulate, with an easy, charming manner. He makes people feel comfortable.

Greg, a handsome, athletic yacht broker, lives in an expensive condominium overlooking a marina. From his sundeck, he can see his sailboat bobbing in its slip as well as the pool and tennis courts crowded with tanned single men and women. At 36, Greg still considers himself young and needing to devote most of his time and energy to building his career. He feels no pressure to marry. In fact, he tells himself, as well as more than an occasional woman, that he needs more time before settling down—time for his work, time for travel, time to "have fun."

Greg describes his life-style as "fun." He jogs and works out daily. He looks youthful, tanned and toned. He dresses fashionably. He tells himself there's no hurry, plenty of time to find his "ideal woman."

Actually, these are excuses for Greg to live in a perpetual adolescence. He talks about responsibility and commitment but runs when a woman starts to demand it. He can be affectionate to a woman and mean it, but he is not willing to grow up and relate to her as an adult. When his relationships get to the stage where it is natural for them to move to a deeper level, Greg becomes frightened and pulls away. He typically dismisses the woman as "dependent, clingy, possessive, demanding," rather than facing his own fear and reluctance to enter adulthood. He is blind to his profound reluctance to mature, for his youthful posture serves as a shield and defense against intimacy.

The Perpetual Adolescent's greatest fear is entrapment, for he doesn't fully trust his own autonomy. "To have to give" and "to be able to receive" both detonate deep, underlying fears of dependency in him. This man hides his fears of intimacy from himself by coming very close to committing in a relationship. But he ultimately wards off those fears by always making sure that "very close" is only that, not marriage.

The Perpetual Adolescent has rather shallow views and interactions with women. For that matter, his friendships with men are equally shallow. He often perceives himself as an adventurer. But the greatest adventure of all—marriage—is an event he is never quite yet ready for.

Initially, he can be captivating, for he has fine-tuned many aspects of his external presence. He can trot out all the phrases that make him sound wonderful and make a woman feel wonderful. The trouble is, he's a deal opener, not a deal closer. The Perpetual Adolescent is extremely frustrating to women, for as they naturally want to deepen what seems like a nicely developing relationship, he slowly pulls away. If he only did something truly rotten, she could free herself and be glad to be rid of him. But he doesn't—maddeningly, his only real flaw is his unwillingness to grow up.

We have said that this man is redeemable, and he is. Given enough time and patience, most men eventually do grow up, marry, and have families. For this type of man, the critical age seems to be about 39. He begins to panic when he is unable to deny being middle-aged. Having learned to trust his own independence more solidly, he is less afraid of entrapment and connection. He has become acutely aware of his own mortality, and he doesn't want to become a lonely old man.

While we wouldn't recommend the younger version of this man, the older model isn't bad at all. Should you know someone like this and want to deepen the relationship, there are a couple of important factors to keep in mind.

This man, even though he fears it, is capable of becoming healthily dependent on a woman. The mistake most women make is in not understanding that he does need a woman and can make a connection. Typically, the woman pushes too quickly and succeeds only in pushing him away. It is not that the impulse to move forward is inappropriate on the woman's part, for it isn't, but the timing is critical. This man is most likely to connect deeply to the woman who has patience to let him develop a strong need for her first. Then, and only then, should she begin to make her healthy demands for commitment. By then, he is so involved that he wants to stay.

THE WALKING WOUNDED

After a separation or divorce, both men and women naturally feel a mixture of hurt, bitterness, and rejection. Fortunately for most of us, these wounds heal over time, and the best medicine is eventually to love again.

Men and women usually suffer equally, but there are wounds unique to men that merit understanding. The Walking Wounded man can drive women crazy for a time, but he does heal and definitely is redeemable. In fact, these men often make fine mates precisely because they are committed to long-term relationships.

There are two basic types of wounds. The most painful is, of course, the loss of one's mate and most likely the loss of family. The other is the loss of financial security resulting from the divorce. The loss of a family structure is devastating to most divorced men. Suddenly, he finds himself alone in an apartment or hotel room, feeling lost, disoriented, and forlorn. He envies his wife, who frequently continues living in the family home, in familiar and, at least in his mind, secure surroundings. For the first time, some men will sadly and poignantly realize how important it was to hear "Daddy" when they came home from work.

Contributing to this sense of isolation that divorced men experience is the constant apprehension that even in his grief, he must continue working hard to make money. There is a line from a western song that goes, "I can't halve my half again." For many men, a divorce means money: the destruction of the financial security and comfortable life-style which they worked so long and hard to create. Women suffer equally from the financial fallout from divorce, but it is our purpose here to acquaint you with the male point of view.

Most men feel "ripped off" after a divorce. Regardless of the validity of this attitude, they are nevertheless embittered by the helplessness they felt during the process of marital dissolution. This helplessness is often in combination with the sense of futility they have regarding child custody. In addition, they have increased financial anxieties related to the demand of separate living expenses. In their anxious and dark moments, they're not sure they can make it.

Even though they may be freer to date than are their wives, they have a sense that it's all a dream. They tend to drink and to abuse drugs, which compounds their depression.

How do these men appear to the women who encounter them? If they are newly separated, they can actually appear quite attractive, because they haven't yet assumed the guarded mantle of men who have been single for a while. They may be vulnerable too, which can be appealing to women, especially those who like to nurture men.

The newly separated man is open, eager to talk and to reveal himself, though too often this evolves into a tedious self-pity which will eventually drive a woman crazy. Even so, his eagerness for contact and relationships is quite appealing to many women.

The recently separated man tends to talk about his ex-wife and bitch about any number of injustices he feels. This facet of him can become so boring that women quickly feel the urge to run. A word of advice: After a while, don't be such a good listener. It's bad for him to wallow in self-pity and definitely not romantic for any woman.

There is a common problem with the Walking Wounded that can break a woman's heart. A woman may be age 32 to 40 and childless and find herself involved with a divorced man of the same age or older who already has children. It is vitally important for that woman, if she wants children of her own, to make this desire known to the man early in the relationship. Many divorced men are well-meaning but frankly have no desire to start another family. Yet they will mutter vaguely, "Well, if it's really going well, I guess I might want to have another kid." That's not good enough. A woman needs a clear answer or else it's time to move on. To invest precious years in a relationship only to end up with a man who has very different dreams is tragic indeed.

Men who have been separated for a year or more are usually less appealing than the very vulnerable, freshly separated ones we've been exploring. But they often have another kind of attractiveness: They're ripe for the picking. This is true in spite of their seemingly hardened outer shell. Though wary and a bit suspicious about being hurt again, they will become involved. They can make good mates, and do wish genuine intimacy, but they are scared. The solution is simple: Don't push for commitment in the beginning, even in the first six months. Women who need reassurances right away will not do well with this type of man. He does need extra time, but not forever. After a period of exclusive involvement, it is appropriate for the relationship to deepen and become more involved. He will commit himself if the woman really means it. But in some cases it may take an ultimatum. The woman who acts as if she will wait forever is making a real mistake, because she will be taken for granted.

One final word on the Walking Wounded. There are women who advise friends and say to themselves, "Stay away from any man who has just come out of a relationship. They just want a nursemaid. As soon as they heal a little, they'll leave you to play the field." It is true that they may be overly dependent at first or need to date around a bit, but some of the best men are not out there very long. Men who have been in a marriage, even a bad marriage, want to be in a relationship again. The best men are not single for long, and shouldn't be dismissed foolishly.

CHAPTER 27

Going to the Therapist
En Route to the Altar

Zoë Wolff

Students commonly make an appointment to speak with a teacher, most often "about grades." More times than one might expect, they end up talking not about grades but about themselves and some particular difficulty they are struggling with. When I am the listener, I try to understand the problem and how they are trying to cope with it. I also try to remind them of their strengths and gifts and that such struggles are common, normal for everyone. They are part of the human condition.

But some of these students, who will say they feel "better" or "relieved" by our conversation together, would balk at saying that what went on in our conversation could be called "therapy." They think, "Therapy is for sick people. If I am in 'therapy,' then I must be sick." They don't realize that healing (therapy) is going on in lots of ordinary communication, just as "hurt and injury" can also be going on in the way people interact. Still because of this misunderstanding, some who could use help and be comforted by talking out a problem don't and, sometimes, won't.

I have met many people who think that if they need to talk out a problem with someone then they are "sick." I have met many students who are very convinced a problem means "sick." In raising the matter in class and applying it to a relationship problem—would you and your beloved seek help if you reached some kind of impasse in your relationship that could actually ruin it—some will say right out—and especially guys—"No way." In my view, that position needs to be rethought. A football player who has found a weakness in some aspect of his on-field performance would have no difficulty admitting the problem and working to get past it. The same player, encountering a problem communicating with his girlfriend, might well say, "If we can't work this out between us, then we should go our separate ways." Not a few students have said this out loud in my classes.

And here we have Zoë Wolff's essay on "relational therapy." She has obviously looked into the matter carefully and suggests that "today couples seek a therapist (a skilled listener) not just to manage a crisis . . . but often, experts say, as validation, a second opinion on whether the relationship has legs." I believe that level-headed friends, who can think and who can care are often wonderful healers, givers of the "second opinion," comforters, sources of wisdom just by being friends and telling the truth in kind ways to those they care about. Some have told me that a relative (aunt, uncle, grandparent, or brother or sister) did just that for them but so did one or both of their own parents. Maybe being a healer is part of being a human. *And of course if there are level-headed people, there are also lame-brained people who have only bad advice leading to bad behavior. We have to protect ourselves from them.*

We have also to protect ourselves from people who can't keep secrets and who will pass on to others we don't know—or don't care to know—private information about us. I have a rule about this that I have used for myself for years: *Tell me one thing about someone else that I have no right to know, and I'll never tell you anything about myself except what I am willing to let everyone know.*

Questions for Discussion

1. How often does a couple break up when they should have and could have remained together but just didn't know how to get the help they needed to communicate with each other about a particular difficulty? And of course, the opposite could be asked: How often does a couple remain in a deep struggle with each other because they have no help, no one to suggest "Maybe you need to find another partner"?

2. Do you find it common among your friends to think that if you need to find "a skilled listener" (therapist), then there's something deeply wrong with you?

3. Can you think of and talk about a time when you needed to confide in someone and found the right person to confide in? How important was that for you?

It was classic: She was anxious to get married. He didn't want to be pressured for the ring.

Liz Naiman and Rich Boardman met two years ago while teaching at a high school in Amherst, N.H. They planned to move in together at the start of the school year. But two weeks before the move Mr. Boardman, 28, dropped a bomb. He didn't want to go ahead with it. In fact he didn't know if he wanted to be with Ms. Naiman at all.

"He couldn't give me any answers as to why he had changed his mind," Ms. Naiman, 27, recalled. "He was completely shut down."

Months of relationship limbo followed. Finally Mr. Boardman decided he wanted to stay together and to marry. Ms. Naiman put forth conditions: He had to write a letter of apology to her parents; he had to cut down on his "frat-boy activities"; and he had to agree to go to couples therapy. He agreed.

Once seen as the province of married people with accrued stock in resentment and stale sex lives, couples therapy for the unmarried has evolved as an acceptable, even desirable, way of navigating modern love for those in their 20's and 30's. Aware of the high price of divorce, comfortable

Copyright © 2005 by the New York Times Co. Reprinted with permission.

with the idea of therapy in general and free from cultural pressures to rush down the aisle, modern couples are turning to professionals earlier in the game to help them work through their relationship problems.

No exact figures exist on the growth of premarital couples therapy, researchers say, but therapists and other marriage and family therapy professionals say that young unwed couples are pursuing therapy more avidly than older generations did.

Dr. Diane H. Ranes, a clinical psychologist at the Carolina Partners Counseling Center in Durham, N.C., said in her practice of 35 clients a week, 10 to 15 are in their late 20's to mid-30's, living together or seriously dating and often considering their first marriage. A decade ago few such couples came through her office, she said.

In Los Angeles, Dr. Marion F. Solomon, a marriage therapist who is also a member of the extension faculty at the University of California, Los Angeles, has counseled about 25 unmarried couples in the last few years. "If I had one young couple 15 years ago, it was a lot," she said.

For unwed couples encountering problems and who have decided, at least for the moment, not to break up, therapy serves as a sort of vetting system for the relationship, a role once taken by parents or religion. Today couples seek a therapist not just to manage a crisis—for volatile arguments, when infidelity has occurred, when one person wants a commitment but the other is reluctant—but often, experts say, as validation: a second opinion on whether the relationship has legs.

The length of therapy depends on the couple, the therapist and the nature of the conflict. Some clients, like Ms. Naiman and Mr. Boardman, have gone for just a few sessions. Others go for months and occasionally years. Psychotherapy techniques for young, unmarried couples are no different from those for marital therapy. For the most part therapists, who charge $75 to $250 a session, think of their work as short term. It is common, however, for couples to return for regular tuneups.

Besides being fluent in therapy talk, people who grew up in the age of divorce, the 1970's and 80's, are all too familiar with broken homes. It is part of contemporary wisdom that relationships are unstable. (Recent studies indicate a marginal decline in divorce rates but show that over 40 percent of marriages fail.) Dr. Solomon said: "A lot of young unmarried couples come in saying: 'I'm not going to have happen to me what happened to my older sister or my parents. We want to see if we can resolve these issues now before we start hating each other.'"

Dr. Ranes said her clients were haunted less by hostile divorces than by seeing parents in stagnant or empty marriages. "When these are contrasted to the idealizations of marriage and love in our culture, the result is very high standards," she said.

Erica, 30, a screenwriter in Manhattan, who, like others interviewed for this article, asked not to have her full name published out of concern for her privacy, has been in therapy with her fiancé since last fall, only a year after they met at a fund-raiser for Senator John Kerry and six months after they became engaged. She credits therapy with breaking what had become a fighting cycle.

"I got tired of saying things that I wanted to take back later," she said. "When you're fighting, you go down the rabbit hole." The presence of a third party, she said, calms things down. "You play better in front of other people. Then you can take that home. It's like, hey, let's do that the next time we're in the kitchen yelling at each other."

Dorian Solot, the executive director of the Alternatives to Marriage Project in Albany and an author of *Unmarried to Each Other: The Essential Guide to Living Together as an Unmarried Couple* (Avalon Publishing Group, 2002), said that most young unmarried couples don't view their relationships as casual but rather as a form of marriage. She cited the 2000 United States Census, which showed a 72 percent increase in the number of unmarried couples living together from 1990 to 2000 and a tenfold increase from 1960 to 2000.

Cohabitants, or couples who spend at least four nights a week together, are likely to face many of the same difficulties as their married counterparts, experts say. "If there's a conflict they can't resolve on their own, it's a no-brainer to many of these couples that they'd seek therapy," Ms. Solot said. "If they think their partner has a lot of potential, but there are kinks to work out first, they'll often seek counseling before they make any lifetime promises."

Couples therapy is a logical solution for a fraying romance, however unromantic that may sound. Rather than enter into a marriage fraught with problems, young couples want to work through the angst before the stakes get too high, experts say. It is a form of preventive medicine.

"The preventive idea is in the air," said Dr. Peter Fraenkel, an associate professor of couples and family therapy in the clinical psychology doctoral program at the City University of New York and a faculty member at the Ackerman Institute for the Family. He was also the director of the prevention and relationship enhancement program at the New York University child studies center, one of the marriage education programs around the country that offer workshops. These programs, which focus on building relationship skills, rather than on psychotherapy, began primarily for newlyweds and engaged couples, but are attracting more young couples who are still figuring out whether to go forward.

"I've seen a growing number of couples like that in my private practice and in this course at N.Y.U., from about one in 12 in the early 90's to one in six by the start of this decade," Dr. Fraenkel said.

Not surprisingly, there are few hard and fast numbers supporting this trend. Bill Northey, the research specialist at the American Association for Marriage and Family Therapy, said, "You're asking people to report on a new transitional period: premarital cohabitation and prolonged engagements." He noted that the age of first marriage is becoming later. (The median age in 2003 was 27.1 for men and 25.3 for women, according to the Census Bureau.)

"It's created a vacuum of what you're supposed to do, so you see a lot more issues coming up in this time period for people in their 20's and 30's," Mr. Northey said. And, he added, this group is more relationship savvy than the previous generation. "So when they see red flags early on, they are more likely to try to do something about it."

Erica, the screenwriter, likens couples therapy to picking out paint colors for the living room. "In our generation, we don't have to be experts at everything anymore," she said. "You don't have to be the decorator. You can get a fabulous decorator and still have a lovely home that's yours. And you can have someone help you with the communication problems in your relationship, and it's still your relationship."

Jesse James, 34, who runs a design showroom in Brooklyn with Constantinos Anagnopoulos, said it took the two of them a long time to work out the problems in their relationship. They only recently quit therapy after five years.

"It was excruciating at times to realize that we couldn't communicate like adults," Mr. James said. "But we always had more to say in the sessions. And that confirmed how much we really wanted to be together."

Mr. Anagnopoulos, 30, said: "Over time the recurring issues started to feel smaller in scope. We realized that the bickering was just part of our relationship."

But it is evident that couples therapy does not always lead to happiness. Sometimes it leads to a breakup.

Alex, 33, a public interest lawyer in San Francisco, said he and his former girlfriend knew they were going to therapy to figure out not just what was going wrong but whether they even wanted to stay together.

"What's surprising is that the cliché adult problems—money, sex, religion—are actually true. We didn't have a sex problem, but religion and money were definitely issues," he said.

He was optimistic because his parents had saved their marriage through couples counseling. But after a few sessions his girlfriend backed out. "I got angry in a session, and I think she felt kind of ambushed," he said. Two months later the relationship was over. Alex has no regrets. "I don't think marrying this person would have been the right thing for me," he said.

Sarah, 35, a Los Angeles film producer, said she wished she had such a realization before she married. Six months into her relationship with the man she was to marry, she suggested they seek counseling to work through what she called his porn addiction. She said he put it off, saying he wanted to do it after the wedding.

They recently did a few sessions with a therapist, but Sarah is fairly certain a separation is imminent. She called therapy "a big step in the process of coming to terms with where we're at," adding "It really helped me gain a lot of clarity." Still, she said, "I'd highly recommend doing it before getting married."

PART SIX

Issues Impacting Marriage

CHAPTER 28

Watching New Love as It Sears the Brain

Benedict Carey

You can't really look into the phenomenon of "love" without wondering what actually happens. There was a quite funny account of "love" in the *New York Times* a few years back, where the writer recounted the "professions of love" given their beloved by a number of well-known Hollywood actors and actresses. I had to admire them for their outrageous demonstrations of affection, things like carving their beloved's initials on their bodies and making outrageously imaginative but wild claims about their own affections for their "love." But about six months or so after the account appeared, the marriages (or relationships) had disappeared, you know, up in smoke. You can find the same sort of thing in most of the Fred Astaire/Ginger Rogers films of the 1930s. "I've *fallen* for you," is the refrain repeated endlessly, sometimes embellished with "head over heels." To fall was to love. But, in fact, to fall is dangerous and in falling one can be seriously injured. Still, "fall" was the metaphor of choice. The metaphor suggests being out of control because that is what happens in a fall. Sometimes a fall puts us where we don't want to be.

And it is not such a bad metaphor either. It has some truth in it. Something is going on in our emotions that we don't exactly have a handle on. In some circumstances, you might actually not want those feeling, but they are there anyway. Here, Benedict Carey offers us a taste of some of the research being done on "love." The research suggests that some of what is called love is not emotional but physical and neurological.

The value of Carey's essay is that it may help us to reflect more deeply on what happens to us in "love" without just falling, and falling, and falling. These last words were used by a student frustrated at finding herself at the end of a series of serious "falls" and being anxious and frustrated at what was happening to her emotions. In the end, she came to "talk to and with her feelings," understanding and appreciating them without being, as she put it, "victimized" over and over again by her own feelings.

Readers may be interested in looking at Niklas Luhmann's *Love as Passion: The Codification of Intimacy*, trans. Jeremy Gaines and Doris L. Jones (Cambridge, MA: Harvard University Press, 1986). Though cast in abstract prose translated from the original German, Luhmann explores how social codes around "love" are socially created and maintained. In other words, they are not entirely emotional and physical. Luhmann shows how the codes have differed in various epochs. Luhmann understands "love" as a feeling but insists we need to examine it from this other angle as a social code. Convincingly he shows love to be also a symbolic code which encourages us to have the appropriate love feelings. Without the code, most people would never have the feelings. These codes can be seen in the novels of Jane Austen, and they are startlingly different from those of the 1930s Astaire Rogers films. In Jane Austen's novels/women have to wait for visible signs of nuptial love before allowing themselves to discover consciously what love is. A good example is Fanny Price's love for her cousin, Edmund, in Part 3 of *Mansfield Park*. Her feelings become explicit only after he confesses to her his love for her. Luhmann's ideas are not some invention of sociological theory but, rather, the naming of love codes energetically working on us whether or not we happen to be aware of them.

Questions for Discussion

1. What examples of "love codes" do you find operating today?
2. Can you name any "love codes" at work today that are in fact false or dangerous?
3. In Carey's essay, do you find any specific passages or even sentences that are especially helpful in thinking about the phenomenon of "love" in new ways?
4. Can you think of any recent movies that offer us particular love codes, good or bad?

New love can look for all the world like mental illness, a blend of mania, dementia and obsession that cuts people off from friends and family and prompts out-of-character behavior—compulsive phone calling, serenades, yelling from rooftops—that could almost be mistaken for psychosis.

Now for the first time, neuroscientists have produced brain scan images of this fevered activity, before it settles into the wine and roses phase of romance or the joint holiday card routines of long-term commitment.

In an analysis of the images appearing today in the *Journal of Neurophysiology,* researchers in New York and New Jersey argue that romantic love is a biological urge distinct from sexual arousal.

It is closer in its neural profile to drives like hunger, thirst or drug craving, the researchers assert, than to emotional states like excitement or affection. As a relationship deepens, the brain scans suggest, the neural activity associated with romantic love alters slightly, and in some cases primes areas deep in the primitive brain that are involved in long-term attachment.

The research helps explain why love produces such disparate emotions, from euphoria to anger to anxiety, and why it seems to become even more intense when it is withdrawn. In a separate, continuing experiment, the researchers are analyzing brain images from people who have been rejected by their lovers.

"When you're in the throes of this romantic love it's overwhelming, you're out of control, you're irrational, you're going to the gym at 6 A.M.

Copyright © 2005 by the New York Times Co. Reprinted with permission.

every day—why? Because she's there," said Dr. Helen Fisher, an anthropologist at Rutgers University and the co-author of the analysis. "And when rejected, some people contemplate stalking, homicide, suicide. This drive for romantic love can be stronger than the will to live."

Brain imaging technology cannot read people's minds, experts caution, and a phenomenon as many-sided and socially influenced as love transcends simple computer graphics, like those produced by the technique used in the study, called functional M.R.I.

Still, said Dr. Hans Breiter, director of the Motivation and Emotion Neuroscience Collaboration at Massachusetts General Hospital, "I distrust about 95 percent of the M.R.I. literature and I would give this study an 'A'; it really moves the ball in terms of understanding infatuation love."

He added: "The findings fit nicely with a large, growing body of literature describing a generalized reward and aversion system in the brain, and put this intellectual construct of love directly onto the same axis as homeostatic rewards such as food, warmth, craving for drugs."

In the study, Dr. Fisher, Dr. Lucy Brown of Albert Einstein College of Medicine in the Bronx and Dr. Arthur Aron, a psychologist at the State University of New York at Stony Brook, led a team that analyzed about 2,500 brain images from 17 college students who were in the first weeks or months of new love. The students looked at a picture of their beloved while an M.R.I. machine scanned their brains. The researchers then compared the images with others taken while the students looked at a picture of an acquaintance.

Functional M.R.I. technology detects increases or decreases of blood flow in the brain, which reflect changes in neural activity.

In the study, a computer-generated map of particularly active areas showed hot spots deep in the brain, below conscious awareness, in areas called the caudate nucleus and the ventral tegmental area, which communicate with each other as part of a circuit.

These areas are dense with cells that produce or receive a brain chemical called dopamine, which circulates actively when people desire or anticipate a reward. In studies of gamblers, cocaine users and even people playing computer games for small amounts of money, these dopamine sites become extremely active as people score or win, neuroscientists say.

Yet falling in love is among the most irrational of human behaviors, not merely a matter of satisfying a simple pleasure, or winning a reward. And the researchers found that one particular spot in the M.R.I. images, in the caudate nucleus, was especially active in people who scored highly on a questionnaire measuring passionate love.

This passion-related region was on the opposite side of the brain from another area that registers physical attractiveness, the researchers found, and appeared to be involved in longing, desire and the unexplainable tug that people feel toward one person, among many attractive alternative partners.

This distinction, between finding someone attractive and desiring him or her, between liking and wanting, "is all happening in an area of the mammalian brain that takes care of most basic functions, like eating, drinking, eye movements, all at an unconscious level, and I don't think anyone expected this part of the brain to be so specialized," Dr. Brown said.

The intoxication of new love mellows with time, of course, and the brain scan findings reflect some evidence of this change, Dr. Fisher said.

In an earlier functional M.R.I. study of romance, published in 2000, researchers at University College London monitored brain activity in young men and women who had been in relationships for about two years. The brain images, also taken while participants looked at photos of their beloved, showed activation in many of the same areas found in the new study—but significantly less so in the region correlated with passionate love, she said.

In the new study, the researchers also saw individual differences in their group of smitten lovers, based on how long the participants had been in the relationships. Compared with the students who were in the first weeks of a new love, those who had been paired off for a year or more showed significantly more activity in an area of the brain linked to long-term commitment.

Last summer, scientists at Emory University in Atlanta reported that injecting a ratlike animal called a vole with a single gene turned promiscuous males into stay-at-home dads—by activating precisely the same area of the brain where researchers in the new study found increased activity over time.

"This is very suggestive of attachment processes taking place," Dr. Brown said. "You can almost imagine a time where instead of going to Match.com you could have a test to find out whether you're an attachment type or not."

One reason new love is so heart-stopping is the possibility, the ever-present fear, that the feeling may not be entirely requited, that the dream could suddenly end.

In a follow-up experiment, Dr. Fisher, Dr. Aron and Dr. Brown have carried out brain scans on 17 other young men and women who recently were dumped by their lovers. As in the new love study, the researchers compared two sets of images, one taken when the participants were looking at a photo of a friend, the other when looking at a picture of their ex.

Although they are still sorting through the images, the investigators have noticed one preliminary finding: increased activation in an area of the brain related to the region associated with passionate love. "It seems to suggest what the psychological literature, poetry and people have long noticed: that being dumped actually does heighten romantic love, a phenomenon I call frustration–attraction," Dr. Fisher said in an e-mail message.

One volunteer in the study was Suzanna Katz, 22, of New York, who suffered through a breakup with her boyfriend three years ago. Ms. Katz said she became hyperactive to distract herself after the split, but said she also had moments of almost physical withdrawal, as if weaning herself from a drug.

"It had little to do with him, but more with the fact that there was something there, inside myself, a hope, a knowledge that there's someone out there for you, and that you're capable of feeling this way, and suddenly I felt like that was being lost," she said in an interview.

And no wonder. In a series of studies, researchers have found that, among other processes, new love involves psychologically internalizing a lover, absorbing elements of the other person's opinions, hobbies, expressions, character, as well as sharing one's own.

"The expansion of the self happens very rapidly, it's one of the most exhilarating experiences there is, and short of threatening our survival it is one thing that most motivates us," said Dr. Aron, of SUNY, a co-author of the study.

To lose all that, all at once, while still in love, plays havoc with the emotional, cognitive and deeper reward-driven areas of the brain. But the heightened activity in these areas inevitably settles down. And the circuits in the brain related to passion remain intact, the researchers say—intact and capable in time of flaring to life with someone new.

CHAPTER 29

You're Getting Married: The Wal-Martization of the Bridal Business

Rebecca Mead

Spring 2005, the country was abuzz about the runaway Georgia bride, Jennifer Wilbanks. Jennifer was due to marry John Mason in a swank ceremony with fourteen bridesmaids and fourteen groomsmen. Six hundred guests were invited to the lavish affair. The news media had a field day when Jennifer got cold feet and disappeared. She bought a bus ticket to Las Vegas, feigned her own kidnapping, and surfaced in Albuquerque, New Mexico. The stress of the wedding had gotten to her. The couple has since parted ways.

Jennifer became the subject of a national joke during the spring and summer of 2005. However, if the public had read Rebecca Mead's article, Jennifer Wilbanks may have evoked a lot more empathy. Mead's piece brilliantly documents the commercialization of weddings. Twenty-two thousand dollars is spent on the wedding day by the average U.S. bride and groom. It should give us all pause. It is worthy of spiritual reflection and discernment.

Questions for Discussion

1. Celebration (fiesta) is legitimate and, indeed, necessary in life. Are there limits to its scope?
2. What three virtues ought to guide choice for one's wedding day?
3. What do you think is a reasonable and just cost for a wedding banquet?
4. Name some imaginative ways of resisting the Wal-martization of the bridal business.

Every year in the United States there are about 2.3 million marriages, and to the members of the North American Bridal Association, a trade orga-

Rebecca Mead is a staff writer for *The New Yorker,* and the author of *Billion Dollar Bride: How the American Wedding Industry Ran Off with the American Wedding* (Penguin Press, January 2007). "Domestic Affairs, You're Getting Married: The Wal-Martization of the Bridal Business" © April 18, 2003 originally appeared in *The New Yorker.* Reprinted by permission of the author.

nization for bridal retailers and wholesalers, each of those marriages represents evidence of the sovereignty of love in a world generally governed by harsher passions, proof of an urge toward commitment in a short-attention-span culture, and a demonstration of the endurance of traditional family structures. It also represents a marketing opportunity. For every vow exchanged there is, it is hoped, a sweeping gown of satin and tulle to be sold; for every aisle walked, a trailing cloud of veil. Every kiss bestowed at the altar, under the huppah, or before the justice of the peace is, potentially, an occasion for the use of a silver-plated wedding-cake knife or a leather-bound guest book or a frilly lace garter threaded with blue ribbon. The average American bride and groom together spend twenty-two thousand dollars on the day that sees them transformed into man and wife, and each new union is filled not just with cordial hope but with the promise of profit.

How is a bridal retailer to make the most of that opportunity? This was the question addressed at a seminar entitled "Winning Bridal Strategies," which was held not long ago at a semiannual trade show in Las Vegas, at which bridal-store owners from around the country view the latest in wedding-dress designs, place orders, share gossip, and pick up business-management skills. The bridal market was held at the Tropicana Hotel—one of the less luxurious of the city's resorts, its main attraction being not a scale model of the Eiffel Tower or an indoor replica of the Grand Canal but a tick-tacktoe-playing chicken against which a challenger stood to win up to ten thousand dollars. For five days last September, the hotel looked like backstage at a Moonie mass wedding. There was a dizzying range of wedding dresses from designers whose exotic names—Janell Berté, Lorrie Kabala, Aurora D'Paradiso—seemed culled from the register at an expensive international school. In display cases, there were enough tiaras to restore every deposed monarchy in history. The endless amount of product appeared, to the untrained eye, deceptively similar and induced, after a few hours, what bridal-store owners call "white blindness." Retailers, however, could discern important distinctions among gowns when it came to stitching, boning, and the ease with which a wearer would be able to "YMCA" at her reception.

The seminar featured a Tennessee-based motivational speaker named Chip Eichelberger, whose résumé noted that he got his start in the business by working for Anthony Robbins, the best-selling author of *Awaken the Giant Within*. "I am excited to be here, and I am challenged to be here," Eichelberger announced, as he bounded to the front of the hotel conference room. He kicked things off by asking the members of the audience—who were, as is typical for the wedding-retail business, mostly women in their middle years—to give their nearest neighbor a back rub. Next, he launched into a peppy exhortation filled with attention-getting, counterintuitive statements.

"People say you should satisfy the customer, but setting out to satisfy the bride is a losing game," he said. The bridal-store owners, who had paid $199 each to listen to Eichelberger, looked puzzled. "Satisfaction is mediocrity. If you set the bar at satisfaction, some people on your team will set out to satisfy. You have to set up a system to exceed expectations. You've got to think,

How can I provide a better experience for the bride?" The store owners scribbled down his words. He explained some of the rudiments of salesmanship, and how they applied to the bridal business. "Some salespeople start at the lower end instead of at the high end," he said. "If you get them excited about the three-hundred-dollar dress, it's hard to get them excited about the thousand-dollar dress." A bride's anxiety—about her dress, about her mother-in-law, about the man she's marrying—should be greeted as providing an opening for the self-assured salesperson. "A lot of people are scared going into marriage, and if you can transfer your certainty, that's good for you," Eichelberger said. Stores should send e-mails to brides who came to browse but have yet to buy—"There's a difference between being pushy and following up," he said—and they should consider traditional seduction techniques. "After every weekend is over, hire some kid with a bike for eight dollars an hour and have him ride around and deliver a single rose to everyone who placed an order," Eichelberger went on. "There's nothing wrong with inducing a little reciprocation, if it's done elegantly. I would wager that's why a lot of brides buy from a salon: because the consultant spent so much time with them. You have to help them buy what they really want, not what they need."

Most of all, he urged, consultants shouldn't let what he called the "'Oh, Mommy' moment" pass them by. "When the bride comes out of the dressing room and looks at herself in the mirror and says, 'Oh Mommy', you need to say, 'Let's write it up,'" Eichelberger said. "You owe it to them. Do they really want to go to nine other appointments at nine other stores? Of course, they don't. You're cheating them if you don't say it." Eichelberger also suggested that retailers should work on themselves. "The best gift you can give your family and your brides is your own personal growth," he said. Store owners should involve their employees in bonding rituals, beginning each day with a football huddle and a declared commitment to go out and do serious business. "Motion creates emotion!" Eichelberger said, and told everyone to stand up and punch her hand in the air and say "Yes!"—at which seventy ladies with blow-dried hair stood up and punched seventy manicured fists skyward.

The wedding industry, like the funeral industry, is something most ordinary people don't think about until it's too late not to. Just as with a funeral, preparing for a wedding is an emotionally charged journey into an unfamiliar territory of arcane practices, all of which appear to be the intimidating preserve of experts and specialists. The bride-to-be, whose initial ignorance of what her nuptial role entails is matched only by her anxiety that she play it to perfection, is one of the most assiduously courted customers in America, where, according to a recent survey by the Condé Nast Bridal Group, the wedding business is worth nearly forty billion dollars a year. That figure includes expenditure not just on long white dresses but on all the accoutrements of the wedding: the catering services and floral arrangements and officiants' fees and rental of banquet halls just large enough to seat all the couple's parents' friends but not quite large enough to fit in most of their own. If you add the national outlay on honeymoons and gifts, wedding-related expenditure comes to fifty billion dollars a year. Bridal-industry sources like to point out that the amount that is spent on weddings is more than the national revenues of McDonald's and PepsiCo; it is also far greater than the gross domestic product of, for example, the Bahamas ($5 billion) or Aruba ($2 billion) or many other island nations to whose beaches the newlyweds are likely to repair after the ceremony is over.

The size and reach of the American wedding industry belies the fact that the bridal business is what Gary Wright, the head of an industry association called the National Bridal Service, describes as "the purest example of an inelastic market." The number of weddings taking place annually has remained static for the past two decades, which troubles bridal retailers. As Wright puts it, "No one yet has found a way to increase the demand. No one ever says, 'This is a great time to get married—the bridal store is having a sale.'" Similarly unnerving to the bridal industry is the changing demographics of marriage. Brides are getting older and are more likely to have been married before, both of which, it is feared, make them less susceptible to the allures of traditional bridal trappings: the "Oh, Mommy" moment may not have quite the same impact when the bride herself is already a mommy.

There are other problems facing the country's three thousand independent bridal retailers, who cling proudly to their mom-and-pop status, even though the stores are usually run only by mom—who, having married off her own daughter, thinks it might be fun to marry off other people's—while pop keeps well out of the way. The biggest threat is presented by a chain store called David's Bridal, which has been greeted by independents with all the enthusiasm shown by small booksellers toward Barnes & Noble or by general stores toward Wal-Mart. David's has a hundred and eighty-one locations around the country and is expanding rapidly: already, twenty percent of all American bridal gowns are purchased at David's. The chain, which is owned by the May Department Stores Company, is the first store to sell wedding dresses in the manner of mass-market ready-to-wear clothing. Although many independent bridal stores do stock some off-the-rack dresses, the traditional method of buying a wedding dress has required the bride to try on the store's sample gowns and place an order for a new dress, which can take as long as six months to be delivered by the manufacturer and will require alterations at additional cost. David's dresses can be bought in sizes 2 through 26, and retail for an average of about five hundred dollars.

Many independent retailers have decided that their only hope for survival is to emphasize their specialized knowledge and to persuade each bride-to-be that dressing herself for her wedding is a project that she is about as well equipped to undertake as she is to remove her own appendix. *Vows*, the trade magazine for bridal retailers, regularly features articles suggesting how such persuasion might be effected. "Pay attention to the verbal and nonverbal clues the wedding party gives," Steve Lang, the president of Mon Cheri Bridals, advises in an article entitled "Seven Steps to Closing a Sale." "You are like a doctor watching vital signs. You adjust the use of selling tools and approach as a doctor would change treatments based on patient response." The undecided bride should be urged to leave a twenty-five-dollar refundable deposit so that the retailer can "continue to research the dress you love" until she returns to the store, because, as Lang points out, "taking money is a much more intimate relationship than just giving a business card to someone."

The average American bride spends eight hundred dollars on her dress, though many gowns retail for thousands, such as those by the designer Vera Wang, who claims to create three new shades of white for every new collection, a feat deserving of a Nobel Prize in Physics. After a bride has been sold on a dress, a retailer should press for further sales: a rule of thumb is that whatever a bride has paid for her dress she should spend over again on shoes, undergarments, jewelry, and other fripperies. The necessity of cumbersome accessories should be explained to the bride, even as she sensibly resists their suggestion. "The most common reason brides don't buy a purse is because they don't want to carry it around on their wedding day," one bridal retailer told *Vows*. "Admittedly, this is a difficult objection to combat, but you still need to try." Long white gloves should be advocated, even though they present an obstruction to the crucial symbolic moment of marrying. The suggested solution: a left-hand glove slit at the fourth finger, so that a groom can put the ring on his bride without messing up her look.

The romance that the retailer is most interested in promoting is not the one between bride and groom but that between bride and gown. Kleinfeld, the wedding-dress retail store in Brooklyn, greets women who make an appointment with a letter that announces, "We believe the day you choose your wedding gown should be as joyful and memorable as the day you wear it."

One evening last fall, hundreds of young women attended a Bridal Expo at the Marriott Marquis Hotel in Times Square. After standing in long lines to enter, they swarmed the scores of booths that were occupied by dress venders, linen and tableware companies, jewellers, tuxedo- and limousine-rental companies, and representatives of every imaginable division of the bridal business. The highlight of the evening was a catwalk show of bridal fashions.

But, before the show began, a mistress of ceremonies poked fun at the few sheepish-looking men who had dared to attend. "Have you noticed how, from the minute you put that ring on her finger, your fiancée starts suffering from P.M.S.?" she said. "I mean premarital syndrome. She has lost all interest in things that aren't to do with her wedding day. You've got to understand: She already had the dress picked out, she had the church picked out, she had the music picked out. You were the last element she picked out."

The contemporary conception of the betrothal period as an extended occasion for retail consumption and elaborate event production is a boon for wedding professionals, among whose gloomier number are those who have feared that the traditional American wedding may be going the way of the traditional American nuclear family. Happily, the opposite seems to be true. Apart from a brief, alarming moment in the nineteen-seventies when dress manufacturers stooped to the demands of hippie brides by offering bridal blouses rather than dresses, weddings have only got bigger and grander, as if the extravagance of the ceremony might keep at bay the hobgoblin of divorce statistics.

However, the bride who approaches her engagement with the fervor of a war planner combined with the giddiness of an Oscar winner is, for the bridal professional, not just an opportunity but a liability. "Brides don't want the fun to end," says Barbara Barrett, the owner of the Bridal Mall, in Niantic, Connecticut, her voice heavy with weariness. When Barrett opened the store, in 1993, her typical customer came in for an average of two visits before she bought her dress. Nowadays, a bride averages five visits before settling on a gown.

The Bridal Mall is the largest bridal store in Connecticut, where brides-to-be can choose among about eight hundred different styles of wedding gowns—from enormous, pouffy productions that weigh twenty pounds and look like bead-encrusted pup tents to flimsy slips with spaghetti straps and layers of chiffon that seem less suited to the altar than to the honeymoon suite. Barrett doesn't just sell wedding dresses: her brides can also order engraved invitations, multitiered cakes, and floral arrangements; they can outfit brides-maids and, from the tuxedo-rental department, intended spouses and their attendants. Barrett also provides, for a fee, services such as pre-ceremony gown storage, with visitation rights included: on busy weekend afternoons, the Bridal Mall looks like a petting zoo, filled with brides-to-be and their friends and relatives, all cooing over the tulle.

For Barrett, as for any bridal-store owner, part of the job's reward is the intangible joy of sending a happy bride into her marital life. Yet the structure of the bridal industry conspires to frustrate both bride and retailer; while they appear to be collaborating on a grand romantic project, their economic interests are very different. The bride is afraid that her naiveté will be exploited; the retailer is on guard against the bride who is shopping but isn't buying. A cycle of resentment can easily be established, which, though it is usually masked by the air of sentimentality that thickens the oxygen in a bridal store, sometimes breaks out into real hostilities. Not long ago, one of the Bridal Mall's customers flung an unwanted garter at Barrett after being reminded of the store's no-returns policy; and last summer Barrett was sued in small-claims court by a bride who contended that the fit of her dress had restricted her ability to dance at her wedding reception twelve months earlier, a trauma that had persisted throughout her first year of marriage.

On a recent Saturday afternoon, a steady flow of brides arrived at the Bridal Mall. First-time visitors were asked to fill out a form including the date of the wedding: a bride without a date is instantly suspect, since she may well also lack a fiancé. Brides are also discreetly asked about their dress budget. More affluent customers are steered to the "couture room," which is spacious and painted purple and furnished with a sofa and chairs and soft lighting and plates of butter cookies, and where the cheapest gown costs twenty-five hundred dollars. On this particular day, Barrett had one customer for the couture room, a twenty-seven-year-old attorney from New Haven who, on an earlier visit, had found a dress she favored and had returned for a second look with her punkish younger sister (and future bridesmaid), who had black-and-blond-dyed hair. The bride's choice was an enormous gown that looked as if it might have been designed by a cartoonist for Disney: it had a scalloped neckline and a crinoline so wide it would have been sufficient to support a parachute jump.

It cost $2,899. "This is the only time in my life I'll be able to wear a big dress," the bride-to-be said. "And this is going to sound gay, but when I was a kid I loved the dresses in *Gone with the Wind* so much."

Brides with fewer resources are directed to the main salon, where dresses cost from $299 to $1,499. A hang tag is attached to each dress, showing three levels of pricing, depending on whether the bride chooses gown storage or post-wedding preservation services; also attached is a booklet of coupons with discounts on items such as cake toppers and toasting glasses. One function of the different pricing levels is to confuse the bride who is bent on comparison shopping. Barbara Barrett cuts the manufacturers' labels out of the dresses in the main salon and won't tell a bride who designed her chosen dress until she has paid for it. She also does not permit cameras or video recorders in the store. "We've had people videotaping through their purses," Barrett says. "Like they were from *60 Minutes*," Barrett's husband, Chris, adds.

Such tactics are intended to discourage brides from using Barrett's as a dressing room before taking their business to a competing store or buying a dress online. "Brides used to come in with their mothers, and their attitude about the bridal consultant was 'This lady is going to help us have the most beautiful wedding, because she is a professional,'" Barrett said. "Now they come in and they're, like, 'Look, lady, I've been on the Internet, and don't tell me you can't go lower than six hundred and nineteen dollars on this dress, because I know you didn't pay that much for it.' This is a scary person to deal with." But because of the chain-store alternative offered by David's Bridal— there are four branches in the geographical area that Barrett serves—Barrett cannot afford to treat her more difficult customers with the sternness she thinks they deserve. Barrett's animus against David's is so strong that she will not allow a garment bag bearing the store's name to enter her shop, even if the bride carrying it is prepared to spend cash on a veil-and-tiara ensemble. "Store owners weren't so down and dirty ten years ago, because there was plenty of business for everyone," Barrett says, bitterly. "It has ceased being a ladies' business."

As happens every weekend, there were, on this occasion, some crises: the bride whose wedding was two weeks off and had been provided with a bridesmaid's dress that was too small (Barrett said they would alter the dress to fit); the first-time visitor who, having undressed in the changing room, informed her consultant that she had no intention of wearing a bra, now or at the ceremony. (Barrett instructed the flustered young consultant to tell the customer that bras are required while trying on gowns, "for health reasons.") There was a cancellation from a girl who had been in five times already to try on gowns, each time with a different set of friends. There was a young bride who, having tried on a Maggie Sottero gown with a beaded bodice and a lace-up back, had been "loaded up," in the parlance of the store, with a cathedral-length veil, chunky-heeled shoes, and a tiara. (Barrett sells between three and five silver-plated crystal tiaras a week, at an average of $249 each. "This is the piece that pays the bills," she says.) The young bride's mother, sister, and cousin all urged her to say yes to the dress, even though her wedding was still sixteen months away. There were lighthearted moments, too, such as the bride who made her selection with the help of two friends armed with paddles marked 1 through 10, like judges at a skating contest. Whenever a sales consultant closed a deal with a bride, she rushed out of the dressing area toward the other consultants clustered at the checkout counter, holding up three fingers above her head in the shape of a W, for "win." A failed sales pitch would end in a sorry L-shaped hand gesture, for "lose."

There was, thankfully, more than one "Oh, Mommy" moment. One customer was a twenty-eight-year-old music teacher who arrived at the store with her mother and sister, needing a dress in a hurry. She'd been engaged for just a week, and the wedding was planned for June, only three and a half months away. The groom was thirty-nine and also a teacher. "He told the priest who's going to marry them, 'I'm not afraid of commitment, I'm afraid of divorce,'" the mother-in-law-to-be said solemnly. The bride, her dark hair piled on top of her head and a string of pearls around her neck, tried on six dresses, the last of which had a scooped, off-the-shoulder neckline, a tight bodice, and a full skirt, and was decorated with white lace flowers. She perched on a footstool provided so that a bride who isn't Julia Roberts's height can get some idea of what she'll look like when she's in her own gown rather than a sample, and gazed at herself in the wall-size mirrors.

"This is my dress," she said dreamily, smoothing the skirt repeatedly with her hands, while her damp-eyed mother looked on. The bride said she was thinking of her fiancé. "I am seeing him in my mind and picturing his reaction," she said. "This is the one that will make him forget to breathe."

The big white dress was firmly established as proper bridal wear in the United States by the end of the nineteenth century. Though brides had worn white in earlier eras, it was Queen Victoria's choice of a white silk-and-lace gown with an eighteen-foot train for her wedding to Prince Albert, in 1840, that confirmed the necessity of the costume. The notion that every woman in the American Republic should look, on her wedding day, like a member of European royalty is the principle upon which David's Bridal was founded. "We basically serve the masses at David's Bridal," explains Robert Huth, David's C.E.O., who is based at David's headquarters, in Conshohocken, just outside Philadelphia. The company occupies a handsomely renovated foundry building with stripped beams and exposed-brick walls, a fancy cafeteria, a staff gymnasium, and cubicles and conference rooms whose calm hum is indistinguishable from that of a prosperous insurance office. "In many cases, this is the most expensive apparel purchase our customer has made to date," Huth says. "It may be the most expensive she will ever make.

She wants to feel special. She is living her dream, in many ways. "David's Bridal was conceived by Phil Youtie, who, in the nineteen-seventies, was the owner of a small chain of traditional bridal stores in Florida, and one of the relatively few men in the business. (The original David was one David Reisberg, who sold Youtie his first bridal store.) In 1990, Youtie joined forces with his best friend from high school, a financier named Steven Erlbaum, to open a wedding-dress outlet store in a warehouse on I-95 outside Hallandale, Florida. Youtie and Erlbaum sold off-price merchandise at a deep discount, and the only frills were the ones on the dresses. "We did no alterations, and if anyone needed a bobby pin we would charge them for it," Youtie explained recently. Within a year, David's Bridal was buying all its dresses directly from manufacturers in Taiwan, where most American wedding dresses originated then. These days, David's dresses are made not only in China but in Vietnam, Thailand, the Philippines, and Sri Lanka, where the company established its own factory a few years ago. "The factory has to be spotless and air-conditioned, because you can't have people perspiring all over white garments," Youtie explains. "Everyone looks like scrub-room nurses, and when we first opened in Sri Lanka the workers kept catching colds because they weren't used to the air-conditioning."

The market of brides who were pleased to have an alternative to the rounds of appointments and ordering and alterations offered by the traditional bridal salons allowed David's to expand dramatically over the next decade, and in 1999 Youtie and Erlbaum took their company public for more than a hundred million dollars. A year later, David's was bought by the May Department Stores Company for four hundred and thirty-six million dollars; the company plans to open about thirty more stores a year for the next five years.

Under May's direction, David's has continued an evolution away from its original, bargain-basement image: the new stores are decorated in peach and sage green, and have the bland conformity of an Ann Taylor store. Some special-order dresses bearing the name of the designer Oleg Cassini have been introduced, but the company's primary appeal remains to the budget bride, with her customary tolerance for the rustle of polyester, the scratch of nylon lace, and the sparkle of plastic beading.

The democratization of princessdom promised by David's has, predictably, a substantial business rationale for the May Company, whose C.E.O., Gene Kahn, intends to build the largest bridal business in the country. After buying David's, the May Company purchased Priscilla's of Boston, a high-end company with a chain of ten stores and a good, if languishing, reputation (the company's last big moment was dressing Tricia Nixon for her White House wedding); a tuxedo-rental chain; and a five-million-dollar stake in the bridal Web site The Knot. Information about every David's bride is gathered and tabulated, so that the company's anticipation of bridal needs can be more precisely refined. "Tuxedos generally get bought five to six months after the wedding gown; bridesmaids' dresses, three to four months," says Gary Schwartz, the senior vice president of marketing for David's. With these data, David's is able to send e-mail reminders to its brides at the appropriate moment, advising them of special offers and urging them to return to the store. "The May Company said, 'Hey, you know what? There are opportunities to influence and generate income from other aspects of the wedding-planning process,'" Schwartz says.

The May Company's intention is not simply to dominate the bridal business. "They bought us for two very solid reasons," Huth says. "One is our ability to grow and be profitable and be a major contributor in our own right. The other is to give them an entrée to a younger customer who is forming a household and needs many of the products they offer." The bride is, in effect, a loss leader for May's bridal registry, which is promoted to David's brides by means of discount coupons and advertising. A David's bride is thus a means by which the department store can tap into her guest list, a much larger pool of potential customers for its cookware and appliances. "The number of brides they can put through our door is a lead generator for all the processes after," as Gary Schwartz puts it. According to the Condé Nast Bridal Group wedding survey, the average American engagement lasts sixteen months, and during this time couples shop for four billion dollars' worth of furniture, three billion dollars' worth of housewares, and four hundred million dollars' worth of tableware. While the bride's fling with a David's store amounts to a brief and heady romance, the May Company is hoping for a retail relationship till death does them part.

Faced with such competition, independent bridal-store owners have been obliged to be imaginative about new marketing possibilities. In particular, they are looking for ways to appeal to the so-called nontraditional bride: divorced brides, older brides, and brides with offspring. To the independent retailer, such customers present a challenge, but one that should be greeted enthusiastically. *Vows'* tipoffs for recognizing the nontraditional bride included the fact that "these women won't change their wedding dates to accommodate dress orders," and they are dangerously apt "to forget the wedding and prepare for marriage."

Bridal specialists have a vested interest in the high incidence of both marriage and divorce, and speak of their returning brides with an exasperated fondness, like an indulgent parent. In the past, a second-time or third-time bride would generally have a low-key ceremony to inaugurate a new marriage, but such modesty has fallen out of fashion, much to the relief of the industry. Cami Hester, a bridal-store owner in Melbourne, Florida, and a frequent contributor to Bridalindustry.com, a bulletin board for the trade, says, "We have one bride we have done seven weddings for already, and every time, the dress gets whiter and the train gets longer."

The bridal industry has taken to promoting the idea that you don't even have to be divorced to enjoy a splashy second wedding. The emerging phenomenon of vow renewal is, potentially, a hopeful sign for retailers, though it should be admitted that, so far, the trend seems largely to exist in the minds of marketing executives at resort hotels, such as the Don Cesar, in St. Petersburg, Florida, which last year hosted a mass renewal of vows on the beach at sunset for two hundred couples and reporters from the *St. Petersburg Times* and the *Tampa Tribune.*

Still, bridal retailers know that such events are rare, and that they would be wise to concentrate on actually sending women to the altar to undergo a legally binding ceremony, not least because a satisfied customer may one day be legally unbound. Retailers are aware of the need to keep in mind the question posed in a recent issue of *Vows*: "Are you reaching the future remarriage market by serving the current generation's brides well?"

On the last evening of the Las Vegas Bridal Market, industry members came together to celebrate a specially orchestrated wedding. Because the market coincided with the first anniversary of the September 11th terrorist attacks, its chairman, Randy Friedman, of the North American Bridal Association, had decided that a fitting way to commemorate the day would be to donate an entire wedding to a Las Vegas firefighter and his bride. Last May, the name of Ken Teeters, Jr., a thirty-five-year-old member of the Las Vegas Fire Department, was drawn out of a firefighter's boot. His fiancée was Destiny Esposito, a thirty-three-year-old editor with the film-advertising company the Ant Farm.

Ken and Destiny were, in many ways, a couple who had made do quite well without marriage or a wedding. They had been dating on and off for fifteen years, and were in the midst of renovating a house they had recently bought together. "I don't think either of us has quite figured out why we didn't get married before," Ken, who is tall and ruddy, said at the wedding rehearsal, as he affably accepted the beers with which his friends kept supplying him. "Hopefully, it won't make any difference to us, being married, because everything works real well as it is. It's really just a piece of paper." Destiny, who has long blond hair and an athletic grace, said, "We've been together forever. We've been engaged a few times, and we've had to put it on hold. But winning this wedding gave us the push we needed."

On the evening of the wedding, a hundred and fifty of Ken and Destiny's friends and relatives gathered on rows of white seats on one side of the Tropicana's large, irregularly shaped pool, while the bridal conventioneers massed on the farther bank, looking on. As dusk fell, a bridal march was struck up on the sound system, and Destiny's five bridesmaids, in dresses provided by Mori Lee, walked down past the hotel's bridal chapel, through the artificial grottoes, past the fake waterfalls, and down to the pool. Destiny, in her donated outfit of an ivory-colored Alfred Angelo gown, a veil by Bel Aire, and Dyeables shoes, and carrying sunflowers and Gerber daisies that had been supplied by Amazon Events, a local décor company, was escorted along the red carpet by her father. Ken, who was wearing his dress uniform, looked on with a grin.

Destiny's sister, Bliss Esposito, read a poem she had written, called "They Won a Wedding," which ribbed the couple for their protracted courtship. "So today here we stand, too late to falter, with Kenny and Des finally at the altar," Bliss read. "They're surrounded by loved ones, some close to tears, and, oh, did I mention the fifteen hundred conventioneers?" Justice Michael

Cherry, who had offered his services after reading about the planned wedding in the local newspaper, pronounced them man and wife.

Bride and groom embraced and kissed, and everyone applauded—both those who actually knew the couple and those for whom Ken and Destiny were an astonishing instance of that which is axiomatically impossible: a couple who had been persuaded to wed by the wedding industry itself. It was a very moving moment, and tears of happiness were shed on both sides of the chlorinated depths.

CHAPTER 30

Money, Marriage, and Making a Future: The Letter to Emily

Michael Warren

A few years ago, I was selected for jury duty. It meant being present in a jury selection room at the county courthouse, not very near my home. So every morning for five days I got to that courthouse early to find a parking space and got into the selection room by 8: 30 A.M. I did that for five days but was never selected, but from our whole group of about seventy-five, only three or four seemed to have been selected. The eight hours in this room milling with people none of whom knew each other was tedious. I had decided I would try to read a notoriously abstract book I needed to read but resisted, Jurgen Habermas's *The Theory of Communicative Action,* Volume I, *Reason and the Rationalization of Society.* I had presumed correctly that among people thrown together who didn't know one another, there would be lots of pretty empty talk. And I was right. Over the five days, every single conversation I overheard (nose-in-book) was about money or some aspect of finances. Every single one. Even accounts of family deaths (and there were some) came around to how much money (or how many bills) were left by the deceased. This experience proved to me something most people don't need to have proved: money is on most people's minds most of the time.

But in my reading on marriage issues, especially in dealing with preparation for marriage, money seems to be a back-counter matter, not an up-front one. Money or the lack of it shapes the structure of one's life. Wisdom about money is at some level wisdom about life. The following is an attempt to speak through a letter to my niece, Emily, about the wedding celebration and money but also about the initial decisions in a marriage that will structure a couple's life for years to come. Read and ponder.

Questions for Discussion

1. What would you judge as the upward limit on a couple's credit debt needed for healthy peace of mind at the start of a marriage?
2. Does the idea of "thinking outside the box" when it comes to a wedding celebration appeal to you? Can you be specific about the rationale behind your answer?
3. Can you describe an innovative (in the sense of less costly but creative) wedding celebration you have been to?

4. What ideas do you have for rethinking wedding celebrations?
5. The writer brings up life structure issues. What do you have to say about this matter? Is it a practical one or just theoretical?

Dear Emmie,

That question you tossed me at the end of your birthday-engagement party was a hot one. I obviously bobbled it. "What advice do you have for a niece who has just gotten engaged?" Of course I shouldn't have been surprised. You have kidded me for years about being "professor marriage," as if you thought it was the only course I taught and maybe a course nobody needed because everybody already knew all they needed to know about it. Basically I don't have any advice for you and Anthony. As a couple you seem so wonderfully matched and wise that I am confident the two of you will find your own way.

Well, I've been thinking about your question and I've decided to try to answer it. But what I can offer you is, not so much advice but some ideas about marriage and money. You may be surprised at the topic. "What does marriage have to do with money? Isn't it all about love?" Yes, it is all about love, but it is interesting how money concerns can throw big obstacles into the way of love. I learned this from my students. Over and over again, they have said openly in class that when their parents have an argument, it is almost always about money. In my head, I name this the M&M issue: money and marriage, and I always bring it up right at the start of my course.

I beg the students to humor me and do something they may have never done before in a university classroom. "I'd like each of you to take out your wallet and then take out any credit cards you have in the wallet. You can do this in a way that nobody is going to know your business. Also do a quick count or guess about the amount of cash in your wallet."

Next I ask a question: "How do you feel about your credit card(s)? Good, bad, comfortable, uncertain, unhappy?" It seems to me that credit cards, which weigh practically nothing, carry big emotional weight for those who hold them. Getting more specific, I ask, "Anyone willing to guess the *average* credit debt in this class? Anyone willing to say out loud what your hunch is about what the average debt might be in this room? Just a guess?" This question has never failed to surface many guesses, which then appear on the blackboard. I don't need to explain (but I still do), if you have no debt on your card(s), then on the debt issue at least, you are at peace. But if you have debt—or let's say "considerable debt"—on your card(s), then each month when the credit bills come in the mail, it can be a time of anxiety. Depending on the amount of the debt, that anxiety can be always in the background of your activities, sort of like the low but constant pain from a pulled muscle.

A neighbor, a psychotherapist, tells me that within the last two years her practice has been entirely given over to helping people deal with a crucial issue today in the lives of many people: credit debt. She has devised approaches that help people understand the spending impulses that got them into what she calls "disruptive debt," the sort that takes away their peace of mind and sometimes undermines their marriages. The final step in the therapy for impulsive spending involves a ritual of destroying all the credit cards and working out a set of "promises to myself" on how to think and act on money issues. The bottom line seems to be: "Because no credit card, then no cash, no buy." She says the habit of putting off paying is the first bad habit to be broken. The next is to be aware of consumer fantasies, or what she calls "need fantasies," and the feeling *I really need this and this and that.*

The final step in this class session is to ask a question I was once certain no student would answer out loud but now find they are very willing to talk about. The question: "What do you think the average credit debt in this class might be? You know much more about credit debt among your crowd and age group than I do, because people talk about this with their friends. Would anyone care to offer a guesstimate of what the average credit card debt might be in our group right here in this room?" Amazingly, students, slowly at first but then as numbers tumble out and are put on the blackboard eagerly, jump to respond. For the most recent group the high figure guess was $6,000.00. I have to stress that this guess is about "the average" credit debt. The lowest figure guess was $500.00. Occasionally, someone will ask: "So what?" An appropriate question. The "so-what" answer is about one's love relationship and moving into marriage.

LAYING OUT THE "WHAT"

Not long ago, three graduate students in my department of theology announced engagements. We were all pleased at the news. I have made a habit of inviting such students to my home for dinner. I'm interested in their plans for the future, but basically I want to celebrate with them this important step. Amazingly, all three couples talked, without any prompting on my part, about the first crisis of their marriages, and in each case it was about money, and specifically about credit debt. In two of the cases, it happened to be the wife who had brought into the marriage credit debt. In one case, her fiancé knew of the debt, was very unhappy about it, but agreed they would pay off the debt as quickly as possible by putting themselves on a stringent budget and by destroying all but a single card they could both sign. The second couple took a different route. The husband felt cheated and deceived that she had not told him of the debt. (It was considerable.) She, of course, was ashamed of the debt and it was mostly out of shame that she hid it. They both had full-time jobs, and their solution, insisted on, it seemed, by the husband, was to keep separate bank accounts until she had paid off her entire credit bill. This seemed to work for them, but to me it was ironic. They slept in the same bed, maybe even shared the same shower; but where their finances were concerned they were in the middle of a serious separation. The third couple that spoke of the debt the husband brought into the marriage did not talk about how they were resolving the problem, and I did not ask.

So, Emily, money and marriage? Oh. Yes. It is definitely an issue. But so far I haven't gotten to the initial expenses of marriage: wedding; first home or apartment; furniture, etc.

FINANCING THE MOVE TO MARRIAGE

In dealing with the move to marriage, I am not going to suppose that a couple's parents are going to be able to foot the bill for the pre-wedding dinners, the wedding, and the reception. The costs of these things are now so astronomical that most people just tremble before them. Each semester I ask students what the current costs are for a reception in "a wedding palace," you know, one of those catering halls that need to be rented up to a full year in advance. But I do know that the expense is forbidding. For some places, someone, often parents, has to put down a very large, non-refundable sum in advance. It puts some parents under great financial stress. A student in my marriage class last year told us all about the gory details of her sister's wedding. The story is tragic. Her sister found out that her fiancé had on the sneak continued during their engagement a relationship with a girlfriend and during that time fathered her child. When her sister found out, a week before the wedding, she was devastated.

She immediately set about to cancel the wedding. But her father who had paid thousands of non-refundable dollars for the wedding insisted she go through with the event. The wedding was five days away, and he had already paid for the whole thing. The wedding had to be held because he had already paid. And so, according to her sister, her wedding was a lie in the sense that it was the opposite of what it seemed on the surface. The annulment was planned before the ceremony. What was most powerful in this articulate account of what she called "the victimization of my sister" was her anger at her sister's being pressured to dramatize a lie in a mock wedding. She endured a double betrayal—by her father and by her fiancé. In the following class, this student brought in a wedding photo of her sister and passed it around for us all to ponder.

And so, Emily, this story (and others) raises for me the following question: Can the wedding torpedo the marriage? Can a wedding be such a "big number" that it interferes in a fundamental way with the relationship of the couple? This questions needs to be carefully considered.

Re-imagining the Wedding Celebration

I might be wrong but one of the things that can easily happen to a couple planning a wedding is that their imagination is locked in by the weddings they have been to. When we have a chance to talk, I'll go into this in detail, if you'd like. The "wedding celebration" challenge is to re-imagine it in a way that is deep fun and festivity and low cost. One recent example is the wedding of two former grad students. They had very little money, as did their parents. So they decided to have the wedding celebration at a summer camp not far from their church. It was May and the camp would not open till July. The camp directors were pleased to have it used, and their main concern was that the space used be fully cleaned up after the wedding. (And it was.) The camp's main building was a big open-sided pavilion that could be used in case of rain, and it was under that roof that the actual wedding vows were exchanged. The wedding dinner was a picnic out on the spacious grassy camp assembly area.

To take care of the celebration, the couple spent several weeks figuring out how many would come to the wedding celebration and what sort of food they thought the celebrants might like. Then they grouped the people they expected to attend by what they knew of their culinary skills. They needed to do this because all the food at the celebration would be cooked or assembled by those who attended the wedding. In other words, everyone was going to be invited to not just attend the celebration but to bring food to it as well. They were invited to make their favorite "specialty dish." My wife and I were asked to bring a garden salad for twelve. The biggest problem with this request was finding a bowl huge enough to accommodate such a salad. (We bought a gigantic plastic bowl from a catering company.) About a hundred persons attended this wedding and everyone brought a dish they decided would add to the joy and festivity of the wedding. We weren't just attending. We are integrally part of the event itself. Each was asked to attach their names to what they brought so that people who wanted to share recipes could.

The "eats" at that wedding are still fondly remembered. But so is the wedding celebration itself, and it has sparked for some a re-imagination of the wedding celebration: low-cost, more fun, more celebration, more mixing, more dancing, etc. than at many weddings. For music we all brought the music we liked and wanted to dance to. There was no band. Unfortunately, no one thought to suggest we bring some original or non-original poetry to commemorate the event. It would have added a wonderful touch. We didn't attend a festival someone else set up for us; we attended a festival we all put together with this couple as a common work of love. After the wedding it was not just "him and her" on their own; they were part of a community of care.

AFTER THE WEDDING: THE NEW PATTERNS

It is hard to generalize about the move to marriage and what it might mean to a couple financially. Some couples have parents who have been saving to help them with this important move, but obviously not all. And today, the cost of housing is extremely high, especially on the East Coast where you now live and in all likelihood will decide to live, at least at the start of your marriage. When I talk about "housing," I'm not talking about buying a home but about renting an apartment. The cost of apartments where you live is out of reach for many people. For first renters, you have to come up with the first month's rent in advance and also a month's "security" deposit. And those costs get you an empty apartment, bare walls and all.

The first household, your first "nest," is important and exciting, and you'll probably have fond memories of it for the rest of your lives. But for all the importance of the apartment itself, its location is just as important. How far will it be from your families and from your places of work? Not everyone considers this question when deciding on the location of their new household. It would seem wise to pick a location where you could stay put for a couple of years at least, so as to avoid another round of moving expenses too quickly.

How far will the first household be from your places of work? The distance of the commute is not the problem; it is the time the commute takes out of your time together. Especially at the beginning of a partnership, most couples need lots of time together, casual time, not rushed time. It is hard to explain exactly why, but that time is needed for the continuing bonding in their relationship. An unwise commute can drain away that precious time for being together. What's an unwise commute? Well, I'd say it is a commute that has not been very carefully considered for its impact on your time together.

I knew a couple who opted after their wedding to buy a home in a new development in New Jersey. She was pregnant and they decided they should sink roots somewhere. The house was spanking new, affordable, and in an area with many young newly-marrieds like themselves. The problem turned out to be this: the location of the development meant for him a two-hour commute each way. So, his workday was not eight hours long but twelve. (And his work was driving a delivery truck.) He came home each night exhausted and hungry. After dinner he was ready to tumble into bed and sleep. With the birth of their second child, the pressures on her as a sort of "single mom" also began to mount. She asked me, "Is this what marriage is meant to be?" To make matters worse, Saturday, the day when she looked forward to some "personal space," with her husband spending some time with the children, was the day he insisted he needed to get out for basketball with friends. For this couple time pressures and the need for more leisure time were sapping the life of their marriage. And those time pressures came from the distance of his work from their home and the four-hour commute. Was it possible for them to have planned more consciously for spending more time together? Could they have rented close to his work, at least for an agreed upon period of time? And did the purchase of a new home put them under financial pressures that renting might have avoided?

THE ISSUE OF LIFE STRUCTURE

Decisions about love, desire and affection surely give direction to our lives. That is something everyone knows. But money and time also tend to structure our lives. Behind "direction" and "structure" are latent metaphors needing attention. Direction suggests movement but structure suggests containment. Both movement and structure need to be in synch with each other. We need a life structure that does not imprison us, and a direction that is wisely set out, as a thoughtful plan for achieving a goal. Money and time are also valuable resources needing watchful care. We cannot take them for granted without peril for ourselves and those we love.

Nurturing a marriage takes time, time together, and time focusing on one another's needs, love time, celebrative time. Such time is "above the price of rubies." Wise planning can help ensure that mundane money matters do not subvert what is, like the rubies, priceless.

PART SEVEN

Commitment, Divorce, and Annulment

CHAPTER 31

What God Has Joined Together . . .

Bernard Cooke

One of the most important essays in this collection is the following one by Bernard Cooke. It deserves and probably will require more than one reading. In addition, most students will probably need to be introduced to some of its technical language and to the process thought on which it is partly based.

Cooke looks at marriage from the points of view of biology, social institution, distinctive personal relationship, and biblically based covenant. He also brings to his discussion the three theological shifts outlined at the start of his essay. Basically, he proposes that marriage as the paradigm form of human friendship should at its best mature into an increasingly indissoluble bond between persons. It is his argument for this position that calls for study. Two sets of questions will aid in examining it, those Cooke himself asks at the very end of his essay and the questions for discussion.

Questions for Discussion

1. Cooke takes very seriously the deep sacramental value of marriage. Which of his statements were for you the clearest expression of this value?

2. What does Cooke mean by saying "The source of whatever indissolubility attaches to a particular marriage must be the character of the marriage itself" and its symbolic import as a Christian sacrament?

3. What do you say to Cooke's point that a marriage becomes increasingly indissoluble as it becomes increasingly Christian?

4. Is Cooke contradicting himself when he says that a couple can be truly married but at the same time still in the process of becoming married to each other?

5. How would you summarize Cooke's position on indissolubility?

6. How would you summarize his position on sexual intercourse?

Among the pastoral problems to which Catholic theology should address attention, few have as widespread impact as the question of the indissolubility of Christian marriages. That we are seriously reexamining this ele-

Copyright © 1987, Commonweal Foundation. Reprinted with permission. For subscriptions: www.commonwealmagazine.org.

ment of Catholic teaching reflects pastoral anxiety for the well-being of the millions of women and men in situations that have separated them from their Catholic roots. But it reflects also the broadened context of doing theology today, and it is to this aspect of reflection on indissolubility that I wish to direct my remarks.

Today's developments in theology constitute a multifaceted phenomenon; within this complex change, it seems to me that three shifts are of special relevance to the topic of our discussion. (1) Today we are using the life experience of believing Christians, as individuals and as communities, as the starting point of our theological reflection. While other sources of insight—Scripture, traditional teaching, liturgy, etc.—enter in as principles of interpretation, it is the providential action of God in people's lives that provides the immediate "word" of revelation with which we must deal as theologians. (2) We are gradually absorbing into our theological process the historical consciousness, the awareness of *process*, and the general acceptance of evolution that are hallmarks of modern Western thought. In doing so, we have rediscovered the eschatological perspective that characterizes biblical thought. (3) We are beginning to theologize ecumenically, realizing that we cannot ignore other Christian traditions—for that matter, religious traditions other than Christian—in our attempts to understand more deeply and accurately the workings of the divine with humans.

Let us, then, draw upon the first of these methodological shifts, namely the use of Christian experience as a basis for reflection. Here we are faced with the concrete and unavoidable reality: according to every ordinary observable measure, large numbers of Catholic marriages do, in fact, dissolve. Can we in the face of this widespread experience justifiably say that these marriages continue to exist?

Any response to that question must distinguish among several meanings of "marriage." For example, at the most elemental biological level, where marriage involves two people mating for the continuation of the race, it is undeniable that in many cases such a strictly biological relationship does not and need not continue beyond a certain point. As a social institution providing stability for the process of begetting and raising children, marriage can take various forms, including, in modern societies, persons being involved in a sequence of marriage–divorce–remarriage. As a distinctive personal relationship involving a unique sexual commitment, marriage does suggest some aspect of indissolubility—at least many people do believe and hope as they marry that this special self-giving is "forever." Nonetheless, the large number of people who have given up this attitude for one of remaining together "as long as things work out" suggests that there is no self-evident and adequate grounding for indissolubility in some promise intrinsic to marital sexual self-giving.

Finally, as a paradigm form of human friendship, marriage at its best should certainly mature into an increasingly indissoluble bond between persons; but human experience teaches us the bitter lesson that friendships, even long-standing and treasured ones, do not always stand the test of time. While it may always be "eternally true" that two married persons *were* close friends, if the friendship does cease, one simply cannot assert that it continues and constitutes indissolubility.

The reproductive drive of the species, society's concern for successful childbearing, marital sexual intimacy, human friendship—all these dimensions of marriage certainly point to some degree of permanence, but not to sufficient grounds for universally attributing indissolubility to all marriages, including Catholic marriages.

We enter a somewhat different realm, however, when we regard Catholic marriage in the light of the bibilical/theological category of covenant. In this context, the contractual aspect of the pledge between woman and man in marriage takes on added dimensions: the couple commit themselves to one another, but they also commit themselves *as a couple* to participate sacramentally and ministerially in the life of the Christian community; they commit themselves to shared discipleship and a life together of working for the establishment of the Kingdom of God. Not that all Catholic couples as they begin their married life are conscious of and open to this broader meaning of their marital contract, but this is the intrinsic reality of Christian marriage which we can hope will become understood and appreciated by people.

Certainly, we are closer to a grounding for indissolubility when we regard Catholic marriage as Christian covenant, for the promise involved has a clearly eschatological orientation; it reaches in its significance to the divine. But what are we to say when the contract has been broken by one or both parties? We might in some cases say that there has been infidelity that extends beyond the two persons to the Christian community and to God, that there has been sinful negligence or malice, that some responsibilities may still remain from the earlier covenant commitment. But can we say, for example, that an innocent and betrayed person in a marriage, a person who has, clearly been irrevocably deserted, is still involved in a one-sided contract? Can a person remain committed to the Christian community to live out a sacramental relationship that is existentially impossible?

One can, of course, give an essentially legal response to this question: we have a law, a law that gives expression to a view of Catholic marriage which we are not free to abandon. Much as it pains us, the overall common good requires that exceptions not be made, so that the indissoluble character of Christian marriage will be safeguarded. But does the preservation of this ideal demand the absolutely universal implementation of this rule? Perhaps this law itself is meant to be the statement of an ideal toward which Catholics should strive with varying degrees of success or failure. Having raised that question, let us bracket it for the moment and come back to it after we have treated some other elements of sacramental theology.

A final possibility for grounding the indissolubility of Christian marriage lies in the sacramentality of the two Christian persons as they live in relationship to one another. They are the sacrament, not simply because they are recognizable in the community as the two who publicly bound themselves by marital contract, but because and *to the extent* that they can be recognized as translating Christian faith into their married and family life. For Christians the parameters, of personal destiny, of personal responsibility and commitment, of personal development and achievement, in brief of human life, are broadened by the revelation contained in the life and death and resurrection of Jesus of Nazareth. This is true of individual human existence; it is true of the shared existence that is marriage.

When two Christians are married they commit not only their growth as persons to one another; they commit their faith, their relation to God in Christ to one another—obviously, not totally, but to a very considerable degree. The concrete interaction with one another in their daily life will unavoidably serve as "word of God" in the light of which they will develop their self-image, their freedom, their values, their faith and hope and love.

But God's word, no matter what the medium of its transmission, has always been a promise of unconditioned divine fidelity. No characteristic is more emphasized in the biblical literature; Israel's God is a faithful God. When we come to the New Testament, the raising of Jesus from the dead is seen as the culminating fulfillment of God's promises, the supreme proof of divine fidelity. And the question comes then: Can a Christian marriage truly sacramentalize, i.e., both speak of and make present, this divine fidelity unless it itself bears the mark of unfailing, irrevocable endurance? Can a marriage speak experientially about a divine love that never fails, unless it itself is lived as a relationship that is indissoluble? Or—to change the question slightly, but perhaps importantly—if it is not lived this way can one speak of it as sacramental?

In this context, we can return to the questions raised earlier about the commitment implicit in marital intercourse. That there is some special personal commitment signified by this action is hard to deny, but it is also hard to deny that it is signified only to the extent that this act is one of genuine personal love, expressive of each person's selfhood and honest respect of the other's selfhood. The extent to which an actual situation of sexual interchange symbolizes an irrevocable, i.e., indissoluble, commitment of each to the other seems, then, to be commensurate with the attitudes, understandings, etc., of the two people engaged in marital intercourse. Apparently we must ask, in a somewhat more restricted form, the question we just raised about the broader reality of Catholic marriage: When are we justified in applying the term "sacramental"?

Without suggesting any final answer to these questions, it does seem that we can associate the indissolubility of Christian marriage more satisfactorily with the sacramentality of marriage than with any other aspect. Historical studies have pointed out how the meaning of "sacrament" as applied to marriage has shifted from the emphasis on "binding promise" which it had in Augustine's explanation of Christian marriage to greater stress in medieval and subsequent centuries on the meaning of "Christian symbol." On the other hand, comtemporary sacramental theology has increasingly broadened the scope of sacrament beyond simply the liturgical ritual; and it has moved away from the "automatic effect" mentality that characterized so much post-Tridentine explanation of sacraments and has instead re-emphasized the extent to which the sanctifying effectiveness of sacraments depends on the awareness and decisions of the Christian people involved in one or other sacramental context.

Inadequate as our understanding of the sacramentality of Christian marriage is, it does seem to provide some focus for the practical pastoral judgments about indissolubility that we face at this moment in Christian history. Perhaps we can sharpen the focus a bit by raising the question: If indissolubility is in some way and to some degree "intrinsic" to Christian marriage, what is the source of this indissolubility *in a particular case?*

Is God the source—or, to put it more bluntly, is God doing something extra to make a particular Christian marriage indissoluble? Unless I misread present theological developments, it seems that we are presently moving toward a reinterpretation of "providence" in terms of the divine *presence* in the lives of humans. But if this is so, and if we then apply this to marriage, it would accentuate the importance of awareness and free decision in the sacramentality of any given marriage, for God's presence to humans is conditioned by their conscious and free acceptance of the divine saving love.

Is the church the source? Does the Christian community, more specifically do the bearers of authority in the church, have the power to make Catholic marriages dissoluble? And if they do have such power, is their exercise of this power the cause of Catholic marriages being indissoluble? I know of no theological voice that would clearly respond "yes," that would go beyond claiming for the church the power to proclaim and defend and socially implement (within the church's own internal life) an indissolubility that already exists in Christian marriage prior to any church action or regulation.

But has not the official church, at least as far back as Trent, claimed the power to govern the *existence* of Catholic marriages by its legal activity? Despite the most Christian self-giving on the part of two devoted Catholics, the absence of the legally established form or of proper delegation on the part of the witnessing cleric rendered their marriage invalid.

For example, years ago, when I was studying the canon law of marriage, the teacher highlighted the importance of "proper form" by repeating a canonical "horror story"—whether factual or not, the story quite clearly made its point. According to the account, a socially prominent young couple, wishing to avoid all the fuss of a big public wedding celebration, went for advice to the chancellor of a large U.S. diocese, since he was a close friend of the woman's family. Sympathetic to the young people's desire, he offered to marry them privately in his office; so, he requested his secretary to join them as witness to the marriage, the marriage was performed, and the young couple on their honeymoon informed their respective families of the fait accompli. However, the next day the chancellor—obviously with great embarrassment—realized the lack of due form because there had been only the one witness to the marriage. Clearly, it would have been catastrophic to contact the newly married in the midst of their honeymoon and ask them to return so that they could be married. Legalism was able, however, to triumph: the chancellor obtained a "sanatio in radice" and the young couple never had to know that they began their married life in a state of material sin.

Common sense seems to say that there is something wrong here. Let us suppose that the diocesan chancellor had never realized his error, and that without any legal "sanation" the two people had lived a life together that reflected to their children and to all who knew them the transforming presence of God's love. Could one truly say that there did not exist a deeply sacramental Christian marriage? My purpose in citing this example is not to ridicule canonical arrangements in the church; rather, it is to raise some basic questions about ecclesiastical claims to make things be or not be. More precisely, it is to question ecclesiastical power to condition the indissolubility of marriages.

We seem to be left, then, with no other clear alternative than the one we have already discovered; the source of whatever indissolubility attaches to a particular marriage must be the character of the marriage itself, more specifically its symbolic import as a Christian sacrament.

Up to this point our reflection together could quite justifiably be faulted for the static way in which it has treated marriage, so let us examine the indissolubility of Christian marriage from the perspective of *marriage as process.* Marriages come into existence over a considerable length of time, conditioned by any number of occurrences and experiences and choices, progressing—if they do progress—through stages of change that find their Christian explanation in terms of the mystery of death and resurrection. Men and women are gradually initiated into marriage as a human relationship and a Christian sacrament; the initiation is never completed in this life—no more than is a person's lifelong initiation into Christianity, for becoming married is for most Christians a major element in the broader initiation into the Christ.

It would seem, then, that one should not talk about a marriage as being completely or absolutely indissoluble but as becoming increasingly indissoluble as it becomes increasingly Christian; the more profoundly Christian a marriage relationship becomes, the more inseparable are the two persons as loving human beings, and the more does their relationship sacramentalize the absolute indissolubility of the divine-human relationship as it finds expression in the crucified and risen Christ. Exactly how all this will occur in a given instance is as diverse and distinctive as are the people involved and the overall social situation of a given culture or historical period.

To put it in biblical terms, a Christian marriage, like any other created realities, does not exist absolutely; like anything in creation, particularly anything in human history, a marriage exists eschatologically; it is tending toward its fulfillment beyond this world. However, the fact that it does not yet have in full fashion the modalities—such as indissolubility—that should characterize it does not mean that it is devoid of them. A Christian marriage is indissoluble, but short of the eschaton it is *incompletely indissoluble.* Perhaps we could profitably borrow a notion from recent New Testament scholarship, namely "realized eschatology." Christian marriage already realizes to some degree the indissolubility which can mirror the divine fidelity to humans, but it cannot yet lay claim to the absoluteness which will come with the fullness of the Kingdom. Similarly, two Christians can be very genuinely and sacramentally married, but they are still being married to one another; their union can become yet richer and stronger.

One wonders if the understanding of Christian marriage has not for centuries suffered the fate of being overly structured and frozen by the use of Greek categories of thought with their presumptions of universality and absoluteness. Since "absolute" is a characteristic reserved to divinity, one cannot strictly speaking apply it to any created reality or to any bit of human knowledge. On the other hand, the view of all creation as eschatological accords with the first of all biblical commands, "I alone am the Lord, your God."

Indissolubility is an aspect of the intrinsic finality of any marriage, more so of a Christian marriage because of its amplified significance. As such, it shares in the responsibility to fulfill that finality which a woman and a man undertake when they enter upon a marriage. Indissolubility is something they should strive to intensify in their shared life. But that does not say that it is impossible for them to fail at this task, impossible for the actual indissolubility of a marriage to gradually weaken and ultimately disappear.

Perhaps we can and must say that the *promise* not to engage in marital intimacy with any other person, the promise that each party made at the time of beginning their marriage, remains in force no matter what happens. Perhaps we can and must say the *responsibility* for the other rests permanently on each of them. But how can we say that a relationship that in its human and existential aspects, and therefore in its sacramentality, has dissolved is indissoluble?

The contemporary church is rapidly regaining its sense of Christian existence as a process, a lifelong initiation into relationship with the Christian community and with the risen Lord. This is the clear import of the post–Vatican II revision of the rite for the initiation of adults. As in the past, liturgical action points the way for our theological reflection and our doctrinal clarification: *lex orandi, lex credendi.* "Being Christian" is something a person only gradually and incompletely achieves.

For Christians, married life is meant to share in this initiation into Christ. The clear conclusion is that an individual Christian marriage does not from its first moments completely reflect the Christ-mystery, completely reflect the indissoluble bond of saving love that links Christ with his spouse, the church, any more than a person is completely Christian with baptism. One *becomes* Christian; one *becomes* married.

By way of corollary, it might be well to extend these remarks to the notion of marital consummation. There is a long history of the role of first sexual intercourse between a couple as establishing a societal bond, and along with this a long history of Christianity considering first marital intercourse as

somehow intrinsic to the marriage contract and therefore to the very existence of the marriage. I have no intention of summarizing, even briefly, that
history. Suffice it to recall the operative church law that regards a marriage
soluble if it is only *ratum* and not *consummatum*.

What I do wish to do is suggest the impropriety of such an abstract
understanding of sexual intercourse, especially of marital intercourse. It is
true that for two people deeply in love, there is often profound meaning in
their first full sexual intimacy, but theirs will be a sad married life if they do
not progress in their self-giving far beyond this first experience. Too much of
the discussion of sexual intercourse among moral theologians and canonists
has forgotten that it is a *human* activity, even though they have verbally nod-
ded in that direction. Precisely because it is so human—distinctive with each
couple, fragilely linked with all the other elements of a couple's relationship
to one another, symbolically expressive of so much that cannot find explicit
verbalization yet is itself in need of communication between persons to make
its meaning clear—truly human sexual intercourse needs to be learned over
a long period of time. And when one introduces Christian significance into
this action so that it can become the heart of the marriage's sacramentality,
the need for lifelong learning becomes only too apparent. Sexual intercourse
does consummate Christian marriage, but only in this context of ongoing
personal intimacy, for it can only authentically say what the two Christians
honestly are for one another.

Tragically, very many marriages are scarcely consummated as personal
relationships; they do not grow. Among these are many that begin in a
Catholic wedding ceremony. If consummation is intrinsic to the establishment of a Christian marriage, one can only wonder how many marriages
qualify as "Christian," and therefore how much claim they can lay to indissolubility.

What can one say by way of conclusion? A list of questions:

- To what extent does modern process view of reality affect the way in
  which we consider a particular Christian marriage as indissoluble?

- If Christian couples themselves are the sacrament of Christian marriage, and couples obviously differ greatly in the extent to which they
  are genuinely Christian, to what extent is a particular marriage truly
  sacramental, to what extent does it actually symbolize the love
  between Christ and the church?

- And if the special indissolubility of *Christian* marriage is tied to sacramentality, in what way does indissolubility pertain to marriages that
  seem to have lost all operative sacramentality?

- Or are we to say that the covenant pledge, with one's partner and with
  the Christian community, which one took at the wedding ceremony
  remains a promise to the community even if the actual human marriage relationship dissolves? In this case the indissolubility attaches to
  the overall ecclesial sacramentality of the institution of Christian mar-

riage rather than to the sacramentality of this or that particular marriage union.

- But, to return to our emphasis on doing theology out of experience, is not the experience of "getting married" and the significance (sacramentality) attached to it one of promise to the other person rather than to the community?

- Finally, it seems that we need a somewhat new though tradition-respecting look at indissolubility to discover whether we are justified in applying it as absolutely as we Catholics have done in more recent centuries. It strikes me that a more flexible and individualized approach will still continue to honor the teaching that Christian marriage is of its nature indissoluble.

CHAPTER 32

The Meaning of Commitment

Margaret Farley

During the 1960s and 1970s, it became fashionable in the United States to call commitment into question. Not only were specific forms and concrete situations critiqued, but commitment "in principle" itself came under challenge. We have never been the same as a society since that social and cultural upheaval. Psychologists, sociologists, philosophers, and novelists have attempted to name and shed some light on our area of "the uncommitted." Farley's essay, from a theological perspective, is the most systematic, sophisticated, and sober treatment of the topic available today.

The author sets the question of commitment in the widest social context. The many different forms of commitment, their complex interconnection, and the elements common to them all are laid out with balance and clarity. But what, precisely, is commitment? What purpose does it service? Are there limitations on its binding force? Are there conditions for release from its promise? These are the foundational questions pursued in this essay. The prime case of the purpose of commitment in human love is presented and brings the issue to the center of marital relations.

Questions for Discussion

1. What is the relation of commitment to the experience of genital sexuality?
2. What counts as a legitimate degree of commitment during the engagement period?
3. What new dimension of commitment is required between partners if they decide also to become parents?
4. What situations or conditions would allow for the release from one's marital commitment-relationship?

T he reason why commitment is such a problem to us is that by it we attempt to influence the future, and by it we bind ourselves to someone or something. Two quite different customs in contemporary society illustrate dramatically how this is done. If I am arrested by the police and wish not to

Excertps from pp. 12–22, 33–35 from *Personal Commitments: Beginning, Keeping, Changing* by Margaret A. Farley. Copyright © 1987 by Margaret A. Farley. Reprinted by permission of Harper-Collins Publishers, Inc.

be in jail while I wait for my trial, I may be able to post bail and so be free until my date in court. In giving money as bail, I am declaring my intention to return for my trial at a future time, and I am binding myself to do so on penalty of forfeiting my bail money. In a wholly different setting, when two persons marry in our society, it is the practice of many to exchange rings. "With this ring, I thee wed . . ." symbolizes the express intention of each to love and to share the life of the other into the future. It symbolizes, moreover, a bonding whereby each gives to the other a claim to the fulfillment of that intention. These examples hold a key to the meaning of commitment. If we look at them closely, we can come to understand what we are doing when we make a commitment.

I find myself hesitant, however, to narrow our focus so quickly to these examples. We need a wider perspective from which to view them. There is, I suspect, something important to be gained from letting our minds roam a bit, trying to see the broadest possible sweep of the forms commitment can take in our lives. This will have the advantage of preventing premature closure on just one meaning for commitment. It will also help to keep any one dilemma of commitment from overwhelming us, or any one celebration of commitment from seducing us into complacency about it.

Indeed, the history of the human race, as well as the story of any one life, might be told in terms of commitments. Civilization's history tends to be written in terms of human discoveries and inventions, wars, artistic creations, laws, forms of government, customs, the cultivation of land, and the conquering of seas. At the heart of this history, however, lies a sometimes hidden narrative of promises, pledges, oaths, compacts, committed beliefs, and projected visions. At the heart of any individual's story, too, lies the tale of her or his commitments—wise or foolish, sustained or broken, fragmented or integrated into one whole.

SURVEYING THE HORIZON

Think again, then, of all the ways in which we experience what we with some seriousness call "commitment." Sometimes these are not immediately evident in one person's life at any one given time. When Sheila, for example, thinks of commitment, she tends to focus only on the one area of commitment which right now is difficult for her. Every day she lives with the more and more pressing question of whether or not she should persuade Joshua that they must divorce. Every day she agonizes over her responsibilities, through marriage, to her husband and to their children, to God, and to herself. But she has many more commitments than these, some that intersect with them, some that compete with them, and some that are not in question in relation to them at all. For instance, Sheila is committed to certain truths, to certain principles. From the day she had her first insight into what she now describes as the "equality" of women and men, her conviction has grown regarding this truth. She can no longer act as if she did not believe it. She cannot turn back and live out the roles in her life as if she had never seen the reality of herself and all women in a new way.

Sheila also believes deeply in the obligation of persons not to harm one another unjustly. Her perception of the value, and the need, of persons in relation to one another goes beyond this, to a desire and a sense of responsibility positively to help others. She has often said, "Life is hard enough for anyone to get through. I figure we can't do it alone. We have to help one another." Her compassion is based on conviction, and it does violence to her not to take account of others' needs—especially Joshua's, her children's, the people she meets in her volunteer work and in the political action groups to which she belongs. Genuine caring and compassion serve to motivate her involvement in organizations that oppose racism and violence and that promote economic rights and peace.

There is a sense, also, in which Sheila is committed to herself, though she is almost afraid to think in these terms. Her growing anger at what she perceives to be Joshua's indifference to her and to the children keeps generating in her mind the question of whether this is how she is meant to live. The frightening realization of how destructive her marriage has been to her keeps pushing her imagination to find alternatives, "ways out."

The story of Sheila's life and commitments could go on and on. But even a brief glimpse into it enables us to begin to see the many different forms, and complex interconnections, possible in our commitments. There are, of course, commitments to other persons—some made explicitly, some assumed implicitly. But there are other kinds of commitments, too. For example, there are what can be called "intellectual" commitments—to specific truths, sometimes to "truth" in general (a commitment that can undergird a pursuit of truth wherever it is to be found). There are commitments to values—the value of an institution, or the life of a family, or to so-called "abstract" values like justice, beauty, peace. There are commitments to plans of action, whether specific projects, or life-plans such as "living in accordance with the Gospel," or programs of vengeance, peaceful revolutions, or "being a good mother."

The appearance of commitment in our lives is even more extensive and nuanced than this, however, and more elusive when we try to encompass it in our overall perspective. There is, for example, a kind of unrecognized commitment, one that serves as an important background for almost everything we do. We are not explicitly aware of it (or of them, for there may be many such commitments). We may never bring it to a level of consciousness where we can reflect on it. This kind of commitment serves to *constitute* part of the very horizon against which we interpret everything. It may be a commitment that psychologists could describe as "basic trust," or one that philosophers could name a "presupposition." It may be one that any of us might recognize, if and when it is brought into focus—as, for example, taking for granted that the law is to be respected, or valuing without question the progress of human education, or assuming that things should "make sense" whether we understand them or not. These kinds of commitments, prior to any explicit recognition of them in our conscious awareness, can be called "pre-reflective" commitments.

But if "commitment" can appear in all these forms, what *is* the common meaning that keeps it from being empty as a term? Some clues emerge from what we have just seen. Commitment seems, in our ordinary language, to include a notion of *willingness to do something* for or about whatever it is we are committed to (at least to protect it or affirm it when it is threatened). Suppose I ask, for example, what truths I am committed to. I soon discover that there are many truths that I hold, affirm, am convinced of, but am not "committed" to. What can this mean? I may say, of some insight of mine or some conviction regarding a state of affairs or a direction to be taken, that "I would not stake my life on it." This could mean that I am not completely certain about it. Or it could mean that, though I am certain, it just is not important enough to me to *do* anything about it. It is not important enough to me to let go of anything else for the sake of it (let alone lay down my life for it); it is not important to me even to use my energy trying to defend it through argument.

A willingness to do something seems, moreover, to follow upon our sense of *being bound* to whomever or whatever is the object of our commitment. Our very selves (in greater or lesser degree) are tied up with this object, so that we do not just appreciate it or desire it, but we are in some way "identified" with it. Our own *integrity* seems to demand that, under certain circumstances, we do something. The object of our commitment has a kind of claim on us, not one that is forced upon us, but that is somehow addressed to our *freedom*. Even when we do not feel very free regarding our commitments, when we feel bound "in spite of ourselves" or against our other desires, there is still a sense in which our own initiative is involved when we act because of that commitment.

We could continue to survey the many forms of commitment and to probe the elements common to them all. We need to ask further about the relation of free choice to commitment and the importance of prereflective commitments for the commitments we are aware of making. Now, however, may be the time when it is more useful to take seriously my lantern metaphor and enter the deeper regions of but one form of commitment. To do that, it helps to identify a kind of "prime case," a central form of commitment—one from which all other forms derive some meaning. *Commitment to persons*, when it is *explicit and expressed*, offers just such a "prime case." And it will bring us back to our two examples: the posting of bail and the exchanging of wedding rings.

"PROMISES TO KEEP . . ."

By explicit, expressed, interpersonal commitment I mean promises, contracts, covenants, vows, etc. These commitments provide a prime case for understanding all of the forms of commitment because the elements of commitment appear more clearly in them. We recognize an obligation to act in a certain way within these commitments more frequently than in any others. Moreover, here we most often confront dilemmas and the inescapability of wrenching decisions. It is in these commitments that questions of love, of time and change, of competing obligations, seem more acute. The very explicitness of promises, or covenants and contracts, places the experience of commitment in bold relief and offers the best chance for understanding it.

There are interpersonal commitments, of course, that are not expressed in any explicit way (at least not in the making of them). For example, some roles that we fill or relationships in which we participate entail commitments, but they become ours without an original choice on our part. We are born into roles such as daughter or son, sister or brother. Some friendships grow spontaneously and seem to need no promises. Other roles we assume by explicit choice and usually through some external expression—familial roles such as husband or wife, sometimes mother or father, and professional roles like physician or teacher. Even roles we do not at first choose, however, can be understood in great part through understanding the roles we explicitly choose; for roles of whatever kind usually at some point require free and explicit "ratification" or "acceptance."

THE MAKING OF PROMISES

The first thing we must do in exploring explicit, expressed commitments is to ask: "What takes place when we commit ourselves in this way?" What did Sheila *do* when she married Joshua? What will actually *happen* in the moment when Karen vows to live a celibate and simple life within a community dedicated to God? What does Ruth *effect* when she signs a business contract? What *takes place* when Dan speaks the Hippocratic Oath as he begins his career as a doctor? What *happens* when heads of state sign an international agreement regarding the law of the seas? What *happens* when Jill and Sharon pledge love and friendship for their whole lives long? What do Barbara and Tim *do* when they place their names on the lease whereby they rent their new apartment for a year? What do any of us do whenever we make a commitment to one another, whenever we promise, whenever we enter or ratify a covenant?

We can ask this question of our examples of posting bail and exchanging wedding rings. What is happening in each of these cases? In both, I am "giving my word" to do something in the future. But what can it mean to "give my word"? It is surely not like other things I could do regarding future actions. It is not, for example, like a *prediction.* If it were, I would not be *responsible* for the future's turning out as I said it would (except perhaps in some limited situations like that of the weather forecaster, who is not responsible in the sense of being able to control the weather, but who might be considered irresponsible if she did not show professional competence in forecasting). "Giving my word" is also not like making a *resolution,* where I may indeed feel responsible to do what I resolved, but where my obligation would be only to myself (to be consistent in carrying out my decisions), not to another to whom I had given my word.

When I post bail, I give my word that I will return for trial. I declare to someone that I will do this in the future, and I bind myself to do so by giving my money as a guarantee of my word. When two persons exchange rings in a marriage ceremony, they declare to each other their intention to act and to be in a certain way in the future, and they give a ring as a sign that their word has been given and that they are thereby obligated to it.

To give my word is to "place" a part of myself, or something that belongs to me, into another person's "keeping." It is to give the other person a claim over me, a claim to perform the action that I have committed myself to perform.[1] When I "give my word," I do not simply give it away. It is given not as a gift (or paid like a fine), but as a pledge. It still belongs to me, but now it is held by the one to whom I have yielded it. It claims my faithfulness, my constancy, not just because I have spoken it to myself, but because it now calls to me from the other person who has received it. My money is still my money when I give it as bail. That is why it binds me to come to trial, lest I lose what is still mine. A wedding ring is not just "given away." It belongs somehow to both partners, for it signifies a word that is "the real" in the speaker, begotten, spoken, first in the heart. Belonging to the speaker, the word now calls from the one who has heard it and who holds it. "What is mine becomes thine," but it is also still mine. It is still mine, or it is still my own self, though I have entrusted it to another. That is why I am bound by it, bound to it, and bound to the other.

What happens, then, when I make a commitment is that I enter a new form of relationship. The root meaning of "commitment" lies in the Latin *mittere*—"to send." I "send" my word into another. Ordinary dictionary uses for "commitment" include "to place" somewhere (as "to commit to the earth," or "to commit to prison," or "to commit to memory"); and "to give in charge," "to entrust," "to consign to a person's care" (as in "to commit all thy cares to God"). When I make a commitment to another person, I dwell in the other by means of my word.

Much of the time "all" that we give is our word—not money, not rings, not special tokens that "stand for" us. We stand in our word. Still, when we give just our word, we search for ways to "incarnate," to "concretize," to make tangible, the word itself. It is as if we need to see the reality of what is happening. For example, we sign our name. Our word within a contract is sealed by placing ourselves—in the form of our name, written by our own hand—on the document. In an ancient Syrian form of blood covenanting, a man was required to write his name in blood on material which was then encased in leather and worn on the arm of his covenant partner.[2] Other rites of blood covenanting went even further, attempting to mingle the blood of one with another. For blood was the sign of life, and it was one's own life that was entrusted to the other in a scared self-binding ritual.

When words seem too weak to carry the whole meaning of a commitment, sometimes we turn the words into chants, as if by repetition they become more solid, more visible in transfer. There is an old betrothal ceremony among the Berber tribes, where the couple alternates in a song that continues for hours:

> I have asked you, I have asked you, I have asked from God and from you.
> I have given you, I have given you, I have given you if you accept my condition.
> I have accepted, I have accepted, I have accepted and agreed. . . . [3]

Commitment, then, entails a new relation in the *present*—a relation of binding and being-bound, giving and being-claimed. But commitment points to the *future*. The whole reason for the present relation as "obligating" is to try to influence the future, to try to determine ourselves to do the actions we intend and promise. Since we cannot completely do away with our freedom in the future (think of the gambler who must choose again and again to keep his promise or not), we seek by commitment to bind our freedom, though not destroy it. How can commitment do this?

By yielding to someone a claim over my future free actions, I give to that person the power to limit my future freedom. The limitation consists in the fact that I stand to lose what I have given in pledge if I fail to be faithful to my promise. I stand to lose the property I have mortgaged, or the bail money I have posted, or my freedom to travel if I am imprisoned for breach of legal agreement. I stand to lose my reputation, or the trust of others, or my own self-respect, if I am unfaithful to even an ordinary and fairly insignificant promise. I stand to lose another's love, or my home, or strong family support, or my sense of honesty and integrity, or my sense of continuity within a culture and religion, if I betray or finally break a profound commitment that is central to my life. I stand to risk the happiness of someone I love, if my fidelity is needed in a commitment made for the sake of another. Sometimes we know fully what we stand to lose, what binds us to our commitments; sometimes we learn what it is or has become only when our fidelity is seriously in question. It is clear that commitments vary, so that in some commitments we stand to lose little but in others we stand to lose everything. Above all, however, as we take our own word seriously, we always stand to lose a part of ourselves if we betray that word.[4]

If we stop here, accepting this as the full meaning of commitment, we are liable to all the dangers regarding commitment. On the one hand, we can see the glorious possibilities of commitment—of gathering up our future in a great love, of belonging to another in a self-expansive way; and we may move too hastily into commitment for commitment's sake. In so doing, our one great commitment can end in a grand, but empty and finally destructive, gesture. On the other hand, the thought of yielding to another a claim over us—great or small—may intimidate us, make us afraid that any commitment we make will narrow our possibilities, leave us with no "way out," give us claustrophobia in a life walled in by obligations and duties.

The essential elements of interpersonal commitment *are* an intention regarding future action and the undertaking of an obligation to another regarding that intended action. But in order to see a reasonable place for it in our lives, and to be able to discern *how* and *when* commitment obligates in specific circumstances, we need to think about the purposes that commitment can reasonably serve and the limitations that it must necessarily have.

A Remedy and a Wager

The primary purpose of explicit, expressed interpersonal commitments is to provide some reliability of expectation regarding the actions of free persons whose wills are shakable. It is to allow us some grounds for counting on one another. As Hannah Arendt observed, "The remedy for unpredictability, for the chaotic uncertainty of the future, is contained in the faculty to make and keep promises."[5]

Commitment as it appears in the human community implies a state of affairs in which there is doubt about our future actions. It implies the possibility of failure to perform acts in the future that are intended, however intensely and whatever firmness, now. "Without being bound to the fulfillment of promises, we would never be able to keep our identities; we would be condemned to wander helplessly and without direction in the darkness of each man's [sic] lonely heart, caught in its contradictions. . . . "[6] Ours is not the instinctually specified and determined course of animals insofar as they have no freedom; ours is not the unshakable course of the freedom of God.

Because our wills are indeed shakable, we need a way to *assure others* that we will be consistent. Because we know our own inconsistencies, we need a way to *strengthen ourselves* for fulfilling our present intentions in an otherwise uncertain future. Yielding to someone else a claim over our future actions provides a barrier against our fickle changes of heart, our losses of vision, our weaknesses and our duplicity. By commitment we give ourselves bonds (and give others a power) which will help us to do what we truly want to do, but might otherwise not be able to do, in the future. A remedy for inconsistency and uncertainty, commitment is our wager on the truth of our present insight and the hope of our present love.

Insofar as promise-making provides assurance to others and strength to ourselves, it facilitates important aspects of human living. It is a device upon which personal relationships depend (in one form or another) and which political life (short of tyranny and total domination by force) requires. It undergirds the very possibility of human communication, for it is the implicit guarantor of truth-telling. As Erik Erikson insisted, "A spoken word is a pact. There is an irrevocably committing aspect to an utterance remembered by others. . . . "[7] It is interpersonal commitment (in a social contract of one kind or another) that has been the instrument of structures designed negatively for *mutual protection*—each person from the other, or a group from an outside threat; or designed positively for *mutual gain*—economic or cultural, through shared labor or property, shared knowledge or aesthetic enjoyment. I need not say again that it is commitment that serves to initiate (sometimes) and sustain (sometimes) *companionship and love.* It is commitment, too, that resides at the center of much of the history of religion, whether in the form of primitive bargainings with feared and hidden gods or of a personally offered covenant: God giving God's word, assuring a people of a divine unshakable will, calling a people to their own consistency in freedom and love.

LIMITATIONS ON BINDING

If we are ever to sort out how and when we are obligated by our commitments, we must have some way of determining their limits. Unless Sheila, for example, decides that there is no way, ever, under any circumstances, that she can justify divorcing Joshua, she needs to be clear about the *extent* of her obligation to him and to their marriage. If all of our commitments are absolutely binding, then we shall expect to be overwhelmed by their competing claims, with no way to resolve them or, ironically, to live them faithfully in peace.

Obviously, not every commitment that we make is of equal importance to us or equally comprehensive in its claim on us. We do set limits to the obligations we undertake. Almost all of our commitments, for example, are provisional in some sense; almost all are partial, conditional, relative. It must be so. In fact, we might well ask whether more than one commitment (at least at one time) can ever be, without contradiction, absolute.

Sometimes there are limits within our commitments of which we are not aware. That is, it is possible for us to think mistakenly that we are committed wholly to something or someone when, in fact, we are not; or the depth of our commitment may be much less than we thought it to be. We are in these instances, like the apostle Peter, surprised at our easy betrayal of what we presumed was our one unquestionable commitment. On the other hand, sometimes we are surprised in the opposite way when we discover, like Judas, that we are more committed, more bound, to someone than we realized; what we assumed was relatively superficial or marginal to our lives, shows itself to be profound and unforgettable. In either case, we may weep bitterly at our discovery and be filled with remorse or with gratitude for what it reveals.

There is perhaps no remedy except time and experience for deficiencies in our own self-knowledge. It is, however, possible to be more reflective about the limits we *intend* (legitimately and necessarily) to include in our commitments. To understand limits is not always to diminish a commitment but may, rather, serve to focus it, to allow it to share in the overall power and hope of a committed life.

It is too soon to try to work out all of the ways in which our commitment-obligations relate to one another. But we can see some general ways in this regard, and at the same time gain an understanding of the possible limits of commitments. The terms that are useful for this are terms like "conditional" and "unconditional," "partial" and "total," and "relative" and "absolute." These pairs of terms are not mutually exclusive, so that they tend to blur into one another at times. Nonetheless, they help to articulate how much we yield in claim to another.

If a commitment is *conditional*, it obligates only under certain conditions. Sometimes we make commitments where we very clearly stipulate the conditions under which they will be binding. I promise to do something *only if*, for example, you reciprocate in kind; or *only when* the building code is met; or *only until* another worker can be transferred to this position; or *only if* my insurance policy will cover my expenses. An *unconditional* commitment, of course, is one in which I commit myself to another "no matter what" conditions prevail. Thus, for example, I may commit myself to "go where you go and stay where you stay," allowing no conditions to justify changing my mind or my sense of being obligated. We may discover that while it is the nature of every commitment to refuse to count some conditions as justifying a change in the commitment, yet most commitments are at least subject to sheer conditions of *possibility* of fulfillment.

A commitment is either *partial* or *total* depending on what is yielded for claim. It may be partial because of a limitation in time: until next week, or until the weather changes, or when I reach retirement age. It may be partial because it simply is "part" of something larger—as a vow of poverty may constitute part of a total commitment to service of one's neighbor. It may be partial because it yields a claim only to my property and not to my person.

We think of commitment as *total* when it somehow involves the whole person of the one who makes it. These are the commitments that constitute fundamental life-options. These may be some of the commitments we make to love other persons. When we try to describe commitments in this way, however, we soon meet difficulties in expressing our complex experiences. For example, how shall we describe the commitment to love another person that arises from the whole of our being, that is affirmed totally with our very lives, and yet does not entail a total availability to the other for the deeds of love? We hesitate to call such a commitment a partial commitment, and the hesitation has its own rich truth.

The notion of "relative" and "absolute" can be extremely helpful for understanding the nature and limits of our commitments. But they, too, hold a variety of possibilities that are not always easy to keep clear. Thus, a *relative* commitment is just that—*related to* another commitment. It is, at least to some extent, dependent for its meaning on the other commitment. It may be derivative from, instrumental to, or a participation in the other commitment. But even these terms, describing modes of relation between commitments, conceal complex possibilities.

There is a vast difference, for example, between purely instrumental commitments (commitments that are solely a means to some other end, some larger commitment) and commitments to love someone who is perceived as an end in herself, though an end (not a means) whose deepest reality is in relation to God. For example, Joshua may be committed to his wife and children purely because they are necessary to him if he is to sustain a certain status with his business associates. Or he may be committed to them because he sees himself as a dependable, responsible husband and father, and he knows that they need his financial and personal support. Or he may be committed to them because he loves them in themselves; but since he believes them to "live and move and have their being" in relation to God, his commitment to them is an intrinsic part of his commitment to God.

The easiest way to think of an "absolute" commitment is to equate it with an "unconditional" commitment. In this sense, however, some relative commitments could be called absolute (if what they are related to is the object of an unconditional commitment, and if the relationship is intrinsic and necessary). We might also equate absolute commitments with "total" commitments; but here we encounter the same sort of uncertainty that we met with the partial/total distinction. To keep the category pure, we might reserve it for commitments that are both unconditional and total. This would be the kind of commitment Gabriel Marcel describes as "entered upon by the whole of myself, or at least by something real in myself which could not be repudiated without repudiating the whole—and which would be addressed to the whole of Being and would be made in the presence of that whole."[8] However Marcel's way of putting it may strike us, it is not difficult to catch the central point of what he is describing.

I could, of course, simply stipulate meanings for these terms. That would be helpful for my use of them hereafter. However, since my real concern is to show the many ways in which we must and do set limits to our commitments. I prefer to leave the terms open to various correlations and to continuing refinement that accords with the many possibilities in our experience.

Distinctions such as I have suggested thus far may seem already overly refined when all we want to do is to live out our commitments faithfully or discern when they no longer bind. Fidelity and betrayal are not simple matters, however, and our lives always prove more complicated than we wish. Not every giving of our word to another is an unlimited yielding of an unlimited claim. Nor is every commitment as circumscribed as our vague promises to "drop in sometime" to visit old friends. Through distinctions we may be surprised by some simple clearings in the forests of complication.

COMMITMENT AND LOVE

Like any other commitment, a commitment to love is not a prediction, not just a resolution. It is the yielding of a claim, the giving of my word, to the one I love—promising what? It can only be promising that I will do all that is possible to keep alive my love and to act faithfully in accordance with it. Like any other commitment, its purpose is to assure the one I love of my ongoing love and to strengthen me in actually loving. Given the challenges we have seen to the wisdom, if not the possibility, of commitments to love, this purpose bears fuller examination.

PURPOSES OF COMMITMENTS TO LOVE

Why should I want commitment if love rises spontaneously, and if I can identify with it by my freedom at every moment? Why should I promise to love if there are risks to the love itself in making it a matter of obligation? Only something at the heart of our experience of loving can explain this.

There are some loves whose very power in us moves us to commitment. "Love's reasons" for commitment are at least threefold, and they go something like this. First, like all commitments, a commitment to love seeks to *safeguard* us against our own inconsistencies, what we perceive to be our possibilities of failure. If we are not naively confident that our love can never die, we sense the dangers of our forgetfulness, the contradictions of intervening desires, the brokenness and fragmentation in even our greatest loves. We sense, too, the powerful forces in our milieu—the social and economic pressures that militate against as well as support our love. We need and want a way to be held to the word of our deepest self, a way to prevent ourselves from destroying everything in the inevitable moments when we are less than this. To give to the one we love our word, to yield to her or him a claim over our love, offers a way.

Love seeks more than this, however. We know that freedom cannot once and for all determine its future affirmation of love. No free choice can settle all future free choices for the continuation of love. Yet sometimes we love in a way that makes us yearn to gather up our *whole future* and place it in affirmation of the one we love. Though we know it is impossible because our lives are stretched out in time, we long to seal our love now and forever. By commitment to unconditional love we attempt to make love irrevocable and to communicate it so. This is the one thing we can do: initiate in the present a new form of relationship that will endure in the form of fidelity or betrayal. We do this by giving a new law to our love. Kierkegaard points to this when he says, "When we talk more solemnly we do not say of two friends: 'They love one another'; we say 'They pledged fidelity' or 'They pledged friendship to one another.'"[9] Commitment is love's way of being whole while it still grows into wholeness.

Finally, love sometimes desires commitment because love wants to express itself as clearly as it can. Commitment is destructive if it aims to provide the only remedy for distrust in a loving relationship. But it can be a ground for *trust* if its aim is honesty about intention, communication of how great are the stakes if intention fails. The decision to give my word about my future love can be part of converting my heart, part of going out of myself truly to meet the one I love (not part of hardening my heart because of excessive fear of sanctions if I break the law that I give to my love). My promise, then, not only verbally assures the one I love of my desire for constancy, but it helps to effect what it assures.

NOTES

1. Of course, not all theorists would describe the meaning of commitment, or of promise-making, in the way I do here. What a promise *is* is closely tied to one's view of how it obligates. There are at least three major positions on this that appear in the history of philosophy and in contemporary discussion of promises: (a) the obligation to keep promises is purely conventional—an agreed upon "practice," or "game" in a given community, sometimes a matter of pretense until it is taken for granted and believed (Hume), sometimes a matter of violent discipline until behavioral conditioning gives it lasting status (Nietzsche); (b) the obligation is produced by the promise itself, for the words of promise are "performative," or "commissive," actually *doing* what they say (Austin, Searle, Melden, Sartre); (c) the obligation to keep promises is ultimately grounded in a more general obligation to respect persons, or to sustain moral community, etc. (Aquinas, Kant, Hegel, Hare). Many philosophers hold a combination of these views—for example, asserting that promising produces its own obligation, but only in a context where the conventions are such that this is possible

(in other words, the "performative" depends on there being a "practice" of promising). My description of what "happens" when we make a commitment can be understood as a description of commitment as a performative. But it also assumes a fundamental ground of moral obligation in the reality of persons. Key treatments of these questions include historical works such as David Hume, *Treatise of Human Nature,* ed. L. A. Selby–Bigge (Oxford: Clarendon Press, 1968), Book III, Part 2, Sec. 5; Georg Hegel, *Philosophy of Right,* trans. T. M. Knox (New York: Oxford University Press, 1967), 57–63; Friedrich Nietzsche, *On a Genealogy of Morals,* trans. W. Kaufman and R. J. Hollingdale (New York: Vintage Books, 1967), 57–61; linguistic approaches such as J. L. Austin, *How To Do Things With Words,* ed. J. O. Urmson (New York: Oxford University Press, 1962); John R. Searle, *Speech Acts* (Cambridge: Harvard University Press, 1970), esp. chaps. 2 and 3; contemporary philosophical discussions such as Pall S. Ardal, "'And That's a Promise'" and "Reply to New on Promises," *The Philosophical Quarterly* 18 and 19 (July 1968 and July 1969); John Rawls, "Two Concepts of Rules," *Philosophical Review* 64 (1955): 3–32; Joseph Raz, "Promises and Obligations," in *Law, Morality and Society: Essays in Honour of H. L. A. Hart,* ed. P. M. S. Hacker and J. Raz (Oxford, 1977); G. J. Warnock, *The Object of Morality* (London: 1971), chap. 7; relevant to contract law, Patrick Atiyah, *The Rise and Fall of Freedom of Contract* (Oxford: Clarendon Press, 1979); Charles Fried, *Contract as Promise: A Theory of Contractual Obligation* (Cambridge: Harvard University Press, 1981). A key treatment important for the whole question of promise-making and promise-keeping is the classic study of Josiah Royce on loyalty: *The Philosophy of Loyalty* (New York: Macmillan, 1924).

2. H. Clay Trumbull, *Blood Covenant: A Primitive Rite and Its Bearings on Scripture* (London: George Redway, 1887), 5 and passim.

3. As quoted in Edward Westermarck, *Marriage Ceremonies in Morocco* (London: Macmillan, 1914), 40–41. This same kind of repetition occurs in pre-1965 ceremonies of vows in Roman Catholic religious communities. "Suscipe me, Domine," sang those making their vows, and they repeated this three times.

4. A further discussion of the nature of this obligation, and of what one risks losing, appears in chap. 7, of *Personal Commitments* (San Francisco: HarperCollins, 1987).

5. Hannah Arendt, *The Human Condition* (Chicago: University of Chicago Press, 1958), 237.

6. Arendt, ibid.

7. Erik Erikson, *Identity, Youth and Crisis* (New York: Norton, 1968), 162.

8. Gabriel Marcel, *Being and Having* (New York: Harper Torchbooks, 1965), 45–46.

9. Søren Kierkegaard, *Works of Love,* trans. Howard and Edna Hong (New York: Harper Torchbooks, 1962), 45.

CHAPTER 33

Annulment: The Process and Its Meaning

Patrick R. Lagges

The annulment process in the Roman Catholic Church remains laden with controversy in spite of some reforms since the Second Vatican Council. It is, as Patrick Lagges writes, a source of healing for some, and a source of scandal for others. It evokes anger and confusion or freedom and reconciliation. Once a rare event in Roman Catholicism, annulments during the past twenty-five years have climbed from fifteen thousand to sixty thousand worldwide—with the majority of those in the United States.

Lagges's essay accepts the current structure and process of annulments. The task he undertakes is to explain it. This he does admirably with clarity and precision.

"Annulment," he believes, is an unfortunate choice of terms. An annulment does not deny a marriage or a relationship existed, or that children born from the union are legitimate. It seeks to indicate that some key elements were missing from the relationship from the very beginning, which prevented a true marriage. The discussion, if it is to shed light rather than heat, then, must take place within the new framework of the church's teaching about marriage and its description of a "true marriage" as an exchange of persons rather than rights.

Lagges lays out the current canonical grounds for annulments and walks us through the process. How well does it work? It varies, he says, from tribunal to tribunal based on available personnel and resources—and we would add competencies.

Questions for Discussion

1. In the popular imagination, is the current annulment process a source of healing or a source of scandal? Give examples.
2. Is there an alternative structure or process you would propose?
3. Is the current process a form of Catholic divorce?
4. How would you compare the process to the Orthodox and the Protestant perspectives on the ending of a marital relationship?

For some, it is a source of healing; for others, a source of scandal. For most, it remains a dark, murky process that is heard about only through rumor and gossip.

The subject of declarations of nullity in the Roman Catholic Church has been a source of misunderstanding for many Catholics, especially those who grew up in the Church prior to the Second Vatican Council. For many people with a traditional Catholic education, annulments were rarely, if ever, obtained, and then only for the most serious reasons. Marriages which produced children or lasted for any length of time were believed to be incapable of being declared null. Much of that had to do with the Church's teaching about the nature of marriage. With the advent of the Second Vatican Council, however, that teaching was re-examined and formulated in a different way.

AN UNFORTUNATE CHOICE OF TERMS

To say that the Church annuls a marriage is not quite correct—for several reasons. First, the term "annulment" implies that the Church is doing something to a marriage. In reality, by granting an annulment, the Church is simply declaring something about a marriage. It says that some key element was missing from the very beginning which rendered the marriage invalid.

Second, the term "annulment" implies that a relationship is being denied or done away with. This is the source of most people's question: "How can you deny that our marriage ever existed?" Once again, declaration of nullity does not mean this. The Church, or anyone else, could never deny that a relationship existed. At the very least, there is a civil document and a Church document that state that these two people joined themselves together on a certain date and in a certain place. However, in declaring a marriage null, the Church states that something was there in the beginning which prevented a true marriage in the first place. Although the relationship resembled a marriage and may have produced children (who, according to Church law, are considered legitimate), there was some key element missing that prevented a real marriage from taking place.

WHAT IS A "TRUE MARRIAGE"?

The Church's description of a "true marriage" has changed in the wake of the Second Vatican Council. Prior to the Council, the Church described marriage as an exchange of rights. Both parties were to bind themselves to the right of their partner to sexual intercourse, to the procreation and education of children, to the permanence and indissolubility of the union, and to fidelity to

Reprinted from *Marriage and Family*, 73, 4 (April 1991): 18–24. Reprinted with permission of Abbey Press.

their spouse. A marriage could be declared null only if something impeded that exchange of rights: if the person excluded the right to sexual acts proper to the procreation of children or the right to permanence or fidelity. Marriages could be declared null if one of the parties entered into the union placing some sort of condition on their consent, was forced into the marriage, or was in error about the person they were marrying. In addition, marriages could be dissolved if they had not been consummated or if one or both of the parties had not been baptized.

In the Second Vatican Council, however, the Church's description of marriage changed. Instead of considering marriage as an exchange of rights, it was talked about as an exchange of persons. In Christian marriage, the parties give and accept each other in a permanent, faithful, fruitful union which is to mirror Christ's relationship to the Church.

Thus, the Council spoke of marriage as an "intimate partnership of life and love," and referred to the marriage covenant rather than the marriage contract. It described marriage as ". . . a means by which a man and a woman render mutual help and service to each other through an intimate union of their persons and of their actions; by which they experience the meaning of their oneness and attain to it with perfection day by day"; and by which "they increasingly advance their own perfection, as well as their mutual sanctification and hence contribute jointly to the glory of God." (These quotations are from paragraph 48 of the *Pastoral Constitution on the Church in the Modern World, Gaudium et spes.*)

In speaking of marriage in this way, the Church acknowledges that marriage is a far more complex reality than had been described previously. It was far more encompassing than two people merely exchanging certain rights and far more personally demanding than we had seen before. It now involves the whole person and is described in terms of the faithful, fruitful love of Yahweh toward the people Israel, and the total self-giving love of Jesus for his people, the Church.

This teaching about marriage forms the whole basis for any discussion about annulments in the Church. It is impossible to understand the concept of annulment unless at the same time you understand the Church's teaching on marriage. This may account for the fact that many people today are confused about the high number of annulments that are granted. The Church's teaching on marriage has changed and unless we understand what the Church teaches about marriage, our understanding of annulments will always be cloudy.

MARRIAGES THAT ARE NULL

In declaring a marriage null, the Church states that there was some key element missing at the time the two people exchanged their consent.

At times, it was the canonical form of marriage that was missing. For Latin-rite Catholics, that means exchanging their consent before a properly delegated priest, deacon, or lay person and two witnesses. For members of the Eastern Orthodox Churches, it means receiving the blessing of the priest within the marriage liturgy. However, these laws apply only to Catholics and to the Eastern Orthodox. The Church recognizes all other marriages as valid, regardless of where they take place. For example, when two non-Catholic Christians marry before a judge or a justice of the peace, the Church looks upon that marriage as a valid, sacramental union. To state otherwise would be to imply that marriages of non-Catholics were of less significance than marriages of Catholics. It would also deny the fact that marriage is first and foremost a human reality which, in the presence of the Lord, becomes the sign of a divine reality.

Sometimes, though, the person's freedom to marry is lacking. This would include people who are bound to a previous valid marriage, those who were not of a certain age, those who were related in certain ways or who had professed permanent vows in a religious community, or received the sacrament of orders. These facts, as well as several others called impediments, restrict a person's freedom to marry within the Church. Some of these impediments, such as a previous bond of marriage, are considered to be of divine law and hence bind all people. Others, like age, are merely Church laws and do not affect those who are not marrying in the Catholic Church.

At still other times, it is the person's actual consent that is called into question. These are the cases that are usually lumped together when people speak of annulments. They are handled by a judicial process which usually takes place over a period of time and requires certain legal procedures.

WHEN CONSENT IS IMPAIRED

The overwhelming majority of cases before Marriage Tribunals in the United States involve some form of defect of consent. Father William Woestman, O.M.I., of Saint Paul University, Ottawa, Ontario, writing in *Studia canonica*, noted that this is a world-wide phenomenon. His statistics indicate the percentages of cases decided in 1987 on the grounds of defect of consent: Australia, Great Britain, and the Republic of South Africa, 100 percent; Canada, the Federal Republic of Germany, Ireland, and the Netherlands, 99 percent; France and the United States, 98 percent; Italy, 96 percent; Poland and Spain, 91 percent. These cases deal with a person's ability to understand and choose marriage—an actual understanding of the commitment and what it is they are choosing. If marriage involves the pledge of two people to commit themselves to each other in an intimate union of life and love, then certain things are necessary. Both parties have to have an adequate understanding of themselves before they give themselves to each other. They have to have an adequate understanding of each other so that they know the person they are accepting as their marriage partner. They have to have a basic capacity for intimacy since this forms the essence of marriage. If either of the parties is seriously lacking in one of these areas, the marriage could be declared null.

Tribunals generally state these reasons as the "grounds" for the case. What follows is a brief explanation of what those grounds might be.

GROUNDS FOR AN ANNULMENT

According to canon law, a person is incapable of entering into marriage if he or she suffers from a "grave lack of discretion of judgment concerning essential matrimonial rights and duties which are to be mutually given and accepted" (Canon 1095.3). Cases heard under these grounds usually deal with a person's maturity, motivation, and understanding of marriage.

Because the commitment to marriage is so all-encompassing, a person has to have a maturity that is proportionate to the decision he or she is making. In a normal developmental process, a child gains the ability to make more and more complex choices based on an ability to understand the consequences of one's actions. Thus, there's usually a certain point when a parent allows the child to cross the street alone or go to the grocery store. Another point is reached when the adolescent is allowed to date or use the family car. Society, too, recognizes this development process when it states certain ages before a person can vote or purchase alcoholic beverages.

A far greater maturity is needed for marriage because the decision to marry has far greater consequences than some of the other choices that people make. It involves a person's whole life and is a commitment to the future as well as to the present. Until a person is able to understand that and is mature enough to make that commitment, he or she is not capable of entering into a valid marriage.

In other cases, though, the person's motivation comes into question. Canon 1057.2 states that the parties mutually give and accept each other "in order to establish marriage." This means that when a person exchanges consent with their partner, it must be motivated by the desire to enter into marriage and not for some other reason. At times, though, people have a different idea in mind. Some people view marriage as a "rite of passage" in society. It's something you do when you're too old to live at home or need to do before you start on a career. Other people marry for the purpose of escaping from a dysfunctional home environment. They suffer the physical or sexual abuse of one of their family members, they've been thrown out of their home, or they can no longer live with the unpredictability of alcoholism or other drug abuse. This consent is not "in order to establish marriage," but "in order to escape from home." Hence, they have not entered into a valid union.

In still other cases, a person fails to understand the implications of their commitment. They see part of the picture and mistake it for the whole thing. A person may see marriage as freedom but fail to see the responsibilities that go along with that. Another person may look to the good times they share with their partner but never realize they must share the struggles as well. They see the good aspects of their partner but overlook the fact that he drinks too much, has been violent on occasion, or has been unable to follow through on his commitments to school or to work. They may see the bad aspects of their partner but believe that marriage changes people and makes them into something they are not. In these cases, too, the person is gravely lacking in discretion of judgment about essential marital rights and duties. They have not formed a correct judgment about those rights and duties, and hence enter into marriage invalidly.

INCAPACITY TO ASSUME THE OBLIGATIONS

A second category of cases is heard under the grounds of one of the parties being "not capable of assuming the essential obligations of matrimony due to causes of a psychic nature" (Canon 1095.3). Some tribunals refer to this as a "lack of due competence" or "lack of canonical competence."

There is some psychological ability needed to enter into Christian marriage. In some cases, the person does not have the psychological ability to enter into Christian marriage. There is some psychological factor in their personality which makes them incapable of establishing a life of intimacy with their partner or of committing themselves to a permanent union or to one that essentially involves fidelity to one's spouse, or to the generation of new life.

For the most part, this includes people who suffer from personality disorders which produce characteristics directly opposed to the nature of marriage. For example, someone suffering from a narcissistic personality would not be capable of entering a relationship which is essentially directed toward the good of another. A person with an anti-social personality would not be capable of forming a relationship which essentially involves permanence, fidelity, and responsibility. And people with a paranoid personality or a schizoid personality would not be capable of the trust or the intimacy essential for a valid marriage. These people, along with those suffering from some of the other personality disorders, would be judged incapable of assuming the essential obligations of marriage. Also included in this category would be those psychosexual disorders or dispositions which would make a normal, heterosexual relationship impossible.

It's important to realize, though, that these must be serious psychological problems. All people have certain quirks and idiosyncrasies. All of us have isolated characteristics associated with certain personality disorders. It's only when those characteristics describe a person's major mode of acting, though, that it can be said that the person is incapable of assuming the essential obligations of marriage. In these cases, the tribunal relies heavily on psychological experts for their understanding of the human personality.

LACK OF INTENTION

Tribunals in the United States use less frequently the grounds that involve the intention of the parties when entering into marriage. These are some of the more traditional grounds used in the past. They include an intention against forming a union that can be dissolved only by the death of one's spouse, an intention against remaining faithful to one's partner, an intention against allowing the marriage to be fruitful or against fulfilling the responsibilities of parenthood, or an intention against working for the mutual good of each other. This also includes an intention against marriage altogether; for example, those who marry to regularize their immigration status, or to get their child baptized or enrolled in a Catholic school. Such people lack the proper intention for marriage since they exclude something essential from the marital commitment.

OTHER FACTORS

Other factors can also influence a person's consent. These include such things as placing a condition on one's consent, entering marriage because of force or fear, entering marriage deceived by fraud, or being in error about the person you are marrying. These factors, however, are difficult to establish. Tribunals use these less frequently, especially when other grounds are clearly evident.

THE PROCESS

One of the unfortunate parts of the 1983 Code of Canon Law is the fact that marriage nullity cases are still treated as contentious cases, even though it's not entirely clear about who the contending parties are. Treating these as contentious trials, the law presumes there are opposing parties. This is not true in most instances. In the majority of the cases before marriage tribunals, both parties agree that the marriage was null from the beginning. This produces the anomaly of having a contentious case with no contending parties. However, since these are the procedures that must be followed at the present time, most tribunals seek to apply these laws as pastorally and as sensitively as possible in order to find just and equitable solutions to the pain of marital breakdown.

The nullity process usually begins within the local parish. This is always going to be the key contact for the person seeking to have a marriage declared null. While at one time, divorced people were excluded from participation in the life of the Church, this is no longer true today. Pope John Paul II, in his *Apostolic Exhortation on the Christian Family in the Life of the World*, has stated: "I earnestly call upon pastors and the whole community of the faithful to help the divorced and with solicitous care to make sure that they do not consider themselves as separated from the Church, for as baptized persons they can, and indeed must, share in her life" (n. 84). Therefore, those who are divorced have a right to be part of their local community of faith. It is for this reason that most tribunals start the nullity process on that level. It helps pastoral ministers become more aware of the needs of their people and helps people become more integrated into their parish community. In many parishes, support groups allow those who have gone through the experience of divorce to come together to share those experiences and to support one another. These groups also assist people in the nullity process. Through sharing their experience of marriage and divorce, people gain a greater understanding of the factors that entered into their decision to marry in the first place.

Once the initial contact is made, tribunals differ on procedure. In some, the person contacts the tribunal directly for an interview; in others, much of the preliminary work is done through a written questionnaire. In either case, the main goal of the tribunal is to have the person tell the story of their relationship with their former spouse from beginning to end, to tell their own life story, and what they know of their former spouse's family history. Through this process, the tribunal gets a better understanding of these two people who entered into marriage: the families, their early life experiences, when and how their relationship began to develop, the factors that entered into their decision to marry, the ways they lived out their marital commitment to each other, and the factors which caused the breakdown of the union.

This is usually the most difficult part of the procedure since it requires the person to reflect upon the events of the past and to see how those events influenced the choices they made. At times, this involves re-living painful experiences of marriage or family life and gives the person the opportunity to gain greater personal insight, understanding, and appreciation for the complexity of Christian marriage. It also gives the Christian community the opportunity to support the person who is going through this process. The sensitive questioning of an interviewer or the discussions in support groups help to share burdens and so fulfill the command of the Lord.

The names of witnesses are also required. Like the term "annulment," the term "witness" is not exactly correct. Unlike the witness in a civil trial who generally testifies for one person and against another, the witnesses in a marriage nullity case are asked to describe the marriage as they saw it. Often, the witnesses can give the tribunal greater insight about the parties in the marriage and into the dynamics of that relationship as they lived it out. Witnesses are usually family members, but they can be nearly anyone who know the parties during the course of their marriage. Since the tribunal focuses on the parties at the time of their marriage, however, it is essential that the witnesses have some knowledge of the marriage from its inception. Tribunals differ in the way they obtain witness testimony. Some require the witnesses to be interviewed in person while others send out written questionnaires. Some tribunals seek the witness testimony before they begin the formal procedure; others wait until the case is actually accepted.

To begin a case, the person presents a formal petition to a tribunal which has jurisdiction over the marriage case. The case is then assigned to a judge, who accepts or rejects the petition. If he accepts it, he must also determine the grounds under which the case will be heard.

At this point, the judge informs both parties that a case has begun. Since there is a presumption in law that the marriage is valid, and since the other party (usually called the respondent or the defendant) has the right to uphold the validity of that union, it is absolutely essential that he or she be contacted and given an opportunity to participate. Failure to do so results in the whole process being null. At times, petitioners have requested that respondents not be contacted because of previous violence or harassment and the fear of a respondent's reaction when informed of the proceedings. This may seem reasonable but the fact is that respondents will generally hear about these proceedings from other sources in addition to the tribunal. Children of the marriage or relatives of one of the parties usually talk about the case long before the tribunal accepts it. Keeping it a secret is not an option that is open to the petitioner. The respondent has a right to know about the proceedings and to participate in them.

In some cases, though, the respondent has disappeared. This is especially true of a marriage which ended a number of years before. The petitioner has no knowledge of the respondent's whereabouts and has made every effort to find a current address. In these cases, the tribunals can proceed with the case but usually appoint an advocate to protect the rights of the respondent.

The judge may also need additional information from the petitioner and will request an additional interview for a psychological evaluation. In addition, he may ask the person to sign a release form so that he has psychological records available. Since many cases today involve psychological grounds, the judge may ask the psychologist specific questions about the maturity of the parties and their ability to enter into marriage.

Once the judge has all this testimony, the case is presented to the advocates (if there are any) and to the defender of the bond, who presents arguments upholding the validity of the marriage. After that, the judge writes his decision and states his reasons for declaring the marriage null or upholding its validity. An affirmative decision is automatically appealed, however, and must pass through a review process where the decision is either confirmed or the case is opened to a new process. If the appeal court confirms the affirmative decision or reaches an affirmative decision on its own, the case is concluded and the parties are free to marry in the Church. If the appeal court overturns the affirmative decision, the case can be appealed to Rome for a third hearing.

The length of time that this takes varies from tribunal to tribunal, based upon available personnel. Some tribunals can conclude cases within eight months while others take several years. Lack of cooperation on the part of the petitioner or the witnesses can also impede the progress of a case. A lack of cooperation on the part of a respondent should not impede the progress of a case. Although the respondent has a right to participate, no one can be forced to exercise a right. Furthermore, the petitioner has a right to have the case heard, and to have it concluded in a timely fashion.

The fees that tribunals request also vary widely. Some tribunals are subsidized through the diocesan tax on parishes or through a special collection for diocesan needs. Other tribunals have a fee based on the petitioner's income, while still others ask the petitioner to determine how much he or she can contribute toward the total cost of the case. Most tribunals have liberal policies for the reduction or total waiver of the fee.

CONCLUSION

It is no secret that more declarations of nullity are being granted today than in the past. Twenty years ago, tribunals heard slightly more than fifteen thousand marriage nullity cases throughout the world. In the present year, the number of affirmative decisions will approach sixty thousand. There are many reasons for this including better staffing of marriage tribunals throughout the world and a greater number of dioceses with functional tribunals. But, in large part, it is due to a greater understanding of the nature of Christian marriage and a greater appreciation of the commitment that couples make to each other when they marry "in the Lord."

CHAPTER 34

Remarried Catholics: Searching for Church Belonging

James J. Young

Paulist Father James Young explains here why so many divorced and remarried Catholics are still living as active Roman Catholics practicing their faith in Catholic parishes. Some of these persons—but far from all—have remarried after receiving annulments declaring their former marriages invalid. Young cites Pope John Paul II's letter, *On the Family*, encouraging divorced and remarried Catholics to remain members of the Church, though officially not allowed to receive communion.

Young points out a way such Catholics may still claim their right to the Eucharist. His discussion of this question deserves careful study.

Questions for Discussion

1. What are the deep conflicts Young claims beset Catholics who remarry without out the Church's approval?
2. What are the reasons Catholic parishes are reaching out to divorced Catholics?
3. If the Pope says divorced and remarried Catholics may not receive Communion, what is the path of good conscience by which they may receive?
4. Explain the theological thinking that permits communion even to those clearly in invalid second marriages?
5. What is your overall reaction to Young's essay?

Note: Jim Young died suddenly in 1987 at a relatively young age. Most of his priestly life, he had worked with tireless creativity in ministry to divorced Catholics.

Sometimes they come to the parish house with a child to be baptized, or appear at parent classes for First Communion preparation. They may volunteer to help with the parish feeding program or sign up to visit the elderly. A husband or wife may be met on a hospital call or at a prayer meeting. At

Reprinted from *Catholic Remarriage: Pastoral Issues and Preparation Models*, edited by Steven Preister and James J. Young. Copyright © 1986 by the North American Conference of Separated and Divorced Catholics, Inc. Used by permission of Paulist Press.

first, they may seem awkward and ill-at-ease, even evasive. They're remarried Catholics, and more of them are surfacing every day in American parishes.

Understandably, they often make other Catholics or those in positions of leadership somewhat nervous. They carry with them the suggestion of marriages abandoned, vows violated, and Church discipline ignored. Some Catholics are anxious that being too friendly or too accommodating to the remarried may undermine the Church's teaching on marital permanence and even encourage divorce. As predictable as these concerns may be, our pastoral experience is painting a far more complex and challenging portrait of remarried Catholics.

We are learning that they typically are men and women who exhausted every resource available to save a failing marriage, and only decided to divorce after prolonged consultation with counsellors and pastors. None divorced easily; the guilt, stress and upset that follows every broken marriage testifies to that. It may well be that because they were so Catholic, shaped by the Church's high valuation of lasting marriage, the pain was even more intense. Even though all divorce recovery programs hold up establishing an autonomous single existence as the major goal for the separated person, it is easy to understand why remarriage emerges so early as the obvious solution to this painful transition. For most people, a new marriage provides the only imaginable way of finding love again, of being happy again, or having a place in society again. Further, somewhat paradoxically, the best parts of a bad marriage may provide the appetite for a better marriage. Daily we meet divorced men and women who have put together a satisfying single life after divorce, but most admit that they would readily marry again if a suitable partner appeared.

The limited surveys we have suggest that, by and large, Catholics are much like the population at large. This means that almost three-fourths of divorced Catholics are dating seriously within a year, and half of them are remarried within three years of the civil divorce. Eventually as many as five out of six of the men and three out of four of the women will remarry.

The benefits of remarriage seem obvious to most. A new marriage brings a new partner with the companionship, sexual intimacy and support marriage provides. For most women, only remarriage helps them return to the financial security they knew in their former marriage. Most single parents are convinced that their children will be better off with a stepfather or stepmother, which is why fully 60% of remarriages bring children into the new household. Even though remarried living and stepparenting are unfamiliar situations with few accepted models of behavior, most will risk the unknown when the opportunity appears rather than continue raising children alone or living alone.

There may be as many as a million Catholics who have remarried over the past fifteen years with the Church's blessing. The increased availability of expeditious annulment procedures has allowed some 800,000 Catholics to receive annulments; many more, who never married as required in a Church ceremony the first time, have been able to marry again with the Church's approval. The Catholic community has worked very hard in recent years, using all the remedies available, to help Catholics remarry and remain in good standing in the community. Yet our best estimates are that well over 75% of remarried Catholics live in presumably invalid second marriages. They are the men and women who are presenting such difficult pastoral problems in Catholic parishes today.

Catholics who remarry without the Church's approval are usually caught in deep conflict. Many of them of lifelong devout Catholics, who attend Mass regularly, pray regularly, and live good Christian lives. When asked how they could go against the Church's discipline which does not provide for such second marriages, they often answer, "I hated to get married outside the Church, but I knew God would understand. I knew he didn't want me to be so lonely, and I knew he wanted my children to have a mother." Others say that though they loved the Church and being Catholic was in their bones, they felt the Church was too strict on divorce and remarriage and didn't appreciate the hardships people endure. Most say they agonized for months, sought spiritual counsel, and prayed at length before deciding to go ahead with a prohibited second marriage. Afterwards many were tormented by fears of "living in sin" and mistaken notions of being excommunicated from the Church. For some such guilt became a burdensome factor working against the success of the second marriage.

Those who have ministered extensively to divorced Catholics insist that the remarried are not men and women who have rejected the Church's teaching on the permanence and indissolubility of marriage. They are not people who promote divorce. Almost unanimously they profess a high regard for lifelong marriage, and insist they would never wish a divorce on anyone. "At times I still can't believe I'm divorced and remarried," a woman told me, "I'm sure if I was still caught in that first marriage, I'd be in a mental hospital now."

Further, surveys indicate that widespread divorce and remarriage among Catholics does not reflect a lessening of traditional Catholic family values among remarried Catholics. Recently, the Notre Dame Study of Parish Life found remarrying Catholics reapproaching and reidentifying with Catholic parishes. The remarried are "normal" again and want to live like ordinary families again. For traditional Catholics that means being part of a parish and raising children in the Church. Social critic Michael Novak believes that widespread divorce among Catholics stems more from the increased pressure on the family rather than lack of commitment to family values. Many commentators cite such contemporary factors as emotional problems, joblessness, addiction, mobility and loss of supportive family relationship, poverty, crime, and effects of Viet Nam—all of which tear marriages apart. To come close to divorced people is to look through a painful window at the dark underside of American life and the many forces that make lasting marriage difficult. For most, remarriage is a second chance to live and love again; another chance to salvage a broken life.

For this reason including these remarried couples in parish life may be an important way of helping the parish ground its life in the realities of Christian living today. The Catholic community has always been close to its people and their pain, and that basic pastoral instinct may be dramatized no more clearly today than in the ever-widening process of reconciliation of the remarried. And as this reconciliation has grown, rather than causing scandal and promoting more divorce and remarriage, the opposite actually has been the case. Since 1981 the U.S. divorce rate has been declining and the remarriage rate slowing. Could it be that understanding divorce better and the difficulties of remarriage has challenged more persons in troubled marriages to work harder at making them last?

The most important reason, however, for reaching out to remarried Catholics is the fact that they remain baptized members of the Church and deserve our pastoral care. Pope John Paul II clearly made this point in his 1980 letter *On the Family.* "I earnestly call upon pastors and the whole community of the faithful to help the divorced (and remarried) and with solicitous care to make sure that they do not consider themselves as separated from the Church, for as baptized persons they can and indeed must share in her life." He calls upon pastors to be especially sensitive to those "who have sincerely tried to save their first marriages and have been unjustly abandoned" and "those who have entered into a second union for the sake of the children's upbringing and who are sometimes subjectively certain in conscience that their previous and irreparably destroyed marriage had never been valid." (*On the Family,* 84) He goes on to say that remarried Catholics should be encouraged to attend Mass, listen to the word of God, persevere in prayer, contribute to works of charity and to community efforts in favor of justice, and to bring up their children in the faith.

In 1977 the American Bishops removed the American Church law which had attached a penalty of automatic excommunication to second marriage for Catholics who had previously been married in a Catholic ceremony and had not obtained an annulment of their first marriage. They wrote about their action, "It welcomes back to the community of believers in Christ all who may have been separated by excommunication. It offers them a share in all the public prayers of the Church community. It restores their right to take part in church services. It removes certain canonical restrictions upon their participation in church life. It is a promise of help and support in the resolution of the burden of family life. Perhaps above all, it is a gesture of love and reconciliation from the other members of the Church."

That love and reconciliation, of which the bishops wrote, is surfacing daily in American Catholic parishes. The papal and episcopal statements indicate the clear pastoral responsibility on the diocesan and parish level to search out and find such alienated remarried Catholics. Sadly some may have no interest in being an active Catholic again, but in recent years diocesan and parish efforts have turned up thousands of married Catholics most interested in being part of the Catholic community again. Pulpit appeals for reconciliation which clarify the place of remarried Catholics in the Church today continue to be needed; some parishes have deputized lay visitors to call on remarried couples who may be alienated and invite them back. There may be several million alienated remarried Catholics in the United States.

In his same 1980 letter, the Pope reaffirmed the Church's general practice of not admitting the remarried to Eucharistic communion. "They are unable to be admitted thereto from the fact that their state and condition of life objectively contradict that union of love between Christ and the Church which is signified and effected by the Eucharist." He added a second reason for the traditional exclusion. "If these people were admitted to the Eucharist the faithful would be led into error and confusion regarding the Church's teaching about the indissolubility of marriage." It must be noted that the Pope has already affirmed the place of remarried Catholics in the Church community and stressed the goodness of many of their lives with a most approving statement of their position in the Church. Yet he feels that the continuing existence of a prior marriage assumed to be binding until death bars them from the Eucharist. Since Eucharistic reception is a sign of accepting the teaching of the Church and living up to that teaching, those who have married a second time without Church approval are not properly disposed to take Communion.

There are two paths which make Eucharistic reception for the remarried possible. The first is an annulment of a prior marriage. Fortunately, this healing remedy is readily available in all of our American dioceses. Where properly explained to remarried Catholics, most choose to pursue an annulment since they have a strong desire to have their new marriage accepted by the Church community and restored to Communion. Catholic belonging always seems incomplete without Eucharist.

The second path is the "good conscience" solution by which a pastoral minister helps the remarried make a judgment about the appropriateness of their taking Communion when an annulment has not been possible. If the Catholics involved have a moral certitude that their first marriage was invalid, i.e., not a true Catholic marriage, then they are not bound by that prior marriage. This means that the second marriage can be considered a true Catholic marriage even though it cannot be publicly celebrated in the Church. This practice was urged on pastors by Cardinal Seper, then Prefect of the Congregation for the Doctrine of the Faith in Rome in 1973.

Where this solution has been applied and where couples in marriages not blessed by the Church have been encouraged by their pastors to take Communion, a compassionate readiness on the part of the Catholic people to welcome them to the Lord's table seems quite common. Even though there is always the danger of scandal in such cases, there seems to be little evidence of such scandal. It may be that given the mobility of our society and the largeness of our congregations people are not well-known enough for their personal marital circumstances to be public knowledge. Or it may be that now that most Catholics know someone who has struggled through divorce and remarriage, often their own family members, there is an understandable desire to see such remarried welcomed and accepted by the Church. Many pastors report a charitable openness on the part of most parishioners in supporting the Church's outreach to the remarried.

All Catholics in second marriages are not covered by the "good conscience" solution. A distinction is made between those who are morally certain that their first marriage was invalid and those who are certain that their first marriage was valid. There are many persons who insist that their first marriage was never a marriage; it was undermined by emotional illness or serious personality defects from the start. Yet others insist that they had a very good Catholic marriage for many years, but it died. Dramatic personality changes in mid-life, some personal tragedy which seemed to destroy the husband–wife relationship, or another person who wins away a spouse—all destroy marriages and lead to divorce. Many sincere Catholics, after the breakup of such marriages, refuse to apply for annulments, convinced they had a good marriage and would still be married, if only . . . The traditional position is that those who are sure their marriage was not a good one from the start, not ever valid, may receive Communion even if they do not have an annulment. Whereas those who are convinced that their first marriage was a good one for a long time, may not. Those in the second category, it is proposed, are bound by the first marriage, and so the second marriage is certainly invalid. Those in invalid second marriages, as we have seen, may not receive Communion.

As might be expected that latter position is being questioned by theologians and canonists today. Must those who have been unable to live up to the Church's teaching and laws on marriage always be excluded from Eucharistic sharing? Those open to the reception of Communion by such remarried persons suggest that where a first marriage is irretrievably lost, and where one or both parties have entered into a stable new marriage where he or she is faithful to obligations which remain from that first marriage—such as raising children in the faith or financial support—they should be offered the Eucharist as a spiritual resource to help them handle the demands of a new marriage. The Pope and bishops have insisted that the remarried are to live up to all the obligations of Christian life. How can they be asked to bear such burdens and not be offered the ordinary food of Christians? There is growing evidence that some pastors are supporting such remarrieds in taking the Eucharist, convinced that they are good people and need the Eucharist. Further, they ask, is not the Eucharist a meal of reconciliation for the flawed and imperfect? Did not the Lord share meals in the Gospels with the outcast and the suffering?

This is the frontier area of ministry to the remarried in the Church today. An enormous amount of progress has been made in cleansing the Catholic community of negative, condemnatory attitudes towards the remarried and a process of reconciliation is underway. How many of these people, and for what reason, can be offered the Eucharist needs much further reflection and lived experience.

Reconciling the remarried has many pastoral benefits for the parish community. It has also saved whole families for the Church; a decade ago many of these families would have been cut off with their children. Further, there are numerous reports of Catholics remarried to persons of no prior religious affiliation who are now coming forward and requesting to be baptized or received into the Catholic Church. Most of all, it brings into the life of the parish the rich Christian experience of men and women who have endured the heartbreak of broken marriage in faith and dared to love again.

CHAPTER 35

Divorce and Remarriage in the Catholic Church: Ten Theses

Michael G. Lawler

Ludwig Wittgenstein spoke of language as a game. To understand a linguistic world, he wrote, you had to get inside its game, know its rules, boundaries, and sanctions. Michael Lawler understands, better than most, the linguistic world of Roman Catholicism, particularly its semantic world of canon law, church councils, and theological doctrine. He knows the Catholic ground rules on divorce and remarriage. He is crystal clear on the current boundaries and clearer still when couples strike out.

Lawler's purpose in the essay is twofold: (1) to explain precisely the rules of the game and, in doing so, to clear up some misconceptions, misunderstandings and misinterpretations, and (2) to propose some new rules—where the spirit of law gives life.

Lawler frames his essay in the form of ten theses. A thesis is a statement in need of defense on the basis of evidence. Lawler concisely states each thesis and proceeds to lucidly and meticulously build a persuasive argument for each. The work is a model of clarity, exposing contradictions between Church practice and preaching, divergent accounts of divorce and remarriage in the New Testament and later Christian traditions, and the regularity of granting divorce in nonsacramental and nonconsummated marriages, although it named the latter *dissolution* rather than *divorce*. Lawler's end game, however, is to propose the ancient Orthodox practice of *oikonomia* as a pastoral care approach to church members in second marriages. The person's second marriage is accepted, without repudiating the second spouse or taking back the first, as a condition for full communion. There is ample warrant, he believes, for *oikonomia*. It is a form of Christian realism and flourishes within a context of spirit and grace. It may also offer thousands of Catholics divorced and remarried the ecclesial peace and communion to which God has called them.

Questions for Discussion

1. What is the origin of the Pauline Privilege and Petrine Privilege—and what is the difference between them?

2. What accounts for the several teachings on divorce and remarriage in the New Testament? Should we take into consideration similar accounts today?

3. Do you agree that, on a case-by-case basis in discussion with a pastoral counselor, Catholics who are divorced and remarried civilly without annulment *must* be admitted to Holy Communion?

4. What is your perspective on the Orthodox Church practice of *oikonomia?* Should the Christian ideal always be at the mercy of human frailty?

THESIS 1
Marriage between baptized believers is a sacrament, that is, a
prophetic symbol of the union between Christ and the Church.

Prophets were fond of symbolic actions. Jeremiah bought an earthen pot, dashed it to the ground, and proclaimed, "Thus says the Lord of Hosts: so will I break this people and this city as one breaks a potter's vessel" (Jer 19:11). Ezekiel took a brick, drew a city on the brick, laid siege to the city, and proclaimed the city "Jerusalem" and his action "a sign for the house of Israel" (Ezek 4:1–3; see also 5:5). Prophetic action-symbols reveal in representation the presence and action of God. Jeremiah's shattering of his pot and Ezekiel's destruction of his city is God's shattering of Jerusalem. The prophet Hosea portrayed marriage, the union of a man and a woman, as a prophetic symbol of the union between God and God's people, a reality not only of law but also of grace. On the one hand, it bespeaks the covenanted love of a man and a woman; on the other hand, it *also* bespeaks the covenanted love of God and God's people. This Jewish view of marriage, with a change of *dramatis personae*, became the Christian view. The Letter to the Ephesians taught that marriage is a prophetic symbol of the new covenant between Christ and Christ's Church; later Christian history taught that it was sacrament (Lawler, 1995, 5–62).

A sacrament, then, is a prophetic symbol in which the Church reveals in representation the grace of God. To say that marriage is a sacrament is to say that it reveals the intimate union of a man and a woman *and* the intimate union of Christ and Christ's Church. A couple entering any marriage says to one another "I love you and I give myself to and for you." A couple entering a sacramental marriage say that too, of course, but also more. Each says "I love you as Christ loves his Church, steadfastly and faithfully." From its beginning, therefore, a sacramental marriage is intentionally more than human covenant; it is *also* religious covenant. It is more than law; it is *also* grace. From its beginning, God and Christ are present in it, gracing it, modeling and challenging its faithfulness. This presence of God, grace in its most ancient Christian meaning, is not something extrinsic to Christian marriage but something intrinsic to it, something without which it would not be *Christian* marriage at all.

From *New Theology Review* 12, 2, May 1999, published by the Order of Saint Benedict.

I note here, and will develop below in Thesis 7, an important sacramental fact. A truly *Christian* marriage is not simply a marriage between two people who *say* they are Christians (Lawler, 1991, 712–31). It is a marriage between two Christian *believers* for whom the steadfast love of God and of God's Christ is consciously present as model for their mutual-love. The love of faith-filled spouses is, indeed, the very matrix of the sacrament of marriage, for it is in and through the spouses' love that God and Christ are prophetically made present. It is a matter for empirical verification, however, that not all Christian marriages become permanent. Some die, and when they die it makes no sense to claim they are still binding ontologically, for the death of a marriage is as definitive as the death of a spouse. When a marriage dies, the Church traditionally deals with it in one of its many canonical processes. Its claim that it is precluded from doing otherwise by "fidelity to the words of Jesus" is not convincing in the honest light of its own ancient tradition.

THESIS 2

The theology and practice of the Catholic Church with respect to divorce and remarriage are not as faithful to the New Testament as is claimed.

On October 14, 1994, the Congregation for the Doctrine of the Faith sent a letter to the bishops of the world entitled "Concerning the Reception of Holy Communion by Divorced and Remarried Members of the Faithful" (CDF, 1994). That letter purported to articulate Catholic doctrine concerning divorce and remarriage and claimed, citing Mark 10:11–12, "fidelity to the words of Jesus Christ." The implication was that, since the doctrine in question is based on fidelity to the words of Jesus, it is irreformable. That argument might be true if the words of Jesus as cited from Mark were the only teaching in the New Testament on divorce and remarriage. That, of course, is not the case.

Paul attributes a prohibition of divorce and remarriage to the Lord (1 Cor 7:10–11), and the Gospels report four times words of Jesus about divorce and remarriage (Mark 10:11–12; Matt 5:32 and 19:9; Luke 16:19). What is critical about these reports for our present purpose is that there are five of them, that they are not in agreement, and that they are not all derived from Jesus. Though Paul reports Jesus' command on divorce and remarriage (1 Cor 7:10–11), he also gives it his own nuance (7:12–16) and that nuance passed into the law of the Catholic Church as the Pauline Privilege. Matthew also nuances Jesus' words with his own exception (5:32; 19:9) which is a genuine exception to Jesus' received words, though "its meaning is not self-evident to modern interpreters" (Collins, 1992, 205). These divergent accounts exist because divergent Christian communities had divergent concerns about marriage and divorce that needed to be addressed. The nuancing of the words of Jesus on the basis of contextual need, initiated by the early Church, was continued in the later Church by Gratian in respect to what consummates a marriage as indissoluble (1140), and by the so-called Petrine Privileges of Popes

Paul III (1537), Pius V (1561), and Gregory XIII (1585) with respect to the circumstances of polygamy and slavery (Lawler, 1993, 92–93). This consistent nuancing of the words of Jesus in the Church makes arguments based exclusively on the words of Jesus at best incomplete and at worst dishonest.

This brief consideration of the traditional data on divorce and remarriage leads to several important conclusions. First, it is incorrect to speak of the New Testament *teaching* on divorce and remarriage; there are several *teachings* which do not all agree. Second, not all these teachings derive from Jesus, as the Catholic Church claims. Third, diverging accounts of divorce and remarriage are an integral part of the New Testament and later Christian traditions because the diverse cultural followers of Jesus sought to translate the meaning of his life, death, and resurrection into their concrete lives. Fourth, though popular unwisdom later singled out one element in those diverging accounts, namely the demand for indissoluble marriage, and allowed that one element to override all the others, that fact should not be allowed to obscure the original divergence.

THESIS 3

The solemn teaching of the Council of Nicea is intimately related to the Church's teaching on divorce and remarriage, and has much to say to its pastoral practice today.

There is a veneration in the Church of ecumenical councils, especially of the first four councils, and most especially of the first of them, the Council of Nicea (325) whose Creed established the doctrinal basis of the Christian faith. Canon 8 of that council goes to the very heart of the question of divorce and remarriage.

> As regards those who define themselves as the Pure and who want to join the Catholic and Apostolic Church, the holy and great Council decrees that they may remain among the clergy once hands have been imposed upon them. But beforehand they will have to promise in writing to comply with the teachings of the Catholic and Apostolic Church and to make them the rule of their conduct. That is to say, they will have to communicate both with *those who married a second time (digamoi)* and with those who failed under persecution but whose time has been established and whose moment of reconciliation has arrived. They will, therefore, be bound to follow the teaching of the Catholic and Apostolic Church completely (Mansi, II, 672, my emphasis).

According to this canon, the "Pure," those who belonged to the rigorous sect called Novatians (Hefele, I, 410), had to promise in writing to accept the teaching of the Catholic Church before they could be reconciled with it. Specifically, they had to accept to live in communion with those who had been married twice *(digamoi)* and those who had apostacized during persecution but who had completed their period of penance and had been reconciled to the Church. We are concerned here only with those *digamoi* who have done penance and have been reconciled to the Church.

Novatian teaching excluded from penance and reconciliation those who were guilty of certain sins "leading to death," among them *digamia* which refers to remarriage either after the death of a spouse or after a divorce. Since, however, remarriage after the death of a spouse was not considered a sin leading to death until long after the Council of Nicea, the council's *digamoi* must be those who have remarried after a divorce or repudiation. That "sin," according to the council, can be forgiven and reconciliation with the Church can be achieved after a period of suitable penance. Acutely relevant is the fact that neither the Church before Nicea nor the council itself required the repudiation of the new spouse as a prerequisite for forgiveness and reconciliation. This was in keeping with the proscriptions of Deut 24:1–4, which was taken to be binding in the Church before Nicea and which forbade a husband to take back his repudiated wife after she had married another (See Origen, PG 13, 1237 and Jerome, PL 22, 563). Basil explicitly reports the treatment of a man who had abandoned his wife and remarried, who had "done penance with tears," and who, after seven years, had been accepted back "among the faithful" (Basil, PG 32, 804–5). The man's second marriage is accepted and neither the repudiation of his second wife nor his taking back of the first is demanded as a prerequisite for full communion. This teaching of Basil is the foundation for the teaching and practice of the Orthodox Church known as *oikonomia*.

THESIS 4

The Catholic Church has never practiced what is enshrined in its law, namely, that "the essential properties of marriage are unity and indissolubility" (1983 Can 1056). The actual number of marriages the Church holds to be indissoluble is very limited.

If the Church truly believed that indissolubility was an essential property not just of Christian marriages but of all marriages, and that by the will of God "from the beginning" (Mark 10:6; Matt 19:4) then it would treat all marriages as indissoluble. It does not and never has. The Church accepts the marriages of the non-baptized as valid when they have been performed according to the laws which govern them and yet, utilizing the Pauline Privilege, it regularly dissolves them "in favor of the faith of the party who received baptism" (1983 Can 1143). It has further extended the Pauline Privilege, as already noted, to embrace the dissolution of valid marriages utilizing the Petrine Privilege. In Christian marriages, indissolubility is said to acquire "a distinctive firmness by reason of the sacrament" (1983 Can 1056), and yet valid sacramental marriages which have not been consummated are dissolved "by the Roman Pontiff for a just reason, at the request of both parties or of either party" (1983 Can 1142). Long-standing church practice with respect to the dissolution of valid marriages demonstrates anything but a belief that an essential property of marriage is indissolubility.

The formal doctrine of the Church on the indissolubility of marriage demonstrates that fidelity to the words of Jesus is not the only criterion for ecclesiastical judgments about divorce and remarriage. Only that marriage "which is ratified (as sacrament) and consummated cannot be dissolved by any human power other than death" (1983 Can 1141). The two conditions which make a marriage indissoluble in the eyes of the Church, that it be both sacramental *and* consummated, are not conditions ever mentioned by Jesus or any of the New Testament writers. They are both the result of historical nuancing long after Jesus, despite the teaching of the recent *Catechism of the Catholic Church* that "the marriage bond has been established by God himself in such a way that a marriage concluded *and consummated* between baptized persons can never be dissolved" (n. 1640, my emphasis). That marriage was created by God no Catholic theologian would debate. That the marriage bond becomes indissoluble, even in a sacramental marriage, only when the marriage is consummated is a nuance added in the twelfth century.

THESIS 5
The Code's claim that "a valid marriage contract cannot exist
between baptized persons without its being by that very fact a
sacrament" (1983 Can 1055,2) contradicts the Catholic dogma
that faith is necessary for the reception of grace and salvation.

The Code presumes something that cannot be theologically presumed, namely, that all that is required for the *sacrament* of marriage is prior baptism and a valid marriage contract. That presumption stands in contradiction to the long tradition about the necessity of personal faith in Catholic teaching. The Gospels record that Jesus both complained about the absence of faith and praised its presence (Matt 8:5–13; 8:23–27; 9:2; 9:20–22; 17:19–21; 21:18–22; Mark 5:25–34; 6:1–6). Paul vehemently defended the necessity of personal faith for salvation (Rom 1:16–17; 3:26–30; 5:1; Gal 3:6–9). That tradition of the necessity of faith continued in the Church and flowered on both sides of the Reformation controversies.

Martin Luther made his stand on "faith alone." Though wishing to combat the Lutheran teaching that faith *alone* was necessary for salvation, the Council of Trent left no doubt about the necessity of personal faith: "Faith is the beginning of man's salvation, the foundation and source of all justification, 'without which it is impossible to please God'" (Heb 11:6) (DS 1532). Baptism is "the sacrament of faith, without which no man has ever been justified" (DS 1529). The Latin text makes clear that "without which" *(sine qua)* qualifies faith and not sacrament or baptism, both of which would require *sine quo.* There is no doubt that the Fathers of Trent wished to affirm solemnly the primacy of active, personal faith for salvation. So also did both the First and Second Vatican Councils: faith is an act by which "a man gives *free* obedience to God by cooperating and agreeing with his grace, which can be resisted" (DS 3010, my emphasis); faith is an act by which "man entrusts his whole self *freely* to God, offering 'the full submission of intellect and will to God who reveals,' and *freely* assenting to the truth revealed by him" (*Dei Verbum,* n. 5). That free, cooperating, personal faith is required for salvation is a solemn dogma of the Catholic Church.

Convinced of the necessity of faith for the validity of baptism, Augustine sought to make good the lack of faith in infant baptism by arguing that *ecclesia fidem supplet,* the Church makes good the faith required (*Epist 98, The Fa-*

thers, 133–38). That argument cannot be applied in the case of marriage, a sacrament for adults who are required to have an active faith to participate in any sacrament. Aquinas never doubted that "every sacrament remains a sign and a proclamation of personal faith. Whoever receives it without believing in his heart places himself in a violent state of 'fiction' and deprives himself of sacramental grace" (Villette, 1964, 40). Bonaventure agrees: the sacrament of marriage can be distinguished only by personal faith (*IV Sent.,* d.26, a.2, q.1. *Opera Omnia,* 6,215).

The 1980 Synod of Bishops gave quasi-unanimous support (201 placet, 3 non placet) to the following proposition: "We have to take into account the engaged couple's degree of faith maturity and their awareness of doing what the Church does. *This intention is required for sacramental validity.* It is absent if there is not at least a minimal intention of believing with the church" (my emphasis). Sacramental intention is critical in sacramental theology. To intend to participate in a sacrament, the participant must intend what the Church intends in the sacrament. The theological question is: Can a person have a real intention to participate in a sacrament without at least minimal personal faith?

Aquinas has no doubt: "Faith directs intention, and without [faith] intention cannot be right" [*Fides intentionem dirigit, et sine ea non potest esse . . . intentio recta (IV Sent.,* d.6, q.1, a.3 ad 5)]. The International Theological Commission continues that tradition: the real intention is born from and feeds on living faith (Malone, 1984, 15). One cannot have a right sacramental intention without at least a minimum of personal faith. When personal faith is absent, so too is right sacramental intention; when right intention is absent, as the tradition universally holds, the sacrament is not valid. No personal faith/no right intention is a well-founded theological judgment. The conclusion that flows from it is equally well founded: without faith no one can enter into a valid sacramental marriage.

The intention required to participate in a sacrament, as distinct from a mere physical rite, is the intention to participate in a rite that offers salvation, a God-in-Christ and Christ-in-Church event. Neither God-in-Christ nor Christ-in-Church can be intended, however, without being at least minimally known and embraced in faith. The connection of personal faith to a valid sacrament is particularly relevant today when Catholic theology distinguishes the baptized as *baptized believers,* those who have been baptized *and* nurtured into active faith, and *baptized non-believers,* those who have been baptized *and* not nurtured into active faith (see Malone, 1984, 14–21). The two should never be confused in law.

Thesis 6

The Catholic Church, which teaches that the only marriage which is indissoluble is the sacramental and consummated marriage, today has no criterion for judging when a marriage has been consummated and therefore made indissoluble.

A theological question is consistently raised about the Catholic teaching on the effect of consummation: What is it that consummation adds to sacrament that makes the consummated sacramental marriage immune to dissolution? Pius XI suggested the answer lies in "the mystical meaning of Christian marriage," namely, its reference to that "most perfect union which exists between Christ and the church" (AAS, 1930, 552). Though it does not specify as precisely as Pius that it is the consummated sacramental marriage that is indissoluble, the International Theological Commission offers the same reason for the indissolubility of Christian marriage. The ultimate basis for the indissolubility of Christian marriage lies in the fact that it is the sacrament, the image, of the indissoluble union between Christ and the Church.

But questions remain. When Pius XI wrote in 1930, he took for granted the 1917 Code of Canon Law that dealt with marriage as a contract (Can 1012), that declared the object of the contract to be the exclusive and perpetual right to the body of the other for acts suitable for the generation of offspring (Can 1081, 2), and that declared the ends of marriage to be primarily procreation and secondarily mutual help and the remedy of concupiscence (Can 1013). In such a legalist and physicalist context, it is easy to see how a single act of sexual intercourse could be taken to be the consummation of a marriage. It is not so easy to see in the changed theological and personalist climate in which the Second Vatican Council rooted its doctrine on marriage.

The council teaches that marriage "is rooted in the conjugal covenant of irrevocable personal consent" (GS,48). Despite insistent demands to retain the legal word *contract* as a precise way to speak of marriage, the council demurred and chose instead the biblical, theological and personal word *covenant*. This choice locates marriage as an *interpersonal* rather than as a *legal* reality, and brings it into line with the rich biblical tradition of covenant between God and God's People and Christ and Christ's Church. The revised Code also preferred *covenant to contract* (1983 Can 1055, 1), though it relapses into contractual language some thirty times.

The council made another crucial change to Catholic teaching about marriage, which is central to any modern theological discussion of consummation and which was later also incorporated into the revised Code. The traditional teaching on the ends of marriage was the primary end–secondary end hierarchy between procreation and spousal love (1917 Can 1013). Despite insistent demands to reaffirm this hierarchical terminology, the council refused to do so. It taught explicitly that procreation "does not make the other ends of marriage of less account," and that marriage "is not instituted solely for procreation" (GS, 50). That this refusal to speak of a hierarchy of ends in marriage was not the result of oversight but a deliberate choice was confirmed when the council's teaching on ends was incorporated into the revised Code (1983 Can 1055, 1).

This change of perspective raises questions about the claim that the spouses' first sexual intercourse is the consummation of their mutual self-gifting and marriage. If the procreation of human life *and* the *consortium–communion* between the spouses are equal ends of marriage, why should an act of sexual intercourse alone be the symbol of the union of Christ and Christ's Church? Why should the extended marital *consortium*, itself symbolized in sexual communion, not be the symbol? These questions have been exacerbated by the change in the way consummation is specified in both the council and the revised Code. A marriage is now said to be "ratified and consummated if the spouses have in a *human manner (humano modo)* engaged together in a conjugal act in itself apt for the generation of offspring" (1983 Can 1061, 1). The phrase I have underscored has placed Catholic teaching on consummation and indissolubility on hold theologically and canonically, for as yet a theology of sexuality elucidating what sexual intercourse *humano modo* means has not been elaborated. Since marital intercourse *humano modo* cannot be precisely defined, neither can the marital consummation it is said to effect. Since consummation cannot be defined, many more valid marriages than heretofore ever imagined are open to dissolution in the Church.

THESIS 7

The Code's claim that "a ratified and consummated marriage cannot be dissolved by any human power" (Can 1141) ignores the more-than-human power in the Church capable of dissolving such marriages.

Though the question of the consummation of a marriage is now moot until the meaning of *humano modo* can be defined, there is still a more-than-human power in the Church to dissolve a failed ratified and consummated marriage. Two things are to be noted. First, the question asks about extrinsic indissolubility, the immunity of a marriage to dissolution by an agent other than the spouses. There is universal agreement that a *marriage* (not only a ratified and consummated marriage) is intrinsically indissoluble, that is, immune to dissolution by the spouses. Second, the extrinsic indissolubility of a ratified and consummated marriage as prescribed in the Code is not a revealed truth. Billot's opinion that it is *de fide catholica* has never found support (Billot, 1929, 440); most theologians judge it to be *doctrina catholica*. Navarrette's claim that Pius XI implicitly and Pius XII explicitly affirm that the ratified and consummated marriage cannot be dissolved, not even by the vicarious power of the Roman pontiff, is an exaggeration (Navarette, 1969, 449). Both popes do no more than cite without comment the legislation then current in Canon 1118. They add nothing that would elevate the teaching to a theological level higher than *doctrina catholica*.

The history of the doctrine and law about ratified and consummated marriage in the Catholic tradition demonstrates three facts. First, it is a compromise between the Roman law in which consent makes marriage and the northern European custom in which sexual intercourse makes marriage. Second, the compromise emerges from a mixed cultural understanding of marriage, the southern culture and the northern culture of twelfth-century Europe. Third, it is not *de fide*; it is *doctrina catholica*. That is not to say that it is not true. It is to say only that it is not irreformable, and to suggest that the agent of reformation is the same agent that introduced the teaching in the first place, namely, the magisterial Church, whose power extends to the binding and loosing of sin, to the transformation of bread and wine, and certainly to the reformation of a reformable doctrine it itself inaugurated. If a non-consummated marriage between baptized believers, that is, a sacramental marriage which falls under God's law, "can be dissolved by the Roman Pontiff for a just reason" (1983 Can 1142), a ratified and consummated marriage which falls under the Church's law can also be dissolved by the Roman Pontiff for a similarly just reason. The bond of a ratified and consummated marriage is far from immune to the more than human power daily exercised in the Church.

THESIS 8

The argument that Catholics who are divorced and remarried civilly without annulment are "in a situation that objectively contravenes God's law (and) consequently they cannot receive holy communion as long as this situation persists" (CDF, 339) is contrary to the universal law of the Catholic Church, obedience to which takes precedence over obedience to a Roman dicastery.

The matter is clear from Book IV, Title III, Chapter I, Article 2 of the current Code, "Participation in the Blessed Eucharist." The relevant canons prescribe the following: "Any baptized person who is not forbidden by law may and must *(debet)* be admitted to holy communion" (1983 Can 912); "those upon whom the penalty of excommunication or interdict has been imposed or declared, and others who obstinately persist in manifest *grave sin*, are not to be admitted to holy communion" (1983 Can 915, my emphasis); "anyone who is conscious of *grave sin* may not celebrate mass or receive the Body of the Lord without previously having been to sacramental confession. . . ." (1983 Can 916, my emphasis).

Since the first part of Canon 915 does not apply to Catholics who have been divorced and civilly remarried without annulment, because they are neither excommunicated nor placed under interdict, that leaves only the question of *grave sin* or *mortal sin* in the terms of Canons 915 and 916. The question can be put succinctly: Does grave sin in the Catholic tradition, and therefore in the mind of the legislator, follow from the fact that an action "objectively contravenes God's law" or constitutes gravely sinful matter? The answer can be put just as succinctly: In Catholic moral theology an objectively serious sinful action does not *ipso facto* result in grave sin.

In addition to objectively grave matter, grave sin requires both full consciousness of the sinfulness of the action *and* fully free consent to the action. The civil remarriage of the Catholic divorced and without annulment may constitute grave matter in the eyes of the Church; it *may* even constitute sin. But it constitutes *grave* sin only when there is full awareness and free consent. Those Catholics who have attempted remarriage after divorce without obtaining an annulment, or who have been unable to obtain an annulment for some formal reason, do not all *necessarily* have the required full awareness and free consent to commit grave sin. They are not, therefore, all guilty of grave sin and are not all, therefore, prohibited by law from receiving holy communion.

Those who are not guilty of grave sin because the traditional conditions for grave sin, objectively grave matter, full consciousness and free consent, have not all been met—and whether or not the conditions have been met will have to be decided on a case by case basis in discussion with a pastoral counselor—*must* be admitted to holy communion according to the universal law of the Catholic Church (1983 Can 912). No undifferentiated pronouncement of any Roman dicastery, or even of the bishop of Rome (AAS, 1982, 185), can bar them from the communion to which they are entitled by faith and by law. And no minister of the Church should either take or be put in the invidious position of refusing them the holy communion to which they are entitled.

THESIS 9

The scandal insinuated in both papal and dicasterial statements if divorced and civilly remarried Catholics are admitted to communion is no different from the scandal one could insinuate in solutions approved by the Church.

Pope John Paul II specifies the scandal that might ensue if the divorced and civilly remarried were admitted to communion: "the faithful would be led into error and confusion regarding the Church's teaching about the indissolubility of marriage" (*Familiaris Consortio,* n. 84). The CDF repeats his judgment without commentary (CDF, 1994, n. 4). The implication is that, if the divorced and civilly remarried were admitted to communion, people could come to believe that the Church no longer teaches that fidelity is required in marriage and that marriage is indissoluble. No one should ever underestimate the possibility of scandal; but neither should anyone overestimate it. No one, in fact, should ever estimate it at all, for real scandal is a fact which can be clarified empirically. Real scandal is in the same category as real sin; it can, and therefore must, be clarified on a case by case basis.

There are two cases in which the Church permits the civilly divorced and remarried to approach communion. The first is the case in which a couple has received the necessary annulment(s) to be free to marry; the second is the case in which a couple agrees to live as brother and sister. Neither case removes the threat of scandal.

The brother-sister case, in which the couple lives together publicly as husband and wife but abstains from all sexual intercourse, provides the same threat of scandal as the case of a couple not living as brother and sister, for no adult conscious of the ways of men and women would ever presume sexual abstention in a couple living together as husband and wife. Kelly notes the obvious: "Unless a couple had a 'brother and sister' logo on their doorstep, neighbors and fellow parishioners would be none the wiser and so the alleged scandal would presumably still be given" (Kelly, 1994, 1374). Given these obvious empirical considerations, it is astonishing to see the pope (AAS, 1982, 186) and the new Catechism (n. 1650) presenting the brother–sister solution as a genuine pastoral option, completely ignoring the weight of theologians and canonists who teach that this option is *res plena periculis* and should be employed *rarissime* and *fere numquam* (Sullivan, 1954, viii). The case of annulment runs the same peril. Unless a couple publicized their annulment from the sanctuary, most fellow-parishioners would never know about its existence. Today, indeed, when annulment has become so commonplace, those fellow parishioners would simply assume that the couple had been granted annulment(s) and think no more of it. Most of them would take the same approach to the divorced and civilly remarried approaching communion.

The scandal given in the case of the divorced and civilly remarried may lie elsewhere, not with the remarried but with the Church which bars them from communion. Based on interviews with priests working with alienated Catholics in Boston, New York, Providence and Wilmington (Del.), Himes and Coriden report that "the single biggest reason people cease active participation in the Church is that they have found themselves in irregular marital situations and feel unwanted and rejected by the Church" (Himes and Coriden, 1996, 118). Cardinal Newman taught that the *consensus fidelium* senses error "which it at once feels as a *scandal*" (Newman, 1986, 73). After a five-year study of divorce and civil remarriage in England, Buckley reports that the consensus of bishops, priests, and people is that "something is seriously wrong with the present teaching and that more than that it is a *scandal*" (Buckley, 1997, 178). There is sound basis for extending that judgment to the United States where, in a 1992 survey, only 23 percent of Catholics agreed that the magisterium *alone* should decide the morality of a divorced Catholic remarrying without an annulment, and 72 percent agreed that divorced and remarried Catholics should be able to receive communion (D'Antonio et al., 1996, 53).

THESIS 10

The Roman Catholic Church should embrace the practice of
oikonomia, declared by the Council of Trent to have certain claim
to the gospel and to the name Christian.

Questions raised today by divorce and remarriage confront all Christian churches in the United States. Not one escapes them. What should the churches do about divorce and remarriage? They should, I suggest, pay closer attention to the ancient Orthodox practice of *oikonomia. Oikonomia* flourishes within a context of spirit and grace, not within a context of law; it grows out of faith in the Spirit of God and of Christ. It heeds the scriptural injunction that "the written code kills, but the Spirit gives life" (2 Cor 3:6).

What does *oikonomia* have to say to the churches about divorce and remarriage? It admonishes them to be realistic, to understand that, though the gospel demands that marriages be lifelong, real men and women sometimes do not fully measure up to the gospel. It instructs them that marriages, even marriages between Christians, sometimes die and that when they die it makes no sense to argue they are still binding. When a marriage is dead, even if the former spouses still live, *oikonomia* moves the churches to be sad, for the death of a marriage is always "the death of a small civilization" (Wallerstein and Blakeslee, xxi), but also to be compassionate, even to the point of permitting the remarriage of an innocent spouse. The ritual of that remarriage, however, is not on a par with the first marriage, now dissolved, as the liturgy makes clear.

There are prayers for the couple now entering into the bond of a second marriage. There are petitions that the spouses be pardoned for their transgressions and confession that there is none sinless save only God. Absent is the unbridled joy of the first-marriage ceremony; present is sorrow and repentance for its failure. Present too is the necessary confession that no one in attendance, including the Church's minister, is without sin. The economy of spirit and grace is always threatened by sin; the Christian ideal is ever at the mercy of human frailty. It is precisely in such an economy that the Church of Christ is summoned to minister and to be compassionate on behalf of the compassionate God.

A reasonable Christian objection arises at this point. Should not what the churches do about divorce and remarriage be based on the tradition of Jesus mediated to them in the New Testament? Yes, it should, and we considered that tradition briefly in Thesis 2 where we found diverging accounts of divorce and remarriage in the New Testament tradition as culturally diverse followers of Jesus sought to translate the meaning of his life, death, and resurrection into their diverse lives.

The early process of interpreting the Lord's command concerning divorce and remarriage continued in the churches of both East and West. The East developed its doctrine of *oikonomia* related to marriage; the West developed its law related to marriage which continues in force today. In the twelfth century, the Bologna canonist, Gratian, developed two pieces of legislation which continue to be a central part of Roman Catholic law. The first was a continuation of Paul's exception, now called the Pauline Privilege, which remains today one of the bases on which the Catholic Church grants the dissolution of a valid marriage. The Pauline Privilege, as noted earlier, has been much extended beyond what Paul ever envisioned by the so-called Petrine Privilege. The second piece of legislation was a compromise solution between the Roman and northern European answers to the question of when a valid marriage came into existence. "Marriage is initiated by betrothal (consent), perfected (or consummated) by sexual intercourse" (Gratian, PL 187, 1429 and 1406). These two pieces of legislation became enshrined in the law of the Roman Catholic Church with respect to the indissolubility of marriage. That Church regards as indissoluble only that marriage which is both sacramental *and* consummated by sexual intercourse (1983 Can 1141). It holds all other marriages to be dissoluble and it dissolves them on occasion "for a just reason" (1983 Can 1142) or "in favor of the faith" (1983 Can 1143).

Several things are clear. First, despite every claim to follow only the Lord's command, the Catholic Church also follows Paul and Matthew in interpreting that command for their ongoing situations. Second, it is not true that the Roman Catholic Church never grants divorces. It grants them regularly in marriages which are not sacramental or not consummated, though it obscures that fact by naming the process *dissolution* rather than *divorce.* Third, though there is no warrant in the New Testament for such canonical processes, there is ample warrant for *oikonomia,* a fact to which the Council of Trent attested. Despite hewing to a rigid line on the question of the indissolubility of marriage, the council steadfastly refused to condemn the practice of *oikonomia* or to declare that it did not have equal claim to the gospel tradition and to the name Christian (DS, 1807).

The 1980 Synod of Bishops presented to Pope John Paul a request that the Orthodox practice of *oikonomia* be carefully studied for any light it might shed on a pastoral approach to Catholics who are divorced and civilly remarried. Many of those second marriages have become so stable, and the families nurtured in them so Christian, that they cannot be abandoned without serious spiritual, emotional, and economic harm. The Catholic Church is summoned to discern whether its understanding of the gospel precludes the development of an *oikonomia* approach to the pastoral care of its members in second marriages. It is summoned to gospel *oikonomia* as a way to alleviate the suffering of those thousands of Catholics divorced and remarried without sin and as a way to attain the ecclesial peace and communion to which God has called all Christians (1 Cor 7:15).

REFERENCES

Aquinas, Thomas. In *IV Sententiarum. Opera Omnia,* vol. VII–I. New York: Musurgia, 1948.

Augustine. *Epistola XCVIII. The Fathers of the Church,* vol. 18. New York: Fathers of the Church, 1953.

Basil the Great. *Epistola LXXVIII.* J. P. Migne, ed., *Patrologiae Cursus Completus: Series Graeca,* vol. 32. Paris, n.d.

Billot, Louis. *De Ecclesiae Sacramentis.* Rome: Gregoriana, 1929.

Bonaventure. *Opera Omnia.* Paris: Ludovicus Vives, 1865.

Buckley, Timothy J. *What Binds Marriage?: Roman Catholic Theology in Practice.* London: Chapman, 1997.

Catechism of the Catholic Church. New York: Paulist, 1994.

Codex Iuris Canonici. Roma: Libreria Editrice Vaticana, 1917.

Codex Iuris Canonici. Roma: Libreria Editrice Vaticana, 1983.

Collins, Raymond F. *Divorce in the New Testament.* Collegeville: The Liturgical Press, 1992.

Congregation for the Doctrine of the Faith (CDF). "Concerning the Reception of Holy Communion by Divorced and Remarried Members of the Faithful." *Origins* 24(October 27, 1994) 337, 339–341.

D'Antonio, William V., et al. *Laity American and Catholic: Transforming the Church.* Kansas City, Mo.: Sheed and Ward, 1996.

Denzinger, Henricus and Adolphus Schönmetzer. *Enchiridion Symbolorum Definitionum et Declarationum de Rebus Fidei et Morum* (DS). Editio XXIII. Roma: Herder, 1965.

Gratian. *Decretum.* J. P. Migne, ed. *Patrologiae Cursus Completus: Series Latina,* vol. 187. Paris, n.d.

Hefele, Charles J. *History of the Christian Councils.* Edinburgh: Clark, 1883.

Himes, Kenneth and James Coriden. "Notes on Moral Theology 1995: Pastoral Care of the Divorced and Remarried." *Theological Studies* 57 (1996) 97–123.

Jerome, Saint. *Epistola LV.* J. P. Migne, ed., *Patrologiae Cursus Completus: Series Latina,* vol. 22. Paris, n.d.

Pope John Paul II. *Familiaris Consortio. Acta Apostolicae Sedis* 74 (1982) 81–191.

Kelly, Kevin T. *Divorce and Second Marriage: Facing the Challenge.* New York: Seabury, 1983.

———, "Divorce and Remarriage: Conflict in the Church." *Tablet* 248 (1994) 1374–1375.

Lawler, Michael G. "Faith, Contract, and Sacrament in Christian Marriage." *Theological Studies* 52 (1991) 712–731.

———. *Marriage and Sacrament: A Theology of Christian Marriage.* Collegeville: The Liturgical Press, 1993.

———. *Symbol and Sacrament: A Contemporary Sacramental Theology.* Omaha: Creighton University Press, 1995.

Malone, Richard and John Connery, eds. *Contemporary Perspectives on Christian Marriage: Propositions and Papers from the International Theological Commission.* Chicago: Loyola Press, 1984.

Mansi, J. D., ed. *Sacrorum Conciliorum Nova Collectio.* Paris: Welter, 1903–1927.

Migne, J. P., ed. *Patrologiae Cursus Completus: Series Graeca* (PG). Paris, n.d.

———, ed. *Patrologiae Cursus Completus: Series Latina* (PL). Paris, n.d.

Navarette, Urban. "Indissolubilitas Matrimonii Rati et Consummati: Opiniones Recentiores et Observationes." *Periodica* 58 (1969) 415–489.

Newman, John Henry. *On Consulting the Faithful in Matters of Doctrine.* London: Collins, 1986.

Pope Pius XI. *Casti Connubii. Acta Apostolicae Sedis* 22 (1930) 539–592.

Origen. *Commentarium in Matthaeum.* J. P. Migne, ed., *Patrologiae Cursus Completus: Series Graeca,* vol. 13. Paris, n.d.

Sullivan, B. *Legislation and Requirement for Permissible Cohabitation as Invalid Marriages.* Washington, D.C.: Catholic University Press, 1954.

Villette, Louis. *Foi et sacrement: de Saint Thomas et Karl Barth.* Paris: Bloud et Gay, 1964.

Wallerstein, Judith S. and Sandra Blakeslee. *Second Chances: Men, Women and Children a Decade after Divorce.* New York: Ticknor and Fields, 1989.

CHAPTER 36

Children after Divorce:
Wounds That Don't Heal

Judith S. Wallerstein

In many discussions of divorce, the question of a breakup's effect on children does not arise. The discussion centers on what divorce means for the divorcing couple. In this section on divorce and annulment, we have put the question of children in divorce first, for two reasons. First of all, some students using this book will themselves be children of divorce or may be dating or engaged to a child of divorce. They may find in the following essay by Judith Wallerstein insight into their own reactions or those of their beloved. Secondly, it seems important to name all those wounded by divorce. Doing so raises the stakes involved in careful preparation for marriage.

Wallerstein reports research among the sons and daughters of divorce, where she finds far more emotional pain than many expected. Apparently, healing the wounds of divorce in children can take many years.

Questions for Discussion

1. Which of the findings of the follow-up studies of children of divorce were for you the most surprising?
2. What is the difference between seeing divorce as a single circumscribed event and seeing it as a process?
3. What does Wallerstein mean by the "sleeper effect" of divorce?
4. What is the diminished parenting consequence and how is it related to the overburdened child?
5. What interpretation do you give to the incident of the boy who piled all the furniture on top of the baby dolls?

A s recently as the 1970s, when the American divorce rate began to soar, divorce was thought to be a brief crisis that soon resolved itself. Young children might have difficulty falling asleep and older children might have

From *The New York Times Magazine*, 22 January 1989, pp. 19–21, 41–44. Copyright © 1989 by Judith Wallerstein and Sandra Blakeslee. Reprinted by arrangement with Virginia Barber Literary Agency, Inc. All rights reserved.

trouble at school. Men and women might become depressed or frenetic, throwing themselves into sexual affairs or immersing themselves in work.

But after a year or two, it was expected, most would get their lives back on track, at least outwardly. Parents and children would get on with new routines, new friends and new schools, taking full opportunity of the second chances that divorce brings in its wake.

These views, I have come to realize, were wishful thinking. In 1971, working with a small group of colleagues and with funding from San Francisco's Zellerbach Family Fund, I began a study of the effects of divorce on middle-class people who continue to function despite the stress of a marriage breakup.

That is, we chose families in which, despite the failing marriage, the children were doing well at school and the parents were not in clinical treatment for psychiatric disorders. Half of the families attended church or synagogue. Most of the parents were college educated. This was, in other words, divorce under the best of circumstances.

Our study, which would become the first ever made over an extended period of time, eventually tracked 60 families, most of them white, with a total of 131 children, for 10, and in some cases 15, years after divorce. We found that although some divorces work well—some adults are happier in the long run, and some children do better than they would have been expected to in an unhappy intact family—more often than not divorce is a wrenching, long-lasting experience for at least one of the former partners. Perhaps most important, we found that for virtually all the children, it exerts powerful and wholly unanticipated effects.

Our study began with modest aspirations. With a colleague, Joan Berlin Kelly—who headed a community mental-health program in the San Francisco area—I planned to examine the short-term effects of divorce on these middle-class families.

We spent many hours with each member of each of our 60 families—hearing their firsthand reports from the battleground of divorce. At the core of our research was the case study, which has been the main source of the fundamental insights of clinical psychology and of psychoanalysis. Many important changes, especially in the long run, would be neither directly observable nor easily measured. They would become accessible only through case studies: by examining the way each of these people processed, responded to and integrated the events and relationships that divorce brings in its wake.

We planned to interview families at the time of decisive separation and filing for divorce, and again 12 to 18 months later, expecting to chart recoveries among men and women and to look at how the children were mastering troubling family events.

We were stunned when, at the second series of visits, we found family after family still in crisis, their wounds wide open. Turmoil and distress had not noticeably subsided. Many adults were angry, and felt humiliated and rejected, and most had not gotten their lives back together. An unexpectedly large number of children were on a downward course. Their symptoms were worse than they had been immediately after the divorce. Our findings were absolutely contradictory to our expectations.

Dismayed, we asked the Zellerbach Fund to support a follow-up study in the fifth year after divorce. To our surprise, interviewing 56 of the 60 families in our original study, we found that although half the men and two thirds of the women (even many of those suffering economically) said they were more content with their lives, only 34 percent of the children were clearly doing well.

Another 37 percent were depressed, could not concentrate in school, had trouble making friends and suffered a wide range of other behavior problems. While able to function on a daily basis, these children were not recovering, as everyone thought they would. Indeed most of them were on a downward course. This is a powerful statistic, considering that these were children who were functioning well five years before. It would be hard to find any other group of children—except, perhaps, the victims of a natural disaster—who suffered such a rate of sudden serious psychological problems.

The remaining children showed a mixed picture of good achievement in some areas and faltering achievement in others; it was hard to know which way they would eventually tilt.

The psychological condition of these children and adolescents, we found, was related in large part to the overall quality of life in the post-divorce family, to what the adults had been able to build in place of the failed marriage. Children tended to do well if their mothers and fathers, whether or not they remarried, resumed their parenting roles, managed to put their differences aside, and allowed the children a continuing relationship with both parents. Only a handful of kids had all these advantages.

We went back to these families again in 1980 and 1981 to conduct a 10-year follow-up. Many of those we had first interviewed as children were now adults. Overall, 45 percent were doing well; they had emerged as competent, compassionate and courageous people. But 41 percent were doing poorly; they were entering adulthood as worried, underachieving, self-deprecating and sometimes angry young men and women. The rest were strikingly uneven in how they adjusted to the world; it is too soon to say how they will turn out.

At around this time, I founded the Center for the Family in Transition, in Marin County, near San Francisco, which provides counseling to people who are separating, divorcing or remarrying. Over the years, my colleagues and I have seen more than 2,000 families—an experience that has amplified my concern about divorce. Through our work at the center and in the study, we have come to see divorce not as a single circumscribed event but as a continuum of changing family relationships—as a process that begins during the failing marriage and extends over many years. Things are not getting better, and divorce is not getting easier. It's too soon to call our conclusions definitive, but they point to an urgent need to learn more.

It was only at the 10-year point that two of our most unexpected findings became apparent. The first of these is something we call the sleeper effect.

The first youngster in our study to be interviewed at the 10-year mark was one who had always been a favorite of mine. As I waited for her to arrive for this interview, I remembered her innocence at age 16, when we had last met. It was she who alerted us to the fact that many young women experience a delayed effect of divorce.

As she entered my office, she greeted me warmly. With a flourishing sweep of one arm, she said. "You called me at just the right time. I just turned 21!" Then she startled me by turning immediately serious. She was in pain, she said.

She was the one child in our study who we all thought was a prime candidate for full recovery. She had denied some of her feelings at the time of divorce, I felt, but she had much going for her, including high intelligence, many friends, supportive parents, plenty of money.

As she told her story, I found myself drawn into unexpected intricacies of her life. Her trouble began, typically, in her late teens. After graduating from high school with honors, she was admitted to a respected university and did very well her freshman year. Then she fell apart. As she told it, "I met my first true love."

The young man, her age, so captivated her that she decided it was time to have a fully committed love affair. But on her way to spend summer vacation with him, her courage failed. "I went to New York instead. I hitchhiked across the country. I didn't know what I was looking for. I thought I was just passing time. I didn't stop and ponder. I just kept going, recklessly, all the time waiting for some word from my parents. I guess I was testing them. But no one—not my dad, not my mom—ever asked me what I was doing there on the road alone."

She also revealed that her weight dropped to 94 pounds from 128 and that she had not menstruated for a year and a half.

"I began to get angry," she said. "I'm angry at my parents for not facing up to the emotions, to the feelings in their lives, and for not helping me face up to the feelings in mine. I have a hard time forgiving them."

I asked if I should have pushed her to express her anger earlier.

She smiled patiently and said, "I don't think so. That was exactly the point. All those years I denied feelings. I thought I could live without love, without sorrow, without anger, without pain. That's how I coped with the unhappiness in my parents' marriage. Only when I met my boyfriend did I become aware of how much feeling I was sitting on all those years. I'm afraid I'll lose him."

It was no coincidence that her acute depression and anorexia occurred just as she was on her way to consummate her first love affair, as she was entering the kind of relationship in which her parents failed. For the first time, she confronted the fears, anxieties, guilt and concerns that she had suppressed over the years.

Sometimes with the sleeper effect the fear is of betrayal rather than commitment. I was shocked when another young woman—at the age of 24, sophisticated, warm and friendly—told me she worried if her boyfriend was even 30 minutes late, wondering who he was with and if he was having an affair with another woman. This fear of betrayal occurs at a frequency that far exceeds what one might expect from a group of people randomly selected from the population. They suffer minute to minute, even though their partners may be faithful.

In these two girls we saw a pattern that we documented in 66 percent of the young women in our study between the ages of 19 and 23; half of them were seriously derailed by it. The sleeper effect occurs at a time when these young women are making decisions with long-term implications for their lives. Faced with issues of commitment, love and sex in an adult context, they are aware that the game is serious. If they tie in with the wrong man, have children too soon, or choose harmful life styles, the effects can be tragic. Overcome by fears and anxieties, they begin to make connections between these feelings and their parents' divorce:

"I'm so afraid I'll marry someone like my dad."

"How can you believe in commitment when anyone can change his mind anytime?"

"I am in awe of people who stay together."

We can no longer say—as most experts have held in recent years—that girls are generally less troubled by the divorce experience than boys. Our study strongly indicates, for the first time, that girls experience serious effects of divorce at the time they are entering young adulthood. Perhaps the risk for girls and boys is equalized over the long term.

When a marriage breaks down, men and women alike often experience a diminished capacity to parent. They may give less time, provide less discipline and be less sensitive to their children, since they are themselves caught up in the maelstrom of divorce and its aftermath. Many researchers and clinicians find that parents are temporarily unable to separate their children's needs from their own.

In a second major unexpected finding of our 10-year study, we found that fully a quarter of the mothers and a fifth of the fathers had not gotten their lives back on track a decade after divorce. The diminished parenting continued, permanently disrupting the child-rearing functions of the family. These parents were chronically disorganized and, unable to meet the challenges of being a parent, often leaned heavily on their children. The child's role became one of warding off the serious depression that threatened the parents' psychological functioning. The divorce itself may not be solely to blame but, rather, may aggravate emotional difficulties that had been masked in the marriage. Some studies have found that emotionally disturbed parents within a marriage produce similar kinds of problems in children.

These new roles played by the children of divorce are complex and unfamiliar. They are not simple role reversals, as some have claimed, because the child's role becomes one of holding the parent together psychologically. It is more than a caretaking role. This phenomenon merits our careful attention, for it affected 15 percent of the children in our study, which means many youngsters in our society. I propose that we identify as a distinct psychological syndrome the "overburdened child," in the hope that people will begin to recognize the problems and take steps to help these children, just as they help battered and abused children.

One of our subjects, in whom we saw this syndrome, was a sweet 5-year-old girl who clearly felt that she was her father's favorite. Indeed, she was the only person in the family he never hit. Preoccupied with being good and helping to calm both parents, she opposed the divorce because she knew it would take her father away from her. As it turned out, she also lost her mother who, soon after the divorce, turned to liquor and sex, a combination that left little time for mothering.

A year after the divorce, at the age of 6, she was getting herself dressed, making her own meals and putting herself to bed. A teacher noticed the dark circles under her eyes, and asked why she looked so tired. "We have a new baby at home," the girl explained. The teacher, worried, visited the house and discovered there was no baby. The girl's story was designed to explain her fatigue but also enabled her to fantasize endlessly about a caring, loving mother.

Shortly after this episode, her father moved to another state. He wrote to her once or twice a year, and when we saw her at the five-year follow-up she pulled out a packet of letters from him. She explained how worried she was that he might get into trouble, as if she were the parent and he the child who had left home.

"I always knew he was O.K. if he drew pictures on the letters," she said. "The last two really worried me because he stopped drawing."

Now 15, she has taken care of her mother for the past 10 years. "I felt it was my responsibility to make sure that Mom was O.K.," she says. "I stayed home with her instead of playing or going to school. When she got mad, I'd let her take it out on me."

I asked what her mother would do when she was angry.

"She'd hit me or scream. It scared me more when she screamed. I'd rather be hit. She always seemed so much bigger when she screamed. Once Mom got drunk and passed out on the street. I called my brothers, but they hung up. So I did it. I've done a lot of things I've never told anyone. There were many times she was so upset I was sure she would take her own life. Sometimes I held both her hands and talked to her for hours I was so afraid."

In truth, few children can rescue a troubled parent. Many become angry at being trapped by the parent's demands, at being robbed of their separate identity and denied their childhood. And they are saddened, sometimes beyond repair, at seeing so few of their own needs gratified.

Since this is a newly identified condition that is just being described, we cannot know its true incidence. I suspect that the number of overburdened children runs much higher than the 15 percent we saw in our study and that we will begin to see rising reports in the next few years—just as the reported incidence of child abuse has risen since it was first identified as a syndrome in 1962.

The sleeper effect and the overburdened-child syndrome were but two of many findings in our study. Perhaps most important, overall, was our finding that divorce has a lasting psychological effect on many children, one that, in fact, may turn out to be permanent.

Children of divorce have vivid memories about their parents' separation. The details are etched firmly in their minds, more so than those of any other experiences in their lives. They refer to themselves as children of divorce, as if they share an experience that sets them apart from all others. Although many have come to agree that their parents were wise to part company, they nevertheless feel that they suffered from their parents' mistakes. In many instances, conditions in the post-divorce family were more stressful and less supportive to the child than conditions in the failing marriage.

If the finding that 66 percent of the 19- to 23-year-old young women experienced the sleeper effect was most unexpected, others were no less dramatic. Boys, too, were found to suffer unforeseen long-lasting effects. Forty percent of the 19- to 23-year-old young men in our study 10 years after divorce, still had no set goals, a limited education and a sense of having little control over their lives.

In comparing the post-divorce lives of former husbands and wives, we saw that 50 percent of the women and 30 percent of the men were still intensely angry at their former spouses a decade after divorce. For women over 40 at divorce, life was lonely throughout the decade; not one in our study remarried or sustained a loving relationship. Half the men over 40 had the same problem.

In the decade after divorce, three in five children felt rejected by one of their parents, usually the father—whether or not it was true. The frequency and duration of visiting made no difference. Children longed for their fathers, and the need increased during adolescence. Thirty-four percent of the youngsters went to live with their fathers during adolescence for at least a year. Half returned to the mother's home disappointed with what they had found. Only one in seven saw both mother and father happily remarried after 10 years. One in two saw their mother or their father undergo a second divorce. One in four suffered a severe and enduring drop in the family's standard of living and went on to observe a lasting discrepancy between their parents' standards of living.

We found that the children who were best adjusted 10 years later were those who showed the most distress at the time of the divorce—the youngest. In general, preschoolers are the most frightened and show the most dramatic symptoms when marriages break up. Many are afraid that they will be abandoned by both parents and they have trouble sleeping or staying by themselves. It is therefore surprising to find that the same children 10 years later seem better adjusted than their older siblings. Now in early and mid-adolescence, they were rated better on a wide range of psychological dimensions than the older children. Sixty-eight percent were doing well, compared with less than 40 percent of older children. But whether having been young at the time of divorce will continue to protect them as they enter young adulthood is an open question.

Our study shows that adolescence is a period of particularly grave risk for children in divorced families. Through rigorous analysis, statistical and otherwise, we were able to see clearly that we weren't dealing simply with the routine angst of young people going through transition but rather that, for most of them, divorce was the single most important cause of enduring pain and anomie in their lives. The young people told us time and again how much they needed a family structure, how much they wanted to be protected, and how much they yearned for clear guidelines for moral behavior. An alarming number of teenagers felt abandoned, physically and emotionally.

For children, divorce occurs during the formative years. What they see and experience becomes a part of their inner world, influencing their own relationships 10 and 15 years later, especially when they have witnessed violence between the parents. It is then, as these young men and women face the developmental task of establishing love and intimacy, that they most feel the lack of a template for a loving relationship between a man and a woman. It is here that their anxiety threatens their ability to create new, enduring families of their own.

As these anxieties peak in the children of divorce throughout our society, the full legacy of the rising divorce rate is beginning to hit home. The new families being formed today by these children as they reach adulthood appear particularly vulnerable.

Because our study was such an early inquiry, we did not set out to compare children of divorce with children from intact families. Lacking fundamental knowledge about life after the breakup of a marriage, we could not know on what basis to build a comparison or control group. Was the central issue one of economics, age, sex, a happy intact marriage—or would any intact marriage do? We began, therefore, with a question—What is the nature of the divorce experience?—and in answering it we would generate hypotheses that could be tested in subsequent studies.

This has indeed been the case. Numerous studies have been conducted in different regions of the country, using control groups, that have further explored and validated our findings as they have emerged over the years. For example, one national study of 699 elementary school children carefully compared children six years after their parents' divorce with children from intact families. It found—as we did—that elementary-age boys from divorced families show marked discrepancies in peer relationships, school achievements and social adjustment. Girls in this group, as expected, were hardly distinguishable based on the experience of divorce, but, as we later found out, this would not always hold up. Moreover, our findings are supported by a litany of modern-day statistics. Although one in three children are from divorced families, they account for an inordinately high proportion of children in mental-health treatment, in special-education classes, or referred by teachers to school psychologists. Children of divorce make up an estimated 60 percent of child patients in clinical treatment and 80 percent—in some cases, 100 percent—of adolescents in inpatient mental hospital settings. While no one would claim that a cause and effect relationship has been established in all of these cases, no one would deny that the role of divorce is so persuasively suggested that it is time to sound the alarm.

All studies have limitations in what they can accomplish. Longitudinal studies, designed to establish the impact of a major event or series of events on the course of a subsequent life, must always allow for the influence of many interrelated factors. They must deal with chance and the uncontrolled factors that so often modify the sequences being followed. This is particularly true of children, whose lives are influenced by developmental changes, only some of which are predictable, and by the problem of individual differences, about which we know so little.

Our sample, besides being quite small, was also drawn from a particular population slice—predominantly white, middle class and relatively privileged suburbanites.

Despite these limitations, our data have generated working hypotheses about the effects of divorce that can now be tested with more precise methods, including appropriate control groups. Future research should be aimed at testing, correcting or modifying our initial findings, with larger and more diverse segments of the population. For example, we found that children— especially boys and young men—continued to need their fathers after divorce and suffered feelings of rejection even when they were visited regularly. I would like to see a study comparing boys and girls in sole and joint custody, spanning different developmental stages, to see if greater access to both parents counteracts these feelings of rejection. Or, does joint custody lead to a different sense of rejection—of feeling peripheral in both homes?

It is time to take a long, hard look at divorce in America. Divorce is not an event that stands alone in children's or adults' experience. It is a continuum that begins in the unhappy marriage and extends through the separation, divorce and any remarriages and second divorces. Divorce is not necessarily the sole culprit. It may be no more than one of the many experiences that occur in this broad continuum.

Profound changes in the family can only mean profound changes in society as a whole. All children in today's world feel less protected. They sense that the institution of the family is weaker than it has ever been before. Even those children raised in happy, intact families worry that their families may come undone. The task for society in its true and proper perspective is to strengthen the family—all families.

A biblical phrase I have not thought of for many years has recently kept running through my head: "Watchman, what of the night?" We are not, I'm afraid, doing very well on our watch—at least for our children. We are allowing them to bear the psychological, economic and moral brunt of divorce.

And they recognize the burdens. When one 6-year-old boy came to our center shortly after his parents' divorce, he would not answer questions; he played games instead. First he hunted all over the playroom for the sturdy Swedish-designed dolls that we use in therapy. When he found a good number of them, he stood the baby dolls firmly on their feet and placed the miniature tables, chairs, beds and, eventually, all the playhouse furniture on top of them. He looked at me, satisfied. The babies were supporting a great deal. Then wordlessly, he placed all the mother and father dolls in precarious positions on the steep roof of the doll house. As a father doll slid off the roof, the boy caught him and, looking up at me, said, "He might die," Soon, all the mother and father dolls began sliding off the roof. He caught them gently, one by one. "The babies are holding up the world," he said.

Although our overall findings are troubling and serious, we should not point the finger of blame at divorce per se. Indeed, divorce is often the only rational solution to a bad marriage. When people ask whether they should stay married for the sake of the children, I have to say, "Of course not." All our evidence shows that children exposed to open conflict, where parents terrorize or strike one another, turn out less well-adjusted than do children from divorced families. And although we lack systematic studies comparing children in divorced families with those in unhappy intact families, I am convinced that it is not useful to provide children with a model of adult behavior that avoids problem-solving and that stresses martyrdom, violence or apathy. A divorce undertaken thoughtfully and realistically can teach children how to confront serious life problems with compassion, wisdom and appropriate action.

Our findings do not support those who would turn back the clock. As family issues are flung to the center of our political arena, nostalgic voices from the right argue for a return to a time when divorce was more difficult to obtain. But they do not offer solutions to the wretchedness and humiliation within many marriages.

Still, we need to understand that divorce has consequences—we need to go into the experience with our eyes open. We need to know that many children will suffer for many years. As a society, we need to take steps to preserve for the children as much as possible of the social, economic and emotional security that existed while their parents' marriage was intact.

Like it or not, we are witnessing family changes which are an integral part of the wider changes in our society. We are on a wholly new course, one that gives us unprecedented opportunities for creating better relationships and stronger families—but one that also brings unprecedented dangers for society, especially for our children.

PART EIGHT

Spirituality of Marriage

CHAPTER 37

Spirituality and Lifestyle

Evelyn Eaton Whitehead
James D. Whitehead

When some people think about their future marriage, their fantasy is not one of "erotic flourishing" in a household with a beloved partner, but this: having in the marriage household all the things they could not afford in the parental household. If this statement is true, it means that the fantasy of marriage is not a relational one at all but a consumerist one, not one of loving but one of having.

There is much in the following essay that may seem to some readers as, to use the authors' own words, "illusory or naive." Here the Whiteheads deal with the sort of attitudes or sense of things that comes from the life and teaching of Jesus of Nazareth. The authors use the word *spirituality* to name the attitudes they describe. Not everyone understands the meaning of this term. The best way of understanding it is this: not thoughts about God but rather a way of living that shows what a person stands for. This can be positive or negative. Some people live out the motto: "Never give a sucker a break" or "Grab all the gusto you can get." Living out either motto gives us a negative dehumanized kind of spirit. Living out the kind of loving stance toward the world and its people that Jesus showed us gives us a very different kind of spirit. You understand a person's spirituality when you stand next to a coffin and ask: what was this person all about; what did this person stand for in his or her life?

One student who read this essay, a young woman, found its proposals so "far out" that she called the authors "religious fanatics." Seen against the depiction of family life found in TV sitcoms, the essay is indeed "far out." However, the authors are proposing that a particular couple have a definite kind of "agency," that is, the power to bring into their home a particular set of values and attitudes that become spelled out in deeds: in ways of speaking to one another; in ways of eating; in the kinds of issues that come up around the dinner table; in the sorts of people invited to gather around that table; in the patterns of prayer or of not praying.

No matter how you see these particular patterns, *there will be patterns of speaking and doing* that will characterize the household. What will they be? Will they be patterns of consumerism, of racism, of sexism, of homophobia, of greed, of hate. Will our attitudes be formed by sitcoms or will there be an alternate set of attitudes? Will the conviction that we are for more than ourselves be basic in our household, or will our conviction be "look out for number one"?

The fanatic is grim, determined, and funless. The proposal here is for a playful marriage. The core of the playful is "a light grasp on things," the opposite of the closed-fist grab for all the gusto you can get. These are the important matters needing discussion that arise in the final pages of this essay.

Questions for Discussion

1. What do you find "way out" in this essay?
2. Are there any particular attitudes or "spirit" you would want your home to have? What might they be?
3. Are there any attitudes you would *not want* your children to pick up in your home?
4. Which of the following do you want to give more thought to:
    • prayer together
    • action for justice
    • the use of time
    • the use of money
    • our participation in the life of a religious group?

The choices that influence our lifestyle are part of the spirituality of our marriage. It is in these choices that we express the values that shape our life together. And we sense that Christianity's most significant contribution to our marriage is in the values to which it calls us. That unselfish love is possible, that sacrifice can have value beyond itself, that pleasure is to be celebrated but not idolized, that I am not for myself alone—these profound truths of human life are not always apparent. There is much in contemporary society, perhaps even much in our own experience, to suggest that these convictions are illusory or naive. Alone, we may feel how fragile is their hold on us. In community with other believers, we can face our doubts with less fear because we do not face them alone. We can nourish the religious vision of life that sustains us in our journey of marriage for a lifetime.

Christianity does not give married love its value; rather it celebrates the deeper meaning of married love that can sometimes be lost or obscured in the hectic pace of life. Christianity gives us insight, vision into what is ordinarily invisible—the power and presence of God's redeeming love all around us and especially in certain privileged, sacramental experiences. And for most Christians, married love and the life commitments that flow from and surround this love are instances of this privileged experience of the power and presence of God. In this chapter we will explore several of the values which help to shape the lifestyle of Christian marriage.

The lifestyle of our marriage is influenced by many forces. Some of these seem beyond our immediate control—economic factors that bring inflation, political factors that shape national policy on child care, cultural factors that affect what is "expected" of women and men. In some marriages the influ-

Copyright © 1981 by Evelyn Eaton Whitehead and James D. Whitehead. Reprinted with permission.

ence of these external factors is so strong that there seems little room for choice. If I am poor, undereducated or chronically unemployed, it will be difficult for me to feel that I am in control of my own life. These burdens of social inequity weigh heavily on many Americans, adding stress in their marriages. A high incidence of divorce and desertion results.

But for most Americans, the lifestyle of marriage is not simply a product of external forces. We are conscious of ourselves as agents. Within certain limits we choose how we shall live. Some of our "choices" may be illusory, more influenced than we would like to admit by factors outside our awareness, but we are nevertheless conscious of ourselves as making decisions that influence the shape of our marriage.

The choices that are most important for our lifestyle are those that touch on the use of our resources. Our resources of concern, of time and of money are the "stuff" of our life together. The choices we make about these resources are not incidental; they are close to the substance of what our marriage is. What do we care about together? What is our money for? How do we spend the time of our life? It is in our response to these questions that we discover the values of our marriage and express them in our lifestyle.

PRAYER AND JUSTICE

Prayer is part of the lifestyle of Christian marriage. This will include the ways that we as a couple, as a family, participate in the prayer of the Church, especially the celebration of the Eucharist. But it will involve as well our developing suitable ways for us to pray together, to share—sometimes as a couple, sometimes with the children as well—the intimate experience of coming into the presence of God in prayer. In recent decades the devotional life of many Catholic homes included the family rosary or prayers honoring the Sacred Heart. Family prayer today is more likely to focus on the reading of Scripture, reflecting together on its meaning for our lives and our actions in the world.

Prayer has been urged in marriage as one of the ways for the family to deepen its own unity: "The family that prays together, stays together." To pray together as a couple and as a family can reinforce, sometimes powerfully, our experience of being together in the ways that matter most. But the prayer of Christians is not simply about unity among us; it is about our community with humankind in the presence of God. Liturgical prayer especially celebrates this larger awareness. It is as the people of God that, in the name of Jesus and through the power of his abiding Spirit, we pray. But family prayer, too, should open us beyond "just us." The needs of the world, concretely the ways in which pain and loss and injustice are part of the world that we can influence, are part of our prayer.

In fall 1978 Archbishop Jean Jadot delivered an address on the implementation of the pastoral plan for family ministry that had been developed by the bishops of the United States. In his talk he spoke of prayer, faith and justice as these touch the family. He said, "The prayer I am speaking about is not so much the recitation of prayers as a shared experience of prayer. This finds its origins in a common reading of the Holy Scriptures and in a concern for those who are in need, for justice and peace in the world, for the coming of the Kingdom of God . . . such prayer quite naturally evokes an awareness of the family's mission to service. It also raises the family's social consciousness."

The conviction that we are for more than ourselves is basic to the Christian world view. This value must find its expression not only in our prayer but in our lifestyle. Most of us know that our marriage is about more than "just us." We need more than "just us" if our family is to thrive. We are aware of how much, as a couple and as a family, we depend on contact with certain relatives and support from special friends. But as Christians we go beyond ourselves not just in what we need but also in what we contribute.

Our life as a family and especially our children carry us into the larger world. As our children grow, we sense how much more they belong to the world and its future than they do to us. Thus, our care for them cannot end at our doorstep. Our first movements to contribute to the world beyond may well be for their sake—to make the world a better place for them, a place worthy of their hopes and conducive to their growth. But it is possible for this initial impulse of generative care, our concern for our children and their future, to stagnate. Our preoccupation with what is good for our family can become a new form of selfishness. The boundaries may be broadened slightly, but it is still "us" against "them."

But for many of us the movement of concern for our children invites us into a concern for the children of the world, for the future of humankind. I become more deeply aware that, by emotion and by action, I am involved in the lives of others. As parent, as worker, as citizen, I am in my own way somehow responsible for the future. The world—its hopes and problems—has a claim on me.

As Christians we hear this invitation to generativity reinforced in the call of Jesus. I am not only my brother's keeper; the category of brother and sister has expanded to include whoever is in need. "I was a stranger and you made me welcome, naked and you clothed me, sick and you visited me, in prison and you came to see me" (Matthew 25:35–36). Christianity expands the boundaries of our concern. We find we belong to a larger community. We hold our resources as stewards: these are not simply our "possessions," but the means of our contribution to a more just world.

Most of us sense, increasingly, that the issues of social value and justice that we face in our own lives are complex. There are not many questions where the "one right answer" emerges quickly and clearly. In any particular case, persons of good will and intelligence may come to different conclusions about what should be done. When the issues at stake touch directly on our own lives or our family's welfare—as in questions of job security or property values or tax reform—it can be even more difficult to determine the just response.

In these situations Christian awareness does not give easy answers but it does give us a starting point. We are not for ourselves alone. Action for justice and the transformation of the world is, as Pope Paul VI proclaimed, constitutive of our response to the gospel. We stand under the gospel challenge that we share the burdens of humankind and participate in its liberation. The way in which we, as a couple and as a family, participate in this mission of Christ may well have to be worked out on our own. But it can be expected that our maturing as Christian adults will involve our developing a lifestyle which expresses our understanding of the mission to which Jesus calls us and supports us in our response.

THE MEANING OF MONEY

Money is a central issue in marriage. What money means to us influences our relationship; how we use money shapes our lifestyle. And in many marriages decisions about money are among the most complex the couple face. Disagreements about money (how to manage it; how to spend it; who should make these decisions) and distress over money (living beyond our means; bills coming due; not having enough money to meet an unexpected expense) are significant sources of marital strain.

Money issues in marriage are troublesome in part because money carries so many different meanings. What is money for? My response here influences the way I answer the other questions. How much money does our family need? Can we ever have enough? How would we even go about determining what would be "enough" money for us?

For some of us, money is mainly for the practical necessities of life—food, clothing, shelter. For others, it is for enjoyment—for leisure or luxury or fun. Sometimes money is for our children's future, their education or financial security. Sometimes it is for self-esteem: "Surely I am worthwhile, just look at how much money I make." Sometimes money is for power: "I can buy anything and anyone I need." And sometimes it is a resource we have to be used for the good of the world.

Most practical decisions about money carry some larger emotional significance. These decisions say something important to us about who we are in the world. If, as a couple, we see money differently, if we each act out of a different sense of "what our money is for," we can anticipate that money issues will be troublesome to bring up between us and difficult to resolve.

The emotional significance of money is not the only source of strain. Inflation and the threat of economic recession are very real factors in the lifestyle of most families. Young couples find they can no longer afford to buy a house and so delay their decision to have a child. Couples with children realize that they both must bring in a paycheck if they wish to send their children to college. Couples who had resolved to retire early now plan to continue to work, unsure that their retirement benefits will remain adequate to living costs. Faced with rising prices, high interest rates and, for some, even unemployment, many families must make difficult decisions about money—decisions that significantly influence the lifestyle of their marriage.

But admitting the reality of these financially uncertain times, the money strain in many marriages is as much influenced by consumerism as by inflation. Even in this inflationary period, American families enjoy one of the highest levels of affluence in the world. We want and expect "the best that money can buy" for ourselves and our families. Advertising expands our sense of what we need, assuring us that "we owe it to ourselves" because "we're worth it." Perhaps especially as Americans we find ourselves susceptible to the temptation to judge our value by what we have—our material possessions, our standard of living, our buying power. This preoccupation with "the things of this world" has always been in tension with deeper religious intuitions: being is more than having; our worth is not grounded in our wealth; we are not "saved" by what we accumulate. The Christian vision has always called us to a certain detachment from wealth. As believers, we know we hold the goods of this world as stewards. Our responsibility is to care for the person in need, even out of our own substance. Today we see that this challenge has even broader scope. We are more aware of the connections between the prosperity of the United States and the poverty that exists elsewhere. It is often at the expense of other peoples that we have enjoyed, as a nation, the abundant resources of food and energy and technology that constitute "the good life." The patterns of this structural injustice are complicated, to be sure. It is not easy to trace our personal responsibility in this or to determine what we, as a family, can do to right the balance in world economics. But the complexity of the problem does not relieve us of responsibility. As Christians, we need to examine our family's standard of living not only in view of the shrinking dollar but in view of our accountability in the world. How we spend our money and where we invest our savings—for the Christian today these are more than practical financial questions to be resolved in terms of prices and interest rates alone. They are issues of religious significance that give shape to a Christian lifestyle.

MARRIAGE AND MINISTRY

For us as Christians, the question of lifestyle ultimately brings us to a discussion of ministry. Ministry is the action of believers undertaken in pursuit of the mission which Jesus entrusted to the Church—the coming of the Kingdom. Formal ministry is activity that is recognized or commissioned by the community of faith. Alongside this formal ministry is that ministry expected of all believers—the daily efforts to shape the world according to Christian values of love and mercy. Some Catholics who are married are part of the Church's formal ministry. The expanding involvement of lay persons in roles of official ministry is a fruit of the new vitality in the Church since the Second Vatican Council. Lay women and men serve in liturgical ministries in parishes as lectors and musicians and ministers of communion. Increasingly, the teaching ministry of parishes and dioceses is carried out by lay persons, some through full-time careers in religious education programs or Catholic school systems, others serving in a volunteer capacity as catechtists, conveners of an adult discussion group or members of the parish school board. There has been a comparable increase in the number of lay persons staffing the service agencies and social policy programs that operate under Church auspices or support.

This expansion of "approved" or "recognized" ministries over the past two decades has blurred many of the earlier distinctions among religious, clergy and lay persons in our Church. Married men ordained to the permanent diaconate, women religious serving as pastoral associates in parishes, women and married men studying in Catholic seminaries in preparation for careers of fulltime ministry—these persons do not fit easily into former categories. In some cases the openness to lay persons in roles of service and leadership has been more a response to personnel shortages ("There just aren't enough brothers, sisters and priests to go around anymore!") than a sign of a deeper appreciation of the scope of the Christian call to ministry. But in any case, a significant number of Catholic lay persons—both married and single— understand their life vocation to be in the formal ministry of the Church.

The involvement of married Catholics as formal ministers in the Church's ministry *to* marriage—as planners and leaders in programs of marriage preparation, marriage enrichment, marriage counseling, and as part of the liturgical celebration of marriage—is on the increase and is good. In our discussion here, however, we wish to look at the relationship of marriage and the general Christian call to ministry.

For some Christians, both those ordained and others who are not, the immediate focus of their own religious action is within the community of faith, a ministry to and through the formal Church. But for most believers the call to live and act in response to the Christian vision will find expression in their family and their work and their other involvements in society. How is the religious experience of marriage related to the religious action or ministry of an adult Christian life? We have discussed this ministry of the mature Christian in terms of religious generativity. Psychological maturity leads me beyond myself and my intimates toward genuine care for the world. So, too, religious generativity leads me beyond the celebration of the "Good News" for myself, toward religious action—ministry—for a world beyond myself and my religious "intimates." We have seen that intimacy can either contribute to generativity (when the experience of our love releases in each of us the psychological resources we need for generosity and self-transcendence) or detract from it (when our love seems so fragile that we must spend our energy and other resources on ourselves, with none to spare for the world beyond). So marriage can have an ambiguous effect in Christian maturity and ministry. There are Christians for whom their own marriage and family occupy their full concern, not only in moments of crisis such as serious illness or the loss of a job, not just during periods of predictable stress like the birth of a child or, for some, the event of retirement—but characteristically. "We are for ourselves—alone." They may take quite seriously their responsibilities as spouses and parents. Their marriage is stable, their children have as many educational opportunities and social advantages as the couple can afford. They may participate actively in the parish. They are regular churchgoers who contribute financially and see to it that their children take part in the religious education program. But through it all, they are "for themselves." They may see the parish in terms of what it has to give them—a satisfying experience of worship, a program of moral education for their children, perhaps even a sense of security and some status in the community. But to be an adult Christian has not brought with it for them the motivating conviction: I am, our family is, for more than ourselves.

Among many other Christians marriage is just such an opening to God and to the world. The lessons of our marriage teach us to care beyond ourselves; our concern for our children links us to the concerns of the world. We sense that our life together as a family not only "uses up" our strengths, but also generates new resources that we can share and spend beyond ourselves. Our home, our love, our joy together, our time, our insights, our concerns, even our money—these resources of our life together do not exist for ourselves alone. At any one point in our marriage we may be overwhelmed with a sense that there is not enough of us to go around, that our resources are deficient, not just in the face of the needs of the world but even for the needs of our own family. But over its life course, if not at every moment, our marriage as maturing Christians will be marked by openness to needs beyond the family and by an active sense of our own contribution to the coming of the Kingdom, the presence of God in justice and love.

There are, of course, many different ways in which this ministry of maturing Christians will be expressed, and so many ways in which the relationship between marriage and ministry will be seen. For some couples, their ministry is through their family life. They open their home to foster children or adopt a handicapped child. In another family the kitchen is always open to the teenagers in the neighborhood and the couple have time to listen to the concerns of their neighbors and friends. A third couple decide in retirement to devote two days a week together to visiting shut-ins or to welcome a recently widowed neighbor to live with them until she can make other plans. Other couples will sense that their involvement in issues of social concern is crucial to the religious education of their children. To take an unpopular stand on a question of racial justice, to become involved in a political campaign, to use part of their family's vacation money to assist those who have suffered in a disaster—these couples see such actions as of religious significance and encourage their children to share this practical understanding of faith.

For many lay Christians the arena of their ministry is the world of their employment. In my professional responsibilities, in my union activities, in a business decision I can influence, in the way I deal with my company subordinates and superiors, I try to bring to bear the convictions of my religious faith. On the job I take a stand that I know is right, even at the risk there may be repercussions. Or as a couple we decide to change jobs and move across country, so that we can participate in a project for economic justice. For many of us, then, our efforts to contribute to the world and to justice among people happen here, in the work that we do in the world. It is here that a sense of personal vocation takes shape. It is here that we work to hasten the coming of the Kingdom.

A PLAYFUL MARRIAGE

The lifestyle of our marriage has much to do with how we are involved beyond ourselves. But our lifestyle also influences and expresses how we are together. Many of the values of Christianity contribute to the way we live our life together by urging us to take marriage seriously. Marriage is for grown-ups; its responsibilities are significant; the honeymoon does not last forever. These sober truths are important for us to hear and the Church serves us well in giving voice to this wisdom. But Christian wisdom also speaks to another side of marriage—the intimate connections between love and play. As our marriage matures, it becomes more playful. Here we will consider several elements that are part of the lifestyle of a playful marriage.

THE TIME OF OUR LIFE

A playful marriage depends on how we spend time together. The demands of careers, children and other involvements can easily overwhelm a marriage relationship. The fatigue and distraction that result can seriously erode our presence to each other. We learn that the playfulness that marked our carefree relationship at the start of our marriage does not endure easily or automatically. We learn, paradoxically, that if we would have a playful marriage we must work at it. Playfulness between us, like our other experiences of intimacy, will have to be cultivated. It will require a discipline in our lifestyle, especially a discipline of our time.

If marriage is a vocation that begins in a resounding "yes," it matures in many "no's." To have quality time for my partner and our family I find I have to say "no" to many outside demands and requests. This discipline helps us structure time for these central commitments of our life. Such disciplined planning and foresight can be experienced as cold calculation or as a canny response to life's multiple demands. Without such an asceticism, we become subject to the endless demands (all of them "worthwhile") of contemporary married life. Gradually exhaustion takes the play out of our marriage, both its flexibility and its fun. Our playfulness can be fostered by planning special times for just the two of us. We set aside times and places with protective boundaries. On our vacation, in days of rest or retreat, we give ourselves permission to play again. Apart from the seriousness of the rest of our life, these occasions invite us to play together and enliven our love.

COMPETITION AND PLAY

A playful marriage also recognizes the connection between competition and play. Our competitiveness can be acknowledged. We can accept the fact that marriage is a contact sport, one in which injury, anger and even loss are sometimes to be expected. But our competitiveness can also enliven us. As we identify together how and when we feel competitive toward one another, these feelings lose some of their force over us. We can share more concretely some of our fears about conflict between us and even feel some of the exhilaration of our struggles.

Competition is often an act of intimacy. It brings us "up close" and engages us with one another, however ambiguously. In competition, as in wrestling, we can come in touch with each other in ways that both excite and threaten us. In our competitive encounters we can learn much about ourselves and each other. We can find unsuspected strengths; we can also come upon unacknowledged weaknesses. To compete does not mean that we must use these strengths to dominate or must exploit these weaknesses. My awareness of your weakness can help me love better, help me to protect or at least not take advantage of your vulnerability. Awareness of a strength can help me love better as well, enabling me to use it to foster rather than control our marriage.

The thought of competition in marriage may still disturb us. It may conjure up images of the professional athlete, concerned only with performance and rating, and with coming out ahead in this encounter. But this is only one narrow interpretation of competition. We may also see competition in our marriage as not necessarily setting us against one another but as bringing us closer together. This "closer together" is, of course, threatening. It may well, on occasion, produce hurt and injury. In love and in competition we take the risk of a very close encounter, trusting that we will both play fair. But when we do—overcoming our fear of being crushed and our need to dominate— we are exhilarated *together;* the winner is our marriage and our intimate lifestyle.

PLAYFUL SEX

Our sexual life together will be part of a playful marriage. Here the Christian tradition has not always been helpful. A central characteristic of play is its uselessness; it is "just for fun." Christians have learned, on the other hand, that sex is very serious business. It has a specific and (even) exclusive purpose: the begetting of children. Only when this goal is dutifully pursued is our sexual activity to be enjoyed. Thus the seriousness and sacredness of sexuality has, for many Christians, overpowered its playfulness. Is not "playful sex" for playmates and libertines? The ambiguity here parallels that of competition. As competition is neither simply destructive nor simply creative, human sexual activity is neither simply purposeful nor simply playful. As Christians we know that sex is sacred: in our sexual sharing we create more life; through it we confirm and increase our love for one another. But this sacredness does not exclude its playfulness. Sex is for Christians very responsible play. The sexual embrace, sometimes generative of new life and much more often generative of our own love, is also fun. Christianity has, to be sure, been cautious in recognizing the value of playfulness in sex. Only recently and even then reluctantly have many of the official voices within the Church been willing to acknowledge the legitimacy of a sexual love whose every act is not intended to bring children into the world. But these developments are happening in our time, in part through the testimony of married Christians. And as they do, it becomes easier for us to celebrate in the lifestyles of Christian marriage the variety and playfulness of sexual love. Sex is not the only place for play in a maturing marriage. But if there is little or no play in our sexual sharing we are likely to find it more difficult to play in the other areas of our common life.

LEARNING TO PLAY FAIR

Another element of a playful marriage is learning to play fair. This means learning the rules that can help our competitiveness and our other intimacies contribute to our marriage, not destroy it. A first rule is that we *need* to contest with one another. To regularly repress our anger, our confusion or disagreement will not reduce these feelings but only store them for later use. Being "a good sport" in our marriage does not mean choosing not to compete with or confront my partner. It means actively engaging in this relationship. "Poor sports" are those who choose not to contest anything with their partners. They may stand on the sidelines and complain, but they do not compete. A marriage in which the partners no longer contest, no longer struggle with each other in any significant way, can be called a stalemate. The partners in such a marriage are likely to experience each other as "stale mates."

If the first rule is simply to play—to compete, to get engaged—the second rule is to play fair. This means playing skillfully, knowing when and how to confront my partner. In marriage, as in every other kind of play, timing is important. And our experience of each other in marriage, the years we have been playing together, should help us to determine the timing of our confrontations. I bring up a sensitive issue when I sense the time is right: when *we* can handle it, not just when I want to take it on. Playing fair is likely to be a part of our lifestyle in marriage the more we are each able to display the skillful behaviors of communication and conflict resolution.

Learning to play fair is a complex virtue, one that most of us acquire only gradually as we mature. Its growth is likely to include the discipline of identifying and cutting away habits of ours that are destructive in our marriage— belittling the other person, striking back indirectly rather than confronting a troublesome issue, using the children as weapons in an effort to win or be right. Finally, play can teach us the importance of compromise and the value of being a good loser. Compromise means finding our way around questions and concerns that threaten a standoff or seem insoluble. The strategies of barter and negotiation will, at times, help us sustain our love and commitment. Learning how to be a good loser is also a sign of maturity. Each of us can expect to fail, even repeatedly, in our efforts at love and mutuality. Play reminds us that we need not be ashamed. Love does not mean never having to say I'm sorry; it means becoming good at it.

In all these ways we mature in love. We learn that play is not just for kids, that being able to trust one another is more important than always being right. In his study of adult maturity, *Adaptation to Life*, George Vaillant summarizes these connections among love, trust and play:

> It is hard to separate capacity to trust from capacity to play, for play is dangerous until we can trust both ourselves and our opponents to harness rage. In play, we must trust enough and love enough to risk losing without despair, to bear winning without guilt, and to laugh at error without mockery. (p. 309)

In our own marriage we can expect to know winning and losing, risk and error, laughter and love. These are the stuff of a playful marriage, the building blocks of a lifestyle of marriage for a lifetime.

CHAPTER 38

Faithful Becoming: Forming Families in the Art of Paradoxical Living in a Fragmented and Pluralistic World

Herbert Anderson

Paradox is at the center of the Christian way. It is also at the heart of every major religious tradition in the world. To die is to live. The first will be last. Become a child to move toward adulthood. Paradox is the capacity to entertain the possibility that two things may be simultaneously true. Marriage is sustained by paradox—by holding in tension the need for intimacy and autonomy.

Herbert Anderson's rich and insightful essay proposes the following: what is necessary for marriage is equally critical for family living. What he proposes is a spirituality of paradox that resonates with our postmodern sensibilities. We are easily tempted to create a family ethos with absolutes that exclude or divide. The family can also become an end in itself—American individualism writ large. However, the path to faithful Christian living involves responding constructively to the challenges of ambiguity, plurality, and uncertainty that are part of our daily lives.

Anderson explores several strategies for dealing with the social, cultural, and religious diversity impacting the Christian family today. He examines (1) balancing the tensions between home and work, resolving which will require a new (just) way of thinking about the marital bond; (2) balancing the tensions with respect to differences in a pluralistic world, which requires a strategy of creating and promoting a family ecology of tolerance and openness; (3) balancing hospitality in a fragmented and dangerous world, which calls for a hospitality that breaks down barriers and creates a common space that is both a haven from the world and a launching pad into the world. Anderson's proposed strategies may seem deceptively simple, but paradoxically, they are also profound.

Questions for Discussion

1. How would you discern the household obligations of each spouse in a just marital bond when both work outside the home?

2. Is tolerance a core value in a time of pluralism? Are there values, policies, worldviews we ought to be intolerant of as Christians?

3. How is hospitality necessary for survival? What is its educational value? Its ethical value? Its spiritual value?

4. Where do you experience the tension between managing forms of contemporary technology and its influence in family, church, and school?

M y mother was raised in rural western Minnesota at the beginning of the twentieth century in a context of ethnic and religious homogeneity. Some of that uniformity still existed when I was a child sixty years ago. Everybody I knew then had been socialized into the same worldview and shared values in which I was being formed. Parents raising children and children growing up at the beginning of the twenty-first century and the third millennium will face a much more diverse context with fewer certainties. Adults in families face the same challenges as they seek to continue to be formed for faithful living. The society in which we live is increasingly less homogeneous, stable, localized, and predictable because we live in increasingly heterogeneous, changing, translocal. and unpredictable globalized contexts. We can no longer assume a common worldview in the primary contexts of our lives, even including the church. When the world appears disjunctive or when we participate simultaneously in very different social or cultural networks, we need to be formed to live in uncertainties, contradictions, ambiguities, and conflicting interests.

The challenge facing families today is to forge patterns of faithful living in a fragmented and pluralistic world. There are at least ten unavoidable tensions that families will face as they learn the art of paradoxical living:

1. How will families balance the demands of the workplace and the obligations of home?

2. How will families foster respect for difference in order to form people for living in an increasingly pluralistic world?

3. How will families of the future continue to be havens of hospitality in a world that has become increasingly dangerous?

4. How will families manage the technology that makes them simultaneously more porous to influence from the world outside the home and more isolated?

5. How will families strengthen the practice of commitment in family living when the society is dubious of the value of long-term commitment?

6. How will families form future citizens with a commitment to the common good in a society that is preoccupied with individualism and privatism?

From *New Theology Review* 18, 3, August 2005, published by the Order of Saint Benedict.

7. How will families respond to the increasing religious and cultural diversity within our own midst?

8. How will multitasking affect the quality of relationships within the family? What will be the effect on childrearing of dictating corporate memos while nursing an infant or consulting by cell phone while watching a child's soccer match?

9. How will marriages be sustained and renewed as the life spam increases and the years of childrearing decrease proportionately?

10. How will families continue to form disciples of Christ for the sake of the world?

Each of these questions is worthy of longer consideration. The intent of this essay is to suggest ways of forming faithful Christians that take seriously the paradoxical nature of family living at the beginning of a new millennium. In the space available for this essay, we will examine only the first three questions.

THE PARADOXICAL SPIRITUALITY OF FAMILY LIVING

The spirituality that embraces paradox is particularly necessary for modern family living. By paradox, I mean a contradiction that does not seem to be true but nonetheless is true. The Cross is the ultimate paradox for the Christian. If we live the way of the Cross, we will live the contradictions that only God can resolve. The last are first, the meek inherit the earth, and in order to live we have to die. Paradox is not only the Christian way: it is inherent in human nature, in human community, and, particularly, in the family. Marriage is sustained by holding in vital, paradoxical tension the fundamental human need for intimacy and the equally fundamental human need for autonomy.

In *The Bonds of Love*, Jessica Benjamin describes a new "logic of paradox" that arises when marital partners see one another as equal subjects. "Perhaps the most fateful paradox is the one posed by our simultaneous need for recognition and independence—that the other subject is outside our control and yet we need him or her" (221). There is no theme more necessary or more complex for a vital marriage than the paradox of mutual recognition of equal subjects. Each person in a marriage may be a fully defined self, but the recognition of that unique self by the other is necessary for the marriage to work. This experience of recognizing and being recognized is not only prerequisite for community; it is fundamental for human growth and identity. Marriages that endure and flourish have achieved a kind of mutual recognition between husband and wife that honors each one as a unique and separate subject.

What is necessary for marriage is equally critical for family living. A family is a community in which the well-being of the whole and the well-being of each part must be held in almost sacred tension. The family's capacity to be intimate and caring and its capacity to be separate and different are para-doxically linked. A family's capacity to be together depends on its ability to be separate and honor the autonomy of each member. Even when we want to be emotionally free, we still depend on others in the family for recognition and intimacy. Solitude and community are paradoxically connected. We leave our families of origin in order to go home again: if we can't go home again, we probably have not left. Couples who are comfortable with the par-adox of marital intimacy and distance will work toward forming families in which commitment to the whole and commitment to each separate person are held as a sacred trust.

Embracing paradox is not easy, even in the safe intimacy of family living. It requires humility about what is right and a willingness to entertain the pos-sibility that two things might be true. Because there is another side to every-thing, as Thomas Merton once observed, we need to practice listening to the other side in our families so that no one's idea or contribution is left out. Embracing paradox is difficult because it is messy and a little like fuzzy-mindedness and too much like ambiguity. Because we would rather believe that things are this way or that way, we are tempted to foster a family belief system with absolutes that exclude or divide.

Pat Parker articulates very clearly what I mean by the truth of paradox in the opening lines of her poem "For the White Person who Wants to Know how to be my Friend."

> The first thing you do is to forget that I'm Black.
> Second, you must never forget that I'm Black (297).

Families need to embrace paradox as a way of faithful Christian living in order to respond constructively to the challenges they face at the beginning of the new millennium. If a family's belief system includes paradox at the center, it will be able to understand that contradiction, ambiguity, and uncer-tainty are part of life and not alien to becoming and being a faithful Christian.

HOW WILL FAMILIES BALANCE THE DEMANDS OF THE WORKPLACE AND THE OBLIGATIONS OF HOME?

Couples who are determined to work toward an equal division of household and parenting responsibilities often find themselves torn by the limits of time. Even when the intent is to establish equality between women and men in marriage, there is simply too much to do and not enough time in which to do it. When both partners in a marriage work outside the home, they often experience a clash of callings—the calling of work and the calling to family living. This conflict is implicit in the organization of modern, industrial, market-driven societies. Although many changes have occurred, like flex-time, job sharing, or personal leaves, the old demands for single-minded devotion to the workplace have not changed significantly. It should not be surprising, therefore, that the family is constantly juggling multiple obligations and expectations to be in several places simultaneously. Sometimes the tensions are of our own making because families have overscheduled their children with too many worthwhile activities. Some couples run out of time because they need to work two, three, or four jobs in order to afford the house they never have time to enjoy. Honoring the vital human needs for community and autonomy is the paradox embedded in the conflict between work and family.

Resolving the tensions between home and work will require a new way of thinking about the marital bond. If we understand equal partnership for women and men at home and in the workplace as a sign of God's longing for justice and mutual respect for all people, then the marital promise will need to include a commitment to be just with one another as well as loving to one another. Pauline Kleingeld, in an essay in *Mutuality Matters: Family, Faith, and Just Love*, has proposed that we reconceive the ideal of marriage as "not only a matter of love, *but also* of justice. On this view, married couples ideally would think of themselves as sharing at least two overarching aims: a loving marriage and a just marriage" (30). What Kleingeld has proposed changes the framework for negotiating role equality in marriage.

Positive changes in some aspects of society and in many marriages have not eliminated injustice from marriage nor have they eradicated injustice toward women in the church and at work. Women are paid less for the same or equivalent work. Household labor studies consistently show that women continue to do more housework than men even when both work outside the home. We need to work for laws and policies that are just, but just laws do not guarantee just action in the privacy of family life. Becoming and being married in a way that honors the unique gifts of each partner in a marriage depends on a commitment to forming a just bond.

A combined sixty-hour workweek for couples with children has been proposed as one way to relieve the tension between work and family. The proponents of this ideal acknowledge that it would only work in wealthier modern societies. To accomplish this ideal, Don S. Browning suggests that "market and government must work with culture-making institutions such as church, synagogue, and mosque to create a new philosophy of leisure and new restraints on the consumerism that drives our compulsion to constantly earn more money" (27). Rather than expecting families to adjust to the demands of the marketplace, the vision embodied in the sixty-hour combined work seeks to reform the world of work so it conforms to the scale of families with children. Even if the demands of a market economy were transformed, the sixty-hour workweek for families with young children would still require couples to be committed to a just distribution of responsibilities within the marital bond.

My wife Phyllis and I made an audiotape twenty-five years ago entitled "One Marriage, Two Ministries." Although the two ministries in our situation were both in the church, the issues we identified around autonomy and community have application for all couples who think of their work in the world as a ministry. We were only beginning to understand then what Klein-geld has identified now as a just marriage. Since then, we have had to make complex choices that included painful sacrifices. Most of the time, the accom-modations have been just, even when they were neither equal nor mutual. Phyllis and I never achieved the ideal of a sixty-hour workweek for couples when the children were at home or after they left home. There is a truth to the ideal, however, that is more important that legislating hours: family life requires time and attention. We have learned in these twenty-five years that the struggle for a just marriage depends on three central commitments: pay-ing attention to one another even if the house is not clean, a willingness to live with the paradoxical reality of autonomy and community, and the desire and commitment to be gracious with one another along the way.

HOW WILL FAMILIES FOSTER RESPECT FOR DIFFERENCE IN ORDER TO FORM PEOPLE FOR LIVING IN AN INCREASINGLY PLURALISTIC CONTEXT?

I was raised in a strong Christian family environment in which difference was regarded as dangerous and sameness was the place of safety. My context was so homogeneous that it was not until much later in life that I was chal-lenged by the religious and ethnic diversity that is now everywhere present. The diversity of religions or cultures is not new, of course. What is new, how-ever, is that human difference is no longer hidden by geographic distance or behind cultural walls or religious imperialism. Encounters with diversity that once were the province of missionaries, the adventurous, the open-minded, or those too poor to live where they wished are now an unavoidable and irreversible dimension of daily living for more and more people. The gift of diversity is that it enlarges our understanding of the world. The challenge of diversity is that there are fewer absolutes. Moreover, we cannot assume that neighbors or even fellow church members will share the same world-view. When honoring difference among us is a core value, disagreement and conflict among the people of God is unavoidable.

Two things are paradoxically true. Children and parents both need to know what they believe and why because our life-contexts are increasingly pluralistic and secular. At the same time, it is important to foster tolerance in everyone in the family toward those who believe differently. There was a telling exchange between John Kerry and President George Bush in the first debate that epitomizes the paradox necessary for families to honor difference and keep core values. John Kerry said, "Sometimes certainty can get you into trouble," to which President Bush responded very quickly that he would con-tinue to hold to his "core values." Most people have core values and most of them would say that they try to keep them. The debate is about which core values to keep. I am suggesting that tolerance must be a core value in this time of pluralism, alongside the commitment to peace, protection of the most vulnerable, and the needs of the poor.

What people believe is increasingly chosen rather than given. This presents families and the church with a new challenge in passing on the faith to the next generation. The authority of church teachings remains but it must be supplemented by age-appropriate internalization of those beliefs as one's own. In order to be intentional about what it teaches, a family needs to be self-conscious and self-critical about its operational belief system. A family is often not aware how its view of life has operationalized a belief system that may or may not be compatible with official church teaching. But family members are more likely to be aware of maxims or sayings that embody family beliefs that are carried from generation to generation. If a sainted member regularly reminds the family that "halitosis is better than no breath at all" or "you can eat with only one spoon at a time," gratitude without complaining is more likely to be fostered than if the family saying is something like "it only costs a little more to go first class" or "schöne Leute, haben schöne Sachen: nice people have nice things."

James Fowler once described the family as an *ecology of faith consciousness* in which the interplay between individual and shared constructions of meaning and purpose honors the age and differences of faith development. "The ecology of consciousness arising from their respective stage-specific ways of contributing to and appropriating from the family's shared meanings will necessarily be quite complex" (14). In order to provide a context in which tolerance of the beliefs of others is encouraged alongside a commitment to one's own faith, families will need to strive for an ecology that is more egalitarian than hierarchical, more including than excluding, and willing to be committed to people and ideas in the midst of uncertainty. Creating a family ecology of openness is critical because the longing for certainty is so deep in this time of terror and uncertainty that people are willing to give up personal autonomy or sacrifice the freedom to doubt in order to feel secure and then pass it on to their children.

HOW SHALL FAMILIES OF THE FUTURE CONTINUE TO BE HAVENS OF HOSPITALITY IN A WORLD THAT HAS BECOME INCREASINGLY DANGEROUS?

I have for some time thought that hospitality is a central theological theme for family living. Husbands and wives are able to be generous and hospitable with one another when they believe they already have enough. "The invisible boundaries that a couple create around their relationship in order to nurture and strengthen it need to be permeable enough to encourage their participation in worlds outside their marital bond" (Anderson & Fite, 157). Families practice hospitality when adult children marry or when a child is born. The characteristics of hospitality essential for welcoming a child continue throughout a family's history. When families are unable to welcome or at least receive new people and ideas, adolescent children may need to run away to grow up, college-age children do not bring home new friends or ideas, and adult children will find endless excuses not to go home if who they love or how they live is unacceptable. Hospitality is the spiritual heart of family living.

When the family offers hospitality to a stranger, it welcomes something new, unfamiliar, and unknown that has the potential to expand the world of the family. In ancient times, because wayside inns were scarce, it was a sacred obligation to show courtesy to the stranger at the gate. In our time, hospitality is not just a sacred obligation; it is necessary for our survival. The Japanese theologian Kosuke Koyama has suggested that "the only way to stop the violence of genocide in our world is by extending hospitality to strangers" (169). Showing hospitality is not only the essence of the Gospel: it is necessary for survival in an increasingly pluralistic world. The family is the first and primary context in which we learn how to practice the art of hospitality.

We may need to redefine hospitality in order to understand how it might be the spiritual heart of family living. I suspect that most of us have had the experience of being in the home of friends who entertained us well with their stories but did not ask anything about our lives. In this pattern of entertaining, the host is the subject and the guest is the object. The problem with this approach to hospitality is that we are too concerned about what we are doing for our guest and not enough concerned about what we are receiving from them. When we extend hospitality in this way, we underscore the power of the host and diminish the guest. Our desire to provide hospitality, noble as it may be, keeps us in the power position and may in the end foster dependency and resentment.

By his table practices, Jesus revealed God's own table practices by being both host and guest. Jesus is both insider and outsider, both stranger and the one who offers hospitality on the road to Emmaus. If we follow the pattern of Jesus, we not only welcome the stranger; we are the stranger who is welcomed. If we are to be a people of hospitality in the spirit of Jesus, we must also be both host and guest to the gifts that the stranger brings. The table may be filled with food but our hearts and minds are empty enough to receive what the guests have to give. Paradoxically, it is emptiness (and even poverty) that makes the fullness of hospitality possible.

Being formed in the practice of hospitality is critical for our time because it invites us to explore different ways of thinking about what is public and what is private. In order to maintain the distinction between the public and private, we have kept separate the public sphere of work from the private domestic sphere, public laws and policies from the personal and private. Roman Catholic lay theologian Rosemary L. Haughton proposes that *home* is a place of encounter between the public and private and *hospitality* is how *home* functions. Here is how she describes her paradoxical vision:

> I use the word *hospitality* in a wide sense that expresses the willingness to make common, at least temporarily, what is in some sense private, which is

how we think of home. But hospitality, even in its most restricted sense, is about breaking down barriers. To invite another person into the space I regard as my own is, at least temporarily, to give up a measure of privacy. It is already to make a breach in the division between the public and the private to create the common—and it happens in the space called home" (208).

Hospitality, as Rosemary L. Haughton describes it, creates something new, something that does not fit the easy separations we make between the public and private spheres of life. And it gives new meaning to *home*. In this sense, hospitality is how we think as well as what we do. It is at the spiritual heart of family living. *Home* is no longer just a private sphere, because hospitality has made it something common. Paradoxically, it is both a haven from the world and a launching place for mission into the world.

CONCLUSION

The question for families becomes this: how will our being together as a family form us and empower us for faithful service in and to the world for the sake of Christ? Faithful becoming for family living in the new millennium must look outside the family as well as inside. Whenever the family becomes an end in itself, it is simply a slightly larger version of American individualism. The family cannot just be a haven from the world if it is understood as *domestic church:* it must also be in mission to the world. It is the vocation of marriage and families, John Paul II wrote in his *Letter to Families,* "to contribute to the transformation of the earth and the renewal of the world, of creation and of all humanity" (1994:653). Each family grows in its understanding of its particular mission in society and in the church through prayer, the study of Scriptures, and a careful reading of the signs of the times. Working toward a just bond, celebrating difference as a gift of God, and practicing hospitality are other ways by which families are formed for ministry in and to the world in the third millennium.

REFERENCES

Anderson, Herbert and Robert Cotton Fite. *Becoming Married.* Louisville, KY: Westminster/John Knox Press, 1993.

Anderson, Herbert, Ed Foley, Bonnie Miller-McLemore, and Robert Schreiter, eds. *Mutuality Matters: Family, Faith, and Just Love.* Lanham, MD: Rowman & Littlefield Publishers, Inc., 2004.

Benjamin, Jessica. *The Bonds of Love: Psychoanalysis, Feminism, and the Problem of Domination.* New York: Pantheon, 1988.

Browning, Don S. *Marriage and Modernization: How Globalization Threatens Marriage and What to Do about It.* Grand Rapids, MI: William B. Eerdmans Publishing Company, 2003.

Fowler, James. "Perspectives on the Family from the Standpoint of Faith Development Theory." In *Perkins School of Theology Journal* 33:1 (Fall, 1979).

Haughton, Rosemary L. "Hospitality: Home and the Integration of Privacy and Community." In Leroy S. Rouner, ed., *The Longing for Home*. Notre Dame. IN: University of Notre Dame Press, 1996.

John Paul II. "Letter to Families." *Origins*. Vol. 23, No. 37 (March 3, 1994).

Kleingeld, Pauline. "Just Love? Marriage and the Question of Justice." In *Mutuality Matters: Family, Faith, and Just Love*. Lanham, MD: Rowman & Littlefield Publishers, Inc., 2004, 23–42.

Koyama, Kosuke. "Extend Hospitality to Strangers." In *Currents in Theology and Mission* (June 1993) 165–76.

Parker, Pat. "For the White Person who wants to know How to be my Friend." Quoted in *Making Face, Making Soul/Hacienda Caras: Creative and Critical Perspectives by Women of Color*. Ed. Gloria Anzaldua. San Francisco: Aunt Lute Foundation Books, 1990.

PART NINE

Religious Traditions: Perspectives on Marriage

CHAPTER 39

Marriage in the Jewish Tradition

Blu Greenberg

To this point, the readings in this volume have been an exploration of marriage (and its set of related issues) mainly from a Christian perspective. This is apt, in light of our primary reading audience. However, a rich examination of marriage today cannot remain sealed within a narrow denominational context. There are two reasons for this: (1) interreligious marriages are flourishing across all boundaries, and (2) viewing marriage from diverse perspectives can foster tolerance, understanding, and appreciation. This section teaches us that comparison and contrast is the spice of life!

Blu Greenberg begins with a detailed sketch of marriage in the Jewish tradition. Marriage is the Jewish way. It is considered an ideal state, a primary community norm, the optimal way to live. It is good, very good. In fact, it is the ultimate paradigm for the relationship between God and the Jewish people.

Greenberg wisely requests a temporary suspension of a feminist critique of the tradition so as to examine the essence of the (biblical and rabbinic) sources—i.e., the centrality of marriage in the literature and life of the people. The voyage is intriguing and illuminating. It is all the more interesting when one compares the Jewish sources, ceremonies, and laws with Christian marital forms, rituals, and codes. Likewise, the impact of the women's movement and intermarriage on Jewish marriage can be seen to bear striking resemblances to the reshaping of marital forms in Christian circles today.

Questions for Discussion

1. What constitutes the core of the traditional Jewish ideal of marriage?
2. What impact has the contemporary women's movement had on Jewish marriages?
3. Name some of the factors involved in the rapid rise in the intermarriage rate for Jews in the United States.
4. If marriage is the primary communal model and norm in Judaism (and the only legitimate adult union), what implications does this hold for other sexual forms that fall outside the marital paradigm?

In Judaism, and from the very moment of origins of the Jewish people, marriage was considered to be the ideal state. Although the institution of marriage has been newly called into question by a marginal few whose values are shaped first and foremost by contemporary culture,[1] marriage nevertheless continues to be a fundamental socio-religious principle of Judaism and a primary community norm. Almost from birth, all things work toward marriage. The greeting recited at a boy's circumcision ceremony, on the eighth day of life, is: "As this child has been entered into the covenant, so may he be entered into a life of Torah study, the wedding canopy, and good deeds."[2]

The marital relationship takes precedence over every other human connection. For example, the Fifth Commandment—filial piety—is of ultimate value and reaches into many areas of life. There is much in the ethical and halachic literature that urges that a child not marry against the parents' will or without consent, but the law is unequivocal: "If the father objects to his son's marriage or woman of his choice, the son is not obliged to listen to his father . . . for the belovedness of the partners is of paramount value."[3]

Marriage is not only the optimal way to live, but it is also central to the theology of Judaism. The entire success of the covenant rests on the marriage premise and its procreative impulse. The biological family, born of marriage, is the unit that carries the promises and the covenant, one generation at a time, toward their full completion and realization.[4]

In this regard—the centrality of marriage—Judaism can be said to be an earthy religion, dealing with intimate relationships, sex, procreation, and the powerful though often untidy bonds of family life. In this regard, too, Judaism differs from more spiritually oriented religions. Or, to put it another way, the spirit comes as much through marriage and family life in Judaism as it does through the individual's experience of *mysterium tremendum.*

Having said all these lovely things about marriage and family in the Jewish tradition, I find myself in an unenviable position, for much of the literature, law, and language surrounding marriage and divorce reflects hierarchy and sexism. As a feminist writing to my own faith cohorts, I feel perfectly uninhibited to point up and critique inherent sexism in the tradition. As a Jew writing to Christians, Muslims, and members of Far Eastern religions—persons who would not naturally feel the love and appreciation an insider feels and who would, therefore, come away with a one-sided and uncorrected view—I feel somewhat constrained.

So I ask the reader to grant me two requests: First, I ask that you suspend for the moment a feminist critique, that you set aside questions of sexism, inequity, and noninclusive language. Let us assume these givens: that imbalance did exist, that patriarchy was the social and psychic mode, that role distinctiveness lent itself too easily to hierarchy. To all this we shall soon return. Second, I ask that you bear in mind these general truths: that the tradition was sexist more in theory than in practice, more in certain cultures than in

From *Journal of Ecumenical Studies,* 22:1 (Winter, 1985) pp. 3–20. Copyright © 1985 by *Journal of Ecumenical Studies.* Reprinted with permission.

others, more in the past than in the present, more in legal formulation than in actual relationships, more in ancient law than in scriptural narrative.[5]

Now, having temporarily set aside this issue, let us proceed to examine the essence of the sources—the centrality of marriage in the literature and life of the people as it moved through 4,000 years of human history.

THE SOURCES

Oddly enough, although marriage is undeniably the only legitimate adult union, we find throughout the Scriptures not a single explicit command to marry. Procreate? Yes. Marry? Not one commandment. Rather, the information comes to us in the form of description and recommendation.[6] In what is surely among the most romantic verses in the Bible, we read: "It is not good that man should live alone . . . therefore, shall a man leave his mother and father and cleave unto his wife, and they shall become as one flesh" (Gen. 2:18, 24). The use of the word "cleave" (*davok*) signifies sensuality, intimacy, interdependency, and a long-term relationship—staples, I would say, of a good marriage.[7]

In contrast to law, biblical narrative is very rich in details of marriage. More than the sacred literature of any other people, the Torah is the story of family, of marriages, and not prettied-up versions, either, but the stuff of real marriages—love, romance, anger, deceit, honor, faithfulness, distrust, infidelity, companionship, intimacy. There is not a single idealized version of marriage in the entire Bible—not one marriage without some flaw or weakness. Perhaps that explains why marriage becomes the ultimate paradigm for the relationship between God and the Jewish people.[8] Just as a good marriage has its high and low points, yet the partners do not sever the bonds, so does a covenantal relationship. This theme—of the lasting marriage between God and the Jewish people despite the latter's backsliding—is sounded repeatedly by the Prophets.

Jewish tradition is often referred to as halacha—the Jewish way. It is the sum of several parts: (a) divine revelation, (b) the Jewish historical experience, and (c) the exegetical enterprise of connecting (a) to (b). What is the process whereby this remarkable feat—of connecting revelation to people's lives through the sweep of generations and in a diversity of cultures—is achieved? That process is none other than rabbinic interpretation, explication, and expansion of the law. Rabbinic literature (Talmud and Midrash), in contrast to the Bible, is much more explicit on all matters concerning marriage and divorce. In fact, six of the sixty-three tractates of the Talmud deal in whole or in large part with such matters.[9]

THE OBLIGATION TO MARRY

Responsibility for marriage rests on everyone—parents, community, and individual:[10]

> What are the essential duties of father to son? ... to circumcise, redeem, teach him Torah, take a wife for him, and teach him a craft. (Kid. 29A)

The tradition goes so far as to say:

> If an orphan wishes to marry [and has no means] the community should purchase for him a dwelling, a bed, and all necessary household utensils and then marry him off. (Ket. 67B)

CHOICE OF MATE

The marriage had to be characterized by *shalom bayit* (a peaceful and harmonious household); consequently, great care had to be taken in selecting a mate:

> A man should be matched to a woman according to the measure of his deeds. (Sot. 2A)

All measures of compatibility were to be considered: character, background, values, the extended family, even genetic makeup.[11] Wealth, however, was not to be a consideration,[12] but mutual desire was a requisite:

> A father is forbidden to betroth his daughter to another while she is a minor. He must wait until she grows up and says, "I want to marry So-and-so." (Kid. 41A)[13]

PREDESTINATION

Still, mere mortals cannot succeed in mate selection without a measure of divine assistance:

> ... What has God been occupied with since the six days of creation? ... with the task of finding appropriate life mates for his earthly creatures ... Though it looks easy to make a match, even for God the task is as difficult as splitting the Red Sea. (Gen. Rab. 67.3)[14]

DUTIES IN MARRIAGE

Many of the obligations of husband to wife were spelled out in the Talmud; some of these were detailed in the *ketubah*, the marriage contract. Though equality did not fully exist, and role distinctions were clearcut, there was nevertheless a kind of complementarianism to the Jewish marriage:

> These are the tasks that a wife must carry out for her husband: She must grind corn, bake, cook, suckle her child, make his bed, and work in wool. (Ket. 5:5)

> Her husband is liable for her support, her ransom, and her burial, Rabbi Judah says even the poorest in Israel must not furnish less than two flutes and one woman wailer [at his wife's funeral]. (Ket. 4:4)

One must always observe the honor due to his wife, because blessings rest
on a man's home only on account of his wife. (B.M. 59A)

SEXUALITY

Sex, in the context of marriage, was of positive value. In contrast to Christianity (Mt. 19:10; 1 Cor. 7), celibates were frowned upon, even if they were
considered to be among the greatest scholars (Yev. 63B). The sexual urge was
considered a basic and normal need that required satisfaction:

> Should a man marry first, or devote himself to Torah and then marry . . .
> Marry first . . . for one who is not married will be possessed the day long
> with sexual thoughts . . . and be unable to concentrate on his studies. (Kid.
> 29B)[15]

PROCREATION

The very first biblical commandment, "Be fruitful and multiply" (Gen. 1:28),
was a fundamental obligation of the marriage partners.[16] The institutions of
polygyny and levirate marriage (a man's obligation to marry his deceased
brother's widow if the brother died childless) can be understood only in the
context of procreation.[17] But procreation had to be balanced with sexual passion in marriage, and mutual desire at that. This explains why (a) polygyny
rarely was practiced and eventually was forbidden; (b) levirate marriages
could be circumvented by a release ceremony of *halitza*; and (c) marital rape
was explicitly forbidden.[18] It also explained why divorce, though not a popular or esteemed option, nevertheless was permitted, for divorce was
deemed to be better than a marriage of unhappy or ill-suited partners.[19] In
sum, then, the ideal was a relationship characterized by romance, sexuality,
compatibility, harmony, fidelity, mutual care, and the business of raising
children. The midrashist summed it up well:

> He who has no wife lives without peace, without help, without joy, without
> forgiveness, without life itself. He is not a whole person; he diminishes the
> image of God in the world. (Gen. Rab. 17:3)

THE ACT OF MARRIAGE

In its most technical sense, marriage in Judaism is a change in personal status. Neither sacrament nor mere legal transaction, it enjoys the trappings of
both: an aura of sacredness, the language of sanctification, the richness of ceremony and rite, the sanction of religious leaders. It also involves a contract, a
formal declaration, witnesses, signatures, and an exchange of monetary
value. To understand how this conglomerate nature came to be, one must
examine the Jewish wedding ceremony from its very beginnings.

The Bible provides relatively few clues to the act of creating a marriage. About all we know is that it is a man's initiative. A man "takes" a woman in marriage (Gen. 29:27; Ex. 2:1; Dt. 22:13). There is hint of preparation, feasting, and celebration (Gen. 24; Gen. 29; Jg. 14:12), but no description whatsoever of an actual ceremony, and no explanation of the verb "take."

The Talmud,[20] reflecting inherited tradition and building upon it, explains the procedures. The Mishnah teaches: "A woman is acquired [in marriage] in three ways and acquires herself [her independence] in two. She is acquired by means of money, deed [document] or cohabitation; she acquires herself by divorce or death of her husband" (Kid. 1:1). In a lengthy discussion of this Mishnah, the Gemara explains that the biblical "take" refers to money; however, this money does not signify purchase but rather is the symbol of a legal transaction.[21] What, then, does acquisition mean? For that, we turn to the next chapter in the Mishnah: "A man betrothes a woman . . ." (Kid. 2:1). The Hebrew for betrothal is *kiddushin*, derived from the root word *kadosh*—holy, set apart, off limits to all others. A woman is set aside for her husband and her husband alone. It is not merely a social commitment such as an engagement is today; rather, it is a halachic procedure. The transfer of an item of monetary value, however small, symbolizes this "setting aside."

A marriage, as mentioned above, can be constituted in two other ways: first, through a deed, a written document drawn to the satisfaction of all parties concerned; second, through cohabitation. What these three methods have in common is a certain privatism for the marriage partners: a man initiates, and a woman consents.[22] Technically, in each instance marriage can be effected in the absence of any sort of control or sanction by community. The sages of Gemara, however, point to the inadmissability of such methods. An exchange of coin of insignificant value was considered inappropriate and hasty for something as serious as marriage; intercourse as a means of betrothal carried the taint of licentious behavior. Thus, the rabbis forbade these procedures as means of effecting a marriage, not by striking the laws from the books, but by interpreting and circumscribing them to bring them more in line with community norms. Those who disregarded community norms could be subject to fines, flogging, and even annulment of the marriage (Yev. 110A). In tracing development of the law, then, we see that control over procedures of marriage was legally shifted from parties of the first part onto the community—probably as it had always been in ancient Jewish life.

Part of this ongoing process was the introduction (circa third century B.C.E. of the *ketubah*—the marriage contract that stipulated obligations of husband to wife during the course of the marriage as well as financial protections in the event of divorce. The *ketubah* was drawn between the parties prior to the betrothal and was witnessed as any other legal document.

To further prevent marriages of whim, the wedding ceremony was divided by rabbinic fiat into two parts: *erusin* (or *kiddushin*), the betrothal; and *nisuin*, the completion of the marriage procedures. The two parts were separated by a period of time, of up to a year. In *erusin* (or *kiddushin*), the groom gave the bride an object of value, in the presence of witnesses, then made a formal declaration to her: "Behold, thou art consecrated unto me, with this ring, according to the law of Moses [inherited tradition] and of Israel [sanction of community]."[23] After the set period of time had elapsed, the couple was joined in *nisuin* under the wedding canopy, and a series of blessings was recited in the presence of a quorum of ten men, the unit that technically constitutes a Jewish congregation. In time, it was observed that the arbitrary separation between betrothal and marriage could lead to problems, so it became standard procedure, and then law (twelfth century), to perform the two ceremonies at the same time. In order to maintain the distinctiveness of each, the *ketubah* was now read aloud between *erusin* and *nisuin*.

Increasingly, then, marriage came under religious control and communal sanction and celebration. Still, it retained its original bi-party transactional nature as described in the Mishnah: a ring as symbol of transaction, the marriage declaration in the presence of witnesses as oral deed, and the bridal canopy as suggestive of intimate relations.

THE WEDDING CEREMONY

A traditional wedding ceremony performed today would likely consist of the following order of events:

1. *Kabbalat kinyan* (acquisition): Prior to the ceremony, the groom formally undertakes the obligations specified in the *ketubah*. He signifies this by holding aloft for a moment a handkerchief held out to him by the officiating rabbi, who stands in for the bride. This action is witnessed by two men who sign their names to the *ketubah*, certifying that the conditions therein were accepted by the parties involved.

2. *Bedeken* (veiling the bride): The groom, accompanied by male family and friends, is escorted to the room where the bride is seated with female members of her party standing about her. The groom and his entourage approach in song. He gently draws the bridal veil over her face. Often, at this moment, the fathers of the couple will each in turn bless the bride, laying their hands on her head as they give blessing. Family and friends look on. It is an indescribably sweet moment, and many eyes glisten in joy.

3. *Chuppah* (bridal canopy): The Jewish wedding has taken on the full coloration of Western culture—including the processional with bridesmaids, ushers, ringbearer, etc. But there are some differences: First, the ceremony must be performed under a *chuppah*, which symbolizes their intimate household. Second, bride and groom do not stand alone during the ceremony; they are accompanied down the aisle by their parents, a symbol that bride and groom do not marry in isolation, nor will they construct their future home in absence of familial or communal support. Third, the last part of the processional at a traditional Jewish wedding is a most unusual one—the bride's

encirclement of the groom. When she reaches the *chuppah*, she walks around the groom seven times, with her mother and mother-in-law following her. Various interpretations have grown around this custom: by drawing a circle with her own body, she creates an invisible wall and then steps inside—a symbol of togetherness and distinctiveness from the rest of society.[24] This tradition is also based on a messianic reference in Jeremiah: "a woman shall encircle a man" (31:22). (Though some consider it a sexist ritual, to me it has always seemed a wonderfully sexual one, as if she is wrapping him up to take him home with her!)

4. *Erusin:* The two betrothal blessings, one over wine and one over the act of betrothal that will follow, are recited by a rabbi. The rabbi does not drink the wine, but gives the goblet to the groom and then to the bride, for each to take a sip. The rabbi is known as the *mesader kiddushin*, one who "arranges" the betrothal rather than performs it. Unlike civil law, where a Justice of the Peace pronounces them husband and wife, Jewish marriage is an act between two partners. The core element of a Jewish marriage remains as it was from the very beginning: man taking woman in marriage. The groom places a ring on the bride's right index finger and recites the ancient declaration, "Behold, thou art consecrated unto me, according to the laws of Moses and of Israel." Her acceptance of the ring is considered assent.

5. *The ketubah:* The marriage contract is read aloud in its original Aramaic. Often, it is read also in translation. The person who reads the *ketubah*—an honored guest—hands it to the groom, who hands it to his bride. It is hers for safekeeping, but for the moment she will likely pass it to a parent or friend during the ceremony. At this juncture, the officiating rabbi often will address the bride and groom.

6. *Nisuin* (marriage): The final part of the ceremony consists of seven different blessings of celebration and hope. Customarily, seven different guests are given the honor, each reciting one blessing. The seventh blessing is as follows:

> Blessed art Thou, Lord our God, creator of the universe Who has created joy and gladness, bridegroom and bride, laughter and exultation, pleasure and delight, love, brotherhood, peace, and fellowship. May it be soon, O Lord our God, that there be heard in the cities of Judah and in the streets of Jerusalem the voice of joy and gladness, the voice of bridegroom and of bride, the jubilant voice of bridegrooms from their canopies and of youths from their feasts of song. Blessed art Thou, O Lord, Who enables bridegroom to rejoice with the bride.

Upon completion of the blessings, of which the first is the benediction over wine, the couple drinks from the wine goblet. Again, in order to distinguish between *erusin* and *nisuin*, a new goblet of wine is used.

Before the couple leaves the *chuppah*, one additional ritual is performed. A glass is wrapped in a napkin and placed on the floor, where the groom shatters it with a well-placed stomp. The breaking of the glass reminds Jews of the destruction of Jerusalem and its ancient holy Temple in the year 70 C.E. The act also suggests to all present that the world is not yet redeemed, and, therefore, our great joy on this day is incomplete—but only for a moment, for now everyone in the audience calls out, "Mazel tov! Congratulations, good luck."

7. *Yichud:* The public ceremony is completed. After the couple return down the aisle, they are escorted to a private room for *yichud,* a few moments of precious privacy. Two witnesses are posted at the door to ensure that no one disturbs them. *Yichud* has both historical and halachic referents. In biblical times, the bride and groom would have their first intercourse immediately after marriage, and the bride would bring forth tokens of her virginity—the sheet with bloodstains—which her family would then display as a badge of honor (Dt. 22:13–17).[25] The reader will remember that according to the Mishnah there were three ways to effect a marriage. Intercourse, the third, was rejected by the rabbis as not being a legitimate mode of marrying and could only consummate a properly performed marriage. Today, of course, no couple consummates marriage at this time, but the privacy of *yichud* symbolically represents consummation and thus finalizes the halachic requirements of a Jewish marriage.

8. *Seudah:* A wedding feast is required. It is a characteristic of Judaism that ritual and rite are formally celebrated with feasting.

9. *Shevah berachot:* The wedding feast closes with a special grace, which includes a repetition of the seven *nisuin* marriage blessings. Here, too, the honors are distributed among the guests.

So what have we in a Jewish wedding? As in much else in Judaism, a dialectic: ancient, yet overlaid with custom that grew in stages; a private transaction, yet one that requires full participation of others and is subject to broad communal norms; a joyous occasion, yet allowing the intrusion of reality and the memory of sorrowful times; straightforward legal procedures, yet replete with rituals of sanctification and tones of sacredness; sexist in structure, yet according honor and deference to the bride. Perhaps it could be no other way in a rite that was shaped over the course of several millennia.

The ceremony I have described is a traditional one. Conservative, Reconstructionist, and Reform Jews observe these procedures in varying degrees. Some assimilated Jews marry in a civil ceremony, but any person who chooses to be married in a Jewish ceremony will follow the core rituals of *erusin* and *nisuin.*

MARRIAGE AND DIVORCE IN RELATION TO THE STATE

Marriage and divorce come wholly under the jurisdiction of the religious courts. In a Jewish state, such as existed prior to the Hurban in 70 B.C.E., and again after 1948 with the rebirth of modern-day Israel, the religious courts were/are an integral part of state machinery. As such, they enjoy a natural autonomy and control in matters of family law.

What about the broad and extensive Diaspora experience, Jews living among the nations of the world as part of, yet distinct from, the host culture? Varied though that experience was, whether under the Zoroastrians of Persia, the Visigoths of Spain, the Muslims of Turkey, or the Roman Catholics of Italy, Jews performed and were married in Jewish marriages.

Under Julius Caesar, Jews were granted status as a *religio licita*, to live according to their own laws.[26] Gradually, as Christianity became the established church throughout Europe, the Jews were relegated increasingly to subordinate status. Life became more difficult and often more oppressive for Jews, but in many areas they were left largely to their own internal devices. Even where their rights and freedoms, including religious ones, were circumscribed, the privilege of regulating marriage was never taken from them.[27]

While internal autonomy was the rule regarding performance of marriage, there were instances where hostile governments imposed their will. In Germany, Austria, and Russia, at various intervals during the eighteenth and nineteenth centuries, the Jews feared the dreaded *familiaten*, government edicts which controlled the number of Jewish marriages that could be contracted in any given locale. Not to be able to marry or to marry off one's children was considered a great tragedy and deprivation. In some communities, child marriages were arranged, for who knew what the morrow would bring?[28]

With emancipation, Jews became citizens of the state and no longer members of a sub-national group with chartered rights, "a state within a state." While emancipation brought with it an end to disabilities, it also brought an end to rights and privileges of self-government and the internal control that this implies. Modern nation-states have continued to respect religious freedoms, and marriage and divorce have continued to be the prerogative of religious corporations. But now there was an alternative—civil procedures. For some Western Jews, emancipation provided the sanction "to reject Jewish civilization in its wider ethnic and cultural implications."[29] Emancipation also spawned the denominations—Reform, Conservative, and Orthodox Judaism—each taking a position regarding the binding nature of religious codes versus civil law. By the 1870's, the liberal branch of Reform Judaism placed marriage in the hands of the civil authorities.[30] In matters of divorce, too, the debate raged loudly between the liberal and traditional wings, the former accepting civil divorce as adequate and legitimate, the Orthodox and Conservative totally rejecting such a view.[31]

MARRIAGE AS A CHANGING INSTITUTION

Many of the halachic dictates regarding marriage come to us as ethical guidelines rather than commandments or prohibitions. Not every Jewish male married, nor did every woman bring joy and light into the home, nor did all couples marry compatibly or forever. Each person is an individual and therefore cannot be pressed into a mold; each relationship has its own dynamic and chemistry. With all its structure, Jewish law accommodated this reality. That is why there is no specific commandment to marry, and why the non-dogmatic regulations and prescriptions could be subject to different interpretations in later generations.

In addition to personal variations, cultural factors affected the nature of Jewish marriage in any given generation. For example, there was greater sexism in Moslem than in Christian cultures. It was Maimonides of Spanish-Arabic culture, and not Rabbi Moses Isserles of the North European Christian one, who enacted more restrictive legislation regarding wives.[32] Polygyny persisted among Yemenite Jews until the twentieth century, for they lived among a people for whom several wives was a sign of status and success. Ashkenazic Jews, living in Christian Europe, never practiced polygamy, and it was formally outlawed in the Middle Ages.[33] Similarly, levirate marriages continued to be enacted in Oriental cultures long after they ceased elsewhere.

What about today? The primary cultural influence on marriage has been the women's movement. Jewish marriages are no less subject to redefinition in light of its far-reaching impact. I will mention five differences in Jewish marriage today.

First, except for the most traditional sectors of a community, Jewish women are now marrying later than ever before, often acquiring professional degrees and securing themselves in a career before they enter into marriage. No more biding one's time, no more waiting around for "Mr. Right" to come along and chart the future. On the one hand, this is a healthy sign of independence; on the other, there is some cause for concern in the Jewish community, because later marriages and the growing number of singles affect population growth. Second, marriages—whether early or late—are producing fewer children. The Jewish community suffers not from zero population growth but from negative population growth, with approximately 1.6 children per couple. This is far below replacement levels, producing a crisis in the community. Birth control is permitted in Jewish law. There are certain restrictions as to method and family requirements, but there is a great deal of room for choice,[34] and many couples make it in favor of smaller and smaller families. Population has always been a serious matter for Jews, particularly so in this generation after the Holocaust.[35]

Third, in view of the fact that most Jewish women also work, there has been an increasing fluidity of roles. Though there is a strong tradition of Jewish women in the workplace, for the past few generations these models were the exception, not the rule.[36] No one wants to rewrite the Mishnah to read, "And *his* duties are to cook, wash, and . . . weave in wool," but this greater sharing of breadwinning and nurturing roles is a fact of life. While the father was an ever-present figure in the medieval Jewish home, and Jewish fathers always instructed their children in a very personal way, the typical nurturing and homemaking tasks were left to the mother.[37] Today, like their non-Jewish counterparts, Jewish couples are restructuring these roles. Fourth, Jews are not much more immune to living in a divorce culture than are other modern Western people. Estimates of divorce among Jews are close to forty percent, compared with a nationwide rate of fifty percent. That represents a body-blow to the once-stable Jewish family. Feminism is surely not the cause, but its emphasis on independence has served as a catalyst—to wit, the great rise in female-initiated divorce.

Fifth, there is a call for equality in religious structures, including those relating to marriage. For example, in the traditional marriage ceremony the woman is a silent partner. In Reform and Conservative Judaism, this has been altered somewhat to incorporate a woman's voice. There are those among the Orthodox who have experimented in this area as well. Without changing the traditional ceremony, they have opened a place for women, such as a female guest reading the *ketubah* or the bride reciting several verses to the groom under the *chuppah*. Similarly, new strides are being made in an attempt to equalize men and women in Jewish divorce law; also, there is increased sharing of rituals in the home. These are relatively small changes, but they are not insignificant in the process of moving toward equality within traditional structures of marriage and divorce.

As the reader can see, it is a two-edged matter. Not all the winds of change blow kindly on Jewish marriages of today. Like all other people, Jews are affected by the erosive forces of contemporary values on marriage and family. And, like all other religious groups, those more anchored to tradition are most resistant to changes. Nevertheless, a balance must be found. Judaism must continue to search for ways to integrate into its permanent structures new rituals that represent the new equity in marriage today.

INTERMARRIAGE

From earliest times, intermarriage was explicitly forbidden to Jews (Dt. 7:3–4, Av. Zar. 36B). Because Judaism, the religion, took root in a family, the concept of Jewish peoplehood was perhaps more central than for most other religions. But it was not purity of bloodlines that was the issue; rather, it was the integrity of the faith community. One could join the faith community through conversion; one could not enter Judaism simply through the act of marrying a Jew. For Jews, exogamy represented not only a violation of halacha but also a dilution of Jewishness of the community. Throughout Jewish history, inter-marriage was kept to a minimum. Several forces were at work. Aside from the laws—which were made very clear—the response that followed such a marriage was an even more powerful preventive. If a Jew married out of the faith, he or she knew what to expect: total banishment from family and community. Parents and siblings would rend their garments and observe the shiva mourning period, as if the child were no longer alive.

Non-Jewish society was similarly opposed to intermarriage. In almost every official Christian document on the Jews throughout the Middle Ages, the injunction against intermarriage with "perfidious Jews" appears.[38] Often, punishment for offenders was harsh. Nor was there any opportunity. In most Christian lands, Jews and non-Jews lived apart, either by mutual desire or by imposed ghettoes. Social interchange between Jews and Christians in non-business settings was the exception, not the rule.

With the dawn of emancipation, the ghetto walls came tumbling down. Jews mainstreamed into the social, cultural, and political life of the nations in which they lived. Intermarriage grew as social contacts grew and as the stigma against Jews was muted. Equality and fraternity were the new and ideal ways to view the "other." Romantic love took precedence over issues of group survival and cohesion. Civil marriages were convenient, for one did not need to convert out of one's own religion to marry a person of another faith.

Until recently, the intermarriage rate for Jews was quite low in the United States. In the decades before 1960, the rate was only six percent. Between 1960 and 1966, it rose to seventeen percent, and by 1971 it had jumped to thirty-two percent.[39] Adjusting for conversion and other factors, the number of Jews in America in 1980 having non-Jewish spouses was approximately 300,000—or five percent of the total Jewish population. Today, it is thought to be considerably higher. The rise is due to many factors: a new age of pluralism and ecumenism has dawned, in which value is placed on every other faith, belief, and style of life; the new fascination with, and therefore desirability of, ethnics; the intense relationships constructed by humanists of all faiths in the course of sharing a crusade such as civil rights, anti-nuclear protest, or feminism; the vast number of Jews on the college campuses[40]; the loss of enforcement power in religious communities; the increasing number of Jews in all professions; and feminism and the increase of female out-marriage.[41] Finally, because of the sheer numbers, the old response of total cut-off is no longer a viable threat.

There are certain new facts about intermarriage that make it no less forbidden according to Jewish law but help to explain some of the contemporary communal responses: First, there is a not-insignificant phenomenon of conversion into Judaism—in fact, more into than out of Judaism. In approximately thirty percent of the intermarriages, the non-Jewish spouse converts to Judaism, either before or after the wedding.[42] Second, even where there is no conversion, intermarriage seems no longer to represent to exogamous Jews a negation of Judaism. Most of them continue to think of themselves as Jews—which they are—and to maintain family and community links.[43] Third, in a recent study of a sample of intermarried couples across the United States, it was found that twenty percent of the families with no conversion had, nonetheless, provided some formal Jewish education for their children, and thirty percent of them celebrated the bar or bat mitzvah rite as well.[44]

The denominational responses to intermarriage are varied. In 1983, the Reform rabbinate formally adopted the principle of Jewishness by patrilineal descent (as well as matrilineal). This is a de jure statement of what Reform Judaism has de facto accepted all along, but the statement represents a more aggressive outreach to the acceptance of intermarried couples. Conservative and Orthodox Jews have strongly objected to the patrilineal-descent motion on the basis of its halachic inadmissibility.

The leaders of Reform Judaism have also called for greater outreach in the area of conversion, and this would apply particularly to non-Jewish spouses. While conversion has always existed in Judaism—and many converts were given the appellation "righteous convert"—there was a controlling ambivalence in tradition and community. Today, Reform Judaism has deemed it the right moment to extend its hand to the "unchurched"; simultaneously, the Central Conference of American Rabbis (Reform) voted to censure rabbis performing a mixed marriage.

Conservative Jews have expanded their educational and rabbinic resources available to potential converts. The procedure for conversion involves several months of study preceding conversion rites, often on a one-to-one basis. This study takes a great deal of time in the life of a rabbi.

In the Orthodox community, the primary response has been one of prevention—to raise children more intensively Jewish, in educational and social settings not conducive to intermarriage, such as yeshiva high school, Jewish summer camps, etc. Orthodox Jews tend also to live in communities that are identifiably Jewish. With community reinforcing home environment, intermarriage remains extremely rare in the Orthodox community. Still, it occasionally does happen, for Orthodox Jews go to college and enter the workplace and are geographically mobile, like everyone else. Moreover, while converts rarely come via an Orthodox partner, many wish to convert through an Orthodox conversion, so that later there will be no questions of acceptability. And, for many, Orthodoxy signifies a certain authenticity of tradition. Once one makes the effort to convert, the rationale seems to be to want to do it in the most "kosher" manner.

Thus, there is today a less resistant attitude to conversion in the Orthodox community. The law has always been that an ulterior motive, such as marriage, is not a valid reason for conversion, which must be based on love of Judaism and not love of a particular Jew. Most rabbis, recognizing reality, have tended to work around that obstacle. More recently, there has been an attempt to point up halachic precedents that validate conversion for the sake of marriage.[45] On the personal level, traumatic though a mixed marriage is in an Orthodox family, the old response of sitting shiva and cutting off all ties no longer seems to be the common response. While an Orthodox Jew would not participate in or attend the wedding ceremony, and while the relationship is surely affected, the connections are often maintained—in part, to encourage that the grandchildren be raised as Jews (converted, if the mother is not Jewish); in part, hoping that with love, time, and familiarity with Judaism the non-Jew will eventually want to convert; in part, because we all live in a culture that places human values above all other claims.

SEXISM IN THE TRADITION

How is one to deal with sexism in sacred and quasi-sacred literature? One cannot rewrite the sources any more than one can rewrite history, nor does one like to tinker excessively with issues of divinity and ancient authority. But neither can one let sexist sources stand uncorrected. One answer lies in the hermeneutic: to teach the richness of tradition and the essence of its message—whether that be the sanctity of marriage or the caring nature of a relationship—yet apply the yardstick of equality. It is possible to point out where the sources, for reasons of sociology, culture, and timing, fall short. It is possible to explain certain texts in the context of those times—hierarchies in all pre-feminist cultures. And because of the conglomerate and cumulative nature of Jewish tradition, it is often possible to find a benign precedent or principle to substitute or counterbalance a sexist one. In other words, it is possible to engage a critical eye and a loving heart at one and the same moment.

Moreover, tradition has much of value to teach—including something important about role distinctiveness in male/female relationships. Role distinctiveness does not necessarily imply hierarchy or inequity. In the long run, role distinctions may be quite healthy for psyche and society. But there are limits to such a gentle and respectful approach. These are reached when outright discrimination affects the lives of real people. In such a case, the second answer lies in the area of politics and power. For example, Jewish divorce law is unequivocally sexist. However, before we explain the law, let us examine the procedure: After all attempts at reconciliation have failed, the couple appear before a *bet din*, a Jewish court of law, consisting of three rabbis who are experts in Jewish divorce law. A scribe and two witnesses are also present. At the instruction of the husband, the scribe hand-letters the *get* (the writ of divorce), filling in name, location, time, and the standard text of the divorce. The core of the *get* is the husband's attestation to divorcing his wife and setting her free to marry any other man. The witnesses sign the *get*, and the rabbi reads it aloud; then the man places it into the woman's hands, acclaiming, "This is your *get*. You are now free to marry another."

No divorce, no matter how amicable, is problem-free. To some extent, Jewish divorce action with its routine methodical procedures and its absence of interpersonal negotiations helps to keep the tensions low; the *get* proceedings lend a note of closure to the relationship, which speeds up the process of psychological closure as well. In that sense, a Jewish divorce proceeding has some positive impact. Moreover, the fact that divorce is permitted at all in Judaism is a fundamental recognition of the human right to happiness.

But, for all that, Jewish divorce law poses problems for women. First, only the husband can issue the *get*. There are cases where the recalcitrant husband, for reasons of spite or blackmail, withholds the *get* from his wife and thereby does not release her to marry. Her life is in limbo. In the closed society of former times, a Jewish court could compel him to authorize the *get* or could punish him under rules of internal autonomy until he acquiesced. Paradoxically, in an open society, the problem is exacerbated. A recalcitrant husband can slip through the cracks between civil and religious jurisdiction.[46] He can refuse to show up at the rabbinic court. A woman faithful to Jewish law is most vulnerable in this situation. Second, if a husband disappears and his whereabouts are not known, his wife remains an *agunah*—a woman anchored to an absentee husband. She, too, is in limbo and cannot get on with her life. While the rabbis in every generation bent their efforts to resolving the problem of an *agunah,* they could do so only within limits, and their efforts were not always successful. Third, the liberal branches of Judaism—Reform and secular Jews—operate by civil law. Jews of Orthodox and Conservative denominations cannot marry Jews divorced according to the laws of the secular state who lack a *get.*

The problems grow directly out of the original sources: "If a man finds something unseemly in his wife, he writes her a writ of divorce, delivers it into her hands, and sends her away" (Dt. 24:1). This principle, the absolute right of the husband in matters of divorce, has been diminished, circumscribed, and, through the process of rabbinic interpretation, whittled away from generation to generation. Moreover, the rights of women in family law have grown through the centuries. A woman may not be divorced against her will, and she has legitimate rights to sue in court for divorce. Yet, despite the many improvements instituted by the rabbis throughout the generations, and despite the new pre-nuptial clauses to prevent abuse, a woman still remains dependent on her husband's willingness to authorize and deliver a *get.* In fact, there are instances of blackmail on the part of recalcitrant husbands. And the community remains divided.

Until such time as Jewish law undergoes reinterpretation, in order to eliminate potential abuse and to incorporate the principle of equity into Jewish divorce proceedings, Jewish law will be subject to charges of sexism. Unless the potential for discrimination is rooted out, much of the credibility of what is good in the tradition, though sexist in language will be eroded.

CONCLUSION

Life in Western society as we approach the year 2000 has indeed changed. Whereas choosing a traditional marriage and family was the ultimate and only legitimate choice, today it is no longer the rule. With a divorce rate of fifty percent, a singles lifestyle, serial marriages—only twenty-four percent of all adult Americans fit the old model! But Judaism, while not forcing everyone into that mold, makes a strong case for traditional marriages: a long-term relationship characterized by love and the bonds of nurturing each other and children, and also bounded by traditional parameters of fidelity, mutual respect, and steadfastness.

I, for one, would hope that these teachings will never be muted, that this paradigm for living will never be replaced by another—no matter how modern or au courant a view of adult relationships might prevail at any given moment in history. I believe a covenantal model works for human relationships. And—just as we have all learned from ecumenism that it is possible for people of different faiths to experience the gifts, the promises, and the covenant uniquely, and without putting down all others—so I believe it is possible to posit a primary model of marriage without demoting to the status of pariah all those who fall outside of it.

What does Judaism teach? That marriage is good, very good: that it is the Jewish way.

NOTES

1. See Ellen Willis' review of *The Second Stage* by Betty Friedan in *The Village Voice*, Literary Supplement, November, 1981, p. 1.

2. The traditional greeting for an infant girl differs: "May she be raised to the wedding canopy and to a life of good deeds." Now that women also study Torah, many modern Jews add that to the female greeting as well.

3. Yoreh Deah 240:25. Yoreh Deah is one of the four tractates of the *Shulkhan Arukh*, which is the most authoritative Jewish legal compendium of the Middle Ages.

4. Irving Greenberg, "The Jewish Family and the Covenant," unpublished manuscript, 1983.

5. For two different approaches to the issue of sexism in the sources, see Leonard Swidlet, *Women in Judaism* (Methuchen, NJ: Scarecrow Press, 1976); and Blu Greenberg, *On Women and Judaism* (Philadelphia: Jewish Publication Society, 1982).

6. There are several other nonnarrative references in the Torah to marriage; among them, see Ex. 21:7–10; Dt. 24:1, 5.

7. It is interesting to note that the Hebrew root, *davok*, to cleave, is the word used to describe the relationship between God and the Jewish people: "And you who cleave unto the Lord your God . . ." (Dt. 4:4).

8. Is. 61:10, 62:5; Ez. 16; Hos. 2:21; Song of Songs.

9. *Yevamot, Kiddushin, Ketubot, Gittin, Niddah, Sotah.*

10. See also Kid. 29B, 30A; Yev. 62b, 113a.

11. Bav. Bat. 110A, Bech 45B, Pes. 49a.

12. Kid. 70A.

13. See further Kid. 41A, Ket. 102B.

14. See also Sot. 2A on predestination of partners.

15. Cf. Yev. 63B; Ket. 63A; Sot. 4B. See also Swidler, *Women in Judaism*, pp. 111–113, for a fuller discussion of wives as a distraction to Torah study.

16. Oddly enough, the formal obligation, "Be fruitful and multiply" (Gen. 1:28), was interpreted by the rabbis to apply only to men, with the defense that a woman could not be commanded to do something that might cause her physical pain.

17. See Chaim Pearl, "Marriage Forms," in Peter Elman, ed., *Jewish Marriage* (London: Soncino, 1967), p. 17. See also Gen. 38 and Ruth 2–3.

18. On circumscribing and then forbidding polygyny, see Yev. 65b and Pes. 113A; also *Shulkhan Aruch*. Even Ha'ezer 1:9–11. On halitzah, see the fine article by Menachem Elon in *Encyclopedia Judaica* (Jerusalem: Keter Publishing, 1971), vol. 11, pp. 122–130. On marital rape, see Eruvin 100b.

19. See Yev. 63B; Git. 90B.

20. The Talmud consists of two layers: the earliest, the Mishnah, is largely a detailed exposition of the law; the second, the Gemara, is an elaboration and explication of the Mishnah, and includes law, history, theology, aphorisms, narrative, debate, etc. The Mishnah was closed in the year 250 C.E.; the Gemara, in 499 C.E.

21. Such a conclusion is derived from two facts: (a) the money specified was so minimal as to eliminate any possibility of constituting a financial transaction; (b) unlike other acquisitions, a wife could not be resold or transferred.

22. The language in rabbinic literature shifts from "he takes" or "he acquires" to "is required," teaching us that the woman has the power of consent or refusal.

23. This declaration is found in the Talmud and is most likely the oral version of what originally constituted "deed" in the Mishnaic reference.

24. Maurice Lamm, *The Jewish Way in Love and Marriage* (San Francisco: Harper & Row, 1982), pp. 213–215.

25. Though it seems primitive to Western sensibilities, the custom of examining the bride's linen after the first night of marriage for spots of blood as proof of her virginity is still practiced in some Oriental communities. See *Encyclopedia Judaica*, vol. 11, p. 1045.

26. See James Parkes, *The Conflict of the Church and the Synagogue* (New York: Atheneum, 1969), ch. 1.

27. See Jacob R. Marcus, *The Jew in the Medieval World* (New York: Harper and Row, 1938), particularly sections 1 and 2. See also Philip and Hanna Goodman, eds., *The Jewish Marriage Anthology* (Philadelphia: Jewish Publication Society, 1965), p. 171; Louis M. Epstein, *The Jewish Marriage Contract* (New York: Jewish Theology Seminary, 1927), pp. 281 ff.; and Zev Falk, *Jewish Matrimonial Law in the Middle Ages* (Oxford: Oxford University Press, 1966).

28. See also Rachel Biale, *Women and Jewish Law* (New York: Schocken Books, 1984), p. 66.

29. See Howard M. Sachar, *The Course of Modern Jewish History* (New York: Dell Publishing, 1957), p. 63.

30. See A. Mielziner, *The Jewish Law of Marriage and Divorce in Ancient and Modern Times and Its Relation to the Law of the State* (Cincinnati: Bloch Publishing, 1884), p. 94.

31. Ibid., chap. 16.

32. See Maimonides, *Mishneh Torah,* Book IV, Laws of Women.

33. In approximately 1025, Rabbenu Gershom, a leading rabbinic light of the Diaspora, formally banned polygamy.

34. It is interesting to note that the responsibility falls upon women; the condom is not permitted. See David M. Feldman, *Marital Relations, Birth Control, and Abortion in Jewish Law* (New York: Schocken Books, 1974).

35. It has been reliably estimated that 6,000,000 Jews were killed in the Holocaust. This represented one-third of world Jewish population. It is now forty years after the Holocaust, and the losses have nowhere been made up.

36. See Paula Hyman, "The Jewish Family: Looking for a Useable Past," in Susannah Heschel, ed., *On Being a Jewish Feminist* (New York: Schocken Books, 1983).

37. See Israel Abrahams, *Jewish Life in the Middle Ages* (New York: Atheneum, 1969), particularly chap. 7, "Monogamy and the Home."

38. See Marcus, *The Jew in the Medieval World,* pp. 4–5, 139.

39. The National Jewish Population Study, Council of Jewish Federations and Welfare Funds, 1972.

40. See Irving Greenberg, "Jewish Survival and the College Campus," in *Judaism* 17 (Summer, 1968): 259–281.

41. Prior to the 1970's, the Jewish male/female outmarriage ratio was three to one. As women have moved increasingly into professional settings, the female outmarriage rate has risen.

42. Egon Mayer, "Intermarriage among American Jews: Consequences, Prospects and Policies" (New York: National Jewish Resource Center, 1979).

43. Ibid., p. 3.

44. Ibid.

45. See Marc Angel, unpublished paper presented at Chevra, National Jewish Resource Center, Spring, 1983, New York City.

46. Normon Solomon, "Jewish Divorce Law in Contemporary Society," *Journal of Jewish Social Sciences*, vol. 25, no. 2 (December, 1983).

CHAPTER 40

The Protestant View of Marriage

Wilson Yates

Wilson Yates's essay represents the very best of the contemporary Protestant theology of marriage. Protestantism, of course, includes a wide range of denominations, but most mainline Protestant bodies, he claims, share a similar focus and meaning. That focal point revolves around the conventional image of marriage. It lies at the heart of its theology, its denominational statements and rituals, and its core meanings. Yes, differences exist among Protestants themselves, but when they gather to celebrate marriage, they are united in a common covenantal perspective.

Yates uses the metaphor of covenant to examine and interpret the major characteristics he deems central to Protestant marriage. He lays out six characteristics that define the contours and meaning of marriage as covenant: (1) to create a life of intimate companionship, (2) to create and sustain a fabric of honesty, trust, openness, and acceptance, (3) to explore and respond to the religious and moral issue in their life's pilgrimage, (4) to live an ethnic of covenantal wholeness, (5) to create appropriate boundaries of behavior, and (6) to break the covenant only as a last resort. Yates acknowledges a contemporary theological convergence in understandings of marriage between Roman Catholic, Orthodox, and Protestant perspectives, but this commonality, however, should be seen within a framework of genuine differences and contrasting emphases.

Questions for Discussion

1. Are the six characteristics of a covenantal marriage, as outlined by Yates, distinctive and unique to Protestant bodies?
2. The principle of intimate companionship lays the basis for a positive ethic of sexual love. What practical implications do you see in this statement for couples?
3. Is the family a "haven in a heartless world" (Lasch) or a "Little Commonwealth"(Morgan)? Discuss in light of an ethic of family social responsibility.
4. What does love expressed as justice mean for marital relations in terms of role patterns and institutional expectations?
5. Yates claims the covenant means breaking the covenant (as a last resort) when the internal life of the relationship has died. Do you agree? Is divorce a moral option?

Protestantism includes a wide range of denominations, each with its own history and theology, but most mainline Protestant bodies that are rooted in the Continental and English Reformation traditions articulate views of marriage which are quite similar in focus and meaning.[1] It is possible, therefore, to speak of a Protestant view of marriage that is in large part shared by all mainline Protestant groups. In this discussion I shall set forth that common perspective while noting major points of divergence.

With the Reformation, Protestant marriage theory began to take shape: the legitimacy and significance of civil authority over the institution was recognized; the sacramental status which the Roman Catholic Church accorded the institution was removed; the biblical basis of marriage was lifted up with frequent references to the wedding at Cana; and certain theological affirmations were made regarding the nature and significance of the institution. Martin Luther considered marriage an order of creation whose origin transcended both church and state. The importance he accorded to the institution, if not his particular view of creation, has remained central to much of Protestant thought. Thus, services speak of marriage as an institution "ordained by God," as a "holy estate," as an institution "established by God." as "an institution of divine origin."

John Calvin and Martin Bucer viewed marriage as a covenant, and down through Protestant history the covenantal nature of marriage has been accented as the pivotal meaning of the relationship. Most important in this history was the work of the English and American Puritans who largely shaped early Protestant understanding in North America: Protestant theology and services of marriage pick up the covenantal character of the institution in our own time. For example, the new, proposed United Church of Christ service states, "God has called you to the covenant of marriage," and the marriage service from *The Lutheran Book of Worship* reflects the essence of the covenant in these words:

> With high praise we recall your acts of unfailing love for the human family, for the house of Israel, and for your people the church. . . . Pour down your grace upon (this couple) that they may fulfill the vows they have made this day and reflect your steadfast love in their lifelong faithfulness to each other.

In this discussion of the Protestant view, I want to examine the metaphor of covenant and to use it to interpret the major characteristics deemed central to Protestant marriage. The concept is deeply embedded in Scripture. God invited the people of Israel to become partners in a divine/human covenant—to become partners in a relationship marked by trust, fidelity, steadfast love, justice, and obedience to the will of God. While the people time and again broke that covenantal relationship, it remained at the heart of their religious calling. In the Hebrew Bible, the covenant had a patriarchal parent/child character. God was the authoritarian Father and the people of

From *Journal of Ecumenical Studies*, 22:1 (Winter, 1985) pp. 41–54. Copyright © 1985 by *Journal of Ecumenical Studies*. Reprinted with permission.

Israel God's children. When early Protestants interpreted the marriage bond as a covenant, they applied the concept to both the husband/wife relationship and the parent/child relationship, with both types of relationship understood to be patriarchal and authoritarian in character.

Down through the history of Protestantism, however, the covenantal bond has taken on a more egalitarian form; the character of both husband/wife and parent/child bonds has accented companionship, love, justice, and intimacy as the moral shape God desires for the relationship. This more egalitarian form, with its emphasis on mutuality and intimacy, is now assumed in modern Protestant services when they speak of "the bond and covenant of marriage" and call the couple to "consider the holy covenant you are about to make." The contemporary United Methodist statement on marriage is typical:

> We affirm the sanctity of the marriage covenant which is expressed in love, mutual support, personal commitment, and shared fidelity, between a man and a woman. We believe that God's blessing rests upon such marriage, whether or not there are children of the union. We reject social norms that assume different standards for women than for men in marriage.[2]

To appreciate more fully the nature of the Protestant covenantal view of the marriage bond, I want to set forth six characteristics that define its contours and meaning. These characteristics constitute the major threads that move through Protestant theories of marriage. In doing so I will touch upon a range of related issues including sexuality and the primary ethical principles which are central to the Protestant image of marriage and the family.

1. The first characteristic is a *commitment by the partners to create a life of intimate companionship.* Companionship lies at the heart of the Protestant view of the marriage covenant. Luther pointed to its importance in his attack on celibacy and his affirmation of the marital relationship. Calvin, in his development of a Protestant theology of marriage, insisted that the essence of the marriage bond was moral and spiritual companionship between two partners; in effect, the primary purpose of marriage was companionship. This Calvinist perspective in the history of the churches' understanding of marriage was a watershed in its theory of marriage: before Calvin the primary purpose of marriage was considered to be procreation; with Calvin, procreation was reinterpreted to be a blessing flowing from companionship; after Calvin the idea of companionship emerged as a central theological focus in all the major Protestant traditions.[3] The Puritans and left-wing sectarian groups such as the Quakers and Congregationalists spoke out most boldly on the significance of companionship, and John Milton set forth the notion that a vital marriage should be a companionable and compatible relationship: "In God's intention a meet and happy conversation is the chiefest and noblest end of marriage." Milton also developed the first major case in Western theology for considering incompatibility, that is, the absence of true companionship, as grounds for divorce.[4]

In this development of the concept, companionship came to mean more than simply moral and spiritual unity, for Puritan writers insisted that love, intimacy, romance, and emotional depth be given due honor. This is delightfully portrayed in a poem by the American Puritan poet, Anne Bradstreet. Writing about her longing for her husband who was away on business, she expressed how she missed him as her romantic partner and companion and friend. She said it all with a touch of humor and irritation at his delay in returning to their home and bed:

My head, my heart, mine eyes, my life—nay more,
My joy, my magazine of earthly store:
If two be one, as surely thou and I,
How stayest thou there, whilst I at Ipswich lie?
So many steps from the heart to sever,
If but a neck, soon should we be together.
I like the earth this season mourn in black;
My sun is gone so far in's Zodiac,
Whom whilst I' joyed, nor storms nor frosts I felt,
His warmth such frigid colds did cause to melt.
My chilled limbs now numbed lie forlorn:
Return, return, sweet sol, from Capricorn.
In this dead time, alas, what can I more
Than view those fruits which through thy heat I bore?
Which sweet contentment yields me for a space
True living pictures of their father's face.
O strange effect! Now thou art southward gone,
I weary grow, the tedious day so long:
But when thou northward to me shalt return,
I wish my sun may never set, but burn
With the Cancer of my glowing breast.
The welcome house of him, my dearest guest.
Where ever, ever, stay, and go not thence
Til nature's sad decree shall call thee hence:
Flesh of thy flesh, bone of thy bone,
I here, thou there, yet both but one.[5]

The value of companionship continued to develop from the seventeenth century to the present, serving as the cornerstone of Protestant covenantal views of marriage. The love and intimacy expressed in Bradstreet's poem became increasingly identified as the inner spirit of companionship. This introduction of companionate love by that rather small community of Puritans in the seventeenth and eighteenth centuries was the major beginning point for Christian theology's accent on the primacy of love and intimacy as the heart of the marriage relationship.[6]

In this development, a positive understanding of sexuality as a means of

expressing marital love, as well as a means of procreation, also emerged.
Major Protestant theology at the time of the Reformation readily affirmed
sexuality as a part of the goodness of creation and denied that the celibate
calling and "spiritual" marriage were of a higher moral order than a marriage
in which the "two became one flesh." But sexual expression was still held
under suspicion by early Protestant theologians, with most insisting that the
only positive purpose of sexual pleasure was the role it played in the procreative process. Thinkers in the late seventeenth and eighteenth centuries, however, linked sexual pleasure with marital love and companionship and
thereby gave sexual companionship a positive function apart from procreation. Protestantism then had the basis for a positive ethic of sexual love and,
in the early twentieth century, a major rationale for accepting contraception,
which, by freeing persons from the fear of pregnancy, permitted fuller enjoyment of marital sexual love.[7]

Recently, a great deal of work has been done in further developing a
Protestant sexual ethic. Such writers as Derrick Sherwin Bailey, Norman Pittenger, Daniel Day Williams, Letty Russell, Phyllis Trible, and, foremost,
James B. Nelson have made major contributions in shaping this ethic.[8] In
their work, they have made a concerted effort at overcoming the remnants of
a body/soul dualism by setting forth a holistic view in which body and spirit
are seen as an integrated whole. Sex is no longer identified as simply a body
function, for it is as much an experience of the spirit as of the body. In turn,
eros is related in an integral way to *agape*. As the British theologian Charles
Williams has written, *eros* need "no longer stand on its knees before *agape*."
James B. Nelson summarizes this integrated holistic understanding of the
different dimensions of love in these terms:

> Agape is not another kind of love. Nor is it, as Tillich rightly notes, a dimen-
> sion strictly comparable to the other three dimensions of our loving. It is the
> transformative quality essential to any true expression of any of love's
> modes. If we define Christian love as agape or self-giving alone—without
> elements of desire, attraction, self-fulfillment, receiving—we are describing
> love which is both impoverished and impoverishing. But the other elements
> of love without agape are ultimately self-destructive. Agape present with
> sexual desire, erotic aspiration and mutuality releases these from self-cen-
> teredness and possessiveness into a relationship that is humanly enriching
> and creative. It does not annihilate or replace the other modes of our loving.
> It undergirds and transforms. And faith knows that agape is a gift, and not
> of our own making.[9]

This important new work in Protestant theology indicates a further
recognition of the importance of intimate, loving companionship and of the
role of sexual expression in manifesting that intimacy within the marital relationship. The ability of persons to use sex for alienating and destructive ends
is certainly recognized, but the accent rests on the way in which sexual
expression can become a means by which intimate companionship is known
and the grace of love experienced.

In the development of the meaning of companionship, there was also an insistence that such companionship include not only a depth of love and intimacy but also a breadth in its range of experiences. Hence, popular Protestant marriage manuals of the nineteenth and early twentieth centuries lifted up the encompassing nature of intimate companionship, insisting that the Christian marriage should realize religious, moral, social, sexual, parental, and intellectual companionship.[10] This perspective remains prominent in contemporary Protestant thought. Charlotte and Howard J. Clinebell's *Intimate Marriage*, for example, holds up sexual, emotional, intellectual, creative, recreational, work, crisis, commitment, and spiritual forms of intimacy as central to a healthy marriage.[11] The Episcopal Church's marriage service picks up in representative fashion this dimension of companionship: "The union of husband and wife in heart, body and mind is intended for their mutual joy, for the help and comfort given one another in prosperity and diversity, and when it is God's will, for the procreation of children and their nurture in the knowledge and love of the Lord."[12] Later in a prayer are the words: "Let their love for each other be a seal upon their hearts, a mantle upon their shoulders, and a crown upon their foreheads. Bless them in their work and in their companionship, in their sleeping and in their waking, in their joys and in their sorrows, in their life and in their death."[13]

2. A second characteristic of a covenantal marriage is *a commitment on the part of the couple to create and sustain a fabric of honesty, trust, openness, and acceptance.* Each of these virtues in Protestant theologies of marriage has its own history, with the latter two a part of more recent marriage theory.

Honesty, in its simplest terms, means truthtelling; it means telling the facts. But there is a deeper level of honesty that is also expected in a religiously shaped marriage, a level at which each person expresses an understanding of a situation with sensitivity for the impact it will have on the other person. In the language of ethics, which is such a dominant part of the Protestant language about marriage, this means being sensitive not only to the factual nature of our truthtelling but also to why we are honest, i.e., our motivations; what we hope to accomplish, i.e., our intentions or aims; and what effect our "telling the truth will have on the other person, i.e., what consequences will result. Dietrich Bonhoeffer expressed this deeper level of truthtelling: "Telling the truth is not solely a matter of moral character, it is also a matter of correct appreciation of real situations and of serious reflection upon them."[14] In Protestant thought, expressed in both theological statements and marriage rituals, such honesty is deemed a significant attribute of a morally mature marriage.

Trust is a second virtue that the literature accents as crucial to the covenantal fabric of marriage. Without it, the marital relationship can easily unravel. Thus, all services of marriage acknowledge the virtue of trust or fidelity, and the theological literature spells out its meaning. In nineteenth-century Protestant thought, the discussion of trust focused primarily on marital fidelity, but in more contemporary literature the concept has been given a much richer meaning. Norman Pittenger, a Protestant theologian who has written widely and representatively on issues of marriage relationships and sexuality, offers an understanding of trust which includes its reciprocity, its life as both trusting and entrusting, and its venturesome nature, its dependence on a leap of faith to reach its fullest depths:

> When I say that I "trust" someone, I am saying that I have a complete confidence in him, certain that what he does and is will never "let me down." And when I "entrust" myself to another, I am saying that I put myself in the other's hands, such that in those hands I am ultimately entirely *safe*, precisely because the other is known to be "trustworthy." Yet it is not quite correct to say that the other is known to be such, for that might suggest that I have some logical proof that such is the case. On the contrary, the situation is much more venturesome. For what I am doing is giving myself into the other's hands in a great act of faith; I do not *know* in any demonstrable fashion that he is what I take him to be. I cannot prove to you that someone to whom in love I thus entrust myself is in very fact what I am confident he is.[15]

The emphasis on trust as dependent, finally, on a "leap of faith" is rooted deeply in Protestant theology and especially its theology of marriage. The partners ought to risk such trust—make such a leap—for trust is a part of the bedrock of their covenant with God. God is trustworthy, and persons are called to trust in God. Equally, in the covenant of marriage, the partners are called to ground their relationship on a steadfast and abiding trust.

A third virtue is that of *openness:* being willing to be self-revelatory and open to the self-revelation of others, to be free to express needs, hopes, feelings, and thoughts in a process of mutual self-disclosure. This understanding of the marital relationship is rooted in a larger theological framework of values, particularly those of individualism and relationality. The Reformers insisted upon the significance of a direct relationship between the individual and God, which offered the individual knowledge about God and a deeper understanding of the person's own soul. Through such a relationship one grew in the love of God and, through the love of God, in the love of self and other. This perspective had a direct bearing on later marriage theology, where it is assumed that marital love and intimacy both help create and depend upon a mutual sharing of the couple's deepest feelings and thoughts. Theologically, then, love—a gift of grace—involves an openness both to receiving disclosure of the other and to disclosing the self to the other.

The virtue of *acceptance* follows from the commitment to openness, for one must accept the other and know that one is accepted. Once again, the model is a larger theological doctrine, that of justifying grace. Justification is the affirmation, as Tillich suggests, that we are accepted by God in spite of what we are. In a marriage neither partner is God, and neither partner is expected to accept unconditionally. Yet, the married couple is called to transcend a limited acceptance that is conditional and calculative and to realize a full and rich acceptance of one another. The couple is called to express in human terms what God offers in divine terms—pardon and acceptance. Such acceptance annuls neither the need for nor the possibility of judgment and forgiveness. Rather, acceptance is that underlying quality in a relationship which frees the partners both to judge and to criticize, to forgive and allow oneself to be forgiven. If such underlying acceptance and affirmation are lacking, judgment takes on the character of rejection, and the possibilities of forgiveness are frozen in the power struggle that follows. Thus, acceptance "for better, for worse, for richer, for poorer, in sickness and in health," as the marriage rituals state, is essential to the health of the marriage covenant.

3. A third element of the covenantal relationship is *the commitment to explore and respond to the religious and moral depths of human existence in light of the affirmations of the Christian faith.* For Protestant theology, one of the major metaphors for interpreting the religious journey is that of "pilgrimage." In this pilgrimage, the Christian encounters religious questions about the meaning of human existence and grapples with the affirmations and doctrines of the Christian faith that can help make sense out of those questions. Marriage is seen as a primary path on which this pilgrimage unfolds, and within its borders Christians are expected to "wrestle with the angels" in their struggle to understand and live out a life of faithfulness to God. Within marriage and the family, those ultimate issues of life and death are confronted; grief over death, suffering from illness, joy from loving, alienation over differences, happiness over success, fear from the threat of loneliness, and sustenance from the routines of marital rhythms are experienced; and the moral issues of truthfulness, promise-keeping, fair play, just dealings, loving acts, protection of freedoms, and demands for social responsibility are encountered and responded to. Thus, marriage is a time and place of pilgrimage, casting its partners into the arena of religious and moral issues which shock them into an awareness of their own limitations and invite them into the experience of fulfillment and wholeness. Marriage demands that some sense be made out of these encounters, that some faith response be given by Christians in light of the Christian faith.

Protestant marriage theory, then, calls married persons to see the relationship of their own marriage to the larger pilgrimage of faith and to accept the responsibility to take seriously the religious and moral issues marriage poses. Such theory goes further, however, for it asks married couples not only to call upon the resources of faith but also to nurture and strengthen one another in the roles of Christian pilgrim and disciple. The eighteenth-century Puritans and sectarians saw marriage as a means by which both partners would be strengthened in their spiritual and moral resolve. It was a vocation whose final goal was to give glory to God through the shaping of the religious and moral life—a theme picked up in the words of a contemporary Presbyterian service of marriage:

> As God's picked representatives of the new humanity, purified and beloved of God himself, be merciful in action, kindly in heart, humble in mind. Accept life, and be most patient and tolerant with one another. Forgive as freely as the Lord has forgiven you. And, above everything else, be truly loving. Let the peace of Christ rule in your hearts, remembering that as mem-

bers of the one body you are called to live in harmony, and never forget to be thankful for what God has done for you.[16]

The married couple also has a responsibility to the larger community to bear children, when such is possible and wise, and to nurture them in the Christian faith. Although contemporary theology and services of marriage lift up the importance of procreation and the nurturance of children, reflecting a certain expectation and goal for marriage, none considers it essential for fulfillment of the marriage covenant or suggests that the primary purpose of marriage is procreation. This is, in part, a recognition that some persons cannot have children; that other persons, given their own personal emotional and social means in life, should not have children; and that all persons should respect the fact that in an overpopulated world the vocation of marriage need not necessarily include bearing or nurturing children.

Finally, the married couple has a responsibility to the larger community to participate actively both in the life of the church which serves the community and as citizens of the community in those actions that contribute to the greatest realization of the common good. Again, it was the Puritans who developed the most elaborate ethic of family social responsibility, seeing the family as a commonwealth writ small which was to care for the larger commonwealth of which it was a part. While nineteenth- and twentieth-century marriage and family literature has highlighted the family's responsibility to its own members, there still remains that strong theme that the couple will "make their life together a sign of Christ's love to this sinful and broken world," will bring up their children "to know you, to love you, and to serve you," and will "reach out in love and concern for others."[17] Thereby, the religious pilgrimage becomes a Christian pilgrimage, and the couple and their family fulfill the vocation they have been given.

4. A fourth element of the covenant is *a commitment to live out an ethic of covenantal wholeness.* The covenantal relationship God created with the people of Israel was interwoven with ethical principles and moral expectations. The Protestant understanding of the marriage covenant is similar. In modern marriage theory, four dominant principles emerge: *love, justice, freedom,* and *order.* As the covenant is interpreted, God calls people to live within the bonds of a loving relationship, to relate in a just and fair manner, to claim and accept the judgment that we are created as free and self-transcending creatures who are responsible for giving moral shape and depth to the covenantal relationship, and to recognize the necessity both for order in life and for the importance of stability and change in maintaining that order.

I referred above to the significance which Protestant marriage theory attributes to the principle of love. Most significantly, contemporary writing recognizes that a healthy marriage needs both romantic and companionate experiences of love (*eros* and *philia*). Romantic love, as the attraction and desire for union with the other, is experienced most intensely in the sexual relationship of the couple, but it should also be present in a full range of relationships as spontaneous and empathetic responsiveness marked by a sense of emotional excitement and heightened awareness. Yet, such romantic love must be complemented or balanced by companionate love, which expresses itself as an ongoing responsiveness in the routines of life together. It is love embued with a respect for the other's privacy, an appreciation for the other's life as a unique blend of limitation and possibility, and a desire for an encompassing relationship of sharing. It is companionate love with its own special respect, appreciation, patience, and steadfastness that provides a foundation for the more emotionally charged expressions of love.

In the past, romantic love was often seen in an unfavorable light, especially in Victorian Protestant writings,[18] but in an earlier Puritan period romance was clearly accepted as a part of the marital relationship, one closely interwoven with companionship. Theologian Thomas Hooker wrote:

> The man whose heart is endeared to the woman he loves, he dreams of her in the night in his eye and apprehension when he awakes, museth on her as he sits at table, talks with her when he travels and parties with her in each place he comes. . . .
>
> That the husband tenders his spouse with an endeared affection above all mortal creatures: This appears by the expressions of his respect, that all he hath, is of her command, all he can do, is wholly improved for her content and comfort, she lies in his bosom and his heart trusts in her, which forceth all to confess, that the stream of his affection, like a mighty current, runs with full tide and strength.[19]

In modern times there is again an appreciation, though in a different voice, of the romantic character of marriage and its importance alongside the extensive emphasis on companionate love.

Justice, and justice as fairness, is a principle which has recently become a very important part of Protestant writings on marriage and the family, paralleling the general cultural interest in justice and equality in the twentieth century, and which is informed by a larger social-justice concern of the church.[20] Justice is concerned with "each receiving his or her due." Its focus, therefore, is on distribution—whether of economic resources, time, work, roles, or other aspects of marital life—which can be seen in terms of either simple equity or special need. In the first, distribution is made on the basis that all receive an equal part or amount of whatever is being distributed; for example, marital roles or money. Creative justice based on special need is concerned with distribution in light of unique needs one partner may have; for example, special medical or career needs.

The question of justice in our own time is particularly manifest in feminist concerns about sexist role patterns and institutional expectations. In response, Protestant thought ranges from a more traditional to a more egalitarian understanding of roles men and women play, with more conservative denominations remaining traditional and more mainline denominations developing egalitarian perspectives. The egalitarian position holds that justice requires us to take very seriously the feminist critique of the traditional division of roles and lift up a new image of marriage in which both parties are invited to choose their own marital and vocational roles in light of their talents, interests, time, and possibilities—rather than simply on the basis of gender. Thus, each partner should be free to choose roles regardless of whether they have been traditionally considered masculine or feminine (with the obvious exceptions of bearing and nursing children). The literature also assumes that married men and women should be free of stereotypes in which women are seen as more relational and men as more autonomous, women as more emotional and men as more rational, women as more passive and men as more active.

There is, then, a new egalitarian image of marriage which has emerged in marriage theory and is making its way into marriage services in such details as the shift from the phrase "man and wife" to "husband and wife." This perspective is an attempt by denominations to grapple with the issue of sexism within marriage and the family. This concern roughly parallels denominational efforts to confront the issue of sexism in other aspects of its life (such as the status and role of women in leadership positions, the use of inclusive language in worship services, and support of the Equal Rights Amendment to the U.S. Constitution). Justice, then, has become an important principle in reasoning about the character of the covenantal relationship.

Freedom is the third principle. Central to Protestant understandings of human nature is the assumption that we are created, as Reinhold Niebuhr has written, both "finite and free." We are limited by the vicissitudes of our natural experience, and yet we are self-transcendent creatures with the power of reflection and choice. We are free to act. This freedom, in turn, implies that persons are responsible for their own actions, since they have chosen them. In terms of a covenantal relationship, a couple is free to respond to that relationship, change it, shape it, violate it, or destroy it. Accordingly, the couple should be held responsible for the quality of relationship that is created.

In marriage theology, freedom is translated in a twofold way: Couples are responsible for exercising their freedom in such a way that they enable each other to realize their own possibilities; at the same time, they are responsible for enabling the marriage to be actualized. Nineteenth-century Protestant marriage theory developed an understanding of marriage as an organic reality with a certain life of its own, a life that is greater than and transcends its individual members. Thus, a marriage has three parties: the two partners and the marriage itself. This theory has developed in late-twentieth-century thought partly in response to the fear that in our time too many couples have exercised their freedom in their own interest rather than that of the marriage. In recent writings, the issue of responsible freedom is often treated in terms of the rights of the individual partners (and children) and the rights of the marriage. Couples are expected to understand and balance these rights.

The fourth principle is that of *order*. The covenant is understood to be a structural order including both stability and change. Within this equation, stability is that sense of ongoingness and predictability within the relationship, undergirded by some significant degree of social, emotional, personal, and economic security. The couple commits itself to realizing such stability. At the same time, order implies change. Order, and its stability, must be dynamic; it must allow for growth so that the life of the relationship will be sustained and developed. The partners, therefore, should attempt to realize a balance between stability and change, such that the covenantal order may avoid either chaos or rigidity.

5. A fifth characteristic of the covenantal relationship is *a commitment to create boundaries or rules of behavior.* When persons marry, they should create certain agreements regarding their common life—agreements that have to do with all significant areas of activity from the personal to the social, from the economic to the parental. These agreements are responses to questions of how the marriage will maintain itself economically; how it will govern itself; how it will express itself sexually; how it will allocate the roles its members shall play; how it will function in the social arena; how it will define its goals regarding vocations, procreation, lifestyles, and social responsibilities; and what values it will hold as central to its life as a marriage.

Protestant marriage theory holds that a couple should take seriously not only the need for such boundaries, rules, or agreements regarding the form and style of their own relationship but also the need to rethink them as the marriage relationship changes, for such rules are necessary if the basic purpose and vision of the marriage covenant are to be realized in concrete patterns of behavior. While Protestant literature does not tend to spell out in detail such rules or guidelines, it does offer concrete advice in such areas of marital life as sex-role fairness, sexual conduct, procreation, church participation, interfaith marriage, and responsible citizenship. Denominations offer guidance on what constitutes responsible boundaries for healthy marital behavior.

6. The sixth element of the covenant has to do with its possible demise. It is that *the couple should commit themselves to breaking the covenant only if its life of intimacy has ceased to exist and all available means have been exhausted in an effort to renew it.* The breakdown of a covenant relationship seldom comes quickly or over a single issue but is the result of a range of negative experiences which increasingly damage and finally destroy the relationship. A couple, therefore, are expected to seek help when negative experiences begin to undercut their intimacy or prevent it from developing.

A breakdown, of course, does not necessarily entail an end to the legal relationship of the marriage nor an end to living together; rather, breakdown occurs when the internal life of the relationship has died. The covenant involves an inner quality of relationship, an internal life of commitment and purpose, an inward expression of virtues and feelings with its own spirit and spirituality. This may be expressed externally, for the covenant is also an external reality, but its life and death are determined by the health of its inner life. When a marriage has reached the point where its members say that "there is no health in us," that the spirit is no more, then the covenant is no longer a "living" reality. In light of this understanding of the covenant, persons should do all in their power to nurture its health and care for it so that it might live—and they should end its life only as a last resort.[21]

It should be noted that Protestantism has shifted over the centuries on the question of divorce. While John Milton's treatise, *On Divorce*, built a case for divorce as early as the seventeenth century, it was not until the twentieth century that Protestant denominations were willing to acknowledge that divorce could be a morally responsible action. It is also significant that there is a growing attempt to develop church rituals that recognize divorce and offer support and hope to the partners in their search for new beginnings, though no denomination has yet formally adopted such a ritual.[22]

I have set forth here a covenantal image of marriage that lies at the heart of Protestantism's theology of marriage and its denominational statements and rituals about the purpose and meaning of marriage.[23] Much of that understanding will also be found in Roman Catholic and Orthodox perspectives. We find in the Vatican II documents on marriage and the family the substantive use and interpretation of the covenantal nature of marriage, and in Protestant writings we discover an appreciation for the sacramental character of marriage insofar as its bonds of love and intimacy are seen as a means of grace. Thus, a certain slow convergence in the understandings of marriage does unfold, albeit within a framework of genuine differences and contrasting emphases among the three major divisions of Christianity.

There are, of course, differences among Protestants themselves. The more liberal mainline groups accent the egalitarian nature of the covenantal bond which has been described here, while conservative and fundamentalist groups tend to accent a more traditional image in which marital and family roles are defined by gender, with the man considered the "head" of the household. Similarly, different positions exist on intermarriage, with more liberal groups counseling the couple to find a church home in which both parties can share, and more conservative groups insisting on marriage "within the fold." Divorce is also treated differently, with all groups accepting divorce but some refusing to remarry divorced members. Sexuality tends to be interpreted differently, with a much stronger emphasis on the procreative function of sex within fundamentalism and less consideration of sexual expression as a means of love and grace. Among those mainline Protestant groups which have given shape to the covenantal image discussed here, however, the bonds of commonality dominate. When Protestants gather together to celebrate a marriage, therefore, their shared commitment to a covenantal perspective unites them.

NOTES

1. Primary source material includes representative Protestant marriage services and official statements from the following mainline denominations: the American Baptist Churches in the U.S.A., the Southern Baptist Convention, the Christian Church (Disciples of Christ), the Episcopal Church, the Lutheran churches (A.L.C., L.C.A.,

A.E.L.C., and Missouri Synod), the Presbyterian Church, U.S.A., the United Church of Canada, the United Church of Christ, and the United Methodist Church.

2. "Social Principles of the United Methodist Church," *The Discipline* (Nashville: The United Methodist Publishing House, 1984).

3. Richard Fagley, *The Population Explosion and Christian Responsibility* (New York: Oxford, 1960). Fagley offers a contrast between and comparison of Luther and Calvin regarding the purposes of marriage and the place of procreation.

4. Roland Bainton, *Sex, Love, and Marriage* (Glasgow: Fontana, 1964), chap. 4–5. See also John Halkett, *Milton and the Idea of Matrimony* (New Haven: Yale University Press, 1970), for an excellent study of Milton's ideas on marriage and divorce.

5. Anne Bradstreet, "A Letter to Her Husband, Absent Upon Publick Employment," in Perry Miller, ed., *The American Puritans* (New York: Doubleday, 1956), pp. 271–272.

6. Two major works explore the role Puritanism played in giving shape to a theory of marriage in which love and companionship are viewed as central to the Christian understanding of marriage: Lawrence Stone, *The Family, Sex, and Marriage in England, 1500–1800* (New York: Harper and Row, 1977); and Edmund Morgan, *The Puritan Family* (New York: Harper and Row, 1966). See also Steven Ozment, *When Fathers Ruled* (Cambridge: Harvard University Press, 1983).

7. Wilson Yates, "Population Ethics: Religious Traditions—Protestant Perspectives," in *Encyclopedia of Bioethics*, vol. 3 (New York: The Free Press, 1978), pp. 1259–1260.

8. E.g., see D. S. Bailey, *The Mystery of Love and Marriage* (New York: Harper and Row, 1952); N. Pittenger, *Making Sexuality Human* (Philadelphia: Pilgrim Press, 1970); D. D. Williams, *The Spirit and Forms of Love* (New York: Harper and Row, 1968); L. Russell, *The Future of Partnership* (Philadelphia: Westminster Press, 1979); P. Trible, "Eve and Adam: Genesis 2–3 Reread," *Andover Newton Quarterly* 13 (March, 1973), and "Two Women in a Man's World." *Soundings* 59 (Fall, 1976); and J. B. Nelson, *Embodiment* (Minneapolis: Ausburg Publishing House; New York: Pilgrim Press, 1978), and *Between Two Gardens* (New York: Pilgrim Press, 1983).

9. Nelson, *Embodiment*, p. 113.

10. Examples of nineteenth-century Protestant marriage manuals include: William Makepeace Thayer, *Hints for the Household* (Boston: John Jewett and Co., 1853); George Weaver, *The Christian Household* (Boston: A. Tompkins and B. B. Mussey, 1856); John Wesley Smith, *Courtship, Love, and Marriage* (New York: Nelson's and Phillip's, 1874); and Charles Hudson, *The Marriage Guide* (Boston: Jewett and Co., 1882).

11. Charlotte and Howard J. Clinebell, Jr., *The Intimate Marriage* (New York: Harper and Row, 1970), pp. 29–33.

12. *The Book of Common Prayer* (New York: Seabury Press, 1977), p. 423.

13. Ibid., p. 430.

14. Dietrich Bonhoeffer, "What Is Meant by Telling the Truth?" in his *Ethics* (New York: The Macmillan Company, 1965), pp. 363–373.

15. Pittenger, *Making Sexuality Human*, p. 43. See also Joseph L. Allen, *Love and Conflict* (Nashville: Abingdon, 1984), pp. 231–234.

16. *The Worshipbook, Services* (Philadelphia: Westminster Press, 1970), p. 67.

17. *Book of Common Prayer*, p. 429.

18. See Charles Franklin Thwing and Carrie F. Butler Thwing, *The Family* (Boston: Lothrop, Lee and Shepard Co., 1886, 1913), for an excellent study that reflects the concerns of the Victorian era regarding "modern" marriage and, particularly, concern over the focus in secular society on romance and individualism.

19. Quoted in Bainton, *Sex, Love, and Marriage*, pp. 104–105.

20. See Jane Cary Peck, *Self and Family* (Philadelphia: Westminster Press, 1984), and William Everett, *Blessed Be the Tie That Binds* (Philadelphia: Fortress Press, 1985).

21. See Allen, *Love and Conflict*, pp. 243–253.

22. The United Church of Christ includes in its proposed marriage services a proposed "Order for Recognition of the End of a Marriage" (*Proposed Services of Marriage* [St. Louis: Office for Church Life and Leadership, United Church of Christ, 1982]).

23. Allen (*Love and Conflict*) provides a good example of a contemporary theologian who uses a covenantal model to interpret a Christian view of marriage. See also Peck, *Self and Family*, and Everett, *Blessed Be the Tie*.

CHAPTER 41

Marriage in Islam

Lois Lamyā' Ibsen al Faruqi

There are a billion Muslims in the world today. Somewhere between two million and three million of that number are in the United States. Islam, currently, is also the fastest-growing religion in the United States and is expected early in the twenty-first century to surpass Judaism as the third-largest religion in the country.

Stereotypes abound in the public perception of Islam in the West. The emergence of a revivalistic Islam strikes bewilderment and terror in many minds and hearts. Prejudice is fueled also by mass ignorance. The result is intolerance, misunderstanding, and chauvinism. This essay should go a long way toward alleviating misperceptions and positively affirming the wisdom of Islam in its marriage teachings and traditions.

The essay falls neatly into four major divisions: (1) the dominant influence of religion on Islamic marriage and the avowed purposes it serves; (2) specific requirements and codes necessary for its legitimacy; (3) mechanisms for the dissolution of marriage are detailed; and, (4) a brief look at the changes and challenges facing Islamic marriage in the future. The essay is a model of clarity and a reservoir of knowledge about our Muslim sisters and brothers.

Questions for Discussion

1. What distinctive differences do you find between the Islamic and the Roman Catholic views of marriage? What common ground do they share?
2. Compare the purposes of marriage in Islam with the twofold purpose as stated in contemporary Roman Catholic theology.
3. Will the meeting of Islam and feminism be confrontation or cooperation in relation to marriage?
4. In what areas will Islamic marriage show resistance and/or assimilation to secular modernity?

I n order to explain how marriage is regarded and manifested in Islamic society, an organization of four major divisions has been utilized here. The first discusses general characteristics and purposes of Islamic marriage; a sec-

From *Journal of Ecumenical Studies*, 22:1 (Winter, 1985) pp. 55–68. Copyright © 1985 by *Journal of Ecumenical Studies*. Reprinted with permission.

ond outlines the specific requirements which legitimize marriage; and a third details the mechanisms for its dissolution. A fourth and final section discusses briefly the issue of change and the future.

GENERAL CHARACTERISTICS OF MARRIAGE IN ISLAM

RELIGION AS DOMINANT FACTOR

Probably the most dominant factor that influences or has influenced Islamic marriage is religion. This is due in part to the Islamic idea that religion (*dīn*) is not a body of ideas and practices which should be practiced or which should influence only that part of human life generally designated as dealing with the sacred. In Islamic culture there is little or no conception of a bifurcation between that which is sacred and that which is secular. Instead, since every aspect of life is the creation of Allah, it carries religious significance. It is the matérial with which humanity works to fulfill the will of God on earth, the ultimate human purpose in creation. Thus, for the Muslim, the ritual prayer conducted in any clean place is as equally valid and acceptable as that performed in the mosque; the commitment to political and social awareness and activity is as much a religious duty as the recitation of prayers; economic pursuits are equally regulated in accordance with religio-ethical pronouncements as the *zakāt* (Islamic levy for social welfare) and the *hajj* (pilgrimage to Makkah). Aesthetic products present not art for art's sake, but art for religion's sake: they are restatements and reminders of religious truth. In fact, every aspect of Islamic life is permeated with the effects of qur'ānic and religious teachings. Marriage is no less affected.

In Islamic society, however, marriage is not a religious sacrament. In other words, it is not a ceremony which necessitates the involvement of any clergy, presupposes a numinous or divine involvement, or, as a consequence, tends to be regarded as an indissoluble commitment.[1] In Islam there are no priests and little notion of sacredness in marriage which surpasses that of any other similarly recommended institution of the culture. Consequently, the religion has delineated accepted procedures for its dissolution.

Although marriage is not regarded as a religious sacrament, Islam recommends it for every Muslim. Commendations are to be found for it in the Qur'ān (4:1, 29; 7:107; 13:38; 24:32–33; 30:20), and the *hadīth* literature—recording sayings and events from the life of the Prophet—contains numerous passages in which celibacy is discouraged and marriage encouraged. For example, "Marriage is of my ways," the Prophet is reported to have taught, as well as, "When a man has married, he has completed one half of his religion," and "Whoever is able to marry, should marry."[2] Such stimulus from religious teachings has made marriage the goal of every Muslim and caused a considerable amount of social pressure to achieve that end for every member of the society.[3] Parents, relatives, and friends all feel committed to assist actively in the process, and few are the individuals who "escape the system."

Religion also guarantees certain rights and imposes certain responsibilities on the participants in marriage. Both men and women are regarded as deriving substantial benefits from the institution of marriage, but they are also bound to its obligations by actual qur'ānic prescriptives and by the legal elaboration and interpretation of the scriptural passages.[4] The religious laws of personal status are therefore crucial to any understanding of Islamic marriage. It is in these laws that the most detailed enunciation of both the woman's and the man's rights and obligations is to be found. Complying with the fulfillment of those mutual responsibilities is therefore regarded as a religious obligation for both parties. The acquiescence of the failure to comply is regarded as an act carrying divine reward or punishment, and therefore it is not a matter to be taken lightly.

Also important is the fact that matrimony in Islam is as much a joining of two families as it is a joining of two individuals. Given the level of interdependence in the Islamic family,[5] Muslims are especially likely to believe marriage necessitates a consideration of the welfare of the familial groups involved rather than merely the desires of the two individuals. For this reason a much larger participation in the choice of marriage partners is regarded as proper and beneficial than would be acceptable in a contemporary Western environment. Even after the marriage, the extended family organization reduces dependence on the single adult relationship of husband and wife and stimulates equally strong relationships between the wife or husband and other members of the family. Despite this heavily "familial" character of the Islamic marriage, the woman maintains her separate legal identity after marriage, her maiden name, her adherence to a particular school of law, and her right to separate ownership of her money, property, or financial holdings.

THE PURPOSES OF MARRIAGE

The importance of marriage in Islamic society and its advocacy by the religious teachings rest on the avowed purposes it serves. First, Muslims regard marriage as providing a balance between individualistic needs and the welfare of the group to which the individual belongs. As such, it is regarded as a social and psychological necessity for every member of the community.

Second, marriage is a mechanism for the moral and mutually beneficial control of sexual behavior and procreation. Islam regards sexual activity as an important and perfectly healthy drive of both males and females. Thus, it is not shameful and should not be denied to members of either sex. Lack of sexual satisfaction is believed to cause personality maladjustments and to "endanger the mental health and efficiency of the society."[6] Islam, therefore, commends sex as natural and good but restricts it to participants of a union which insures responsibility for its consequences.[7]

A third purpose of marriage is its provision of a stable atmosphere for the rearing of children. Islam sees this purpose as inextricably tied to an extended family system. The extended family may vary in size, even in residential proximity, as is evidenced in different regions of the Muslim world, but the cohesion of its members is inextricably bound to qur'ānic prescriptions and Islamic law. These explicity enunciate the rights and obligations of its members and the legal extent of those benefits and responsibilities.[8]

Fourth, marriage assures crucial economic benefits for women during their child-bearing and child-rearing years. Self-support during this period is difficult, if not impossible, for mothers who have no outside help. Even if sustained by the "supermom," of which we hear so much in recent times, the physical and emotional toll on such persons is beyond what most individuals can tolerate.

Fifth, the close companionship of the marital partners provides emotional gratification for both men and women. The importance of this purpose of marriage in Islam is evidenced by repeated references in the Qur'ān and *ḥadīth* literature to the quiescence (Qur'ān 30:21; 7:189) and protective nature (Qur'ān 9:71) of the bond between the husband and wife. The man and woman are considered to be so close that they are described as garments of one another (Qur'ān 2:187). The kindness, love, and consideration enjoined on the partners appears repeatedly in both religious and legal texts.

SPECIFIC REQUIREMENTS FOR MARRIAGE IN ISLAM

Given its general characteristics and purposes as outlined above, Islamic marriage also entails certain specific features which are regarded necessary for its legitimacy. Let us first specify the criteria which must be met by the participants themselves.

LIMITATION OF PARTICIPANTS

Applying to both parties are the Islamic boundaries of incestuous union. The list of acceptable persons whom one can marry rests on a firm ground of conformity since the basic exogamy/endogamy[9] patterns are fixed by the Qur'ān and *ḥadīth*.[10] Islam prescribes limits on marriages between certain blood (consanguine) relatives, between others closely related through marriage (affinal relatives), and between lactational relatives, that is, those who have been nursed by the same woman.[11] Since the institution of the wet nurse and the reciprocal nursing of their babies by women with close familial or affinal ties have often been widespread, the lactational limits have proved very influential for discouraging inbreeding. The jurists of the different schools have unanimously adhered to that prohibition and accepted the authenticity of the *ḥadīth*s on this matter,[12] although the details of how much nursing and how much milk constitutes a prohibiting amount, the ages of affected children, etc., were sometimes disputed.

The definition of allowable marriage partners is considered by Muslims to fulfill two major purposes: to prevent the biological effects of inbreeding, and to guard against excessive familiarity between sexual partners. Such familiarity is regarded as cause for sexual indifference in the partners. Therefore, marriage with someone as close as a mother, sister, daughter, or aunt would result, in most cases, in a denial of sexual gratification for the marriage partners. In the Muslim village, young people of the opposite sex are separated from the age of puberty or before. If they are to realize a sexually successful marriage in the village, the possibilities for familiarity must be limited and the aura of mystery and excitement engendered by marriage candidates of the opposite sex preserved. Whether consciously or unconsciously pursued by the Muslim peoples, this concern seems to be at the base of the preference—or, in some parts of the Muslim world, the demand—for segregation of the sexes. That is a much more logical underlying purpose for segregation than the need to curb sexual promiscuity. The latter is almost an impossibility in the close quarters and intensive interaction of the village.[13]

There are also religious affiliation boundaries for participation in an Islamic marriage. The male must be a Muslim; the female may be a Muslim, Jew, or Christian (Qur'ān 5:6). Sometimes the religious requirements for the female have been interpreted more widely to include anyone who is not idolatrous. The prohibition against a non-Muslim man's marrying a Muslim woman is, however, qur'ānic and has been unequivocally adhered to by all the legal schools.

Though a few early jurists rejected completely the idea of intermarriage, most Muslims have considered it permissible under certain conditions.[14] The qur'ānic and legal directives on intermarriage tended to be reinforced by the circumstances of the early centuries of Islamic history. As traders, warriors, missionaries, teachers, administrators, and religious or education-seeking pilgrims, many Muslim men traveled to live in different parts of the world. They often lived in predominantly non-Muslim societies where Muslim women were not available for marriage partners. Women, on the other hand, tended to remain in their predominantly Muslim societies and therefore had access to Muslim male partners.

There were no age limitations for marriage partners in Islamic culture until recent times. Since the individuals remained part of a larger family structure which did not call upon them to support themselves, to set up their own home, or to cope unaided with the problems of parenting children, Islam held a much more relaxed view of the prior preparedness for marriage. As the extended family of certain urban environments has been weakened in recent times, a greater emphasis has been placed on the readiness of the married couple to live a more isolated and self-sufficient existence. This has stimulated an appeal by certain individuals and groups in a number of Muslim countries to call for the setting of minimum age limits for marriage.[15] Since marriage in Islam means the signing of a contract, with consummation following perhaps at a much later time, marriage of minors did not raise the same sort of problems it might in another societal complex. This does not mean that the custom of child marriage was never abused; it does mean that this Islamic custom need not be detrimental if practiced in tandem with a properly functioning Islamic society. Not its use but its misuse in an Islamically inconsistent social complex has generated Muslim concern and the recent need for a minimum-age limitation for marriage partners.

Some writers have attributed the recent calls for minimum-age requirements to Western influences on Islamic thinking and customs. In fact, that argument has been the main thrust of conservative opposition to the initiation of age restrictions on marriage. It seems much more likely that this so-called Westernization would not have taken root unless the misuse and/or imbalance within the system had not made some sort of change necessary.

Another requirement which relates to the qualifications of the marriage participants is that the Muslim woman must be unmarried. If she has formerly been married, she should not be pregnant or in the first three months following her previous marriage, a period known as *'iddah,* in which she may not be aware of a possible pregnancy. The former husband is obliged to support her during the *'iddah* or until the birth of her child, after which she may remarry. Such restrictions help verify paternity of a child resulting from the earlier marriage.

The male partner in marriage, however, is not limited to a single marriage. Islam can be described as permitting polygynous marriage, that is, it is a society in which plural marriages for males are possible. In Islamic society, however, only a small portion of the males practice polygyny. If those that do are known to have no valid reason for taking another wife,[16] or do not treat their wives with the complete equality commanded by the Qur'ān (4:3; 129), Muslims judge such instantiation of this form of marriage as unIslamic and religiously and morally reprehensible. As an excuse for sexual promiscuity, the practice is unconditionally condemned, but, if practiced according to Islamic moral exhortations and legal provisions, Muslims regard polygyny as a more equitable and humane solution to certain situations than the unconditional demand for monogamy.[17] In some schools of law, a woman who wishes to prevent her husband's future second marriage can ask that such a stipulation be written into the marriage agreement.

Mechanistic Requirements

Other specific requirements of Islamic marriage pertain to the actual execution of the marriage rather than to the qualities of its participants. These are designated here as "mechanistic requirements."

A WRITTEN CONTRACT   Marriage in Islam constitutes an agreement between a man and a woman which is embodied in a written contract. The marriage agreement includes specification of the dower (both an initial and delayed portion, see the section on Dower, below), signatures of the two participants and of their respective witnesses, and other terms agreed upon by the parties concerned. The contract is a legal document, which is filed with the local Islamic registry of the government and upholdable in a court of law.

The occasion for the signing of the contract is called *'aqd nikāḥ* ("marriage contract"). It usually takes place at the home of the bride's parents, in the presence of members of the family and close friends. The *'nikāḥ* is accompanied by the surrender of the agreed-upon initial dower and the exchange of gifts by the marriage partners. It also marks the beginning of preparations for the consummation of the marriage. The actual marriage requirements are fulfilled in the *'aqd nikāḥ,* and the marriage is complete, but it is not until the *'urs* or actual wedding party that the marriage is consummated and the bride moves to the home of her husband. This may take place shortly after the contract signing or at a much later time, as the parties desire.

The 'urs may be a simple party or an elaborate occasion. Refreshments, activities, and entertainment vary according to tastes, financial capabilities, and regional preferences. It may take place at the groom's home or at a public place reserved for the occasion. It is the common practice not only for gifts to be presented to the bride and groom by guests on this occasion but also for the couple to reciprocate with a token of their gratitude—usually a small dish or platter for carrying sweets or an item of clothing for closer relatives. These vary in extravagance to match the economic situation of the wedding participants.

The clothing of the bride and groom varies from one level of society to another and from one region to another. In the Arab Mashriq (near the eastern end of the Mediterranean Sea), for example, the wedding dress may be a white gown and headcovering similar to that common in Western societies or an elaborate example of the local style. Men wear Western-style suits or traditional dress. In the Indian subcontinent, brides are clothed in crimson saris elaborately decorated with gold, while grooms don the traditional "Nehru jacket" with its high collar and buttoned front. In Malaysia the typical attire for both bride and groom is a traditionally styled outfit made of the locally produced brocade woven with gold threads. If the wedding couple come from wealthy families, the clothing may be so heavily decorated with the precious metal that the pair have difficulty in moving. But this does not present too much of a problem since the function of the 'urs is an elaborate reception at which the bride and groom and their families accept the congratulations and best wishes of friends and relatives.

TWO ADULT WITNESSES   Two witnesses—one representing the bride, the other representing the groom—are a necessary feature of the marriage-contract signing. Where possible, these are the two fathers of the couple, but any other adult Muslim could legitimately fill this role. No other intermediary is required for the performance of a marriage. Any person who is chosen by the parties may make and accept the marriage proposal. Often, however, a qāḍī or Muslim lawyer attends as a registrar of the marriage.

SU'ĀL AND ĪJĀB ("QUESTION AND CONSENT")   Another element of a legitimate marriage in Islamic society is an explicit request by the groom and his family or representatives and an explicit consent to marriage by the bride and her family or representatives, which may be either in writing or oral. The Qur'ān does not deal specifically with this matter, but there are a number of instances from the ḥadīth literature which pertain to this question.[18] The story is told of a woman in the time of Muhammad who demanded and was accorded by the Prophet the right to repudiate her marriage because she had not been asked and therefore had not given her consent to the bond.[19] Despite strongly authenticated instances in the sunnah ("example") of the Prophet Muhammad, Muslim jurists have varied in their interpretations of the guardian's powers in arranging marriage for his wards or children. Some deem it a necessary condition for the father to seek the consent of his daughter before he gives her in marriage. Others argue that it is commendable rather than necessary. Still others limit the need for the consent of the bride to the mature woman who is a widow or divorcee.[20]

DOWER A fourth requirement of the Islamic marriage is a marriage gift or dower to the bride by the groom. This gift may consist of anything deemed suitable by the participants—money, real estate, or other valuable items. In some cases it has entailed the transfer of great wealth to the bride; in others, it has been as modest as an iron ring or a token coin.[21] No maximum has been set by Islamic law, though some schools have specified minimums.[22] Such details are worked out by the representatives of the bride and groom prior to the *'aqd nikāḥ* and are specified in the written contract.

The dower may be immediate, that is, given at the time of signing the *'aqd nikāḥ* More often, the parties agree that the dower be divided into two parts: one portion (the *mahr*) surrendered to the bride at the time of marriage, and another delayed portion (the *mu' akhkhar*) which falls due in case of death or divorce. If a man dies, Islamic law provides that his widow's *mu' akhkhar* settlement be paid before any other commitment on his estate is honored.

The immediate dower may be used for the trousseau and the household purchases needed for the newly married couple. At other times it is a kind of economic insurance for the future welfare of the bride, in which case she invests it and draws benefits from it. In the case of poor people, the amounts are so negligible that they can be viewed as little more than a symbol of the groom's willingness to take on financial responsibility for this future wife. Amounts of dower vary not only with the difference in the economic capabilities of different grooms and their families but also according to regional practices and social levels within a particular society.

It is clear that the Islamic marriage is not a "ceremony." Although it may be associated with a number of elaborate activities (procession of the bride to her new husband's home, beautification of the bride prior to marriage with henna decorations, gift-giving and well-wishing of friends and relatives, elaborate clothing, refreshments, and entertainment), marriage in Islam is essentially a legal agreement between two individuals and two families. While carrying the sanction and blessing of the religion, it cannot be considered a sacred ceremony. Marriage, like so many other aspects of Islamic culture, is neither wholly sacred nor wholly secular, neither religious nor nonreligious.

DISSOLUTION OF MARRIAGE

DISSOLUTION THROUGH DEATH

Dissolution of marriage occurs either by death of one of the parties or by divorce. In the case of the woman's death, there are inheritance laws which pertain to her wealth since her property remains separate from that of her husband. There are similarly specific requirements for the distribution of his wealth following the death of the husband. Other requirements pertain to the female survivor. These include payment of the *mu' akhkhar* dower to the widow and the illegality of the widow's remarriage before completion of the three-month *'iddah* period in which the possibility of pregnancy can be determined. During this time, the widow is financially supported by her late husband's estate. If she is pregnant, maintenance is guaranteed until birth of the child or the end of the nursing period, but she must not remarry until the birth of her child.

DIVORCE

More complicated is the dissolution of marriage through legal divorce. Although it is generally believed that dissolution of marriage takes place in Islam only by male repudiation of the wife—that is, by his pronouncing three times, "I divorce you"—the fact is that Islamic law provides various mechanisms and channels for ending a marriage. Despite the variety of means for divorce, it has remained a repugnant act in Islamic society,[23] to be invoked only when all methods of reconciliation have been exhausted. Some types of divorce are male-instigated, others female-instigated; still others are the result of mutual agreement or judicial process.

MALE-INSTIGATED DIVORCE   The most common form of divorce initiated by Muslim males is known as *ṭalāq* ("letting go free"), which involves a series of three statements by the husband that he divorces his wife. Contrary to common opinion, these repudiation statements cannot legally be rendered at a single time. In fact, very strict rules have been established in Islamic law to prevent misuse.[24] Unfortunately, these laws have not always been enforced.

Ṭalāq is to be pronounced with specific terms before two qualified witnesses. Each pronouncement must be made at a time when the wife is not incapacitated for sexual activity by menstrual flow. Having made the first statement of divorce, the man must wait to make the second statement until the woman completes her next monthly period. The third pronouncement must be similarly spaced. Only after the third repudiation is the divorce considered final. Each of the other two statements is revocable. The wife continues to live in her home, and she is provided full maintenance throughout the divorce proceedings. During this time, attempts are made to achieve reconciliation through the counseling and arbitration of family and friends. Only if this is not possible is the final pronouncement made and the marriage considered irrevocably broken. From that point, husband and wife are forbidden to live together or to remarry each other unless and until the woman has remarried someone else from whom she becomes widowed or divorced. Any Islamic divorce, like the dissolution of marriage by death, requires a three-months' waiting period in order to determine whether the divorcee is pregnant. She is not free to remarry until that period is completed or, in case of pregnancy, until she gives birth. As in the case of dissolution of marriage by death, maintenance of the wife is incumbent upon the husband for the *'iddah* the period of child-bearing.

Any *ṭalāq* divorce not made in accordance with these rules is considered to be an aberration, or *bid'ah*. Such practice is regarded as sinful, but unfortunately the actions of some Muslims and the positions of certain jurists have not always accorded with the ideal.[25]

FEMALE-INSTIGATED DIVORCE   In the Qur'ān it is stated that women have equitable rights in divorce to those of men (2:228). As in other Islamic matters, equitable does not mean equivalence or identity. Therefore, there are different procedures which apply to women in their initiation of divorce proceedings. The wife is entitled to originate dissolution of her marriage under four circumstances.

First, in a delegated divorce, the right of *ṭalāq*, or repudiation, by the wife may be agreed upon prior to marriage and stipulated as a condition of the marriage contract.[26] Second is a conditional divorce, a stipulation in the marriage contract that the wife will be free to divorce her husband if he does certain things contrary to his pre-marriage promises. This type of divorce is accepted by some jurists but rejected by others.[27] Third is a court divorce, in which freedom from the marriage bond is granted to a woman for any of the inadequacies of the husband which are generally regarded as legitimate causes for divorce: long absence or desertion, impotence, failure to provide adequate support, physical or mental mistreatment, serious physical or mental illness, apostasy, and proved debauchery. As noted earlier, a wife may also be granted a divorce if, upon reaching maturity, she rejects a marriage contracted by a guardian on her behalf while she was still a child. A fourth type of divorce instigated by the wife is known as *khul'*. It involves a release of the wife from the marriage contract on her agreement to pay compensation to the husband.

MUTUAL CONSENT OR *MUBĀRA'AH*   When a husband and wife reach mutual agreement to dissolve their marriage, it is called *mubāra'ah*. It differs from the *khul'* in being effected by mutual desire on the part of the marriage partners.[28]

JUDICIAL PROCESS   *Li'ān* or "double testimony" is the dissolution of marriage which results from the husband's accusation that his wife has committed adultery. If he proves his case (four eye-witnesses are necessary in Islamic law!), it it considered valid reason for divorce. If he has no witnesses other than himself, he must swear by God four times that his statement is true. The wife is called upon to admit her guilt or to testify in a similar way that her husband has lied about her. Both also invoke divine curses for false swearing. If no further proof either for or against the accusation can be substantiated, reconciliation between the two parties is deemed impossible, and the marriage is dissolved by judicial process.[29] Certain types of divorce instigated by women are also dealt with by the Islamic courts (see "court divorce," above).

CHANGE AND THE FUTURE

An increase in the number of women in the work force, increased education for women and men, the development of Islamic awareness and identity among Muslims in all parts of the world, increased mobility, concentration of populations in urban centers, increased contact with alien cultures, as well as many other contemporary facts of life may require certain adjustments in marriage practice in any society. Whether such adjustments will prove disastrous to the institution of Islamic marriage as it is now known—and, therefore, to Muslim society—or merely productive of a new synthesis of twentieth- and twenty-first-century influences with the core premises depends on the ability of society to react with a strong and intelligent social conscience. Social change as such need not be unduly disruptive of Islamic marriage practices. In fact, the magnitude of the Muslim identity (nearly 1,000,000,000 persons) and the diversity of geographic, ethnic, linguistic, and cultural backgrounds out of which these people moved toward Islamization have resulted in an extremely rich and varied tradition in marriage as in all other aspects of the civilization.

Islam has been particularly tolerant of its new converts, and those converts have been particularly ingenious in adapting their local customs to basic Islamic premises wherever possible. At the same time, there were basic premises of the faith as expressed in the Qur'ān and exemplified in the teachings and example of Muhammad which provided a religio-cultural core with which the more superficial variations could be sympathetically related. History has confirmed that, along with a maintenance of the core, Islamic society has been flexible enough to allow regional variations as well as changes accompanying the passage of time and the variation of circumstances. Each period has had to make its "peace" with those variations of circumstances, to take that which was acceptable and combinable with the Islamic core, to reject those which were culturally and religiously "indigestible," and to adapt—that is, to Islamize—still others before adopting them. This process must, of course, be carried on in the present day and into the future. To rule it out would be to kill the culture and the religion.

A society's proper reaction to change implies two prerequisites. First, it needs a study and awareness of the total societal complex, each of whose institutions and factors is integrally interwoven with and dependent upon the others. Any suggestion for change regarding marriage practices, therefore, should not be investigated in isolation. It should be studied in relation to the other factors of individual and group welfare which those factors may affect. It might be argued, for instance, that, because of increased participation of women in the work force in many Muslim countries, the Islamic custom of mandatory male support for women should be abolished; yet such a shortsighted view fails to take into account anything but the material aspects of the question. It might be counter-argued that much more important in this Islamic stipulation is the reinforcement it gives to the interdependence of the marriage partners; to break those bonds of rights for women and obligations for men would cut deeply into the strength of the marriage bond.

Similarly, some contemporaries might argue that Islam is old-fashioned in its unshakable condemnation of sex outside of marriage. They would cite contraceptive devices and new attitudes toward the sexual freedom of women as demanding a reappraisal of an old Islamic "fixation." But Islam's reason for rejecting greater sexual freedom was not that no adequate contraceptives were available in earlier times to prevent children born out of wedlock, nor did it insist on the importance of female virginity in order to discriminate against women or set a "double standard." Rather, Islam promoted this idea in order to strengthen the institutions of marriage and the family by making them carry benefits that could not be achieved elsewhere. To destroy the uniqueness of such marital benefits in an attempt to provide complete sexual equity would carry widespread and debilitating effects, not only for those institutions, but equally for the individuals who make up those institutions. We do not have to surmise about the effect on women that this innovation might have, for a living example is available in Western society. The consequences are already glaringly apparent. The increased sexual dispensability of the wife which this new promiscuity produces is one of the factors leading to the increased divorce rate. It also has drastically adverse effects on both the financial and emotional security of middle-aged and older women. Proper reaction of a society to change, therefore, demands a careful screening of the elements of change and their results for compatibility with the rest of the culture's goals and institutions.

Second, in order for Muslims to avoid rash acceptance of drastic and harmful changes in their marriage laws and customs, they must purge their society of the misuse of existent laws and customs. Often it is the widespread neglect or circumvention of the qur'ānic or legal prescriptives which are at the root of the problem, rather than the institutions and practices themselves. A case in point is the misuse of the institution of *ṭalāq*, many instances of which fail to comply with the regulations and restrictions which have been established for it. Adherence to those regulations and restrictions would obviate the need for drastic changes in the institution.

The imbalances caused by rapid social change are probably inevitable factors in any society. At this period of history, they are particularly challenging. Without careful reappraisal of the side-effects of contemplated innovation and its compatibility with other aspects of the religion and culture, and without a purging of misapplications of extant institutions, massive social disorientation and deleterious effects on the members of any society are inevitable. This is the contemporary challenge, not only for Muslim society, but also for every other society in the world.

NOTES

1. In Christianity, marriage was first recognized as a sacrament in the twelfth century, when Peter Lombard's "Sentences" (Book 4, dist. 1, num. 2) enumerated marriage as one of the seven sacraments. That work became the standard textbook of Catholic theology during the Middle Ages and was formally accepted by the Councils of Florence (1439) and Trent (1545–1563).

2. Muhammad ibn Isma'il al Bukhārī, *Saḥīḥ Al-Bukhārī*, tr. Muhammad Muhsin Khān, Al-Medina al-Munauwara: Islamic University, 1974, Vol. 7, pp. 2–5, 8.

3. To this day, in the highly Westernized society of Beirut, Lebanon, unmarried young people are often embarrassed by the constant social pressures on them to marry.

4. The Muslim maintains that the Qur'ān is the word of God dictated verbatim to the Prophet Muḥammad. Its basic ethical principles and prescriptive laws, therefore, carry the authenticity of divine provenance. These principles and laws are designated as the *sharī'ah* ("path"). The human elaboration and interpretation of the *sharī'ah*, i.e., its development into specific laws by the jurists of the five schools of law (four Sunnī and one Shī'ī *madhāhib*, s. *madhhab*), is the subject matter of Islamic jurisprudence or *fiqh*.

5. See Lois Lamyā' (Ibsen) al Faruqi, "An Extended Family Model from Islamic Culture," *Journal of Comparative Family Studies* 9 (Summer, 1978): 243–256; and "Islamic Traditions and the Feminist Movement: Confrontation or Cooperation?" *The Islamic Quarterly*, vol. 27, no. 3 (1983), pp. 132–139.

6. Hammūdah 'Abd al 'Atī, *The Family Structure in Islam* (Indianapolis: American Trust Publications, 1977), p. 50.

7. The Qur'ān and Islamic law, reflecting the practice of slavery which existed in the pre- and early Islamic periods, also condoned cohabitation of a master with his slave girls (Qur'ān 23:5–7; 70:29–31). Although most Muslims would try to rationalize the existence of the passages sanctioning this form of extramarital sex (see 'Abd al 'Atī, *Family Structures*, pp. 41–49) and draw attention to the companion mechanisms which legitimized the children of such unions, enjoined emancipation for the mothers, and generally controlled and regulated the practice, few, if any, Muslims today would regard sex as legitimate except within the bonds of marriage.

8. The Qur'ān contains not only repeated references to the rights of kin (17:23–26; 4:7–9; 8:41; etc.) but also inheritance and support provisions which are stipulated as reaching far beyond the nuclear family (2:180–182; 4:33, 176; eitc.). Dire punishment is threatened for those who ignore these measures for intra-family support (4:7–12).

9. Exogamy is the custom of marrying only outside one's own tribe, clan, or family, i.e., outbreeding; endogamy is the opposite, i.e., inbreeding.

10.
> Prohibited to you
> (For marriage) are:
> Your mothers, daughters,
> Sisters; father's sisters,
> Mother's sisters; brother's daughters,
> Sister's daughters; foster-mothers;
> (Who gave you suck), foster-sisters;
> Your wives' mothers;
> Your step-daughters under your
> Guardianship, born of your wives
> To whom ye have gone in,
> No prohibition if ye have not gone in;
> (Those who have been)
> wives of your sons proceeding
> From your loins;
> And two sisters in wedlock
> At one and the same time,
> Except for what is past;
> For God is Oft-forgiving
> Most Merciful. (Qur'ān 4:23)

See also al Bukhārī, *Saḥīḥ Al-Bukhārī*, pp. 28–34.

11. The qur'ānic passage stating that it is unlawful for men to marry their "milk rela-

tives" is to be found in 4:23. See note 10 above and al Bukhārī, *Saḥīḥ Al-Bukhārī,* pp. 24–28.

12. 'Abd al 'Atī, *Family Structure,* p. 131; al Bukhārī, *Saḥīḥ Al-Bukhārī,* pp. 28–34.

13. The ever-widening problems of impotence in contemporary males may in large part be a result of the excessive sexual freedom and familiarity which pertains in many of the societies of this century. See G. L. Ginsberg, et al., "The New Impotency," *Archives of General Psychology* 28 (1972): 218; and G. F. Gilder, *Sexual Suicide* (New York: Quadrangle/The New York Times Book Co., 1973).

14. See 'Abd al 'Atī, *Family Structure,* p. 139.

15. In Turkey and Pakistan, men and women can marry at eighteen and sixteen years of age, respectively; in Egypt, at nineteen and seventeen; in Jordan, at eighteen and seventeen; in Morocco and Iran, at eighteen and fifteen; and in Tunisia, at twenty for both sexes. Marriage of younger persons must have the consent of guardians and the permission of the court.

16. E.g., barrenness of the first wife, disbalance of male/female population, chronic illness of the wife, large numbers of helpless widows and orphans in the community, etc.

17. See Tanzil-ur-Rahman, *A Code of Muslim Personal Law* (Karachi: Hamdard Academy, 1978), pp. 94–101, for a summary of modern legislation pertaining to polygyny. The Tunisian Law of 1956 prohibits it outright, while other countries have placed various restrictions on having more than one wife—e.g., financial ability of the husband, just cause, consent of the first wife or wives, and/or permission of a court or ad hoc council.

18. Al Bukhārī, *Saḥīḥ Al-Bukhārī, Al-Bukhārī,* pp. 51–53.

19. Tanzil-ur-Rahman, *Code,* pp. 51–52.

20. 'Abd al 'Atī, *Family Structure,* pp. 76–84. Tanzil-ur-Rahman, *Code,* chap. 3, see especially pp. 71–74, for modern legislation in various Muslim countries relating to consent to marriage.

21. Al Bukhārī, *Saḥīḥ Al-Bukhārī,* pp. 51, 55, 59–61.

22. Asaf A. A. Fyzee, *Outlines of Muhammadan Law,* 2nd ed. (London: Oxford University Press, 1955), pp. 112–113; Tanzil-ur-Rahman, *Code,* pp. 218–221.

23. This paraphrases a *ḥadīth* from the life of the Prophet Muhammad: "Of all the permitted acts the one disliked most by God is divorce" (S. Ameenul Hasan Rizvi, "Women and Marriage in Islam," *The Muslim World League Journal,* vol. 12, no. 1 (Muharram. 1404 A. H. [October, 1984], p. 26).

24. Tanzil-ur-Rahman, *Code,* pp. 313–316; Fyzee, *Outlines,* pp. 128–130.

25. Fyzee, *Outlines,* pp. 130–131.

26. Tanzil-ur-Rahman, *Code,* chap. 12, pp. 339ff.; Fyzee, *Outlines,* pp. 134–135.

27. Tanzil-ur-Rahman, *Code,* pp. 346–350.

28. Ibid., pp. 552ff.; Fyzee, *Outlines,* pp. 138–139; Alhaji A. D. Ajijola, *Introduction to Islamic Law* (Karachi: International Islamic Publishers for Ajijola Memorial Islamic Publishing Co. [Nigeria], 1981), pp. 172ff.

29. Tanzil-ur-Rahman, *Code,* pp. 504ff.; Ajijola, *Introduction,* pp. 176–177; Fyzee, *Outlines,* pp. 141–142.